A4 DM.

KV-620-883

Cassell's
Dictionary
of Abbreviations

Cassell's Dictionary of Abbreviations

Compiled by
J. W. GURNETT
and
C. H. J. KYTE

Revised and Enlarged Edition

CASSELL · LONDON

Cassell & Company Ltd.

35 Red Lion Square, London, W.C.1.
and at Melbourne, Sydney, Toronto, Johannesburg, Cape Town, Auckland

© Cassell & Company Ltd., 1966, 1972

First Published 1966
2nd edition (revised and enlarged) 1972

I.S.B.N. 0 304 93879 3

Printed in Great Britain by C. Tinling & Co. Ltd.,
London and Prescot.

Preface
to the First Edition

Today, in this era of space travel and automation, we find more than ever the need for abbreviations to save time in both business and pleasure. Having compiled a dictionary of over 21,000 abbreviations, we find ourselves in the rather ironic position of having to resort to prose to explain our work. Could we not have invented some ingenious contraction to enlighten the reader? Scarcely a day passes without some newspaper or journal printing a new abbreviation that has to be assimilated into the language, and although the meanings of some of them are easily decipherable, there are many others that are not. It is to meet this need that this volume has been compiled.

Our main consideration has been to include abbreviations that have gained some degree of general currency both nationally and internationally. Although it is not always easy to differentiate between an abbreviation and a symbol, we have as a rule omitted pure symbols except those in common use. Neither have we included popular diminutives of christian names except in special cases, such as books of the Bible and English monarchs.

A common failing with abbreviations is that they can have more than one meaning but this is unavoidable. We hope, nevertheless, that visitors to Rome will not think that 'S.P.Q.R.' stands for 'Small Profits—Quick Returns.'

In a work of this size it is inevitable that there will be a number of errors and omissions and we will gladly receive any corrections, amendments or additional material which will add to the usefulness of this dictionary.

Finally we should like to thank the many libraries and newspaper information departments for their generous help, in particular *The Times* Intelligence Department, the Library Association and the B.B.C. News Information Officer. Our thanks also to the Union of International Associations for permission to use the list of international abbreviations contained in the *Yearbook of International Organisations*.

Note to the Revised Edition

In the five years which have elapsed since this Dictionary was first published, a considerable body of new abbreviations has come into common use, while the process of time has rendered others obsolete. We have, therefore, carefully revised the text of the original edition, deleting those abbreviations no longer in common use, and adding new abbreviations, with the result that this new edition has expanded from some 21,000 entries to over 23,000.

J.W.G.

C.H.J.K.

Notes to the User

1. The entries are set out in alphabetical order, but where they contain the same letters or combinations of letters, the following rules of precedence have been observed.

(i) Capitals precede lower case:
   viz 'A.' precedes 'a.' and 'A.B.' precedes 'a.B.' and 'a.b.'

(ii) Unpunctuated entries precede punctuated entries:
   viz 'A' precedes 'A.'

(iii) Single words precede two or more words:
   viz 'abc.' precedes 'ab.c.' which precedes 'a.b.c.'

(iv) The full-stop precedes all other forms of punctuation:
   viz 'A.B.' precedes 'A.–B.' and 'A/B.'

2. Where the use of capitals or lower case or punctuation is optional in an abbreviation, the user may not always find all forms of the abbreviation included. In the interests of economy these variants have been excluded where such abbreviation has only one meaning.

3. Brackets in heavy type '( )' are part of the abbreviation. Letters in an abbreviation enclosed by light brackets '( )' may either be optional, or plural forms of the abbreviation.

A

A Alcohol
Argon
Atomic weight
A Angström, unit of measurement
A. Absolute
Academy
Academician
Ace
Acre
Acting
Active
Adjective
Adjutant
Admiral
Adult
Advance(d)
Afternoon
Air
Altesse (Highness)
Alto
Amateur
America(n)
Ampère
Anna
Anode
Answer
Area
Armoured
Arrive
Arriving
Art
Article
Artillery
Associate
Athletic
Atomic
a. acid
active
actual
address
age
ampère
anno (in the year)
ante (before)
aqua (water)
area
A.A. Achievement Age
Advertising Agency
Advertising Association
Air Attaché
Alcoholics Anonymous
All Along
Anti-Aircraft
Architectural Association
Army Act
Associate in Arts
Audio-animatronics
Augustinians of the Assumption
Automobile Association
a.a. always afloat
A.A.A. Amateur Athletic Association
American Automobile Association *cont.*

Association of Attenders any
Alumni of the Hague Academd
of International Law
Australian Automobile Association
A.A.A.A. Australian Association of Advertising Agencies
A.A.A.L. American Academy of Arts and Letters
A.A. & G.M. Anti-Aircraft and Guided Missiles Branch
A.A. & Q.M.G. Assistant Adjutant and Quartermaster General
A.A.A.S. American Academy of Arts and Sciences
American Association for the Advancement of Science
Associate of the American Antiquarian Society
A.A.B. Association of Applied Biologists
A.A.B.L. Associated Australasian Banks in London
Associated Australian Banks in London
A.A.B.M. Australian Association of British Manufacturers
A.A.C. Agricultural Advisory Council for England and Wales
Amateur Athletic Club
anno ante Christum (in the year before Christ)
Army Air Corps
Austrian Alpine Club
Automatic Amplitude Control
A.A.C.C.A. Associate of the Association of Certified and Corporate Accountants
A.A.C.E. Aberdeen Association of Civil Engineers
A.A.C.L. Association of American Correspondents in London
A.A.C.O.B.S. Australian Advisory Council on Bibliographical Services
A.A.C.P. Anglo-American Council on Productivity
A.A.C.R. Association for the Advancement of Civil Rights (Gibraltar)
A.A.C.S. Aberdeen-Angus Cattle Society
Airways and Air Communications Service (U.S.)
A.A.D.C. Air Aide-de-Camp
A.A.E. American Association of Engineers
A.A.E.A. African Adult Education Association
A.A.E.C. Australian Atomic Energy Commission
A.A.E.E. Aircraft and Armament Experimental Establishment
A.A.E.S. Association of Agricultural Education Staffs of Local Authorities *cont.*

Australian Army Education Service

A.A.F. Army Air Force(s) (U.S.)
Auxiliary Air Force (*now* R.Aux.A.F.)

A.A.F.A. Anglo-American Families Association

A.A.F.C.E. Allied Air Forces Central Europe

A.A.F.I.S. Army and Air Force Intelligence Staff

A.A.F.N.E. Allied Air Forces Northern Europe

A.A.F.S.E. Allied Air Forces Southern Europe

A.A.F.S.S. advanced aerial fire support system

A.A.G. Aslib Aeronautical Group
Assistant Adjutant-General
Association of American Geographers

A.A.I. Architectural Association of Ireland
Associate of the Chartered Auctioneers' and Estate Agents' Institute
Association of Advertisers in Ireland

A.A.I.A. Associate of the Association of International Accountants

A.A.I.I. Associate of the Australian Insurance Institute

A.A.L. Academy of Art and Literature
Association of Assistant Librarians

A.A.L.D. Australian Army Legal Department

A.A.L.P.A. Associate of the Incorporated Society of Auctioneers and Landed Property Agents

A.A.M. Anti-Apartheid Movement
Association of Assistant Mistresses in Secondary Schools

A.A.M.C. Australian Army Medical Corps

A.A.M.W.S. Australian Army Medical Women's Service

A.A.N.A. Australian Association of National Advertisers

A. & A. Additions and Amendments

A. & A.EE. Aircraft and Armament Experimental Establishment

A. & C. Addenda and Corrigenda
Antony and Cleopatra (Shakespeare)

A. & C.P. Anchors and Chains Proved

A. & M. Ancient and Modern (Hymns)

A. & N. Army and Navy Club
Army and Navy Stores

A. & P. Agricultural and Pastoral

A. & S.H. Argyll and Sutherland Highlanders

A.A.N.S. Australian Army Nursing Service

A.A.N.S.W. Archives Authority of New South Wales

a.a.O. am angeführten Orte (at the place quoted)

A.A.O.C. Australian Army Ordnance Corps

A.A.P. Australian Associated Press

A.A.P.A. Advertising Agency Production Association

A.A.P.C. All African Peoples' Conference

A.A.P.H.I. Associate of the Association of Public Health Inspectors

A.A.P.O. All African Peoples' Organization

A.A.P.S. American Association for the Promotion of Science

A.A.P.S.O. Afro-Asian People's Solidarity Organisation

A.A.P.S.S. American Academy of Political and Social Science

A.A.P.S.W. Associate of the Association of Psychiatric Social Workers

A.A.P.T. American Association of Physics Teachers

A.A.Q.M.G. Assistant Adjutant and Quartermaster General

a.a.r. against all risks

A.A.S. Aberdeen Art Society
Academiae Americanae Socius (Fellow of the American Academy)
Acta Apostolicae Sedis (Acts of the Apostolic See)
Agnostics' Adoption Society
American Astronautical Society
American Astronomical Society
Associate in Applied Science
Association for Archery in Schools
Association of Architects and Surveyors
Australian Academy of Science
Auxiliary Ambulance Service

A.A.S.A. Associate of the Australian Society of Accountants

A.A.S.C. Australian Army Service Corps

A.A.S.F. Advanced Air Striking Force

A.A.S.R. Ancient Accepted Scottish Rite

A.A.S.S. Americanae Antiquarianae Societatis Socius (Fellow of the American Antiquarian Society)

A.A.S.T.C. Associate in Architecture of the Sydney Technical College

A.A.T.A. Anglo-American Tourist Association

A.A.T.N.U. Administration de l'assistance technique des Nations Unies (United Nations Technical Assistance Administration)

A.A.T.T.A. Arab Association of Tourism and Travel Agents

A.A.T.U.F. All-African Trade Union Federation

A.A.U. Amateur Athletic Union (U.S.)

A.A.U.P. American Association of University Professors

A.A.U.Q. Associate in Accountancy of the University of Queensland

A.A.U.W. American Association of University Women

A.A.V.C. Australian Army Veterinary Corps

A.A.Y.P.L. Atlantic Association of Young Political Leaders

ab. about
A.B. Able-bodied
Advisory Board
Air Board
Alliance balkanique (Balkan Alliance)
Army Book
Artium Baccalaureus (Bachelor of Arts)
Asthmatic Bronchitis
A/B. Aktiebolaget (limited company)
a.B. auf Bestellung (on order)
a/b. airborne
A.B.A. Amateur Boxing Association
American Bankers' Association
American Bar Association
American Booksellers' Association
Antiquarian Booksellers' Association
Associate of the British Archaeological Association
A.B.A.A. Antiquarian Booksellers' Association of America
Associate of the British Association of Accountants and Auditors
A.B.A.C. Association of British Aero Clubs and Centres
A.B.A.S. Amateur Basketball Association of Scotland
Abb. Abbess
Abbey
Abbot
A.B.B.A. Amateur Basket Ball Association
abb(rev). abbreviation
A.B.B.F. Association of Bronze and Brass Founders
A.B.C. Aerated Bread Company
Air Bridge to Canada
Alphabet
America, Britain, Canada
American Book-prices Current
American Broadcasting Company
Animal Birth Control
Argentina, Brazil, Chile
Associated British Cinemas
Association of Building Centres
Audit Bureau of Circulations
Australian Bankruptcy Cases
Australian Broadcasting Commission
Automatic Binary Computer
A.B.C.A. Army Bureau of Current Affairs (*later* B.C.A.)
A.B.C.B. Association of Birmingham Clearing Banks
A.B.C.C. Association of British Chambers of Commerce
Association of British Correspondence Colleges
A.B.C.D. America, Britain, China, Dutch East Indies
Atomic Biological and Chemical Protection and Damage Control
A.B.C.M. Associate of the Bandsman's College of Music
Association of British Chemical Manufacturers

A.B.D. Association of British Detectives
Abd. Abdias
abd. abdicate(d)
A.B.D.A. American, British, Dutch, Australian
Aber. Aberdeen
A.B.F. Actors' Benevolent Fund
Associated British Foods
A.B.F.L. Association of British Foam Laminators
A.B.F.M. American Board of Foreign Missions
A.B.G.B. Allgemeines bürgerliches Gesetzbuch (Austrian Civil Code)
ABH Alpha-benzene-Hexachloride
A.B.H.M. Association of Builders' Hardware Manufacturers
A.B.I. Associate of the Institute of Book-keepers
A.B.I.A. Associate of the Bankers' Institute of Australasia
A.B.I.M. Association of British Insecticide Manufacturers
A.B.I.S. Association of Burglary Insurance Surveyors
ab init. ab initio (from the beginning)
Abl. Abril (April)
abl. ablative
A.B.L.C. Association of British Launderers and Cleaners
A.B.L.S. Association of British Library Schools
A.B.M. Anti-ballistic Missile
Australian Board of Missions
Automatic Batch Mix
A.B.M.A.C. Association of British Manufacturers of Agricultural Chemicals
A.B.M.E.X. Association of British Mining Equipment Exporters
A.B.M.P.M. Association of British Manufacturers of Printers Machinery
A.B.M.S. Ayurvedacharya, Bachelor of Medicine and Surgery
A.B.N. Anti-bolshevik Bloc of Nations
A.B.O.C.F. Association of British Organic and Compound Fertilisers
A.B.O.F. Association of British Organic Fertilisers
Abp. Archbishop
A.B.P. Arterial Blood Pressure
Associated Book Publishers
A.B.P.C. American Book Publishers' Council
Association of British Packing Contractors
A.B.P.I. Association of the British Pharmaceutical Industry
A.B.P.N. Association of British Paediatric Nurses
A.B.Ps.S. Associate of the British Psychological Society
A.B.P.T. Association of Blind Piano Tuners
A.B.P.V.M. Association of British Plywood and Veneer Manufacturers
abr. abridge(d)
A.B.R.F.M. Association of British Roofing Felt Manufacturers

A.B.R.O. Animal Breeding Research Organisation
    Army in Burma Reserve of Officers
A.B.R.R.M. Association of British Reclaimed Rubber Manufacturers
A.B.R.S. Association of British Riding Schools
A.B.R.S.M. Associated Board of the Royal Schools of Music
ABS Acrylonitrile butadiene styrene
    Sodium alkyl benzene sulphonate
Abs. Absorbent
abs. absence
    absolute(ly)
    abstract
A.B.S. American Bible Society
    American Bureau of Shipping
    Architects' Benevolent Society
    Associate of the Building Societies Institute
    Association of Broadcasting Staff
A.B.S.C. Association of Boiler Setters, Chimney and Furnace Constructors
abse. re. absente reo (the defendant being absent)
A.B.S.I. Associate of the Boot and Shoe Institution
A.B.S.M. Associate of the Bendigo School of Mines
    Associate of the Birmingham School of Music
A.B.S.M.G.P. Associate Member of the British Society of Master Glass-Painters
absol. absolute(ly)
abstr. abstract
A.B.S.W. Association of British Science Writers
abt. about
A.B.T. Association of Building Technicians
A.B.T.A. Allied Brewery Traders' Association
    Association of British Travel Agents
    Australian British Trade Association
A.B.T.A.P.L. Association of British Theological and Philosophical Libraries
A.B.T.I.C.S. Abstract and Book Title Index Card Service
A.B.T.S.A. Association of British Tree Surgeons and Arborists
A.B.T.T. Association of British Theatre Technicians
A.B.U. Alliance biblique universelle (United Bible Societies)
    Assembly of the Baptist Union
A.-B.U. Anglo-Belgian Union
A.B.Y.A. Association of British Yacht Agents
A.B.Z. Association of British Zoologists
Ac Actinium
ac. acre
    activity
A.C. Advisory Committee
    Aero Club
    Air Command
    Air Commodore

    Air Control
    Air Corps
    Air Council
    Aircraftman
    Alpine Club
    Ambulance Corps
    Analogue Computer
    Analytical Chemist
    Annual Conference
    ante Christum (before Christ)
    Appeal Case
    Appeal Court
    Army Corps
    Army Council
    Artillery College
    Arts Council of Great Britain
    Assistant Commissioner
    Athletic Club
    Atlantic Charter
    Auditor Camerae (Auditor of the Papal Treasury)
    Auto Carriers, Limited
    Azione Cattolica (Catholic Action)
(A.C.) Army Co-operation (Squadron)
a.c. à compte (on account)
    alternating current
    anno corrente (this year)
    ante cibo (before meals)
    author's correction
a/c. account current
A.C.A. Adjacent-channel Attenuation
    Advertisement Contractors' Association
    Agricultural Cooperative Association
    American Composers' Alliance
    Amusement Caterers' Association
    Anglers' Co-operative Association
    Associate of the Institute of Chartered Accountants in England and Wales
    Australian Council for Aeronautics
Acad. Academy
    Academical
A.C. & A.E. Association of Chemical and Allied Employers
A.C.A.O. Assistant County Advisory Officer
A.C.A.S. Assistant Chief of Air Staff
A.C.A.T.S. Association of Civil Aviation Technical Staffs
A.C.B. Association of Clinical Biochemists
a/c. Bk. Account Book
acc. acceleration
    accent
    acceptance
    according
    account
    accusative
A.C.C. Administrative Co-ordination Committee
    Advanced Communications Course
    Air Co-ordinating Committee (U.S.)

cont.

Army Catering Corps
Associated Chemical Companies
A.C.C.A. Agricultural Central Co-operative Association
Association of Certified and Corporate Accountants
Accad. Accademia (Academy)
A.C.C.A.S.T. Advisory Committee on Colonial Colleges of Arts, Science and Technology (*now* C.O.C.A.S.T.)
accel. accelerando (faster)
access. accessory
ACCHAN Allied Command Channel
A.C.C.O. Associate of the Canadian College of Organists
Association of Child Care Officers
A.C.C.P. American College of Chest Physicians
Accred. Accredited
Acct. Accountant
acct. account
acctd. accented
A.C.D.C.M. Archbishop of Canterbury's Diploma in Church Music
A.Cdre. Air Commodore
ACE alcohol-chloroform-ether
A.C.E. Advisory Centre for Education
Allied Command Europe
American Council on Education
Association of Circulation Executives
Association of Consulting Engineers
Association of Cultural Exchange
Australian College of Education
Automatic Computing Engine
A.C.E.N. Assembly of Captive European Nations
A.C.E.O. Association of Chief Education Officers
A.C.E.R. Australian Council for Educational Research
Acet. Acetone
A.C.F. Académie Canadienne Française (French Canadian Academy)
Active Citizen Force (South Africa)
Army Cadet Force
Army Council Form
Australian Comforts Fund
Automobile Club de France
A.C.F.A. Army Cadet Force Association
A.C.F.A.S. Association Canadienne) Française pour l'avancement des sciences (French Canadian Association for the Advancement of Sciences)
A.C.F.C. Anglo-Cypriot Friendship Council
ac. ft. acre foot *or* feet
Acft. C. Aircraft-carrier
A.C.G. Assistant Chaplain-General
Automatic Control Gear
A.C.G.B. Arts Council of Great Britain
A.C.G.F.C. Associate of the City and Guilds Finsbury College (London)
A.C.G.I. Associate of the City and Guilds of London Institute

A.C.G.U. Alchemists Club Glasgow University
ACh acetylcholine
A.Ch.S. Associate of the Society of Chiropodists
A.C.H. Association of Contemporary Historians
A.C.I. Alliance coopérative internationale (International Co-operative Alliance)
Alloy Castings Institute
Army Council Instruction
Associate of the Clothing Institute
Associate of the Institute of Commerce
Association of Chambers of Commerce of Ireland
Automobile Club d'Italia
a.c.i. assuré contre l'incendie (insured against fire)
A.C.I.A. Associate of the Corporation of Insurance Agents
A.C.I.A.A. Australian Commercial and Industrial Artists' Association
A.C.I.B. Associate of the Corporation of Insurance Brokers
A.C.I.C. Aeronautical Charting and Information Center (U.S.)
ACICAFE Association du commerce et de l'industrie du café dans la C.E.E. (Association for the Coffee Trade and Industry in the E.E.C.)
A.C.I.G.S. Assistant Chief of the Imperial General Staff
A.C.I.I. Associate Member of the Chartered Insurance Institute
A.C.I.O.P.J.F. Association catholique internationale des œuvres de protection de la jeune fille (International Catholic Girls' Society)
A.C.I.S. Associate of the Chartered Institute of Secretaries
A.C.I.V. Associate of the Commonwealth Institute of Valuers
A.C.J.P. Airways Corporations Joint Pensions
ack. acknowledge
ACLANT Allied Command Atlantic
A.C.L.M. Association of Contact Lens Manufacturers
A.C.L.P. Association of Contact Lens Practitioners
A.Cl.S. Additional Clergy Society
A.C.L.S. American Council of Learned Societies
Automatic Carrier Landing System
A.C.M. Air Chief Marshal
Association of Crane Makers
A.C.M.A. Agricultural Co-operative Managers' Association
Asbestos Cement Manufacturers' Association
Asphalt and Coated Macadam Association
Athletic Clothing Manufacturers' Association
A.C.M.E.T. Advisory Council on Middle East Trade
A.C.M.F. Australian Commonwealth Military Forces

5

A.C.M.L. Anti-Common Market League
A.C.M.M. Associate of the Conservatorium of Music, Melbourne
A.C.M.P. Assistant Commissioner of the Metropolitan Police
A.C.N. ante Christum natum (before the birth of Christ)
A.C.N.S. Assistant Chief of Naval Staff
A.C.O. Admiralty Compass Observatory
　　　Association of Children's Officers
A.Comm. Associate in Commerce
A.Comm.A. Associate of the Society of Commercial Accountants
A.C.O.P. Association of Chief Officers of Police
A.C.O.R.D. Advisory Council on Research and Development
A.C.O.R.N. Automatic Check-out and Recording Network
A.C.O.S. American College of Osteopathic Surgeons
　　　Assistant Chief of Staff
A.C.P. American College of Physicians
　　　Associate of the College of Preceptors
　　　Association of Circus Proprietors of Great Britain
　　　Association of Clinical Pathologists
　　　Association of Correctors of the Press
A.-C.P. Anti-Concorde Project
A.C.P.A. Associate of the Institution of Certified Public Accountants
A.C.P.M. Association of Corrugated Paper Makers
A.C.P.O. Association of Chief Police Officers of England and Wales
A.C.R. Admiral Commanding Reserves
A/C.R.E. Acting Commander Royal Engineers
A.C.R.R. American Council on Race Relations
A.C.R.S. Advisory Committee on Reactor Safeguards (U.S.)
A.C.S. Additional Curates' Society
　　　Admiral Commanding Submarines
　　　Admiralty Computing Service
　　　American Chemical Society
　　　American College of Surgeons
a.c.s. anodal closing sound
a/c. s. aircraft security vessel
A.C.S.E.A. Allied Command South East Asia
A.C.S.I.L. Admiralty Centre for Scientific Information and Liaison
A.C.S.M. Associate of the Camborne School of Metalliferous Mining
A.C.S.N. Association of Collegiate Schools of Nursing
A.C.S.P. Advisory Council on Scientific Policy
Act. Acting
　　　Actuary
act. active
　　　activities

A.C.T. Agricultural Central Trading
　　　Aid Committee for Technion
　　　Air Council for Training
　　　Australian Capital Territory
　　　Australian College of Theology
A.C.T.A.T. Association of Cinematograph, Television and Allied Technicians
A.C.T.C. Art Class Teacher's Certificate
Actg. Acting
ACTH adrenocorticotrophic hormone (or corticotrophin)
A.C.T.O. Advisory Council on the Treatment of Offenders
A.C.T.S. Associate of the Society of Certificated Teachers of Shorthand
　　　Australian Catholic Truth Society
A.C.T.T. Association of Cinematograph, Television and Allied Technicians
A.C.T.U. Australian Council of Trade Unions
A.C.U. Actors' Church Union
　　　American Congregational Union
　　　Association of Commonwealth Universities
　　　Association of Cricket Umpires
　　　Auto-Cycle Union
A.C.U.A. Association of Cambridge University Assistants
A.C.V. Air Cushion Vehicle(s)
　　　Associate of the College of Violinists
　　　Associated Commercial Vehicles
A.C.W. Aircraftwoman
a.c.w. alternating continuous waves
A.C.W.A. Associate of the Institute of Cost and Works Accountants
A.C.W.W. Associated Country Women of the World
ad. adapted
　　　addatur (let there be added)
　　　adverb
　　　advertisement
A.D. Administrative Department
　　　Air Defence
　　　Anno Domini (in the year of our Lord)
　　　Armament Depot
　　　Autograph Document
　　　Average Deviation
A/D. Aerodrome
a.D. ausser Dienst (retired on half pay)
a.d. after date
　　　ante diem (day before)
ADA Acetone-dicarboxylic acid
A.D.A. Action Data Automation
　　　Agricultural Development Association
　　　Aluminium Development Association
　　　American Dental Association
　　　Americans for Democratic Action
　　　Australian Dental Association
adag. adagio (leisurely)
A.D. and C. Advice Duration and Charge

A.D.A.W.S. Assistant Director of Army Welfare Services
A.D.B. Accidental Death Benefit
Asia Development Bank
A.D.B.M. Association of Dry Battery Manufacturers
A.D.C. Aerodrome Control
Agricultural Development Corporation (Jamaica)
Aid to Dependent Children
Aide-de-Camp
Air Defence Command (U.S.)
Amateur Dramatic Club
Army Dental Corps (*now* R.A.D.C.)
Art Directors' Club
Automatic Digital Calculator
Cambridge Amateur Dramatic Club
A.D.C.T. Art Directors' Club, Toronto
Add. Addenda
Address(ed)
A.D.D.C. Air Defence Direction Center (U.S.)
addl. additional
Add.MS(S). Additional Manuscript(s)
addns. additions
adds. address
A.D.D.S. Assistant Director of Dental Services
addsd. addressed
Adel. Adelaide
ADELA Atlantic Community Development Group for Latin America
a des. a destra (to the right)
A.D.E.S. Association of Directors of Education in Scotland
ad eund. ad eundem gradum (to the same degree)
A.D.F. Alexandra Day Fund
Automatic Direction Finder
ad fin. ad finem (towards the end)
A.D.F.W. Assistant Director of Fortifications and Works
A.D.G. Anti-Decimal Group
Assistant Director-General
A.D.G.B. Air Defence of Great Britain
A.D.G.M.S. Assistant Director-General of Medical Services
A.D.H. Assistant Director of Hygiene
Association of Dental Hospitals of Great Britain and Northern Ireland
ad inf. ad infinitum (without limit)
ad init. ad initium (at the beginning)
ad int. ad interim (for the meanwhile)
Adj. Adjutant
adj. adjacent
adjective
adjourned
adjustment
A.D.J.A.G. Assistant Deputy Judge Advocate General
Adjt. Adjutant
A.D.L. Activities of Daily Living
Assistant Director of Labour
A.D.L.A. Art Directors' Club, Los Angeles
ad lib. ad libitum (to the extent desired)
A.D.L.P. Australian Democratic Labour Party

A.D.L.R.I. Arthur D. Little Research Institute
Adm. Administration
Admiral
Admiralty
Admission
adm. admitted
A.D.M. Annual Delegate Meeting
Ad. Man. Advertisement Manager
Admin. Administration
admin. administrator
administratrix
Admin. Apost. Administrator Apostolic
A.D.M.M. Association of Dandy Roll and Mould Makers
A.D.M.O.(C.A.) Assistant Director of the Meteorological Office (Civil Aviation)
Admon. Administration
Adm. Rev. Admodum Reverendus (Very Reverend)
A.D.M.S. Assistant Director Medical Services
A.D.M.T. Association of Dental Manufacturers and Traders of the United Kingdom
admx. administratrix
A.D.N.A. Assistant Director of Naval Accounts
A.D.N.C. Assistant Director of Naval Construction
A.D.N.I. Assistant Director of Naval Intelligence
A.D.O. Air Defence Officer
Assistant District Officer
Association of Dispensing Opticians
A.D.O.F. Assistant Director of Ordnance Factories
A.D.O.S. Assistant Director of Ordnance Service
ADP Adenosine disphosphate
A.D.P. Air Defence Position
Association of Dental Prosthesis
Automatic Data Processing
A.D.P.R. Assistant Director of Public Relations
A.D.R. and M.M. Association of Dandyroll and Mould Makers
A.D.R.A. Animal Diseases Research Association
ads. advertisements
Ad.S. Académie des Sciences (Academy of Science)
ad s. ad sectam (at the suit of)
A.D.S. Advanced Dressing Station
a.d.s. autograph document signed
ad saec. ad saeculum (to the century)
A.D.S.& T. Assistant Director of Supplies and Transport
A.D.T. an demselben Tage (the same day)
Assistant Director of Transport
A.D.Tn. Assistant Director of Transportation
ad us. ad usum (according to custom)
Adv. Advance
Advent
Advertisement
Advice
Advocate

adv. advance
    adverb
    adversus (against)
    advisory
ad val. ad valorem (in proportion to (estimated) value of goods)
advb. adverb
Adv. Bse. Advanced Base
advert. advertisement
advl. adverbial
A.D.V.S. Assistant Director of Veterinary Services
Advt. Advertisement
advv. adverbs
A.D.W. Assistant Director of Works
A.D.W.E. & M. Assistant Director of Works Electrical and Mechanical
A.E. Adult Education
    Aeronautical Engineer(ing)
    Agricultural Engineer(ing)
    All England
    Army Education
    Atomic Energy
    Pen-name of George William Russell
A.E.A. Actors' Equity Association (U.S.)
    Agricultural Education Association
    Agricultural Engineers' Association
    Air Efficiency Award
    Atomic Energy Authority (also U.K.A.E.A.)
A.E.A.A. Asociación de Escritores y Artistas Americanos (Association of American Writers and Artists)
A.E.A.F. Allied Expeditionary Air Force
A.E.B. Area Electricity Board
A.E.C. Agricultural Executive Committee
    American Express Company
    Army Educational Corps (now R.A.E.C.)
    Associated Equipment Company
    Association européenne de céramique (European Ceramic Association)
    Association of Education Committees
    Atomic Energy Commission
A.E.C.A. Anglican and Eastern Churches Association
A.E.C.L. Atomic Energy of Canada Limited
A.E.C.M. Association of Exhibitors and Conference Managers
A.Ed. Associate of Education
A.E.D. Association of Engineering Distributors
A.E.D.E. Association européenne des enseignants (European Teachers' Association)
A.E.D.T. Association européenne des organisations nationales des commerçants-détaillants en textiles (European Association of National Organizations of Textile Retailers)
A.E.D.U. Admiralty Experimental Diving Unit

A.E.E. Atomic Energy Establishment(s)
A.E.E.C. Airlines Electronic Engineering Committee
A.E.E.F. Association européenne des exploitations frigorifiques (European Association of Refrigeration Enterprises)
A.E.F. Afrique Equatoriale Française (French Equatorial Africa)
    Allied or American Expeditionary Force(s)
    Australian Expeditionary Force(s)
    Centre d'action européenne fédéraliste (European Centre for Federalist Action)
A.E.F.M. Association européenne des festivals de musique (European Association of Music Festivals)
A.e.g. All edges gilt
AEGIS Aid for the Elderly in Government Institutions
A.E.G.M. Anglican Evangelical Group Movement
A.E.H.A. Association of Electrical Housecraft Advisers
A.E.I. Associated Electrical Industries
    Association des écoles internationales (International Schools Association)
A.E.I.O.U. Austriae Est Imperare Orbi Universi (It is given to Austria to rule the whole world)
A.E.J.I. Association of European Jute Industries
A.E.L. Admiralty Engineering Laboratory
    Associated Engineering, Limited
A.E.L.E. Association européenne de libre-échange (European Free Trade Association)
A.E.L.T.C. All England Lawn Tennis Club
A.E.M.T. Association of Electrical Machinery Trades
Aen. The Aeneid
A.E.N.A. All-England Netball Association
Aen. Nas. Aenei Nasi (Brazen Nose i.e. Brasenose College, Oxford)
A.E.O. Assistant Experimental Officer
Aeol. Aeolic
A.E.O.S. Ancient Egyptian Order of Sciots
A.E.P. Association of Embroiders and Pleaters
aeq. aequalis (equal)
aer. aeronautics
    aeroplane
A.E.R. Army Emergency Reserve
A.E.R.A. Associate-Engraver of the Royal Academy
Aer. E. Aeronautical Engineer
A.E.R.E. Atomic Energy Research Establishment
A.E.R.I. Agricultural Economics Research Institute
AERNO Aeronautical Equipment Reference Number
aero. aeronautic(al)

A.E.R.T.E.L. Association européenne rubans, tresses, tissus élastiques (European Ribbon, Braid and Elastic Material Association)

Aes. Aesop

A.E.S. Agricultural Economics Society
Amateur Entomologists' Society

Aesth. Aesthetics

A.E.S.N. Association of Export Subscription Newsagents

aet(at). aetatis (of *or* at the age of)

A.E.T. Association of Auto-Electrical Technicians

A.E.T.F.A.T. Association pour l'étude taxonomique de la flore d'Afrique tropicale (Association for the Taxonomic Study of Tropical African Flora)

A. et M. Arts et Métiers (Arts and Crafts)

A.E.U. Amalgamated Engineering Union (ion now A.U.E.W.)

A.E.W. Admiralty Experimental Works
Airborne Early Warning

A.E.W.H.A. All England Women's Hockey Association

A.E.W.L.A. All England Women's Lacrosse Association

Af. Africa(n)

A.F. Académie Française (French Academy)
Action Française
Admiral of the Fleet
Advanced Freight(s)
Armée Française (French Army)
Army Form
Associate Fellow
Associated Fisheries
Automatic Smoke Filter

A.-F. Anglo-French

a.f. anno futuro (next year)
audio frequency

A.F.A. Air Force Act
Amateur Fencing Association
Amateur Football Alliance
Amateur Football Association
Associate in Fine Arts
Associate of the Faculty of Actuaries in Scotland
Associate of the Faculty of Auditors

A.F.A.D. Association of Fatty Acid Distillers

A.F.A.I.M. Associate Fellow of the Australian Institute of Management

A.F.A.M. Ancient Free and Accepted Masons

A.F.A.S. Associate Architect Member of the Faculty of Architects and Surveyors
Association française pour l'avancement des sciences (French Association for the Advancement of the Sciences)

A.F.A.S.I.C. Association for All Speech Impaired Children

A.F.B.M.D. Air Force Ballistic Missile Division (U.S.)

A.F.B.S. American and Foreign Bible Society

A.F.C. Air Force Cross
Amateur Football Club
Association of Flooring Contractors
Association Football Club
Australian Flying Corps (*now* R.A.A.F.)

a.f.c. automatic frequency control

A.F.C.A.I. Associate Fellow of the Canadian Aeronautical Institute

A.F.C.E. Associate in Fuel Technology and Chemical Engineering

AFCENT Allied Forces Central Europe

A.F.C.M.A. Aluminium Foil Container Manufacturers Association

A.F.C.O. Admiralty Fleet Confidential Order

A.F.C.U. American and Foreign Christian Union

A.F.C.W. Association of Family Case Workers

A.F.D. Accelerated Freeze Drying
Doctor of Fine Arts

A.F.D.S. Air Fighting Development Squadron

A.F.E.E. Airborne Forces Experimental Establishment

A.F.E.S. Admiralty Fuel Experimental Station

AFEX Armed Forces Exchange (U.S.)

aff. affiliated
affirmative

affd. affirmed

affec. affectionate

affil. affiliated

A.F.F.M. Association of Folding Furniture Manufactures

afft. affidavit

Afgh. Afghanistan

A.F.H.Q. Allied Forces Headquarters

A.F.I. Associate of the Faculty of Insurance

A.F.I.A. American Foreign Insurance Association
Apparel and Fashion Industry's Association
Associate of the Federal Institute of Accountants (Australia)

A.F.I.A.S. Associate Fellow of the Institute of the Aerospace Sciences (U.S.)

A.F.I.I.M. Associate Fellow of the Institute of Industrial Managers

A.F.L. Air Force List
American Federation of Labour (*now* A.F.L.—C.I.O.)

A.F.L.A. Asian Federation of Library Associations
Associate of the Association of Fire Loss Adjusters

A.F.L.-C.I.O. American Federation of Labour and Congress of Industrial Organisations (U.S.)

A.F.L.E. Association of Film Laboratory Employers

A.F.M. Air Force Medal

A.F.M.A. Artificial Flower Manufacturers' Association of Great Britain

A.F.M.E. American Friends of the Middle East

AFMED Allied Forces Mediterranean

A.F.M.M. Association of Fish Meal Manufacturers
A.F.N. American Forces Network
A.F.N.E. Allied Forces Northern Europe
AFNOR Association française de normalisation (French Association for Standardisation)
AFNORTH Allied Forces Northern Europe
A.F.O. Admiralty Fleet Order
　Army Forwarding Officer
A.F.P. Agence France-Presse
A.F.P.A. Advertising Film Producers Association
Afr. Africa(n)
A.F.R. Air-Fuel Ratio
A.F.R.A. Average freight rate assessment
A.F.R.Ae.S. Associate Fellow of the Royal Aeronautical Society
AFRASEC Afro-Asian Organization for Economic Co-operation
Afrik. Afrikaan(s)
A.F.R.T.S. Armed Forces Radio and Television Service (U.S.)
A.F.S. Advanced Flying School
　American Field Service
　Army Fire Service
　Associate Surveyor Member of the Faculty of Architects and Surveyors
　Atlantic Ferry Service
　Auxiliary Fire Service
afsd. aforesaid
A.F.S.I.L. Accommodation for Students in London
AFSOUTH Allied Forces Southern Europe
A.F.S.W.P. Armed Forces Special Weapons Project (U.S.)
aft. after
A.F.T. American Federation of Teachers
A.F.T.A. Atlantic Free Trade Area
aftn. afternoon
A.F.T.N. Aeronautical Fixed Telecommunications Network
A.F.T.S. Aeronautical Fixed Telecommunications Service
A.F.U. Advanced Flying Unit
A.F.V. Armoured Fighting Vehicle
A.F.V.G. Anglo-French Variable Geometry Aircraft
A.F.W. Army Field Workshop
Ag Argentum (Silver)
　Atomgewicht (Atomic weight)
Ag. Agent
　Agreement
　Agriculture
A.G. Action Group Party (Nigeria)
　Adjutant-General
　Agent-General
　Aktiengesellschaft (joint stock company)
　Argovia
　Art Gallery
A.-G. Attorney-General
A.g. Air Gunner
a/g. airgraph
a.-g. anti-gas

A.G.A. Amateur Gymnastics Association
　Architectural Granite Association
　Australian Garrison Artillery
A.G.A.C.S. Air-Ground-Air Communications System
A.G.A.R.D. Advisory Group for Aeronautical Research and Development
a.g.b. a good brand
A.G.B.I. Artists' General Benevolent Institution
A.G.C. Automatic Gain Control
A.G.C.A. Automatic Ground-controlled-Approach
A.G.C.M. Association of Glass Container Manufacturers
Agcy. Agency
agd. agreed
A.G.D.C. Assistant Grand Director of Ceremonies
A.G.D.L. Attorney-General of the Duchy of Lancaster
A.G.E. Admiralty Gunnery Establishment
A.G.F. Adjutant-General to the Forces
agg. aggregate
A.G.H. Australian General Hospital
A.G.I. Associate of the Institute of Certificated Grocers
A.G.I.P. Agenzia Generale Italiana Petroli (Italian Oil General Company)
A.G.M. Annual General Meeting
　Association of Good Motorists
A.G.M.A. American Guild of Musical Artists
　Athletic Goods Manufacturers' Association
agn. again
A.G.P. Aviation General Policy
Agr. Agriculture
A.G.R. Advanced Gas-Cooled Reactor
A.G.R.A. Association of Genealogists and Record Agents
　Australian Garrison Royal Artillery
Agric. Agriculture
A.G.R.M. Adjutant-General, Royal Marines
A.G.S. Air Gunnery School
　Alpine Garden Society
　American Geographical Society
A.G.S.M. Associate of the Guildhall School of Music and Drama
A.G.S.R.O. Association of Government Supervisors and Radio Officers
agst. against
Agt. Agent
A.G.T. Associate in Glass Technology
A.G.U. All Got Up (*i.e.* all set in type)
　American Geophysical Union
a.g.v. anilin gentian violet
A.G.V.A. American Guild of Variety Artists
a.g.w. actual gross weight
A.G.W.A.C. Australian Guided Weapons and Analogue Computer
agy. agency
A.H. Anno Hebraico (in the Jewish Year)
　Anno Hegirae (the year of the Hegira)

a.h. after hatch
   ampère hour
A.H.A. American Historical Association
   American Hotel Association
   American Humane Association
   Associate of the Institute of Hospital Administrators
A.H.B.A. Association of Hotel Booking Agents
A.H.C. Accepting Houses Committee
A.H.E.M. Association of Hydraulic Equipment Manufacturers
a.h.l. ad hunc locum (at this passage *or* place)
A.H.M. Association of Head Mistresses
A.H.M.C. Association of Hospital Management Committees
A.H.M.P.S. Association of Headmistresses of Preparatory Schools
A.H.P.R. Association of Health and Pleasure Resorts
A.H.Q. Air Headquarters
   Army Headquarters
A.H.R. Academy of Human Rights
A.H.R.I.H.(N.Z.) Associate of Honour of the Royal New Zealand Institute of Horticulture
A.H.R.I.S. Association of Heads of Recognised Independent Schools
A.H.S. Anno Humanae Salutis (in the year of human salvation)
   Antiquarian Horological Society
A.H.T. Animal Health Trust
a.h.v. ad hunc vocem (at this word)
A.H.W.A. Association of Hospital and Welfare Administrators
A.H.W.C. Associate of the Heriot-Watt College, Edinburgh
A.I. Admiralty Instruction
   Altesse impériale (Imperial Highness
   American Institute
   Amnesty International
   Anno Inventionis (in the year of Discovery)
   Anthropological Institute (*now* R.A.I.)
   Chartered Auctioneers' and Estate Agents' Institute
a.i. ad interim (for the meantime)
A.I.A. Abrasive Industries Association
   Aerospace Industries Association of America
   American Institute of Architects
   Anglo-Indian Association
   Anglo-Israel Association
   Artists International Association
   Associate of the Institute of Actuaries
   Association internationale d'allergologie (International Association of Allergology)
   Association of International Accountants (I.U.K.)
   Aviation Industry Association (New Zealand)
A.I.A.A. Associate Architect Member of the Incorporated Association of Architects and Surveyors *cont.*

Association of International Advertising Agencies
A.I.A.C. Association internationale d'archéologie classique (International Association for Classical Archaeology)
A.I.A.G. Association internationale des assureurs contre la grêle (International Association of Hail Insurance Companies)
A.I.Agr.E. Associate of the Institution of Agricultural Engineers
A.I.A.L. Associate Member of the International Institute of Arts and Letters
A.I.A.N.Z. Associate of the Incorporated Institute of Accountants, New Zealand
A.I.Arb. Associate of the Institute of Arbitrators
A.I.A.S. Associate Surveyor Member of the Incorporated Association of Architects and Surveyors
   Australian Institute of Agriculture and Science
A.I.A.S.Quan. Quantity Surveyor Member of the Incorporated Association of Architects and Surveyors
A.I.B. Accidents Investigation Branch
   Associate of the Institute of Bankers
   Associate of the Institute of Building
   Association of Insurance Brokers
A.I.B.A. Association internationale de boxe amateur (International Amateur Boxing Association)
A.I.B.C. Architectural Institute of British Columbia
A.I.B.C.M. Association of Industrialised Building Component Manufacturers
A.I.B.D. Associate of the Institute of British Decorators and Interior Designers
A.I.B.E. Associate of the Institute of Building Estimators
A.I.B.M. Associate of the Institute of Baths Management
   Association internationale des bibliothèques musicales (International Association of Music Libraries)
A.I.B.P. Associate of the Institute of British Photographers
A.I.B.S. Associate of the Institute of Building Societies (South Africa)
A.I.C. Académie internationale de la céramique (International Academy of Ceramics)
   Advertising Inquiry Council
   Agricultural Improvement Council for England and Wales
   Agricultural Institute of Canada
   American Institute of Chemists
   Asbestos Information Committee
   Associate of the Institute of Chemistry (*now* A.R.I.C.)
   Association of Independent Cinemas
   Association of Investment Clubs

A.I.C.A. Associate Member of the Commonwealth Institute of Accountants
Associate of the Institute of Company Accountants

A.I.C.B. Association internationale contre le bruit (International Association Against Noise)

A.I.C.B.M. Anti-Intercontinental Ballistic Missile

A.I.C.C. All-India Congress Committee

A.I.C.C.F. Association internationale du congrès des chemins de fer (International Railway Congress Association)

A.I.C.D.T. International Advisory Committee on Documentation and Terminology in Pure and Applied Science

A.I.C.E. American Institute of Consulting Engineers
Associate of the Institution of Civil Engineers

A.I.Ceram. Associate of the Institute of Ceramics

A.I.Ch.E. American Institute of Chemical Engineers

A.I.C.M.A. Association internationale des constructeurs de matériel aérospatial (International Association of Aerospace Equipment Manufacturers)

A.I.C.M.R. Association internationale des constructeurs de matériel roulant (International Association of Rolling Stock Builders)

A.I.C.S. Associate of the Institute of Chartered Shipbrokers
Association internationale du cinéma scientifique (International Scientific Film Association)

A.I.C.T.A. Associate of the Imperial College of Tropical Agriculture (Trinidad)

A.I.D. Advertisement Investigation Department
Aeronautical Inspection Directorate
Agency for International Development
Agricultural Industrial Development
Aircraft Intelligence Department
Alliance internationale de la diffusion par fil (International Alliance for Distribution by Wire)
American Institute of Decorators
Army Intelligence Department
Artificial Insemination by Donor
Association Internationale pour le développement (International Development Association)

A.I.D.A. Association internationale de droit africain (International African Law Association)
Association internationale de la distribution des produits alimentaires (International *cont.*

Association of Food Distribution)

A.I.D.E. Association internationale des distributions d'eau (International Water Supply Association)

A.I.D.I.A. Associate of the Industrial Design Institute of Australia

A.I.D.I.S. Asociación Interamericana de Ingeniería Sanitaria (Inter-American Association of Sanitary Engineering)

A.I.D.L. Auckland Industrial Development Laboratory

A.I.D.P. Association internationale de droit pénal (International Association of Penal Law)

A.I.D.T. Association interparlementaire du tourisme (Interparliamentary Association for Tourism)

A.I.E.A. Agence internationale de l'énergie atomique (International Atomic Energy Agency)
Association internationale des étudiants en agriculture (International Association of Agricultural Students)

A.I.E.D. Association internationale des étudiants dentaires (International Association of Dental Students)

A.I.E.E. American Institute of Electrical Engineers
Associate of the Institution of Electrical Engineers
Association des instituts d'études européennes (Association of Institutes for European Studies)

A.I.E.J.I. Association internationale des éducateurs de jeunes inadaptés (International Association of Workers for Maladjusted Children)

A.I.E.P. Association internationale des usagers d'embranchements particuliers (International Association of Users of Private Sidings)

A.I.E.R.I. Association internationale des études et recherches sur l'information (International Association for Mass Communication Research)

A.I.E.S.E.C. Association internationale des étudiants en sciences économiques et commerciales (International Association of Students of Economics and Commercial Sciences)

A.I.E.S.S. Association internationale des écoles de service social (International Association of Schools of Social Work)

A.I.E.S.T. Association internationale des experts scientifiques du tourisme (International Association of Scientific Experts in Tourism)

A.I.F. Alliance internationale des femmes (International Alliance of Women)
Australian Imperial Force(s)

A.I.F.A. Associate of the International Faculty of Arts

A.I.F.M. Associate of the Institute of Factory Managers *cont.*

Association internationale des femmes médicins (International Association of Women Doctors)

A.I.F.S. American Institute for Foreign Study

A.I.G. Adjutant Inspector-General
Alliance of Individual Grocers
Assistant Inspector-General
Association internationale de géodésie (International Association of Geodesy)

A.I.G.A. American Institute of Graphic Arts
Association internationale de géomagnétisme et d'aéronomie (International Association of Geomagnetism and Aeronomy)

A.I.G.C.M. Associate of the Incorporated Guild of Church Musicians

A.I.G.M. Associate of the Institute of General Managers
Association internationale de grands magasins (International Association of Department Stores)

A.I.G.T. Association for the Improvement of Geometrical Teaching

A.I.H. All in hand
Artificial Insemination by Husband
Association internationale de l'hôtellerie (International Hotel Association)
Association of Independent Hospitals

A.I.H.A. Associate of the Institute of Hospital Administrators

A.I.H.S. Association internationale d'hydrologie scientifique (International Association of Scientific Hydrology)

A.I.Hsg. Associate of the Institute of Housing

A.I.H.V.E. Associate of the Institution of Heating and Ventilating Engineers

A.I.I. Air India International

A.I.I.A. Associate of the Indian Institute of Architects
Associate of the Insurance Institute of America
Australian Institute of International Affairs

A.I.I.A.L. Associate of the International Institute of Arts and Letters

A.I.I.C. Association internationale des interprètes de conférence (International Association of Conference Interpreters)

A.I.J.P. Association Internationale des Journalistes Philatéliques (International Association of Philatelic Journalists

A.I.I.R.M. Association internationale des intérêts radio-maritimes (International Association of Marine Radio Interests)

A.I.I.S.U.P. Association internationale d'information scolaire, universitaire et professionnelle (International Association for Educational and Vocational Information)

A.I.I.Tech. Associate Member of the Institute of Industrial Technicians

A.I.J.D. Association internationale des juristes démocrates (International Association of Democratic Lawyers)

A.I.J.E. Association des industries du jute européennes (Association of European Jute Industries)

A.I.L. Air Intelligence Liaison
Associate of the Institute of Linguists
Association internationale de limnologie théorique et appliquée (International Association of Theoretical and Applied Limnology)

A.I.L.A. Associate of the Institute of Landscape Architects

A.I.L.C. Association internationale de littérature comparée (International Comparative Literature Association)

A.I.L.O. Air Intelligence Liaison Officer

A.I.Loco.E. Associate of the Institution of Locomotive Engineers

A.I.M. Africa Inland Mission
American Institute of Management
Associate of the Institution of Metallurgists
Association internationale de la mutualité (International Association for Mutual Assistance)
Association of Industrial Machinery Merchants
Australian Inland Mission (Presbyterian)

a.i.m.a. as interest may appear

A.I.Mar.E. Associate of the Institute of Marine Engineers

A.I.M.E. Associate of the Institute of Municipal Entertainment

A.I.Mech.E. Associate of the Institution of Mechanical Engineers

A.I.M.I. Associate of the Institute of the Motor Industry

A.I.M.I.C. Association of Insurance Managers in Industry and Commerce

A.I.Min.E. Associate of the Institution of Mining Engineers

A.I.M.M. Australasian Institute of Mining and Metallurgy
Associate of the Institution of Mining and Metallurgy

A.I.M.O. Association of Industrial Medical Officers

A.I.M.P.A. Association internationale de météorologie et de physique de l'atmosphère (International Association of Meteorology and Atmospheric Physics)

A.I.M.P.E. Australian Institute of Marine and Power Engineers

A.I.M.S. Association for Improvement in the Maternity Services
Association for Improving Moral Standards

A.I.M.T.A. Associate of the Institute of Municipal Treasurers and Accountants

A.I.N.A. Associate of the Institution of Naval Architects (*now* A.R.I.N.A.)

A.I.N.E.C. All-India Newspaper Editors' Conference

A.I.N.P. Association internationale des numismates professionnels (International Association of Professional Numismatists)

A.Inst.B.C.A. Associate of the Institute of Burial and Cremation Administration

A.Inst.C.E. Associate of the Institution of Civil Engineers

A.Inst.Ex.E. Associate of the Institute of Executive Engineers and Officers

A.Inst.H.E. Associate of the Institution of Highway Engineers

A.Inst.M.O. Associate of the Institute of Market Officers

A.Inst.M.S.M. Associate of the Institute of Marketing and Sales Management

A.Inst.P. Associate of the Institute of Physics

A.Inst.P.A. Associate of the Institute of Park Administration

A.I.O.B. Associate of the Institute of Building

A.I.O.C.C. Association internationale d'organisateurs de courses cyclistes (International Association of Organizers of Cycle Competitions)

A.I.O.S.P. Association internationale d'orientation scolaire et professionnelle (International Association for Educational and Vocational Guidance)

A.I.P. American Institute of Physics

A.I.P.A. Associate Member of the Institute of Practitioners in Advertising

Association internationale de psychologie appliquée (International Association of Applied Psychology)

A.I.P.C. Association internationale de prophylaxie de la cécité (International Association for the Prevention of Blindness)

Association internationale des palais des congrès (International Association of Congress Centres)

Association internationale des ponts et charpentes (International Association for Bridge and Structural Engineering)

A.I.P.C.E.E. Association des industries du poisson de la C.E.E. (Assocation of Fish Industries of the E.E.C.)

A.I.P.C.N. Association internationale permanente des congrès de navigation (Permanent International Association of Navigation Congresses)

A.I.P.C.R. Association internationale permanente des congrès de la route (Permanent International Association of Road Congresses)

A.I.P.E. Associate of the Institution of Production Engineers

A.I.P.E.P.O. Association internationale de presse pour l'étude des problèmes *cont.*

d'outre-mer (International Press Association for the Study of Overseas Problems)

A.I.Pet. Associate of the Institute of Petroleum

A.I.P.H. Association internationale des producteurs de l'horticulture (International Association of Horticultural Producers)

A.I.P.H.E. Associate of the Institution of Public Health Engineers

A.I.P.P.I. Association internationale pour la protection de la propriété industrielle (International Association for the Protection of Industrial Property)

A.I.P.S. Association internationale de la presse sportive (International Sporting Press Association)

Association internationale pour le progrès social (International Association for Social Progress)

A.I.Q. Associate of the Institute of Quarrying

A.I.Q.S. Associate of the Institute of Quantity Surveyors

A.I.R. All-India Radio

A.I.R.B.R. Association internationale du registre des bateaux du Rhin (International Association for the Rhine Ships Register)

A.I.R.G. Agency for Intellectual Relief in Germany

A.I.R.H. Association internationale de recherches hydrauliques (International Association of Hydraulic Research)

A.I.R.I. Associate of the Institution of the Rubber Industry

A.I.R.M.A. All-India Radio Manufacturers' Association

AIRPASS Airpass interception radar and pilots attack sight system

A.I.R.T.E. Associate of the Institute of Road Transport Engineers

A.I.S. Anglo-Italian Society

Association internationale de la savonnerie et de la détergence (International Association of the Soap and Detergent Industry)

Association internationale de la soie (International Silk Association)

Association internationale de sociologie (International Sociological Association)

Australian Illawarra Shorthorn

A.I.San.E. Associate of the Institution of Sanitary Engineers (*now* A.I.P.H.E.)

A.I.S.E. Association internationale des sciences économiques (International Economic Association)

A.I.S.I. Associate of the Iron and Steel Institute

A.I.S.J. Association internationale des sciences juridiques (International Association of Legal Science)

A.I.S.M. Association internationale de signalisation maritime (International Association of Lighthouse Authorities)

A.I.S.P.I.T. Association internationale de séismologie et de physique de l'intérieur de la terre (International Association of Seismology and Physics of the Earth's Interior)

A.I.S.S. Association internationale de la sécurité sociale (International Social Security Association)
Association internationale de la science du sol (International Association of Soil Science)

A.I.Struct.E. Associate of the Institution of Structural Engineers

A.I.T. Alliance internationale de tourisme (International Tourist Alliance)
Association of H.M. Inspectors of Taxes
Association of Investment Trusts

A.I.T.A. Association internationale du théâtre d'amateurs (International Amateur Theatre Association)

A.I.T.I.T. Association internationale de la teinture et de l'impression textile (International Association of Textile Dyers and Printers)

A.I.U. Alliance israélite universelle
Association internationale des universités (International Association of Universities)

A.I.V. Association internationale de volcanologie (International Association of Volcanology)
Method of preserving fodder (*named after its inventor Prof. A. I. Virtanen*)

A.I.V.M. Association internationale pour les voiles minces (International Association for Shell Structures)

A.I.W.C. All-India Women's Conference

A.I.W.E. Associate of the Institution of Water Engineers

A.I.W.M.A. Associate Member of the Institute of Weights and Measures Administration

A.I.W.O. Agudas Israel World Organization

A.J.A. Amateur Judo Association of Great Britain
Anglo-Jewish Association
Australian Journalists' Association

A.J.A.G. Assistant Judge Advocate General

A.J.C. Australian Jockey Club

AJEX Association of Jewish Ex-Service Men and Women

A.J.P.M. Ad Jesum per Mariam (To Jesus through Mary)

A.J.R. Association of Jewish Refugees
Australian Jurist Reports, Victoria

A.J.Y. Association for Jewish Youth

A.K. Above Knee

Akad. Akademie

A.K.C. American Kennel Club
Associate of King's College, London

A.K.C.(N.S.) Associate of the University of King's College, Nova Scotia

Akc.Spal. Akciova společnost (joint stock company)

A.K.E.L. Anorthotion Komma Ergazomanou Laou (Reform Party of the Working People, Cyprus)

A.K.O.E. Anti-killer Organization of Expatriates (Cyprus)

Aktb. Aktiebolaget (Joint stock company)

Al Aluminium

A.L. Admiralty Letter
American Legion
Anno Lucis (in the year of Light)
Army List
Autograph Letter

a.l. après livraison (after delivery)
autograph letter

Ala. Alabama

A.L.A. Air Licensing Authority
American Library Association
Associate of the Library Association

A.L.A.I. Association littéraire et artistique internationale (International Literary and Artistic Association)

A.L.A.L.E. Association latino-américaine de libre échange (Latin-American Free Trade Association)

A.L.A.M. Associate of the London Academy of Music

A.L.A.R. Association of Light Alloy Refiners and Smelters

Alas. Alaska

A.L.A.S. Associate of the Land Agents' Society

Alb. Albania(n)

Alba. Alberta

A.L.B.E.S. Association of London Borough Engineers and Surveyors

A.L.B.M. Air-launched Ballistic Missile

alc alcohol

A.L.C. Agricultural Land Commission
Associate of Loughborough College of Advanced Technology

a.l.c. à la carte

ALCAN Aluminum Company of Canada

A.L.C.D. Associate of the London College of Divinity

Alch. Alchemy

A.L.C.L. Association of London Chief Librarians

A.L.C.M. Associate of the London College of Music

Ald. Alderman

ALDEV African Land Development

A.L.F. Automatic Letter Facer

ALFSEA Allied Land Forces South-East Asia

Alg. Algebra

A.L.G. Advanced Landing Ground

A.L.G.E.S. Association of Local Government Engineers and Surveyors

A.L.G.F.O. Association of Local Government Financial Officers

A.L.H.E. Association of London Housing Estates

A.L.I. American Library Institute

A.L.J.R. Australian Law Journal Reports

Al.-L. Alsace-Lorraine
A.L.L. Association for Latin Liturgy
Alleg. Allegory
All H. All Hallows
allo. allegro (sprightly
All S. All Souls
All SS. All Saints
A.L.M. Artium Liberalium Magister (Master of the Liberal Arts)
A.L.M.A. Association of London Model Agencies
A.L.M.T. Association of London Master Tailors
A.L.O. Air Liaison Officer
A.L.O.E. A Lady of England (pseudonym of Charlotte M. Tucker)
A.L.P. Association of Little Presses
Australian Labour Party
A.L.P.O. Association of Land and Property Owners
Association of Lunar and Planetary Observers
alr. aliter (otherwise)
A.L.R. Aden Law Reports
Argus Law Reports, Victoria
A.L.R.A. Abortion Law Reform Association
A.L.R.C. Anti-Locust Research Centre
A.L.S. Agricultural Land Service
Associate of the Linnean Society of London
a.l.s. autograph letter signed
Alt. Alternate
Altesse (Highness)
Alto (high)
alt. alternating
altitude
Alta. Alberta
alt.dieb. alternis diebus (on alternate days)
alter. alteration
alt. hor. alternis horis (every two hours)
alt. noc. alternis noctibus (every other night)
A.L.T.P.R. Association of London Theatre Press Representatives
A.L.T.U. Association of Liberal Trade Unionists
alum. aluminium
alumnus
Am Americium
Am. America(n)
Ammeter
Ammunition
A.M. Air Mail
Air Marshal
Air Ministry
Albert Medal
Anno Mundi (in the year of the world)
Annus Mirabilis (1660, the Restoration of Charles II)
Army Manual
Artium Magister (Master of Arts)
Assistant Manager
Associate Member
Ave Maria (Hail Mary)
A.-M. Alpes-Maritimes
a.m. amplitude modulation
ante meridiem (before noon)
A.M.A. Accumulator Makers' Association *cont.*

Against Medical Advice
American Medical Association
Associate of the Museums Association
Auckland Mathematical Association
Australian Medical Association Incorporated Association of Assistant Masters in Secondary Schools
A.M.A.B. Army Medical Advisory Board
A.L.T. Association of Law Teachers
A.L.T.M. Association of Lifting Tackle Manufacturers
A.M.A. Abstaining Motorists' Association
Adhesive Manufacturers' Association
Australian Musical Association
A.M.A.I.M.M. Associate Member of the Australasian Institute of Mining and Metallurgy
Amal. Amalgamated
A.M. Am. I.E.E. Associate Member of the American Institute of Electrical Engineers
Amb. Ambassador
Ambulance
A.M.B. Air Ministry Bulletin
A.M.B.A.C. Associate Member of the British Association of Chemists
Amb.Ex. Ambassador Extraordinary
Amb.Ex. & Plen. Ambassador Extraordinary and Minister Plenipotentiary
A.M.B.I.M. Associate Member of the British Institute of Management
A.M.Brit.I.R.E. Associate Member of the British Institution of Radio Engineers (*now* A.M.I.E.R.E.)
A.M.C. Army Medical Corps (*now* R.A.M.C.)
Art Master's Certificate
Associated Motor Cycles
Association of Municipal Corporations
A.M.C.A. Amateur Motor-Cycle Association
Architectural Metal Craftsmen's Association
A.M.C.I.A. Associate Member of the Association of Cost and Industrial Accountants
A.M.C.I.B. Associate Member of the Corporation of Insurance Brokers
A.M.C.L. Association of Metropolitan Chief Librarians
A.M.C.T. Associate of the Manchester College of Science and Technology
am. cur. amicus curiae (a friend of the court)
A.M.D. Admiralty Machinery Depot
A.M.D.B. Agricultural Machinery Development Board
A.M.D.E.A. Associated Manufacturers of Domestic Electrical Appliances
A.M.D.E.C. Agricultural Marketing Development Executive Committee
Associated Manufacturers of Domestic Electric Cookers

A.M.I.Plant E.

A.M.D.G. Ad majorem Dei gloriam (For the greater glory of God)
amdt. amendment
A.M.E. African Methodist Episcopal
A.M.E.C.U.S.D. Association of Manufacturers and Exporters of Concentrated and Unconcentrated Soft Drinks
A.M.E.E. Association of Managerial Electrical Executives
A.M.E.I.C. Associate Member of the Engineering Institute of Canada
A.M.E.M. African Methodist Episcopal Mission
A.M.E.M.E. Association of Mining, Electrical and Mechanical Engineers
A.M.E.N.D. Association for Relatives of the Mentally, Emotionally and and Nervously Disturbed
amendt. amendment
Amer. America(n)
A.M.E.S. Air Ministry Experimental Station
A.Met. Associate of Metallurgy
A.M.E.W.A. Associated Manufacturers of Electric Wiring Accessories
A.M.E.Z.C. African Methodist Episcopal Zion Church
A.M.F. Australian Military Force(s)
amg. among
A.M.G. Allied Military Government Audio Manufacturers' Group
A.M.G.O. Assistant Master-General of Ordnance
A.M.G.O.T. Allied Military Government of Occupied Territory (*later* A.M.G.*)
A.M.H.C.I. Associate Member of the Hotel and Catering Institute
A.M.I. Ancient Monuments Inspectorate
　　Association Montessori internationale (International Montessori Association)
A.M.I.A. Associate Member of the Institute of Almoners
A.M.I.A.M.A. Associate Member of the Incorporated Advertising Managers' Association
A.M.I.Brit.F. Associate Member of the Institute of British Foundrymen
A.M.I.C.E. Associate Member of the Institution of Civil Engineers
A.M.I.C.E.I. Associate Member of the Institution of Civil Engineers of Ireland
A.M.I.Chem.E. Associate Member of the Institution of Chemical Engineers
A.M.I.E.A. Associate Member of the Institution of Engineers, Australia
A.M.I.E.D. Associate Member of the Institution of Engineering Designers
A.M.I.E.E. Associate Member of the Institution of Electrical Engineers
A.M.I.E.I. Associate Member of the Institution of Engineering Inspection
A.M.I.E.(Ind.) Associate Member of the Institution of Engineers, India
A.M.I.E.R.E. Associate Member of the Institution of Electronic and Radio Engineers

A.M.I.Fire E. Associate Member of the Institution of Fire Engineers
A.M.I.Gas E. Associate Member of the Institution of Gas Engineers
A.M.I.H. Associate Member of the Institute of Housing
A.M.I.H.V.E. Associate Member of the Institution of Heating and Ventilating Engineers
A.M.I.I. Association of Musical Instrument Industries
A.M.I.Loco.E. Associate Member of the Institution of Locomotive Engineers
A.M.I.Mar.E. Associate Member of the Institute of Marine Engineers
A.M.I.M.E. Associate Member of the Institution of Mining Engineers
A.M.I.Mech.E. Associate Member of the Institution of Mechanical Engineers
A.M.I.M.I. Associate Member of the Institute of the Motor Industry
A.M.I.Min.E. Associate Member of the Institution of Mining Engineers
A.M.I.M.M. Associate Member of the Institution of Mining and Metallurgy
A.M.I.Mun.E. Associate Member of the Institution of Municipal Engineers
A.Minls.Tech. Associate in Minerals Technology
A.M.Inst.B.&C.A. Associate Member of the Institute of Burial and Cremation Administration
A.M.Inst.B.E. Associate Member of the Institution of British Engineers
A.M.Inst.C.E. Associate Member of the Institution of Civil Engineers (*now* A.M.I.C.E.)
Am.Inst.E.E. American Institute of Electrical Engineers
A.M.Inst.H.E. Associate Member of the Institution of Highway Engineers
A.M.Inst.P.C. Associate Member of the Institute of Public Cleansing
A.M.Inst.R. Associate Member of the Institute of Refrigeration
A.M.Inst.T. Associate Member of the Institute of Transport
A.M.Inst.T.E. Associate Member of the Institution of Transport Engineers
A.M.I.Nuc.E. Associate Member of the Institution of Nuclear Engineers
A.M.I.O.B. Associate Member of the Institute of Building
A.M.I.O.P. Associate Member of the Institute of Printing
A.M.I.P.A. Associate Member of the Institute of Park Administration
　　Associate Member of the Institute of Practitioners in Advertising
A.M.I.P.E. Associate Member of the Institution of Production Engineers
A.M.I.P.H.E. Associate Member of the Institution of Public Health Engineers
A.M.I.PlantE. Associate Member of the Institution of Plant Engineers

17

A.M.I.Prod.E. Associate Member of the Institution of Production Engineers

A.M.I.Ptg.M. Associate Member of the Institute of Printing Management

A.M.I.San.E. Associate Member of the Institution of Sanitary Engineers (*now* A.M.I.P.H.E.)

A.M.I.Struct.E. Associate Member of the Institution of Structural Engineers

A.M.I.T.A. Associate Member of the Industrial Transport Association

A.M.I.W.E. Associate Member of the Institution of Water Engineers

A.M.I.W.M. Associate Member of the Institution of Works Managers

A.M.J. Assemblée mondiale de la jeunesse (World Assembly of Youth)

A.M.L. Admiralty Materials Laboratory
Applied Mathematics Laboratory (New Zealand)
Association of Master Lightermen and Barge Owners

a.m.l. amplitude modulation with noise limiter

A.M.M. Association médicale mondiale (World Medical Association)
Association of Manipulative Medicine

A.M.M.I. American Merchant Marine Institute

ammo. ammunition

amn. ammunition

A.M.N.Z.I.E. Associate Member of the New Zealand Institution of Engineers

A.M.O. Air Ministry Order
Area Milk Officer

A.M.O.R.C. Ancient Mystical Order Rosae Crucis (Rosicrucian Order)

AMP adenosine monophosphate

Amp. Amplitude

amp. amperage
ampère

A.M.P. Advanced Management Programme
Air Member for Personnel (Air Council)
Associated Master Plumbers and Domestic Engineers
Association of Multiracial Playgroups
Australian Mutual Provident Society

A.M.P.A. Agricultural Machine Parts Association
Associate of the Master Photographers Association of Great Britain

A.M.P.A.S. Academy of Motion Picture Arts and Sciences (U.S.)

amph. amphibian

Amp.-hr. Ampère-hour

A.M.P.M. Association of Malt Products Manufacturers

A.M.P.S.S. Advanced Manned Precision Strike System

A.M.Q. American Medical Qualification

A.M.R. Atlantic Missile Range)

A.M.R.A. Accessory Manufacturers' Racing Association

A.M.R.I.N.A. Associate Member of the Royal Institution of Naval Architects

Amrit. Amritsar

A.M.R.O. Association of Medical Record Officers

A.M.R.S. Air Ministry Radio Station

A.M.R.T.S. Associate Member of the Royal Television Society

A.M.S. Ancient Monuments Society
Army Map Service
Army Medical Services
Army Medical Staff
Assistant Military Secretary
Association of Medical Secretaries
Association of Metal Sprayers
Assurance Medical Society
Australian Medical Services

A.M.S.E. Associate Member of the Society of Engineers
Association of Media Sales Executives

A.M.S.E.F. Anti-mine-sweeping explosive float

A.M.S.G.A. Association of Manufacturers and Suppliers for the Graphic Arts

A.M.S.H. Association for Moral and Social Hygiene

A.M.S.O. Air Member for Supply and Organisation (Air Council)
Association of Market Survey Organisations

A.M.S.S.F.G. Association of Manufacturers of Small Switch and Fuse Gear

Amst. Amsterdam

amt. amount

A.M.T. Academy of Medicine, Toronto
Air Mail Transfer
Air Member for Training (Air Council)
Association of Marine Traders

A.M.T.C. Academic Member of the Trinity College of Music
Art Master's Teaching Certificate

A.M.T.D.A. Agricultural Machinery and Tractor Dealers' Association

A.M.T.D.S. Agricultural Machinery Training Development Society

A.M.T.P.I. Associate Member of the Town Planning Institute

A.M.U. Association of Master Upholsterers
Atomic Mass Unit

A.M.U.A. Associate of Music, University of Adelaide

A.Mus. Associate in Music

A.M.V. Association mondiale vétérinaire (World Veterinary Association)

A.M.V.A.P. Associated Manufacturers of Veterinary and Agricultural Products

AMVETS American Veterans of World War II and Korea

A.M.Y. Automatic Monitor of Yarn

An Actinon

an. anno (in the year)

A.N. Ante-natal
A.-N. Anglo-Norman
a.n. above-named
A.N.A. Associate National Academician (U.S.)
    Australian National Airways
    Australian Natives' Association
Anac. Anacreon
anaes. anaesthesia
    anaesthetic
anag. anagram
anal. analogy
    analyse(d)
    analytical
A.N.A.R.E. Australian National Antarctic Research Expedition
Anat. Anatomical
    Anatomy
anc. Ancient
A.N.C. African National Congress
    All Numbers Calling
    Australian Newspapers Council
A.N.C.E. Assemblée des nations captives d'Europe (Assembly of Captive European Nations)
A.N.C.U.N. Australian National Committee for the United Nations
And. Andorra
and. andante (moderately slow)
A.N.E.C. Inst. Associate of the North-East Coast Institution of Engineers and Shipbuilders
A.N.F. Atlantic Nuclear Force
Ang. Anglesey
ang. angle
A.N.G.A.U. Australian New Guinea Administrative Unit
Angl. Angleterre (England)
    Anglican
Anhyd. Anhydrous
a.n.i. atmosphère normale internationale (International normal atmosphere)
Anm. Anmerkung (note)
A.N.M. Admiralty Notices to Mariners
Ann. Annal
ann. annals
    annual
anniv. anniversary
annot. annotation
Annuit. Annuitant
Annunc. Annunciation
anny. annuity
anon. anonymous
A.N.P. Australian Nationalist Party
A.N.P.A. American Newspaper Publishers' Association
anr. another
A.N.R.C. Australian National Research Council
    American National Red Cross
ans. answer
A.N.S. Army Nursing Services
a.n.s. autograph note signed
A.N.S.A. Agenzia Nazionale Stampa Associata (Italian Press Agency)
A.N.S.L. Australian National Standards Laboratory
A.N.S.P. Australian National Socialist Party
Ant. Antigua
    Antrim

ant. antenna
    antiquarian
    antique
    antonym
A.N.T.A. American National Theatre and Academy
    Australian National Travel Association
A.N.T.C. Association of Nursery Training Colleges
anthol. anthology
Anthrop. Anthropology
Antig. Antigua
Antiq. Antiquarian
Ant. Lat. Antique Latin
Ant. Ld. Antique Laid
anton. antonym
A.N.T.O.R. Association of National Tourist Office Representatives in Great Britain
Ant. O.S. Antique Old Style
Antr. Antrim
Ant. Wo. Antique Wove
A.N.U. Australian National University (Canberra)
A.N.Z.A.A.S. Australian and New Zealand Association for the Advancement of Science
A.N.Z.A.C. Australian and New Zealand Army Corps
A.N.Z.A.M. Australia, New Zealand and Malaya
A.N.Z.I.A. Associate of the New Zealand Institute of Architects
A.N.Z.I.C. Associate of the New Zealand Institute of Chemists
A.N.Z.L.A. Associate of the New Zealand Library Association
A.N.Z.U.S. Australia, New Zealand and United States (Treaty)
A.O. Accountant Officer
    Air Ordnance
    Anno Ordinis (In the year of the Order)
    Area Officer
    Army Order
A/o. Account of
A.O.A. Accident Offices Association
    Aerodrome Owners' Association
    Air Officer in charge of Administration
    Association of Official Architects
A.O.B. Antediluvian Order of Buffaloes
A.O.C. Air Officer Commanding
    Anno Orbis Conditi (in the year of the Creation)
    Artists of Chelsea
A.O.C. in C. Air Officer Commanding-in-Chief
A.O.D. Advanced Ordnance Depot
    Ancient Order of Druids
    Army Ordnance Department
A.O.E.R. Army Officers' Emergency Reserve
A.O.F. Ancient Order of Foresters
A. of F. Admiral of the Fleet
A. of S. Academy of Science
A.O.H. Ancient Order of Hibernians
A.o.I. Aims of Industry

a.o.i.v. automatically operated inlet valve
A.O.L. Absent over leave (U.S.)
A.O.P. Association of Optical Practitioners
aor. aorist
A/or and/or
A.O.R.G. Army Operational Research Group
A.O.S. Ancient Order of Shepherds
A.O.S.M. Associate of the Otago School of Mines
A.O.S.S. Americanae Orientalis Societatis Socius (Fellow of the American Oriental Society)
A.O.S.W. Association of Official Shorthandwriters
A.O.T. Association of Occupational Therapists
A.O.U.D. Alliance universelle des ouvriers diamantaires (Univeral Alliance of Diamond Workers)
Ap. Apostle
    April
ap. apparent
A.P. Additional Premium
    Advanced Post
    American Pharmacopoeia
    Andhra Pradesh
    Armour-piercing
    Associated Presbyterian
    Associated Press
    Atomic Power
    Author's Proof
A/P. Additional premium
    Authority to purchase
a.p. above proof
    author's proof
A.P.A. All Parties Administration (Australia)
    American Philological Association
    American Protestant Association
    Army Parachute Association
    Association for the Prevention of Addiction
    Association of Public Analysts
    Australian Physiotherapy Association
A.P.A.C. Association of Patternmakers and Allied Craftsmen
A.P.A.C.L. Asian Peoples' Anti-communist League
A.P.A.E. Association of Public Address Engineers
A.P.A.N.Z. Associate of the Public Accountants of New Zealand
a.-part. alpha particle
Aparts. Apartments
A.P.B.F. Accredited Poultry Breeders' Federation
A.P.B.S. Accredited Poultry Breeding Stations Scheme
A.P.C. Advertising Press Club
    Assistant Principal Chaplain
    Associated Portland Cement
    Automatic Phase Control
    Automatic pitch control
A.P.C.A. Anglo-Polish Catholic Association

A.P.C.A.P.C. Association of Postal Controllers and Assistant Postal Controllers
A.P.C.M. Association of Plastic Cable Makers
A.P.C.N. Anno post Christum natum (in the year after the birth of Christ)
A.P.C.O. Association of Pleasure Craft Operators on inland waterways
A.P.C.O.L. All-Pakistan Confederation of Labour
A.P.D. Administrative Planning Division
    Admiralty Press Division
    Army Pay Department
    Authors' and Printers' Dictionary
A.P.D.E. Association of Painting and Decorating Employers
Ap. Deleg. Apostolic Delegate
A.P.E.R. Association of Publishers' Educational Representatives
A.P.F. Association for the Propagation of the Faith
    Association of Professional Foresters
A.P.F.C. Asia-Pacific Forestry Commission
A.P.F.O. Association of Playing Fields' Officers
A.P.G.L. All Parties Government League (Australia)
aph. aphorism
A.P.H. Anterior Pituitary Hormone
    Sir Alan Herbert
A.P.H.I. Association of Public Health Inspectors
A.P.I. Air-position Indicator
    Associate of the Plastics Institute
    Association phonétique internationale (International Phonetic Association)
A.P.I.S. Army Photographic Intelligence Service
Apl. April
A.P.L.E. Association of Public Lighting Engineers
A.P.M. Assistant Paymaster
    Assistant Provost Marshal
A.P.M.C. Allied Political and Military Commission
A.P.M.G. Assistant Postmaster General
A.P.M.I. Association of Printing Machinery Importers
A.P.N. Agentstvo Pechati Novosti (News Press Agency (Russia))
A.P.O. Acting Pilot Officer
    African People's Organization
    Army Post Office
    Asian Productivity Organization
Apoc. Apocalypse
    Apocrypha(l)
A.P.O.C. Anglia and Prefect Owners' Club
apos. apostrophe
Apost. Del. Apostolic Delegate
Apoth. Apothecary
App. Appeal
    Apostles

app. apparent
appended
appendix
appointed
apprentice
approval
approved
approximate
appar. apparatus
apparent
A.P.P.I.T.A. Australian Pulp and Paper Industries Technical Association
appl. appeal
appellant
applied
applicable
Appr. Apprentice
A.P.P.R. Army Package Power Reactor (U.S.)
appro. approval
approx. approximately
Apptd. Appointed
appurts. appurtenances
Appx. Appendix
Apr. April
A.P.R.A. Air Public Relations Association
A.P.R.C. Anno post Romam conditam (in the year after the building of Rome)
A/Prin. Assistant Principal
A.P.R.L. Association for the Preservation of Rural Life
A.P.R.S. Association for the Preservation of Rural Scotland
Association of Professional Recording Studios
A.P.S. Aborigines' Protection Society (Australia)
American Peace Society
American Physical Society
American Protestant Society
Army Postal Services
Assistant Private Secretary
Associate of the Pharmaceutical Society of Great Britain
Associate of the Philosophical Society of England
a.p.s. autograph poem signed
A.P.S.A. Association for Point of Sale Advertising
Australian Political Studies Association
A.P.S.L. Acting Paymaster Sub-Lieutenant
A.P.S.S. Army Printing and Stationery Services
A.P.S.W. Association of Psychiatric Social Workers
A.P.T. Advanced passenger train
Association of Printing Technologists
Association of Private Traders
A.P.T.C. Army Physical Training Corps
A.P.T.I. Association of Principals of Technical Institutions
Apts. Apartments
A.P.T.U. African Postal and Telecommunications Union
Association of Public Transport Users

A.P.U. Arab Postal Union
Auxiliary Power Unit
A.P.U.C. Association for Promoting the Unity of Christendom
A.P.W.A. All Pakistan Women's Association
aq. aqua (water)
A.Q. Accomplishment *or* Achievement Quotient
aq. bull. aqua bulliens (boiling water)
A.Q.C. Associate of Queen's College, London
aq. cal. aqua calida (hot water)
aq. com. aqua communis (tap water)
aq. dest. aqua destillata (distilled water)
aq. ferv. aqua fervida (hot water)
aq. fluv. aqua fluvialis (river water)
aq. font. aqua fontana (spring water)
aq. gel. aqua gelida (cold water)
aq. mar. aqua marina (sea water)
A.Q.M.G. Assistant Quartermaster-General
aq. niv. aqua nivalis (snow water)
aq. pluv. aqua pluvialis (rain water)
aq. pur. aqua pura (pure water)
aq. tep. aqua tepida (tepid water)
Ar Argon
Ar. Arabia
ar. arrive
A.R. Accomplishment *or* Achievement Ratio
Advice of Receipt
Altesse Royale (Royal Highness)
Anno Regni (in the year of the reign)
Annual Register
Annual Return
Assistant Resident
Associated-Rediffusion
Augmented Roman (alphabet)
A/r. all risks
A.R.A. Aerial Ropeways Association
Aircraft Research Association
Amateur Rowing Association
Army Rifle Association
Asphalt Roads Association
Associate of the Royal Academy
Association of River Authorities
Arab. Arabia(n)
A.R.A.C. Associate of the Royal Agricultural College
Arach. Arachnology
A.R.A.C.I. Associate of the Royal Australian Chemical Institute
A.R.A.D. Associate of the Royal Academy of Dancing
A.R.Ae.S. Associate of the Royal Aeronautical Society
A.R.A.I.A. Associate of the Royal Australian Institute of Architects
Aram. Aramaic
A.R.A.M. Associate of the Royal Academy of Music
A.R.A.N. Association for the Reduction of Aircraft Noise
A.R.A.S. Associate of the Royal Astronomical Society
Arb. Arbitrator
arb. arbiter
A.R.B. Air Registration Board
Air Research Bureau

A.R.B.A. Associate of the Royal Society of British Artists
A.R.B.E. Académie Royale des Beaux-Arts, École Supérieure des Arts Décoratifs et École Supérieure d'Architecture de Bruxelles (Brussels Royal Academy of Fine Arts)
A.R.B.M. Association of Radio Battery Manufacturers
Arbor. Arboriculture
A.R.B.S. Associate of the Royal Society of British Sculptors
A.R.C. Aeronautical Research Council
    Agricultural Research Council
    Anthropological Research Club
    Arthritis and Rheumatism Council
    Asthma Research Council
    Automatic Relay Calculator
A.R.C.A. Associate of the Royal Canadian Academy of Arts
    Associate of the Royal College of Art
A.R. Cam. A. Associate of the Royal Cambrian Academy
A.R.C.E. Academical Rank of Civil Engineers
Arch. Archdeacon
    Archipelago
    Architecture
arch. archaic
    archery
    architect
ARCH Articulated Computer Hierarchy
Archaeol. Archaeological
    Archaeologist
    Archaeology
Archbp. Archbishop
Archd. Archdeacon(ry)
    Archduke
Archdioc. Archdiocese
Archt. Architect
A.R.C.M. Associate of the Royal College of Music
A.R.C.O. Associate of the Royal College of Organists
A.R.C.O.(CHM) Associate of the Royal College of Organists (Diploma of Choir Master)
ARCOS Anglo-Russian Co-operative Society
A.R.C.R.L. Agricultural Research Council Radiobiological Laboratory
A.R.C.S. Associate of the Royal College of Science
    Associate of the Royal College of Surgeons of England
    Australian Red Cross Society
A.R.C. Sc. Associate of the Royal College of Science
A.R.C.S.T. Associate of the Royal College of Science and Technology (Glasgow)
A.R.C.U.K. Architects' Registration Council of the United Kingdom
A.R.C.V.S. Associate of the Royal College of Veterinary Surgeons
A.R.D. Armament Research Department
A.R.D.C. Air Research and Development Command (U.S.)

A.R.D.C.S. Association of Rural District Council Surveyors
A.R.D.E. Armament Research and Development Establishment
A.R.D.I. Association of Registered Driving Instructors
A.R.E. Associate of the Royal Society of Painter-Etchers and Engravers
    Association for Religious Education
A.R.E.E. Admiralty Regional Electrical Engineer
A.R.E.L.S. Association of Recognised English Language Schools
A.R.F. Advertising Research Foundation
    Aid to Russia Fund
Arg Argentum
Arg. Argent
    Argentina
    Argyll(shire)
A.R.H. Ammunition Railhead
A.R.H.A. Associate of the Royal Hibernian Academy of Painting, Sculpture and Architecture
A.R.I. Aircraft Research Association
A.R.I.B.A. Associate of the Royal Institute of British Archdects
A.R.I.C. Associate of the Royal Institute of Chemistry
A.R.I.C.S. Professional Associate of the Royal Institution of Chartered Surveyors
A.R.I.N.A. Associate of the Royal Institution of Naval Architects
A.R.I.P.H.H. Associate of the Royal Institute of Public Health and Hygiene
Arist. Aristotle
Aristoph. Aristophanes
Arith. Arithmetic(al)
Ariz. Arizona
Ark. Arkansas
A.R.L. Admiralty Research Laboratory
    Aeronautical Research Laboratory
Arm. Armagh
    Armenia(n)
Ar.M. Architecturae Magister (Master of Architecture)
A.R.M. Alliance réformée mondiale (Alliance of the Reformed Churches Throughout the World Holding the Presbyterian Order)
A.R.M.C.M. Associate of the Royal Manchester College of Music
Armd. Armoured
Armid. Armidale
A.R.M.I.T. Associate of the Royal Melbourne Institute of Technology
A.R.M.S. Associate of the Royal Society of Miniature Painters, Sculptors and Gravers
    Association of Representatives and Marketing Salesmen
A.R.N.O. Association of Retired Naval Officers
A.R.(N.S.W.) Industrial Arbitration Reports, New South Wales

A.R.O. Army Routine Order
Asian Relations Organisation (India)
Associate Member of the Register of Osteopaths
A.R.O.-I.C.F.T.U. Asian Regional Organization - International Confederation of Free Trade Unions
A.R.P. Air-Raid Precautions
Ammunition Refilling Point
Associated Reformed Presbyterian
Australian Republican Party
A.R.P.A. Advanced Research Projects Agency (U.S.)
A.R.P.I.Co. Air Raid Protection Institute Company
A.R.P.O. Association of Resort Publicity Officers
A.R.P.S. Associate of the Royal Photographic Society of Great Britain
Association of Railway Preservation Societies
arr. arrange(d)
arrive(d)
A.R.R. Anno Regni Regis *or* Reginae (in the year of the king's *or* queen's reign)
Association for Radiation Research
A.R.R.C. Associate of the Royal Red Cross
Arrond. Arrondissement (administrative district)
A.R.S. Anno Reparatae Salutis (in the year of our redemption)
Army Radio School
A.R.S.A. Associate of the Royal Scottish Academy
Associate of the Royal Society of Arts
A.R.San.I. Associate of the Royal Sanitary Institute (*now* A.R.S.H.)
A.R.S.D. Association of Road Surface Dressing Contractors
A.R.S.H. Associate of the Royal Society for the Promotion of Health
A.R.S.L. Associate of the Royal Society of Literature of the United Kingdom
A.R.S.M. Associate of the Royal School of Mines
Art. Artemis
Artificer
art. article
artificial
artist
A.R.T.C. Air Route Traffic Control
Associate of the Royal Technical College, Glasgow (*now* A.R.C.S.T.)
Artif. Artificer
Art. Pf. Artist's Proof
arts. articles
A.R.T.S.M. Association of Road Traffic Sign Makers
A.R.V. American (Standard) Revised Version (Bible)
A.R.V.A. Associate of the Rating and Valuation Association
A.R.V.I.A. Associate of the Royal Victorian Institute of Architects

A.R.V.N. Army of the Republic of Vietnam
A.R.W.S. Associate of the Royal Society of Painters in Water Colours
As Arsenic
As. Asia
A.S. Academy of Science(s)
Account Sales
Admiral Superintendent
Air Staff
Anno Salvatoris (in the year of the Saviour)
Assistant Secretary
Assistant Surgeon
Association of Surgeons of Great Britain and Ireland
A.-S. Anglo-Saxon
A/S Account Sales
After Sight
Alongside
Anti-submarine
A.S.A. Advertising Standards Authority
Amateur Swimming Association
American Standards Association
American Statistical Association
Atomic Scientists Association
A.S.A.A. Associate of the Society of Incorporated Accountants and Auditors
A.S.A.B. Association for the Study of Animal Behaviour
A.S.A.L.A. Associate of the South African Library Association
A.S.A.M. Associate of the Society of Art Masters
a.s.a.p. as soon as possible
A.S.A.U.K. African Studies Association of the United Kingdom
asb. asbestos
A.S.B. Africaans Studentebond (South African Union of Students)
A.Sc. Associate in Science
A.S.C. Air Service Command (U.S.)
American Society of Cinematographers
Anglo-Soviet Committee
Army Service Corps (*later* R.A.S.C. *now* R.C.T.)
Asian Socialist Conference
Association of Superannuation Committees
A.S.C.A.P. American Society of Composers, Authors and Publishers
A.S.C.B. Army Sports Control Board
A.S.C.C. Association of Scottish Climbing Clubs
A.S.C.E. American Society of Civil Engineers
Ascen. Ascension
A.S.C.M. Association of Ships' Compositions Manufacturers
Association of steel conduit Manufacturers
Association of Steel Conduit Movement
ASCOFAM Association mondiale de lutte contre la faim (World Association for the Struggle Against Hunger)
ASCOMACE Association des constructeurs de machines à coudre de la C.E.E. (Association of Sewing Machine Manufacturers of the E.E.C.)

A.Sc.W. Association of Scientific Workers (*now*) A.S.T.M.S.)
A.S.D. Admiralty Salvage Department
Armament Supply Department
a/s. de aux soins de (care of)
A.S.D.I.C. Allied Submarine Detection Investigation Committee
A.S.D.M. Association of Steel Drum Manufacturers
A.S.D.S.F.B. Association of Scottish District Salmon Fishery Boards
A.S.E. Admiralty Signal Establishment
American Stock Exchange
Army School of Education
Association for Science Education (*formerly* A.W.S.T.)
Associate of the Society of Engineers
Association for Special Education
Astronomical Society of Edinburgh
a.s.e. air standard efficiency
A.S.E.A. Association of South East Asia
A.S.E.A.N. Association of South East Asian Nations
A.S.E.D. Army School of Education and Depot
A.S.E.E. Association of Supervising Electrical Engineers
Association of Supervisory and Executive Engineers
A.S.F. Associate of the Institute of Shipping and Forwarding Agents
ASFALEC Association des fabricants de laits de conserve des pays de la C.E.E. (Association of Powdered Milk Manufacturers of the E.E.C.)
A.S.F.P. Association of Specialized Film Producers
A.S.G. Acting *or* Assistant Secretary-General
A.S.G.B. Adlerian Society of Great Britain
Anthroposophical Society in Great Britain
A.S.G.B.I. Anatomical Society of Grea Britain and Ireland
asgd. assigned
ashp. airship
A.S.I. Air Speed Indicator
Association soroptimiste internationale (Soroptimist International Association)
Augmented Spark Igniter (Rocketry)
A.S.I.A. Airlines Staff International Association
A.S.I.C.A. Association internationale pour le calcul analogique (International Association for Analogue Computation)
A.S.I.F. Amateur Swimming International Federation
A.S.I.F.A. Association Internationale du Film d'animation (International Animated Film Association)
A.S.L. Acting Sub-Lieutenant
Advanced Student in Law
Architectural Society of Liverpool

A.S.L.E.C. Association of Street Lighting Erection Contractors
A.S.L.E.F. Associated Society of Locomotive Engineers and Firemen
A.S.L.I.B. Association of Special Libraries and Information Bureaux
A.S.L.O. Australian Scientific Liaison Office
A.S.L.P. Amalgamated Society of Lithographic Printers
A.S.L.W. Amalgamated Society of Leather Workers
A.S.M. Acting Sergeant-Major
Air-to-Surface Missile
Assistant Stage-Manager
Assistant Station Master
A.S.M.C. Association of Stores and Materials Controllers
A.S.M.E. American Society of Mechanical Engineers
Association for the Study of Medical Education
As.Mem. Associate Member
A.S.M.P. American Society of Magazine Photographers
A.S.N. Army Service Number
A.S.N.D.E. Associate of the Society of Non-Destructive Examination
A.S.N.E. American Society of Newspaper Editors
A.S.N.E.M.G.E. Association des sociétés nationales européennes et méditerranéennes de gastro-entérologie (Association of National European and Mediterranean Societies for the Study of Gastro-enterology)
A.S.N.H.S. Association of School Natural History Societies
A.S.O. Air Staff Officer
Area Specialist Officer
A.S.P. African Special Project (of the International Union for the Conservation of Nature and Natural Resources)
American Selling Price
a.s.p. accepté sous protêt (accepted under protest)
A.S.P.A. Australian Sugar Producers' Association
A.S.P.A.C. Asia and Pacific Co-operation Council
A.S.P.A.D.S. Associated Sheep, Police and Army Dog Society
A.S.P.C. Association of Swimming Pool Contractors
a.s.p.c. accepté sous protêt pour à compte (accepted under protest for account)
A.S.P.C.A. American Society for the Prevention of Cruelty to Animals
A.S.P.F. Association of Superannuation and Pension Funds
A spol. A spolecnost (and company)
A.S.P.S. African Succulent Plant Society
A.S.R.E. Admiralty Signal and Radar Establishment
A.S.R.S. Amalgamated Society of Railway Servants (*now* N.U.R.)
A/S.R.S. Air-Sea Rescue Service
A.S.R.T. Atlantic Salmon Research Trust
Ass. Assembly
Assessóre (Alderman *or* Assessor)

ass. assistant
A.S.S.A. Astronomical Society of South Australia
Ass. Com.-Gen. Assistant Commissary-General
A.S.S.E.T. Aerothermodynamic-elastic Structural Systems Environmental Tests
Association of Supervisory Staffs, Executives and Technicians (*now* A.S.T.M.S.*)
A.S.S.G.B. Association of Ski Schools in Great Britain
assigt. assignment
assim. assimilated
A.S.S.M. Association of Shopfront Section Manufacturers
assmt. assessment
Assn. Association
Assoc. Associate(d)
Association
Assocd. Associated
Assoc. Eng. Associate of Engineering
Assoc. Met. Associate of Metallurgy
Assocn. Association
Assoc. Sci. Associate in Science
A.S.S.R. Autonomous Soviet Socialist Republic
Asst. Assistant
Ass/t. Assistant
A.S.S.U. American Sunday School Union
ASSUC Association des organisations professionnelles de commerce des sucres pour les pays de la C.E.E. (Association of Sugar Trade Organizations for the E.E.C. Countries)
assy. assembly
Assyr. Assyrian
A.S.T. Air Service Training
Astronomical Society of Tasmania
A.S.T.A. American Society of Travel Agents
Association of Short-Circuit Testing Authorities
Auckland Science Teachers Association (New Zealand)
A.S.T.C. Associate of the Sydney Technical College
A.S.T.I. Association of Secondary Teachers, Ireland
A.S.T.I.A. Armed Services Technical Information Agency (U.S.)
A.S.T.M. American Society for Testing and Materials
Association of Sanitary Towel Manufacturers
A.S.T.M.S. Association of Scientific, Technical and Managerial Staffs
A.S.T.O.R. Anti-submarine Torpedo Ordnance Rocket
Astro. Astronautics
A.S.T.R.O. Air Space Travel Research Organisation (U.S.)
Astrol. Astrology
Astron. Astronomy
astrophys. astrophysical
Ast.T. Astronomical Time
A.S.T.U.C. Anglo-Soviet Trades Union Committee

A.S.U. Arab Socialist Union
A.S.U.A. Amateur Swimming Union of the Americas
A.S.V. American Standard Version (Bible)
A.S.V.A. Associate of the Incorporated Society of Valuers and Auctioneers
A.S.W. Amalgamated Society of Woodworkers
Anti-submarine Work
Anti-submarine Warfare
Association of Scientific Workers
Association of Social Workers
A.S.W.B. Association of Solid Woven Belting Manufacturers
A.S.W.D. and K.W. Amalgamated Society of Wire Drawers and Kindred Workers
A.S.W.D.U. Air Sea Warfare Development Unit
A.S.W.M. Amalgamated Society of Woodcutting Machinists
Asyl. Asylum
At Astatine
at. atomic
A.T. Achievement Test
Altes Testament (Old Testament)
Anti-Tank
Apparent Time
A/T. American Terms
A.t. Atlantic time
A.T.A. Air Transport Association
Air Transport Auxiliary
Amusement Trades' Association
Animal Technicians' Association
Atlantic Treaty Association
A.T.A.C. Air Transport Advisory Council
A.T.A.E. Association of Tutors in Adult Education
A.T.A.F. Allied Tactical Air Force
A.T.A.M. Association for Teaching Aids in Mathematics
A.T.A.R. Anti-tank Aircraft Rocket
A.T.A.S. Air Transport Auxiliary Service
A.T.B. Aeration Test Burner
A.T.C. Air Traffic Control
Air Training Corps
Annotated Tax Cases
A.T.C.C. Air Traffic Control Centre
A.T.C.D.E. Association of Teachers in Colleges and Departments of Education
A.T.C.E.U. Air Traffic Control Experimental Unit
atchd. attached
A.T.C.L. Associate of the Trinity College of Music, London
A.T.C.O. Air Traffic Control Officer
A.T.D. Art Teacher's Diploma
Association of Tar Distillers
Australian Tax Decisions
A.T.D.S. Association of Teachers of Domestic Science
A.T.E. Automatic Telephone and Electric Company
A.T.E.C. Air Transport Electronics Council

A.T.F.G.F. Association of Toy and Fancy Goods Factors
A.T.F.S. Association of Track and Field Statisticians
Ath. Athabasca
Athletic(s)
Athen. Athenian
A.T.I. Air Technical Intelligence
Associate of the Textile Institute
Association of Technical Institutions
A.T.I.B.T. Association technique internationale des bois tropicaux (International Technical Tropical Timber Association)
A.Tk. Anti-tank
Atl. Atlantic
A.T.L.B. Air Transport Licensing Board
atm. atmosphere
atmospheric
A.T.M. Air Training Memorandum
Anti-tank Missile
Association of Teachers of Management
Association of Teachers of Mathematics
A.T.M.A. Adhesive Tape Manufacturers' Association
A.T.N.A. Australasian Trained Nurses' Association
At.No. Atomic Number
A.T.O. African Telecommunications Union
Area Training Organisation
Assisted Take-off
a.t.o. Qualified on an Ammunition Technical Officers' Course at the School of Ammunition
A. to A. Air-to-Air
A.T.O.A. Air Taxi Operators Association
ATP Adenosine triphosphate
A.T.P. Air Technical Publications
Associated Theatre Properties
A.T.P.A.S. Association of Teachers of Printing and Allied Subjects
A.T.P.M. Association of Toilet Paper Manufacturers
Association of Touring and Producing Managers
A.tps. Army troops
a.t.r.i.m.a. as their respective interests may appear
A.T.S. American Tract Society
American Travel Service
Animal Tub Sized
Associate of Theological Study
Auxiliary Territorial Service (*now* W.R.A.C.)
a.t.s. anti-tetanic serum
at the suit of
A.T.S.C. Associate of the Tonic Sol-Fa College
att. attached
Att.-Gen. Attorney-General
A.T.T.I. Association of Teachers in Technical Institutions
attrib. attributed
A.T.U.C. African Trade Union Confederation
A.T.V. Associated Television

26

at.wt. atomic weight
A.Typ.I. Association typographique internationale (International Typographic Association)
AU Angstrom Unit
Au Aurum (Gold)
A.U. Actors' Union (U.S.)
All Up (*i.e.* all set in type)
Astronomical Unit
A.U.A. American Unitarian Association
Associate of the University of Adelaide
A.U.A.W. Amalgamated Union of Asphalt Workers
A.U.B.C. Association of Universities of the British Commonwealth
A.U.B.T.W. Amalgamated Union of Building Trade Workers
A.U.C. Anno Urbis Conditae (in the year of the founding of the city)
Association of Underwater Contractors
Aud.-Gen. Auditor-General
A.U.E.W. Amalgamated Union of Engineering and Foundry Workers
A.U.F.W. Amalgamated Union of Foundry Workers of Great Britain and Ireland (*now* A.U.E.W.)
Aug. August
Augustine
aug. augmentative
Augm. Augmentation
A.U.M. Air-to-Underwater Missile
A.U.M.L.A. Australian Universities Modern Language Association
a.u.n. absque ulla nota (with no identifying mark)
Auntie Automatic Unit for National Taxation and Insurance
A.U.O. African Unity Organisation
Aus. Australia
Austria
A.U.S. Army of the United States
Assistant Under-Secretary
A.U.S.A. Association of the U.S. Army
Ausg. Ausgabe (edition)
Aust. Australia
Austria
Austral. Australasia
Aut. Autriche (Austria)
aut. autograph
autòre (author)
A.U.T. Association of University Teachers
A.U.T.E.C. Atlantic Underwater Test Evaluation Centre
auth. authentic
author
authority
authorized
A.U.T.M. Association of Unit Trust Managers
Association of Used Tyre Merchants
auto. automatic
automobile
automotive
autog. autograph
a.u.w. all-up-weight
Aux. Auxiliary

Av. Avenue
Avocat (Barrister)
Avril (April)
av. average
avoirdupois
A.V. Authorised Version
A.v. Atomic volume
a.v. annos vixit (he *or* she lived for . . . years)
a/v. a vista (at sight)
A.V.A. Academy of Visual Arts
Alberta Veterinary Association
Amateur Volleyball Association of Great Britain
Australian Veterinary Association
A.V.A.B. Automatic Vending Association of Britain
A.V.A.S. Association of Voluntary Aided Secondary Schools
A.V.C. Army Veterinary Corps (*now* R.A.V.C.)
Av.Cert. Aviator's Certificate
avdp. avoirdupois
Ave. Avenue
A.V.E. Association of Vermiculite Exfoliators
avg. average
A.V.G. Association of Voluntary Groups
A.V.I. Association of Veterinary Inspectors
Association universelle d'aviculture scientifique (World Poultry Science Association)
Avia. Aviation
A.V.L.A. Audio Visual Language Association
A.V.M. Air Vice-Marshal
A.V.M.A. Automatic Vending Machine Association
A.V.O. Administrative Veterinary Officer
avp. avoirdupois
Avr. Avril (April)
A.V.R. Army Volunteer Reserve
AVRO A. V. Roe and Company
A.V.S. Anti-Vivisection Society
Association of Veterinary Students of Great Britain and Ireland
A.V.T. Added Value Tax
A.V.T.R.W. Association of Veterinary Teachers and Research Workers
Avv. Avvocato (Barrister)
A.W. Armstrong Whitworth
Atomic Warfare
a.w. atomic weight
a/w. airworthy

A.W.A. Amalgamated Weavers' Association
A.W.A.M. Association of West African Merchants
A.W.A.S. Australian Women's Army Service
A.W.B. Agricultural Wages Board
Australian Wool Board
A.W.B.A. American World's Boxing Association
A.W.C. Allied Works Council
Army War College (U.S.)
A.W.D. Air Worthiness Division of the International Civil Aviation Organisation
A.W.G. American Wire Gauge
Art Workers' Guild
A.W.H.A. Australian Women's Home Army
A.W.L. Absent without Leave
Association of Women Launderers
A.W.L.A. Association of Welsh Local Authorities
A.W.L.L.A. All Wales Ladies Lacrosse Association
A.W.M.C. Association of Workers for Maladjusted Children
A.W.N.L. Australian Women's National League
A.W.O. Association of Waterworks Officers
A.W.O.L. Absent without Leave
A.W.R. Association for the Study of the World Refugee Problem
A.W.R.A. Australian Wool Realisation Agency
A.W.R.E. Atomic Weapons Research Establishment
A.W.S. Agricultural Wholesale Society
Automatic Warning System
a.w.s. Qualified at the R.A.F. Flying College *or* the U.S. Air Warfare College
A.W.S.T. Association of Women Science Teachers (*now* A.S.E.)
A.W.U. Atomic Weight Unit
Australian Workers' Union
A.W.W.M. Association of Wholesale Woollen Merchants
ax. axiom
A.Y.L.I. As You Like It (Shakespeare)
A.Y.M. Ancient York Masons
Ayr. Ayrshire
A.Y.R.S. Amateur Yacht Research Society
Az. Azimuth
Azure
Az.Ld. Azure Laid
Az.Wo. Azure Wove

B

B Boron
Soft (pencils
B. Bachelor
Bacillus

Bag
Bale
Baptist
Baron

cont.

B.

Base
Bass
Battle
Baumé
Bay
Beam
Beatus (Blessed)
Belgium
Benediction
Bey
Bible
Bishop
Black
Bloody
Board
Boatswain
Bomber
British
Building
b. bag
bale
ball
base
bath
batsman
bedroom
before
bis (twice
bitch
blue sky
book
born
bound
bowled
breadth
brother
bust
by
bye
Ba Barium
B.A. Bachelor of Arts
Basses-Alpes
Board of Agriculture
Bombe Atomique (Atomic Bomb)
Booksellers' Association of Great
Britain and Ireland
British Academy
British Association for the Advancement of Science
Bronchial Asthma
Buenos Aires
B.A.A. Bachelor of Art and Architecture
Booking Agents' Association of
Great Britain
British Acetylene Association
British Agrochemicals Association
British Alsatian Association
British Archaeological Association
British Astronomical Association
B.A.A.B. British Amateur Athletic Board
B.A.A. & A. British Association of Accountants and Auditors
B.A. & C.C. Billiards Association and Control Council
B.A.A.S. British Association for the Advancement of Science

Bab. Babylonian
B.A.B.S. British Aluminium Building Service
Bac. Baccalaureus (bachelor)
B.A.C. Boiler Availability Committee
British Aircraft Corporation
British Association of Chemists
British Atlantic Committee
British Automatic Company
Business Archives Council
B.A.C.A.H. British Association of Consultants in Agriculture and Horticulture
B.A.C.A.N. British Association for the Control of Aircraft Noise
B.A.C.C. British-American Chamber of Commerce
B.A.C.E. British Association of Corrosion Engineers
Bach. Bachelor
B.A.C.I.E. British Association for Commercial and Industrial Education
Back. Backwardation
B.A.C.M. British Association of Colliery Management
B.A.C.M.A. British Aromatic and Compound Manufacturers' Association
B.A.C.R. British Association for Cancer Research
Bact. Bacteriology
B.A.D. Base Air Depot
British Association of Dermatology
B.A.D.A. British Antique Dealers' Association
B.Admin. Bachelor of Administration
B.A.E. Badminton Association of England
Belfast Association of Engineers
Board of Architectural Education
B.A.E.A. British Actors' Equity Association
B.A.E.F. Belgian-American Educational Foundation
B.A.F.M. British Association of Forensic Medicine
B.A.F.M.A. British and Foreign Maritime Agencies
B.A.F.O. British Air Forces of Occupation
British Army Forces Overseas
B.A.F.R.A. British Aluminium Foil Rollers Association
B.A.F.S.C. British Association of Field and Sports Contractors
B.A.F.T.M. British Association of Fishing Tackle Makers
B.A.G. British Animation Group
B.A.G.A. British Amateur Gymnastic Association
B.A.G.D.A. British Advertising Gift Distributors' Association
B.Agr. Bachelor of Agriculture
B.Agr.(Hort.) Bachelor of Agriculture (Horticulture)
B.Agr.Sc. Bachelor of Agricultural Science
Bah. Bahamas

B.A.H.O. British Association of Helicopter Operators
B.A.H.O.H. British Association of the Hard of Hearing
B.A.H.S. British Agricultural History Society
B.A.I. Baccalaureus Artis Ingeniariae (Bachelor of Engineering)
Book Association of Ireland
B.A.I.E. British Association of Industrial Editors
B.A.(J.) Bachelor of Arts in Journalism
Bal. Balance
Ballarat
B.A.L. British Anti-Lewisite
Ball. Balliol College, Oxford
Ballistics
ball. ballast
B.A.L.P.A. British Air Line Pilots' Association
B.-Alpes Basses-Alpes
bals. balsam
Balt. Baltimore
BALTAP Allied Command Baltic Approaches
B.A.M. Bachelor of Ayurvedic Medicine
Brothers to All Men
B.A.M.A. British Aerosol Manufacturers' Association
British Amsterdam Maritime Agencies
British Army Motoring Association
B.A.M.M. British Association of Manipulative Medicine
B.A.M.M.A.T.A. British Animal Medicine Makers' and Allied Traders' Association
B.A.M.S. Bachelor of Ayurvedic Medicine and Surgery
British Air Mail Society
B.A.M.T.M. British Association of Machine Tool Merchants
B.A.M.W. British Association of Meat Wholesalers
Ban. Bangor
B.A.N. British Association of Neurologists
Banc.Sup. Bancus Superior (King's or Queen's Bench)
b. & b. bed and breakfast
b. & e. beginning and ending
B. & F.B.S. British and Foreign Bible Society
b. & s. brandy and soda
B. & W. Bath and Wells
b. & w. black and white
B. & W.E. Bristol and West of England
B.A.N.S. British Association of Numismatic Societies
B.A.N.Z.A.R.E. British-Australian-New Zealand Antarctic Research Expedition
B.A.O. Baccalaureus Artis Obstetricae (Bachelor of Obstetrics)
Bankruptcy Annulment Order
British American Oil
British Association of Otolaryngologists
B.A.O.F.R. British Association of Overseas Furniture Removers

B.A.O.L.P.E. British Association of Organisers and Lecturers in Physical Education
B.A.O.R. British Army of the Rhine
bap. baptize(d)
b.à.p. billets à payer (bills payable)
B.A.P.A. British Airline Pilots' Association
British Amateur Press Association
BAPCO Bahrain Petroleum Company
B.A.(P.E.) Bachelor of Arts in Physical Education
B.A.P.M. British Association of Physical Medicine
B.A.P.P. British Association of Pig Producers
B.App.Sc. Bachelor of Applied Science
B.A.P.S. British Association of Paediatric Surgeons
British Association of Plastic Surgeons
Bapt. Baptist
B.A.P.T. British Association for Physical Training
Bar. Baruch
bar. barleycorn
barometer
barrel
B.A.R. Book Auction Records
Browning Automatic Rifle
b.à.r. billets à recevoir (bills receivable)
Barb. Barbados
B.A.R.C. British Automobile Racing Club
B.Arch. Bachelor of Architecture
B.Arch. & T.P. Bachelor of Architecture and Town Planning
barg. bargain
B.A.R.M.A. Boiler and Radiator Manufacturers Association
Barn. Barnabas
B.Arp. Bachelier en arpentage (Bachelor of Surveying)
B.A.R.P. British Association of Retired Persons
Barr. Barrister
B.A.R.S. British Association of Residential Settlements
Bart. Baronet
Bartholomew
B.A.R.T.G. British Amateur Radio Teleprinter Group
Bart's St. Bartholomew's Hospital, London
B.A.S. Bachelor in Agricultural Science
British Acoustical Society
British Antarctic Survey
Building Advisory Service
B.A.S.A. British Architectural Students' Association
B.A.S.A.F. British and South Africa Forum
B.A.Sc. Bachelor of Applied Science
B.A.S.E.E.F.A. British Approvals Service for Electrical Equipment in Flammable Atmospheres
B.A.S.E.S. British Anti-Smoking Education Society
B.A.S.F. Badische Anilin und Soda-Fabrik (German Chemical Company)

29

B.A.S.I. British Association of Ski Instructors

B.A.S.L.C. British Association of Sportsground and Landscape Contractors

B.A.S.M.A. Boot and Shoe Manufacturers' Association and Leather Trades Protection Society

B.A.S.M.N. British Association of Sewing Machine Manufacturers

BASOMED Basutoland Socio-Medical Services

B.A.(S.S.) Bachelor of Arts in Social Studies

B.A.S.R.A. British Amateur Scientific Research Association

B.A.S.R.M. British Association of Synthetic Rubber Manufacturers

Bat. Batavia

bat. battalion
battery
battle

B.A.T. British-American Tobacco Company
Bureau de l'assistance technique (Technical Assistance Bureau)

B.A.T.A. Bakery and Allied Traders Association

B.A.(Theol.) Bachelor of Arts in Theology

B.A.T.M.A. Bookbinding and Allied Trades Management Association

B.A.T.O. Balloon Assisted Take-off

B.A.(T.P.) Bachelor of Arts in Town and Country Planning

Batt. Battery

Battn. Battalion

Batty. Battery

B.A.U. British Association Unit

B.A.U.A. Business Aircraft Users' Association

B.A.U.S. British Association of Urological Surgeons

Bav. Bavaria(n)

b.à.v. bon à vue (good at sight i.e. bills etc.)

B.A.W.A. British Amateur Wrestling Association

B.A.W.E. British Association of Women Executives

B.A.W.L.A. British Amateur Weight-Lifters' Association

B.A.W.R.A. British Australian Wool Realization Association

B.A.Y.S. British Association of Young Scientists

BB Double Black (pencils)

bb books

Bb. Bishops

B.B. Bail Bond
Balloon Barrage
Bank Book
Basket Ball
Below Bridges
Bill Book
Blue Book
B'nai B'rith
Boys' Brigade
Branch Bill
Burton and Bitter (Beer)

b.b. ball bearing
bearer bonds
beer barrel

B.B.A. Bachelor of Business Administration
Big Brothers of America
British Bankers' Association
British Bee-keepers' Association
British Bobsleigh Association

BBB Treble Black (pencils)

B.B.B. Bach, Beethoven and Brahms

B.B.B.A. British Bird Breeders' Association

B.B.B.C. British Boxing Board of Control

BBC Bromo-benzyl cyanide

B.B.C. Baseball Club
British Broadcasting Corporation

B.B.C.F. British Bacon Curers' Federation

B.B.C.M. Bandmaster, Bandsman's College of Music

B.B.C.M.A. British Baby Carriage Manufacturers' Association

B.B.C.S. British Beer Mat Collectors Society

B.B.E.A. Brewery and Bottling Engineers Association

B.B.F.C. British Board of Film Censors

B.B.F.O. Bardsey Bird and Field Observatory

B.B.G.A. British Broiler Growers' Association

B.B.I. British Bottlers' Institute
Builders' Benevolent Institution

B.Bibl. Bachelier en bibliothéconomie (Bachelor in Library Science)

B.B.I.R.A. British Baking Industries' Research Association

B.B.K.A. British Bee-keepers' Association

bbl. barrel

B.Bldg. Bachelor of Building

B.Bld.Sc. Bachelor of Building Science

bbls. barrels

B.B.M.A. British Bath Manufacturers' Association
British Brush Manufacturers' Association
British Button Manufacturers' Association
Building Board Manufacturers' Association of Great Britain

B.B.M.R.A. British Brush Manufacturers' Research Association

B.B.M.S. British Battery Makers Society

B.B.O. British Ballet Organisation

B.B.R.S. Blair Bell Research Society

B.B.S. British Biophysical Society
British Bryological Society

B.B.S.A. British Blind and Shutter Association

B.B.S.I. British Boot and Shoe Institution

B.B.S.R. Bermuda Biological Station for Research

B.B.T.A. British Bureau of Television Advertising

correct own entry

B.C. Baccalaureus Chirurgiae (Bachelor of Surgery)
Bad Character
Badminton Club
Bank Clearing
Bankruptcy Court
Basket Ball Club
Battery Commander
Battle Cruiser
Before Christ
Billiards Club
Bills for Collection
Bishop and Confessor
Board of Control
Boating Club
Bomber Command
Borough Council
Bowling Club
Bowls Club
Boxing Club
Boys' Club
Bristol Channel
British Columbia
British Commonwealth
British Council
Budgeted Cost
Building Centre
Burnham Committee

B.C.A. British Carton Association
British Chicken Association
British Chiropractors' Association
British College of Accountancy
British Confectioners' Association
Bureau of Current Affairs

B.C.A.B. Birth Control Advisory Bureau

B.C.A.C. British Conference on Automation and Computation

B.C.A.R. British Civil Airworthiness Requirements
British Council for Aid to Refugees

B.C.A.S. British Compressed Air Society

B.C.C. Birth Control Campaign
British Colour Council
British Council of Churches
Bureau central de compensation (Central Bureau of Compensation, of U.I.C.)

B.C.C.C.U.S. British Commonwealth Chamber of Commerce in the United States

B.C.E.L. British Commonwealth Ex-Services League

B.C.C.F. British Cast Concrete Federation

B.C.C.G. British Cooperative Clinical Group

B.C.D. British Crop Driers, Limited

B.C.D.T.A. British Chemical and Dyestuffs Traders' Association

B.C.E. Bachelor of Chemical Engineering
Bachelor of Civil Engineering
Board of Customs and Excise

B.C.E.C.C. British and Central-European Chamber of Commerce

B.C.F. Battle Cruiser Force
British Chess Federation
British Cycling Federation

B.C.F.A. British-China Friendship Association

B.C.F.G. British Camp Fire Girls

B.C.F.G.A. British Columbia Fruit Growers' Association

B.C.F.K. British Commonwealth Forces in Korea

B.C.F.L. British Czechoslovak Friendship League

B.C.F.S. British Columbia Forestry Society

B.C.F.T.E. British Commonwealth Forest Translation Exchange

B.C.G. Bacillus-Calmette Guérin

B.C.G.A. British Commercial Gas Association
British Cotton Growing Association

Bch. Branch

B.Ch. Baccalaureus Chirurgiae (Bachelor of Surgery)

B.Ch.D. Baccalaureus Chirurgiae Dentalis (Bachelor of Dental Surgery)

B.Ch.E. Bachelor of Chemical Engineering

B.C.H.F.A. British-Canadian Holstein-Friesian Association

B.Chir. Baccalaureus Chirurgiae (Bachelor of Surgery)

B.Chrom. Bachelor of Chromatics

B.C.I.A. British Coking Industry Association
British Columbia Institute of Agrologists

B.C.I.N.A. British Commonwealth International Newsfilm Agency

B.C.I.P.P.A. British Cast Iron Pressure Pipe Association

B.C.I.R.A. British Cast Iron Research Association

B.C.L. Bachelor of Canon Law
Bachelor of Civil Law

B.C.L.M.A. British Columbia Lumber Manufacturers' Association

B.C.M. Blackheath Conservatoire of Music
British Catalogue of Music
British Chess Magazine
British Commercial Monomark
British Consular Mail

B.C.M.A. British Chip Board Manufacturers' Association
British Columbia Medical Association
British Colour Makers' Association
British Council of Maintenance Associations
British Country Music Association

B.C.M.S. Bible Churchmen's Missionary Society

B.C.N. British Commonwealth of Nations

B.C.O.F. British Commonwealth Occupation Force

B.Comm. Bachelor of Commerce

B.Com.Sc. Bachelor of Commercial Science

B.C.P. Book of Common Prayer
B.C.P.A. British Copyright Protection Association
B.C.P.I.T. British Council for the Promotion of International Trade
B.C.P.M.A. British Chemical Plant Manufacturers' Association
B.C.P.O. British Commonwealth Producers' Organization
B.C.R.A. British Ceramic Research Association
British Coke Research Association
B.C.R.C. British Columbia Research Council
B.C.R.D. British Council for the Rehabilitation of the Disabled
B.C.S. Bachelor of Chemical Science
Bachelor of Commercial Science
Battle Cruiser Squadron
Bengal Civil Service
British Cardiac Society
British Cartographic Society
British Ceramic Society
British Computer Society
B.C.S.A. British Constructional Steelwork Association
B.C.S.H. British Committee for Standards in Haematology
B.C.S.O. British Commonwealth of Nations Scientific Liaison Offices
B.C.T. Belfast Chamber of Trade
B.C.T.A. British Canadian Trade Association
British Children's Theatre Association
B.C.T.C. British Ceramic Tile Council
B.C.U. Big Close Up
British Canoe Union
British Commonwealth Union
B.C.U.R.A. British Coal Utilization Research Association
B.C.V.A. British Cattle Veterinary Association
British Columbia Veterinary Association
B.C.W.A. British Cotton Waste Association
B.C.W.M.A. British Clock and Watch Manufacturers' Association
Bd. Band (book *or* volume)
Board
Boulevard
bd. bold
bond
bound
broad
B.D. Bachelor of Divinity
Battle Dress
Bill Discounted
Bishop and Doctor
Bomb Disposal
Boom Defence
Bundesrepublik Deutschland (German Federal Republic)
B/D. Bank Draft
Bar Draft
b.d. bis in die (twice daily
b/d. brought down
B.D.A. Brick Development Association
British Dental Association *cont.*

British Diabetic Association
British Door Association
B.D.B.J. Board of Deputies of British Jews
B.D.C. Bachelier en droit canonique (Bachelor of Canon Law)
Bedford Drivers' Club
Book Development Council
Bureau international de documentation des chemins de fer (International Office of Railway Documentation)
b.d.c. bottom dead centre
B.D.C.C. British Defence Co-ordinating Committee
B.D.D.A. British Deaf and Dumb Association
Bde. Bände (books *or* volumes)
Brigade
B.D.F.A. British Dairy Farmers' Association
bdg. binding
B.D.H. British Drug Houses
B.D.H.A. British Dental Hygienists Association
B.Di. Bachelor of Didactics
B.D.I. Bundesverband der Deutschen Industrie (Federation of German Industries)
b.d.i. bearing deviation indicator
both days included *or* inclusive
B.D.L. British Drama League
bdle(s) bundle(s)
B.D.M. Births, Deaths, Marriages
Bomber Defence Missile
Branch Delegates' Meeting
B.D.M.A. British Disinfectant Manufacturers' Association
B.D.M.A.A. British Direct Mail Advertising Association
Bdmr. Bandmaster
B.D.O. Boom Defence Officer
Bdr. Bombardier
Brigadier
B.D.R.A. British Drag Racing Association
bds. boards
B.D.S. Bachelor of Dental Surgery
Bomb Damage Survey
Bomb Disposal Squad
British Debt Services
British Deer Society
British Display Society
British Driving Society
b.d.s. bis in die sumendus (to be taken twice a day)
B.D.S.A. British Dental Students' Association
B.D.Sc. Bachelor of Dental Science
B.D.S.T. British Double Summer Time
B.D.U. Bomb Disposal Unit
Bdx. Bordeaux
Be Beryllium
Bé. Baumé
be. bezüglich (with reference to)
B.E. Bachelor of Education
Bachelor of Engineering
Bank of England
Borough Engineer
British Element
British Embassy *cont.*

British Empire
Buddhist Era
Building Exhibition

B/E. Bill of Entry
Bill of Exchange

b.e. binding edge

B.E.A. British Egg Association
British East Africa
British Electricity Authority
(*later* C.E.A.)
British Engineers' Association
(*now* B.M.E.F.)
British Esperanto Association
British European Airways

B.E.A.B. British Electric Approvals Board

B.E.A.C. British European Airways Corporation

B.E.A.I.R.E. British Electrical and Allied Industries' Research Association: *see* E.R.A.

B.E.A.M.A. British Electrical and Allied Manufacturers' Association Incorporated

B.E. & C.W.L.C. British Empire and Commonwealth Weight-Lifting Council

bec. because

B.Ec. Bachelor of Economics

B.E.C. British Employers' Confederation (*now* C.B.I.)
Bureau européen du café (European Coffee Bureau)

B.E.C.C. British Empire Cancer Campaign

B.E.C.G.C. British Empire and Commonwealth Games Council

B.E.C.G.F. British Empire and Commonwealth Games Federation

Bech. Bechuanaland

B.E.Chem. Bachelor of Chemical Engineering

B.E.C.M. British Electric Conduit Manufacturers

B.E.C.M.A. British Electro-Ceramic Manufacturers' Association

B.Econ. Bachelor of Economics

B.Econ.(I.A.) Bachelor of Economics in Industrial Administration

B.Econ.(P.A.) Bachelor of Economics in Public Administration

B.E.C.W.L.C. British Empire and Commonwealth Weight Lifting Council

B.Ed. Bachelor of Education

B.E.D.A. British Electrical Development Association

B.Ed.N. Bachelor of Education in Nursing

B.Ed.(P.E.) Bachelor of Education in Physical Education

B.Ed.P.R. Bachelier en éducation physique et récréative (Bachelor of Physical and Recreational Education)

Beds. Bedfordshire

beds. bedrooms

B.Ed.Sc. Bachelor of Educational Science

B.E.E. Bachelor of Electrical Engineering

B.E.E.P. Bureau européen de l'éducation populaire (European Bureau of Adult Education)

bef. before

B.E.F. British Expeditionary Force

beg. beginning

B.E.G. Brush Export Group

B.E.H.A. British Export Houses Association

B.E.I. Banque européenne d'investissement (European Investment Bank)

B.E.I.A. Bureau d'éducation ibéro-américain (Ibero-American Bureau of Education)

Beibl. Beiblatt (Supplement)

beif. beifolgend (enclosed)

B.E.I.S. British Egg Information Service

B.E.J.E. Bureau européen de la jeunesse et de l'enfance (European Bureau for Youth and Childhood)

bel.ex. bel exemplaire (a fine copy of book or engraving)

Belf. Belfast

Belg. Belgian
Belgium

B.E.L.R.A. British Empire Leprosy Relief Association

B.E.M. British Empire Medal
Bug-eyed Monster

B.E.M.A. Bristol and West of England Engineering Manufacturers' Association
British Essence Manufacturers' Association

B.E.M.A.C. British Exports Marketing Advisory Committee

B.E.M.B. British Egg Marketing Board

B.E.M.S. Bakery Equipment Manufacturers Society

B.E.M.S.A. British Eastern Merchant Shippers' Association

Ben. Benedictio (blessing)
Bennet

Bend. Bendigo

B. en Dr. Bachelier en droit (Bachelor of Laws)

Bened. Benedict

Benef. Benefice

BENELUX Belgium, Netherlands, Luxembourg Treaty

Benev. Benevolent

Beng. Bengali

B.Eng. Bachelor of Engineering

B.Eng.Sc. Bachelor of Engineering Science

B.en H. Bachelier en Humanidades (Bachelor of Humanities)

B.Ep.A. British Epilepsy Association

B.E.P.C. British Electrical Power Convention

B.E.P.O. British Experimental Pile O

beq. bequeath(ed)

beqt. bequest

ber. berechnen (compute)

BERCO British Electric Resistance Company

Berks. Berkshire

Berm. Bermuda

Berw. Berwickshire

bes. besonders (especially)

B.E.S. Bank Education Service
Biological Engineering Society
British Ecological Society
B.ès A. Bachelier ès arts (Bachelor of Arts)
B.E.S.A. British Engineering Standards Association (*now* B.S.I.)
British Esperanto Scientific Association
B.E.S.I. Bus Electronic Scanning Indicator
B.ès L. Bachelier ès lettres (Bachelor of Letters)
B.E.S.L. British Empire Service League
B.ès S. Bachelier ès sciences (Bachelor of Science)
Best. Bestellung (order)
bet. between
B.E.T. Baccalauréat en enseignement technique (Bachelor in Technical Teaching)
British Electric Traction Company
B.E.T.A. Business Equipment Trades' Association
B.E.T.A.A. British Export Trade Advertising Association
B.E.T.R.O. British Export Trade Research Organisation
B.E.U. Benelux Economic Union
British Empire Union (*now* B.C.U.)
bev. bevelled
B.e.v. Billion electron volt(s)
bez. bezüglich (respecting)
bezw. beziehungsweise (respectively)
bf. brief
B.F. Banque de France
Belgian francs
British Funds
b.f. bankruptcy fee
base frequency
beer firkin
bloody fool
bold face
bona fide (genuine(ly) *or* sincere(ly))
b/f. brought forward
B.F.A. Bachelor of Fine Arts
British Fellmongers' Association
British Film Academy (*now* S.F.T.A.)
B.F.A.C. British Federation of Aesthetics and Cosmetology
B.F.A.P. British Forces Arabian Peninsular
B.F.B.P.W. British Federation of Business and Professional Women
B.F.B.S. British and Foreign Bible Society
B.F.C. British Falconers' Club
Bureau international du film pour les chemins de fer (International Railway Film Bureau)
B.F.C.A. British Federation of Commodity Associations
B.F.C.S. British Friesian Cattle Society
B.F.E.B.S. British Far Eastern Broadcasting Service
B.F.E.S. British Families Education Service
B.F.F.A. British Film Fund Agency

B.F.H.M.F. British Felt Hat Manufacturers' Federation
B.F.I. British Film Institute
B.F.I.A. British Flower Industry Association
B.F.M. British Furniture Manufacturers Federated Associations
B.F.M.A. British Farm Mechanization Association
B.F.M.C. British Friction Materials Council
B.F.M.F. British Federation of Music Festivals
B.F.M.I.R.A. British Food Manufacturing Industries' Research Association
B.F.M.P. British Federation of Master Printers
B.F.M.S.A. British Firework Manufacturers Safety Association
Bfn. Bloemfontein
B.F.O. Beat-frequency Oscillator
B.For. Bachelor of Forestry
B.For.Sc. Bachelor of Forestry Science
B.F.P.A. British Film Producers' Association
B.F.P.C. British Farm Produce Council
B.F.P.M. British Federation of Plumbers' Merchants (*now* N.F.B.P.M.)
B.F.P.O. British Forces Post Office
B.F.S. Branded Furniture Society
British Frontier Service
British Fuchsia Society
B.F.S.A. British Fire Services' Association
B.F.S.S. British and Foreign Sailors' Society
British Field Sports Society
B.F.T.A. British Fur Trade Alliance
B.F.U.W. British Federation of University Women
bg. bag
B.G. Birmingham Gauge
Blood Group
British Guiana
b.g. bay gelding
b/g. bonded goods
B.G.A. British Gliding Association
British Grit Association
Business Graduates Association
Irish Sugar Beet Growers' Association
B.G.B. Booksellers' Association of Great Britain and Ireland
B.Gen. Brigadier-General
B.G.F. Banana Growers' Federation (Australia)
B.G.G.A. British Golf Greenkeepers' Association
B.G.G.R.A. British Gelatine and Glue Research Association
B.G.G.S. Brigadier-General, General Staff
B.G.I.R.A. British Glass Industry Research Association
B.G.M. Bethnal Green Museum
B.G.M.A. British Gear Manufacturers' Association
bgs. bags
B.G.S. Brigadier, General Staff
British Geriatrics Society *cont.*

British Goat Society
British Grassland Society
Brothers of the Good Shepherd
B.G.S.A. British Gas Staff Association
(*now merged with* N.A.L.G.O.)
B.G.W.F. British Granite and Whinestone Federation
B.H. Base Hospital
British Honduras
Burlington House
B/H. Bill of Health
b.h. bougie-heure(s) (candle-hour(s))
B.H.A. British Homeopathic Association
British Horse Association
British Humanist Association
B.H.A.F.R.A. British Hat and Allied Feltmakers' Research Association
B'ham Birmingham
BHC benzene hexachloride
B.H.C. British Herdsmen's Club
British High Commissioner
B.H.Cross Brotherhood of the Holy Cross
B.H.C.S.A. British Hospitals Contributory Schemes Association
bhd. billhead
bulkhead
B.H.E. Bachelor of Home Economics
B'head Birkenhead
B.H.Ec. Bachelor of Home Economics
Bachelor of Household Economics
B.H.F. Baptist Holiday Fellowship
B.H.H.I. British Home and Hospital for Incurables
B.H.I. British Horological Institute
British Humanities Index
Bureau hydrographique international (International Hydrographic Bureau)
B.H.L. Barnardo Helpers' League
British Housewives League
B.H.M.A. British Hard Metal Association
B.H.M.E.A. British Hard Metal Export Association
B.H.M.R.A. British Hydromechanics' Research Association
B.H.N. Brinell Hardness Number
b.h.p. brake horse power
bhpric. bishopric
B.H.Q. Brigade Headquarters
B.H.R.A. British Hotels and Restaurants Association
British Hydromechanics Research Association
B.H.S. Boys' High School
British Herpetological Society
British Home Stores
British Horse Society
B.H.Sc. Bachelor of Household Science
B.H.T.A. British Herring Trade Association
B.Hy. Bachelor of Hygiene
Bi Bismuth
B.I. Balearic Islands
Bulk Issue
B.I.A. British Institute of Acupuncture
British Insurance Association
British Ironfounders' Association

B.I.A.A. British Industrial Advertising Association
B.I.A.C. Business and Industry Advisory Committee (of O.E.C.D.)
B.I.A.D. Bureau international d'anthropologie différentielle (International Bureau of Differential Anthropology)
B.I.A.T.A. British Independent Air Transport Association
Bib. Bible
b.i.b. baby incendiary bomb
Bibl. Biblical
bibl. bibliographer
bibliographical
bibliography
B.I.B.R.A. British Industrial Biological Research Association
B.I.C. Bahá'í International Community
Bureau international des containers (International Container Bureau)
Bureau international du cinéma (International Cinema Bureau)
B.i.C. bibas in Christo (live in Christ)
bicarb. bicarbonate of soda
B.I.C.C. British Insulated Callender's Cables
B.I.C.E. Bureau international catholique de l'enfance (International Catholic Child Bureau)
B.I.C.E.M.A. British Internal Combustion Engine Manufacturers' Association
B.I.C.E.P. British Industrial Collaborative Exponential Programme
B.I.C.E.R.A. British Internal Combustion Engine Research Association
B.I.C.S(c). British Institute of Cleaning Science
B.I.C.T.A. British Investment Casters' Technical Association
B.I.D. Bachelor of Interior Design
Banque interaméricaine de développement (Inter-American Development Bank)
Building Industry Distributors (*now* N.F.B.P.M.)
b.i.d. bis in die (twice daily)
B.I.E. British Institute of Embalmers
Bureau international d'education (International Bureau of Education)
Bureau international des expositions (International Exhibition Bureau)
B.I.E.M. Bureau international de l'édition mécanique (International Bureau of the Societies administering the Rights of Mechanical Recording and Reproduction)
bien. biennial
B.I.E.T. British Institute of Engineering Technology
B.I.F. British Industries Fair
B.I.F.A. British Industrial Film Association
B.I.F.U.S. British, Italian, French and United States
B.I.G. Blind Integration Group
B.I.H.A. British Ice Hockey Association
B.I.H.F.S. British Institute of Hardwood Flooring Specialists

35

B.I.M. Bachelor of Indian Medicine
Bord Iascaigh Mhara
(Irish Sea Fisheries Board)
British Institute of Management
— British Insulin Manufacturers
B.I.M.C.A.M. British Industrial Measuring and Control Apparatus Manufacturers' Association
B.I.N. Bulletin of International News
B.I.N.C. Building Industries' National Council
Bio. Biophysics
biochem. biochemistry
biog. biographer
biographical(ly)
biography
Biogeog. Biogeography
Biol. Biological
Biologist
Biology
B.I.O.S. British Intelligence Objectives Sub-Committee
B.I.O.T. British Indian Ocean Territories
B.I.P. British Industrial Plastics
British Institute in Paris
B.I.P.C.A. Bureau international permanent de chimie analytique pour les matières destinées à l'alimentation de l'homme et des animaux (Permanent International Bureau of Analytical Chemistry of Human and Animal Food)
B.I.P.M. Bureau international des poids et mesures (International Bureau of Weights and Measures)
B.I.P.P. British Institute of Practical Psychology
B.I.P.A.R. Bureau International des Producteurs d'Assurances et de Réassurances (International Bureau of Insurance Assessors)
B.I.P.A.V.E.R. Bureau International Permanent des Associations des Vendeurs et Rechapeurs de Pneumatiques (Permanent International Bureau of Tyre Dealers and Retreaders Associations)
B.I.P.O. British Institute of Public Opinion
B.I.R. Board of Inland Revenue
British Institute of Radiology
Bureau International de la Récupération (International Salvage Bureau)
B.I.R.D. Banque internationale pour la reconstruction et le développement (International Bank for Reconstruction and Development)
B.I.R.E. British Institution of Radio Engineers
B.I.R.F. Brewing Industry Research Foundation
B I.R.S. British Institute of Recorded Sound
— **B.I.R.U.** British Ideology Research Unit
bis. bissextile
B.I.S. Bank for International Settlements
British Ichthyological Society *cont.*

British Information Services
British Interplanetary Society
British Iris Society
B.I.S.A.K.T.A. British Iron, Steel and Kindred Trades Association
B.I.S.F. British Iron and Steel Federation
B.I.S.F.A. British Industrial and Scientific Film Association
Bureau international pour la standardisation de la rayonne et des fibres synthétiques (International Bureau for the Standardisation of Man-Made Fibres)
B.I.S.I.T.S. British Iron and Steel Industry Translation Service
B.I.S.P.A. British Independent Steel Producers Association
B.I.S.R.A. British Iron and Steel Research Association
B.I.T. Bureau international du travail (International Labour Office)
B.I.T.A. British Industrial Truck Association
B.I.T.U. Bustamante Industrial Trade Union (Jamaica)
B.I.U. British Import Union
Bureau international des universités (International Universities Bureau)
biv. bivouac
B.I.W.F. British-Israel World Federation
B.J. Bachelor of Journalism
B.J.A. British Joint Association of Gold, Silver, Horological and Allied Trades
— British Judo Association
B.J.C.C. British Junior Chambers of Commerce
B.J.C.E.B. British Joint Communications Electronics Board
B.J.C.G. British Joint Corrosion Group
B.J.S. British Society for the Propagation of the Gospel Among the Jews
B.J.S.M. British Joint Services Mission
B.J.T.R.A. British Jute Trade Research Association
B.Jur. Bachelor of Jurisprudence
Bk Berkelium
bk. backwardation
bank
book
Bkg. Banking
bklt. booklet
bkm. buckram
bkrpt. bankrupt
Bks. Barracks
bks. books
B.K.S. British Kinematograph Society
— **B.K.S.T.S.** British Kinematograph, Sound and Television Society
bkt. basket
Bl. Blessed
Bölük (company)
bl. bale
barrel
B.L. Bachelor of Law
Barrister-at-Law   *cont.*

36

Base Line
Bill Lodged
Bill of Lading
Black Letter
Boatswain Lieutenant
Bodleian Library, Oxford
Breech-loader
Breech-loading
British Legion (*now* R. B. L.)
B.L.A. British Legal Association
British Liberation Army (*now* B.A.O.R.*)
B.L.A.C. British Light Aviation Centre
B.L.A.C.C. British and Latin American Chamber of Commerce
B.L.C. British Lighting Council
bld. bold
bldg(s). building(s)
Bldg.E. Building Engineer
B.L.E.S.M.A. British Limbless Ex-Servicemen's Association
B.L.E.U. Belgo-Luxembourg Economic Union
Blind Landing Experimental Unit
B.L.F. British Leather Federation
B.L.G. Burke's Landed Gentry
B.L.H. British Legion Headquarters
B.L.H.A. British Linen Hire Association
B.Lib. Bachelor of Librarianship
B.Lib.Sc. Bachelor in Library Science
B.L.I.C. Bureau de liaison des industries du caoutchouc de la C.E.E. (Rubber Industries Liaison Bureau of the E.E.C.)
B.Lit. Bachelor of Literature
B.Litt. Baccalaureus Literarum (Bachelor of Letters)
blk. black
blank
block
bulk
B.LL. Bachelor of Laws
B.L.M.A. British Lead Manufacturers' Association
B.L.M.A.S. Bible Lands Missions' Aid Society
B.L.M.C. British Leyland Motor Corporation
B.L.M.R.A. British Leather Manufacturers' Research Association
B.L.O.F. British Lace Operatives' Federation
b.l.r. breech-loading rifle
B.L.R.A. British Launderers' Research Association
bls. bales
barrels
B.L.S. Bachelor of Library Science
Benevolenti lectori salutem (greeting to the well-wishing reader)
Branch Line Society
Bureau of Labor Statistics (U.S.)
B.L.S.G.M.A. British Lampblown Scientific Glassware Manufacturers' Association
blt. built
B.L.V. British Legion Village
Blvd. Boulevard

B.L.W.A. British Laboratory Ware Association
B.M. Bachelor of Medicine
Bachelor of Music
Beata Maria (Blessed Virgin)
Beatae Memoriae (of blessed memory)
Bench Mark
Bending Moment
Binding Margin
Bishop and Martyr
Bonae Memoriae (of happy memory)
Brigade Major
British Monomark
British Museum
Bronze Medallist
b.m. bene merenti (to the well-deserving)
breech mechanism
broad measure
B.M.A. British Manufacturers' Association
British Medical Association
B.M.C. British Match Corporation
British Metal Corporation
British Motor Corporation
British Mountaineering Council
Catalogue of books printed in the xv century now in the British Museum
B.M.C.R.C. British Motor Cycle Racing Club
B.M.D. Births, Marriages and Deaths
B.M.D.M. British Museum Department of Manuscripts
B.M.E. Bachelor of Mechanical Engineering
Bachelor of Mining Engineering
B.Mech.E. Bachelor of Mechanical Engineering
B.Med.Sc. Bachelor of Medical Science
B.M.E.F. British Mechanical Engineering Federation (*formerly* B.E.A.)
b.m.e.p. brake mean effective pressure
B.Met. Bachelor of Metallurgy
B.Met.E. Bachelor of Metallurgical Engineering
B.M.E.W.S. Ballistic Missile Early Warning System *or* Station
B.M.F.F. British Man-Made Fibres Federation
B.M.I. Ballistic Missile Interceptor
Birmingham and Midland Institute
B.M.J. British Medical Journal
B.M.L.A. British Maritime Law Association
B.M.M. Baptist Men's Movement
B.M.M.A. British Mantle Manufacturers' Association
B.M.M.F. Bible and Medical Missionary Fellowship
B'mouth Bournemouth
B.M.P. National Council of Building Material Producers
b.m.p. brake mean power
B.M.P.M.A. British Metalworking Plant Makers Association
B.M.P.S. British Musicians' Pension Society

B.M.R. Basal Metabolic Rate
B.M.R.A. British Manufacturers' Representatives' Association South Africa
B.M.R.B. British Market Research Bureau
B.M.R.M.C. British Motor Racing Marshals' Club
B.M.S. Baptist Missionary Society
Birmingham Metallurgical Society
British Mycological Society
B.M.S.A. British Medical Students Association
B.M.S.E. Baltic Mercantile and Shipping Exchange
B.M.T. British Mean Time
B.M.T.A. British Motor Trade Association
B.M.T.F.A. British Malleable Tube Fittings Association
B.Mus. Bachelor of Music
British Museum
B.M.V. Blessed Mary the Virgin
B.M.W.S. Ballistic Missile Weapon System
Bn. Baron
Battalion
bn. been
born
B.N. Bachelor of Nursing
Bank Note
B.N.A.F. British North Africa Force
B.N.B. British National Bibliography
B.N.B.C. British National Book Centre
B.N.C. Brasenose College, Oxford
British National Committee on Surface Active Agents
B.N.C.C. British National Committee for Chemistry
B.N.C.S. British National Carnation Society
B.N.C.S.A.A. British National Committee on Surface Active Agents
B.N.C.S.R. British National Committee for Scientific Radio
British National Committee on Space Research
Bndr.S.L. Bandmaster Sub-Lieutenant
B.N.E.C. British National Export Council
British Nuclear Energy Conference
B.N.E.S. British Nuclear Energy Society
B.N.F. British National Formulary
B.N.F.M.F. British Non-Ferrous Metals Federation
B.N.F.M.R.A. British Non-Ferrous Metals Research Association
B.N.F.S.A. British Non-Ferrous Smelters' Association
B.N.G.A. British Nursery Goods Association
B.N.G.M. British Naval Gunnery Mission
BNHQ Battalion Headquarters
Bnkg. Banking
B.N.O.A. British Naturopathic and Osteopathic Association

B.N.O.C. British National Opera Company
B.N.P. British National Party
B.N.S. British Numismatic Society
British Nylon Spinners
B.N.Sc. Bachelor of Nursing Science
B.O. Bachelor of Oratory
Box Office
Branch Office
Broker's Order
Bulletin officiel
Buyer's Option
b.o. body odour
bowels open
b/o. brought over
B.O.A. British Olympic Association
British Optical Association
British Orthopaedic Association
British Osteopathic Association
B.O.A.C. British Overseas Airways Corporation
B.O.A.F.G. British Order of Ancient Free Gardeners
B.O.B.A. British Overseas Banks' Association
B.O.B.M.A. British Oil Burner Manufacturers' Association
B.O.C. British Ornithologists' Club
British Oxygen Company
B.O.C.E. Board of Customs and Excise
B.O.C.M. British Oil and Cake Mills
Bod. Bodleian Library, Oxford
B.O.D. Biochemical Oxygen Demand
B.O.E. Board of Education
B.O.E.C. British Oil Equipment Credits
B.O.F. British Overseas Fairs, Limited
B.of E. Bank of England
B.of H. Band of Hope Union
B.O.G.A. British Onion Growers' Association
Boh. Bohemia
B.O.H.S. British Occupational Hygiene Society
Bol. Bolivar
Bolivia(no)
bol. bolus
B.O.L. Bachelor of Oriental Learning
Bom. Bombay
B.O.M.A. British Overseas Mining Association
Bomb. Bombadier
bon. bataillon (battalion)
B.O.P. The Boy's Own Paper
B.Optom. Bachelor of Optometry
Bor. Borough
B.Or. Bachelor of Orientation
B.O.R.A.D. British Oxygen Research and Development Association
Boro. Borough
Bos'n Boatswain
B.O.S.S. Bureau of State Security (South Africa)
Bot. Botanical
Botanist
Botany
bot. bottle
bought
B.o.T. Board of Trade
B.O.T.A.C. Board of Trade Advisory Committee

B.O.T.U. Board of Trade Unit
B.O.U. British Ornithologists' Union
Boul. Boulevard
B.O.W.O. Brigade Ordnance Warrant Officer
Bp. Bishop
bp. birthplace
B.P. Bachelor of Painting
    Back Projection
    Baden-Powell (1st Baron)
    Behaviour Pattern
    Between Perpendiculars
    Black Power
    Blood Pressure
    Borough Polytechnic, London
    British Petroleum
    British Pharmacopoeia
    British Public
    Buckingham Palace
b.p. below proof
    boiling point
    bonum publicum (the public good)
b/p. bill of parcels
    bills payable
    blueprint
B.P.A. Bahnpostamt (Railway Post Office)
    Bookmaker's Protection Association
    British Paediatric Association
    British Parachute Association
    British Philatelic Association
    British Ploughing Association
B.P.A.A. British Poster Advertising Association
B.Paed. Bachelor of Paediatrics
B.P.B. Bank Post Bill
B.P.B.F. British Paper Box Federation
B.P.B.I.R.A. British Paper and Board Industry Research Association (now Pira)
B.P.B.M.A. British Paper and Board Makers' Association
B.P.C. Book Prices Current
    British Pharmaceutical Codex
    British Pharmacopoeia Commission
    British Productivity Council
B.P.C.F. British Precast Concrete Federation
B.Pd. Bachelor of Pedagogy
B.P.D. Boots Pure Drug Company
B.P.E. Bachelor of Physical Education
B.Ped. Bachelor of Pedagogy
B.P.F. Bachelière en pédagogie familiale (Bachelor of Family Pedagogy)
    British Plastics Federation
    British Polio Fellowship
b.p.f. bon pour francs (good for francs)
B.Pharm. Bachelor of Pharmacy
B.P.H.E. Bachelor of Physical and Health Education
B.Phil. Bachelor of Philosophy
B.Phty. Bachelor of Physiotherapy
B.P.I. Booksellers' Provident Institution
B.P.I.C.A. Bureau permanent international des constructeurs d'automobiles (International Permanent Bureau of Motor Manufacturers)
bpl. birthplace

B.P.M.A. British Premium Manufacturers Association
    British Pump Manufacturers' Association
B.P.M.F. British Postgraduate Medical Federation
    British Pottery Manufacturers' Federation
B.P.N.M.A. British Plain Net Manufacturers' Association
B.P.O. Base Post Office
    Berlin Philharmonic Orchestra
B.P.O.E. Benevolent and Protective Order of Elks
B.P.P. Bechuanaland People's Party
B.P.P.M.A. British Power-Press Manufacturers' Association
B.P.R.A. Book Publishers' Representatives' Association
B.Ps. Bachelor in Psychology
B.P.S. British Paper Stock Merchants Association
    British Pharmacological Society
    British Phrenological Society
    British Printing Society
    British Psychological Society
B.P.S.A. British Pharmaceutical Students' Association
B.Ps.S. British Psychological Society
Bp. Suff. Bishop Suffragan
B.P.T. Battle-practice Target
B-Pyr. Basses-Pyrénées
Bq. Barque
B.Q. Bene quiescat (may he or she rest in peace)
B.Q.M.S. Battery Quartermaster Sergeant
Br. Brazil
    British
    Bromine
    Brother
br. branch
    bridge
    brig
    brown
B.R. Bancus Reginae (Queen's Bench)
    Bancus Regis (King's Bench)
    Book of Reference
    British Railways (now British Rail)
    Bureau des Renseignements (Information or Intelligence Office)
B/R. Bills Receivable
    Builders' Risks
b.r. bank rate
bra. brassière
B.R.A. Beef Recording Association
    Bee Research Association
    Brigadier Royal Artillery
    British Radiesthesia Association
    British Records Association
    British Refrigeration Association
    British Resorts' Association
    British Rheumatism and Arthritis Association
Branc. Brancardier (Stretcher-bearer)
BRASTACS Bradford Scientific, Technical and Commercial Service
Braz. Brazil(ian)
B.R.B. British Railways Board
B.R.C. British Rabbit Council
    British Radio Corporation

B.R.C.A. British Roller Canary Association

B.R.C.C. British Roller Canary Club

Brch. Branch

B.R.C.M.A. British Radio Cabinet Manufacturers' Association

B.R.C.S. British Railways Catering Service
British Red Cross Society

B.R.D. Bundesrepublik Deutschland (German Federal Republic)

B.R.D.C. British Racing Drivers' Club

B.R.E. Bachelor of Religious Education

Brec. Brecknockshire *or* Brecon

b. rec. bills receivable

B.R.E.M.A. British Radio Equipment Manufacturers' Association

Bret. Breton

Brev. Brevet

brev. breveté (patent(ed))

B.R.F. Bible Reading Fellowship
British Road Federation

Brg. Bearing

B.Rh. Bas-Rhin

B.R.I. Banque des règlements internationaux (Bank for International Settlements)

Brig. Brigade
Brigadier

BRIMAFEX British Manufacturers of Malleable Tube Fittings Export Group

Brisb. Brisbane

Brit. Britannia
Britannica
Britain
British

Brit.I.R.E. British Institution of Radio Engineers (*now* I.E.R.E.)

Brit. Mus. British Museum

Britt. Britannorum (of the Britons)

brl. barrel

B.R.M. British Racing Motor

B.R.M.A. Board of Registration of Medical Auxiliaries

B.R.M.C.A. British Ready Mixed Concrete Association

B.R.M.F. British Rainwear Manufacturers' Federation

Bro. Brotherhood

bro. brother

B.R.O. Brigade Routine Order

Brom. bromide

Bros. Brothers

brot. brought

B.R.R.A.M.A. British Rubber and Resin Adhesive Manufacturers' Association

B.R.S. British Record Society
British Road Services
Building Research Station

B.R.S.A. British Railways Staff Association

B.R.S.C.C. British Racing and Sports Car Club

Br. T. British Time

B.R.T.A. British Racing Toboggan Association
British Regional Television Association
British Road Tar Association

Brunsw. Brunswick

B.Rur.Sc. Bachelor of Rural Science

Brush British Representative Unit for Style Hair

B.R.V.M.A. British Radio Valve Manufacturers' Association

B.R.W. British Relay Wireless

Bry. Bryology

brz. bronze

bs. bags
bales

B.S. Bachelor of Science
Bachelor of Surgery
Balance Sheet
Battle Ship
Bibliographical Society
Bill of Sale
Biochemical Society
Biometric Society
Blackfriars Settlement
Blessed Sacrament
Boiler Survey
Boy Scouts
Bristol Siddeley
British Standard
Budgerigar Society
Building Society

B/S. Bill of Store

b.s. back stage
balance sheet

B.S.A. Bachelor of Science in Agriculture
Bibliographical Society of America
Birmingham Small Arms Company
Botanical Society of America
Boy Scouts' Association
Boy Scouts of America
British School at Athens
British Shipbreakers' Association
British Society of Aesthetics
British Sociological Association
British Speleological Association
Building Societies' Association

B.S.A.A. British School of Archaeology at Athens

B.S.-A.C. British Sub-Aqua Club

B.S.A.F. British Sulphate of Ammonia Federation

B.S.A.P. British Society of Animal Production
British South Africa Police

B.S.A.S. Bakery Students Associations of Scotland
British Ship Adoption Society

B.S.A.V.A. British Small Animal Veterinary Association

B.S.B. British Standard Beam

B.S.B.A. British Starter Battery Association

B.S.B.C. British Social Biology Council

B.S.B.I. Botanical Society of the British Isles

B.Sc. Bachelor of Science

B.S.C. Bengal Staff Corps
Bibliographical Society of Canada
British Safety Council
British Samoyed Club
British Shippers' Council *cont.*

British Shoe Corporation
British Standard Channel
British Stationery Council
British Steel Corporation
British Sugar Corporation

B.Sc.A. Bachelier ès sciences appliquées (Bachelor of Applied Sciences)

B.S.C.A. British Sulphate of Copper Association

B.Sc.Ag. Bachelor of Science in Agriculture

B.Sc.(Ag.eng.) Bachelor of Science in Agricultural Engineering

B.Sc.(A.H.) Bachelor of Science (Animal Husbandry)

B.Sc.App. Bachelor of Applied Science

B.S.C.C. British Society for Clinical Cytology
British Synchronous Clock Conference

B.Sc.(C.E.) Bachelor of Science in Civil Engineering

B.Sc.Com. Bachelier ès sciences commerciales (Bachelor of Commercial Science)

B.Sc.D. Bachelor of Science in Dentistry

B.Sc.Dom. Bachelier en sciences domestiques (Bachelor of Household Science)

B.Sc. (Econ.) Bachelor of Science in the Faculty of Economics

B.Sc.Ed.Inf. Bachelière en sciences de l'éducation des infirmières (Bachelor of Science in Nursing Education)

B.Sc.(E.E.) Bachelor in Science in Electrical Engineering

B.Sc.El.Ed. Bachelor of Science in Elementary Education

B.Sc.(Eng.) Bachelor of Science in Engineering

B.Sc.F. Bachelor of Science in Forestry

B.Sc.Fam. Bachelier ès sciences familiales (Bachelor of Science in Home Economics)

B.Sc.For. Bachelor of Science in Forestry

B.Sc.(Hort.) Bachelor of Science (Horticulture)

B.Sc.Hosp. Bachelier en sciences hospitalières (Bachelor of Nursing)

B.Sc.Inf. Baccalauréat ès sciences infirmières (Bachelor of Science in Nursing Education)

B.Sc.L.A. Bachelor of Science (Laboratory Assistant)

B.Sc.(M.E.) Bachelor of Science in Mechanical Engineering

B.Sc.Med. Bachelor of Science in Medicine

B.Sc.Met. Bachelor of Science in Metallurgy

B.Sc.Min. Bachelor of Science in Mining

B.Sc. (M.L.S.) Bachelor of Science in Medical Laboratory Science

B.Sc.N. Bachelor of Science in Nursing

B.Sc.(Nutr.) Bachelor of Science (Nutrition)

B.Sc.P. Bachelier ès sciences (pêcheries) (Bachelor of Fisheries)

B.Sc.(P. and O.T.) Bachelor of Science in Physical and Occupational Therapy

B.Sc.(P.Ed.) Bachelor of Science in Physical Education

B.Sc.(Pharm.) Bachelor of Science in Pharmacy

B.Sc.(Q.S.) Bachelor of Science in Quantity Surveying

B.S.C.R.A. British Steel Castings Research Association

B. Sc.Rel. Bachelier en sciences religieuses (Bachelor of Religious Science)

B.Sc.(R.S.) Bachelor of Science (Rural Science)

B.Sc.R.T. Bachelor of Science in Radiologic Technology

B.Sc.(Soc.) Bachelor of Science (Sociology)

B.Sc.S.P. Bachelier ès sciences sociales et politiques (Bachelor of Social and Political Sciences)

B.Sc.S.S. Bachelor of Science in Secretarial Studies

B.Sc.Sur. Bachelor of Science in Land Surveying

B.Sc.(T.E.) Bachelor of Science in Textile Engineering

B.Sc.(Tech.) Bachelor of Science in Technology

B.Sc.(Text.) Bachelor of Science (Textiles)

B.Sc.(Vet.) Bachelor of Science (Veterinary)

B.S.D. British Society of Dowsers

B.S.D.A. British Spinners' and Doublers' Association

B.S.E. Bachelor of Science in Education
Bachelor of Science in Engineering
Base Support Equipment
British Shipbuilding Exports

B.Serv.Soc. Bachelier en service social (Bachelor of Social Service)

B.S.E.S. British Schools' Exploring Society

B.S.F. Bachelor of Science in Forestry
Baptist Students' Federation
British Salonica Force
British Slag Federation
British Standard Fine
British Stone Federation

B.S.F.A. British Sanitary Fireclay Association
British Science Fiction Association
British Steel Founders' Association

B.S.F.S. Bachelor of Science in Foreign Service
British Soviet Friendship Society

B.S.G. British Standard Gauge

b.s.g.d.g. breveté sans garantie du gouvernement (patented without government guarantee)

bsh. bushel

B.S.H. British Society of Hypnotherapists

B.S.H.Ec. Bachelor of Science in Home Economics

B.S.H.S. British Society for the History of Science

D

41

B.S.I. British Standards Institution
    Building Societies' Institute
B.S.I.B. Boy Scouts International
    Bureau
    British Society for International Bibliography (*now* A.S.L.I.B.)
B.S.I.P. British Solomon Islands Protectorate
B.S.I.R.A. British Scientific Instrument Research Association
B.S.I.U. British Society for International Understanding
B.S.J.A. British Show Jumping Association
Bs.L. Bills of Lading
B.S.L. Boatswain Sub-Lieutenant
B.S.Litt. Bachelor of Sacred Letters
B.S.L.S. Bradford Small Livestock Society
B.S.M. Battery Sergeant-Major
    Bronze Star Medal (U.S.)
B.S.M.A. British Skate Makers' Association
B.S.M.G.P. British Society of Master Glass-Painters
B.S.N. Bachelor of Science in Nursing
B.S.O. Boston Symphony Orchestra (U.S.)
    Bournemouth Symphony Orchestra
B.Soc.Sc. Bachelor of Social Science
B.Soc.St. Bachelor of Social Studies
B.S.P. Bachelor of Science in Pharmacy
    Birmingham School of Printing
    British Standard Pipe-thread
    Bureau sanitaire panaméricain (Pan-American Sanitary Bureau)
B.S.P.A. Basic Slag Producers' Association
B.S.R. Birmingham Sound Reproducers
    British School at Rome
B.S.R.A. British Ship Research Association
    British Society for Research on Ageing
    British Sound Recording Association
    British Sugar Refiners' Association
B.S.R.A.E. British Society for Research in Agricultural Engineering
B.S.S. British Sailors' Society (At Home and Abroad)
    British Standard Sizes
    British Standard Specification
B.S.Sc. Bachelor of Sanitary Science
B.S.S.O. British Society for the Study of Orthodontics
B.S.S.S. British Society of Soil Science
B/St. Bill of Sight
B.S.T. British Standard Time
    British Summer Time
B.S.T.A. British Surgical Trades' Association
B.S.T.F. British Student Tuberculosis Foundation
B.Surv. Bachelor of Surveying
B.S.W. Bachelor of Social Work
    British Standard Whitworth

B.S.W.B. Boy Scouts World Bureau
B.S.W.I.A. British Steel Wire Industries' Association
Bt. Baronet
    Benefit
    Brevet
bt. beat
    bought
B.T. Bachelor of Teaching
    Bishop's Transcript
B.T.A. Billiards Trade Association
    Boot Trades' Association
    British Travel Association
    British Troops in Austria
B.T.B.A. British Ten Pin Bowling Association
    British Twinning and Bi-lingual Association
B.T.B.S. Boot Trade Benevolent Society
B.T.C. British Transport Commission
B.T.C.S. British Transport Catering Service
B.T.E. British Troops in Egypt
B.Tech. Bachelor in Technology
B.T.E.F. Book Trade Employers' Federation
B.Tel.E. Bachelor of Telecommunication Engineering
B.T.E.M.A. British Tanning Extract Manufacturers' Association
B.Text. Bachelor of Textiles
B.T.F. British Tarpaviors' Federation
    British Trawlers' Federation
    British Turkey Federation
bth. bath(room)
B.Th. Bachelor of Theology
B.T.H. British Thomson-Houston Company
B.T.H.A. British Travel and Holidays Association (*now* B.T.A.)
B.Th.U. British Thermal Unit(s)
B.T.I. British Technology Index
B.T.M. British Theatre Museum
B.T.M.A. British Toy Manufacturers' Association
    British Typewriter Manufacturers' Association
B.T.N. Brussels Tariff Nomenclature
B.T.O. British Trust for Ornithology
B.T.R. British Tax Review
    British Telecommunications Research
B.T.R.A. Bombay Textile Industry's Research Association
B.T.R.P. Bachelor of Town and Regional Planning
B.T.S. Blood Transfusion Service
B.T.U. Board of Trade Unit
B.t.u. British thermal unit
B.T.U.C. Bahamas Trade Union Congress
bu. bushel
B.U. Baptist Union of Great Britain and Ireland
B.U.A. British United Airways
B.U.A.F. British United Air Ferries
B.U.A.V. British Union for the Abolition of Vivisection
Bucks. Buckinghamshire
B.U.C.O.P. British Union Catalogue of Periodicals

B.U.F.O.R.A. British Unidentified Flying Objects Research Association
B.U.J. Baccalaureus Utriusque Juris (Bachelor of Canon and Civil Law)
Bulg. Bulgaria(n)
Bull. Bulletin
B.U.L.V.A. Belfast and Ulster Licensed Vintners' Association
B.U.N.A.C. British Universities' North American Club
B.U.P. British United Press
B.U.P.A. British United Provident Association
bur. buried
burl. burlesque
Burm. Burma
   Burmese
bus. business
B.U.S.F. British Universities' Sports Federation
B.V. Beatitudo Vestra (Your Holiness)
   Bible Version (of Psalms)
   Blessed Virgin
   Blood Volume
b.v. bene vale (farewell)
   book value
   by voorbeeld (for example)
B.V.A. British Radio Valve Manufacturers' Association
B.V.A. British Veterinary Association
   British Vigilance Association
B.V.H. British Van Heusen Corporation
B.V.J. British Veterinary Journal
B.V.K. Bundesverdienstkreuz (Federal Cross of Merit, Germany)
B.V.M. Blessed Virgin Mary
B.V.M.A. British Valve Manufacturers' Association
B.V.M.S. Bachelor of Veterinary Medicine and Surgery
B.V.O. Bundesverdienstorden (Federal Order of Merit, Germany)
B.V.P. British Volunteer Programme
B.V.Sc. Bachelor of Veterinary Science
B.W. Black Watch
   Bonded Warehouse
   British Waterways
B/W. Black and White
b.w. biological warfare
   bitte wenden (please turn the page)

B.W.A. Baptist World Alliance
   British Waterworks Association
B.W.B. British Waterways Board
B.W.C. British War Cabinet
B.W.C.C. British Weed Control Conference
B.W.F. British Wool Federation
B.W.G. Birmingham Wire Gauge
B.W.L. British West Indies
   British Workmen's Institute
B.W.I.A. British West Indian Airways
B.W.I.R. British West India Regiment
B.W.I.S.A. British West Indies Sugar Association
B.W.L. Baptist Women's League
B.W.M. British War Medal
B.W.M.A. British Woodwork Manufacturers' Association
B.W.M.B. British Wool Marketing Board
B.W.O. Backward-wave Oscillator
B.W.P.A. British Waste Paper Association
   British Wood Preserving Association
B.W.P.U.C. British Wastepaper Utilisation Council
B.W.R. Boiling Water Reactor
B.W.R.A. British Welding Research Association
B.W.R.R.A. British Wire Rod Rollers' Association
B.W.S. British Water-colour Society
B.W.S.F. British Water Ski Federation
B.W.T.A. British Women's Temperance Association
   British Wood Turners' Association
B.W.W.A. British Waterworks Association
bx. box
B.X. British Xylonite
bxs. boxes
By. Barony
b—y bloody
B.Y.N.A. British Young Naturalists' Association
Byo. Bulawayo
Byz. Byzantine
Bz Benzene

C

C Capacitance
   Carbon
   100 (Roman numerials)
C. Caesar
   Canon
   Cape
   Captain
   Catechism
   Catholic
   Centigrade
   Central
   Chancellor
   Chancery
   Chapter
   Chief
   Church
   Circuit
   Collected
   Commander
   Common Metre
   Compound
   Confessor
   Confidential
   Congregational

cont.

Congress
Conservative
Constable
Consul
Consultum (legislative decree)
Contralto
Contrast
Coulomb
Count
Counter-tenor
County
Coupon
Court
Cross
Cruiser
Cubic
Curacy
Curate

c. case
    cathode
    caught
    centigramme(s)
    cent(s)
    centime(s)
    centimetre(s)
    central
    century
    chapter
    charge
    chest
    child
    cibus (meal)
    circa (about, approximately)
    city
    class
    cloudy
    clubs
    cold
    colt
    conductor
    constable
    contra (against)
    convection
    coupon
    court
    cousin
    creation
    crowned
    cubic
    currency
    current

Ca Calcium
Ca. Compagnia (company)
ca. case(s)
    cathode
    circa (about, approximately)
C.A. Canadian Army
    Caterers' Association of
      Great Britain
    Catholic Association
    Central America
    Chartered Accountant
    Chemical Abstracts
    Chief Accountant
    Chronological Age
    Church Army
    Church Assembly
    City Attorney
    Civil Aviation
    Classical Association
    College of Arms
    Command Accountant

Commercial Agent
Community Association
Companies Act
Constituent Assembly
Consumers' Association
Corps d'Armée (Army Corps)
Council Accepted (American
    Medical Association)
County Alderman
County or City Architect
Court of Appeal
Credit Account
Croquet Association
Crown Agent
Cruising Association
Current Account
Member of the Institute of
    Chartered Accountants of Scot-
    land

C/A. Capital, Credit or Current Account,
C/a. cuenta abierta (open account)
c.a. chronological age
    courant alternatif (alternating cur-
    rent)
C.A.A. Cambrian Archaeological As-
    sociation
    Canadian Authors' Association
    Central African Airways Cor-
    poration
    Cold Asphalt Association
    Concert Artists' Association
    Cost Accountants' Association
C.A.A.A. Canadian Association of Ad-
    vertising Agencies
C.A.A.E.O. Commission des affaires
    d'Asie et d'Extrême-Orient de la
    chambre de commerce internationale
    (Commission on Asian and Far East-
    ern Affairs of the International
    Chamber of Commerce)
C.A.A.R.C. Commonwealth Advisory
    Aeronautical Research Council
C.A.A.V. Central Association of Agri-
    cultural Valuers
Cab. Cabinet
C.A.B. Canadian Association of Broad-
    casters
    Citizens' Advice Bureau(x)
    Civil Aeronautics Board (U.S.)
    Commonwealth Agricultural
    Bureaux
    Corrosion Advice Bureau
C.A.B.A.S. City and Borough Archi-
    tects' Society
C.A.B.E.I. Central American Bank for
    Economic Integration
C.A.B.M. Commonwealth of Australia
    Bureau of Meteorology
C.A.B.M.A. Canadian Association of
    British Manufacturers and Agencies
C.A.C. Central Advisory Committee
    Colonial Advisory Council
    Comité administratif de co-
      ordination (des Nations
      Unies) (Administrative Co-
      ordination Committee (of the
      United Nations))
    Consumer's Advisory Council
    (U.S.)
    County Agricultural Com-
    mittee(s)

cont.

C.A.C.A. Cement and Concrete Association
Central After-Care Association
C.A.C.C. Civil Aviation Communications Centre
C.A.C.E. Central Advisory Council for Education
C.A.C.T.M. Central Advisory Council of Training for the Ministry (*now* Central Advisory Council for the Ministry)
Cad. Cadet
cad. cadenza
C.A.D. Comité d'aide au développement (Development Assistance Committee)
c.a.d. cash against documents
c-à-d c'est-à-dire (that is to say)
C.A.D.F. Commutated Antenna Direction Finder
C.A.E. Canadian Aviation Electronics
Chartered Automobile Engineer
C.A.E.A. Central American Economics Association
C.A.E.A.I. Chartered Auctioneers' and Estate Agents' Institute
C.A.E.C. Committee of the Acta Endocrinologica Countries
County Agricultural Executive Committee
C.A.E.M. Conseil d'assistance économique mutuelle (Council for Mutual Economic Assistance)
Caern(s). Caernarvonshire
Caes. Caesar
C.A.F. Central African Federation
Curates' Augmentation Fund
C.A.F.E.A.-I.C.C. Commission on Asian and Far Eastern Affairs of the the International Chamber of Commerce
C.A.F.I.C. Combined Allied Forces Information Centre
C.A.F.M.N.A. Compound Animal Feeding Stuffs Manufacturers' National Association
C.A.G. Commercial Artists' Guild
CAH Cyanacetic Hydrazide
C.A.I. Canadian Aeronautical Institute
Club Alpino Italiano (Italian Alpine Club)
C.A.I.B. Certified Associate of the Institute of Bankers
C.A.I.S.M. Central Association of Irish Schoolmistresses
Caith. Caithness
Cal. Calcutta
Calends
California
Calorie (large)
cal. calendar
calibre
calorie (small)
C.A.L. Cocoa Association of London
C.A.L.A. Civil Aviation (Licensing) Act
Calc. Calcutta
calcd. calculated
C.A.L.E. Canadian Army Liaison Executive
Calg. Calgary

Calif. California
C.A.L.S. Christadelphian Auxiliary Lecturing Society
Cam. Camouflage
C.A.M.A. Coated Abrasives Manufacturers' Association
Camb. Cambridge(shire)
Cambs. Cambridgeshire
C.A.M.C. Canadian Army Medical Corps
C.A.M.D.A. Car and Motorcycle Drivers' Association
C.A.M.E. Conference of Allied Ministers of Education
Cam.Seg. Cameriere segrete di spada e cappa (Privy Chamberlain of Sword and Cape)
Can. Canada
Canadian
Canon
Canonically
Canonry
Canto
Canc. Cancellarius (Chancellor)
CANCIRCO Cancer International Research Cooperative
Cand. Candidate
c. & b. caught and bowled
c. & c. carpets and curtains
c. & d. collection and delivery
c. & f. cost and freight
C. & F.A. Cookery and Food Association
c. & i. cost and insurance
c. & p. carriage and packing
c. & p. collated and perfect
CANDU Canadian Deuterium Uranium Reactor
C. & W. Country and Western
C.A.N.G.O. Committee for Air Navigation and Ground Organization
CANS Citizens Advice Notes
C.A.N.S.G. Civil Aviation Navigational Services Group
Cant. Canterbury
Canticles
Cantonese
Cantab. Cantabrigiensis (of Cambridge)
cantab. cantabile
CANTAT Canadian Transatlantic Telephones
Canton. Cantonment
Cantuar. Cantuariensis (of Canterbury)
CANUSPA Canada and United States Parents' Association
C.A.O. Canadian Association of Optometrists
Chief Accountant Officer
County Advisory Officer
County Agricultural Officer
CAOBISCO Association d'industries de produits sucrés de la C.E.E. (Association of the Confectionery Industries of the E.E.C.)
C.A.O.R.B. Civil Aviation Operational Research Branch
C.A.O.R.G. Canadian Army Operational Research Group
C.A.O.T. Canadian Association of Occupational Therapy
CAP Chloro-aceto-phenone

45

Cap. Capital Letter
    Captain
cap. capital
    capitalized
    caput (chapter)
C.A.P. Canadian Association of Physicists
    Civil Air Patrol (U.S.)
    Code of Advertising Practice
C.A.P.A.C. Composers', Authors' and Publishers' Association of Canada
C.A.P.O. Canadian Army Post Office
Caps. Capital Letters
caps. capsule
Capt. Captain
capt. caption
Car. Carlow
    Carolus (Charles)
car. carat
C.A.R. Canadian Association of Radiologists
    Commonwealth (Australia) Arbitration Reports
C.A.R.A.C. Civil Aviation Radio Advisory Committee
Carb. Carbon
    Carbonate
Card. Cardiganshire
    Cardinal
C.A.R.D. Campaign Against Racial Discrimination
C.A.R.D.E. Canadian Armament Research and Development Establishment
Cards. Cardiganshire
C.A.R.E. Co-operative for American Relief Everywhere
    Cottage and Rural Enterprises, Ltd.
Carib. Caribbean
Carm(s). Carmarthenshire
Carn. Caernarvonshire
carp. carpentry
carr. carriage
C.A.R.S. Canadian Arthritis and Rheumatism Society
cart. cartage
Cartog. Cartography
Cas. Castle
cas. casual
C.A.S. Cathcart Art Society
    Chief of the Air Staff
    Children's Aid Society
    Connecticutensis Academiae Socius (Fellow of the Connecticut Academy of Arts and Sciences)
    County Architects Society
ca. sa. capias ad satisfaciendum (a writ of execution)
C.A.S.A. Contemporary Art Society of Australia
C.A.S.E. Confederation for the Advancement of State Education
C.A.S.I.G. Careers Advisory Service in Industry for Girls
Ca.S.L. Catering Sub-Lieutenant
Cast. Castile
    Castilian
C.A.S.T. Cartoon Archetypal Slogan Theatre

C.A.S.T.E. Civil Aviation Signals Training Establishment
C.A.S.U. Co-operative Association of Suez Canal Users
Cat. Catalan
    Catalogue
    Catholic
cat. cataplasm
    catapult
    cattle
    catalogue(d)
C.A.T. Child's Apperception Test
    Civil Air Transport
    Clear air turbulence
    College of Advanced Technology
    Comité de l'assistance technique de l'O.N.U. (Technical Assistance Committee, U.N.)
    Compagnie Air Transport (French Air Line)
    Compressed Air Tunnel
Catal. Catalan
    Catalonia
C.A.T.C. Commonwealth Air Transport Commission
    Commonwealth Air Transport Council
Cath. Cathedral
    Catholic
cath. cathode
C.A.T.O.R. Combined Air Transport Operations Room
C.A.T.R.A. Cutlery and Allied Trades Research Association
C.A.T.S.A. Confectionery and Allied Trades Sports Association
C.A.U. Community Action Union
caus. causation
    causative
Cav. Cavaliere (Knight)
    Cavalry
cav. caveat (a form of writ)
C.A.V. Curia Advisari Vult (the court wishes to consider the matter)
C.A.V.D. Completion, Arithmetic Problems, Vocabulary, Following Directions (intelligence test)
C.A.V.I. Centre audio-visuel international (International Audio-Visual Centre)
C.A.W.C. Central Advisory Water Committee
C.A.W.G. Christian Alliance of Women and Girls
C.A.W.U. Clerical and Administrative Workers' Union
Cb Columbium
C.B. Cape Breton
    Cash Book
    Centre of Buoyancy
    Coal Board
    Common Bench
    Companion of the Order of the Bath
    Confidential Book
    Confined to Barracks
    County Borough
    C. B. Cochran
c.b. cash book
C.B.A. Commercial Bank of Australia
    Council for British Archaeology

C.B.A.B.G. Commonwealth Bureau of Animal Breeding and Genetics
C.B.A.H. Commonwealth Bureau of Animal Health
C.B.A.N. Commonwealth Bureau of Animal Nutrition
C.B.A.T. Central Bureau for Astronomical Telegrams
C.B.C. Canadian Broadcasting Corporation
    Christian Brothers' College (Australia)
    County Borough Council
C.B.C.S. Commonwealth Bureau of Census and Statistics (Australia)
C.B.C.S.M. Council of British Ceramic Sanitaryware Manufacturers
c.b.d. cash before delivery
C.B.D.S.T. Commonwealth Bureau of Dairy Science and Technology
C.B.E. Commander of the Order of the British Empire
    Council for Basic Education
C.B.E.L. Cambridge Bibliography of English Literature
C.B.E.V.E. Central Bureau For Educational Visits and Exchanges
C.B.F. Central Board of Finance
    Confectioners Benevolent Fund
C.B.H. Commonwealth Bureau of Helminthology
C.B.H.P.C. Commonwealth Bureau of Horticulture and Plantation Crops
C.B.I. Central Bureau of Identification (U.S.)
    China, Burma, India
    Confederation of British Industry
    Cumulative Book Index
C.B.J.O. Co-ordinating Board of Jewish Organizations
CBK Cheque Book
c.bl. carte blanche (full discretionary power)
C.B.M.C. Communauté de travail des brasseurs du marché commun (Working Committee on Common Market Brewers)
C.B.M.M. Council of Building Materials Manufacturers
C.B.M.P.E. Council of British Manufacturers of Petroleum Equipment
C.B.O. Counter-Battery Officer
C.B.P.B.G. Commonwealth Bureau of Plant Breeding and Genetics
C.B.P.F.C. Commonwealth Bureau of Pastures and Field Crops
C.B.R. Chemical, Biological, Radiological (warfare)
C.B.R.I. Central Building Research Institute (India)
C.B.S. Christian Brothers School
    Columbia Broadcasting System (U.S.)
    Commonwealth Bureau of Soils
    Confraternity of the Blessed Sacrament
    Incorporated Church Building Society
C.B.S.O. City of Birmingham Symphony Orchestra
C.B.U. Container bomb unit
CC. Clarissimus (Most Illustrious)

Cc. Confessors
cc. capita (Chapters)
C.C. Caius College, Cambridge
    Carbon Copy
    Caribbean Commission
    Cash Credit
    Central Committee
    Chamber of Commerce
    Charity Commission
    Chess Club
    Chest Complaint
    Circuit Court
    City Council
    Civil Commotions
    Civil Court
    Common Councillor
    Community Council
    Compass Course
    Confined to Camp
    Consular Clerk
    Consumer Council
    Continuation Clause
    County Clerk
    County Council
    County Court
    Credit Card
    Cricket Club
    Croquet Club
    Crown Clerk
    Cruising Club
    Cycling Club
c.c. compte courant (current account)
    courant continu (direct current)
    cubic centimetres
    cubic contents
c/c. compte courant (current account)
C.C.A. Cement and Concrete Association
    Chief Clerk of the Admiralty
    Circuit Court of Appeals
    Commonwealth Correspondents' Association
    Copper Conductors' Association
    Council for Colored Affairs (U.S.)
    County Councils' Association
    Court of Criminal Appeal
    Covered Conductors' Association
C.C.A.A.P. Central Committee for the Architectural Advisory Panels
C.C.A.B. Canadian Circulations Audit Board
C.C.A.H.C. Central Council for Agricultural and Horticultural Co-operation
c.c.b. cubic capacity of bunkers
C.C.B.M. Copper Cylinder and Boiler Manufacturers' Association
C.C.B.N. Central Council for British Naturism
C.C.B.S.A. Central Council of Bank Staff Associations
C.C.B.V. Comité professionnel des coopératives des pays du marché commun pour le bétail et la viande (Committee of Cattle and Meat Co-operatives in the Common Market Countries)
C.C.C. Canoe Camping Club
    Central Criminal Court   *cont.*

Club Cricket Conference
Conseil de coopération culturelle (European Council for Cultural Cooperation)
Corpus Christi College, Oxford
Council for the Care of Churches
County Cricket Club
Cross Country Club
Customs Co-operation Council

C.C.C.A. Cocoa Chocolate and Confectionery Alliance

C.C.C.B.R. Central Council of Church Bell Ringers

C.C.C.C. Central Council for the Care of Cripples
Corpus Christi College, Cambridge

C.C.C.P. Soyuz Sovietskikh Sotsialisticheskikh Respublik (Union of Soviet Socialist Republics)

C.C.C.S. Commonwealth and Continental Church Society

C.C.D. Conseil de coopération douanière (Customs Co-operation Council)

C.C.E. Conseil des communes d'Europe (Council of European Municipalities)

C.C.E.P. Commission Consultative des Études Postales (De l'union postale universelle) (Consultive Commission For the Study of Postal Services)

C.C.E.T.I. Commission Consultative des Employés et des Travailleurs (Advisory Committee on Salaried Employees and Professional Workers)

C.C.F. Combined Cadet Force
Concentrated Complete Fertiliser
Co-operative Commonwealth Federation (Canada)

C.C.F.A. Combined Cadet Force Association

C.C.F.C. Circus Clown Friends Club
Continental Car Ferry Centre

C.C.F.R. Commonwealth Committee on Fuel Research

C.C.G. Control Commission Germany

C.C.G.(B.E.) Control Commission, Germany (British Element)

c.c.h. cubic capacity of holds

C.C.H.E. Central Council for Health Education

C.C.I. Chambre de commerce internationale (International Chamber of Commerce)

C.C.I.A. Commission of the Churches on International Affairs

C.C.I.C. Comité consultatif international du coton (International Cotton Advisory Committee)

C.C.I.R. Catholic Council for International Relations
Comité consultatif international des radiocommunications (International Radio Consultative Committee)

C.C.I.T.T. Comité consultatif international télégraphique et téléphonique (International Telegraph and Telephone Consultative Committee)

C.C.J. Circuit *or* County Court Judge

C.C.J.O. Consultative Council of Jewish Organizations

C.C.L. Caribbean Congress of Labour

c.cm. cubic centimetre(s)

C.C.M.D. Carnegie Committee for Music and Drama

C.C.M.T.C. Crown Cork Manufacturers' Technical Council

C.C.N.Y. Carnegie Corporation of New York

C.C.O. Central Coding Office
Country Clearing Office

C.C.O.A. County Court Officers' Association

C.C.O.K. Central Chancery of the Orders of Knighthood

C.C.P. Chinese Communist Party
Code of Civil Procedure
Committee on Commodity Problems (F.A.O.)
Commonwealth Centre Party (Australia)
Court of Common Pleas

C.C.P.E. Canadian Council of Professional Engineers

C.C.P.F. Comité central de la propriété forestière de la C.E.E. (Central Committee on Forest Property for the E.E.C.)

C.C.P.I.T. China Committee for the Promotion of International Trade

C.C.P.O. Comité central permanent de l'opium (Permanent Central Opium Board)

C.C.P.R. Central Council of Physical Recreation

C.C.P.S. Consultative Committee for Postal Studies

C.C.P.W. Catholic Council for Polish Welfare

C.C.R. Commission centrale pour la navigation du Rhin (Central Commission for the Navigation of the Rhine)
Common Centre of Research

C.C.R.A. Commander Corps Royal Artillery

C.Cr.P. Code of Criminal Procedure

C.C.R.T.D. Committee for Coordination of Cathode Ray Tube Development

C.C.S. Canadian Cancer Society
Canadian Ceramic Society
Casualty Clearing Station
Ceylon Civil Service
Child Care Service

C.C.S.A. Canadian Committee on Sugar Analysis

C.C.S.A.T.U. Co-ordinating Council of South African Trade Unions

C.C.T. Correct Corps Time

C.C.T.A. Commission de coopération technique pour l'Afrique (Commission for Technical Co-operation in Africa)
Coordinating Committee of Technical Assistance

c.c.tks. cubic capacity of tanks

C.C.T.V. Closed circuit television

CC.VV. Clarissimi viri (most illustrious men)

C.C.Y. Camping Club Youth
Cd Cadmium
Cd. Command
    Commissioned
    Could
cd. could
C.D. Canadian Forces Decoration
    Chancery Division
    Civil Defence
    Clearance Diving
    College Diploma
    Commission du Danube (Danube Commission)
    Contagious Disease(s)
    Corps Diplomatique
    County Development
C/D. Commercial Dock
    Consular Declaration
c.d. carried down
    cum dividend (with dividend)
    current density
C.D.A. Canadian Dental Association
    Civil Defence Act
    College Diploma in Agriculture
    Colonial Dames of America
    Copper Development Association
C.D.A.A.A. Committee to Defend America by Aiding the Allies
Cd.A.Eng. Commissioned Air Engineer
C.D.& W. Colonial Development and Welfare
Cd.Armn. Commissioned Airman
C.D.A.S. Civil Defence Ambulance Service
Cd.B. Commissioned Boatswain
cdbd. cardboard
Cd.Bndr. Commissioned Bandmaster
Cd.B.(P.R.) Commissioned Boatswain (Plotting and Radar)
C.D.C. Commonwealth Development Corporation
    Cost Determination Committee
Cd.Cmy.O. Commissioned Commissary Officer
Cd.C.O. Commissioned Communication Officer
Cd.Con. Commissioned Constructor
C.D.E. Coal Development Establishment
C.D.E.E. Chemical Defence Experimental Establishment
C.de G. Croix de Guerre
Cd.El.O. Commissioned Electrical Officer
Cd.Eng. Commissioned Engineer
C.D.F.C. Commonwealth Development Finance Company
C.D.G.M.A. Cornish and Devon Granite Masters Association
Cd.Gr. Commissioned Gunner
C.D.H. College Diploma in Horticulture
Cd.In.O. Commissioned Instructor Officer
c.div. cum dividend (with dividend)
C.D.L. Council of the Duchy of Lancaster
    Country and Democratic League (Australia)
C.D.M. Cadbury's Dairy Milk

Cd.M.A.A. Commissioned Master-at-Arms
Cd.O. Commissioned Officer
Cd.Obs. Commissioned Observer
Cd.O.E. Commissioned Ordnance Engineer
Cd.O.O. Commissioned Ordnance Officer
C.D.P.E. Continental Daily Parcels Express
Cdr. Commander
    Conductor
Cd.Rad.O. Commissioned Radio Officer
C.D.R.B. Canadian Defence Research Board
C.D.R.C. Civil Defence Regional Commissioner
Cdre. Commodore
C.D.R.F. Canadian Dental Research Foundation
C.D.R.I. Central Drug Research Institute (India)
C.D.R.S. Civil Defence Rescue Service
C.D.S. Chief of the Defence Staff
    Civil Defence Services
Cd.Sh. Commissioned Shipwright
Cd.S.O. Commissioned Stores Officer
C.D.S.O. Companion of the Distinguished Service Order
Cdt. Cadet
    Commandant
C.D.T. Carnegie Dunfermline Trust
Cdt.Mid. Cadet Midshipman
C.D.U. Christlich-Demokratische Union (Christian Democratic Union, Germany)
C.D.U.C.E. Christian Democratic Union of Central Europe
C.D.V. Civil Defence Volunteers
c.d.v. carte-de-visite (visiting-card)
Cd.Wdr. Commissioned Wardmaster
Cd.W.O. Commissioned Writer Officer
C.D.W.S. Civil Defence Wardens' Service
Ce Cerium
C.E. Canada East
    Chancellor of the Exchequer
    Chemical Engineer
    Chief Engineer
    Christian Endeavour
    Church of England
    Civil Engineer
    Common Era
    Compression Engine
    Council of Europe
    Counter-espionage
c.e. caveat emptor (let the buyer beware)
C.E.A. Canadian Electrical Association
    Central Electricity Authority (*now* E.C. *and* C.E.G.B.)
    Cinematograph Exhibitors' Association of Great Britain and Ireland
    Combustion Engineering Association
    Comité européen des assurances (European Insurance Committee)
    Confédération des éducateurs américains (Confederation of Latin American Teachers)

cont.

49

Confédération européenne de l'agriculture (European Confederation of Agriculture)
Conference of Educational Associations
Control Electronics Assembly (Autopilot)
Council of Economic Advisers

C.E.A.A. Centre européen d'aviation agricole (European Agricultural Aviation Centre)
Council of European-American Associations

C.E.A.C. Commission européenne de l'aviation civile (European Civil Aviation Commission)

C.E.A.F. Comité Européen des associations de fonderies (European Committee of Foundry Associations)

C.E.B. Confédération européenne de billard (European Billiards Confederation)

C.E.C. Canadian Electrical Code (of Standardization)
Centre européen de la culture (European Cultural Centre)
Church Education Corporation
Commonwealth Economic Committee
Commonwealth Education Conference

C.E.C.A. Communauté européenne du charbon et de l'acier (European Coal and Steel Community)

C.E.C.B. Conseil européen du cuir brut (Comité des Six) (European Hide Council (Six Countries Committee))

C.E.C.C. Communauté européenne de crédit communal (European Municipal Credit Community)

C.E.C.E. Committee for European Construction Equipment

C.E.C.H. Comité européen de la culture du houblon (European Hops Culture Committee)

C.E.C.L.E.S. Conseil européen pour la construction de lanceurs d'engins spatiaux (European Launching Development Organization)

CECOMAF Comité européen des constructeurs de matériel frigorifique (European Committee of Manufacturers of Refrigeration Equipment)

C.E.C.S. Church of England Children's Society
Communications Electronics Co-ordination Section

C.E.C.T. Comité européen de la chaudronnerie et de la tôlerie (European Committee for Boilermaking and Kindred Steel Structures)

C.E.D. Centro de Exploración y Documentación (Research and Documentation Centre of the U.E.A.)
Committee for Economic Development

C.E.D.I. Centre européen de documentation et d'information (European Documentation and Information Centre)

C.E.E. Central Engineering Establishment
Commission économique pour l'Europe (Economic Commission for Europe)
Commission internationale de réglementation en vue de l'approbation de l'équipement électrique (International Commission on Rules for the Approval of Electrical Equipment)
Common Entrance Examination
Communauté économique européenne (European Economic Community)

C.E.E.A. Communauté européenne de l'energie atomique (European Atomic Energy Community)

C.E.E.P. Centre européen d'études de population (European Centre for Population Studies)

C.E.F. Canadian Expeditionary Force
Children's Entertainment Films

C.E.F.A.C.D. Comité européen des fabricants d'appareils de chauffage et de cuisine domestiques (European Committee of Manufacturers of Domestic Heating and Cooking Appliances)

C.E.F.I.C. Centre européen des fédérations de l'industrie chimique (European Centre of Chemical Manufacturers' Federations)

C.E.F.S. Comité européen des fabricants de sucre (European Committee of Sugar Manufacturers)

CEFTRI Central Food Technological Research Institute (India)

C.E.G. Catholic Evidence Guild

C.E.G.B. Central Electricity Generating Board

C.E.G.G.S. Church of England Girls' Grammar School

CEGROB Communauté européenne des associations du commerce de gros de bière des pays membres de la C.E.E. (European Community of Associations of the Wholesale Beer Trade for the E.E.C. Countries)

C.E.G.S. Church of England Grammar School

C.E.H. Conférence européenne des horaires des trains de voyageurs (European Passenger Time-Table Conference)

C.E.I. Commission électrotechnique internationale (International Electro-technical Commission)
Council of Engineering Institutions

C.E.I. Bois Confédération européenne des industries du bois (European Confederation of Woodworking Industries)

C.E.I.F. Council of European Industrial Federations

C.E.I.R. Corporation for Economic and Industrial Research

cel. celibate
celebrated

C.E.L.A. Council for Exports to Latin America

CELAM Conseil episcopal latino-américain (Latin-American Episcopal Council)

C.E.L.C. Commonwealth Education Liaison Committee

CELNUCO Comité européen de liaison des nagociants et utilisateurs de combustibles (European Liaison Committee of Fuel Merchants and Users)

Celt. Celtic

Cem. Cemetery

C.E.M. Christian Education Movement
College of Estate Management
Council of European Municipalities

C.E.M.A. Canadian Electrical Manufacturers' Association
Catering Equipment Manufacturers' Association
Council for Encouragement of Music and the Arts

C.E.M.A.P. Commission européenne des méthodes d'analyse des pesticides (Collaborative Pesticides Analytical Committee)

C.E.M.F. Counter-electromotive Force

C.E.M.L.A. Centro de Estudios Monetarios Latino-americanos (Latin-American Centre for Monetary Studies)

C.E.M.S. Church of England Men's Society

C.E.M.T. Conférence européenne des ministres des transports (European Conference of Ministers of Transport)

Cen. Eccl. Censura Ecclesiastica (Ecclesiastical Censure)

Cent. Centigrade
Central

cent. centavo
centesimo
centime
central
centrifugal
century

CENTAG Central Army Group (N.A.T.O.)

CENTO Central Treaty Organization

C.E.O. Chief Education Officer

C.E.O.A. Central European Operating Agency (N.A.T.O.)

C.E.P. Confédération Européenne D'Études Phytosanitaires (European Confederation for Plant Protection Research)

C.E.P.C. Central European Pipeline Committee
Comité européen pour les problèmes criminels (European Committee on Crime Problems)

C.E.P.C.E.O. Comité d'étude des producteurs de charbon d'Europe occidentale (Western European Coal Producers' Association)

C.E.P.E.S. Comité européen pour le progrès économique et social (European Committee for Economic and Social Progress)

C.E.P.O. Central European Pipeline Office

C.E.P.T. Conférence européenne des administrations des postes et des télécommunications (European Conference of Postal and Telecommunications Administrations)

Cer. Ceramics

C.E.R.A. Civil Engineering Research Association

C.E.R.L. Central Electricity Research Laboratories

C.E.R.N. Conseil européen pour la recherche nucléaire (*now* European Organisation for Nuclear Research)

C.E.R.P. Centre européen des relations publiques (European Centre of Public Relations)

Cert. Certificate
Certified

cert. certain
certificate
certified
certify

Certif. Certificate(d)

cert.inv. certified invoice

C.E.S. Centre for Environmental Studies
Christian Evidence Society

C.E.S.O. Canadian Executive Service Overseas

C.E.S.S.A.C. Church of England Soldiers', Sailors' and Airmen's Clubs

Cestr. Cestrensis (of Chester)

C.E.T. Central European Time
Centre Européen de Traduction (European Translation Centre)
Common External Tariff

C.E.T.O. Centre for Educational Television Overseas

C.E.T.O.P. Comita Européen des Transmissions Oléohydrauliques et Pneumatiques (European Hydraulic and Pneumatic Committee)

cet. par. ceteris paribus (other things being equal)

C.E.T.S. Church of England Temperance Society

C.E.U. Christian Endeavour Union
Constructional Engineering Union

C.E.U.S.A. Committee for Exports to the United States of America

C.E.W.C. Council for Education in World Citizenship

C.E.Y.C. Church of England Youth Council

Cey. Ceylon

C.E.Z.M.S. Church of England Zenana Missionary Society (*now merged with the* Church Missionary Society)

Cf Californium

Cf. Calf
Confessions

cf. confer (compare)

C.F. Centre Forward
Centre of Flotation

cont.

Chaplain to the Forces
Clarissima Femina (Most Illustrious Woman)
Comédie Française
Commonwealth Fund
c.f. chemin-de-fer (railway)
cost and freight
cubic feet
c/f. carried forward
C.F.A. Canadian Federation of Agriculture
Canadian Field Artillery
Canadian Forestry Association
Circus Fan Association of Great Britain
Commonwealth Forestry Association
Communauté Financière Africaine
Cookery and Food Association
Council of Iron Foundry Associations
C.F.A.E. Centre de formation en aérodynamique expérimentale (Training Centre for Experimental Aerodynamics)
C.F.A.L. Current Food Additives Legislation
C.F.A.P. Canadian Foundation for the Advancement of Pharmacy
C.F.A.T. Carnegie Foundation for the Advancement of Teaching
C.F.B. Commonwealth Forestry Bureau
Council of Foreign Bondholders
C.F.B.A. Chinchilla Fur Breeders' Association
C.F.C. Cinematographic Films Council
C.F.C.E. Conseil des fédérations commerciales d'Europe (Council of European Commercial Federations)
C.F.E. Central Fighter Establishment
C.F.F. Chemins de fer fédéraux Suisses (Swiss National Railway)
Children's Film Foundation
C.F.I. Chaplain to Foreign Immigrants
Chief Flying Instructor
Christian Friends of Israel
c.f.i. cost, freight and insurance
C.F.L. Cease-fire Line
Central Film Library
cfm. confirm(ation)
C.F.M. Cadet Forces Medal
Council of Foreign Ministers
c.f.m. cubic feet per minute
C.F.M.A. Chair Frame Manufacturers' Association
C.F.O. Central Forecasting Office
Chief Fire Officer
C.f.o. Channel or Coast for Orders
C.F.O.A. Chief Fire Officers' Association
C.F.P. Colonies Françaises du Pacifique
C.F.S. Central Flying School
Clergy Friendly Society
c.f.s. cubic feet per second
Officers who have qualified as flying instructors at the Central Flying School or a recognised flying instructors' school

c.ft. cubic foot or feet
C.F.T.B. Commonwealth Forestry and Timber Bureau
C.F.X. Congregatio Fratrum Xaverianorum (Xaverian Brothers)
cg. centigram(s)
C.G. Centre of Gravity
Coastguard
Coldstream Guards
Commerce en gros wholesale trade)
Commissary General
Consul General
Croix de Guerre
C.-G. Captain-General
c.g. centre of gravity
C.G.A. Canadian Gas Association
Cargo's proportion of General Average
Certified General Accountant
Community of the Glorious Ascension
Country Gentlemen's Association
cge. carriage
charge
C.-Gen. Chaplain-General
C.G.H. Cape of Good Hope
C.G.I. Chief Ground Instructor
Chief Gunnery Instructor
Congrès Géologique International (International Geological Congress)
c.g.i. corrugated galvanized iron
C.G.I.A. City and Guilds of London Insignia Award
C.G.I.L. Confederazione Generale Italiana del Lavoro (Italian Workers' General Confederation)
C.G.L.I. City and Guilds of London Institute
C.G.M. Conspicuous Gallantry Medal
cgo. cargo
contango
C.G.P. College of General Practitioners
C.G.P.M. Conseil général des pêches pour la Méditerranée (General Fisheries Council for the Mediterranean)
C.G.R.M. Commandant General, Royal Marines
C.G.S. Canadian Geographical Society (now R.C.G.S.)
Chief of General Staff
Central Gunnery School
c.g.s. centimetre gramme second(s)
C.G.S.B. Canadian Government Specifications Board
c.g.s.e. centimetre gramme second electromagnetic
C.G.T. Compagnie Générale Transatlantique (The French Line)
Confédération Générale du Travail (General Confederation of Labour, France)
Ch. Chairman
Chamber
Champion
Chancellor
Chancery   *cont.*

Chaplain
Chapter
Chief
China
Chinese
Chirurgia (Surgery)
Christ
Church
ch. chain
chambre (room)
chapter
charts
check
chemical
chemistry
chestnut
cheval-vapeur (horsepower)
chevaux (horses)
chief
choice
choir
C.H. Centre Half
Clearing House
Court House
Custom House
Member of the Order of the Companions of Honour
c.h. candle hour(s)
central heating
C.H.A. Chest and Heart Association
Country-Wide Holidays Association
C.H.A.C. Central Housing Advisory Committee
chal. chaleur (heat)
Chald. Chaldean
Chamb. Chamberlain
Chambers
Champ. Champion
Chanc. Chancellor
Chancery
CHANCOM Channel Committee (N.A.T.O.)
Chap. Chaplain
Chaplaincy
Chapel
Chapter
Chap.-Gen. Chaplain General
Chap.St.J. Chaplain of the Order of Saint John of Jerusalem (now Ch.St.J.)
char. character
charter
charity
charwoman
chars. characters
Chas. Chambers
Ch.B. Baccalaureus Chirurgiae (Bachelor of Surgery)
Ch.B.S. Incorporated Church Building Society
CHC Cyclohexylamine Carbonate
C.H.C. Clerk to the House of Commons
ch.cent. chauffage central (central heating)
Ch.Ch. Christ Church
Ch.Coll. Christ's College, Cambridge
Ch.D. Chancery Division
Doctor of Chemistry
C.H.D. Coronary Heart Disease
Ch.E. Chemical Engineer
Chief Engineer

CHEKA Chrezvychainaya Kommissia (All Russian Extraordinary Commission for Fighting Counter-Revolution and Sabotage)
C.H.E.L. The Cambridge History of English History
Chem. Chemical
Chemist(ry)
Ches. Cheshire
Chev. Chevalier (knight)
chev. chevron
chf. chief
Ch.F. Chaplain of the Fleet
C.H.F.T. Carnegie Hero Fund Trust
ch/fwd. charges forward
chg. change
charge
Chi. Chicago
China
Chinese
Chiv. Chivalry
Ch.J. Chief Justice
Ch.K. Christ the King
ch.-l. chef-lieu (chief town)
C.H.L. Cambridge Higher Loca
chlo. chloride
chloroform
Chm. Chairman
Choirmaster
Ch.M. Chirurgiae Magister (Master of Surgery)
C.H.M. Diploma of Choir Master of the Royal College of Organists
Cho. Choral
C.H.O. Crop Husbandry Officer
choc. chocolate
Ch. of F. Chaplain of the Fleet
Ch. of S. Chamber of Shipping
Chor. Choral
Chorus
Chorister
C.H.P. Certificat en hygiène publique (Certificate in Public Health)
ch/ppd. charges prepaid
chq. cheque
Chris. Christian
Chrm. Chairman
Chron. Chronicles
Chronometry
chron. chronicle
chronological(ly)
chronology
Chrs. Chambers
C.H.S. Church Historical Society
Ch.Skr. Chief Skipper
Ch.St.J. Chaplain of the Order of Saint John of Jerusalem
C.H.U. Centigrade Heat Unit
ch.v. cheval-vapeur (horsepower)
c.h.w. constant hot water
chwdn. churchwarden
C.I. Channel Islands
Chief Inspector
Chief Instructor
Commonwealth Institute
Communist International
Consular Invoice
Counter Intelligence
Imperial Order of the Crown of India
c.i. cast iron
compression ignition

Cia. Compagnia (Company)
C.I.A. Central Intelligence Agency(U.S.)
   Chief Inspector of Armaments
   Collegium Internationale Allergologicum
   Comité international d'Auschwitz (International Auschwitz Committee)
   Confédération internationale des accordéonistes (International Confederation of Accordionists)
   Conseil international des archives (International Council on Archives)
   Corporation of Insurance Agents
C.I.A.A. Centre international d'aviation agricole (International Agricultural Aviation Centre)
C.I.A.B. Conseil international des agences bénévoles (International Council of Voluntary Agencies)
C.I.A.F.M.A. Centre International de l'Actualité Fantastique et Magique (International Magic Circle)
C.I.A.I. Comité international d'aide aux intellectuels (International Relief Committee for Professional Workers)
C.I.A.L. Communauté internationale des associations de la librairie (International Community of Booksellers' Associations)
   Corresponding Member of the International Institute of Arts and Letters
C.I.A.O. Conférence internationale des africanistes de l'ouest (International West African Conference)
C.I.A.P.G. Confédération internationale des anciens prisonniers de guerre (International Confederation of Former Prisoners of War)
C.I.A.S. Conference of Independent African States
C.I.B. Communauté internationale Baha'ie (Bahá'í International Community)
   Conseil international du bâtiment pour la recherche, l'étude et la documentation (International Council for Building Research, Studies and Documentation)
   Criminal Investigation Branch
C.I.B.C. Commonwealth Institute of Biological Control
C.I.C.R.A. Centre International pour la coordination des Recherches en Agriculture (International Centre for the Coordination of Research in Agriculture)
C.I.B.E. Confédération internationale des betteraviers européens (International Confederation of European Sugar-Beet Growers)
C.I.B.E.P. Section des six pays du commerce international de bulbes à fleurs et de plantes ornementales (International Flower, Bulb and Ornamental Plant Trade Section for the Six Countries)

C.I.C. Capital Issues Committee
   Chemical Institute of Canada
   Commonwealth Information Centre
   Commercial Instruments Conference
   Confédération internationale de la coiffure (International Confederation of the Hairdressing Trade)
   Confédération internationale des cadres (International Confederation of Executive Staffs)
   Conseil international de la chasse (International Hunting Council)
   Conseil international des compositeurs (International Council of Composers)
   Counter Intelligence Corps (U.S.)
C.I.C.A. Confédération internationale du credit agricole (International Confederation for Agricultural Credit)
C.I.C.A.E. Confédération internationale des cinémas d'art et d'essai (International Experimental and Art Film Theatres Confederation)
C.I.C.C. Conférence internationale des charités catholiques (International Conference of Catholic Charities)
Cicestr. Cicestrensis (of Chichester)
C.I.C.G. Centre international du commerce de gros (International Centre for Wholesale Trade)
C.I.C.I.A.M.S. Comité internationale catholique des infirmières et assistantes médico-sociales (International Committee of Catholic Nurses)
C.I.C.I.H. Confédération internationale catholique des institutions hospitalières (International Catholic Confederation of Hospitals)
C.I.C.J. Comité international pour la coopération des journalistes (International Committee for Co-operation of Journalists)
C.I.C.P. Comité Internacional para la Cooperación de los Periodistas (International Committee for the Co-operation of Journalists)
   Confédération internationale du crédit populaire (International Confederation for Small-Scale Credit)
C.I.C.R. Comité international de la Croix Rouge (International Committee of the Red Cross)
C.I.C.R.C. Commission internationale contre le régime concentrationnaire (International Commission Against Concentration Camp Practices)
C.I.C.R.I.S. Co-operative Industrial and Commercial Reference and Information Service
C.I.C.T. Conseil international du cinéma et de la télévision (International Film and Television Council)
C.I.C.Y.P. Consejo Interamericano de Comercio y Producción (Inter-American Council of Commerce and Production)

54

C.I.D. Comité international de Dachau (Dachau International Committee)

Comité International de la Détergence (International Committee of Surface Activity)

Council of Industrial Design

Criminal Investigation Department

C.I.D.A. Comité Interamericano de Desarrollo Agricola (Inter-American Committee for Agricultural Development)

Comité intergouvernemental du droit d'auteur (Intergovernmental Copyright Committee)

CIDADEC Confédération internationale des associations d'experts et de conseils (International Confederation of Associations of Experts and Consultants)

CIDALC Comité international du cinéma d'enseignement et de la culture (International Committee of Film Education and Culture)

C.I.D.E.S.A. Centre international de documentation économique et sociale africaine (International Centre for African Social and Economic Documentation)

CIDESCO Comité international d'esthétique et de cosmétologie (International Committee for Aesthetics and Cosmetology)

C.I.D.G. Civilian Irregular Defence Group

C.I.D.S.S. Comité international pour la documentation des sciences sociales (International Committee for Social Sciences Documentation)

Cie. compagnie (company)

C.I.E. Captain's Imperfect Entry

Centre international de l'enfance (International Children's Centre)

Commission internationale de l'éclairage (International Commission on Illumination)

Commonwealth Institute of Entomology

Companion of the Order of the Indian Empire

Coras Iompair Eireann (Transport Organisation of Ireland)

C.I.E.C. Centre international d'études crimonologiques (International Centre of Criminological Studies)

Commission internationale de l'état civil (International Commission on Civil Status)

Confederación Interamericana de Educación Católica (Inter-American Confederation of Catholic Education)

Conseil international des employeurs du commerce (International Council of Commerce Employers)

C.I.E.E. Companion of the Institution of Electrical Engineers

C.I.E.M. Conseil international pour l'exploration de la mer (International Council for the Exploration of the Sea)

C.I.E.N. Commission interaméricaine d'énergie nucléaire (Inter-American Nuclear Energy Commission)

C.I.E.O. Catholic International Education Office

C.I.E.P.S. Conseil international de l'éducation physique et sportive (International Council of Sport and Physical Education)

C.I.E.S. Comité international des entreprises à succursales (International Association of Chain Stores)

C.I.E.T.A. Centre international d'études des textiles anciens (International Research Centre on Ancient Textiles)

C.I.F. Commission interaméricaine des femmes (Inter-American Commission of Women)

Conseil international des femmes (International Council of Women)

c.i.f. cost, insurance, freight

c.i.f. & c. cost, insurance, freight and commission

c.i.f.c.i. cost, insurance, freight, commission and interest

C.I.F.E. Conseil international du film d'enseignement (International Council for Educational Films)

Conseil des fédérations industrielles d'Europe (Council of European Industrial Federations)

c.i.f.e. cost, insurance, freight and exchange

c.i.f.i. cost, insurance, freight and interest

C.I.F.E.J. Centre international du film pour l'enfance et la jeunesse (International Centre of Films for Children)

c.i.f.L.t. cost, insurance and freight, London terms

C.I.G. Comité international de géophysique (International Geophysical Committee)

C.I.G.B. Commission internationale des grands barrages de la Conférence mondiale de l'énergie (International Commission of Large Dams of the World Power Conference)

C.I.G.R. Commission internationale du génie rural (International Commission of Agricultural Engineering)

C.I.G.R.E. Conférence internationale des grands réseaux électriques (International Conference on Large Electric Systems)

C.I.G.S. Chief of the Imperial General Staff

C.I.H.A. Comité international d'histoire de l'art (International Committee on the History of Art)

C.I.I. Chartered Insurance Institute

Confederation of Irish Industry

cont.

Conseil international des infirmières (International Council of Nurses)

C.I.I.A. Canadian Institute of International Affairs

Commission internationale des industries agricoles (International Commission for Agricultural Industries)

C.I.I.T.C. Confédération Internationale des Industries Techniques du Cinéma (International Confederation of the Cinema Industry)

C.I.J. Commission internationale de juristes (International Commission of Jurists)

C.I.L.B. Commission internationale de lutte biologique contre les ennemis des plantes (International Committee for Biological Control)

C.I.L.C. Confédération internationale du lin et du chanvre (International Linen and Hemp Confederation)

C.I.L.P.E. Conférence internationale de liaison entre producteurs d'énergie électrique (International Liaison Conference for Producers of Electrical Energy)

C.I.M. China Inland Mission

Commission for Industry and Manpower

Conférence islamique mondial (World Muslim Conference)

Conseil international de la musique (International Music Council)

Consejo Internacional de Mujeres (International Council of Women)

Convention internationale concernant le transport des merchandises par chemins de fer (International Convention Concerning the Carriage of Goods by Rail)

C.I.M.A.C. Congrès international des machines à combustion (International Congress on Combustion Engines)

C.I.Mar.E. Companion of the Institute of Marine Engineers

C.I.M.C.E.E. Comité des industries de la moutarde de la C.E.E. (E.E.C. Committee for the Mustard Industries)

C.I.M.E. Comité intergouvernemental pour les migrations européennes (Intergovernmental Committee for European Migration)

C.I.Mech.E. Companion of the Institution of Mechanical Engineers

C.I.M.M. Canadian Institute of Mining and Metallurgy

C.I.M.P. Conseil international de la musique populaire (International Folk Music Council)

C.I.M.P.M. Comité international de médecine et de pharmacie militaires (International Committee of Military Medicine and Pharmacy)

C.I.M.S.C.E.E. Comité des industries des mayonnaises et sauces condimentaires de la C.E.E. (Committee of *cont.*

the Mayonnaise and Sauce Industries of the E.E.C.)

C.I.M.T.P. Congrès international de médecine tropicale et de paludisme (International Congress of Tropical Medicine and Malaria)

C.I.N. Commission internationale de numismatique (International Numismatic Commission)

C.-in-C. Commander-in-Chief

Curate in Charge

CINCAFMED Commander-in-Chief Allied Forces Mediterranean

C.I.N.C.C. Coal Industry National Consultative Council

CINCEASTLANT Commander-in-Chief Eastern Atlantic Area

CINCENT Commander-in-Chief Allied Forces Central Europe

CINCHAN Commander-in-Chief Channel and South North Sea

CINCLANT Commander-in-Chief Atlantic Fleet (U.S.)

CINCMED Commander-in-Chief British Naval Forces in the Mediterranean

CINCNELM Commander-in-Chief U.S. Naval Forces in Europe, the East Atlantic and the Mediterranean

CINCNORTH Commander-in-Chief Allied Forces Northern Europe

CINCPAC Commander-in-Chief Pacific Fleet (U.S.)

CINCSOUTH Commander-in-Chief Allied Forces Southern Europe

CINCWESTLANT Commander-in-Chief Western Atlantic Area

Cinn. Cincinnati

C.I.N.O. Chief Inspector of Naval Ordnance

C.I.N.O.A. Confédération internationale des négociants en oeuvres d'art (International Confederation of Art Dealers)

C.Inst. R.E. (Aust.) Companion of the Institution of Radio Engineers (Australia)

C.I.O. Church Information Office

Commission internationale d'optique (International Commission for Optics)

Comité international olympique (International Olympic Committee)

Congress of Industrial Organisations (*now* A.F.L.-C.I.O.)

C.I.O.M.R. Comité Interallié des Officiers Médicins de Réserve (Interallied Committee of Medical Reserve Officers)

C.I.O.M.S. Council for International Organizations of Medical Sciences

C.I.O.S. Combined Intelligence Objectives Sub-Committee

Comité international de l'organisation scientifique (International Committee of Scientific Management)

C.I.O.S.L. Confederación Internacional de Organizaciones Sindicales Libres (International Confederation of Free Trade Unions)

C.I.O.S.T.A. Commission internationale pour l'organisation scientifique du travail en agriculture (International Agricultural Labour Science Group)

C.I.O.T.F. Conseil international des organismes de travailleuses familiales (International Council of Home-Help Services)

C.I.P. Collège international de podologie (International College of Podology)
Comité international de photobiologie (International Committee of Photobiology)
Commission internationale du peuplier (International Poplar Commission
Council of Iron Producers

C.I.P.A. Chartered Institute of Patent Agents

C.I.P.B.C. Church of India, Pakistan, Burma and Ceylon

C.I.P.C. Comité international permanent de la conserve (Permanent International Committee on Canned Foods)

C.I.P.C.E. Centre d'information et de publicité des chemins de fer européens (Information and Publicity Centre of the European Railways

C.I.P.C.I. Conseil International des Praticiens du Plan Comptable International (International Council of Practitioners of the International Plan of Accounts)

C.I.P.E. Consejo Internacional de la Película de Enseñanza (International Council for Educational Films)

C.I.P.L. Comité international permanent de linguistes (Permanent International Committee of Linguists)

C.I.P.O. Comité international pour la préservation des oiseaux (International Committee for Bird Preservation)

C.I.P.P. Conseil indo-pacifique des pêches (Indo-Pacific Fisheries Council)

C.I.P.R. Commission internationale de protection contre les radiations (International Commission on Radiological Protection)

C.I.P.S.H. Conseil international de la philosophie et des sciences humaines (International Council for Philosophy and the Humanities)

C.I.Q. Confoederatio internationalis ad qualitates plantarum edulium perquirendas (International Association for Quality Research on Food Plants)

Cir. Circus

cir. circuit
circular
circulation

C.I.R. Canada-India Reactor
Commission on Industrial Relations
Consejo Interuniversitario Regional (Regional Inter-University Council)

circ. circa (about *or* approximately)
circumference

C.I.R.C.C.E. Confédération internationale de la représentation commerciale de la Communauté européenne (International Confederation of Commercial Representation in the European Community)

circum. circumference

C.I.R.F. Centre international d'information et de recherche sur la formation professionnelle (International Vocational Training Information and Research Centre)

C.I.R.F.S. Comité international de la rayonne et des fibres synthétiques (International Rayon and Synthetic Fibres Committee)

C.I.R.I.E.C. Centre international de recherches et d'information sur l'économie collective (International Centre of Research and Information on Public and Collective Economy)

C.I.R.M. Comité International Radio-Maritime (International Radio-Maritime Committee)

C.I.R.P. Collège international pour l'étude scientifique des techniques de production mécanique (International Institution for Production Engineering Research)

C.I.S. Chartered Institute of Secretaries
Conference of Internationally-Minded Schools

C.I.S.A.C. Confédération internationale des sociétés d'auteurs et compositeurs (International Confederation of Societies of Authors and Composers)

C.I.S.B.H. Comité international de standardisation en biologie humaine (International Committee for Standardization in Human Biology)

C.I.S.C. Confédération internationale des syndicats chrétiens (International Federation of Christian Trade Unions)
Conférence internationale du scoutisme catholique (International Catholic Scouters Conference)

C.I.S.F. Confédération internationale des sages-femmes (International Confederation of Midwives)

C.I.S.H. Comité international des sciences historiques (International Committee of Historical Sciences)

C.I.S.I.R. Ceylon Institute of Scientific and Industrial Research

C.I.S.J.A. Comité international de solidarité avec la jeunesse algérienne (International Solidarity Committee with Algerian Youth)

C.I.S.L. Confédération internationale des syndicats libres (International Confederation of Free Trade Unions)
Confederazione Italiana Sindacati Lavoratori (Italian Confederation of Workers' Trade Unions

E

C.I.S.M. Conseil international du sport militaire (International Military Sports Council)

C.I.S.N.A.L. Confederazione Italiana dei Sindacati Nazionali dei Lavoratori (National Italian Confederation of Workers' Trade Unions)

C.I.S.O. Comité international des sciences onomastiques (International Committee of Onomastic Sciences)

C.I.S.P.M. Confédération internationale des sociétés populaires de musique (International Confederation of Popular Music Societies)

C.I.S.P.R. Comité international spécial des perturbations radioélectriques (International Special Committee on Radio Interference)

C.I.S.S. Comité international des sports silencieux (International Committee for Silent Games)
Conférence internationale de service social (International Conference of Social Work)
Conferencia Interamericano de Seguridad Social (Inter-American Conference on Social Security)
Conseil international des sciences sociales (International Social Science Council)

C.I.S.S.B. Civil Service Selection Board

C.I.S.V. Children's International Summer Village Association

C.I.S.W.O. Coal Industry Social Welfare Organisation

cit. citadel
citation
cited
citizen
citrate

C.I.T. California Institute of Technology
Carnegie Institute of Technology
Comité international des transports par chemins de fer (International Railway Transport Committee)
Conseil international des tanneurs (International Council of Tanners)

c.i.t. compression in transit

C.I.T.A. Confederación Internacional de Ingenieros y Técnicos de la Agricultura (International Confederation of Technical Agricultural Engineers)

C.I.T.C.E. Comité international de thermodynamique et de cinétique électro-chimiques (International Committee of Electro-Chemical Thermodynamics and Kinetics)

C.I.T.E.N. Comité international de la teinture et du nettoyage (International Committee for Dyeing and Dry Cleaning)

C.I.T.I. Confédération internationale des travailleurs intellectuels (International Confederation of Professional and Intellectual Workers)

C.I.T.S. Commission internationale technique de sucrerie (International Commission of Sugar Technology)

C.I.T.T.A. Comité international des fabricants de tapis et de tissues d'ameublement (International Committee of Manufacturers of Carpets and Furnishing Fabrics)

C.I.U. Club and Institute Union

C.I.U.S. Conseil international des unions scientifiques (International Council of Scientific Unions)

C.I.U.S.S. Catholic International Union for Social Service

civ. civil(ian)
civilisation

C.I.V. City Imperial Volunteers
Commission internationale du verre (International Commission on Glass)
Convention internationale concernant le transport des voyageurs et des bagages par chemins de fer (International Convention Concerning the Carriage of Passengers and Baggage by Rail)

Civ.E. Civil Engineer(ing)

C.I.W. Carnegie Institute of Washington

cj. conjectural

C.J. Chief Justice

C.J.C.C. Commonwealth Joint Communications Committee

C.J.M. Code de justice militaire (Code of Military Justice)
Congregation of Jesus and Mary (Eudist Fathers)
Congrès juif mondial (World Jewish Congress)

ck. cask
check

ckw. clockwise

Cl Chlorine

Cl. Class
Classical
Classics
Clergy(man)
Cloth
Council

cl. centilitre(s)
class
classical
clause
clergy(man)
clerk
clove

C.L. Calendar Line
Centre Line
Civil Law
Civil Lord
Commander of the Order of Leopold (Belgium)
Common Law
Communication Lieutenant
Craft Loss
Critical List

c.l. cut lengths

c/l. cash letter
craft loss

Cla. Clackmannan

58

C.L.A. Canadian Library Association
Church Literature Association
Country Landowners' Association
C.L.A.I.R.A. Chalk Lime and Allied Industries Research Association
C.L.A.M. Comité Permanent de Liaison de l'Agriculture Méditerranéenne (Permanent Committee for Liaison of Mediterranean Agronomists)
Clar. Clarenceux (King of Arms)
Clarendon
Clarinet
C.L.A.R.C. Consejo Latino-Americano de Radiación Cósmica (Latin-American Council for Cosmic Rays)
C.L.A.S.P. Consortium of Local Authorities Special Programme
class. classic(al)
classification
C.L.A.S.S. Computer-based Laboratory for Automated School Systems
C.L.A.W. Consortium of Local Authorities in Wales
C.L.B. Church Lads' Brigade
C.L.C. Chartered Life Underwriter of Canada
Commonwealth Liaison Committee
C.L.C.B. Committee of London Clearing Bankers
C.L.C.C.R. Comité de liaison de la construction de carrosseries et de remorques (Liaison Committee of Coachwork and Trailer Builders)
C.L.Cr. Communication Lieutenant-Commander
cld. called
cleared
coloured
could
C.L.E. Council of Legal Education
Clean California League Enlisting Action Now
C.L.E.A.P.S.E. Consortium of Local Education Authorities for the Provision of Science Equipment
CLEPA Comité de liaison de la construction d'équipements et de pièces d'automobile (Liaison Committee for the Manufacture of Automobile Equipment and Spare Parts)
Cler. Clerical
C.L.H. Croix de la Légion d'Honneur (Cross of the Legion of Honour)
C.L.I.M.M.A.R. Centre de liaison international des marchands de machines agricoles et réparateurs (International Liaison Centre for Agricultural Machinery Distributors and Maintenance)
Clin. Clinic(al)
C.Litt. Companion of Literature
C.L.J. Cambridge Law Journal
clk. clerk
clock
clkw. clockwise
C.L.M.L. Current List of Medical Literature
C.L.O. Chief Liaison Officer
Cod Liver Oil

C.L.P.A. Central London Productivity Association
Common Law Procedure Acts
clr. colour
C.L.R.U. Cambridge Language Research Unit
C.L.S. Certificate in Library Science
Courts of London Sessions
C.L.T. Canadian Law Times
C.L.U. Chartered Life Underwriter
Cm Curium
cm. centimetre(s)
C.M. Canadian Militia
Catholic Mission
Certificate of Merit
Certificated Master or Mistress
Chirurgiae Magister (Master of Surgery)
Church Mission(ary)
Circulation Manager
Common Market
Common Metre
Congregation of the Mission (Vincentian Fathers)
Corporate Membership
Corresponding Member
Court Martial
c.m. causa mortis (in case of or because of death)
circular mil
classes moyennes (middle classes)
C.M.A. Cable Makers' Association
Canadian Medical Association
Church Music Association
Corset Manufacturers' Association
C.M.A.C. Catholic Marriage Advisory Council
C.M.A.C.P. Conseil mondial pour l'assemblée constituante des peuples (World Council for the Peoples' World Convention)
C.M.A.S. Clergy Mutual Assurance Society
Confédération mondiale des activités subaquatiques (World Underwater Federation)
C.M.B. Central Medical Board
Central Midwives' Board
Coastal Motor Boat
C.M.B.H.I. Craft Member British Horological Institute
C.M.C. Canadian Marconi Company
Collective Measures Committee (U.N.)
Groupement des producteurs de carreaux céramiques du Marché Commun (Common Market Group of Ceramic Tile Producers)
C.M.C.W. Calvinistic Methodist Church of Wales
Cmd. Command
C.M.D. Common Metre Double
C.M.D.C. Central Milk Distributive Committee
Cmdg. Commanding
Cmdr. Commander
Comdre. Commodore
Cmdt. Commandant

C.M.E. Conférence mondiale de l'énergie (World Power Conference)
C.M.E.A. Council for Mutual Economic Aid (Comecon)
C.M.F. Central Mediterranean Force
Ceylon Military Force(s)
Commonwealth Military Force(s)
Cordis Mariae Filius (Missionary Sons of the Immaculate Heart of Mary)
C.M.G. Companion of the Order of Saint Michael and Saint George
C.M.H. Combined Military Hospital
Congressional Medal of Honor (U.S.)
C.M.H.A. Canadian Mental Health Association
C.M.I. Comité maritime international (International Maritime Committee)
Commission mixte internationale pour la protection des lignes de télécommunication et des canalisations (Joint International Committee for the Protection of Telecommunication Lines and Ducts)
Commonwealth Mycological Institute
C.M.J. Church's Ministry among the Jews
C.M.L. Central Music Library
C.M.M. Chief Metropolitan Magistrate
Congregation of the Missionaries of Mariannhill
C.M.M.A. Concrete Mixer Manufacturers' Association
C.M.O. Chief Medical Officer
C.M.O.P.E. Confédération mondiale des organisations de la profession enseignante (World Confederation of Organizations of the Teaching Profession)
cmp. compromise
C.M.P. Commissioner of the Metropolitan Police
Corps of Military Police (*now* C.R.M.P.)
cm. pf. cumulative preferred *or* preference shares
cm. p. s. centimetres per second
C.M.R.O. County Milk Regulations Officer
C.M.R.S.S. Conseil méditerranéen de recherches en sciences sociales (Mediterranean Social Sciences Research Council)
C.M.S. Church Missionary Society
c.m.s. cras mane sumendus (to be taken tomorrow morning)
C.M.Z.S. Corresponding Member of the Zoological Society
CN Chloracetophenone
Cn. Canon
C.N. Circular Note
Code Napoléon
Consignment Note
Country Note
C/N. Circular Note
Consignment Note
Contract Note
Cover Note
Credit Note

C.N.A.A. Council for National Academic Awards
C.N.A.S. Chief of Naval Air Services
C.N.D. Campaign for Nuclear Disarmament
C.N.D.A. Clapham Notre Dame Association
C.N.(Eng.)O. Chief Naval Engineering Officer
C.N.I. Chief of Naval Information
C.N.I.P.A. Committee of National Institutes of Patent Agents
C.N.L. Commonwealth National Library (Australia)
C.N.M.A. Cordage and Net Manufacturers' Association
C.N.O. Chief of Naval Operations
C.N.P. Chief of Naval Personnel
C.N.R. Canadian National Railways
Civil Nursing Reserve
C.N.S. Chief of the Naval Staff
C.N.S.S.O. Chief Naval Supply and Secretariat Officer
C.N.T. Canadian National Telegraphs
Co Cobalt
Columbium
Co. Colon
Company
County
Course
C.O. Cabinet Office
Cash Order
Central Office
Chief Office
Clerical Officer
Colonial Office
Command Order
Commanding Officer
Conscientious Objector
Criminal Office
Crown Office
C/O. Case Oil
Certificate of Origin
c.o. change over
c/o. care of
carried over
cash order
C.O.A. Condition on Admission
coad. coadjutor
Coal. Coalition
C.O.A.S. Council of the Organisation of American States
C.O.B.C.C.E.E. Comité des organisations de la boucherie et charcuterie de la C.E.E. (Committee of Meat Trade Organizations of the E.E.C.)
c.o.b.q. cum omnibus bonis quiescat (may he *or* she rest with all good souls)
C.O.C. Chamber of Commerce
Clerk of the Chapel
Corps of Commissionaires
C.O.C.A.S.T. Council for Overseas Colleges of Arts, Science and Technology
C.O.C.É.M.A. Comité des constructeurs européens de matériel alimentaire (Committee of European Manufacturers of Food Machinery)
coch. cochleare (a spoonful)
COCOM Coordinating Committee Controlling East-West Trade

cod. codex
 codicil
 codification
C.O.D. Chamber of Deputies
 Collect *or* Cash on Delivery
 Concise Oxford Dictionary
C.O.E. Conseil œcuménique des
 églises (World Council of Churches)
Co.Ed. Co-Educational
Co.-ed. Co-editor
C.O.E.D. Concise Oxford English Dict-
 ionary
coeff. coefficient
C.O.F. Comité Olympique Française
 (French Olympic Committee)
C. of A. Certificate of Airworthiness
 College of Arms
COFALEC Comité des fabricants de
 levure de panification de la C.E.E.
 (Committee of Bread Yeast Manufact-
 urers of the E.E.C.)
C. of B. Confirmation of Balance
C. of C. Coefficient of Correlation
C. of E. Church of England
 Council of Europe
 Coefficient of Elasticity
C. of E.C.S. Church of England Child-
 ren's Society
C. of F. Chaplain of the Fleet
 Coefficient of Friction
c. of g. centre of gravity
C. of I. Church of Ireland
C. of L. City of London
C. of S. Chief of Staff
 Church of Scotland
 Conditions of Service
cog. cognate
 cognisant
 cognomen
C.O.G. Cleansing Officers' Guild
c.o.g. centre of gravity
COGECA Comité général de a co-
 opération agricole des pays de la
 C.E.E. (General Committee for Agri-
 cultural Co-operation in the E.E.C.
 Countries)
coh. coheir
C.O.H.S.E. Confederation of Health
 Service Employees
C.O.I. Central Office of Information
 Certificate of Origin and Interest
 Commission océanographique
 intergouvernementale (Inter-
 governmental Oceanographic
 Commission)
C.o.I.D. Council of Industrial Design
C.O.I.F. Control of Intensive Farming
COIN Counter-insurgency
C.O.I.N.S. Committee on the Improve-
 ment of National Statistics
C.O.I.S.M. Conseil des Organisations
 Internationales des Sciences Médi-
 cales (Council of International Org-
 anisations of Medical Science)
C.O.J.O. Conference of Jewish Organ-
 isations
Col. Colon
 Colonel
 Colonial
 Colony
 Colorado   *cont.*

Colossians
 Colour
col. cola (strain)
 coloured
 column
Co. L. Coalition Liberal
C.O.L.B. Cost of Living Bonus
Col.Comdt. Colonel Commandant
Cold. Coloured
COLIPED Commission de liaison des
 pièces et équipements de deux roues
 (Liaison Committee for Motor Cycle
 and Bicycle Equipment and Spare
 Parts)
Coll. Collateral
 College
 Collegiate
coll. collateral
 colleague
 collect(ion)
 collegiate
 colloquial
collab. collaborate
 collaborator
collat. collateral
Colloq. Colloquial
Colo. Colorado
colog. cologarithm
Col.-Sgt. Colour-Sergeant
Com. Comedy
 Commander
 Commemoration
 Commerce
 Commissary
 Commissioner
 Commodore
 Commonwealth
 Commune
 Communist
com. comic
 commentary
 commerce
 commission
 committee
 common
 communication
 community
C.O.M.A. Coke Oven Managers' Asso-
 ciation
COMACA Corresponding Member of
 the Academy of Arts of the U.S.S.R.
COMAF Comité des constructeurs de
 matériel frigorifique de la C.E.E.
 (Committee of Refrigerating Plant
 Manufacturers of the E.E.C.)
COMAIRCENTLANT Air Command-
 er Central Atlantic Sub-area
COMAIRCHAN Maritime Air Commander Channel
COMAIREASTLANT Air Commander Eastern Atlantic Area
COMAIRLANT Commander Air
 Force, Atlantic (U.S.)
COMAIRNORLANT Air Commander
 Northern Atlantic Sub-area
comb. combination
 combined
 combining
 combustible
COMBISLANT Commander Bay of
 Biscay Atlantic Sub-area
combs. combinations

COMCANLANT Commander Canadian Atlantic Sub-area
COMCENTLANT Commander Central Atlantic Sub-area
COMCRULANT Commander Cruisers, Atlantic (U.S.)
Comd. Command(er)
    Commanding
COMDEV Commonwealth Development Finance Company
Comdg. Commanding
Comdr. Commander
Comdt. Commandant
C.O.M.E. Chief Ordnance Mechanical Engineer
COMECON Council for Mutual Economic Assistance
Com. Err. The Comedy of Errors (Shakespeare)
COMET Committee for Middle East Trade
C.O.M.E.T. Council on Middle East Trade
COMTEC-GAZ Comité d'études économiques de l'industrie du gaz (Economic Research Committee of the Gas Industry)
COMEXO Committee for Oceanic Exploration
Com.-Gen. Commissary-General
Cominform Communist Information Bureau
Comintern Communist International
COMISCO Committee of International Socialist Conference
coml. commerical
Comm. Commerce
    Commercial
    Commission
commd. commissioned
commem. commemorative
Commiss. Commissary
Commn. Commission
Commr. Commissioner
Commun. Community
commun. communication
COMNAVNORTH Commander Allied Naval Forces Northern Europe
COMNORASDEFLANT Commander North American Anti-Submarine Defence Force Atlantic
COMNORLANT Commander Northern Atlantic Sub-area
COMOCEANLANT Commander Ocean Atlantic Sub-area
comp. companion
    comparative
    compare
    comparison
    compensation
    competitative
    competitor
    compiler
    composer
    composition(s
    compositor
    compound(ed)
    comprehensive
Compa. Compañia (Company
COMPAC Commonwealth Trans-Pacific Telephone Cable

compar. comparative
compd. compound
Comp.Gen(l). Comptroller-General
compl. complement
    complete(d)
    compliment(ary)
complt. complainant
    complaint
compo. composition
compt. compartment
Comptr. Comptroller
Comr. Commissioner
COMSAT Communications Satellite
COMSTRIKEFLTLANT Commander Striking Fleet Atlantic
COMSUBEASTLANT Commander Submarine Force Eastern Atlantic
Comy.-Gen. Commissary-General
Con. Consolidate(d)
    Constructor
    Consul
    Convict
con. concentration
    concerning
    concerto
    conclusion
    continued
    contra (against)
    convenience
    conversation
ConAC Continental Air Command (U.S.)
ConAD Continental Air Defense Command (U.S.)
ConARC Continental Army Command (U.S.)
conbd. contributed
conc. concentrate(d)
    concentration
Con.C. Constructor Captain
Conch. Conchology
concr. concrete(ly)
Con.Cr. Constructor Commander
cond. condense(r)
    condition(al)
    conduct(ed)
    conductivity
    conductor
CONELRAD Control of Electromagnetic Radiation
con esp. con espressione (with expression)
Conf. conference
conf. confectionery
    confer (compare)
Confd. Confederated
    Confederation
Conf. Pont. Confessor Pontifex (Confessor and Bishop)
Cong. Congregation(al)
    Congregationalist
    Congress(ional)
cong. congius (gallon)
Cong. R. Congressional Record (U.S.)
Cong.U. Congregational Union of England and Wales
C.O.G.N.U. Council of National Golf Unions
C.O.N.I. Comitato Olimpico Nazionale Italiano (Italian National Olympic Committee)

conj. conjugation
    conjunction
    conjunctive
Con.L. Constructor Lieutenant
Con.L.Cr. Constructor Lieutenant-Commander
Conn. Connecticut
conn. connected
    connection
    connotation
conq. conquer
    conqueror
Cons. Consecrated
    Conservative
    Constable
    Consul
cons. consecrated
    consecration
    consecutive
    consequence
    conservation
    consigned
    consignment
    consolidated
    consonant
    constitutional
    construction
    consulting
Conserv. Conservatoire *or* Conservatory
cons. et prud. consilio et prudentia (by counsel and prudence)
consgt. consignment
consid. consideration
Con. S.L. Constructor Sub-Lieutenant
consol. consolidated
Const. Constitution
const. constable
    constant
    constituency
    constitution(al)
    construction
Constl. Constitutional
Constn. Constitution
constr. constructed
    construction
Cont. Containing
    Contemporary
    Contents
    Continental
    Continue
cont. continent
    continuum
    contra (against)
    contract
    control(ler)
contag. contagious
contbd. contraband
contbg. contributing
cont. bon. mor. contra bonos mores (contrary to good habits)
contd. contained
    continued
contemp. contemporary
contg. containing
contn. continuation
contr. contract(ed)
    contraction
    contrary
contrib. contribution
    contributor

Conv. Convent
    Convocation
conv. convenient
    conventional
    conversation
    converter
convce. conveyance
co-op. co-operation
    co-operative
Co-Op.U. Co-operative Union
co-ord. co-ordinate(s)
    co-ordination
Cop. Coptic
cop. copper
C.O.P.A. Comité des organisations professionnelles agricoles de la C.E.E. (Committee of Agricultural Organizations in the E.E.C.)
COPEC Conference on Politics, Economics and Citizenship (1924)
COPERS Preparatory Commission for European Space Research (*now* E.S.R.O.)
COPMEC Comité des petites et moyennes entreprises commerciales des pays de la C.E.E. (Committee of Small and Medium Sized Commercial Enterprises of the E.E.C. Countries)
C.O.P.P.S.O. Conference of Professional and Public Service Organisations
Copt. Coptic
Cor. Corinthians
    Coriolanus (Shakespeare)
    Coroner
cor. cornet
    coroner
    corpus
    correct(ion)
    correlative
    correspondence
    correspondent
    corrupt
CORDS Civil Operations and Revolutionary Development Support (Vietnam)
C.O.R.E. Congress of Racial Equality (U.S.)
CORESTA Centre de coopération pour les recherches scientifiques relatives au tabac (Cooperation Centre for Scientific Tobacco Research)
Corn. Cornish
    Cornwall
corol. corollary
Corp. Corporal
    Corporation
Corpn. Corporation
Corr. Corrigenda
corr. correct(ed)
    correction
    correlative
    correspondence
    correspondent
    corrugated
C.O.R.R.A. Combined Overseas Rehabilitation Relief Appeal
Cors. Corsica(n)
C.O.R.S. Chief of the Regulating Staff
cort. cortex

C.o.R.T. Council of Repertory Theatres
Cos. Companies
    Consul
    Counties
cos. cosine
C.O.S. Chamber of Shipping
    Charity Organisation Society
      (*now* F.W.A.)
    Chief of Staff
c.o.s. cash on shipment
co.sa. come sopra (as above)
COSEC Coordinating Secretariat of the National Unions of Students
cosec. cosecant
cosh hyperbolic cosine
C.O.S.M.D. Combined Operations Signals Maintenance Division
cosmog. cosmographical
    cosmography
    cosmogony
COSPAR Committee on Space Research of the International Council of Scientific Unions
Coss. Consules (Consuls)
C.O.S.S.A.C. Chief of Staff to Supreme Allied Commander
C.O.S.V.(N.) Central Office for South Vietnam
cot. cotangent
C.o.T. College of Technology
C.O.T.A.L. Confédération des organisations touristiques de l'Amérique latine (Latin American Confederation of Travel Organizations)
COTAR Correlation Tracking and Ranging (System)
C.O.T.C. Canadian Overseas Telecommunications Corporation
coth hyperbolic cotangent
Co.U. Coalition Unionist
couch. couchant
Coun. Counsellor
    Council(lor)
cour. courant (of the current month)
cov. covenant
C.O.W.T. Council of World Tensions
Cox. Coxswain
Coy. Company
Cp Cassiopeium
Cp Compline
cp. centipoise
    compare
C.P. Book of Common Prayer
    Cape Province
    Cardinal Point
    Carter Paterson
    Central Provinces (*now* Madhya Pradesh, India)
    Charter Party
    Chemical Practitioner
    Chief Patriarch
    Chief of Police
    Civil Procedure
    Clarendon Press
    Clerk of the Peace
    Code of Procedure
    College of Preceptors
    Communist Party
    Congregatio Passionis (Passionist Fathers)
    Court of Common Pleas
    Court of Probate   *cont.*

    Concert Party
    Convict Prison
C/P. Custom of Port
c.p. candle power
    carriage paid
    centre of pressure
    chemically pure
    common pleas
    constant pressure
C.P.A. Calico Printers' Association
    Canadian Pacific Airlines
    Canadian Pharmaceutical Association
    Canadian Psychological Association
    Certified Public Accountant
    Chartered Patent Agent
    Chick Producers' Association
    Children's Play Activities
    Church Pastoral-Aid Society
    Commonwealth Parliamentary Association
    Contractors' Plant Association
C.P.A.C. Collaborative Pesticides Analytical Committee
C.P.A.G. Child Poverty Action Group
C.Pal. Crystal Palace
C.P.A.S. Catholic Prisoners' Aid Society
    Church Pastoral-Aid Society
C.P B. Casual Payments Book
C.P.C. City Police Commissioner
    Clerk of the Privy Council
    Clinical Pathological Conference
    Coffee Promotion Council
    Conservative Political Centre
C.P.C.I.Z. Comité permanent des congrès internationaux de zoologie (Permanent Committee of International Zoological Congresses)
C.P.C.U. Chartered Property and Casualty Underwriter
cpd. compound
C.P.D. Charterers Pay Dues
C.P.E. College of Physical Education
    Congrès du peuple européen (Congress of European People)
C.P.E.A. Catholic Parents' and Electors' Association
c.pén. code pénal (penal code)
C.P.E.Q. Corporation of Professional Engineers of Quebec
C.P.F. Contributory Pension Fund
C.P.F.S. Council for the Promotion of Field Studies
C.P.G.B. Communist Party of Great Britain
C.P.H. Certificate in Public Health
C.P.H.A. Canadian Public Health Association
C.P.I. Chief Pilot Instructor
    Commission permanente internationale de l'acétylène, de la soudure autogène et des industries qui s'y rattachent (Permanent International Committee on Acetylene, Oxy-Acetylene Welding and Allied Industries)

C.P.I.T.U.S. Comité permanent international des techniques et de l'urbanisme souterrains (Permanent and International Committee of Underground Town Planning and Construction)

C.P.I.U.S. Comité permanent Internacional de Tecnicos y de Urbanismo Subterráneo (Permanent and International Committee of Underground Town Planning and Construction)

C.P.J.I. Cour permanente de justice internationale (Permanent Court of International Justice)

Cpl. Corporal

C.P.L. Central Public Library
Colonial Products Laboratory

C.P.M. Common Particular Metre
Critical Path Method

c.p.m. cycles per minute

C.P.M.A. Chinchilla Pelt Marketing Association

C.P.M.E. Conseil Parlementaire du Mouvement Européen (Parliamentary Council of the European Movement)

cpn. coupon

C.P.N.R.C. Crystal Palace National Recreation Centre

C.P.O. Chief Petty Officer
Command Pay Office
Commonwealth Producers' Organization
County Planning Office(r)

C.P.P. Convention People's Party (Ghana)

C.P.P.A. Canadian Pulp and Paper Association

C.P.P.C.C. Chinese People's Political Consultative Conference

C.P.P.S. Congregatio Pretiosissimi Sanguinis (Fathers of the Most Precious Blood)

C.P.P.S. Comisión permanente para la Explotación y Conservación de las Riquezas Marítimas del Pacífico Sur (Permanent Commission for the Conservation of the Maritime Resources of the South Pacific)

cpr. copper

C.P.R. Canadian Pacific Railway

C.P.R.C. Central Price Regulation Committee

C.P.R.E. Council for the Preservation of Rural England

C.P.R.S. Central Policy Review Staff

C.P.R.W. Council for the Preservation of Rural Wales

C.P.S. Cambridge Philosophical Society
Church Patronage Society
Clerk of Petty Sessions
Committee for Penicillin Sensitivity
Commonwealth Public Service
Custos Privati Sigilli (Keeper of the Privy Seal)

c.p.s. cycles per second

C.P.S.A. Clay Pigeon Shooting Association

C.P.S.M. Council for Professions' Supplementary to the Medicine Act, 1960

C.P.S.S. Certificate in Public Service Studies

C.P.S.U. Communist Party of the Soviet Union

C.P.T. Canadian Pacific Telegraphs

C.P.T.B. Clay Products Technical Bureau

C.P.U. Central Processing Unit
Coloured People's Union
Commonwealth Press Union

C.Q.A. Chalk Quarrying Association

C.Q.M. Chief or Company Quartermaster

C.Q.M.S. Company Quartermaster-Sergeant

Cr Chromium

Cr. Commander
Crown
Cruiser

cr. created
credit(or)
crown

C.R. Carolina Regina (Queen Caroline)
Carolus Rex (King Charles)
Carrier's Risk
Central Registry
Chief Ranger
Civis Romanus (Roman Citizen)
Conditioned Reflex
Commendation Ribbon (U.S.)
Community of the Resurrection
Company's Risk
Compression Ratio
Credit Rating
Current Rate
Custos Rotulorum (Keeper of the Rolls)

c/r. company's risk

C.R.A. Canadian Rheumatism Association
Commander, Royal Artillery
Commercial Rabbit Association

Cr.A.A. Commander-at-Arms

C.R.A.C. Careers Research Advisory Centre
Central Religious Advisory Committee

C.R.A.M. Card Random Access Memory

Cran. Craniology

C.R.A.S.C. Commander, Royal Army Service Corps

C.R.B. Central Radio Bureau

C.R.C. Composing Room Chapel
Continental Railway Circle

C.R.C.C. Canadian Red Cross Committee

C.R.D. Centre de recherches et de documentation (Research and Documentation Centre of the W.E.A.)
Chronic Respiratory Disease

C.R.D.F. Cathode-Ray Direction-Finding

C.R.E. Coal Research Establishment
Commander, Royal Engineers
Commercial Relations Export Department

C.R.E.D.O. Centre for Curriculum Renewal and Educational Development Overseas

Cres. Crescent

cresc. crescendo (increasing)
C.R.G. Cave Research Group of Great Britain
C.R.I. Children's Relief International
Coconut Research Institute (Ceylon)
Croce Rossa Italiana (Italian Red Cross)
C.R.I.C. Canon Regular of the Immaculate Conception
C.R.I.L.C. Canadian Research Institute of Launderers and Cleaners
crim.con. criminal conversation
Criminol. Criminology
crit. criterion
critical
criticism
C.R.L. Canon Regular of the Lateran
Certified Record Librarian
Chemical Research Laboratory
C.R.M.A. Cotton and Rayon Merchants' Association
C.R.M.P. Corps of Royal Military Police (*formerly* C.M.P.)
Crn. Crown
C.R.N.S.S. Chief of the Royal Naval Scientific Service
C.R.O. Cathode-ray Oscilloscope *or* Oscillograph
Chief Recruiting Officer
Commonwealth Relations Office (*now* part of Foreign Office)
Criminal Records Office
Croat. Croatia(n)
Cr.P. Criminal Procedure
C.R.P. Calendarium Rotulorum Patentium (Calendar of the Patent Rolls)
Canon Regular of Prémontré
C.R.P.L. Central Radio Propagation Laboratory (U.S.)
C.R.R. Commercial Reference Room, Guildhall Library
Curia Regis Roll
C.R.S. Catholic Record Society
Cereals Research Station
Cold-rolled Steel
C.R.S.A. Cold Rolled Section Association
Crt. Court
C.R.T. Cathode Ray Tube
crtkr. caretaker
C.R.T.S. Commonwealth Reconstruction Training Scheme
C.R.U. Civil Resettlement Unit(s)
Collective Reserve Union
Composite Reserve Unit(s)
Cruz. Cruzeiro
C.R.W.P.C. Canadian Radio Wave Propagation Committee
Crypto. Cryptographic
Cryptography
cryst. crystal
crystalline
crystallized
crystallog. crystallography
Cs Caesium
Cs. cours (quotation price)
cs. cases
census
consul

66

C.S. Capital Stock
Cast Steel
Certificate in Statistics
Chemical Society
Chief Secretary
Christian Science
City Surveyor
Civil Servant
Civil Service
Clerk of Session
Clerk to the Signet
Close Shot
Colliery Screened
College of Science
Commissary of Subsistence
Common Serjeant
Conchological Society of Great Britain and Ireland
Co-operative Society
Cotton Seed
County Surveyor
Court of Session
Cruiser Squadron
Custos Sigilli (Keeper of the Seal)
c/s. cycles per second
C.S.A. Canadian Standards Association
Civil Service Alliance
Commonwealth Sugar Agreement
Confederate States of America
C.S. & E.U. Confederation of Shipbuilding and Engineering Unions
C.S.A.P. Canadian Society of Animal Production
C.S.B. Bachelor of Christian Science
Central Statistical Board
C.S.B.G.M. Committee of Scottish Bank General Managers
csc. cosecant
C.S.C. Charles Stuart Calverley
Church Schools Company
Civil Service Commission
Comprehensive Schools Committee
Conspicuous Service Cross (*now* D.S.C.)
C.S.C.A. Civil Service Clerical Association
C.S.C.B.S. Commodore Superintendent Contract Built Ships
C.S.C.C. Council of Scottish Chambers of Commerce
C.S.D. Commonwealth Society for the Deaf
Doctor of Christian Science
C.S.D.E. Central Servicing Development Establishment (R.A.F.)
Cse. Course
C.S.E. Central Signals Establishment
Certificate of Secondary Education
Council of the Stock Exchange, London
C.S.E.U. Confederation of Shipbuilding and Engineering Unions
C.S.F. Cerebro-Spinal Fluid
Coil Spring Federation
C.S.F.A. Canadian Scientific Film Association
C.S.F.E. Canadian Society of Forest Engineers

C.S.G. Catholic Social Guild
 Combined Studies Group (C.I.A.)
C.S.G.A. Canadian Seed Growers' Association
C.S.I. Church of South India
 Commission séricicole internationale (International Sericultural Commission)
 Commission Sportive Internationale (International Sports Commission)
 Companion of the Order of the Star of India
C.S.I.E.J.B. Certificate of the Sanitary Inspectors Examination Joint Board
C.S.I.R. Council for Scientific and Industrial Research (*now* C.S.I.R.O.)
 Council of Scientific and Industrial Research (India)
C.S.I.R.O. Commonwealth Scientific and Industrial Research Organization
C.S.I.T. Comité sportif international du travail (International Workers Sport Association)
csk. cask
C.S.L. Commonwealth Serum Laboratories (Australia)
 Communication Sub-Lieutenant
C.S.L.A.T.P. Canadian Society of Landscape Architects and Town Planners
C.S.L.O. Canadian Scientific Liaison Office
 Combined Services Liaison Officer
C.S.L.T. Canadian Society of Laboratory Technologists
C.S.M. Cerebro-spinal Meningitis
 Christian Socialist Movement
 Commission for Synoptic Meteorology
 Company Sergeant-Major
C.S.M.A. Civil Service Motoring Association
C.S.M.F.R.A. Cotton, Silk and Man-Made Fibres Research Association
C.S.M.M. Camborne School of Metalliferous Mining
C.S.M.M.G. Chartered Society of Massage and Medical Gymnastics
C.S.O. Central Selling Organisation
 Central Statistical Office
 Chief Signal Officer
 Chief Staff Officer
 Colonial Secretary's Office
 Command Signals Officer
 Commonwealth Scientific Office
C.S.P. Chartered Society of Physiotherapy
 Civil Service of Pakistan
 Congregation of Saint Paul
C.S.P.A. Civil Service Pensioners' Alliance
C.S.P.A.A. Conférence de solidarité des pays afro-asiatiques (Afro-Asian Peoples' Solidarity Conference)
C.S.R. Czechoslovak Socialist Republic

C.S.S.A. Civil Service Sailing Association
 Civil Service Supply Association
C.S.S.C. Civil Service Sports Council
C.S.S.M. Children's Special Service Mission
 Compatible Single-sideband Modulation System
C.SS.R. Congregatio Sanctissimi Redemptoris (Redemptorist Fathers)
C.SS.S. Congregatio Sanctissimi Salvatoris (Brigittine Congregation)
C.S.T. Central Standard Time
 College of Science and Technology
 College of Speech Therapists
C.S.T.A. Canadian Society of Technical Agriculturists
 Canterbury Science Teachers Association (New Zealand)
C.S.T.I. Council of Science and Technology Institutes
C.St.J. Commander of the Order of Saint John of Jerusalem
C.S.U. Central Statistical Unit
 Christlich-Soziale Union (Christian Social Union, Germany)
 Civil Service Union
 Constant Speed Unit
C.S.U.C.A. Consejo Superior Universitario Centroamericano (Supreme Council of the Central American Universities)
C.S.V. Congregation of St. Victor
C.S.W. Christlicher Studenten-Weltbund (World Student Christian Federation)
Ct. Count
 Court
ct. carat
 caught
 cent
 centum (hundred)
 circuit
 courant (the present month)
 court
 credit
 current
C.T. Cable Transfer
 Californian Terms
 Candidate in Theology
 Cape Town
 Central Time
 Certified Teacher
 Civic Trust
 Code Telegrams
 College of Technology
 Commercial Traveller
C.T.A. Camping Trade Association
 Camping Trade Association of Great Britain
 Canadian Tuberculosis Association
 Caribbean Travel Association
 Chain Testers' Association of Great Britain
 Channel Tunnel Association
 Chaplain Territorial Army
 Chicago Transit Authority
 Commercial Travellers' Association *cont.*

Conurbation Transport Authorities

c.t.a. cum testamento annexo (with will annexed)

C.T.A.C. Creative Tourist Agents' Conference

C.T.B. Commonwealth Telecommunications Board

C.T.B.A. Catering Trades' Benevolent Association

C.T.B.F. Cinematograph Trade Benevolent Fund

CTC Carbon Tetrachloride

C.T.C. Civil Technical Corps
Corn Trade Clauses
Cyclists' Touring Club

C.T.D. Central Training Depot
Classified Telephone Directory

Cte. Comte (Count)

Ctesse. Comtesse (Countess)

C.T.E.T.O.C. Council for Technical Education and Training for Overseas Countries

ctf. certificate
certify

C.T.F. Chaplain to the Territorial Forces

ctge. cartage
cottage

C.T.H. Corporation of Trinity House

C.Theod. Codex Theodosianus (Theodosian Code)

ctl. cental
central

c.t.l. constructive total loss

c.t.l.o. constructive total loss only

C.T.M. Conférence Technique Mondiale (World Engineering Conference)

C.T.M.A. Collapsible Tube Manufacturers' Association

ctn. cotangent

Cto. Concerto

C.T.O. Central Telegraph Office
Central Tractor Organisation (India)
—— Central Treaty Organisation
Chief Technical Officer

c. to c. (from) centre to centre

Ctr. Contributor
Contributions

ctr. centre

C.T.R. Controlled Thermonuclear Reaction

C.T.R.A. Coal Tar Research Association

C.T.R.U. Colonial Termite Research Unit

cts. carats
centimes
cents
crates

C.T.S. Incorporated Catholic Truth Society

C.T.S.A. Crucible and Tool Steel Association

C.T.T. Coras Trachtala (Irish Export Board)

C.T.T.B. Central Trade Test Board (R.A.F.)

C'tte. Committee

C.T.T.S.C. Certificate in the Teaching and Training of Subnormal Children

C.T.U.S. Carnegie Trust or the Universities of Scotland

Cu Cuprum (Copper)

cu. cubic
cumulus

C.U. Cambridge University
Casualties Union
Church Union
Close Up
Congregational Union of England and Wales
Co-operative Union
Cornell University (U.S.)
Customs Union

C.U.A. Colour Users' Association

C.U.A.C. Cambridge University Athletic Club

C.U.A.F.C. Cambridge University Association Football Club

C.U.A.S. Cambridge University Agricultural Society
Cambridge University Air Squadron

cub. cubic

C.U.B.C. Cambridge University Boat Club
Cambridge University Boxing Club

C.U.C. Canberra University College
Coal Utilization Council

C.U.C.C. Cambridge University Cricket Club

cu. cm. cubic centimetre(s)

C.U.E. Cornell University Extender

C.U.E.W. Congregational Union of England and Wales

C.U.F. Catholicarum Universitatum Foederatio (Federation of Catholic Universities)

cu. ft. cubic foot or feet

C.U.G.C. Cambridge University Golf Club

C.U.H.C. Cambridge University Hockey Club

cu.in. cubic inch(es)

cuis. cuisine

cuj. cujus (of which or of whom)

C.U.K.T. Carnegie United Kingdom Trust

Cul. Culinary

C.U.L. Cambridge University Library

C.U.L.T.C. Cambridge University Lawn Tennis Club

cum. cumulative

C.U.M. Cambridge University Mission

Cumb. Cumberland

C.U.M.D.S. Cambridge University Marlowe Dramatic Society

Cum. Pref. Cumulative Preference (Shares)

C.U.M.S. Cambridge University Musical Society

C.U.N.A. Credit Union National Association

C.U.O.G. Cambridge University Opera Group

C.U.P. Cambridge University Press

cur. currency
current

CURE National Addiction and Research Bureau

C.U.R.F.C. Cambridge University Rugby Football Club
C.U.S. Catholic University School
    Congregational Union of Scotland
cu. sec. cubic feet per second
C.U.S.O. Canadian University Service Overseas
C.U.S.R.P.G. Canada-United States Regional Planning Group (NATO)
custod. custodian
C.U.W.B.C. Cambridge University Women's Boat Club
C.V. Common Version (Bible)
c.v. cheval-vapeur (horsepower)
    chief value
    cursus vitae (course of life)
C.V.A. Cerebro-vascular Stroke
c.v.d. cash against (versus) documents
C.V.E. Council for Visual Education
C.V.K. Centre Vertical Keel
C.V.M. Company of Veteran Motorists
C.V.O. Commander of the Royal Victorian Order
Cvt.Gdn. Covent Garden
C.W. Canada West
    Chemical Warfare
    Child Welfare
    Clerk of Works
    Commercial Weight
    Commissions and Warrants Department of the Admiralty
c.w. continuous or carrier wave
C.W.A. Catering Wages Act
    Country Women's Association (Australia)
    Crime Writers' Association
C.W.B. Canadian Wheat Board
    Central Wages Board
C.W.C. Catering Wages Commission
    Commonwealth of World Citizens
C.W.D. Civilian War Dead
C'wealth Commonwealth
C.W.G.C. Commonwealth War Graves Commission
C.W.I.N.C. Central Waterways, Irrigation and Navigation Commission (India)

C.W.L. Catholic Women's League
C.W.L.C. Captive Women's Luncheon Club
C.W.M. Caribbean Workers' Movement
C.W.M.E. Commission on World Mission and Evangelism of the World Council of Churches
C.W.N.A. Canadian Weekly Newspapers Association
C.W.O. Chief Warrant Officer
c.w.o. cash with order
C.W.O.I.H. Conference of World Organisations interested in the Handicapped
C.W.R. Continuous welded rail
C.W.S. Co-operative Wholesale Society
cwt. hundredweight
C.W.T. Central War Time
C.W.U. Chemical Workers' Union
C.W.W.A. Coloured Workers' Welfare Association
cx. convex
Cy cyanide
cy. capacity
    currency
Cyber. Cybernetics
cyc. cycles
    cycling
    cyclopaedia
C.Y.C. Company of Young Canadians
C.Y.C.A. Clyde Yacht Clubs Association
C.Y.F.A. Club for Young Friends of Animals
cyl. cylinder
    cylindrical
Cym. Cymric
Cymb. Cymbeline (Shakespeare)
C.Y.M.S. Catholic Young Men's Society
Cyp. Cypress
    Cyprian
    Cyprus
C.Z. Canal Zone
Czech. Czechoslovak(ian)

D

D 500 (Roman numerals)
    Deuterium
d density
    diameter
    differential
D. Deacon
    Decision
    Deliver(ed)
    Delivery
    Democrat
    Demy
    Deputy
    Destroyer

cont.

Deus (God)
Deutschland (Germany)
Diretto (slow train in Italy)
Distinguished
Doctor
Dogana (Customs or Custom House)
Dominus (Lord or Master)
Douane (Customs or Custom House)
Dowager
Duchess
Duke
Dump
Dutch

d. damn
  date
  daughter(s)
  day
  dead
  deceased
  deci
  deciduous
  decree
  degree
  delete
  delta
  denarii (pence)
  denarius (a penny)
  depart(s)
  depth
  desert(ed)
  deserter
  destra (the right hand)
  diamonds (playing cards)
  died
  dime
  diopter
  discharged
  distance
  dollar
  dose
  drama
  drizzle
  drizzling
  droite (the right hand)
Da Davyum
Da. Danish
D.A. Defence Act
  Department of the Army
  Deposit Account
  Deputy Advocate
  Deputy Assistant
  Diploma in Anaesthetics
  Dissolved Acetylene
  District Attorney (U.S.)
  Doesn't Answer
  Doctor of Arts
D/a. Deposit account
  Discharge afloat
d/a. days after acceptance
  documents against acceptance
D.A.A. Défense anti-aérienne (Anti-
  Aircraft Defence)
  Diploma of the Advertising
  Association
D.A.A. & Q.M.G. Deputy Assistant
  Adjutant and Quartermaster-General
D.A.A.G. Deputy Assistant Adjutant
  General
D.A.B. Daily Audience Barometer
  Deutsches Apothekerbuch (Ger-
  man Pharmacopoeia)
  Dictionary of American Biog-
  raphy
D.A.C. Development Assistance Com-
  mittee (O.E.C.D.)
d.a.c. deductible average clause
D.A.C.G. Deputy Assistant Chaplain
  General
D.A.D. Deputy Assistant Director
D.A.D.A. Designers' and Art Directors'
  Association
D.A.D.G.M.S. Deputy Assistant Direc-
  tor General of Medical Services
D.A.D.M.E. Deputy Assistant Director
  of Military Engineering

D.A.D.M.S. Deputy Assistant Director
  of Medical Services
D.A.D.O.S. Deputy Assistant Director
  of Ordnance Services
D.A.D.Q. Deputy Assistant Director of
  Quartering
D.A.D.S. Deputy Assistant Director of
  Supplies
D.A.D.S.T. Deputy Assistant Director
  of Supplies and Transport
D.A.E. Dictionary of American English
  Diploma in Advanced Engineer-
  ing
  Director of Army Education
D.A.E.P. Division of Atomic Energy
  Production
D.A.E.R. Department of Aeronautical
  and Engineering Research (Admiralty)
D.A.F.S. Department of Agriculture
  and Fisheries for Scotland
dag. decagram(s)
D.A.G. Deputy Adjutant-General
  Development Assistance Group
D.Agr. Doctor of Agriculture
D.Agr.Sc. Doctor of Agricultural
  Science
Dah. Dahomey
D.A.H. Disordered Action of the Heart
D.A.J.A.G. Deputy Assistant Judge
  Advocate General
dal. decalitre(s)
D.A.L.T.A. Dramatic and Lyric
  Theatres' Association
dam. decametre(s)
D.A.M. Diploma in Ayurvedic Medicine
D.A.M.S. Deputy Assistant Military
  Secretary
Dan. Danish
D. & C. Dean and Chapter
D. & D. Drunk and Disorderly
D. & E.G. Development and Engineer-
  ing Group
D. & H.A.A. Dock and Harbour
  Authorities' Association
d. and p. development and printing
d. and s. demand and supply
D.A.O. District Advisory Officer (of
  N.A.A.S.)
D.A.O.T. Director of Air Organization
  and Training (Navy)
D.A.P. Director of Administrative Plan-
  ning
d.a.p. documents against payment
D.A.P. & E. Diploma in Applied
  Parasitology and Entomology
D.A.P.D. Directorate of Aircraft Pro-
  duction Development
D.A.P.H.N.E. Dido and Pluto Hand-
  maiden for Nuclear Experiments
D.A.P.I.S. Danish Agricultural Pro-
  ducers' Information Service
D.A.P.M. Deputy Assistant Provost
  Marshal
D.A.P.S. Director of Army Postal Ser-
  vices
D.A.Q.M.G. Deputy Assistant Quarter-
  master-General
D.A.R. Daughters of the American
  Revolution
D.Arch. Doctor of Architecture
D.A.R.D. Directorate of Aircraft Re-
  search and Development

D.A.S. Development Advisory Service
   Director of Armament Supply
d.a.s. delivered alongside ship
D.A.Sc. Doctor in Agricultural Sciences
D.A.S.D. Director of Army Staff Duties
D.A.S.M. Delayed Action Space Missile
dat. dative
D.A.T.A. Draughtsmen's and Allied Technicians' Association
D.A.T.A.C. Development Areas Treasury Advisory Committee
dau. daughter
D.A.V. Disabled American Veteran(s)
D.A.W.S. Director of Army Welfare Services
dB decibel(s)
D.B. Bachelor of Divinity
   Dark Blue
   Day Book
   Deals and Battens
   Dock Brief
   Domesday Book
   Double-barrelled
d.b. double-breasted
   draw bar
d.b.a. doing business at
D.B.B. Deals, Battens and Boards
D.B.E. Dame Commander of the Order of the British Empire
D.B.I.U. Dominion Board of Insurance Underwriters (Canada)
dbk. drawback
dble. double
D.B.M. Diploma in Business Management
Dbn. Durban
D.B.O. Diploma of the British Orthoptic Board
D.B.R. Division of Building Research (Canada)
D.Bs. Double Bottoms
D.B.S.T. Double British Summer Time
D.C. da capo (repeat from the beginning)
   Death Certificate
   Decimal Classification
   Depth Charge
   Deputy Chief
   Deputy Commissioner
   Deputy Consul
   Deputy Counsel
   Deviation Clause
   Diagnostic Centre
   Diplomatic Corps
   Disarmament Conference
   Disciples of Christ
   District Commissioner
   District Court
   District of Columbia
   Doctor of Chiropractics
   Double Crochet
   Double Crown
D/C. Deviation Clause
d.C. dopo Cristo (after Christ)
d.c. da capo (repeat from the beginning)
   dead centre
   direct current
   double column
D.C.Ae. Diploma of the College of Aeronautics

D.C.A.O. Deputy County Advisory Officer
D.C.A.S. Deputy Chief of the Air Staff (Air Council)
D.C.B. Decimal Currency Board
D.C.C. Diocesan Consistory Court
D.C.C.C. Domestic Coal Consumers' Council
D.C.C.P. Directorate of Communications Components Production
D.C.D. Directorate of Communications Development
D.C.E. Diploma in Chemical Engineering
D.C.E.P. Diploma of Child and Educational Psychology
D.C.F. Discounted cash flow
dcg. dancing
   decigram(s)
D.C.G. Deputy Chaplain-General
D.C.G.S. Deputy Chief of the General Staff
D.Ch. Doctor Chirurgiae (Doctor of Surgery)
D.C.H. Diploma in Child Health
D.Ch.O. Diploma in Ophthalmic Surgery
D.C.I. Directorate of Chemical Inspection
D.C.I.G.S. Deputy Chief of the Imperial General Staff
D.C.J. District Court Judge (U.S.)
dcl. decalitre(s)
   declaration
D.C.L. Distillers' Company, Limited
   Doctor of Civil Law
D.C.L.I. Duke of Cornwall's Light Infantry
D.Cl.Sc. Doctor of Clinical Science
dcm. decametre(s)
D.C.M. Department of Coins and Medals (British Museum)
   Distinguished Conduct Medal
   District Court Martial
D.C.M.S. Deputy Commissioner Medical Services
D.C.N.I. Department of the Chief of Naval Information
D.Cn.L. Doctor of Canon Law
D.C.N.S. Deputy Chief of Naval Staff
D.C.O. Dominions, Colonies, Overseas (Department of Barclays Bank)
   Duchy of Cornwall Office
D.C. of S. Deputy Chief of Staff
D-Col. Double-Column
D.Com. Doctor of Commerce
D.Com.L. Doctor of Commercial Law
D.Comm. Doctor of Commerce
D.C.P. Diploma of Clinical Pathology
D.C.R. District Chief Ranger (Ancient Order of Foresters)
D.C.R.A. Dyers' and Cleaners' Research Association
D.C.R.E. Deputy Commandant, Royal Engineers
D.C.S. Deputy Chief of Staff
   Deputy Clerk of Session
   Doctor of Commercial Sciences
D.C.S.O. Deputy Chief Scientific Officer

71

D.C.S.T. Deputy Chief of Supplies and Transport
dct. document
D.C.T. Depth-Charge Thrower
Doctor of Christian Theology
Drapers' Chamber of Trade
D.C.T.Batt. Diploma of the Battersea College of Technology
D.C.V.O. Dame Commander of the Royal Victorian Order
dd. dated
dedicated
delivered
D.D. Department of Defense (U.S.)
Deputy Director
Devonshire and Dorset Regiment
Direttissima (Italian category of train)
Discharged Dead
Doctor of Divinity
Dono Dedit (gave as a gift)
Double Demy
D/D. Delivered at Docks
Demand Draft
D.d. Deo dedit (gave to God)
D/d. Days' date
d.d. days after date
delivered dock
demand draft
dono dedit (gave as a gift)
dry dock
d----d damned
D.D.A. Dangerous Drugs Act
Disabled Drivers' Association
D.D. & Shpg. Dock Dues and Shipping
D.D.C. Dewey Decimal Classification
Docteur en droit canonique (Doctor of Canon Law)
D.D.D. Dat, Dicat, Dedicat (gives, devotes and dedicates)
Deadline Delivery Date
Direct Distance Dialling
Dono Dedit Dedicavitque (He gave and consecrated as a gift)
D.D.D.S. Deputy Director of Dental Services
D.D.E.M. Directorate of Design of Equipment and Mechanisation
D.D.F. Dental Documentary Foundation
D.D.G. Deputy Director-General
D.D.G.S.E. Deputy Director-General of Signals Equipment
D.D.G.S.R. Division of the Director-General of Scientific Research
D.D.I. Divisional Detective Inspector
d.d. in d. de die in diem (from day to day)
D.D.L. Deputy Director of Labour
D.D.M. Difference in Depth Modulation
Diploma in Dermatological Medicine
Doctor of Dental Medicine
D.D.M.C. Disabled Drivers' Motor Club
D.D.M.E. Deputy Director of Mechanical Engineering
D.D.M.I. Deputy Director of Military Intelligence

D.D.M.O.I. Deputy Director of Military Operations and Intelligence
D.D.M.S. Deputy Director of Medical Services
D.D.M.T. Deputy Director of Military Training
D.D.N.I. Deputy Director of Naval Intelligence
D.D.O. Diploma in Dental Orthopaedics
D.D.O.S. Deputy Director of Ordnance Services
D.D.P. Declaration of Design Performance
D.D.P.H. Diploma in Dental Public Health
D.D.P.R. Deputy Director of Public Relations
D.D.P.S. Deputy Director of Personal Services
Deputy Director of Postal Services
D.D.R. Deutsche Demokratische Republik (German Democratic Republic)
Diploma in Diagnostic Radiology
D.D.R.A. Deputy Director, Royal Artillery
D.D.R.D. Deputy Directorate of Research and Development
D.D.R.M. Deputy Directorate of Repair and Maintenance
dd/s. delivered sound
D.D.S. Deputy Directorate of Science
Director of Dental Services
Doctor of Dental Surgery
D.D.Sc. Doctor of Dental Science
D.D.S.D. Deputy Director of Staff Duties
D.D.S.R. Deputy Directorate of Scientific Research
D.D.S.T. Deputy Director of Supplies and Transport
DDT Dichlorodiphenyltrichlorethane
D.D.V.S. Deputy Director of Veterinary Services
D.D.W.E. & M. Deputy Director of Works Electrical and Mechanical
D.E. Dáil Eireann (House of Representatives, Eire)
Deflection Error
Doctor of Engineering
Doctor of Entomology
Double Elephant
Dynamical Engineer
Dynamite Engineer
d.e. double entry
deckle edge
Dea. Deacon
D.E.A. Dairy Engineers' Association
Davis Escape Apparatus
Department of Economic Affairs
D.E.A.U.A. Diesel Engineers' and Users' Association
deb. debenture
debit
debut(ante)
Dec. Decanus (Dean)
December
Declination
Decorate(d)

dec. deceased
decimal
declaration
declare
declension
decoration
decrease
decreasing
decrescendo (becoming softer)
D.E.C. Disaster Emergency Committee
Dollar Exports Council
decd. deceased
decid. deciduous
decim. decimetre(s)
decl. declension
decn. decontamination
decomp. decomposition
D.Econ. Doctor of Economics
Ded. Dedicated
Dedication
ded. deduced
D.Ed. Doctor of Education
D.E.E. Diploma in Electrical Engineering
def. defence
defendant
deferred
deficit
define
definite
definition
defunctus (deceased)
deft. defendant
deflection
deg. degree(s)
Dekag. Dekagramme(s)
Dekal. Dekalitre(s)
Dekam. Dekametre(s)
Del. Delaware
Delegate
Delegation
del. delete
delineavit (drew this)
deld. delivered
Deleg. Delegate
Delegation
delv. deliver(ed)
dely. delivery
Dem. Democrat
dem. demand
democracy
democratic
demurrage
demy
D.E.M.E. Director of Electrical and
Mechanical Engineering
demob(bed). demobilize(d)
demon. demonstrate
D.E.M.S. Defensively Equipped Merchant Ship(ping)
Den. Denbighshire
Denmark
den. denotation
denotative(ly)
denouement
D. en D. Docteur en droit (Doctor of Laws)
D.Eng. Doctor of Engineering
D. en M. Docteur en médecine (Doctor of Medicine)
denom. denomination
dent. dental

Dep. Department
Dependent
Deposits
Depot
Deputy
dep. depart
deponent
deposed
deposit
depuis (since)
D.E.P. Deflection Error, Probable
Department of Employment and Productivity
Director of Equipment and Policy
Dep.-Dir. Deputy-Director
Dept. Department
Dept. of A. Department of Agriculture
der. derivation
derivative
derived
Derbys. Derbyshire
D.E.R.E. Dounreay Experimental Reactor Establishment
D.E.R.R. Duke of Edinburgh's Royal Regiment
D.E.R.V. Diesel-engined Road Vehicle
D.E.S. Department of Education and Science
desc. descendant
describe(d)
desid. desideratum (wanted)
desig. designate
D. ès. L. Docteur ès lettres (Doctor of Letters)
desp. despatch(ed)
Des.R.C.A. Designer of the Royal College of Art
Dest. Destroyer
destn. destination
Det. Detective
det. detach(ed)
detachment
Det. Con. Detective Constable
Det. Insp. Detective Inspector
Det. Sgt. Detective Sergeant
D.E.U.A. Diesel Engineers' and Users' Association
D.E.U.C.E. Digital Electronic Universal Computing Engine
Deut. Deuteronomy
Dev. Development
Deviation
Devon. Devonshire
devs. devotions
D.E.W. Distant Early Warning Radar Line
DEXAN Digital Experimental Airborne Navigator
Dez. Dezembre (December)
df. draft
D.F. Dean of Faculty
Defender of the Faith
Doctor of Forestry
Double Foolscap
Drop Forging
D/F. Direction Finding (by radio)
d. f. dead freight
D.F.A. Doctor of Fine Arts
Diploma in Foreign Affairs
Dairy Farmers' Association
D.F.C. Distinguished Flying Cross

F

D.F.H. Diploma of the Faraday House Engineering College
D.F.I. Directorate of Food Investigation
D.F.L.S. Day Fighter Leaders School
D.F.M. Diploma in Forensic Medicine
Distinguished Flying Medal
DFP Diisopropylphosphorofluoridate
D.F.R. Dounreay Fast Reactor
D.F.R.A. Drop Forging Research Association
D.F.Sc. Doctor of Financial Science
dft. defendant
draft
D.F.W. Director of Fortifications and Works
dg. decigram(s)
D.G. Déclaration de guerre (Declaration of War)
Dei Gratia (by the Grace of God)
Deo Gratias (thanks to God)
Director General
Dragoon Guards
durch Güte (by favour of)
D.G.A. Director General Aircraft
Directors Guild of America
D.G.A.A. Distressed Gentlefolk's Aid Association
D.G.A.M.S. Director General of Army Medical Services
D.G.B. Deutscher Gewerkschaftsbund (German Federation of Trade Unions)
D.G.C. Diploma in Guidance and Counselling
D.G.C.A. Director General of Civil Aviation
D.G.C.E. Directorate General of Communications Equipment
D.G.C.St.J. Dame Grand Cross of the Order of Saint John of Jerusalem
D.G.D. Director Gunnery Division
D.G.D.&M. Director General Dockyards and Maintenance
D.G.D.C. Deputy Grand Director of Ceremonies
D.G.E. Directorate General of Equipment
D.G.I. Director General of Information
D.G.M. Director General of Manpower
D.G.M.S. Director General of Medical Services
D.G.M.T. Director General of Military Training
D.G.M.W. Director General of Military Works
Dgn. Dragoon
D.G.O. Diploma in Gynaecology and Obstetrics
D.G.O.S. Dublin Grand Opera Society
D.G.P. Director General of Personnel
Director General of Production
D.G.P.S. Director General of Personal Services and Officer Appointments
D.G.R. Director of Graves Registration
D.G.S. Director General, Ships
Directorate General of Signals
D.G.S.R.D. Directorate General of Scientific Research and Development
D.G.St.J. Dame of Grace of the Order of Saint John of Jerusalem (*now* D.St.J.)
D.G.T. Director General of Training

D.G.T.A. Dry Goods Trade Association
D.G.W. Director General of Weapons
Director General of Works
D.H. De Havilland
d.h. das heisst (that is to say)
dead heat
D.H.A.A. Dock and Harbour Authorities Association
D.H.D.P. Diplôme en hygiène publique dentaire (Diploma in Dental Public Health)
D.H.L. Doctor of Hebrew Literature
D.H.M. Diocesan Home Missionary
D.H.M.P.G.T.S. Department of His *or* Her Majesty's Procurator General and Treasury Solicitor
D.H.P. Diplôme en hygiène publique (Diploma in Public Health)
D.H.Q. District *or* Divisional Headquarters
D.H.S. Department of Health for Scotland
Diploma in Horticultural Science
District High School
D.Hum.Lit. Doctor of Humane Letters
D.H.V.P. Diplôme en hygiène publique vétérinaire (Diploma in Veterinary Public Health)
D.Hy. Doctor of Hygiene
Di Didymium
Di. Dinar(s)
D.I. Defence Intelligence
Director of Infantry
District *or* Divisional Inspector
Double Imperial
d.i. diplomatic immunity
das ist (that is)
dia. diagram
dialect
diameter
D.I.A. Design and Industries Association
Diploma in International Affairs
dial. dialect(ic)
dialogue
diam. diameter
diap. diapason
Dic. Dicembre (December)
D.I.C. Diploma of Membership of the Imperial College of Science and Technology
D.I.C.E. Dairy and Ice Cream Equipment Association
D.I.Chem. Diploma of Industrial Chemistry
Dict. Dictionary
dict. dictation
dictated
dictator
dictionary
dicta. dictaphone
D.I.C.T.A. Diploma of the Imperial College of Tropical Agriculture (Trinidad)
Did. Didactics
D.I.D.A.S. Dynamic Instrumentation Data Automobile System

D.I.E. Diploma of the Institute of Engineering
Diploma in Industrial Engineering
dieb. alt. diebus alternis (on alternate days)
D.I.E.M.E. Directorate of Inspection of Electrical and Mechanical Equipment
Diet. Dietetics
D.I.F. District Inspector of Fisheries
diff. difference
difference(ial)
dig. digest
digit(al)
D.I.G. Deputy Inspector-General
Disabled Income Group
D.I.H. Diploma in Industrial Health
dil. dilute
dilet. dilettante
Dim. Dimanche (Sunday)
dim. dimension
diminished
diminuendo (becoming softer)
diminutive
D.I.M. Diploma in Industrial Management
DIMPLE Deuterium Moderated Pile Low Energy
din. dinner
dining-room
D.I.N. Deutsche Industrie-Normen (German Industry Standards)
D.Ing. Doctor Ingeniariae (Doctor of Engineering)
D.Inst.P.A. Diploma of the Institute of Park Administration
D.I.O. District Intelligence Officer
Dioc. Diocesan
Diocese
Dioc.Syn. Diocesan Synod
Dip. Diploma
Dip.A.D. Diploma in Art and Design
Dip.Agr. Diploma in Agriculture
Dip.A.Ling. Diploma in Applied Linguistics
Dip.A.M. Diploma in Applied Mechanics
Dip.App.Sc. Diploma of Applied Science
Dip.Arch. Diploma of Architecture
Dip. Arts Diploma in Arts
Dip.Ass.Sc. Diploma in Association Science
Dip. Bac. Diploma in Bacteriology
Dip.B.M.S. Diploma in Basic Medical Sciences
Dip.Card. Diploma in Cardiology
Dip.C.D. Diploma of Civic Design
Dip.Com. Diploma of Commerce
Dip.D.Hus. Diploma in Dairy Husbandry
Dip.D.P. Diploma in Drawing and Painting
Dip.Econ. Diploma of Economics
Dip. Ed. Diploma of Education
Dip.Eng. Diploma in Engineering
Dip.F.A. Diploma in Fine Arts
Dip.For. Diploma of Forestry
Dip.G.T. Diploma in Glass Technology
Dip.H.A. Diploma in Hospital Administration

Dip.H.E. Diploma in Highway Engineering
Dip.H.Sc. Diploma in Home Science
Dip.J. Diploma of Journalism
Dipl. Diploma
Diplomatic
dipl. diplomacy
diplomat
Dip.L. Diploma in Languages
Dip.Lib. Diploma of Librarianship
Dipl.Ing. Diplôme Ingénieur (Diploma in Engineering)
Dipl.R.T.C. Diploma of the Royal Technical College, Glasgow
Dip.L.Sc. Diploma of Library Science
Dip.Mech.E. Diploma of Mechanical Engineering
Dip.M.F.O.S. Diploma in Maxial, Facial and Oral Surgery
Dip.N.A. & A.C. Diploma in Numerical Analysis and Automatic Computing
Dip.N.Ed. Diploma in Nursery School Education
Dip.N.Z.L.S. Diploma of the New Zealand Library Society
Dip. O. & G. Diploma in Obstetrics and Gynaecology
Dip.O.L. Diploma in Oriental Learning
Dip. Orth. Diploma in Orthodontics
Dip.P.A. Diploma in Public Administration
Dip.P. & O.T. Diplôme en physiothérapie et occupation thérapie (Diploma in Physiotherapy and Occupational Therapy)
Dip.Pharm. Diploma of Pharmacy
Dip.P.Hus. Diploma in Poultry Husbandry
Dip.Phys.Ed. Diploma of Physical Education
Dip.Q.S. Diploma in Quantity Surveying
Dip. R.A.D.A. Diploma of the Royal Academy of Dramatic Art
Dip.S. & P.A. Diploma in Social and Public Administration
Dip.S.S. Diploma in Social Studies
Dip.S.W. Diploma in Social Work
Dip.T. Diploma in Teaching
Dip. T.C.P. Diploma in Town and Country Planning
Dip.Tech. Diploma in Technology
Dip.Th. Diploma in Theology
Dip.T.P. Diploma in Town Planning
Dip.V.F.M. Diploma in Valuation and Farm Management
Dir. Dirham
dir. direction
director
Dir.-Genl. Director-General
dis. discharge
disciple
disconnect(ed)
discontinue(d)
discount
dispensed
dispensing
distribute
D.I.S. Development and Information Service
disab. disability

disbs. disbursements
disc. disciple
    discipline
    discount
    discovered
    discoverer
    discovery
disch. discharge(d)
disct. discount
dishon. dishonourable
    dishonourably
dismd. dismissed
disp. dispensary
    dispensation
    dispensed
    disperse
displ. displacement
Diss. Dissenter
diss. dissolved
Dist. Distance
    District
dist. distant
    distilled
Dis.T.P. Distinction in Town Planning
distr. distribution
DISTRIPRESS Fédération internationale des distributeurs de presse (International Association of Wholesale Newspaper, Periodical and Book Distributors)
D.I.T. Detroit Institute of Technology
Div. Dividend
    Divine
    Divinity
    Division
div. divide
    division
    divisor
    divorce
Divn. Division
Divnl. Divisional
divs. dividends
divvy dividend
D.I.Y. Do-it-Yourself
D.J. Department of Journalism
    Dinner Jacket
    Diploma in Journalism
    Disc Jockey
    Divorce Judge
D.-j. Dust-jacket
d.j. diesjährig (of this year)
D.J.A.G. Deputy Judge Advocate General
D.J.St.J. Dame of Justice of the Order of Saint John of Jerusalem (now D.St.J.)
Dk. Dock
dkg. decagram(s)
dkl. decalitre(s)
dkm. decametre(s)
D.K.S. Deputy Keeper of the Signet
dkyd. dockyard
dl. decilitre(s)
D.L. Deputy Lieutenant
    Doctor of Law
    Double Ledger
    Driving Licence
d---l devil
D.Lat. Difference of Latitude
D.L.C. Diploma of the Loughborough College of Technology
    Doctor of Celtic Literature

dld. delivered
D.L.E.S. Doctor of Letters in Economic Studies
D.L.I. Durham Light Infantry
D.-Lib. Liberal Democrat (U.S.)
D.L.I.S. Desert Locust Information Service
D.Lit. Doctor of Literature
D.Litt. Doctor Literarum (Doctor Letters)
D.L.J. Dame of Justice of the Order of Saint Lazarus of Jerusalem
d.l.M. des laufenden Monats (of the current Month)
D.L.M.A. Decorative Lighting Manufacturers' Association
D.L.O. Dead Letter Office (now R.L.O.)
    Diploma in Laryngology and Otology
    Divisional Legal Officer
d.l.o. dispatch loading only
D.Long. Difference of Longitude
D.L.O.Y. Duke of Lancaster's Own Yeomanry
D.L.P. Double Large Post
D.L.R. Doctor of Library Science
    Dominion Land Surveyor
    Driving Licences Regulations
    Dominion Law Reports
dlvd. delivered
D.L.W. Diploma in Labour Welfare
dly. daily
dm. decimetre(s)
D.M. The Daily Mail
    Deputy Master
    Deutsche Mark
    Director of Music
    District Manager
    Doctor of Mathematics
    Doctor of Medicine
    Doctor of Music
    Double Medium
d.m. dieses Monats (of the instant)
D.M.A. Diploma in Municipal Administration
D.M. & C.W. Diploma in Maternity and Child Welfare
D.M.D. Doctor Medicinae Dentalis (Doctor of Dental Medicine)
    Doctor of Mathematics and Didactics
D.M.E. Diploma in Mechanical Engineering
    Director of Mechanical Engineering
    Distance-measuring Equipment
D.Med. Doctor of Medicine
D.Met. Doctor of Metallurgy
    Diploma of Meteorology
D.M.F. Decorative Marble Federation
    Dyers of Man-Made Fibre Fabrics Federation
D.M.G.O. Divisional Machine Gun Officer
D.M.H.S. Director of Medical and Health Services
D.M.I. Director of Military Intelligence
D.Miss. Doctor of Missiology
D.M.J. Diploma of Medical Jurisprudence
D.M.L. Defence Medal for Leningrad

D.M.L.T. Diploma in Medical Laboratory Technology
D.M.M. Defence Medal for Moscow
D.M.O. Defence Medal for Odessa
 Director of Military Operations
 District Medical Officer
D.M.O. & I. Director Military Operations and Intelligence
D.M.P. Diploma in Medical Psychology
 Director of Manpower Planning
D.M.P.A. Direct Mail Producers' Association
 Dublin Master Printers' Association
D.M.P.I. Desired Mean Point of Impact
D.M.R. Diploma in Medical Radiology
 Director of Materials Research
D.M.R. & E. Diploma in Medical Radiology and Electrology
D.M.R.D. Diploma in Medical Radio-Diagnostics
 Directorate of Materials Research and Development
D.M.R.E. Diploma in Medical Radiology and Electricity *or* Electrology
D.M.R.(T.) Diploma in Radiotherapy
D.M.S. Director of Medical Services
 Directorate of Military Survey
 Dis manibus sacrum (consecrated to the souls of the departed)
 Doctor of Medical Science
 Documentation of Molecular Spectroscopy
D.M.Sc. Doctor of Missionary Science
D.M.S.S. Director of Medical and Sanitary Services
dmstr. demonstrator
D.M.S.V. Defence Medal for Sevastopol
D.M.T. Director of Military Training
D.M.T.R. Dounreay Materials Testing Reactor
D.Mus. Doctor of Music
D.M.V. Docteur en médecine vétérinaire (Doctor of Veterinary Medicine)
D.N. Debit Note
 Diploma in Nutrition
 Dominus Noster (Our Lord)
d--n damn
DNA deoxyribonucleic acid
Dña. Doña
D.N.A. Director of Naval Accounts
 District Nursing Association
D.N.A.D. Director of Naval Air Division
D.N.A.R. Director of Naval Air Radio
D.N.B. Deutsches Nachrichten-Büro (Nazi news agency)
 Died (Nonbattle)
 Dictionary of National Biography
D.N.C. Director of Naval Construction
D.N.C.L. Diploma of the Northampton College of Advanced Technology
D.N.D. Director of Navigation and Direction
D.N.E. Diploma in Nursing Education
 Director of Naval Equipment
D.N.E.S. Director of Naval Education Service

D.N.I. Director of Naval Intelligence
D.N.J.C. Dominus noster Jesus Christus (Our Lord Jesus Christ)
D.N.M.S. Director of Naval Medical Services
D.N.O. Director of Naval Ordnance
 District Naval Officer
DNOC Dinitro-ortho-cresol
DNP di-iso-octyl phthalate
D.N.PP. Dominus noster Papa (Our Lord the Pope)
D.N.R. Director of Naval Recruiting
D.N.S.A. Diploma in Nursing Service Administration
D.N.T. Director of Naval Training
D.N.W.S. Director of Naval Weather Service
do. ditto (the aforesaid)
D.O. Defence Order
 Deferred Ordinary (Shares)
 Delivery Order
 Design Office
 Diploma in Ophthalmology
 Direct Order
 District Office
 Divisional Officer
 Doctor of Oratory
 Doctor of Osteopathy
 Drawing Office
d/o. delivery order
D.O.A. Dead on Arrival
D.O.A.E. Defence Operational Analysis Establishment
Doc. Doctor
 Document(s)
D.O.C. District Officer Commanding
Doc.Eng. Doctor of Engineering
D.O.D. Department of Defense (U.S.)
D.o.D. Department of Defence
D.Oec. Doctor Oeconomiae (Doctor Economics)
D. of H. Degree of Honour
D. of L. Duchy of Lancaster
D. of P. Director of Plans Division
D. of S. Director of Stores
dogm. dogmatic
D.O.H. Department of Health (Ireland)
D.O.I. Died of Injuries
 Director of Information
dol. dollar
D.O.L. Doctor of Oriental Learning
dols. dollars
Dom. Dominion
 Dominus (Lord, Master)
dom. domestic
 domicile
 dominant
D.O.M. Domino *or* Deo optimo maximo (to the Lord *or* God, the supreme and mighty ruler of the world)
D.O.M.M.D.A. Drawing Office Material Manufacturers' and Dealers' Association
D.O.M.S. Diploma in Ophthalmic Medicine and Surgery
Dom. Sc. Domestic Science
Don(eg). Donegal
DOP Dioctyl phthalate
D.O.P. Developing-out Paper
D.O.P.B.M. Department of Oriental Printed Books and Manuscripts (British Museum)

D.Opt. Diploma in Ophthalmics
Dor. Doric
D.Or. Doctor in Orientation
D.O.R. Directorate of Operational Research
D.O.R.A. Defence of the Realm Act(s)
Dorna desoxyribose nucleic acid
Dors. Dorset
D.Orth. Diploma in Orthoptics
D.O.S. Day of Sale
　　Diploma in Orthopaedic Surgery
　　Director of Ordnance Services
　　Directorate of Overseas Surveys
dot. dotation
D.O.T. Department of Overseas Trade
　　Department of Transport
　　Diploma in Occupational Therapy
D.o.T. Department of Telecommunications
Dott. Dottore (Doctor)
Dow. Dowager
D.O.W. Died of Wounds
doz. dozen(s)
dp. deep
D.P. by Direction of the President
　　Delivery point
　　Democratic Party (Australia)
　　Diametral Pitch
　　Diploma in Psychiatry
　　Disabled Person
　　Displaced Person
　　Doctor of Philosophy
　　Documents against Payment
　　Domestic Prelate
　　Domus Procerum (House of Lords)
　　Duty Paid
D/p. Documents against payment
d.p. direct port
D.P.A. Deutsche Presse-Agentur (German Press Agency)
　　Diary Publishers' Association
　　Diploma in Public Administration
　　Discharged Prisoners' Aid
D.P. & S.P.A. Display Producers' and Screen Printers' Association
D.P.A.S. Royal London Discharged Prisoners' Aid Society
D.P.B. Department of Printed Books (British Museum)
　　Deposit Pass Book
D.P.D. Department of Prints and Drawings (British Museum)
　　Diploma in Public Dentistry
D.P.Ec. Doctor of Political Economy
D.Ph. Doctor of Philosophy
D.P.H. Department of Public Health
　　Diploma in Public Health
　　Doctor in Public Health
D.Pharm. Doctor of Pharmacy
D.Phil. Doctor of Philosophy
D.P.H.N. Diploma in Public Health Nursing
D.P.I. Director of Public Instructions
D.P.M. Deputy Prime Minister
　　Deputy Provost Marshal
　　Diploma in Psychological Medicine

D.P.O. Distributing Post Office
　　District Pay Office
D.Pol.Sc. Doctor of Political Science
D.P.P. Diploma in Plant Pathology
　　Director of Public Prosecutions
D.P.R. Director of Public Relations
D.P.S. Department of Political Science
　　Director of Personal Services
　　Director of Postal Services
D.P.S.A. Display Producers' and Screen Printers' Association
　　Diploma in Public and Social Administration
D.Ps.Sc. Doctor of Psychological Science
D.Psych. Diploma of Psychiatry
dpt. department
　　deponent
　　deposit
　　depot
d.p.t. distributed profit tax
Dpty. Deputy
Dpx. Duplex
D.Q. Development quotient
D.Q.M.G. Deputy Quartermaster-General
D.Q.M.S. Deputy Quartermaster-Sergeant
Dr. Debit
　　Debtor
　　Director
　　Doctor
　　Drachma
　　Drawer
　　Drive(r)
dr. debit
　　debtor
　　door
　　drachma
　　dram
　　drama
　　draw(n
　　dresser
　　drive(r)
　　drum
D.R. Daughters of the Revolution
　　Dead Reckoning
　　Defence Regulation(s)
　　Despatch Rider
　　Deutsches Reich (German Empire)
　　Diploma in Radiology
　　District Railway
　　District Registry
　　Double Royal
　　Dutch Reformed
D/R. Deposit Receipt
d.r. dead reckoning
D.R.A. De-Rating Appeals
D.R.A.C. Director Royal Armoured Corps
Dr.Agr. Doctor of Agriculture
dram. drama
　　dramatic
　　dramatist
dram. pers. dramatis personae (characters in a play)
D.R.B. Defence Research Board (Canada)
D.R.C.O.G. Diploma of the Royal College of Obstetricians and Gynaecologists

D.R.E. Doctor of Religious Education
Directorate of Radio Equipment
drg. drawing
D.R.G.M. Deutsches Reichsgebrauchs-muster (German registered design)
Dr.h.c. Doctor honoris causa (Honorary Doctor)
Dr.Ing. Dottore in Ingegneria (Doctor of Engineering)
D.R.L.S Despatch Rider Letter Service
D.R.M. Diploma in Resource Management
DRNA desoxyribose nucleic acid
D.R.O. Disablement Resettlement Officer
Divisional *or* Daily Routine Order(s)
D.R.P. Deutsches Reichspatent (German Patent)
Directorate of Radio Production
D.R.P.C. Defence Research Policy Committee
D.R.P.P. Directorate of Research Programmes and Planning
D.R.S.A.M. Diploma of the Royal Scottish Academy of Music
D.R.T. Director of Railway Transport
D.R.T.E. Defence Research Telecommunications Establishment (Canada)
D.R.U. Design Research Unit
Dr.u.Vrl. Druck und Verlag (printed and published by)
D.R.V.(N.) Democratic Republic of Vietnam
Ds. Dominus (Lord, Master)
D.S. dal segno (repeat from the sign)
Debenture Stock
Dental Surgeon
Department of State
Deputy Secretary
Document Signed
D/S Days after sight
Day's Sight
D.S.A. Diploma in Social Administration
Docteur en sciences agricoles (Doctor of Agriculture)
D.S.A.S.O. Deputy Senior Air Staff Officer
D.S.B. Drug Supervisory Body
d.s.b. double sideband
D.Sc. Doctor of Science
D.S.C. Distinguished Service Cross
d.s.c. down stage centre
D.Sc.A. Docteur en sciences agricoles (Doctor of Agriculture)
Docteur en sciences appliquées (Doctor of Sciences)
D.Sc.Agr. Doctor of Science in Agriculture
D.Sc.Com. Docteur en sciences commerciales (Doctor of Commerce)
D.Sc.D. Doctor of Science and Didactics
D.Sc.(Econ.) Doctor of Science (Economics)
D.Sc.For. Doctor of Science in Forestry
D.Sc.Mil. Doctor of Military Science
D.Scn. Doctor of Scientology
D.Sc.Pol. Docteur ès sciences politiques (Doctor of Political Sciences)

D.Sc.Soc. Docteur en Science sociale (Doctor of Social Science)
D.Sc.Tech. Doctor of Technical Science
D.S.D. Director of Signals Division
Director of Staff Duties
D.S.E. Derby Society of Engineers
D.S.I. Dairy Society International
D.S.I.R. Department of Scientific and Industrial Research (*now* S.R.C.)
D.S.L(s). Deep Scattering Layer(s)
D.S.M. Distinguished Service Medal
Directorate of Servicing and Maintenance
D.S.O. Distinguished Service Order
D.Soc.Sc. Doctor of Social Science
D.S.P. Director of Selection of Personnel
d.s.p. decessit sine prole (died without issue)
D.S.P.C.A. Dublin Society for the Prevention of Cruelty to Animals
d.s.p.l. decessit sine prole legitima (died without legitimate issue)
d.s.p.m. decessit sine prole mascula (died without male issue)
d.s.p.m.s. decessit sine prole mascula superstite (died without surviving male issue)
d.s.p.s. decessit sine prole superstite (died without surviving issue)
d.s.p.v. decessit sine prole virile (died without male issue)
D.S.Q. Discharged to Sick Quarters
D.S.R. Director of Scientific Research
D.S.R.D. Directorate of Signals Research and Development
D.S.S. Dental Students' Society
Doctor Sacrae Scripturae (Doctor of Holy Scripture)
D.S.S.A. Direct Sales and Service Association
D.S.Sc. Diploma in Sanitary Science
Doctor of Social Science
D.S.T. Daylight Saving Time
Director of Supplies and Transport
Doctor of Sacred Theology
Double Summer Time
D.St.J. Dame of Justice *or* Grace of the Order of Saint John of Jerusalem
dstn. destination
D.S.W. Doctor of Social Work
D.T. The Daily Telegraph
Delirium Tremens
Doctor Theologiae (Doctor of Divinity)
D.T.A. Dance Teachers' Association (*now* I.D.T.A.)
Diploma in Tropical Agriculture
Distributive Trades' Alliance
D.T.A.S.W. Department of Torpedo and Anti-Submarine Warfare
D.T.C. Department of Technical Co-operation
Diploma in Textile Chemistry
D.T.C.D. Diploma in Tuberculosis and Chest Diseases
D.T.D. Dekoratie voor Trouwe Dienst (Decoration for Distinguished Service)   *cont.*

79

iploma in Tuberculosis *or*
Tuberculous Diseases
Director of Technical Development
D.Tech. Doctor in Technology
D.T.F. Dental Traders' Federation
Domestic Textiles Federation
D.Th. Doctor of Theology
D.T.H. Diploma in Tropical Hygiene
D.Th.P.T. Diploma in Theory and Practice of Teaching
D.T.I. Department of Trade and Industry
D.T.L. Dictograph Telephones Limited Down the Line
D.T.M. Diocesan Travelling Mission
Diploma in Tropical Medicine
D.T.M. & H. Diploma in Tropical Medicine and Hygiene
D.T.O.D. Director of Trade and Operations Division
D.T.P.S. Dublin Typographical Provident Society
D.T.R. Diploma in Therapeutic Radiology
D.T.R.P. Diploma in Town and Regional Planning
D.T's. Delirium Tremens
D.T.V.M. Diploma in Tropical Veterinary Medicine
D.T.W.P. Director of Tactical and Weapons Policy Division
Du. Duchy
Duke
Dutch
D.U. Doctor of University
Dub. Dublin
dub. dubious
D.U.M. Dublin University Mission
Dumb. Dumbarton
Dumf. Dumfries
Dun. Dunedin
dun. dunnage
duo. duodecimo
dup. duplicate
D.U.P. Docteur de l'Université de Paris
Dur. Durham
D.U.S.W. Director of Undersurface Warfare Division
Dut. Dutch
D.V. Defective Vision
Deo Volente (God willing)
Diploma in Venereology *cont.*

Distinguished Visitor
Douay Version (Bible)
D.V. & D. Diploma in Venereology and Dermatology
D.V.H. Diploma in Veterinary Hygiene
D.V.L.R. Derwent Valley Light Railway
D.V.M. Doctor of Veterinary Medicine
d.v.m. desessit vita matris (died in the lifetime of the mother)
D.V.M. & S. Doctor of Veterinary Medicine and Surgery
D.V.O. Divisional Veterinary Officer
d.v.p. decessit vita patris (died in the lifetime of the father)
D.V.P.H. Diploma in Veterinary Public Health
Dvr. Driver
D.V.S. Director of Veterinary Services
D.V.Sc. Doctor of Veterinary Science
D.V.S.M. Diploma in Veterinary State Medicine
D.W. Dock Warrant
d.w. dead weight
delivered weight
dock warrant
D.-w. Dust-wrapper
d.w.c. deadweight capacity
dwg. drawing
dwelling
D.W.R. Duke of Wellington's Regiment
dwt. pennyweight
d.w.t. dead weight tons
D.X.R. Deep x-ray
D.X.R.T. Deep x-ray Therapy
Dy Dysprosium
Dy. Demy
dy. delivery
D.Y. Dockyard
Dyd. Dockyard
Dyn. Dynasty
dyn. dynamics
dynamite
dynamo
D.Y.S. Duke of York's Royal Military School
D.Z. Doctor of Zoology
Dropping Zone
D.Z.F. Deutsche Zentrale für Fremdenverkehr (German Central Tourist Association)
D.Zool. Doctor of Zoology
D.-Zug. Durchgang-Zug through train)

E

E Erbium
E. Earl
Earth
East(erly)
Eastern
Efficiency
Elocution
Eminence
Enemy *cont.*

Engineer
England
English
Espagne (Spain)
Excellency
Excellent
e. eccentricity
economics
educated *cont.*

elasticity
elder
eldest
electric(ity)
electromotive
errors
excellence
excellent
ea. each
E.A. Economic Adviser
    Electrical Artificer
    Ente Autonomo (Autonomous Corporation)
    Evangelical Alliance
E/A. Enemy Aircraft
E.A.A. Edinburgh Architectural Association
    Electrical Appliance Association
E.A.A.A. European Association of Advertising Agencies
E.A.A.C. European Agricultural Aviation Centre
E.A.A.F.R.O. East African Agriculture and Forestry Research Organisation
E.A.A.P. European Association for Animal Production
E.A.C. Engineering Advisory Council
E.A.C.A. East Africa Court of Appeal Reports
E.A.C.C. East Asia Christian Conference
E.A.C.S.O. East African Common Services Organisation
E.A.E.G. European Association of Exploration Geophysicists
E.A.E.N.F. Engineering and Allied Employers' National Federation (*now* E.E.F.)
E.A.E.S. European Atomic Energy Society
E.A.F. Employment Agents' Federation
E.A.F.R.O. East African Fisheries Research Organisation
E.A.G. Economists Advisory Group
E.A.H.C. East African High Commission
E.A.H.T.M.A. Engineers' and Allied Hand Tool Makers' Association
E.A.M.F. European Association of Music Festivals
E.A.M.P.A. East Anglian Master Printers' Alliance
E.A.M.S. Empire Air Mail Scheme
E.A.M.T.C. European Association of Management Training Centres
E.& O.E. Errors and Omissions Excepted
e.a.o.n. except as otherwise noted
E.A.P. East Africa Protectorate
E.A.P.R. European Association for Potato Research
E.A.R.B. European Airlines Research Bureau
E.A.R.C.C.U.S. East African Regional Committee for Conservation and Utilisation of Soil
E.A.R.O.P.H. East Asia Regional Organization for Planning and Housing
E.A.S. Estimated Air Speed
E.A.S.A. Entertainment Arts Socialist Association
East L. East Lothian

E.A.T.R.O. East African Trypanosomiasis Research Organisation
E.A.V.R.O. East African Veterinary Research Organisation
E.A.W. Electrical Association for Women
Eb. Eisenbahn (Railway)
E.B. Electricity Board
    Encyclopaedia Britannica
eb. point d'ébullition (boiling point)
E.B.A. English Bowling Association
E.B.& R.A. Engineer Buyers' and Representatives' Association
E.B.C. European Billiards Confederation
    European Brewery Convention
E.B.L. European Bridge League
E. boat Eil (fast) boat
Ebor. Eboracum (York)
E.B.R. Electron Beam Recorder
    Experimental Breeder Reactor
E.B.R.A. Engineer Buyers' and Representatives' Association
E.B.S. Emergency Bed Service
    English Bookplate Society
E.B.U. English Bridge Union
    European Boxing Union
    European Broadcasting Union
E.B.Y.C. European Bureau for Youth and Childhood
E. by N. East by North
E. by S. East by South
Ec. Ecuador
E.C. East Central
    East Coast
    Eastern Command
    Ecclesiastical Commissioner
    Education Committee
    Electricity Council (*formerly* C.E.A.)
    Emergency Commission
    Engineer Captain
    Episcopal Church
    Established Church
    Executive Committee
e.c. enamel-covered
    exempli causa (for example)
E.C.A. Economic Commission for Africa
    Economic Co-operative Administration (*later* M.S.A.)
    Educational Centres Association
    Electrical Contractors' Association
    European Confederation of Agriculture
    European Congress of Accountants
E.C.A.C. European Civil Aviation Conference
E.C.A.F.E. Economic Commission for Asia and the Far East
E.C.A.S. Electrical Contractors' Association of Scotland
ecc. eccetera (etcetera)
E.C.C. European Cultural Centre
eccl. ecclesiastic(al)
Eccl(es). Ecclesiastes
Ecclus. Ecclesiasticus

E.C.C.M. Electronic counter counter measures
E.C.C.P. East Coast Coal Port
European Committee on Crime Problems
E.C.C.U. English Cross Country Union
E.C.E. Economic Commission for Europe
Export Council for Europe
E.C.F. Eastern Counties Farmers
European Commission on Forestry and Forest Products
E.C.F.M.G. Educational Council for Foreign Medical Graduates
E.C.F.M.S. Educational Council for Foreign Medical Students
E.C.G. Electrocardiogram
Electrocardiograph
Export Credit Guarantee(s)
E.C.G.B. East Coast of Great Britain
E.C.G.C. Empire Cotton Growing Corporation
E.C.G.D. Export Credits Guarantee Department
Ech. Echelon
E.C.I. East Coast of Ireland
E.C.I.T.O. European Central Inland Transport Organization
Ecl. Eclogue(s)
E.C.L.A. Economic Commission for Latin America
eclec. eclectic
ECLOF Ecumenical Church Loan Fund
E.C.M. Electronic Counter measures
European Common Market
E.C.M.A. European Computer Manufacturers' Association
E.C.M.B.R. European Committee on Milk-Butterfat Recording
E.C.M.F. Electric Cable Makers' Federation
E.C.M.T. European Conference of Ministers of Transport
ecol. ecological
ecology
econ. economics
economist
economy
ECOSOC Economic and Social Council (U.N.)
E.C.P. European Committee of Crop Protection
E.C.P.S. Eastern Counties Poultry Society
E.C.R.L. Eastern Caribbean Regional Library
E.C.R.U. Eastern Counties Rugby Union
E.C.S.C. European Coal and Steel Community
E.C.T. Electroconvulsive Therapy
E.C.T.A. Electrical Contractors' Trading Association
E.C.U. English Church Union
European Chiropracts Union
E.C.U.K. East Coast of United Kingdom
Ed. Edinburgh
Edited
Edition
Editor
Education

ed. edited
edition
editor
educated
E.D. Doctor of Engineering
Education Department
Efficiency Decoration
Employment Department
Entertainments Duty
Estate Duties
Existence Doubtful
Extra Dividend
E.D.A. British Electrical Development Association (*also* B.E.D.A.)
Educational Development Association
Educational Drama Association
Ed.B. Bachelor of Education
E.D.C. Economic Development Committee(s)
Educational Development Centre
European Defence Community
Expected Date of Confinement
Express Dairy Company
e.d.c. extra dark colour
Edcn. Education
Ed.D. Doctor of Education
E.D.D. English Dialect Dictionary
Expected Date of Delivery
Edin. Edinburgh
edit. edited
edition
editor
E.D.I.T. Estate Duties Investment Trust
e.d.l. edition de luxe
Ed.M. Master of Education
Edn. Edition
E.D.O.N. Eniaia Demokratiki Organosis Neolaias (United Democratic Youth Organisation, Cyprus)
E.D.P. Electronic Data Processing
Emergency Defence Plan
E.D.P.S. Electronic Data Processing System
E.D.R. European Depositary Receipts
E.D.S.A.C. Electronic Delayed Storage Automatic Computer
E.D.T. Eastern Daylight Time
Edu. Education
educ. educated
Educn. Education
E.E. Electronic Engineer(ing)
Employment Exchange
Envoy-Extraordinary
Errors Excepted
Euer Ehrwürden (your Reverence)
E.-E. Early English
Envoy-Extraordinary
e.e. errors excepted
E.E.A. Ecurie Ecosse Association
Educational Exhibitors' Association
Electronic Engineering Association
E.-E.& M.P. Envoy-Extraordinary and Minister Plenipotentiary
E.E.B. Eastern Electricity Board
E.E.C. English Electric Company
European Economic Community

E.E.F. Egyptian Expeditionary Force
Engineering Employers' Federation (*formerly* E.A.E.N.F.)
E.E.G. Electroencephalogram
Electroencephalograph
➤ Essence Export Group
E.Eng. Early English
E.E.S. Egypt Exploration Society
European Exchange System
➤ **E.E.T.C.** East Europe Trades Council
E.E.T.S. Early English Text Society
E.E.U.A. Engineering Equipment Users' Association
➤ **E.E.V.C.** English Electric Valve Company
E.F. Elevation Finder
Expeditionary Force
Extra Fine
E.F.A. Empire Forestry Association
Eton Fives Association
E.F.B.T.E. Eastern Federation of Building Trades' Employers
E.F.C. European Federation of Corrosion
European Forestry Commission
E.F.C.E. European Federation of Chemical Engineering
E.F.D.S.S. English Folk Dance and Song Society
eff. efficiency
E.F.F. European Furniture Federation
E.F.M. European Federalist Movement
E.F.P. European Federation of Purchasing
E.F.P.M.B. Employers' Federation of Papermakers and Boardmakers
➤ **E.F.P.W.** European Federation for the Protection of Waters
E.F.S.C. European Federation of Soroptimist Clubs
E.F.T.A. European Free Trade Association
➤ **E.F.T.C.** Electrical Fair Trading Council
E.F.T.S. Elementary Flying Training School
E.F.U. Europäische Frauenunion (European Union of Women)
European Football Union
E.F.V.A. Educational Foundation for Visual Aids
Eg. Egypt(ian)
E.G. Engineers' Guild
e.g. ejusdem generis (of a like kind)
exempli gratia (for example)
E.G.B. Eastern Gas Board
➤ **E.G.C.I.** Export Group for the Construction Industries
E.G.C.S. English Guernsey Cattle Society
E.Ger. East Germany
E.G.M. Empire Gallantry Medal (*superseded by the* George Cross)
European Glass Container Manufacturers' Committee
e.G.m.b.H. eingetragene Gesellschaft mit beschränkter Haftung (registered company with limited liability)
E.G.O. Eccentric Geophysical Observatories
E.G.S.P. Electronics Glossary and Symbol Panel

E.G.U. English Golf Union ➤
Egyptol. Egyptologist
Egyptology
e.h. ehrenhalber (for the sake of honour)
E.H.C.C. European Hops Culture Committee
E.H.F. Experimental Husbandry Farms
E.H.G.C. European Hops Growers' Convention
E.H.L. Effective Half-Life
e.h.p. effective horsepower
electric horsepower
E.H.V. Extra-high Voltage
E.I. East India
East Indies
Endorsement Irregular
E.I.A. Engineering Industries' Association
E.I.B. European Investment Bank
E.I.B.A. Electrical Industries' Benevolent Association
E.I.C. Electrical Industries' Club
Engineering Institute of Canada
E.I.C.S. East India Company's Service
E.I.D. East India Dock
Electrical Inspection Directorate
E.I.F.I. Electrical Industries Federation of Ireland
E.I.J.C. Engineering Institutions Joint Council
E.-in-C. Engineer-in-Chief
E.I.S. Educational Institute of Scotland
E.I.U. Economist Intelligence Unit
E.I.V.T. European Institute for Vocational Training
E.J.C. Engineers' Joint Council
E.J.M.A. English Joinery Manufacturers' Association ➤
ejusd. ejusdem (of the same)
EKCO E. K. Cole, Limited
E.K.G. Electrocardiogram
Electrocardiograph
E.K.S. Etaireia Kypriakon Spoudon (Society of Cyprus Studies)
el. elected
electric(ity)
element
elevated
elevation
E.L. Engineer Lieutenant
E.L.A.A. Electric Light Fittings Association
E.L.A.N.E. Electronics Association for ➤ the North East
E.L.Cr. Engineer Lieutenant-Commander
eld. elder
eldest
E.L.D.O. European Space Vehicle Launcher Development Organisation
elec. electric(al)
electricity
electuary
E.L.E.C. European League for Economic Cooperation
ELECO Engineering and Lighting Equipment Company
Electron. Electronics
elem. elementary
elev. elevation
E.L.F. European Landworkers' Federation

E.L.F.A. Electric Light Fittings Association
E.L.I.C. Electric Lamp Industry Council
ELINTS Electronic Intelligence Ships
El.L. Electrical Lieutenant
E.L.L.A. European Long Lines Agency
El.L.Cr. Electrical Lieutenant-Commander
ellipt. elliptical
ELMA Electro-mechanical Aid
E.L.M.A. Electrical Lamp Manufacturers' Association
E.L.R. Export Licensing Regulations
El.S.L. Electrical Sub-Lieutenant
E.L.T. European Letter Telegram
E.L.U. English Lacrosse Union
Ely. Easterly
Elz. Elzevir
Em. Eminence
em. emanation
    embargo
    eminent
E.M. Earl Marshal
    Edward Medal
    Efficiency Medal
    Electrical and Mechanical
    Electron Microscope
    Engineer Manager
    Engineer of Mining
    Enlisted Man
    Equitum Magister (Master of the Horse)
    État-Major (General Staff)
    European Movement
    Expanded Metal
e.m. electro-magnetic
    expanded metal
E.M.A. Educational maintenance allowances
    European Monetary Agreement
    Evangelical Missionary Alliance
    Exhibition Manufacturers' Association
E.M.A.I.A. Electrical Meter and Allied Industries' Association (Australia)
E.M.A.P. European Marketing and Advertising Press
Emb. Embankment
    Embassy
emb. embargo
embr. embroidered
    embroidery
Embry. Embryology
E.M.C.C. European Municipal Credit Community
E.M.C.C.C. European Military Communications Co-ordinating Committee
E.M.D.P. Electromotive Difference of Potential
E.M.E.B. East Midlands Electricity Board
Emer. Emeritus
emer. emergency
E.M.F. European Motel Federation
e.m.f. electro-motive force
E.M.G. État-Major-Général (General Staff)
    Electromyogram
E.M.G.B. East Midlands Gas Board

E.M.I. Electric and Musical Industries
E.M.I.C. Emergency Maternity and Infant Care
E.M.K. elektromotorische Kraft (electromotive force)
E.M.L. Everyman's Library
Emm. Emmanuel College, Cambridge
E.M.M.S. Edinburgh Medical Missionary Society
E.M.M.S.A. Envelope Makers' and Manufacturing Stationers' Association
Emp. Emperor
    Empire
    Empress
empld. employed
E.M.R. Eastern Mediterranean Region
E.M.R.L.S. East Midlands Regional Library System
E.M.S. Emergency Medical Service
E.M.T.A. Electro-Medical Trade Association
e.m.u. electromagnetic unit(s)
En. Engineer
en. enemy
E.N.A. English Newspaper Association
    European Nuclear Agency
E.N.A.B. Evening Newspaper Advertising Bureau
enam. enamelled
E.N. & T. Ear, Nose and Throat
enc. enclosed
    enclosure(s)
E.N.C.A. European Naval Communications Agency
Ency. Encyclopaedia
Ency. Brit. Encyclopaedia Britannica
Endon. Endowment
Endp. Endpaper
E.N.E. East-North-East
E.N.E.A. European Nuclear Energy Agency
E.N.E.F. English New Education Fellowship
E.N.F. European Nuclear Force
Eng. Engineering
    England
    English
    Engraved
    Engraving(s)
Engin. Engineering
Engl. England
    English
Engr. Engineer
    Engraver
E.N.I. Ente Nazionale Idrocarburi (Hydrocarbons National Corporation)
E.N.I.A.C. Electronic Numerical Integrator and Calculator
E.N.I.T. Ente Nazionale Industrie Turistiche (Italian State Tourist Department)
enl. enlarged
    enlargement
    enlisted
En.L. Engineer Lieutenant
En.L.Cr. Engineer Lieutenant-Commander
Ens. Ensign
E.N.S.A. Entertainments National Services Association
En.S.L. Engineer Sub-Lieutenant

Ent. Entered
    Entertainment
    Entomology
E.N.T. Ear, Nose and Throat
entd. entered
Entom. Entomology
Env. Envoy
env. envelope
    environs
Env-Extr. Envoy-Extraordinary
e.n.z. en zoo voort (and so forth)
E.O. Education Officer
    Emergency Operation
    Employers' Organisation
    Engineer Officer
    Executive Officer
    Experimental Officer
E.o. Easter offerings
e.o. ex officio (by virtue of office)
E.O.A. Examination, Opinion and
    Advice
E.O.A.R.D.C. European Office of the
    Air Research and Development Com-
    mand (U.S.)
e.o.d. every other day
e.o.h.p. except otherwise herein pro-
    vided
E.O.K.A. Ethniki Organosis Kyprion
    Aganiston (National Organization of
    Cypriot Combatants)
E.O.M. Egyptian Order of Merit
    end of month
    every other month
E.O.N.R. European Organisation for
    Nuclear Research
e.o.o.e. erreur ou omission exceptée
    (errors and omissions excepted)
E.O.Q.C. European Organization for
    Quality Control
E.O.S. European Orthodontic Society
E.O.T.P. European Organisation for
    Trade Promotion
Ep. Episcopus (Bishop)
    Epistle
    Electro-plate(d)
    European Plan
    Estimated Position
    Expanded Polystyrene
e.p. editio princeps (first edition)
    end paper(s)
    en passant (in passing)
    estimated position
E.P. Easy Projection
    Extended Play
E.P.A. Educational priority areas
    Educational Puppetry Associ-
    ation
    Emergency Powers Act
    Environmental Protection
    Agency
    European Productivity Agency
E.P.A.C.C.I. Economic Planning and
    Advisory Council for the Construct-
    ion Industries
E.P.C. Economic and Planning Council
E.P.C. Economic Policy Committee
    (O.E.C.D.)
    Export Publicity Council
E.P.D. Earliest Practicable Date
    Excess Profits Duty
E.P.D.A. Emergency Powers (Defence)
    Act

E.P.E.A. Electrical Power Engineers'
    Association
E.P.F. European Packaging Federation
E.P.G. Eggs per gramme
    European Press Group
Eph. Ephesians
E.P.I. Electronic Position Indicator
    (system)
E.P.I.C. End Poverty in California
    (Upton Sinclair's Campaign)
Epict. Epictetus
E.P.I.D.C. East Pakistan Industrial
    Development Corporation
epil. epilogue
Epiph. Epiphany
Episc. Episcopal(ian)
epit. epitome
E.P.M. Evolution Protest Movement
E.P.N.S. Electro-plate on Nickel Silver
    English Place-Name Society
E.P.P.O. European and Mediterranean
    Plant Protection Organization
E.P.T. Excess Profits Tax
E.P.T.A. Electro-Physiological Tech-
    nologists' Association
    Expanded Programme of
    Technical Assistance
E.P.U. Empire Press Union
    European Payments Union
    European Press Photo Agencies
    Union
Epus. Episcopus (Bishop)
Eq. Equator(ial)
    Equerry
eq. equal
    equate
    equation
    equipment
    equitable
    equity
eqn. equation
eqpt. equipment
equiv. equivalent
Er Erbium
er. elder
E.R. Eastern Region (British Rail)
    East Riding (Yorkshire)
    Edwardus Rex (King Edward)
    Elizabeth Regina (Queen Eliza-
    beth)
    Engine Room
E.R.A. British Electrical and Allied
    Industries Research Associ-
    ation (*also* B.E.A.I.R.A.)
    Electronic Reading Automation
    Electronic Rentals Association
    Engine-Room Artificer
    Evangelical Radio Alliance
Erb Erbium
Erb. Erbitten (request)
E.R.C. Economic Research Council
    Empire Rheumatism Council
E.R.D. Army Emergency Reserve Dec-
    oration
E.R.D.A. Electrical and Radio Develop-
    ment Association (Australia)
E.R.D.E. Engineering Research and
    Development Establishment
E.R.et.I. Edwardus Rex et Imperator
    (Edward King and Emperor)
E.R.F.A. European Radio Frequency
    Agency

erg. ergon (work)
Ergon. Ergonomics
erm. ermine
E.R.N.I.E. Electronic Random Number Indicating Equipment
E.R.O. European Regional Organization of the International Confederation of Free Trade Unions
E.R.O.P.A. Eastern Regional Organization for Public Administration
E.R.P. European Recovery Programme
e.r.p. effective radiated power
erron. erroneous(ly)
E.R.S. Electric Railway Society
    Elizabethan Railway Society
    Engine Repair Section
    Ergonomics Research Society
E.R.U. English Rugby Union
E.R.V. English Revised Version (Bible)
Es Einsteinium
es. esémpio (example)
E.S. Econometric Society
    Eldest Son
    Electrostatic
    Engine-sized
    Entomological Society
e.s. electric starting
    eldest son
E.S.A. Educational Settlements Association
    Educational Supply Association
    Engineer Surveyors' Association
    European Schoolmagazine Association
E.S.A.A. English Schools' Athletic Association
E.S.A.N.Z. Economic Society of Australia and New Zealand
E.S.B. Electricity Supply Board (Ireland)
    English Speaking Board
Esc. Escudo
E.S.C. Economic and Social Council
    Electronic Structural Correlator
E.S.C.A. English Schools' Cricket Association
eschat. eschatological
    eschatology
E.S.C.M.A. Electric Steel Conduit Manufacturers' Association
Esco. Escocia (Scotland)
E.S.C.O. Educational, Scientific and Cultural Organisation (U.N.)
ESCOM Electricity Supply Commission of South Africa
Esd. Esdras
E.S.D. Echo Sounding Device
E.S.E. East-South-East
    Engineers Stores Establishment
E.S.E.F. Electrotyping and Stereotyping Employers' Federation
E.S.G. English Standard Gauge
E.S.H. European Society of Haematology
Esk. Eskimo
E.S.M.A. Electrical Sign Manufacturers' Association
E.S.N. Educationally Subnormal
E.S.N.Z. Entomological Society of New Zealand
ESOMAR European Society for Opinion Surveys and Market Research

Esp. Esparto
    Esperanto
esp. especially
E.S.P. Extra-Sensory Perception
Esq. Esquire
E.S.R. Estimated Sedimentation Rate
E.S.R.O. European Space Research Organization
E.S.R.S. European Society for Rural Sociology
E.S.R.U. English Schools Rugby Union
ess. essence(s)
E.S.S.A. English Schools Swimming Association
Est. Estonia(n)
    Estuary
est. established
    estimated
E.S.T. Eastern Standard Time
Estab. Establishment
estab. established
estd. established
    estimated
ESTEC European Space Technology Centre
Esth. Esther
E.S.T.I. European Space Technology Institute
E.S.T.R.A. English Speaking Tape Respondents Association
E.S.U. English-Speaking Union
e.s.u. electrostatic unit(s)
E.S.V. Earth Satellite Vehicle
E.T. Educational Therapy
    Electric Telegraph
    English Text
    English Translation
    Entertainment Tax
    Equation of Time
    Exchange Telegraph
e.t. en titre (in title)
E.T.A. Estimated Time of Arrival
    European Teachers' Association
Étabs. Établissements (Establishments)
et al. et alia (and other things)
    et alibi (and elsewhere)
etc. et cetera (and the rest *or* and so on)
E.T.C. Eastern Telegraph Company
    European Travel Commission
E.T.C.T.A. Electrical Trades Commercial Travellers' Association
E.T.E. Experimental Tunnelling Establishment
Eth. Ethic
    Ethiopia
E.T.H. Eidgenössische Technische Hochschule (Swiss Federal Institute of Technology)
ethnog. ethnography
ethnol. enthnology
E.T.I.C. English-Teaching Information Centre
E.T.J.C. Engineering Trades Joint Council
E.T.L. Ericsson Telephones, Limited
E.T.M.A. English Timber Merchants' Association
E.T.O. European Theatre of Operations
e.t.o. en tout cas (in any case *or* in emergency)

E.T.O.U.S.A. European Theatre of Operations, United States Army
E.T.P.S. Empire Test Pilots' School
E.T.S. Electrodepositors' Technical Society
Expiration of Time of Service
E.T.S.A. Electricity Trust of South Australia
et seq. et sequentia (and what follows)
E.T.T.A. English Table Tennis Association
E.T.T.U. European Table Tennis Union
E.T.U. Electrical Trades Union
et ux. et uxor (and wife)
E.T.V. Educational Television
(jet) Engine Test Vehicle
Etym. Etymological
Etymology
Eu Europium
E.U. États-Unis (United States)
Evangelical Union
Experimental Unit
E.U.A. États-Unis d'Amérique (United States of America)
Euc. Euclid
EUCARPIA European Association for Research on Plant Breeding
EUCEPA Comité européen de liaison pour la cellulose et le papier (European Liaison Committee for Pulp and Paper)
Eucl. Euclid
Eugen. Eugenics
E.U.P. English Universities Press
euphem. euphemistic(ally)
Eur. Europe(an)
E.U.R. Esposizione Universale Roma (Rome Universal Exhibition)
EURATOM European Atomic Energy Community
Eurip. Euripides
EUROCAE European Organization for Civil Aviation Electronics
EUROCHEMIC European Company for the Chemical Processing of Irradiated Fuels
EUROCOM European Fuel Merchants' Union
EUROFIMA Societé européenne pour le financement de matériel ferroviaire (European Company for the Financing of Railway Rolling Stock)
EUROFINAS Association of European Finance Houses
EUROMAISIERS Groupement des associations des maisiers des pays de la C.E.E. (Maize Industry Association Group for the E.E.C. Countries)
EUROMALT Comité de travail des malteries de la C.E.E. (Working Committee of the Malt-Houses of the E.E.C.)
EUROP European Railway Wagon Pool
EUROPECHE Association des organisations nationales d'entreprises de pêche de la C.E.E. (Association of National Organizations of Fishing Enterprises of the E.E.C.)

EUROPHOT Association européenne des photographes professionnels (Council of the Professional Photographers of Europe)
EUROSAC Fédération européenne des fabricants de sacs en papier à grande contenance (European Federation of Manufacturers of Multiwall Paper Sacks)
EUROSPACE European Industrial Space Study Group
EUROTOX European Committee for the Protection of Populations against the Hazards of Chronic Toxicity
E.U.S.A. Evangelical Union of South America
Eus(eb). Eusebius
EUSEC Conference of Representatives from the Engineering Societies of Western Europe and the United States of America
E.U.W. European Union of Women
e.v. electron volt(s)
en ville (local)
E.V.A. Electric Vehicle Association of Great Britain
Engineer Vice Admiral
evac. evacuation
Evang. Evangelical
Evangelist
evg. evening
evid. evidence
E.V.L. E. V. Lucas
evng. evening
evol. evolution
E.V.R. Electronic video recording and reproduction
E.V.T. Educational and Vocational Training
Europäische Vereinigung für Tierzucht (European Association for Animal Production)
E.V.W. European Volunteer Worker(s)
evy. every
E.W. England and Wales
e.w. each way
E.W.F. Electrical Wholesalers' Federation
E.W.O. Essential Work(s) Order
E.W.O.N.A. Education Welfare Officers' National Association
E.W.R. Early-warning Radar
E.W.R.C. European Weed Research Council
E.W.S. Emergency Water Supply
E.W.S.F. European Work Study Federation
Ex. Exchange
Exeter
Exodus
Extension
ex. examined
example
excellent
except(ion)
exchange
excluding
exclusive
excursion
executed
executive
executor   *cont.*

87

exempt
exercise
export
extra
extract
exag. exaggerated
    exaggeration
Exam. Examiner
    Examining
exam. examination
Exc. Excellency
exc. excellent
    except(ion)
    excommunication
    excudit (has engraved this)
Exch. Exchequer
exch. exchange
excl. exclamation
    exclude
    excluding
    exclusive
ex cp. without coupon
Exd. Examined
ex div. without dividend
Exec. Executive
    Executor
exec. executed
    execution
execx. executrix
exel. exclusive(ly)
exes. expenses
Exet. Exeter College, Oxford
ex. g. exempli gratia (for example)
exh. exhibition
    exhaust
Exhbn. Exhibition
Exhib. Exhibit(ed)
    Exhibition(er)
Ex.Im. United States Export-Import
  Bank
ex int. without interest
ex-l. ex libris (from the library of)
Ex-Mer. Ex-Meridian
ex. new. exclusive of right to participate
  in new issue
Exod. Exodus
ex off. ex officio (by virtue of office)
exor(s). executor(s)
EXP Exchange of Persons Office
  (U.N.E.S.C.O.)

Exp. Express
exp. expanded
    expansion
    expedition
    expense
    experienced
    experiment
    export(ation)
    exported
    express(ion)
ex p. ex parte (on one side only
expdn. expedition
Exped. Expeditionary
Exper. Experimental
expl. explained
    explanatory
    explosion
    explosive
explan. explanatory
exploit. exploitation
expn. exposition
exp. o. experimental order
expr. express
ex-Pres. ex-President
expt. experiment
exptl. experimental
exptr. exporter
expurg. expurgate(d
exr. executor
exrx. executrix
exs. expenses
ext. extend
    extension
    extent
    exterior
    external
    extinct
    extra
    extract
    extreme
extn. extension
extr. extraordinary
extrad. extradition
exx. examples
    executrix
Exz. Exzellenz (Excellency)
E.Y.C. European Youth Campaign
E.Y.R. East Yorkshire Regiment
Ez. Ezra
Ezek. Ezekiel

F

F Fluorine
F. Fahrenheit
    Fair
    Family
    Fast
    Father
    Fellow
    Felon
    Ferrovia (Railway)
    Fiction
    Fighter

    Finance
    Firm
    Fleet
    Folio
    Foreign Member
    France
    French
    Frequency
    Frère (Brother)
    Friday
f. fair

cont.

cont.

farad(s)
farthing
fathom
feet
felon
female
feminine
filly
fine
focal length
fog
folgende Seite (next page)
following
foot
for
force
formula
fortasse (perhaps)
forte (loud)
founded
franc(s)
from
function
furlong(s)
furlough
F.A. Factory Act
Faculty of Actuaries
Fanny Adams (nothing at all)
Field Allowance
Field Artillery
Financial Advisor
Football Association
f.a. free alongside
F.A.A. Federal Aviation Agency (U.S.)
Fellow of the American Association for the Advancement of Science
Fellow of the Australian Academy of Science
Film Artistes' Association
Fleet Air Arm
f.a.a. free of all average
F.A.A.A.S. Fellow of the American Association for the Advancement of Science
Fellow of the American Academy of Arts and Sciences
F.A.A.O.S. Fellow of the American Academy of Orthopaedic Surgeons
Fac. Faculty
F.A.C. Federation of Agricultural Co-operatives
f.a.c. fast as can
F.A.C.A. Fellow of the American College of Anaesthetists
F.A.C.C. Fellow of the American College of Cardiology
F.A.C.C.A. Fellow of the Association of Certified and Corporate Accountants
F.A.C.D. Fellow of the American College of Dentistry
F.A.C.E. Fellow of the Australian College of Dentistry
Field Artillery Computer Equipment
F.A.C.E.M. Federation of Associations of Colliery Equipment Manufacturers
facet. facetious
F.A.C.I.A.A. Fellow of the Australian Commercial and Industrial Artists' Association

G

F.A.C.O.G. Fellow of the American College of Obstetricians and Gynaecologists
F.A.C.P. Fellow of the American College of Physicians
F.A.C.R. Fellow of the American College of Radiology
Facs. Facsimile
F.A.C.S. Fellow of the American College of Surgeons
Fellow of the Association of Certified Secretaries of South Africa
F.A.C.T. Flanagan Aptitude Classification Test
f.a.d. free air delivered
F.A.D.O. Fellow of the Association of Dispensing Opticians
fag. fagotto (bassoon)
F.A.G.O. Fellow of the American Guild of Organists
F.A.G.S. Federation of Astronomical and Geophysical Services
Fellow of the American Geographical Society
Fahr. Fahrenheit
F.A.I. Fédération abolitionniste internationale (International Abolitionist Federation)
Fédération aéronautique internationale (International Aeronautical Federation)
Football Association of Ireland
F.A.I.A. Fellow of the American Institute of Architects
Fellow of the Association of International Accountants
F.A.I.A.S. Fellow of the Australian Institute of Agricultural Science
F.A.I.B. Fédération des associations internationales établies en Belgique (Federation of International Associations Established in Belgium)
Fellow of the Australian Institute of Builders
F.A.I.C. Fellow of the American Institute of Chemists
F.A.I.H.A. Fellow of the Australian Institute of Hospital Administration
F.A.I.I. Fellow of the Australian Insurance Institute
F.A.I.M. Fellow of the Australian Institute of Management
F.A.I.S. Fellow of the Amalgamated Institute of Secretaries
fam. familiar
family
F.A.M. Free and Accepted Mason(s)
f.a.m. free at mill
F.A.M.A. Fellow of the American Medical Association
Foundation for Mutual Assistance in Africa
F.A.M.E.M. Federation of Associations of Mine Equipment Manufacturers
F.A.M.N.Z. Fellow of the Arts Galleries and Museums Association of New Zealand
F.A.M.S. Fellow of the Ancient Mounments Society *cont.*

Fellow of the Indian Academy of Medical Sciences

f.& a. fore and aft

F.& C. Full and Change (high-water)

f.& d. freight and demurrage

f. and f. fittings and fixtures

f.& t. fire and theft

F.A.N.Y. First Aid Nursing Yeomanry

F.A.N.Y.S. First Aid Nursing Yeomanry Service

F.A.N.Z.A.A.S. Fellow of the Australian and New Zealand Association for the Advancement of Science

F.A.O. Fleet Accountant Officer
Food and Agriculture Organisation

f.a.o. finish all over

F.A.P. First Aid Post

F.A.P.H.A. Fellow of the American Public Health Association

F.A.P.I. Fellow of the Australian Planning Institute

F.A.P.S. Fellow of the American Physical Society

f.a.q. fair average quality
free alongside quay

f.a.q.s. fair average quality of season

Far. Faradic

far. farthing

FARELF Far East Land Forces

F.A.S. Faculty of Architects and Surveyors

f.a.s. firsts and seconds
free alongside ship

F.A.S.A. Fellow of the Acoustical Society of America
Fellow of the Australian Society of Accountants
First Auditor of Sheriff's Accounts

fasc. fascicolo (number *or* part)

F.A.S.C.E. Fellow of the American Society of Civil Engineers

F.A.S.E. Fellow of the Antiquarian Society, Edinburgh

F.A.S.S. Federation of Associations of Specialists and Sub-Contractors

F.A.T.I.P.E.C. Fédération d'associations de techniciens des industries des peintures, vernis, émaux et encres d'imprimerie de l'Europe continentale (Federation of Associations of Technicians in the Paint, Varnishes, Enamels and Printing-Ink Industries of Continental Europe)

F.A.T.I.S. Food and Agriculture Technical Information Service (O.E.E.C.)

F.A.U. Friends' Ambulance Unit

F.A.W.A. Federation of Asian Women's Associations

F.B. Faculty of Building
Fenian Brotherhood
Fire Brigade
Fishery Board
Flying Boat
Free Baptists
Full Back
Full Bore

f.b. flat bar
fog bell

F.B.A. Farm Buildings Association
Federal Bar Association (U.S.)
Federation of British Astrologers
Fellow of the British Academy
Freshwater Biological Association

F.B.A.A. Fellow of the British Association of Accountants and Auditors

F'ball Football

F.B.B.M. Federation of Building Block Manufacturers

F.B.B.D.O. Fibre Building Board Development Organization

f.b.c. fallen building clause

F.B.C.A. Federation of British Cremation Authorities

F.B.C.A.E.I. Federation of Builders Contractors and Allied Employers of Ireland

F.B.C.P. Fellow of the British College of Physiotherapists

f.b.c.w. fallen building clause waiver

F.B.E.A. Fellow of the British Esperanto Association

F.B.F.M. Federation of British Film Makers

F.B.G. Federation of British Growers

F.B.H. Fire Brigade Hydrant

F.B.H.I. Fellow of the British Horological Institute

F.B.H.T.M. Federation of British Hand Tool Manufacturers

F.B.I. Federal Bureau of Investigation
Federation of British Industries (*now* C.B.I.)

F.B.I.A. Fellow of the Bankers' Institute of Australasia

F.B.I.M. Fellow of the British Institute of Management

F.B.I.S. Fellow of the British Interplanetary Society

F.B.K.S. Fellow of the British Kinematograph Society

F.B.L. Foreign Bird League

F.B.M. Fleet Ballistic Missile

F.B.O.A. Fellow of the British Optical Association

F.B.O.U. Fellow of the British Ornithologists' Union

F.B.P.M.C. Federation of British Police Motor Clubs

F.B.P.S. Fellow of the British Phrenological Society
Forest and Bird Protection Society of New Zealand

F.B.Ps.S. Fellow of the British Psychological Society

F.B.R.A.M. Federation of British Rubber and Allied Manufacturers

F.Brit.I.R.E. Fellow of the British Institution of Radio Engineers (*now* F.I.E.R.E.)

F.B.S. Fellow of the Botanical Society of the British Isles
Fellow of the Building Societies Institute

F.B.S.C. Fellow of the British Society of Commerce

F.B.S.E. Fellow of the Botanical Society of Edinburgh

F.B.S.I. Fellow of the National Institution of the Boot and Shoe Industry

F.B.S.M. Fellow of the Birmingham School of Music

F.B.S.M.G.P. Fellow of the British Society of Master Glass-Painters

F.B.T.R.C. Federation of British Tape Recording Clubs

F.B.U. Federation of Bone Users and Allied Trades
Fire Brigades Union

F.B.U.A. Franco-British Union of Architects

F.C. Federal Cabinet
Fellow Craft
Fencing Club
Fifth Column
Fighter Command
Fire Control
Fisheries' Convention
Fishmongers' Company
Football Club
Forestry Commission
Free Church

f.c. fidei commissum (bequeathed in trust)
follow copy
foot candle

F.C.A. Farm Credit Administration (U.S.)
Federation of Canadian Artists
Fellow of the Institute of Chartered Accountants in England and Wales
Forsa Cosanta Aitiuil (Local Defence Force) (Ireland)

F.C.A.A. Fellow of the Australasian Institute of Cost Accountants

F.C.A.(Aust.) Fellow of the Institute of Chartered Accountants in Australia

f.c.& s. free of capture and seizure

F.C.A.P. Fellow of the College of American Pathologists

F.C.B. Frequency Co-ordinating Body (I.C.A.O.)

F.C.B.A. Fellow of the Canadian Bankers' Association

F.C.B.M. Federation of Clinker Block Manufacturers

F.C.C. Federal Communications Commission (U.S.)
First Class Certificate

F.C.C.A. Floor Covering Contractors' Association

F.C.C.O. Fellow of the Canadian College of Organists

F.C.C.S. Fellow of the Corporation of Certified Secretaries

F.C.D.A. Federal Civil Defense Administration (U.S.)

F.C.E.C. Federation of Civil Engineering Contractors

F.C.F.C. Free Church Federal Council

F.C.G.I. Fellow of the City and Guilds of London Institute

F.C.G.P. Fellow of the College of General Practitioners

F.Ch.S. Fellow of the Society of Chiropodists

F.C.I. Fédération cynologique internationale (International Federation of Kennel Clubs)
Fellow of the Clothing Institute
Fellow of the Institute of Commerce
Finance Corporation for Industry

F.C.I.A. Fellow of the Corporation of Insurance Agents

F.C.I.B. Fellow of the Corporation of Insurance Brokers

F.C.I.C. Fellow of the Chemical Institute of Canada

F.C.I.I. Fellow of the Chartered Insurance Institute

F.C.I.P.A. Fellow of the Chartered Institute of Patent Agents

F.C.I.S. Fellow of the Chartered Institute of Secretaries

F.C.M.A. Flushing Cistern Makers' Association

F.C.M.I.E. Fellow of the Colleges of Management and Industrial Engineering

F.C.N.A. Fellow of the College of Nursing (Australia)

fco. franco (post free)

F.C.O. Farmers' Central Organisation
Fellow of the College of Organists (now F.R.C.O.)
Fire-Control Officer
Foreign and Commonwealth Office

F.C.O.G. Fellow of the College of Obstetricians and Gynaecologists (now F.R.C.O.G.)

F.Comm.A. Fellow of the Society of Commercial Accountants

fcp. foolscap

F.C.P. Federation of Calico Printers
Fellow of the College of Preceptors

F.C.P.A. Fellow of the Canadian Psychological Association

F.C.R.A. Fellow of the College of Radiologists of Australasia

F.C.R.O.A. Fellow of the Civic Recreation Officers' Association

fcs. francs

F.C.S. Fellow of the Chemical Society
Fellow of the Corporation of Secretaries

f.c.s. free of capture and seizure

f.c.s.r.c.c. free of capture, seizure, riots and civil commotions

F.C.S.T. Fellow of the College of Speech Therapists

F.C.T. Federal Capital Territory

F.C.T.B. Fellow of the College of Teachers of the Blind

F.C.T.U. Federation of Associations of Catholic Trade Unionists

F.C.U. Fighter Control Unit

F.C.W.A. Fellow of the Institute of Cost and Works Accountants

fd. forward
found(ed)

F.D. Fidei Defensor (Defender of the Faith)
Fire Department
Fleet Duties

cont.

Free Delivery
Free Democrat
F/d. Free docks
f.d. focal distance
    free delivery
    free discharge
    free dispatch
F.D.A. Association of First Division Civil Servants
    Food and Drug Administration (U.S.)
F.D.C. Furniture Development Council
f.d.c. fleur de coin (mint condition)
F.D.D. Foundation Documentaire Dentaire (Dental Documentation Foundation)
F.D.F. Footwear Distributors' Federation
    Francis Drake Fellowship
F.D.F.U. Federation of Documentary Film Units
F.D.H.O. Factory Department, Home Office
F.D.I. Fédération dentaire internationale (International Dental Federation)
F.D.I.F. Fédération démocratique internationale des femmes (Women's International Democratic Federation)
F.D.I.M. Federación Democrática Internacional de Mujeres (Women's International Democratic Federation)
F.D.L. Fast Development Logistic Ships
F.D.O. Fleet Dental Officer
F.D.P. Freie Demokratische Partei (Free Democratic Party (Germany))
Fdr. Founder
F.D.R. Franklin Delano Roosevelt
Fdry. Foundry
F.D.S. Fellow in Dental Surgery
F.D.S.R.C.S. Fellow in Dental Surgery of the Royal College of Surgeons of England
F.D.S.R.C.S.Ed. Fellow in Dental Surgery of the Royal College of Surgeons of Edinburgh
Fe Ferrum (iron)
F.E. Far East
    Foreign Editor
f.e. first edition
    for example
F.E.A. Federation of European Aerosol Associations
    Fédération internationale pour l'éducation artistique (International Federation for Art Education)
F.E.A.F. Far East Air Force
F.E.A.I.C.S.M.T. Fédération européenne des associations d'ingénieurs et chefs de services de sécurité et des médecins du travail (European Federation of Associations of Engineers and Heads of Industrial Safety Services)
F.E.A.N.I. Fédération européenne d'associations nationales d'ingénieurs (European Federation of National Associations of Engineers)
Feb. February
fec. fecit or fecerunt (made)

F.E.C. First Edition Club
    Fondation européenne de la culture (European Cultural Foundation)
F.E.C.B. Foreign Exchange Control Board
F.E.C.E.P. Fédération européenne des constructeurs d'équipement pétrolier (Federation of European Petroleum Equipment Manufacturers)
F.E.C.M. Fellowship of the Elder Conservatorium of Music
F.E.C.S. Fédération européenne des fabricants de céramiques sanitaires (European Federation of Ceramic Sanitaryware Manufacturers)
Fed. Federal(ist)
    Federation
F.E.D.C. Federation of Engineering Design Consultants
FEDECAME Féderación Cafetalera de America (Federation of Coffee Growers of America)
FEDIOL Fédération de l'industrie de l'huilerie de la C.E.E. (Federation of the Oil Industry of the E.E.C.)
F.E.F.A.C. Fédération européenne des fabricants d'aliments composés pour animaux (European Federation of Manufacturers of Composite Foodstuffs for Animals)
F.E.F.C.E.B. Fédération européenne des fabricants de caisses et emballages en bois (European Federation of Packing Case and Wooden Crate Manufacturers)
F.E.F.C.O. Fédération européenne des fabricants de carton ondulé (European Federation of Corrugated Container Manufacturers)
F.E.G.R.O. Fédération européenne du commerce de l'horlogerie en gros (European Federation for the Wholesale Watch Trade)
F.E.I. Fédération équestre internationale (International Equestrian Federation)
F.E.I.E.A. Federation of European Industrial Editors' Associations
F.E.I.S. Fellow of the Educational Institute of Scotland
F.E.L.F. Far East Land Forces
Fell. Fellow
fem. female
    feminine
F.E.M. Fédération européenne des motels (European Motel Federation)
    Fédération européenne de la manutention (European Mechanical Handling Confederation)
F.E.N.S.A. Film Entertainments National Service Association
F.E.O. Fleet Engineer Officer
F.E.P.E. Fédération européenne pour la protection des eaux (European Federation for the Protection of Waters)
F.E.P.E.M. Federation of European Petroleum Equipment Manufacturers

F.E.P.F. Fédération européenne des industries de porcelaine et de faïence de table et d'ornementation (European Federation of the Industries of Earthenware and China Tableware and Ornamental Ware)

Fer. Fermanagh

F.E.R.D.Y. For Extracting Random Daughter Yields

FERES Fédération internationale des instituts de recherches sociales et socio-religieuses (International Federation of Institutes for Social and Socio-Religious Research)

ferv. fervens (boiling)

F.E.S.F.P. Fédération européenne des syndicats de fabricants de parquets (European Federation of Parquet Manufacturers)

FESYP Fédération Européenne des Syndicats de Fabricants de Panneaux de Particules (European Federation of Associations of Particle Board Manufacturers)

F.E.T.A. Fire Extinguisher Trades Association

F.E.T.A.P. Fédération Européenne des Transports Aériens Privés (European Federation of Independent Air Transport)

Feud. Feudal

F.E.Z. Fédération européenne de zootechnie (European Association for Animal Production)

FF Thick Fog

ff. fecerunt (made)
folios
following
fortissimo(very loud)
thick fog

F.F. Felicissimi Fratres (Most Fortunate Brothers)
Fianna Fáil (Eire)
Field Force
Fixed Focus
Ford Foundation
Frontier Force

F.f. Fortsetzung folgt (to be continued)

f.f. fixed focus

F.F.A. Fellow of the Faculty of Actuaries in Scotland

f.f.a. free foreign agency
free from alongside

F.F.A.R.A.C.S. Fellow of the Faculty of Anaesthetists of the Royal Australasian College of Surgeons

F.F.A.R.C.S. Fellow of the Faculty of Anaesthetists of the Royal College of Surgeons of England

F.F.A.S. Fellow of the Faculty of Architects and Surveyors

F.F.B. Fellow of the Faculty of Building

fff fortissimo plus (as loudly as possible)

F.F.F. Furnishing Fabrics Federation

F.F.G. Far from Gruntled

F.F.H.C. Freedom From Hunger Campaign

F.F.Hom. Fellow of the Faculty of Homoeopathy

F.F.I. Free from Infection
French Forces of the Interior

F.F.J. Franciscan Familiar of Saint Joseph

F.F.R. Fellow of the Faculty of Radiologists

F.F.S. Fellow Surveyor Member of the Faculty of Architects and Surveyors
Fellow of the Franklin Society

F.F.U. Federation of Film Unions

F.F.V. First Families of Virginia

ffy. faithfully

F.F.Y. Fife and Forfar Yeomanry

F.G. Federal Goverment
Fine Gael (Eire)
Fine Grain
Fire Guards
Foot Guards
Friction-glazed
Full Gilt

f.g. fine grain

F.G.A. Family Grocer Alliance
Fellow of Gemmological Association of Great Britain

f.g.a. free of general average

F.G.A.J. Fellow of the Guild of Agricultural Journalists

F.G.B. Fireclay Grate Back Association

F.G.C.M. Federation of Gellatine and Glue Manufacturers
Field General Court Martial

f.g.f. fully good, fair

F.G.I. Fédération graphique internationale (International Graphical Federation)
Fellow of the Institute of Certificated Grocers

Fgn. Foreign

F.G.O. Fleet Gunnery Officer

F.G.S. Fellow of the Geological Society of London

F.G.S.A. Fellow of the Geological Society of America

F.G.S.M. Fellow of the Guildhall School of Music and Drama

F.G.Y.A. Franco-German Youth Agency (Deutsch-Französisches Jugendwerk)

F.H. Field Hospital
Fire Hydrant

f.h. fog horn
fore hatch

F.H.A. Federal Housing Administration (U.S.)
Fellow of the Institute of Hospital Administrators
Finance Houses Association

F.H.A.S. Fellow of the Highland and Agricultural Society of Scotland

f.h.b. family hold back

F.H.C.I. Fellow of the Hotel and Catering Institute

F.H.F. Federation of Hardware Factors

f'hold freehold

F.H.R. Federal House of Representatives

F.H.S. Forces Help Society and Lord Roberts Workshops

F.H.T.A. Federated Home Timber Associations

F.H.W.C. Fellow of the Heriot-Watt College, Edinburgh

F.I. Faroe Islands
Fire Insurance
f.i. for instance
free in
F.I.A. Fédération internationale des acteurs (International Federation of Actors)
Fédération internationale de l'automobile (International Automobile Federation)
Fellow of the Institute of Actuaries
f.i.a. full interest admitted
F.I.A.A. Fédération internationale athlétique d'amateur (International Amateur Athletic Federation)
Fellow Architect Member of the Incorporated Association of Architects and Surveyors
F.I.A.B. Fédération internationale des associations de bibliothécaires (International Federation of Library Associations)
F.I.A.B.C.I. Fédération internationale des administrateurs de biens conseils immobiliers (International Real Estate Federation)
F.I.A.C. Fédération interaméricaine des automobile-clubs (Inter-American Federation of Automobile Clubs)
Fellow of the Institute of Company Accountants
F.I.A.F. Fédération internationale des archives du film (International Federation of Film Archives)
F.I.A.I. Fédération internationale des associations d'instituteurs (International Federation of Teachers' Associations)
F.I.A.I.I. Fellow of the Incorporated Australian Insurance Institute
F.I.A.J. Fédération internationale des auberges de la jeunesse (International Youth Hostel Federation)
F.I.A.L. Fellow of the International Institute of Arts and Letters
F.I.A.M.A. Fellow of the Incorporated Advertising Managers' Association
F.I.A.M.C. Fédération internationale des associations des médecins catholiques (International Federation of Associations of Catholic Doctors)
F.I.A.N.E.I. Fédération internationale d'associations nationales d'élèves ingénieurs (International Federation of National Associations of Engineering Students)
F.I.A.N.Z. Fellow of the Institute of Actuaries of New Zealand
F.I.A.P. Fédération internationale de l'art photographique (International Federation of Photographic Art)
F.I.A.P.F. Fédération internationale des associations de producteurs de films (International Federation of Film Producers' Associations)
F.I.Arb. Fellow of the Institute of Arbitrators

F.I.A.R.P. Federación interamericana des Asociaciones de Relaciones Públicas (Inter-American Federation of Public Relations Associations)
F.I.A.S. Fellow of the Institute of the Aerospace Sciences (U.S.)
Fellow Surveyor Member of the Incorporated Association of Architects and Surveyors
F.I.A.T. Fabbrica Italiana Automobile Torino (Italian Automobile Manufacturers, Turin)
F.I.A.T.A. Fédération internationale des associations transitaires et assimilées (International Federation of Forwarding Agents' Associations)
F.I.A.T.C. Fédération internationale des associations touristiques de cheminots (International Federation of Railwaymen's Travel Associations)
F.I.B. Fédération internationale de boules (International Bowling Federation)
Fellow of the Institute of Bankers
Fellow of the Institute of Building
f.i.b. free into barge *or* bunkers
F.I.B.A. Fédération internationale de basketball amateur (International Amateur Basketball Federation)
F.I.B.C.A. Fellow of the Institute of Burial and Cremation Administration
F.I.B.C.M. Fellow of the Institute of British Carriage and Automobile Manufacturers
F.I.B.D. Fellow of the Incorporated Institute of British Decorators and Interior Designers
F.I.B.E. Fellow of the Institute of Building Estimators
F.I.B.E.P. Fédération internationale des bureaux d'extraits de presse (International Federation of Press Cutting Agencies)
F.I.B.M. Fellow of the Institute of Baths Management
F.I.B.T. Fédération internationale de bobsleigh et de tobogganing (International Bobsleighing and Tobogganing Federation)
F.I.B.T.P. Fédération internationale du bâtiment et des travaux publics (International Federation of Building and Public Works)
F.I.C.A. Fédération internationale des cheminots antialcooliques (International Railway Temperance Union)
Fellow of the Commonwealth Institute of Accountants
F.I.C.C. Fédération internationale des ciné-clubs (International Federation of Film Societies)
Fédération internationale de camping et de caravanning (International Federation of Camping and Caravanning)

F.I.C.C.I.A. Fédération Internationale des Cadres de la Chimie et Industries Annexées (International Federation of Technicians in the Chemical and Allied Industries)

F.I.C.D. Fellow of the Institute of Civil Defence

F.I.C.E. Fédération internationale des communautés d'enfants (International Federation of Children's Communities)

F.I.C.E.P. Fédération internationale catholique d'éducation physique et sportive (Catholic International Federation for Physical and Sports Education)

F.I.Ceram. Fellow of the Institute of Ceramics

F.I.C.I. Fellow of the Institute of Chemistry of Ireland

F.I.C.I.C. Fédération internationale du commerce et des industries du camping (International Federation for the Camping Trade and Industry)

F.I.C.J.F. Fédération internationale des conseils juridiques et fiscaux (International Federation of Legal and Fiscal Consultants)

F.I.C.M. Fellow of the Institute of Credit Management

F.I.C.P. Fédération internationale des clubs de publicité (International Federation of Advertising Clubs)

F.I.C.S. Fédération internationale des chasseurs de sons (International Federation of Sound Hunters)
Fellow of the Institute of Chartered Shipbrokers
Fellow of the International College of Surgeons

F.I.C.S.A. Federation of International Civil Servants' Associations

fict. fiction(al)
fictitious

F.I.C.T. Fédération internationale de centres touristiques (International Federation of Tourist Centres)

F.I.C.W.A. Fellow of the Institute of Cost and Works Accountants

fid. fiduciary

F.I.D. Fédération internationale de documentation (International Federation for Documentation)
Fédération internationale du diabète (International Diabetes Federation)
Fellow of the Institute of Directors
Field Intelligence Department

F.I.D.A.F. Federación Internacional de Asociaciones de Ferreteros y Almacenistas de Hierros (International Federation of Ironmongers' and Iron Merchants' Associations)

F.I.D.A.Q. Fédération internationale des associations de quincailliers et marchands de fer (International Federation of Ironmongers' and Iron Merchants' Associations)

Fid. Def. Fidei Defensor (Defender of the Faith)

F.I.D.E. Fédération internationale des échecs (World Chess Federation)
Fédération de l'industrie dentaire en Europe (Federation of the European Dental Industry)

F.I.D.E.M. Fédération internationale des éditeurs de médailles (International Federation of Medal Producers)

F.I.D.H. Fédération internationale des droits de l'homme (International Federation for the Rights of Man)

F.I.D.I. Fédération internationale des déménageurs internationaux (Federation of International Furniture Removers)

F.I.D.I.C. Fédération internationale des ingénieurs-conseils (International Federation of Consulting Engineers)

F.I.D.J.C. Fédération internationale des directeurs de journaux catholiques (International Federation of Directors of Catholic Publications)

F.I.D.O. Film Industry Defence Organisation
Fog, Intensive, Dispersal of

FIDOR Fibre Building Board Development Organisation

F.I.D.S. Falkland Islands Dependencies Survey

FIDUROP Commission du marché commun de la Fédération européenne des utilisateurs de fibres dures (Common Market Committee of the European Federation of Hard Fibre Users)

F.I.E. Fédération internationale d'escrime (International Fencing Federation)

F.I.E.C. Fédération Internationale des Associations d'Études Classiques (International Federation of the Societies of Classical Studies)
Fellowship of Independent Evangelical Churches

F.I.E.D. Fellow of the Institution of Engineering Designers

F.I.E.J. Fédération internationale des éditeurs de journaux et publications (International Federation of Newspaper Publishers)

F.I.E.M. Fédération internationale de l'enseignement ménager (International Federation of Home Economics)

F.I.E.P. Fédération internationale d'éducation physique (International Federation for Physical Education)

F.I.E.R.E. Fellow of the Institute of Electronic and Radio Engineers (*formerly* F. Brit. I.R.E.)

F.I.E.S. Fellow of the Illuminating Engineering Society

F.I.E.T. Fédération internationale des employés et des techniciens (International Federation of Commercial, Clerical and Technical Employees)

F.I.E.V. Fédération des Industries des Équipments pour Véhicules (Federation of Motor Equipment Manufacturers)

F.I.F. Fellow of the Institute of Fuel

fi.fa. fieri facias (that you cause to be done)

F.I.F.A. Fédération internationale de Football Association (International Association Football Federation)
Fédération internationale du film d'art (International Federation of Art Films)
Fellow of the International Faculty of Arts

F.I.F.C.L.C. Fédération internationale des femmes de carrières libérales et commerciales (International Federation of Business and Professional Women)

F.I.F.D.U. Fédération internationale des femmes diplômées des universités (International Federation of University Women)

F.I.F.E. Fellow of the Institution of Fire Engineers

F.I.F.M. Fellow Institute of Factory Managers

F.I.F.S.P. Fédération internationale des fonctionnaires supérieurs de police (International Federation of Senior Police Officers)

fig. figurative(ly)
figure

F.I.G. Fédération internationale des géomètres (International Federation of Surveyors)
Fédération internationale de gymnastique (International Gymnastic Federation)

F.I.G.C.M. Fellow of the Incorporated Guild of Church Musicians

F.I.G.E.D. Fédération internationale des grandes entreprises de distribution (International Federation of Distributors)

F.I.G.M. Fellow of the Institute of General Managers

F.I.G.O. Fédération international de gynécologie et d'obstétrique (International Federation of Gynaecology and Obstetrics)

F.I.G.R.S. Fellow of the Irish Genealogical Research Society

F.I.H. Fédération internationale de hockey sur gazon (International Lawn Hockey Federation)
Fédération internationale des hôpitaux (International Hospital Federation)

F.I.H.C. Fédération internationale haltérophile et culturiste (International Weightlifting and Physical Culture Federation)

F.I.Hsg. Fellow of the Institute of Housing

F.I.H.U.A.T. Fédération internationale pour l'habitation, l'urbanisme et l'aménagement des territoires (International Federation for Housing and Town Planning)

F.I.H.V.E. Fellow of the Institution of Heating and Ventilating Engineers

F.I.I. Federation of Irish Industries
Fellow of the Imperial Institute

F.I.I.A. Fellow of the Indian Institute of Architects

F.I.I.G. Fédération des institutions internationales semi-officielles et privées établies à Genève (Federation of Semi-Official and International Private Institutions Established in Geneva)

F.I.I.M. Fellow of the Institute of Industrial Managers

F.I.Inst. Fellow of the Imperial Institute

F.I.I.Tech. Fellow of the Institute of Industrial Technicians

F.I.J. Fédération internationale des journalistes (International Federation of Journalists)
Fédération internationale de judo (International Judo Federation)

F.I.J.C. Fédération internationale de la jeunesse catholique (International Catholic Youth Federation)

F.I.J.E.T. Fédération internationale des journalistes et écrivains du tourisme (International Federation of Travel Journalists and Writers)

F.I.J.L. Fédération internationale des journalistes libres de l'Europe centrale et orientale et des pays baltes et balkaniques (International Federation of Free Journalists of Central and Eastern Europe and Baltic and Balkan Countries)

F.I.J.M. Fédération Internationale des Jeunesses Musicales (Youth and Music)

F.I.L. Fédération internationale de laiterie (International Dairy Federation)
Fellow of the Institute of Linguists

F.I.L.A. Fédération internationale de lutte amateur (International Amateur Wrestling Federation)
Fellow of the Institute of Landscape Architects

F.I.L.D.I.R. Fédération internationale libre des déportés et internés de la résistance (International (Free) Federation of Deportees and Resistance Internees)

F.I.L.E. Fellow of the Institute of Legal Executives

F.I.L.T. Fédération internationale de lawn tennis (International Lawn Tennis Federation)

F.I.M. Fédération internationale motocycliste (International Motorcycle Federation)
Fédération internationale des musiciens (International Federation of Musicans)
Fellow of the Institution of Metallurgists

F.I.M.A. Fellow of Institute of Municipal Administration (Australia)

Forging Ingot Makers' Association

F.I.M.Ent. Fellow of the Institute of Municipal Entertainment

F.I.M.F. Federación Internacional de Medicina Física (International Federation of Physical Medicine)

F.I.M.I. Fellow of the Institute of the Motor Industry

F.I.M.I.T. Fellow of the Institute of Musical Instrument Technology

F.I.M.I.T.I.C. Fédération internationale des mutilés et invalides du travail et des invalides civils (International Federation of Disabled Workmen and Civilian Cripples)

F.I.M.L.T. Fellow of the Institute of Medical Laboratory Technology

F.I.M.O.C. Fédération internationale des mouvements ouvriers chrétiens (International Federation of Christian Workers' Movements)

F.I.M.P. Fédération internationale de médecine physique (International Federation of Physical Medicine)

F.I.M.S. Fédération internationale de médecine sportive (International Federation of Sporting Medicine)

F.I.M.T. Fellow of the Institute of the Motor Trade

F.I.M.T.A. Fellow of the Institute of Municipal Treasurers and Accountants

F.I.M.Wood.T. Fellow of the Institute of Machine Woodworking Technology

Fin. Finland

fin. finis (the end)

final

finance

financial

F.I.N. Fellow of the Institute of Navigation

F.I.N.A. Fédération internationale de natation amateur (International Amateur Swimming Federation)

F.I.N.A.T. Fédération internationale des fabricants et transformateurs d'adhésifs et thermo-collants sur papiers et autres supports (International Federation of Manufacturers and Converters of Pressure-Sensitive and Heatseal Materials on Paper and Other Base Materials)

Finn. Finnish

Fin.Sec. Financial Secretary

F.Inst.Arb. Fellow of the Institute of Arbitrators

F.Inst.Ch. Fellow of the Institute of Chiropodists

F.Inst.D. Fellow of the Institute of Directors

F.Inst.F. Fellow of the Institute of Fuel

F.Inst.H.E. Fellow of the Institution of Highway Engineers

F.Inst. Met. Fellow of the Institute of Metals

F.Inst.M.S.M. Fellow of the Institute of Marketing and Sales Management

F.Inst.P. Fellow of the Institute of Physics

F.Inst. P.C. Fellow of the Institute of Public Cleansing

F.Inst.Pet. Fellow of the Institute of Petroleum

F.Inst.P.I. Fellow of the Institute of Patentees and Inventors

F.Inst.R.E. (Aust.) Fellow of the Institution of Radio Engineers (Australia)

F.Inst.T. Fellow of the Institute of Transport

F.I.O. Fédération internationale d'oléiculture (International Olive Growers' Federation)

Fellow of the Institute of Ophthalmology

Food Investigation Organisation

f.i.o. free in and out

F.I.O.B. Fellow of the Institute of Building

F.I.O.C.C. Fédération internationale des ouvriers de la chaussure et du cuir (International Shoe and Leather Workers' Federation)

F.I.O.C.E.S. Fédération internationale des organisations de correspondances et d'échanges scolaires (International Federation of Organizations for School Correspondence and Exchange)

F.I.O.M. Fédération internationale des ouvriers sur métaux (International Metalworkers' Federation)

F.I.O.P. Fellow of the Institute of Plumbing or Printing

F.I.O.P.P. Federación Interamericana de Organizaciones de Periodistas Profesionales (Inter-American Federation of Working Newspapermen's Organisations)

F.I.O.Q. Fellow of the Institute of Optometrists of Queensland

F.I.O.Sc. Fellow of the Institute of Optical Science

F.I.O.W. First International Organisation of Welcome

F.I.P. Fédération internationale pharmaceutique (International Pharmaceutical Federation)

Fédération internationale de la précontrainte (International Federation of Prestressing)

Fédération internationale de philatélie (International Philatelic Federation)

F.I.P.A. Fédération internationale des producteurs agricoles (International Federation of Agricultural Producers)

Fellow of the Institute of Practitioners in Advertising

F.I.P.A.C.E. Fédération internationale des producteurs auto-consommateurs industriels d'électricité (International Federation of Industrial Producers of Electricity for Own Consumption)

FIPAGO Fédération internationale des fabricants de papiers gommés (International Federation of Gummed *cont.*

Paper Manufacturers)

F.I.P.E.S.O. Fédération internationale des professeurs de l'enseignement secondaire officiel (International Federation of Secondary Teachers)

F.I.Pet. Fellow of the Institute of Petroleum

F.I.P.H.E. Fellow of the Institution of Public Health Engineers

F.I.P.J.F. Fédération internationale des producteurs de jus de fruits (International Federation of Fruit Juice Producers)

F.I.Plant.E. Fellow of the Institution of Plant Engineers

F.I.P.M. Fédération internationale de psychothérapie médicale (International Federation for Medical Psychotherapy)
Fellow of the Institute of Personnel Management

F.I.P.P. Fédération internationale de la presse périodique (International Periodical Press Federation)
Fondation internationale pénale et pénitentiaire (International Penal and Penitentiary Foundation)

F.I.P.R. Fellow of the Institute of Public Relations

FIPRESCI Fédération internationale de la presse cinématographique (International Cinematographic Press Federation)

F.I.Ptg.M. Fellow of the Institute of Printing Management

F.I.Q.S. Fellow of the Institute of Quantity Surveyors

fir. firkin(s)

F.I.R. Fédération internationale des résistants (International Federation of Resistance Movements)
Flight Information Region

f.i.r. floating-in rates

F.I.R.A. Fédération internationale de rugby amateur (International Amateur Rugby Federation)
Furniture Industry Research Association

F.I.R.E. Fellow of the Institute of Radio Engineers (U.S.)

F.I.R.E.C. Fédération Internationale des Rédacteurs en Chef (International Federation of Chief Editors)

F.I.R.I. Fellow of the Institution of the Rubber Industry

F.I.R.S. Fédération internationale de roller-skating (International Roller Skating Federation)

F.I.S. Fédération internationale de sauvetage (International Life Saving Federation)
Fédération internationale des centres sociaux et communautaires (International Federation of Settlements and Neighbourhood Centres) *cont.*

Fédération internationale de ski (International Ski Federation)
Fellow of the Institute of Statisticians

F.I.S.A. Fédération internationale des semaines d'art (International Art Weeks Federation)
Fédération internationale des sociétés d'aviron (International Rowing Federation)
Fellow of the Incorporated Secretaries Association
Fellow of the Institute of Shops Acts Administration

F.I.S.A.I.C. Fédération internationale des sociétés artistiques et intellectuelles de cheminots (International Federation of Railwaymen's Art and Intellectual Societies)

F.I.San.I. Fellow of the Institution of Sanitary Engineers (*now* F.I.P.H.E.)

F.I.S.C. Foundation for International Scientific Co-ordination

F.I.S.C.C. Fruit Industry Sugar Concession Committee (Australia)

F.I.S.C.E.T.C.V. Fédération internationale des syndicats chrétiens d'employés, techniciens, cadres et voyageurs de commerce (International Federation of Christian Trade Unions of Salaried Employees, Technicians, Managerial Staff and Commercial Travellers)

F.I.S.C.M. Fédération internationale des syndicats chrétiens de la métallurgie (International Federation of Christian Metalworkers' Unions)

F.I.S.C.O.A. Fédération internationale des syndicats chrétiens d'ouvriers agricoles (International Federation of Christian Agricultural Workers' Unions)

F.I.S.C.O.B.B. Fédération internationale des syndicats chrétiens d'ouvriers du bâtiment et du bois (International Federation of Christian Trade Unions of Building and Wood Workers)

F.I.S.C.T.T.H. Fédération internationale des syndicats chrétiens des travailleurs du textile et de l'habillement (International Federation of Christian Trade Unions of Textile and Garment Workers)

F.I.S.D. Fédération internationale de sténographie et de dactylographie (International Federation of Shorthand and Typewriting)

F.I.S.E. Fédération internationale syndicale de l'enseignement (World Federation of Teachers' Unions)
Fellow of the Institution of Sanitary Engineers (*now* F.I.P.H.E.)
Fellow of the Institution of Structural Engineers
Fonds des Nations Unies pour l'enfance (United Nations Children's Fund)

F.I.S.E.M. Fédération internationale des sociétés d'écrivains médecins (International Federation of Doctor-Authors)

F.I.S.I.T.A. Fédération internationale des sociétés d'ingénieurs des techniques de l'automobile (International Federation of Automobile Engineers' and Technicians' Associations)

F.I.S.P. Fédération internationale des sociétés de philosophie (International Federation of Philosophical Societies)
    Fellow of the Institute of Sewage Purification

F.I.S.U. Fédération internationale du sport universitaire (International University Sports Federation)

F.I.S.W. Fellow of the Institute of Social Welfare

F.I.T. Fédération internationale des traducteurs (International Federation of Translators)

f.i.t. fabrication in transit
    free in truck
    free of income tax

F.I.T.A. Fédération internationale de tir à l'arc (International Federation for Archery)

F.I.T.A.P. Fédération Internationale des Transports Aériens Privés (International Federation of Independent Air Lines)

F.I.T.B.B. Fédération internationale des travailleurs du bâtiment et du bois (International Federation of Building and Woodworkers)

F.I.T.C.E. Fédération des ingénieurs des télécommunications de la communauté européenne (Federation of Telecommunications Engineers in the European Community)

F.I.T.E.C. Fédération internationale du thermalisme et du climatisme (International Federation of Thermalism and Climatism)

F.I.T.H. Fédération Internationale des Travailleurs d'Habillement (International Federation of Garment Workers)

F.I.T.I.M. Federación Internacional de Trabajadores de las Industrias Metalurgicas (International Metalworkers' Federation)

F.I.T.P. Fédération internationale des travailleurs du pétrole (International Federation of Petroleum Workers)

F.I.T.P.A.S.C. Fédération internationale des travailleurs des plantations, de l'agriculture et des secteurs connexes (International Federation of Plantation, Agricultural and Allied Workers)

F.I.T.T. Fédération internationale de tennis de table (International Table Tennis Federation)

Fitzw. Fitzwilliam

F.I.V.B. Fédération internationale de volley-ball (International Volley-Ball Federation)

F.I.V.Z. Fédération internationale vétérinaire de zootechnie (International *cont.*

Veterinary Federation of Zootechnics)

f.i.w. free in wagon

F.I.W.E. Fellow of the Institution of Water Engineers

F.I.W.M. Fellow of the Institution of Works Managers

F.I.W.M.A. Fellow of the Institute of Weights and Measures Administration

F.J.I. Fellow of the Institute of Journalists

F.K.C.(L.) Fellow of King's College London

Fl. Flanders
    Flemish
    Fleuve (River)
    Florin(s)

fl. flauto (flute)
    florin(s)
    floruit (flourished)
    fluid

F.L. Flag Lieutenant
    Flight Lieutenant
    Football League

f.l. falsa lectio (false reading)

Fla. Florida

F.L.A. Fellow of the Library Association
    Fiat Lege Artis (let it be done by rules of the art)
    Film Laboratory Association

flag. flageolet

flak Flugzeugabwehrkanone (anti-aircraft gunfire)

F.L.A.S. Fellow of the Chartered Land Agents' Society

F.L.C.M. Fellow of the London College of Music

F.L.D. Friends of the Lake District

Flem. Fleming
    Flemish

flex. flexible

Flexo. Flexographic

F.L.G.A. Fellow of the Local Government Association

F.L.I. Fédération lainière internationale (International Wool Textile Organization)

Flint. Flintshire

FLIP Floating Instrument Platform

Flli. Fratelli (Brothers)

F.L.M. Fédération luthérienne mondiale (Lutheran World Federation)

F.L.N. Front de liberation nationale (National Liberation Front, Algeria)

f.l.n. following landing numbers

F.L.Q. Front de Libération du Québec ⟵

flr. florin(s)

F.L.R. Fiji Law Reports

F.L.S. Fellow of the Linnean Society

Flt. Flight

fluor. fluorescent

Fm Fermium

Fm. Farm

fm. fathom(s)
    from

F.M. Field Magnet
    Field Marshal
    Flight Mechanic
    Foreign Mission
    Fraternitas Medicorum (Fraternity of Physicians) *cont.*

Fraternité mondiale (World Brotherhood)
Frequency Modulation
Friars Minor

f.m. femmes mariées (married women)
fine measure
frequency modulation

F.M.A. Fan Manufacturers' Association
Fellow of the Museums Association
— Fertiliser Manufacturers' Association
File Manufacturers' Association
Food Machinery Association

F.M.A.C. Fédération mondiale des anciens combattants (World Veterans' Federation)

F.M.A.N.U. Fédération mondiale des associations pour les Nations Unies (World Federation of United Nations Associations)

F.M.A.O. Farm Machinery Advisory Officer

F.M.B. Federation of Master Builders

F.M.C. Fatstock Marketing Corporation
— Federal Maritime Commission (U.S.)
Forces Motoring Club
Ford Motor Company
Section des fleuristes du marché commun de la fédération européenne des unions professionelles de fleuristes (Common Market Florists' Section of the Federation of European Professional Florists)

F.M.C.E. Federación Mundial Cristiana de Estudiantes (World Student Christian Federation)
Federation of Manufacturers of Construction Equipment

F.M.C.P. Federation of Manufacturers of Contractors' Plant

fmd. formed

F.M.D. Foot and Mouth Disease

F.M.F. Food Manufacturers' Federation

F.M.I. Fellow of the Motor Industry
Filii Mariae Immaculatae (Sons of Mary Immaculate)

F.M.I.G. Food Manufacturers' Industrial Group

F.M.J.D. Fédération mondiale de la jeunesse démocratique (World Federation of Democratic Youth)

F.M.J.F.C. Fédération mondiale des jeunesses féminines catholiques (World Federation of Young Catholic Women and Girls)

fmn. formation

F.M.O. Fleet Medical Officer

F.M.P.A. Fédération mondiale pour la protection des animaux (World Federation for the Protection of Animals)
Fellow of the Master Photographers Association of Great Britain

F.M.P.E. Federation of Master Process Engravers

fmr. former

fmrly. formerly

F.M.S. Federated Malay States
Fédération mondiale des sourds (World Federation of the Deaf)
Fellow of the Medical Society of London

F.M.S.M. Fédération mondiale pour la santé mentale (World Federation for Mental Health)

F.M.T. Federation of Merchant Tailors of Great Britain

F.M.T.A. Farm Machinery and Tractor Trade Association of New South Wales

F.M.T.S. Fédération mondiale des travailleurs scientifiques (World Federation of Scientific Workers)

F.M.V.J. Fédération mondiale des villes jumelées (United Towns Organization)

fn. footnote

f.n.a. for necessary action

F.N.A.A. Fellow of the National Association of Auctioneers, Rating Surveyors and Valuers (S. Africa)

fnd. found(ed)

fndr. founder

F.N.E.C.Inst. Fellow of the North East Coast Institution of Engineers and Shipbuilders

F.N.F. Flying Needle Frame

F.N.F.H.F.T.M. Federation of Needle, Fish Hook and Fishing Tackle Makers

F.N.I. Fédération naturiste internationale (International Naturist Federation)
Fellow of the National Institute of Sciences in India

F.N.L. Friends of the National Libraries

F.N.O. Fleet Navigation Officer

F.N.U. Forces des Nations Unies (United Nations Forces)
Fonds des Nations Unies pour les réfugiés (United Nations Refugee Fund)

F.N.Z.I.A. Fellow of the New Zealand Institute of Architects

F.N.Z.I.C. Fellow of the New Zealand Institute of Chemistry

F.N.Z.I.M. Fellow of the New Zealand Institute of Management

F.N.Z.L.A. Fellow of the New Zealand Library Association

F.N.Z.S.A. Fellow of the New Zealand Society of Accountants

fo. folio

F.O. Federal Official
Field Officer
First Officer
Flag Officer
Flying Officer
Foreign Office (now F.C.O.)
Full Organ

F/O. Flying Officer

f.o. firm offer
free overside
fuel oil

f/o. for orders
    free overside
    full out
f.o.b. free on board
F.O.B. Forward Operating Base
F.O.B.F.O. Federation of British Fire Organisations
F.O.B.S. Fractional Orbital Bombardment System
F.O.C. Father of the Chapel
f.o.c. free of charge
F.O.C.A.P. Federación Odontológica Centro América Panama (Odontological Federation of Central America and Panama)
F.O.C.T. Flag Officer Carrier Training
F.O.C.U.S. Federation of Colleges United for Sport
f.o.d. free of damage
F.O.E. Fraternal Order of Eagles
F.O.F.A.T.U.S.A. Federation of Free African Trade Unions of South Africa
F.O.H. Front of House
F.O.I.C. Flag Officer in Charge
fol. folio
foll. follow(ing)
F.O.O. Forward Observation Officer
F.O.P. Forward Observation Post
f.o.q. free on quay
For. Foreign
    Forestry
    Forint
F.O.R. Fellowship of Reconciliation
    Fellowship of Riders (Motorcyclists)
f.o.r. free on rail
FORATOM Forum atomique européen (European Atomic Forum)
formn. formation
fort. fortification
    fortified
f.o.r.t. full out rye terms
F.O.S. Fisheries Organisation Society
f.o.s. free on station *or* steamer
FOSDIC Film Optical Sensing Device for Input to Computer
f.o.t. free of tax
    free on trucks
Found. Foundation
f.o.w. first open water
    free on wagon
F.O.Y. Fellowship of Youth
Fp. Frontispiece
F.P. Federal Parliament
    Field Punishment
    Fine Paper
    Fire Plug
    Fire Policy
    Floating *or* Open Policy
    Former Pupil
    Fowl Pest
    Free Presbyterian
    Fresh Paragraph
    Fully Paid
f.p. fine paper
    fixed price
    flame-proof
    flash-point
    foot pound
    forte piano (loud then soft)   *cont.*

    freezing point
    full point
F.P.A. Family Planning Association
    Fire Protection Association
    First Point of Aries
    Foreign Press Association
    Franklin P. Adams
f.p.a. free of particular average
F.P.A.N.Z. Fellow Public Accountant Member of the New Zealand Society of Accountants
F.P.C. Federal Power Commission (U.S.)
    Federation of Painting Contractors
    First Part of the Contention (Shakespeare)
    Flowers Publicity Council
f.p.c. for private circulation
F.P.C.E.A. Fibreboard Packing Case Employers' Association
F.P.C.M.A. Fibreboard Packing Case Manufacturers' Association
F.P.G. Film Producers Guild
F.Pharm.S. Fellow of the Pharmaceutical Society of Great Britain
F.Ph.S.(Eng.) Fellow of the Philosophical Society of England
F.Phy.S. Fellow of the Physical Society
F.P.I. Fédération prohibitionniste internationale (World Prohibition Federation)
    Fellow of the Plastics Institute
F.P.I.S. Forward Propagation Ionosphere Scatter
f.p.m. feet per minute
F.P.O. Field Post Office
    Fire Prevention Officer
F.P.R.C. Flying Personnel Research Committee
F.P.R.L. Forest Products Research Laboratory
F.P.S. Fauna Preservation Society
    Fellow of the Pharmaceutical Society of Great Britain
    Fellow of the Philological Society
    Fellow of the Philosphical Society of England
    Fellow of the Physical Society
f.p.s. feet per second
    foot-pound-second
f.p.s.p.s. feet per second per second
F.P.T. Fixed Price Tenders
F.P.T.S. Forward Propagation Troposphere Scatter
F.Q. Faerie Queen (Spenser)
F.Q.A. Floor Quarry Association
Fr Francium
Fr. Father
    France
    Fratelli (Brothers)
    Frau
    Free
    French
    Friar
    Friday
fr. fragments
    franc(s)
    from

F.R. Federal Republic
  Forum Romanum (the Roman Forum)
  Freight Release
f.r. folio recto (right hand page)
F.R.A.C.I. Fellow of the Royal Australian Chemical Institute
F.R.A.C.P. Fellow of the Royal Australasian College of Physicians
F.R.A.C.S. Fellow of the Royal Australasian College of Surgeons
F.R.A.D. Fellow of the Royal Academy of Dancing
F.R.Ae.S. Fellow of the Royal Aeronautical Society
F.R.A.H.S. Fellow of the Royal Australian Historical Society
F.R.A.I. Fellow of Royal Anthropological Institute of Great Britain and Ireland
F.R.A.I.A. Fellow of the Royal Australian Institute of Architects
F.R.A.I.C. Fellow of the Royal Architectural Institute of Canada
F.R.A.M. Fellow of the Royal Academy of Music
f.r.&c.c. free of riots and civil commotions
Frank. Frankish
F.R.A.N.Z. Fellow Registered Accountant Member of the New Zealand Society of Accountants
F.R.A.S. Fellow of the Royal Asiatic Society of Great Britain and Ireland
F.R.B.S. Fellow of the Royal Society of British Sculptors
F.R.C. File Research Council
F.R.C.A. Fellow of the Royal College of Art
F.R.C.A.B. Felt Roofing Contractors' Advisory Board
F.R.C.M. Fellow of the Royal College of Music
F.R.C.O. Fellow of the Royal College of Organists (*formerly* F.C.O.)
F.R.C.O.(CHM) Fellow of the Royal College of Organists (with Diploma of Choir Mastership)
F.R.C.O.G. Fellow of the Royal College of Obstetricians and Gynaecologists (*formerly* F.C.O.G.)
F.R.C.P. Fellow of the Royal College of Physicians of London
F.R.C.P.Ed. Fellow of the Royal College of Physicians of Edinburgh
F.R.C.P.I. Fellow of the Royal College of Physicians of Ireland
F.R.C.S. Fellow of the Royal College of Surgeons of England
  Fellow of the Royal Commonwealth Society (*formerly* F.R.E.S.)
F.R.C.Sc.I. Fellow of the Royal College of Science for Ireland
F.R.C.S.Ed. Fellow of the Royal College of Surgeons of Edinburgh
F.R.C.S.I. Fellow of the Royal College of Surgeons in Ireland
F.R.C.V.S. Fellow of the Royal College of Veterinary Surgeons

F.R.Econ.S. Fellow of the Royal Economic Society
FRED Fantastically Reliable Electronic Device (Jersey)
F.R.E.D. Fast Reactor Experiment, Dounreay
  Figure Reading Electronic Device
FRELIMO Frente de Libertação de Moçambique
F.R.Ent.S. Fellow of the Royal Entomological Society of London
freq. frequent(ly)
F.R.E.S. Fellow of the Royal Empire Society (*now* F.R.C.S.)
  Fellow of the Royal Entomological Society of London
F.R.F.P.S.G. Fellow of the Royal Faculty of Physicians and Surgeons of Glasgow
F.R.G.S. Fellow of the Royal Geographical Society
F.R.H.B. Federation of Registered House-Builders
F.R.Hist.S(oc). Fellow of the Royal Historical Society
F.R.Hort.S. Fellow of the Royal Horticultural Society
F.R.H.S. Fellow of the Royal Historical Society
  Fellow of the Royal Horticultural Society
Fri. Friday
F.R.I. Fellow of the Royal Institution of Great Britain
  Fulmer Research Institute
F.R.I.A. Fellow of the Royal Irish Academy
F.R.I.A.S. Fellow of the Royal Incorporation of Architects in Scotland
F.R.I.B.A. Fellow of the Royal Institute of British Architects
F.R.I.C. Fellow of the Royal Institute of Chemistry
F.R.I.C.S. Fellow of the Royal Institution of Chartered Surveyors (*formerly* F.S.I.)
F.R.I.I.A. Fellow of the Royal Institute of International Affairs
F.R.I.P.A. Fellow of the Royal Institute of Public Administration
F.R.I.P.H.H. Fellow of the Royal Institute of Public Health and Hygiene
Fris. Frisian
Frl. Fräulein
frld. foreland
  freehold
frm. from
F.R.M.A. Floor Rug Manufacturers' Association
F.R.M.C.M. Fellow of the Royal Manchester College of Music
F.R.M.C.S. Fellow of the Royal Medico-Chirurgical Society of Glasgow
F.R.Met.S. Fellow of the Royal Meteorological Society
F.R.M.S. Fellow of the Royal Microscopical Society
F.R.N.S. Fellow of the Royal Numismatic Society
F.R.N.Z.I.H. Fellow of the Royal New Zealand Institute of Horticulture

F.R.O. Fellow of the Register of Osteopaths
Fire Research Organisation
f.r.o.f. fire risk on freight
F.R.P.S. Fellow of the Royal Photographic Society of Great Britain
F.R.P.S.L. Fellow of the Royal Philatelic Society, London
frs. francs
F.R.S. Federal Reserve System (U.S.)
Fellow of the Royal Society
Fuel Research Station
F.R.S.A. Fellow of the Royal Society of Arts
F.R.S.A.I. Fellow of the Royal Society of Antiquaries of Ireland
F.R.San.I. Fellow of the Royal Sanitary Institute (*now* F.R.S.H.)
F.R.S.C. Fellow of the Royal Society of Canada
F.R.S.E(din). Fellow of the Royal Society of Edinburgh
F.R.S.G.S. Fellow of the Royal Scottish Geographical Society
F.R.S.H. Fellow of the Royal Society of Health (*formerly* F.R.San. I.)
F.R.S.L. Fellow of the Royal Society of Literature of the United Kingdom
F.R.S.M. Fellow of the Royal Society of Medicine
F.R.S.N.Z. Fellow of the Royal Society of New Zealand
F.R.S.S. Fellow of the Royal Statistical Society
F.R.S.S.A. Fellow of the Royal Society South Africa
F.R.S.T.M. & H. Fellow of the Royal Society of Tropical Medicine and Hygiene
frt. freight
frt/fwd. freight forward
frt/ppd. freight prepaid
F.R.T.S. Fellow of the Royal Television Society
FRUCOM Fédération européenne des importateurs de fruits secs, conserves, épices et miels (European Federation of Importers of Dried Fruits, Preserves, Spices and Honey)
F.R.U.I. Fellow of Royal University of Ireland
frum. fratrum (of the brothers)
F.R.V.A. Fellow of the Rating and Valuation Association
F.R.V.I.A. Fellow of the Royal Victorian Institute of Architects
F.R.Z.S.(Scot.) Fellow of the Royal Zoological Society of Scotland
fs. facsimile
F.S. Fabian Society
Faraday Society
Fathers of Sion
Ferrovie dello Stato (Italian State Railway)
Field Security
Financial Secretary
Financial Statement
Fleet Surgeon
Flight Sergeant
Friendly Society
f.s. faire suivre (please forward)   *cont.*

film strip
foot-second
F.S.A. Fellow of the Society of Antiquaries of London
Flax Spinners' Association
Friendly Societies Act
F.S.A.A. Fellow of the Society of Incorporated Accountants and Auditors
F.S.A.G. Fellow of the Society of Australian Genealogists
F.S.A.L. Fellow of the Society of Antiquaries of London
F.S.A.L.A. Fellow of the South African Library Association
F.S.Arc. Fellow of the Society of Architects (*now* F.R.I.B.A.)
F.S.A.S. Fellow of the Society of Antiquaries of Scotland
F.S.A.S.M. Fellow of the South Australian School of Mines
F.S.C. Federal Supreme Court (U.S.)
Fellow of the Society of Chiropodists
Field Studies Council
Fratres Scholarum Christianorum (Brothers of the Christian Schools, Christian Brothers)
Friends Service Council
F.S.C.J. Figli del Sacro Cuore de Gesu (Sons of the Sacred Heart of Jesus, Verona Fathers)
F.S.D.C. Fellow of the Society of Dyers and Colourists
F.S.E. Fellow of the Society of Engineers
F.S.F. Fellow of the Institute of Shipping and Forwarding Agents
F.S.F.A. Federation of Specialised Film Associations
F.S.G. Fellow of the Society of Genealogists
F.Sgt. Flight Sergeant
F.S.G.T. Fellow of the Society of Glass Technology
F.S.H.M. Fellow of the Society of Housing Managers
F.S.I. Federation of Sussex Industries
Fédération spirite internationale (International Spiritualist Federation)
Fellow of Chartered Surveyors' Institution (*now* F.R.I.C.S.)
Free Sons of Israel
F.S.I.A. Fellow of the Society of Industrial Artists
F.S.K. Frequency-Shift Keying
F.S.L. First Sea Lord
F.S.M. Fédération syndicale mondiale (World Federation of Trade Unions)
Flying Spot Microscope
Free Speech Movement (U.S.)
F.S.M.C. Freeman of the Worshipful Company of Spectaclemakers
F.S.O. Field Security Officer
Fleet Signals Officer
F.S.P. Field Security Police
F.S.P.B. Field Service Pocket Book
F.S.R. Field Service Regulations
F.S.S.U. Federated Superannuation Scheme for Universities

F.S.T.D. Fellow of the Society of Typographic Designers
F.S.U. Family Service Unit(s)
F.S.V.A. Fellow of the Incorporated Society of Valuers and Auctioneers
f.s.w. Completed satisfactorily a short war course at R.A.F. Staff College
Ft. Fort
ft. feet
   flat
   foot
   fortified
f.t. full terms
F.T.A. File Trade Association
F.T.B. Fleet Torpedo Bomber
F.T.B.A. Furniture Trades Benevolent Association
F.T.C. Federal Trade Commission (U.S.)
   Flying Training Command (R.A.F.)
   Full Technological Certificate
F.T.C.D. Fellow of Trinity College, Dublin
F.T.C.L. Fellow of the Trinity College of Music, London
F.T.D.A. Fellow of the Theatrical Designers' and Craftsmen's Association
F.T.D.C. Fellow of the Society of Typographic Designers of Canada
F.T.E.S.A. Foundry Trades Equipment and Supplies Association
fthm. fathom(s)
F.T.I. Fellow of the Textile Institute
F.T.I.T. Fellow of the Institute of Taxation
F.T.M. Flying Training Manual
F.T.O. Fleet Torpedo Officer
F.T.P.A. Fellow of the Town and Country Planning Association
F.T.S. Flying Training School
F.T.S.C. Fellow of the Tonic Sol-Fa College
F.T.U. Federation of Trade Unions (Hong Kong)
F.T.W. Free Trade Wharf
F.U. Farmers' Union
F.U.A.C.E. Fédération universelle des associations chrétiennes d'étudiants (World Student Christian Federation)
F.U.C.U.A. Federation of University Conservative and Unionist Associations
F.U.E. Federated Union of Employers (Ireland)
F.U.E.N. Federal Union of European Nationalities

F.U.E.V. Föderalistische Union Europäischer Volksgruppen (Federal Union of European Nationalities)
fund. fundamental
F.U.N.U. Force d'urgence des Nations Unies (United Nations Emergency Force)
fur. furlong(s)
   further
Fus. Fusilier(s)
F.u.S.f. Fortsetzung und Schluss folgen (to be continued and concluded)
fut. future
F.U.W. Farmers' Union of Wales
f.v. folio verso (left hand page)
F.V.C.Q.F.R.A. Fruit and Vegetable Canning and Quick Freezing Research Association
F.V.D.E. Fighting Vehicles Design Establishment
F.V.R.D.E. Fighting Vehicles Research and Development Establishment
F.W. Fresh Water
F.W.A. Factories and Workshops Act
   Family Welfare Association
   Free Wales Army
F.W.B. Free Will Baptists
f.w.b. four wheel brake
F.W.C.C. Friends' World Committee for Consultation
fwd. forward
f.w.d. four wheel drive
   free water damage
F.Weld.I. Fellow of the Welding Institute
F.W.I. Federation of West Indies
F.W.M.B. Federation of Wholesale and Multiple Bakers
F.W.O. Federation of Wholesale Organisations
   Fleet Wireless Officer
F.W.R.M. Federation of Wire Rope Manufacturers of Great Britain
F.W.S. Fighter Weapons School
   Fleet Work Study
fwt. featherweight
F.X. Francis Xavier
f.x. foreign exchange
fxg. fixing
fxle. forecastle
F.Y.P. Five or Four Year Plan
F.Z.G. Federation of Zoological Societies of Great Britain and Northern Ireland
F.Z.S. Fellow of the Zoological Society of London

G

G. German
   Gilt
   Goal(keeper)
   Government   *cont.*
   Grand
   Gravity
   Green
   Ground colour   *cont.*

Guardian
Guernsey
Guide
Gulf
g. gravity
garage
gauche (left)
gauge
gelding
general factor
general intelligence
genitive
gloomy
good
grain
gramme
green
guinea
gun(nery)
the suffix -*ing*
Ga Gallium
Ga. Gallic
Georgia
G.A. Garrison Artillery
General Agent
General Assembly
General Assignment
Geologists' Association
Geographical Association
Government Actuary
Graphic Arts
g/a. general average
G.A.A. Gaelic Athletic Association
G.A.B. General Arrangements to Borrow
Gabr. Gabriel
G.A.C. General Advisory Council
Gael. Gaelic
G.A.F.L.A.C. General Accident Fire and Life Assurance Corporation
G.A.G.B. Gemmological Association of Great Britain
G.A.I. Guild of Architectural Ironmongers
G.A.J. Guild of Agricultural Journalists
Gal. Galations
Galen
Galway
Général
gal(s). gallon(s)
G.A.L.H. General Association of Ladies Hairdressers
galv. galvanic
galvanized
G.A.M. Guided Aircraft Missile
gam. gamut
G.A.O. General Accounting Office
G.A.P.A.N. Guild of Air Pilots and Air Navigators
G.A.P.C.E. General Assembly of the Presbyterian Church of England
gar. garage
G.A.R. Grand Army of the Republic (U.S.)
Guided Aircraft Rocket
G.A.R.I.O.A. Government Aid and Relief in Occupied Areas
gastroent. gastroenterological
G.A.T. Greenwich Apparent Time
G.A.T.C.O. Guild of Air Traffic Control Officers

H

G.A.T.T. General Agreement on Tariffs and Trade
G.A.U.F.C.C. General Assembly of Unitarian and Free Christian Churches
G.A.U.K. Gamekeepers' Association of the United Kingdom
Gaul. Gaulish
gaz. gazette(d)
gazetteer
G.B. Gas Board
Great Britain
Guide Book
Guild of Bricklayers
Gunboat
G.B.A. Association of Governing Bodies of Public Schools
G.B.A.D. Great Britain Allied and Dominion
G.B. and I. Great Britain and Ireland
G.B.C. Green Belt Council of Greater London
G.B.C.W. Governing Body of the Church in Wales
G.B.D.O. Guild of British Dispensing Opticians
G.B.E. Knight *or* Dame Grand Cross of the Order of the British Empire
g.b.e. gilt bevelled edge(s)
G.B.G.S.A. Association of Governing Bodies of Girls Public Schools
G.B.I. Governesses' Benevolent Institution
G.B.M.C. Golf Ball Manufacturers' Conference
G.B.N.E. Guild of British Newspaper Editors
gbr. gebräuchlich (usual)
G.B.R.E. General Board of Religious Education
G.B.S. George Bernard Shaw
G.B.S.M. Graduate of the Birmingham School of Music
G.C. Gas Council
Gentleman Cadet
George Cross
Gesu Cristo (Jesus Christ)
Gliding Club
Golf Club
Good Conduct
Goldsmiths' College
Government Chemist
Grand Chancellor
Grand Chaplain
Grand Chapter
Gyro-Compass
Gun Carriage
G.C.A. Grand Central Association
Ground Control Approach
g.cal. gramme calorie(s)
G.Capt. Group Captain
G.C.B. Good Conduct Badge
Knight Grand Cross of the Order of the Bath
G.C.C. Girton College, Cambridge
Gonville and Caius College, Cambridge
G.C.D. Great Circle Distance
g.c.d. greatest common divisor
G.C.E. General Certificate of Education
g.c.f. greatest common factor

G.C.H. Knight Grand Cross of the Hanoverian Order
G.C.H.Q. Government Communications Headquarters
G.C.I. Ground Controlled Interception
G.C.I.E. Knight Grand Commander of the Order of the Indian Empire
G.C.L.H. Grand Cross of the Legion of Honour
G.C.M. General Court Martial
g.c.m. greatest common multiple
G.C.M.A. Glazed Cement Manufacturers Association
G.C.M.G. Knight Grand Cross of the Order of Saint Michael and Saint George
G.C.N. Greenwich Civil Noon
G.C.O. Gun Control Officer
G.C.R. Ground Controlled Radar
G.C.R.I. Glasshouse Crops Research Institute
G.C.S.G. Knight Grand Cross of the Order of Saint Gregory the Great
G.C.S.I. Knight Grand Commander of the Order of the Star of India
G.C.S.S. Knight Grand Cross of the Order of Saint Sylvester
G.C.St.J. Bailiff *or* Dame Grand Cross of the Order of Saint John of Jerusalem
G.C.T. Greenwich Civil Time
G.C.V.O. Knight *or* Dame Grand Cross of the Royal Victorian Order
Gd Gadolinium
Gd. Guard
gd. good
   granddaughter
   ground
G.D. General Duties
   Graduate in Divinity
   Grand Duchess
   Grand Duchy
   Grand Duke
   Gunnery Division
g.d. good delivery
g.-d. gravimetric density
G.D.A.(Com.) Government Diploma in Commercial Art
G.D.B.A. Guide Dogs for the Blind Association
G.D.C. General Dynamics Corporation
   Guild of Dyers and Cleaners
g.d.e. gilt deckled edge(s)
G.D.E.S. Government Department Electrical Specification
Gdn(s). Garden(s)
gdn. guardian
G.D.R. German Democratic Republic
Gds. Guards
gds. goods
Gdsm. Guardsman
Ge Germanium
G.E. Garrison Engineer
   General Election
g.e. gilt edge(s)
Geb(r). Gebrüder (Brothers)
geb. geboren (born)
   gebunden (bound)
G.E.C. General Electric Company
G.E.D.A. Goodyear Electronic Differential Analyser

106

GEFAP Groupement européen des associations nationales des fabricants de pesticides (European Group of National Pesticide Manufacturers' Associations)
Geh. Gehalt (contents)
   Geheimrat (Privy Councillor)
G.E.M.A. Gymnastic Equipment Manufacturers' Association
Gen. Genealogical
   General
   Generating
   Genesis
gen. gender
   genera
   general(ly)
   generic
   genetics
   genitive
   genuine
   genus
Gend. Gendarme
Geneal. Genealogy
Genl. General
Genn. Gennaio (January)
gent gentleman
gents. gentlemen
Geo. Georgia
Geod. Geodesy
geod. geodetic
Geog. Geographer
   Geographical
   Geography
Geol. Geological
   Geologist
   Geology
Geom. Geometrical
   Geometry
Geophys. Geophysics
Ger. German(y)
ger. gerund(ive)
G.E.R. German Educational Reconstruction
Ges. Gesellschaft (Association *or* Company)
ges. gesetzlich geschützt (registered trade mark)
Gesch. Geschichte (History)
gest. gestorben (deceased, died)
GESTAPO Geheime Staatspolizei
G.E.T. Gratuitous Enrichment Tax
G.e.v. Giga electron volt(s)
G.F. Government Form
   Guggenheim Foundation
G.F.A. Good Freight Agent
g.f.a. good fair average
G.F.C.M. General Fisheries Council for the Mediterranean
G.F.R. German Federal Republic
G.F.S. Girls' Friendly Society
G.F.T.U. General Federation of Trade Unions
G.F.W.C. General Federation of Women's Clubs
G.G. Gamma Globulin
   Gas Generator
   Georgian Group
   Girl Guide
   Grenadier Guards
G.G.A. Girl Guides' Association
g.gd. great granddaughter
g.gr. great gross

G.G.R.A. Gelatine and Glue Research Association
g.gs. great grandson
G.G.S.M. Graduate of the Guildhall School of Music and Drama
G.H. General Hospital
　　Green Howards
G.H.M.S. Graduate in Homoeopathic Medicine and Surgery
Gh.N. Ghana Navy
G.H.I. Good Housekeeping Institute
G.H.Q. General Headquarters
G.H.S. Girls' High School
gi. gill(s)
G.I. General Issue
　　Government Issue
　　Government of India
　　Royal Glasgow Institute of the Fine Arts
g.i. galvanised iron
Gib. Gibraltar
G.I.C. Guilde internationale des coopératrices (International Co-operative Women's Guild)
G.I.E.E. Graduate of the Institution of Electrical Engineers
G.I.I.P. Groupement international de l'industrie pharmaceutique des pays de la C.E.E. (International Pharmaceutical Industry Group for the E.E.C. countries)
G.I.Mech.E. Graduate of the Institution of Mechanical Engineers
G.Inst.T. Graduate of the Institute of Transport
G.I.O. Guild of Insurance Officials
G.I.P. Great Indian Peninsular Railway
G.I.R.P. Groupement international de la répartition pharmaceutique des pays de la communauté européenne (International Group for Pharmaceutical Distribution in the Countries of the European Community)
G.J.A.B. Groups Joint Administration Board
G.J.A.C. Groups Joint Administration Committee
G.J.C. Grand Junction Canal
G.J.D. Grand Junior Deacon
Gk. Greek
G.K. Gomei Kaisha (unlimited partnership)
G.K.A. Garter King of Arms
G.K.C. Gilbert Keith Chesterton
G.K.D. Gordon-Kendall-Davison Notation
G.K.N. Guest, Keen and Nettlefolds
Gl Glucinum
gl. gill(s)
　　glass
　　gloss
G.L. Gothic Letter
　　Government Laboratories
　　Grand Lodge
　　Ground Level
　　Gun Layer
　　Gun Licence
G.L.A.F.A.M.S. Grand Lodge of Ancient Free and Accepted Masons of Scotland
Glam. Glamorgan

Glas. Glasgow
G.L.B. Girls' Life Brigade
G.L.C. Greater London Council(lor)
　　Guild of Lettering Craftsmen
G.L.C.M. Graduate of the London College of Music
G.L.E.E.P. Graphite Low Energy Experimental Pile
G.L.F.B. Greater London Fund for the Blind
G.L.I.S. Greater London Information Service
Glock. Glockenspiel
Glos. Gloucestershire
Gloss. Glossary
Glouc. Gloucester
G.L.P. Greater London Plan
G.L.S. Gypsy Lore Society
　　Grand Lodge of Scotland
glt. gilt
G.L.T. Greetings Letter Telegram
gm. gram(me)
G.M. General Manager
　　General Merchandise
　　General Mortgage
　　Geological Museum
　　George Medal
　　Gold Medal(list)
　　Grand Master
　　Grand Medallist
　　Gruppo Misto (Mixed Group)
　　Guided Missile
G.M.A.T. Greenwich Mean Astronomical Time
G.M.B. Grand Master of the Order of the Bath
g.m.b. good merchantable brand
G.M.B.E. Grand Master of the Order of the British Empire
G.m.b.H. Gesellschaft mit beschränkter Haftung (limited liability company)
Gmc. Germanic
G.M.C. General Medical Council
　　Guild of Memorial Craftsmen
G.M.F. Glass Manufacturers' Federation
G.M.I.E. Grand Master of the Order of the Indian Empire
G.M.K.P. Grand Master of the Knights of Saint Patrick
G.M.M.G. Grand Master of the Order of Saint Michael and Saint George
G.M.P. Grand Master of the Order of Saint Patrick
　　Gurkha Military Police
g.m.q. good merchantable quality
gms. gram(me)s
G.M.S.C. General Medical Services Council
G.M.S.I. Grand Master of the Order of the Star of India
G.M.T. Greenwich Mean *or* Meridian Time
Gn. Guinea
g.n. grandnephew
　　grandniece
G.N.A.S. Grand National Archery Society
G.N.C.(E.W.) General Nursing Council for England and Wales
gnd. ground

G.N.P. Gross National Product
Gnr. Gunner
gns. guineas
G.N.S.R.A. Great North of Scotland Railway Association
G.N.T.C. Girl's Nautical Training Corps
G.O. Gas Operated
General Office(r)
General Order
Grand Officier
Grand Organ
Group Officer
g.o.b. good ordinary brand
G.O.C. General Officer Commanding
Greek Orthodox Church
G.O.C. in C. General Officer Commanding in Chief
G.O.D.A. Guild of Drama Adjudicators
G.O.E. General Ordination Examination
G.O.L.D. Guild of Lady Drivers
G.O.M. Grand Old Man (William Ewart Gladstone)
GOMAC Groupement des opticiens du marché commun (Common Market Opticians' Group)
G.O.P. Grand Old Party (Republican Party, U.S.)
Goth. Gothic
Gou. Gourde
Gov. Governor
Gov.-Gen. Governor-General
Govt. Government
G.O.W.R. Grand Order of Water Rats
Gp. Group
G.P. Gallup Poll
General Paralysis (see also G.P.I.)
General Pause
General Practitioner
General Purpose
Gloria Patri (Glory be to the Father)
Graduate in Pharmacy
Grand Prix
g.p. galley proofs
great primer
G.P.A. General Practitioners' Association
Gp.C. Group Captain
G.P.C. General Purposes Committee
Gp.Comdr. Group Commander
g.p.d. gallons per day
G.P.D.A. Grand Prix Drivers' Association
Gypsum Products Development Association
G.P.D.S.T. Girls' Public Day School Trust
G.P.E. Guided Projectile Establishment
G.Ph. Graduate in Pharmacy
g.p.h. gallons per hour
G.P.H.I. Guild of Public Health Inspectors
G.P.I. General Paralysis of the Insane
G.P.K.T. Grand Priory of the Knights of the Temple
G.P.L.C. Guild of Professional Launderers and Cleaners
G.P.M. Grand Past Master

g.p.m. gallons per minute
G.P.O. General Post Office
Government Printing Office (U.S.)
G.P.P. Guild of Public Pharmacists
G.P.R. Genio Populi Romani (to the genius of the Roman People)
Glider Pilot Regiment
G.P.S. Graduated Pension Scheme
Great Public Schools (Australia)
g.p.s. gallons per second
G.P.T. Guild of Professional Toastmasters
G.P.U. Gosudarstvennoye Politicheskoe Upravleniye (State Political Administration (Russia))
G.Q.G. Grand Quartier Général (General Headquarters)
G.Qs. General Quarters
Gr. Grade
Grammar
Grecian
Greece
Greek
Gunner
gr. grain
gramme(s)
grand
gravity
great(er)
grind
gross
G.R. General Reconnaissance
General Reserve
Georgius Rex (King George)
Grand Recorder
Ground Rent
Guillelmus Rex (King William)
Gurkha Rifles
G.R.A. Game Research Association
Greyhound Racing Association
G.R.A.C.E. Group Routing and Charging Equipment
Grad. Graduate
Gram. Grammar
Grammatical
G.R.B. Gas Research Board
G.R.B.I. Gardeners' Royal Benevolent Institution
G.R.C.M. Graduate of the Royal College of Music
Greg. Gregorian
Gregory
G.R. et. I. Georgius Rex et Imperator (George, King and Emperor)
G.R.I. Grassland Research Institute
Gr.L. Gunner Lieutenant
grm. gramme(s)
G.R.N.C. German Radio Navigation Committee
gro. gross
G.R.O. General Register Office
G.R.O.B.D.M. General Register Office for Births, Deaths and Marriages
Gros. Grosvenor
Grp. Group
grs. grains
grandson
G.R.S.E. Guild of Radio Service Engineers
Gr.S.L. Gunner Sub-Lieutenant

G.R.S.M. Graduate of the Royal Schools of Music
g.r.t. gross registered tons
gr.t.m. gross ton-mile
gr.wt. gross weight
gs. grandson
  guineas
G.S. General Secretary
  General Service
  General Staff
  Geographical *or* Geological Survey
  Gold Standard
  Grammar School
  Grand Sentinel
  Grand Scribe
  Grand Sentry
  Grand Steward
  Ground Speed
g.s. grandson
G.S.A. Glasgow School of Art
G.S.B. Government Savings Bank
G.S.C. General Service Corps
  Girls' School Company
G.S.G.B. Geological Survey of Great Britain
G.S.G.S. Geographical Section, General Staff
G.S.I. Geological Survey of India
G.S.L. Geological Society of London
  Geological Survey of London
G.S.M. Garrison Sergeant-Major
  Geological Survey of Great Britain and Museum of Practical Geology
  Grammes per Square Metre
g.s.m. good sound merchantable
  grammes per square metre
G.S.M.D. Guildhall School of Music and Drama
G.S.O. General Staff Officer
G.S.P. Good Service Pension
G.S.R. Galvanic Skin Response
g.-st. garter-stitch
G.S.T. Greenwich Sidereal Time
G.S.W. Gunshot Wound
gt. gilt
  great
  gutta (drop)
G.T. General Transire
  Good Templars
  Grand Tiler
  Grand Tourer *or* Touring   *cont.*

  Grand Treasurer
  Greetings Telegram
G.t. Gilt top(s)
g.t. gas tight
  gilt top(s)
  gross tonnage
G.T.A. Gun Trade Association
G.T.B.C. Guild of Teachers of Backward Children
G.T.C. General Teaching Council
  Girls' Training Corps
  Government Training Centre
G.T.C.L. Graduate of the Trinity College of Music, London
gtd. guaranteed
g.t.e. gilt top edge(s)
G.T.M. General Traffic Manager
g.t.m. good this month
G.T.M.A. Galvanized Tank Manufacturers' Association
  Gauge and Tool Makers' Association
G.T.P.D. Guild of Television Producers and Directors (*now* S.F.T.A.)
Gtr. Greater
G.T.S. Greenwich Time Signal
gtt. guttae (drops)
g.t.w. good this week
Gu. Gules
  Guinea
G.U. Gastric Ulcer
Gua. Guarani
guar. guarantee(d)
Guat. Guatemala
Gui. Guiana
Guil. Guilder(s)
Gun. Gunnery
G.U.S. Great Universal Stores
g.u.v. gerecht und vollkommen (correct and complete)
G.V. Grande vitesse (Express train)
g.v. gravimetric volume
g.w. Completed successfully a Guided Weapons Course
G.W.O.A. Guerilla Warfare Operating Base
G.W.P. Government White Paper
G.W.R. Great Western Railway (*now* Western Region of British Rail)
Gym. Gymnasium
  Gymnastics
Gyn. Gynaecology
G.Y.P. Guild of Young Printers

H

H Hydrogen
H. Harbour
  Hard(ness)
  Heft (number, *or* part)
  Henry
  Holy
  Hommes men)   *cont.*

  Horizontal
  Hydrant
  Hydraulics
h. habitants
  hail
  harbour
  hard(ness)   *cont.*

has
have
hearts
heat
heavy
height
high
hips
hits
horizontal
horse
hour(s)
house
hull
hundred
husband

Ha. Hawaii
    Hectare(s)

H.A. Hautes-Alpes
    Heavy Artillery
    High Angle
    Highway(s) Act
    Historical Association
    Hockey Association
    Horse Artillery
    Hostile Aircraft
    Hour Angle
    Hydraulic Association of Great Britain

h.a. heir apparent
    hoc anno (this year)

H.A.A. Heavy Anti-Aircraft

H.A. & M. Hymns Ancient and Modern

Hab. Habakkuk

hab. habitat(ion)

H.A.B. High Altitude Bombing

H.A.B.A. Hardwood Agents' and Brokers' Association

habt. habeat (let him have)

H.A.C. Honourable Artillery Company
    Horticultural Advisory Council for England and Wales

HAFMED Headquarters Allied Forces Mediterranean

H.A.F.R.A. British Hat and Allied Feltmakers' Research Association

Hag. Haggai

H.A.G.B. Helicopter Association of Great Britain (*now incorporated with the Royal Aeronautical Society*)

H.A.L.T.A.T.A. High and Low Temperature Accuracy Testing Apparatus

Ham. Hamlet (Shakespeare)

H.A.M.S.A. Hearing Aid Manufacturers' and Suppliers' Association

Han. Hanover(ian)

h. & c. hot and cold

h. & t. hardened and tempered

Hants. Hampshire

H.A.O. Horticultural Advisory Officer

H.app. Heir apparent

Har. Harbour

Harv. Harvard University (U.S.)

H.A.S. Headmasters' Association of Scotland

H.A.S.R. High-Altitude Sounding Rocket

H.A.T.R.A. Hosiery and Allied Trades Research Association

H.A.T.S. Hour Angle of the True Sun

hav. haversine

Hb. Haemoglobin

H.B. Hard Black
    House of Bishops

H.B.C. Hudson's Bay Company

H.B.M. His *or* Her Britannic Majesty

H.C. Habitual Criminal
    Hague Convention
    Headmasters' Conference
    Health Certificate
    Held Covered
    High Church
    High Commission(er)
    Higher Certificate
    Highway Code
    Hockey Club
    Holy Communion
    Home Counties
    Hors concours (not for competition)
    House of Clergy
    House of Commons
    House Corrections
    House of Correction
    Housing Centre
    Housing Corporation

h.c. hot and cold
    honoris causa (for the sake of the honour)

H.C.A. High Conductivity Copper Association
    Horder Centre for Arthritics
    Hospital Caterers' Association

H.C.A.A.S. Homeless Children's Aid and Adoption Society

H.C. & E.S. Hull Chemical and Engineering Society

H'cap Handicap

H.C.B. House of Commons Bill

H.C.F. Honorary Chaplain to the Forces

h.c.f. highest common factor

H.Ch.D. Diploma in Higher Chiropody

H.C.I. Hotel and Catering Institute

H.C.J. High Court of Justice
    Holy Child Jesus

H.C.M. High Court Master
    His *or* Her Catholic Majesty

H.C.M.P.A. Home Counties Master Printers' Alliance

H.C.O. Higher Clerical Officer

hcp. handicap

H.C.P.T. Historic Churches Preservation Trust

H.C.R. High Chief Ranger

H.C.S. Home Civil Service

H.C.T. High Commission Territories

H.C.T.B.A. Hotel and Catering Trades Benevolent Association

H.C.V.C. Historic Commercial Vehicle Club

hd. head
    hogshead(s)

H.D. Heavy Duty
    Hilda Doolittle
    Home Defence
    Horse-drawn
    Hourly Difference

H.d. Hochdruck (high pressure)

h.d. Hora decubitus (on going to bed)

H.D.A. Diploma of the Hawkesbury Agricultural College (Australia)
    Hydrographic Department, Admiralty

hdbk. handbook
H.D.D. Diploma of Dairying, Hawkesbury Agricultural College (Australia)
Higher Dental Diploma
H.D.G.A. Hot Dip Galvanizers' Association
H.Dip.E. Higher Diploma in Education
hdkf. handkerchief
hdn. harden
Hdqrs. Headquarters
H.D.R.A. Henry Doubleday Research Association
H.D.R.I. Hannah Dairy Research Institute
He Helium
H.E. Hammerless ejector
Heat Engine
Height of Eye
High Explosive
His Eminence
His Excellency
Home Establishment
Hydraulic Engineer
h.e. horizontal equivalent
H.E.A. Horticultural Education Association
H.E.A.C. Higher Education Advisory Centre
Heb. Hebraic
Hebrew(s)
hebd. hebdomadal
Hebr. Hebrides
hectog. hectogram(s)
hectol. hectolitre(s)
hectom. hectometre(s)
H.E.C.T.O.R. Heated Experimental Carbon Thermal Oscillator Reactor
H.E.F. High-energy Fuel
H.E.H. His or Her Exalted Highness
H.E.I.C. Honourable East India Company
H.E.I.C.N. Honourable East India Company Navy
H.E.I.C.S. Honourable East India Company's Service
heir app. heir apparent
Hel. Helvetia (Switzerland)
HELEN Hydrogenous Exponential Liquid Experiment
heli. helicopter
Hellen. Hellenic
Hellenistic
H.E.L.P. Haulage Emergency Link Protection
H.E.O. Higher Executive Officer
H.E.P.C.C. Heavy Electrical Plant Consultative Council
Her. Heraldry
Herefordshire
HERALD Highly Enriched Reactor Aldermaston
Herefs. Herefordshire
HERMES Heavy Element and Radioactive Material Electromagnetic Separator
H.E.R.O. Hot Experimental Reactor of O Power
Herod. Herodotus
herpet. herpetology
herst. herstellung (manufacture)

HERTIS Hertfordshire Information Service
Herts. Hertfordshire
Hesych. Hesychius
H.E.T.M.A. Heavy Edge Tool Manufacturers' Association
HETP Hexaethyl Tetraphosphate
Hex. uranium hexafluoride
hex. hexachord
hexagon(al)
Hf Hafnium
Hf. Half
H.F. Hard Firm
High Frequency
Holy Father
Home Fleet
Home Forces
h.f. high frequency
H.F.A.R.A. Honorary Foreign Associate of the Royal Academy
hf.bd. half bound
hf.cf. half calf
hf.cl. half cloth
H.F.D.F. High Frequency Detecting and Finding
hf.-mor. half-morocco
H.F.R.O. Hill Farming Research Organisation
Hg Hydrargyrum
hg. hectogram(s)
heliogram(s)
H.G. Haute-Garonne
High German
High Grade
His or Her Grace
Holy Ghost
Home Guard
Horse Guards
H.-G. High German
H.G.D.H. His or Her Grand Ducal Highness
H.G.H. Human Growth Hormone
H.G.J.P. Henry George Justice Party (Australia)
H.G.M.M. Hereditary Grand Master Mason
HH Heavy Hydrogen
Double Hard
H.H. His or Her Highness
His Holiness
His Honour
H.H.B.S. Hereford Herd Book Society
hhd. hogshead(s)
HHH Treble Hard
H.I. Hawaiian Islands
Hic Iacet (here lies)
High Intensity
Horizontal Interval
H.I.A. Housing Improvement Association
H.I.B. Herring Industry Board
Hib(s). Hibernian(s)
H.I.E. Hibernation Information Exchange
Hier. Hierosolyma (Jerusalem)
HIFAR High Flux Australian Reactor
Hi. Fi. High Fidelity
H.I.H. His or Her Imperial Highness
Hil. Hilary
H.I.M. His or Her Imperial Majesty

Hind. Hindi
 Hindu(stan)
Hipp. Hippocrates
H.I.S. Hardwood Importers' Section of the T.T.F.
 Hic Iacet Sepultus (here lies buried)
 Horticulture Improvement Scheme
Hist. Historical(ly)
 History
histn. historian
Histol. Histology
Hitt. Hittite
H.J.S. hic jacet sepultus (here lies buried)
H.K. Handelskammer (Chamber of Commerce)
 Hong Kong
 House of Keys
hkf. handkerchief
hl. hectolitre(s)
 heilig (holy)
H.L. Hard Labour
 Haute-Loire
 Honours List
 House of Laity
 House of Lords
H.L.I. Highland Light Infantry
H.L.P.R. Howard League for Penal Reform
H.L.R.S. Homosexual Law Reform Society
hls. holes.
hl.S. heilige Schrift (Holy Scripture)
Hlw. Halbleinwand (half bound cloth)
hm. hectometre(s)
H.M. Hand Made
 Harbour Master
 Haute-Marne
 Headmaster or Headmistress
 His or Her Majesty
 Home Mission(s)
h.m. hand made
 headmaster or headmistress
 hoc mense (this month)
H.M.A. Hardware Manufacturers' Association
H.M.A.C. His or Her Majesty's Aircraft Carrier
H.M.A.S. His or Her Majesty's Australian Ship
H.M.B.D.V. His or Her Majesty's Boom Defence Vessel
H.M.B.I. His or Her Majesty's Borstal Institution
H.M.C. Headmasters' Conference
 His or Her Majesty's Customs
 Historical Manuscripts Commission
 Horticultural Marketing Council
 Hospital Management Committee
H.M.C.S. His or Her Majesty's Canadian Ship
H.M.C.S.C. His or Her Majesty's Civil Service Commissioners
H.M.D. His or Her Majesty's Destroyer
H.M.F. Haslemere Music Festival
 His or Her Majesty's Forces

H.M.G. His or Her Majesty's Government
 Higher Middle German
H.M.H.S. His or Her Majesty's Hospital Ship
H.M.I. His or Her Majesty's Inspector
H.M.L. His or Her Majesty's Lieutenant
H.M.L.R. His or Her Majesty's Land Registry
H.M.M.L. His or Her Majesty's Motor Launch
H.M.M.M.S. His or Her Majesty's Motor Mine Sweeper
H.M.O.C.S. His or Her Majesty's Overseas Civil Service
H.M.P. Hoc Monumentum Posuit (erected this monument)
h.m.p. handmade paper
H.M.R.T. His or Her Majesty's Rescue Tug
H.M.S. His or Her Majesty's Service
 His or Her Majesty's Ship
 His or Her Majesty's Steamer
H.M.S.O. His or Her Majesty's Stationery Office
H.M.T. His or Her Majesty's Trawler
 His or Her Majesty's Tug
 His or Her Majesty's Treasury
H.M.V. His Master's Voice
H.M.W.A. Hairdressing Manufacturers and Wholesalers' Association
H.N.C. Higher National Certificate
H.N.D. Higher National Diploma
hnos. hermanos (brothers)
Hnrs. Honours
Ho Holmium
ho. house
H.O. Head Office
 Home Office
 Hostilities Only
h.o. hold over
H.O.C. Heavy Organic Chemicals
h.o.c. held on charge
H.o.D. Head of Department
H. of C. House of Commons
H. of K. House of Keys
H. of L. House of Lords
H. of R. House of Representatives
Holl. Holland
Hom. Homer
homeo. homeopathic
hon. honorary
 honourable
 honourably
Hond. Honduras
Hons. Honours
H.O.P.E. Help Organise Peace Everywhere
Hor. Horace
hor. horizon(tal)
HORACE H_2O Reactor Aldermaston Critical Experiment
HoReCa International Union of National Associations of Hotel, Restaurant and Café Keepers
horol. horological
 horology
H.O.R.S.A. Hut Operation Raising School-leaving Age
Hort. Horticulture
H.O.R.U. Home Office Research Unit

Hos. Hosea
Hosp. Hospital
How. Howitzer
H.P. Half Pay
High Power
High Pressure
High Priest
Hire Purchase
Horizontal Parallax
Horse Power
Hot-pressed
House Physician
Houses of Parliament
h.p. half pay
heir presumptive
horizontal parallax
H.P.A. Hospital Physicists' Association
Hurlingham Polo Association
H.P.C. High Performance Club
History of Present Complaint
H.P.F. Horace Plunkett Foundation
hp.-hr. horsepower-hour
h.p.n. horse power nominal
H.P.P.A. Horses' and Ponies' Protection Association
H.P.R. Hungarian People's Republic
H.P.T.A. Hire Purchase Trade Association
H.Q. Headquarters
h.q. hoc quaere (look for *or* see this)
H.Q.B.A. Headquarters Base Area
H.Q.E. High Quality Environment
Hr. Herr
hr. hour
H.R. Highland Regiment
Home Rule(r)
House Record
House of Representatives
H.R.A. Historical Records of Australia
H.R.C. Hairdressers' Registration Council
Holy Roman Church
Hop Research Centre
H.R.C.A. Honorary Member of the Royal Cambrian Academy of Art
H.R.E. Holy Roman Empire *or* Emperor
H.R.H. His *or* Her Royal Highness
H.R.H.A. Honorary Member of the Royal Hibernian Academy of Arts
H.R.I. Honorary Member of the Royal Institute of Painters in Water Colours
H.R.I.P. Here Rests in Peace
H.R.O.I. Honorary Member of the Royal Institute of Oil Painters
hrs. hours
H.R.S. Hydraulics Research Station
H.R.S.A. Honorary Member of the Royal Scottish Academy
H.R.S.W. Honorary Member of the Royal Scottish Society of Painters in Water Colours
Hs. Handschrift (Manuscript)
H.S. Hakluyt Society
Hansard Society
Harleian Society
Haute-Saône
Hic Sepultus (here is buried)
High School
Home Secretary
Home Service
Hospital Ship   *cont.*

House Surgeon
h.s. highest score
hoc sensu (in this sense)
H.S.A. Hospital Saving Association
H.S.C. Higher School Certificate
Honourable Society of Cymmrodorion
H.Sch. High School
H.S.E. Hic Sepultus Est (here is buried)
H.S.F. Hospital Saturday Fund
hsg. housing
H.S.H. His *or* Her Serene Highness
H.S.L. Huguenot Society of London
H.S.M. His *or* Her Serene Majesty
H.S.Q. Historical Society of Queensland
H.S.S. History of Science Society (U.S.)
H.S.S.A. High Speed Steel Association
H.S.T. Highest Spring Tide
ht. heat
height
H.T. High Tide
High Treason
h.t. half time
halftone
high tension
hoc tempore (at this time
hoc titulo (in *or* under this title)
H.T.A. Horticultural Traders' Association
Household Textile Association
H.T.B. Horserace Totalisator Board
Hte. Gar. Haute-Garonne
Hte.L. Haute-Loire
Hte.M. Haute-Marne
Hte.Saô. Haute-Saône
Hte.Sav. Haute-Savoie
Htes.Pyr. Hautes-Pyrénées
H.T.G.C.R. High Temperature Gascooled Reactor
H.T.M.A.E.W. Home Timber Merchants Association of England and Wales
Ht.-Rhin. Haut-Rhin
H.Trin. Holy Trinity
h.t.s. half time survey
high-tensile steel
H.T.V. Hypersonic Test Vehicle
ht. wkt. hit wicket
H.U. Harvard University (U.S.)
H.U.D. Head-up Display System
H.U.G.O. Highly Unusual Geophysical Operations
HULTIS Hull Technical Interloan Scheme
Hum. Humanities
Humanity
hum. humble
humorous
Hun(g). Hungarian
Hungary
Hunts. Huntingdonshire
H.V. Haute-Vienne
High Vacuum
High Velocity
High Voltage
hoc verbum (at this word)
H.V.A. Health Visitors' Association
H.V.A.R. High-velocity Aircraft Rocket
H.V.C.A. Heating and Ventilating Contractors' Association
H.V.R.A. Heating and Ventilating Research Association

hw. hwan
H.W. High Water
h.w. hit wicket
h/w. herewith
Hwb. Handwörterbuch (pocket dictionary)
H.W.L.B. High Water, London Bridge
H.W.M. High Water Mark
H.W.N.T. High Water, Neap Tide
H.W.O.N.T. High Water, Ordinary Neap Tide
H.W.O.S.T. High Water, Ordinary Spring Tide
H.W.S.T. High Water, Spring Tide
hy. heavy

hyb. hybrid
hyd. hydraulic
hydrographic
hydrostatic
Hydr. Hydrographer
Hydro. Hydropathic
Hydrostatics
hydrog. hydrographic
hydt. hydrant
Hyg. Hygiene
hyp. hypothesis
hypothetical
hypoth. hypothesis
hypothetical

I

I Iodine
I. Idaho
Iesus
Imperial
Imperator (Emperor)
Imperatrix (Empress)
Imperium (Empire)
Incumbent
Independent
Infidelis (unbeliever, infidel)
Inspector
Institute
Instructor
Intelligence
Interceptor
Interpreter
Ireland
Irish
Island
Isle
Italian
Italy
i. id (that)
indicated
intransitive
Ia. Iowa
I.A. Incorporated Accountant
Indian Army
Infected Area
Institute of Actuaries
i.A. im Auftrage (by order of)
I.A.A. Institute of Automobile Assessors
International Advertising Association
International Aerosol Association
International Apple Association
International Association of Allergology
I.A.A.A. Irish Association of Advertising Agencies
I.A.A.B. Inter-American Association of Broadcasters
I.A.A.C. International Agricultural Aviation Centre

I.A.A.C.C. Inter-Allied Aeronautical Commission of Control
I.A.A.F. International Amateur Athletic Federation
International Association of Agricultural Economists
I.A.A.L.D. International Association of Agricultural Librarians and Documentalists
I.A.A.M. Incorporated Association of Assistant Masters in Secondary Schools
I.A.A.P. International Association of Applied Psychology
I.A.A.S. Incorporated Association of Architects and Surveyors
I.A.B. Imperial Agricultural Bureaux (*now* C.A.B.)
Industrial Advisers to the Blind
Industrial Advisory Board
International Council of Scientific Unions Abstracting Board
I.A.B.A. International Amateur Boxing Association
International Association of Aircraft Brokers and Agents
Irish Amateur Boxing Association
I.A.B.L.A. Inter-American Bibliographical and Library Association
I.A.B.S.E. International Association for Bridge and Structural Engineering
I.A.C. Institute of Amateur Cinematographers
I.A.C. Institute of Amateur Cinematographers
International Athletes Club
I.A.C.D. International Association of Clothing Designers
I.A.C.C.P. Inter-American Council of Commerce and Production
I.A.C.M.E. International Association of Crafts and Small and Medium-sized Enterprises
I.A.C.P. International Association for Child Psychiatry and Allied Professions

I.A.C.S. International Annealed Copper Standard

I.A.D.B. Inter-American Defence Board

I.A.D.F. Inter-American Association for Democracy and Freedom

I.A.D.L. International Association of Democratic Lawyers

I.A.D.R. International Association for Dental Research

I.A.D.S. International Association of Dental Students
International Association of Department Stores

I.A.E. Institute of Automobile Engineers

I.A.E.A. Indian Adult Education Association
International Atomic Energy Agency

I.Ae.E. Institution of Aeronautical Engineers (*now incorporated with the Royal Aeronautical Society*)

I.A.E.E. International Association for Earthquake Engineering

I.A.E.S.T.E. International Association for the Exchange of Students for Technical Experience

I.A.F. Indian Air Force
Indian Auxiliary Force
International Abolitionist Federation
International Astronautical Federation

I.A.F.C. International Association of Fire Chiefs

I.A.F.D. International Association of Food Distribution

I.A.F.W.N.O. Inter-American Federation of Working Newspapermen's Organizations

I.A.G. International Association of Geodesy
International Association of Gerontology

I.A.G.A. International Association of Geomagnetism and Aeronomy

I.A.G.B.& I. Ileostomy Association of Great Britain and Ireland

I.Agr.E. Institution of Agricultural Engineers

I.A.H. International Association of Hydrology

I.A.H.A. Inter-American Hotel Association

I.A.H.M. Incorporated Association of Head Masters

I.A.H.P. International Association of Horticultural Producers

I.A.H.R. International Association for the History of Religions
International Association for Hydraulic Research

I.A.H.S. International Academy of History of Science

I.A.I. International African Institute

I.A.I.A.S. Inter-American Institute of Agricultural Sciences

I.A.J.E. Internacio Asocia de Juristoj Esperantistoj (International Association of Esperantist Jurists)

I.A.L. International Aeradio, Limited
International Arbitration League
International Association of Theoretical and Applied Limnology
Irish Academy of Letters

I.A.L.A. International African Law Association
International Association of Lighthouse Authorities

I.A.L.L. International Association of Law Libraries

I.A.L.P. International Association of Logopedics and Phoniatrics

I.A.L.S. International Association of Legal Science

I.A.M. Institute of Advanced Motorists

I.A.M.A. Incorporated Advertising Managers' Association
International Abstaining Motorists' Association
Irish Association of Municipal Authorities

I.A.M.A.P. International Association of Meteorology and Atmospheric Physics

I.A.M.B. International Association of Macrobiologists
Irish Association of Master Bakers

I.A.M.C. Indian Army Medical Corps

I.A.M.C.R. International Association for Mass Communication Research

I.A.M.L. International Association of Music Libraries

I.A.M.M. International Association of Medical Museums

I.A.M.S. International Association of Microbiological Societies

I.A.M.W.F. Inter-American Mine Workers Federation

I.A.N.C. International Airline Navigators' Council

I.& C.L.Q. International and Comparative Law Quarterly

I.A.N.E.C. Inter-American Nuclear Energy Commission

I.A.O. Incorporated Association of Organists

I.A.O.C. Indian Army Ordnance Corps

I.A.O.S. Irish Agricultural Organisation Society

I.A.P. International Academy of Pathology

I.A.P.A. Inter-American Press Association

I.A.P.B. International Association for the Prevention of Blindness

I.A.P.C.C. International Association of Political Campaign Consultants

I.A.P.H. International Association of Ports and Harbours

I.A.P.I.P. International Association for the Protection of Industrial Property

I.A.P.N. International Association of Professional Numismatists

I.A.P.S.O. International Association for the Physical Sciences of the Ocean

I.A.P.S. Incorporated Association of Preparatory Schools
International Academy of Political Science

I.A.P.S.C. Inter-African Phytosanitary Commission

I.A.P.T. International Association for Plant Taxonomy

I.A.Q.R. International Association on Quaternary Research

I.A.R.A. Inter-Allied Reparation Agency

I.Arb. Institute of Arbitrators

I.A.R.C. Indian Agricultural Research Council

I.A.R.F. International Association for Liberal Christianity and Religious Freedom

I.A.R.I.W. International Association for Research into Income and Wealth

I.A.R.O. Indian Army Reserve of Officers

I.A.R.U. International Amateur Radio Union

I.A.S. Indian Administrative Service
Institute of the Aerospace Sciences (U.S.)

I.A.S.C. Indian Army Service Corps
International Association of Seed Crushers

I.A.S.H. International Association of Scientific Hydrology

I.A.S.I. Inter-American Statistical Institute

I.A.S.L.I.C. Indian Association of Special Libraries and Information Centres

I.A.S.P. International Association for Social Progress

I.A.S.P.E.I. International Association of Seismology and Physics of the Earth's Interior

I.A.S.S. International Association for Shell Structures
International Association of Soil Science

I.A.S.S.W. International Association of Schools of Social Work

I.A.S.T.A. Institute for Advanced Studies in the Theatre Arts

I.A.T.A. International Air Transport Association
International Amateur Theatre Association

I.A.T.E. International Association for Temperance Education

I.A.T.M.E. International Association of Terrestrial Magnetism and Electricity

I.A.T.R. International Association of Teachers of Russian

I.A.T.U.L. International Association of Technical University Libraries

I.A.U. International Academic Union
International Association of Universities
International Astronomical Union

I.A.U.P.L. International Association of University Professors and Lecturers

I.A.V. International Association of Volcanology

I.A.V.C.E.I. International Association of Volcanology and Chemistry of the Earth's Interior

I.A.V.F.H. International Association of Veterinary Food Hygienists

I.A.V.G. International Association for Vocational Guidance

I.A.W. International Alliance of Women

i.a.w. in accordance with

I.A.W.A. International Association of Wood Anatomists

I.A.W.M. Industrial Association of Wales and Monmouthshire

I.A.W.M.C. International Association of Workers for Maladjusted Children

I.A.W.R.T. International Association of Women in Radio and Television

I.A.W.S. Irish Agricultural Wholesale Society

ib. ibidem (in the same place)

I.B. In Bond
Incendiary Bomb
Infectious Bronchitis
Information Bureau
Institute of Bankers
Institute of Building
Instruction Book
Intelligence Branch
International Bank
Invoice Book
Ivor Brown

I.B.A. Independent Broadcasting Authority
Industrial Bankers' Association
International Bar Association
International Brigade Association

I.B.A.E. Institution of British Agricultural Engineers

I.B.A.H. Inter-African Bureau for Animal Health

I.B.B. Institute of British Bakers

I.B.C.A. Institute of Burial and Cremation Administration
International Bureau for Culture Activities

I.B.C.A.M. Institute of British Carriage and Automobile Manufacturers

I.B.D. Incorporated Institute of British Decorators and Interior Designers

I.B.E. Institute of British Engineers
Institute of Building Estimators
Institution of Body Engineers
Institution of British Engineers
International Bureau of Education

I.B.E.G. Internationaler Bund der Erziehungsgemeinschaften (International Federation of Children's Communities)

I.B.E.N. Incendiary Bomb with Explosive Nose

I.B.F. Institute of British Foundrymen
International Badminton Federation

I.B.F.M.P. International Bureau of the Federations of Master Printers

I.B.G. Incorporated Brewers Benevolent Society and Guild
Institute of British Geographers

I.B.H.A. Insulation, Building and Hard Board Association

I.B.I. International Broadcasting Institute
Internationales Burgen-Institut (International Castle Research Institute)

i.b.i. invoice-book inwards
I.B.I.C.C. Incorporated British Institute of Certified Carpenters
ibid. ibidem (in the same place)
I.Biol. Institute of Biology
I.B.K. Institute of Bookkeepers
I.B.L. Institute of British Launderers
I.B.M. Intercontinental Ballistic Missile
  Institute of Baths Management
  International Business Machines
I.B.M.R. International Bureau for Mechanical Reproduction
i.b.o. invoice-book outwards
I.B.O.A. Irish Bank Officials' Association
I.B.P. Institute of British Photographers
  International Biological Programme
i.b.p. initial boiling point
I.B.R.D. International Bank or Reconstruction and Development
I.B.R.O. International Brain Research Organization
I.B.S. Institute of Bankers in Scotland
I.B.(Scot.) Institute of Bankers in Scotland
I.B.S.M. Institute of Building Site Management
I.B.S.T. Institute of British Surgical Technicians
I.B.W.M. International Bureau of Weights and Measures
I.B.W.S. International Bureau of Whaling Statistics
I.B.Z. Internationale Bibliographie der Zeitschriften-Literatur
I.C. Indentity Card
  Iesus Christus (Jesus Christ)
  Imperial College of Science and Technology, London
  Imperial Conference
  Index Correction
  Industrial Court
  Information Centre
  Institute of Charity (Rosminian)
  Intelligence Corps
  Internal Combustion Engine
  Internal Communication
I.-C. Indo-China
i.c. index correction
i/c. in charge *or* command
I.C.A. Fédération internationale chrétienne des travailleurs de l'alimentation, du tabac et de l'hôtellerie (International Christian Federation of Food, Drink, Tobacco and Hotelworkers)
  Ice Cream Alliance
  Industrial Catering Association
  Institute of Chartered Accountants in England and Wales
  Institute of Company Accountants
  Institute of Contemporary Arts
  International Cartographic Association   *cont.*

International Chiropractors' Association
International Co-operative Alliance
International Council on Archives
Irish Countrywomen's Association
I.C.A.A. Invalid Children's Aid Association
I.C.A.B. International Council Against Bullfighting
I.C.A.C. International Confederation for Agricultural Credit
  International Cotton Advisory Committee
I.C.A.E. International Commission on Agricultural Engineering
  International Conference of Agricultural Economists
I.C.A.E.S. International Congress of Anthropological and Ethnological Sciences
I.C.A.I. Internationa Commission or Agricultural Industries
I.C.A.M. Institute of Corn and Agricultural Merchants
I.C. & C.Y. Inns of Court and City Yeomanry
I.C.A.O. International Civil Aviation Organisation
I.C.A.P. Institute of Certified Ambulance Personnel
I.C.A.R. Indian Council of Agricultural Research
I.C.A.S. Institute of Chartered Accountants of Scotland
  International Council of the Aeronautical Sciences
I.C.B. Indian Coffee Board
  International Container Bureau
I.C.B.A. International Community of Booksellers' Associations
I.C.B.P. International Council for Bird Preservation
I.C.B.D. International Council of Ballroom Dancing
I.C.B.M. Intercontinental Ballistic Missile
I.C.B.P. International Committee for Bird Preservation
I.C.B.S. Incorporated Church Building Society
I.C.C. International Cricket Conference
  International Association for Cereal Chemistry
  International Chamber of Commerce
  International Children's Centre
  International Congregational Council
I.C.C.A. Intercontinental Corrugated Case Association
I.C.C.B. International Catholic Child Bureau
I.C.C.C. Inter-Council Co-ordination Committee
  International Conference of Catholic Charities
  International Council of Christian Churches

I.C.C.D. Institute of Chocolate and Confectionery Distributors

I.C.C.E. International Council of Commerce Employers

I.C.C.F. International Committee on Canned Foods
International Correspondence Chess Federation

I.C.C.I.C.A. Interim Co-ordinating Committee for International Commodity Arrangements

I.C.C.J. International Committee for Co-operation of Journalists

I.C.C.L. International Committee of Comparative Law

I.C.C.P. International Council for Children's Play

I.C.C.S. International Centre of Criminological Studies

I.C.C.T.A. International Consultative Council of Travel Agents

I.C.C.U. International Cross Country Union

I.C.D. Iesu Christo Duce (with Jesus Christ as leader)
Institute of Civil Defence

I.C.D.O. International Civil Defence Organization

Ice. Iceland

I.C.E. Institution of Chemical Engineers
Institution of Civil Engineers
Internal Combustion Engine
International Cultural Exchange

I.C.E.F. International Committee for Ethnographic Films
International Council for Educational Films

I.C.E.G. Insulated Conductors' Export Group

I.C.E.I. Institution of Civil Engineers of Ireland

Icel. Icelandic

I.C.E.M. Intergovernmental Committee for European Migration

I.C.E.R. Information Centre of the European Railways

I.Ceram. Institute of Ceramics

I.C.E.S. International Council for the Exploration of the Seas

I.C.E.T. International Council on Education for Teaching

I.C.E.T.T. Industrial Council for Educational Training and Technology

I.C.F. Ice Cream Federation
Industrial Christian Fellowship
International Canoe Federation

I.C.F.C. Industrial and Commercial Finance Corporation
International Centre of Films for Children

I.C.F.P.W. International Confederation of Former Prisoners of War

I.C.F.T.A. International Committee of Foundry Technical Associations

I.C.F.T.U. International Confederation of Free Trade Unions

I.C.F.W. International Christian Federation of Food, Drink, Tobacco and Hotelworkers

I.C.G. International Commission on Glass

I.C.G.A. International Classic Guitar Association

I.C.G.S. International Catholic Girls' Society

Ich. Ichthyology

I.C.H.C. International Committee for Horticultural Congresses

I.C.H.C.A. International Cargo Handling Co-ordination Association

I.Chem.E. Institution of Chemical Engineers

I.C.H.E.O. Inter-University Council for Higher Education Overseas

I.C.H.P.E.R. International Council for Health, Physical Education and Recreation

I.C.H.S. International Committee Historical Sciences

Ichth. Ichthyology

I.C.I. Imperial Chemical Industries
Institute of Chemistry of Ireland
International Commission on Illumination

I.C.I.A. International Credit Insurance Association

I.C.I.D. International Commission on Irrigation and Drainage

I.C.I.T.A. International Chain of Industrial and Technical Advertising Agencies

I.C.J. International Commission of Jurists
International Court of Justice

I.C.J.W. International Council of Jewish Women

I.C.L. International Computers Limited

I.C.L.A. International Committee on Laboratory Animals
International Comparative Literature Association

I.C.L.S. Irish Central Library for Students

I.C.M. Institute of Credit Management
International Confederation of Midwives
Irish Church Missions

I.C.M.A. Independent Cable Makers' Association
International City Managers' Association
International Congresses for Modern Architecture

I.C.M.C. International Catholic Migration Commission

I.C.M.I.C.A. Pax Romana, International Catholic Movement for Intellectual and Cultural Affairs

I.C.M.L.T. International Congress of Medical Laboratory Technologists

I.C.M.M.P. International Committee of Military Medicine and Pharmacy

I.C.M.S.A. Irish Creamery Milk Suppliers' Association

I.C.N. in Christi nomine (in the name of Christ)
International Council of Nurses

I.C.N.A.F. International Commission for the Northwest Atlantic Fisheries

I.C.O. Intergovernmental Commission on Oceanography
International Commission for Optics
International Congess of Otolaryngology

ICOGRADA International Council of Graphic Design Associations

I.C.O.M. International Council of Museums

I.C.O.M.I.A. International Council of Marine Industry Associations

icon. iconographical
iconography

I.C.O.R. Inter-governmental Conference on Oceanic Research

I.C.O.S. International Committee of Onomastic Sciences

I.C.O.U. Office international des unions de consommateurs (International Office of Consumers' Unions)

I.C.P.A. International Commission for the Prevention of Alcoholism
International Co-operative Petroleum Association

I.C.P.H.S. International Council for Philosophy and Humanistic Studies

I.C.P.I.G.P. Internationale chrétienne professionnelle pour les industries graphiques et papetières (International Federation of Christian Trade Unions of the Graphical and Paper Industries)

I.C.P.O. International Criminal Police Organisation (Interpol)

I.C.P.U. International Catholic Press Union

I.C.R. International Congress of Radiology

I.C.R.C. International Committee of the Red Cross

I.C.R.F. Imperial Cancer Research Fund

I.C.R.I.C.E. International Centre of Research and Information on Collective Economy

I.C.R.O. International Cell Research Organisation

I.C.R.P. International Commission on Radiological Protection

I.C.R.S.C. International Council for Research in the Sociology of Co-operation

I.C.S. Imperial College of Science and Technology, London
Indian Chemical Society
Indian Civil Service
Institute of Chartered Shipbrokers
International Chamber of Shipping
International College of Surgeons
International Correspondence Schools

I.C.S.B. International Centre of School-Building

I.C.S.C.H.M. International Commission for a History of the Scientific and Cultural Development of Mankind

I.C.S.E. Intermediate Current Stability Experiment

I.C.S.H.B. International Committee for Standardization in Human Biology

I.C.S.I.D. International Council of Societies of Industrial Design

I.C.S.P.E. International Council of Sport and Physical Education

I.C.S.S.D. International Committee for Social Sciences Documentation

I.C.S.T. Imperial College of Science and Technology, London

I.C.S.U. International Council of Scientific Unions

I.C.S.W. International Conference of Social Work

I.C.T. Iesu Christo Tutore (Jesus Christ being our protector)
Institute of Clay Technology
International Computers and Tabulators (now I.C.L.)
International Council of Tanners

I.C.T.A. Imperial College of Tropical Agriculture, Trinidad
International Confederation of Technical Agriculturists
International Council of Travel Agents

I.C.T.A.A. Imperial College of Tropical Agriculture Association

I.C.T.M.M. International Congresses on Tropical Medicine and Malaria

I.C.T.U. Irish Congress of Trade Unions

Ictus. Iurisconsultus (Counsellor-at-law)

I.C.U. International Code Use

I.C.U.A.E. International Congress of University Adult Education

I.C.U.M.S.A. International Commission for Unified Methods of Sugar Analysis

I.C.V.A. International Council of Voluntary Agencies

I.C.W. Institute of Clayworkers
Institute of Clerks of Works of Great Britain
Inter-American Commission of Women
International Council of Women

i.c.w. in connexion with
interrupted continuous wave

I.C.W.A. Indian Council of World Affairs
Institute of Cost and Works Accountants

I.C.W.G. International Co-operative Women's Guild

I.C.W.P. International Council of Women Psychologists

I.C.Y.F. International Catholic Youth Federation

I.C.Z.N. International Commission on Zoological Nomenclature

Id. Idaho

id. idem (the same)

I.D. Induced Draught
Infectious Disease(s)
Information Department
Institute of Directors
Intelligence Department
Iraqui Dinar(s)

i.d. inside diameter
Ida. Idaho
I.D.A. Immortalis Dei Auspicio (with the guidance of Immortal God)
Industrial Development Authority (Ireland)
International Development Association
➤ International Drummers Association
Irish Dental Association
Irish Drug Association
I.D.A.C. Import Duties Advisory Committee
IDACE Association des industries des aliments diététiques de la C.E.E. (Association of Dietetic Foodstuff Industries of the E.E.C.)
I.D.B. Illicit Diamond Buying *or* Buyer
Inter-American Development Bank
I.D.C. Imperial Defence College *or* Committee
Industrial Development Certificate(s)
International Dermatologica Committee
i.d.c. has completed course at, or served for a year on the staff of, the Imperial Defence College
I.D.C.S.P. Interim Defence Communication Satellite Programme
I.D.E.S. Irmandade do Divino Espirito Santo (Brotherhood of the Divine Holy Ghost)
I.D.E.S.T. Irmandade do Divino Espirito Santo e da Trinidade (Brotherhood of the Divine Holy Ghost and Trinity)
I.D.F. International Dairy Federation
International Democratic Fellowship
International Diabetes Federation
I.D.F.F. Internationale Demokratische Frauenföderation (Women's International Democratic Federation)
I.D.I. Institut de droit international (Institute of International Law)
➤ **I.D.I.A.** Industrial Design Institute of Australia
I.D.I.B. Industrial Diamond Information Bureau
I.D.L. International Date Line
I.D.L.I.S. International Desert Locust Information Service
➤ **I.D.M.A.** International Dancing Masters' Association (*now* I.D.T.A.)
I.D.N. In Dei Nomine (in the name of God)
I.D.P. International Driving Permit
I.D.R. Infantry Drill Regulations
I.D.R.A. Irish Dinghy Racing Association
I.D.S. Institute of Dental Surgery
I.D.S.A. Indian Dairy Science Association
I.D.S.M. Indian Distinguished Service Medal
I.D.T. Industrial Design Technology

➤ **I.D.T.A.** International Dance Teachers' Association
I.E. Index Error
Indian Empire
Indo-European
Institute of Export
Institution of Electronics
Order of the Indian Empire
i.e. id est (that is)
I.E.A. Institute of Economic Affairs
Institution of Engineers, Australia
International Economic Association
International Electrical Association
International Ergonomics Association
I.E.C. Imperial Economic Committee (*now* C.E.C.)
International Electrotechnical Commission
I.E.D. Institution of Engineering Designers
I.E.E. Institution of Electrical Engineers
I.E.F. Indian Expeditionary Force
I.E.I. Industrial Education International ➤
Institution of Engineering Inspection
I.E.I.C. Institution of Engineers-in-Charge
I.E.K.V. Internationale Eisenbahn-Kongress-Vereinigung (International Railway Congress Association)
➤ **I.E.M.C.S.** Industrial Estates Management Corporation for Scotland
I.E.R.E. Institute of Electronic and Radio Engineers
➤ **I.E.R.F.** Industrial Educational and Research Foundation
I.E.S. Illuminating Engineering Society
Indian Educational Service
Institution of Engineers and Shipbuilders in Scotland
I-et-L Indre-et-Loire
I-et-V Ille-et-Vilaine
I.F. Imperial Father
Ingénieur forestier (Forest Engineer)
Institute of Fuel
i.f. intermediate frequency
ipse fecit (he did it himself)
I.F.A. Incorporated Faculty of Arts
International Federation of Actors
International Fertility Association
International Fiscal Association
Irish Football Association
I.F.A.C. International Federation of Automatic Control
I.F.A.L.P.A. International Federation of Air Line Pilots' Associations
I.F.A.P. International Federation of Agricultural Producers
I.F.A.T.C.A. International Federation of Air Traffic Controllers' Associations
I.F.A.T.C.C. International Federation of Associations of Textile Chemists and Colourists

I.F.O.R.S.

I.F.B.B.F. Imported Fibre Building Board Federation
I.F.B.P.W. International Federation of Business and Professional Women
I.F.B.W.W. International Federation of Building and Woodworkers
I.F.C. International Finance Corporation
International Fisheries Convention
I.F.C.A.T.I. International Federation of Cotton and Allied Textile Industries
I.F.C.A.W.U. International Federation of Christian Agricultural Workers' Unions
I.F.C.C. International Federation of Camping and Caravanning
International Federation of Children's Communities
I.F.C.C.A. International Federation of Community Centre Associations
I.F.C.C.T.E. International Federation of Commercial, Clerical and Technical Employees
I.F.C.J. International Federation of Catholic Journalists
I.F.C.L. International Faculty of Comparative Law
I.F.C.M. International Federation of Christian Metalworkers' Unions
I.F.C.M.U. International Federation of Christian Miners' Unions
I.F.C.P. International Federation of Catholic Pharmacists
I.F.C.T.U. International Federation of Christian Trade Unions
I.F.C.T.U.B.W.W. International Federation of Christian Trade Unions of Building and Wood Workers
I.F.C.T.U.G.P.I. International Federation of Christian Trade Unions of the Graphical and Paper Industries
I.F.C.T.U.S.E.T.M.S.C.T. International Federation of Christian Trade Unions of Salaried Employees, Technicians, Managerial Staff and Commercial Travellers
I.F.C.T.U.T.G.W. International Federation of Christian Trade Unions of Textile and Garment Workers
I.F.C.U.A.W. International Federation of Christian Unions of Agricultural Workers
I.F.D. International Federation of Documentation
I.F.E. Institution of Fire Engineers
I.F.E.E.S. International Federation of Electroencephalographic Societies
I.F.E.M.S. International Federation of Electron Microscope Societies
I.F.F. Indicator Friend or Foe
International Film Fund
I.F.F.A. International Federation of Film Archives
I.F.I.P.S. Interntioanal Federation for Information Processing Societies
I.F.F.J. International Federation of Free Journalists of Central and Eastern Europe and Baltic and Balkan Countries

I.F.F.J.P. International Federation of Fruit Juice Producers
I.F.F.P.A. International Federation of Film Producers' Associations
I.F.F.S. International Federation of Film Societies
I.F.F.T.U. International Federation of Free Teachers' Unions
I.F.G.A. International Federation of Grocers' Associations
I.F.G.O. International Federation of Gynecology and Obstetrics
I.F.H.E. International Federation of Home Economics
I.F.H.P. International Federation for Housing and Planning
I.F.I.A. International Federation of Ironmongers' and Iron Merchants' Associations
I.F.I.F. Internationale Föderation von Industriegewerkschaften und Fabrikarbeiterverbänden (International Federation of Industrial Organisations and General Workers' Unions)
I.F.I.P. International Federation for Information Processing
I.F.I.W.A. International Federation of Importers' and Wholesale Grocers' Associations
I.F.J. International Federation of Journalists
I.F.K.A.B. Internationale Federatie van Katholieke Arbeiders Bewegingen (International Federation of Christian Workers' Movements)
I.F.K.M. Internationale Föderation für Kurzschrift und Maschinenschreiben (International Federation of Shorthand and Typewriting)
I.F.L. Institute of Fluorescent Lighting
International Friendship League
I.F.L.A. International Federation of Landscape Architects
International Federation of Library Associations
International Federation of Lithographers, Process Workers and Kindred Trades
I.F.L.F.F. Internationale Frauenliga für Frieden und Freiheit (Women's International League for Peace and Freedom)
I.F.M. International Falcon Movement
I.F.M.C. International Folk Music Centre
International Folk Music Council
I.F.M.E. International Federation for Medical Electronics
International Federation of Municipal Engineers
I.F.M.P. International Federation for Medical Psychotherapy
I.F.M.S.A. International Federation of Medical Students' Associations
I.F.O.F.S.A.G. International Fellowship of Former Scouts and Guides
I.F.O.R. International Fellowship of Reconciliation
I.F.O.R.S. International Federation of Operational Research Societies

I.F.O.S.A. International Federation of Stationers' Associations

I.F.P.A.A.W. International Federation of Plantation, Agricultural and Allied Workers

I.F.P.C.S. International Federation of Unions of Employees in Public and Civil Services

I.F.P.C.W. International Federation of Petroleum and Chemical Workers

I.F.P.I. International Federation of the Phonographic Industry

I.F.P.L.V.B. Internationale Föderation der Plantagen- und Landarbeiter und verwandter Berufsgruppen (International Federation of Plantation, Agricultural and Allied Workers)

I.F.P.M. International Federation of Physical Medicine

I.F.P.W. International Federation of Petroleum Workers

I.F.R. Instrument Flight Rules
Internationaler Frauenrat (International Council of Women)

I.F.R.B. International Frequency Registration Board

I.F.R.U. Institut Français du Royaume-Uni (French Institute of the United Kingdom)

I.F.S. Indian Forest Service
International Federation of Settlements and Neighbourhood Centres
International Federation of Surveyors
Irish Free State

I.F.S.C.C. International Federation of Societies of Cosmetic Chemists

I.F.S.D.A. International Federation of Stamp Dealers' Associations

I.F.S.D.P. International Federation of the Socialist and Democratic Press

I.F.S.E.M. International Federation of Societies for Electron Microscopy

I.F.S.P. International Federation of Societies of Philosophy

I.F.S.P.O. International Federation of Senior Police Officers

I.F.S.T. Institute of Food Science and Technology
International Federation of Shorthand and Typewriting

I.F.S.W. International Federation of Social Workers

I.F.T. International Frequency Tables

I.F.T.A. International Federation of Teachers' Associations

I.F.T.C. International Film and Television Council
International Fine Technics Association

Iftus. Inhabitants friendly to us

I.F.T.W.A. International Federation of Textile Workers' Associations

I.F.U.W. International Federation of University Women

I.F.W.A. International Federation for Weeks of Art

I.F.W.E.A. International Federation of Workers' Educational Associations

I.F.W.L. International Federation of Women Lawyers

I.F.W.R.I. Institute of the Furniture Warehousing and Removing Industry

I.F.W.T.A. International Federation of Workers' Travel Associations

I.F.Y.C. International Federation of Young Co-operators

ig. ignition

I.G. Indo-Germanic
Industrial Group
Inertial Guidance
Inner Guard
Inside Guardian
Inspector-General
Instructor of Gunnery
Interessengemeinschaft (Combine)
Irish Guards

I.G.A. Insulation Glazing Association
International Geographical Association (Esperantist)
International Grains Arrangement
Irish Gas Association

I.G.A.P. Internationale Gesellschaft für Ärztliche Psychotherapie (International Federation for Medical Psychotherapy)

I.G.C. International Geophysical Committee
International Grassland Congress

I.G.C.C. Inter-Governmental Copyright Committee

I.G.C.M. Incorporated Guild of Church Musicians

i.g.d. illicit gold dealer

I.G.E. Institution of Gas Engineers

I.G.F. International Graphical Federation
International Gymnastic Federation

I.G.M. Internationale Gesellschaft für Moorforschung (International Society for Research on Moors)

ign. ignition
ignotus (unknown)

I.G.O. Inter-Governmental Organisation

I.G.P.M.S. International Grand Prix Medical Service

igr. igitur (therefore)

I.G.R.O.F. Internationale Rorschach-Gesellschaft (International Rorschach Society)

I.G.R.S. Irish Genealogical Research Society

I.G.T. Inspector-General to the Forces for Training

I.G.U. International Gas Union
International Geographical Union
Internationale Gewerbeunion (International Association of Crafts and Small and Medium-Sized Enterprises)

I.G.V. Internationaler Gemeindeverband (International Union of Local Authorities)

I.G.W.F. International Garment Workers' Federation

I.G.Y. International Geophysical Year

I.H. Diplôme d'infirmière hygiéniste (Diploma in Public Health Nursing)
Infective Hepatitis
I.h. Iacet hic (Here lies)
I.H.A. Institute of Hospital Administrators
International Hotel Association
International House Association
Issuing Houses' Association
I.H.A.T.I.S. International Hide and Allied Trades' Improvement Society
I.H.B. International Hydrographic Bureau
I.H.C. International Help for Children
I.H.C.A. International Hebrew Christian Alliance
I.H.E. Institution of Highway Engineers
I.H.E.U. International Humanist and Ethical Union
I.H.F. International Hospital Federation
International Lawn Hockey Federation
I.H.K. Internationale Handelskammer (International Chamber of Commerce)
I.H.L. International Homeopathic League
I.H.M. Iesus Mundi Salvator (Jesus the Saviour of the World)
Institute of Housing Managers
I.H.O.U. Institute of Home Office Underwriters
i.h.p. indicated horsepower
I.H.R. Institute of Historical Research
I.H.R.M.A. Irish Hotel and Restaurant Managers' Association
I.H.S. symbol representing IHΣ, the first three letters of the Greek name of Jesus; *also* Iesus Hominum Salvator (Jesus, Saviour of Mankind)
I.H.T. Institute of Handicraft Teachers
I.H.V.E. Institution of Heating and Ventilating Engineers
I.I. Ikebana International
I.I.A.I. Indian Institution of Art in Industry
I.I.A.L. International Institute of Arts and Letters
I.I.A.S. International Institute of Administrative Sciences
I.I.B. Institut international des brevets (International Patent Institute)
I.I.B.D.& I.D. Incorporated Institute of British Decorators and Interior Designers
I.I.C. International Institute for the Conservation of Historic and Artistic Works
I.I.C.A. Instituto Internacional de Ciencias Administrativas (International Institute of Administrative Sciences)
I.I.C.C. International Institute for Study and Research in the Field of Commercial Competition
I.I.E. Institut international de l'épargne (International Thrift Institute)
International Institute of Embryology

I.I.E.L. Institut international d'études ligures (International Institute for Ligurian Studies)
I.I.F. Institut international du froid (International Institute of Refrigeration)
I.I.F.A. International Institute of Films on Art
I.I.H.F. International Ice Hockey Federation
I.I.I. Inter-American Indian Institute
International Isostatic Institute
I.I.M. Institute of Industrial Managers
I.Inf.Sc. Institute of Information Scientists
I.I.N.S. Interuniversity Institute of Nuclear Sciences
I.I.O.E. International Indian Ocean Expedition
I.I.P. Institut international de la presse (International Press Institute)
International Institute of Philosophy
I.I.P.A. Institute of Incorporated Practitioners in Advertising
I.I.P.E.R. International Institution of Production Engineering Research
I.I.P.F. International Institute for Public Finance
I.I.R. International Institute of Refrigeration
I.I.R.B. Institut international de recherches betteravières (International Institute for Sugar Beet Research
I.I.S. Institut international de la soudure (International Institute of Welding)
Institut international de statistique (International Statistical Institute)
Institute of Industrial Supervisors
Internationales Institut des Sparwesens (International Thrift Institute)
International Institute of Sociology
Irish Institute of Secretaries
I.I.S.A. Institut international des sciences administratives (International Institute of Administrative Sciences)
I.I.S.L. International Institute of Space Law
Istituto Internazionale di Studi Liguri (International Institute for Ligurian Studies)
I.I.S.O. Institution of Industrial Safety Officers
I.I.S.W.M. Institute of Iron and Steel Wire Manufacturers
I.I.T. Indian Institute of Technology
Institut international du théâtre (International Theatre Institute)
Institute of Industrial Technicians
I.I.T.S. International Institute of Theoretical Sciences
I.I.W. International Institute of Welding
I.J. Irish Jurist
i.J. im Jahre (in the year)

i.J.d.W. im Jahre der Welt (in the year of the World)

I.J.I. International Juridical Institute

I.J.K. Internationale Juristen-Kommission (International Commission of Jurists)

I.K.G. Internationale Kommission für Glas (International Commission on Glass)

I.K.H. Ihre königliche Hoheit (Her Royal Highness)

I.K.I. Internationales Kali-Institut (International Potash Institute)

I.K.M.B. Internationale Katholische Mittelstands bewegung (International Catholic Union of the Middle Classes)

I.K.N. Internationale Kommission für Numismatik (International Numismatic Commission)

I.K.R.K. Internationales Komitee vom Roten Kreuz (Internationale Committee of the Red Cross)

I.K.U.E. Internacia Katolika Unuigo Esperantista (International Union of Catholic Esperantists)

I.K.V. Internationaler Krankenhausverband (International Hospital Federation)

I.K.V.S.A. Internationale Katholische Vereinigung für Soziale Arbeit (Catholic International Union for Social Service)

Il. Iliad

I.L. Inside Left
L'Internationale libérale (Union libérale mondiale) (Liberal International (World Liberal Union))

i.l. inside leg

I.L.A. Institute of Landscape Architects
International Laundry Association
International Law Association
International Leprosy Association

I.L.A.A. International Legal Aid Association

I.L.A.A.S. Integrated light attack avionics system

I.L.A.B. International League of Antiquarian Booksellers

I.L.A.F.A. Instituto Latinoamericano del Fierro y el Acero (Latin-American Iron and Steel Institute)

I.L.C. International Law Commission

I.L.C.O.P. International Liaison Committee of Organisations for Peace

I.L.E. Institution of Locomotive Engineers

I.L.E.A. Inner London Education Authority

I.L.E.I. Internacia Ligo de Esperantistaj Instruistoj (International League of Esperantist Teachers)

I.L.F. International Landworkers' Federation

I.L.F.I. International Labour Film Institute

I.L.G.A. Institute of Local Government Administration

I.L.I. Inter-African Labour Institute

Ill. Illustrated

ill. illustrissimus (most distinguished) illustration

illit. illiterate

I.L.N. Illustrated London News

I.L.P.H. International League for the Protection of Horses

ills. illustrations

illum. illuminated

illust. illustration

Ilmo. Illustrissimo (most illustrious)

I.L.O. International Labour Office
International Labour Organisation

i.l.o. in lieu of

I.L.O.A. Industrial Life Officers' Association

I.Loco.E. Institution of Locomotive Engineers

I.L.P. Independent Labour Party

I.L.R.I. Indian Lac Research Institute

I.L.R.M. International League for the Rights of Man

I.L.S. Incorporated Law Society
Industrial Locomotive Society
Instrument Landing System
International Latitude Service
International Lunar Society

I.L.T. Infectious Laryngo-tracheitis

I.L.T.F. International Lawn Tennis Federation

I.L.U. Institute of London Underwriters

I.M. Ihre Majestät (Your Majesty)
Institute of Metals
Institution of Metallurgists
Interceptor Missile

I.M.A. Indian Military Academy
Institutional Management Association
International Mineralogical Association
International Music Association
Irish Medical Association

IMACE Association des industries margarinières des pays de la C.E.E. (Association of Margarine Industries of the E.E.C.)

I.Mar.E. Institute of Marine Engineers

I.M.A.U. International Movement for Atlantic Union

I.M.B. Internationaler Metallarbeiterbund (International Metalworkers' Federation)

I.M.B.L. Independent Meat Buyers, Ltd.

I.M.C. Institutum Missionum a Consolata (Consolata Fathers)
Instrument Meteorological Conditions
International Maritime Committee
International Missionary Council
International Music Council

I.M.C.O. Inter-Governmental Maritime Consultative Organization

I.M.C.S. Pax Romana, International Movement of Catholic Students

I.M.D. Indian Medical Department

I.M.E. Institution of Mechanical Engineers
Institution of Mining Engineers
Institution of Municipal Engineers
I.Mech.E. Institution of Mechanical Engineers
I.M.E.D.E. Institut pour l'Etude des Méthodes de Direction de l'entreprise (Institute for Management Study)
I.Meth. Independent Methodist(s)
I.M.F. Institute of Metal Finishing
International Marketing Federation
International Metalworkers' Federation
International Monetary Fund
International Motorcycle Federation
I.M.H. Institute of Materials Handling
I.M.I. Imperial Metal Industries
Imperial Mycological Institute (*now* C.M.I.)
Improved Manned Interceptor
Institute of the Motor Industry
Irish Management Institute
I.Min.E. Institution of Mining Engineers
imit. imitation
imitative
I.M.L.T. Institute of Medical Laboratory Technology
I.M.M. Institution of Mining and Metallurgy
I.M.M.T.S. Indian Mercantile Marine Training Ship
immun. immunology
I.M.N.S. Imperial Military Nursing Service
I.M.O. Inter-American Municipal Organisation
Imp. Imperial
imp. imperative
imperator (emperor)
imperfect
impersonal
implement
import(ed)
importer
impression
imprimatur (let it be printed)
imprimé (printed)
imprimeur (printer)
I.M.P. International Match Point(s)
Interplanetary Monitoring Platforms
impce. importance
imper. imperative
imperf. imperfect
imperforate
impersonal
Impft. Imperfect
imposs. impossible
impreg. impregnated
improp. improper
impt. important
imptr. importer
I.M.R.A. Industrial Marketing Research Association
I.M.R.C. International Marine Radio Company, Limited

I.M.S. Independent Medical Services
Indian Medical Service
Industrial Methylated Spirit
International Musicological Society
I.M.S.M. Institute of Marketing and Sales Management
I.M.T.A. Imported Meat Trade Association
Institute of Municipal Treasurers and Accountants
I.M.T.D. Inspectors of the Military Training Directorate
I.M.U. Inertial Measurement Unit
International Mathematical Union
I.Mun.E. Institution of Municipal Engineers
I.M.V.S. Institute of Medical and Veterinary Science (Australia)
In Indium
In. Instructor
in. inch
I.N. Indian Navy
I.N.A. Indian National Army
International Newsreel Association
inaug. inaugurate(d)
inc. included
including
inclusive
income
incorporated
increase
increasing
incumbent
In.C. Instructor Captain
I.N.C. in nomine Christi (in the name of Christ)
Indian National Congress
International Nickel Company
International Numismatic Commission
Ironfounders' National Confederation
I.N.C.A. International Newspaper Colour Association
I.N.C.A.P. Institute of Nutrition of Central America and Panama
incho. inchoate
INCIDI Institut international des civilisations différentes (International Institute of Differing Civilizations)
incl. incline
including
inclusive
incog. incognito
Incorp. Incorporated
Incorporation
incorr. incorrect
incr. increase
increasing
increment
In.Cr. Instructor Commander
INCREF International Children's Rescue Fund
incun. incunabula
Ind. India(n)
Indiana
Industries
Industry

ind. independent
 index
 indicated
 indication
 indicative
 indirect(ly)
 industry
I.N.D. in nomine Dei (in the name of God)
I.N.D.E.C. Independent Nuclear Disarmament Election Committee
indecl. indeclinable
indef. indefinite
Ind.et-L. Indre-et-Loire
indic. indicative
Ind. Imp. Indiae Imperator (Emperor of India)
indiv. individual
Ind.L. Independent Liberal
Indo-Eur. Indo-European
indre. indenture
Ind.Rep. Independent Republican
Ind.T. Indian Territory
induc. induction
ined. inedita (unpublished)
in ex. in extenso (at length)
Inf. Infantry
inf. inferior
 infinitive
 information
 infra (below)
I.N.F. International Naturist Federation
Infirm. Infirmary
infl. inflated
 influence(d)
Infm. Information
info. information
INFORFILM International Information Film Service
infra dig. infra dignitatem (beneath one's dignity)
Ing. Ingegnere (Engineer)
Ingl. Inghilterra (England)
I.N.G.O. International Non-Governmental Organisation
Inh. Inhaber (proprietor)
I.N.I. in nomine Iesu (in the name of Jesus)
init. initial(ly)
I.N.J. in nomine Jesu (in the name of Jesus)
In.L. Instructor Lieutenant
In.L.Cr. Instructor Lieutenant-Commander
in lim. in limine (at the outset)
in loc. in loco (in place of)
in loc. cit. in loco citato (in the place cited)
inns. innings
Inorg. Inorganic
inorg. inorganic
I.N.P.C. Irish National Productivity Committee
I.N.P.F.C. International North Pacific Fisheries Commission
in pr. in principio (in the beginning)
Inq. Inquisition
INQUA International Union on Quaternary Research

I.N.R.I. Iesus Nazarenus Rex Iudaeorum (Jesus of Nazareth, King of the Jews)
 Imperator Napoleon Rex Italiae (Emperor Napoleon, King of Italy)
Ins. Inspector
 Insulate(d)
ins. inches
 inscribed
 inscription
 inspector
 insular
 insurance
in s. in situ (in original place)
Inscr. Inscribed
 Inscription
INSDOC Indian National Scientific Documentation Centre
I.N.S.E.A. International Society for Education through Art
insep. inseparable
In.S.L. Instructor Sub-Lieutenant
insol. insoluble
insolv. insolvent
Insp. Inspection
 Inspector
Inspec.-Gen. Inspector-General
Inst. Institute
 Institution
 Instructor
inst. instant
 instrument
I.N.S.T. in nomine Sanctae Trinitatis (in the name of the Holy Trinity)
Inst.Act. Institute of Actuaries
Inst.C.E. Institution of Civil Engineers
Inst.D. Institute of Directors
Inst.E.E. Institution of Electrical Engineers
Inst.F. Institute of Fuel
Inst.Gas.E. Institution of Gas Engineers
Inst.H.E. Institution of Highway Engineers
instl. installation
Inst.M.E. Institute of Marine Engineers
Inst.Mech.E. Institution of Mechanical Engineers
Inst.Met. Institute of Metals
Inst.M.M. Institution of Mining and Metallurgy
Instn. Institution
Inst.P. Institute of Physics
Inst.Pckg. Institute of Packing
Inst.Pet. Institute of Petroleum
Inst.P.I. Institute of Patentees and Inventors
Instr. Instructor
 Instrument(al)
Inst.R. Institute of Refrigeration
Inst.W. Institute of Welding
Inst.W.E. Institution of Water Engineers
in sum. in the summary
Int. Intercept
int. intelligence
 interest
 interim
 interior
 interjection

cont.

intermediate
internal
international
interpretation
interpreted
interval
intransitive
intag. intaglio
int. al. inter alia (amongst other things)
INTAPUC International Association of Public Cleansing
intcl. intercoastal
int.comb. internal combustion
intens. intensive
Inter. Intermediate
INTERASMA International Association of Asthmology
intercom. intercommunication
INTEREXPO Comité des organisateurs de participations collectives nationales aux manifestations économiques internationales (Committee of Collective National Participation in International Fairs)
INTERFILM International Inter-Church Film Centre
INTERFRIGO International Railway-Owned Company for Refrigerated Transport
INTERLAINE Comité des industries lainières de la C.E.E. (Committee for the Wool Industries of the E.E.C.)
Internat. International
INTERPHOTO Fédération internationale des négociants en photo et cinéma (International Federation of Photograph and Cinema Dealers)
INTERPOL International Criminal Police Organisation
interrog. interrogation
interrogatively
INTERSTENO International Federation of Shorthand and Typewriting
I.N.T.O. Irish National (Primary) Teachers' Organisation
intr(ans). intransitive
in trans. in transit
introd. introduced
introduction
I.N.T.U.C. Indian National Trade Union Congress
I.Nuc.E. Institution of Nuclear Engineers
Inv. Inverness
Investment
inv. invented
inventor
inverted
invoice
Io. Iowa
I.O. India Office
Inspecting Officer
Intelligence Officer
I/O. Inspecting Order
I.O.A.T. International Organisation Against Trachoma
I.O.B. Institute of Bookkeepers
Institute of Brewing
I.o.B. Institute of Bankers
Institute of Builders
I.O.B.I. Institute of Bankers in Ireland

I.O.B.S. Institute of Bankers in Scotland
I.O.C. Initial or Interim Operational Capability
Inter-Governmental Oceanographic Commission
International Olympic Committee
I.O.C.U. International Organisation of Consumers' Unions
I.O.C.V. International Organisation of Citrus Virologists
I.O.D.E. Independent Order of Daughters of the Empire (Canada)
I.O.E. International Office of Epizootics
International Organisation of Employers
I.O.F. Independent Order of Foresters
Institute of Fuel
I.o.F. Institute of Fuel
I. of A. Instructor of Artillery
I. of Arb. Institute of Arbitrators
I. of E. Institute of Export
I. of M. Isle of Man
I.O.F.S.I. Independent Order of the Free Sons of Israel
I.O.G.T. International Order of Good Templars
I.O.J. International Organisation of Journalists
I.o.J. Institute of Journalists
I.O.M. Institute of Metals
Institute of Office Management
Institution of Metallurgists
Isle of Man
Indian Order of Merit
I.O.M.E. Institute of Marine Engineers
I.O.M.T.R. International Office for Motor Trades and Repairs
Ion. Ionic
I.o.N. Institute of Navigation
I.O.O. Inspecting Ordnance Officer
I.O.O.F. Independent Order of Odd Fellows
I.O.O.T.S. International Organisation of Old Testament Scholars
International Organisation for Old Testament Studies
I.O.P. Institute of Packaging
Institute of Petroleum
Institute of Physics
Institute of Plumbing
Institute of Printing
I.O.P.A.B. International Organisation of Pure and Applied Biophysics
I.O.Q. Institute of Quarrying
I.O.R. Independent Order of Rechabites
I.O.R.S. International Orders' Research Society
I.O.S. International Organisation for Standardisation
I.O.S.A. Incorporated Oil Seed Association
I.O.S.M. Independent Order of the Sons of Malta
I.O.S.O.T. International Organization for the Study of the Old Testament
I.o.T. Institute of Transport
I.o.T.A. Institute of Traffic Administration

127

I.O.U.

I.O.U. Industrial Operations Unit
 I owe You
I.O.V.P.T. Internationale Organisation für Vakuum-Physik und -Technik (International Organisation for Vacuum Science and Technology)
I.O.V.S.T. International Organisation for Vacuum Science and Technology
I.O.W. Institute of Welding
I.o.W. Isle of Wight
I.O.Z.V. Internationale Organisation für Zivilverteidigung (International Civil Defence Organisation)
I.P. Imperial Preference
 India Paper
 Input Primary
 Instalment Plan
 Institute of Petroleum
I.P.A. India Pale Ale
 Institute of Park Administration
 Institute of Practitioners in Advertising
 Institute of Public Administration
 Institute of Public Affairs (Australia)
 International Phonetic Alphabet or Association
 International Police Association
I.P.A.A. International Prisoners' Aid Association
I.P.A.R.A. International Publishers' Advertising Representatives' Association
I.P.B.A.M. International Permanent Bureau of Automobile Manufacturers
I.P.B.M.M. International Permanent Bureau of Motor Manufacturers
I.P.C. Institute of Public Cleansing
 Inter-African Phytosanitary Commission
 International Poplar Commission
 International Publishing Corporation
I.P.C.A. Industrial Pest Control Association
 International Petroleum Co-operative Alliance
I.P.C.C.I.O.S. Indo-Pacific Council of the International Committee of Scientific Management
I.P.C.L. Institut du petrole, des carburants et lubrifiants (French Fuel Research Institute)
I.P.C.S. Institution of Professional Civil Servants
I.P.D. Individual Package Delivery
 In Praesentia Dominorum (in presence of the Lords of Session)
I.P.E. Institution of Plant Engineers
 Institution of Production Engineers
Ipecac. Ipecacuanha
IPEX International Printing Machinery and Allied Trades' Exhibition
I.P.F. Irish Printing Federation
I.P.F.C. Indo-Pacific Fisheries Council
I.P.G. Independent Publishers' Group
 Industrial Painters' Group
 Industrial Policy Group

i.p.h. impressions per hour
I.P.H.C. International Pacific Halibut Commission
I.P.H.E. Institution of Public Health Engineers
I.P.I. Institute of Patentees and Inventors
 International Press Institute
i.p.i. in partibus infidelium (in the region of the unbelievers)
I.Plant E. Institution of Plant Engineers
I.P.M. Immediate Past Master
 Institute of Personnel Management
I.P.M.S. International Polar Motion Service
I.P.O.E.E. Institution of Post Office Electrical Engineers
I.P.P.F. International Penal and Penitentiary Foundation
 International Planned Parenthood Federation
I.P.R. Institute of Pacific Relations
 Institute of Public Relations
I.P.R.A. Indian Paint Research Association
 International Public Relations Association
I.P.R.E. Incorporated Practitioners in Radio and Electronics
I.Prod.E. Institution of Production Engineers
I.P.S. Incorporated Phonographic Society
 Indian Police Service
 Institute of Public Supplies
 International Confederation for Plastic Surgery
I.P.S.A. International Political Science Association
I.P.S.F. International Pharmaceutical Students' Federation
I.P.T.P.A. International Professional Tennis Players' Association
I.P.T.T. Internationale du personnel des postes, télégraphes et téléphones (Postal, Telegraph and Telephone International)
I.P.U. International Paleontological Union
 International Peasant Union
 International Population Union
 Inter-Parliamentary Union
I.Q. Institute of Quarrying
 Intelligence Quotient
i.q. idem quod (the same as)
i.q.e.d. id quod erat demonstrandum (that which was to be proved)
I.Q.S. Institute of Quantity Surveyors
I.Q.S.Y. International Year of the Quiet Sun
Ir Iridium
Ir. Ireland
 Irish
I.R. Infra-Red
 Inland Revenue
 Inside Right
 Institute of Refrigeration
 Irish Reports
i.r. infra-red

I.R.A. Institute of Registered Architects
International Reading Association
International Recreation Association
Irish Republican Army
I.R.A.S.A. International Radio Air Safety Association
I.R.B. Irish Republican Brotherhood
I.R.B.M. Intermediate Range Ballistic Missile
I.R.C. Industrial Reorganisation Corporation
Infantry Reserve Corps
International Rainwear Council
International Red Cross
International Rice Commission
I.R.C.A. International Railway Congress Association
I.R.D.A. Industrial Research and Development Authority
I.R.D.C. International Rubber Development Committee
Ire. Ireland
I.R.E. Institute of Radio Engineers (U.S.)
I.R.E.C. Irrigation Research and Extension Advisory Committee (Australia)
I.R.E.R. Infra-Red Extra Rapid
I.R.F. International Road Federation
International Rowing Federation
I.R.F.A.A. International Rescue and First Aid Association
I.R.F.V. Internationaler Regenmantelfabrikantenverband (International Rainwear Council)
I.R.G. Internationale des résistants à la guerre (War Resisters' International)
I.R.I. Institution of the Rubber Industry
I.R.I.S. Industrial Research and Information Services
Infra Red Intruder System
I.R.L. Internationaler Ring für Landarbeit (International Agriculture Labour Science Group)
International Registration Letters
I.R.L.C.S. International Red Locust Control Service
I.R.M.C. International Radio-Maritime Committee
Inter-Services Radio Measurements Committee
I.R.M.R.A. Indian Rubber Manufacturers' Research Association
I.R.O. Industrial Relations Officer
Inland Revenue Office
iron. ironic(ally)
I.R.R.D.B. International Rubber Research and Development Board
irreg. irregular
I.R.R.I. International Rice Research Institute
I.R.R.S. Irish Railway Record Society
I.R.S. International Rorschach Society
Irrigation Research Station
I.R.S.E. Institution of Railway Signal Engineers
I.R.S.F. Inland Revenue Staff Federation
I.R.S.F.C. International Rayon and Synthetic Fibres Committee

I.R.S.G. International Rubber Study Group
I.R.T. Institute of Reprographic Technology
I.R.T.E. Institute of Road Transport Engineers
I.R.T.U. International Railway Temperance Union
I.R.U. Industrial Rehabilitation Unit
International Relief Union
International Road Transport Union
I.R.W.C. International Registry of World Citizens
Is. Isaiah
Islands
Isles
I.S. Industrial Society
Information Service
Input Secondary
International Socialists
International Society of Sculptors, Painters and Gravers
Irish Society
Isa. Isaias
Isaiah
I.S.A. Incorporated Society of Authors, Playwrights and Composers
International Schools' Association
International Silk Association
International Sociological Association
I.S.A.B. International Scholastic Advisory Bureau
I.S.A.E. Internacia Scienca Asocio Esperantista (International Esperantist Scientific Association)
I.S.A.L.P.A. Incorporated Society of Auctioneers and Landed Property Agents
I.S.A.P.C. Incorporated Society of Authors, Playwrights and Composers
I.S.A.R. International Society for Astrological Research
I.S.A.S. International Screen Advertising Services
I.S.A.W. International Society of Aviation Writers
I.S.B. Internationaler Studentenbund (International Union of Students)
International Society of Biometeorology
i.s.b. independent sideband
I.S.B.A. Incorporated Society of British Advertisers
I.S.B.B. International Society for Bioclimatology and Biometeorology
I.S.C. Imperial Service College
Indian Staff Corps
Interamerican Society of Cardiology
International Sericultural Commission
International Society of Cardiology
International Statistical Classification
International Student Conference
International Sugar Council

I.S.C.A.Y. International Solidarity Committee with Algerian Youth
I.S.C.B. International Society for Cell Biology
I.S.C.E. International Society of Christian Endeavour
I.S.C.E.H. International Society for Clinical and Experimental Hypnosis
ISCERG International Society for Clinical Electroretinography
I.S.C.M. International Society for Contemporary Music
I.S.C.P. International Society of Clinical Pathology
I.S.C.T.R. International Scientific Committee for Trypanosomiasis Research
I.S.D. International Subscriber Dialling
I.S.E. Indian Service of Engineers
Institution of Sanitary Engineers (*now* I.P.H.E.)
Institution of Structural Engineers
I.S.E.C.W. Incorporated Society of Estate Clerks of Works
I.S.F. International Shipping Federation
International Society for Fat Research
International Spiritualist Federation
I.S.F.A. Institute of Shipping and Forwarding Agents
International Scientific Film Association
I.S.G.E. International Society of Gastroenterology
I.S.H. International Society of Haematology
I.S.H.A.M. International Society for Human and Animal Mycology
I.S.H.R.A. Iron and Steel Holding and Realisation Agency
I.S.H.S. International Society for Horticultural Science
I.S.I. Indian Standards Institution
International Statistical Institute
Iron and Steel Institute
I.S.I.B. Inter-Services Ionospheric Bureau
I.S.I.C. International Solvay Institute of Chemistry
I.S.I.M. International Society of Internal Medicine
I.S.I.O. Institute for the Study of International Organisation
Isl. Island
I.S.L.F.D. Incorporated Society of London Fashion Designers
I.S.L.W. Indian Spring Low Water
I.S.L.W.F. International Shoe and Leather Workers' Federation
I.S.M. Iesus Salvator Mundi (Jesus, Saviour of the World)
Imperial Service Medal
Incorporated Society of Musicians
Institute of Service Management
I.S.M.A. Incorporated Sales Managers' Association (*now* I.M.S.M.)
Industrial Safety (Personal Equipment) Manu- *cont.*

facturers' Association
International Superphosphate Manufacturers' Association
I.S.M.E. Institute of Sheet Metal Engineering
International Society for Music Education
I.S.M.H. International Society of Medical Hydrology
I.S.M.I. Institute for the Study of Mental Images
I.S.M.R.C. Inter-Services Metallurgical Research Council
I.S.M.U.N. International Student Movement for the United Nations
I.S.N.P. International Society of Naturopathic Physicians
I.S.O. Companion of the Imperial Service Order
International Shopfitting Organisation
International Standardization Organisation
isol. isolation
I.S.P. Institute of Sewage Purification
Internationale des services publics (Public Services International)
I.S.P.A. International Screen Publicity Association
International Small Printers' Association
International Sporting Press Association
I.S.P.C.C. Irish Society for the Prevention of Cruelty to Children
I.S.P.E. Institute and Society of Practitioners in Electrolysis
I.S.P.E.M.A. Industrial Safety (Personal Equipment) Manufacturers' Association
I.S.P.P. Inter-Services Plastic Panel
I.S.R. Institute of Social Research
International Society of Radiology
I.S.R.B. Inter-Services Research Bureau
I.S.R.C.S.C. Inter-Service Radio Components Standardisation Committee
I.S.R.D. International Society for Rehabilitation of the Disabled
I.S.R.F.C.T.C. Inter-Services Radio-Frequency Cables Technical Committee
I.S.R.R. International Society for Rorschach Research
I.S.R.U. International Scientific Radio Union
I.S.S. Institute for Strategic Studies
International Seismological Summary
International Social Service
I.S.S.A. International Ship Suppliers' Association
International Social Security Association
I.S.S.B. Inter-Service Security Board
I.S.S.C. International Social Science Council
I.S.S.C.B. International Society for Sandwich Construction and Bonding

I.S.S.C.T. International Society of Sugar Cane Technologists
I.S.S.M.F.E. International Society of Soil Mechanics and Foundation Engineering
I.S.S.S. International Society for Socialist Studies
International Society of Soil Science
I.S.T. Institute of Science Technology
I.S.T.A. International Seed Testing Association
I.S.T.C. Iron and Steel Trades' Confederation
I.S.T.D. Imperial Society of Teachers of Dancing
Institute for the Study and Treatment of Delinquency
International Society of Tropical Dermatology
Inter-Services Topographical Department
I.S.T.E.A. Iron and Steel Trades Employers' Association
Isth. Isthmus
I.Struct.E. Institution of Structural Engineers
I.S.T.U. International Student Theatre Union
I.S.U. International Skating Union
I.S.U.S.E. International Secretariat for the University Study of Education
I.S.V. International Scientific Vocabulary
I.S.W.C. International Society for the Welfare of Cripples (*now* I.S.R.D.)
I.S.W.G. Imperial Standard Wire Gauge
It. Italian
Italy
I.T. Income Tax
Indian Territory (U.S.)
Infantry Training
Inner Temple
i.t. in transit
I.T.A. Independent Television Authority
Industrial Transport Association
Institut du transport aérien (Institute of Air Transport)
Institute of Travel Agents
i.t.a. initial teaching alphabet
I.T.A.C. Imperial Three Arts Club
Ital. Italian
Italic
I.T. & T. International Telephone and Telegraph Corporation
I.T.B. Internationaler Turnerbund (International Gymnastic Federation)
International Time Bureau
Irish Tourist Board
I.T.C. Imperial Tobacco Company
Industrial Training Council
Infantry Training Centre
International Tin Council
I.T.C.A. Independent Television Companies' Association
I.T.C.R.M. Infantry Training Centre, Royal Marines
I.T.D.A. Indirect Target Damage Assessment

I.T.F. Internationale Transportarbeiter-Föderation (International Transport Workers' Federation)
I.T.G.W.F. International Textile and Garment Workers' Federation
I.T.G.W.U. Irish Transport and General Workers Union
I.T.I. International Technical Institute of Flight Engineers
International Theatre Institute
International Thrift Institute
itin. itinerary
I.T.M. Institute of Travel Managers
I.T.M.A. Institute of Trade Mark Agents
It's That Man Again
I.T.M.E.B. International Tea Market Expansion Board
I.T.M.R.C. International Travel Market Research Council
I.T.N. Independent Television News
I.T.N.V. Internationaler Transport-Versicherungs-Verband (International Union of Maritime Insurance)
I.T.O. India Tourist Office
International Trade Organisation
Irish Tourist Office
I.T.P.S. Income Tax Payers' Society
I.T.R.C. International Tin Research Council
I.T.S. International Technogeographical Society
International Tracing Service
International Trade Secretariats' Liaison Committee
I.T.T.F. International Table Tennis Federation
I.T.T.T.A. International Technical Tropical Timber Association
I.T.U. International Telecommunication Union
International Temperance Union
I.T.W. Initial Training Wing (R.A.F.)
I.T.X. Inclusive tour excursion
I.T.Z.N. International Trust for Zoological Nomenclature
I.U. Interlingue-Union
International Union
I.U.A. International Union Against Alcoholism
International Union of Advertising
International Union of Architects
I.U.A.A. International Union of Advertisers' Associations
International Union of Alpine Associations
I.U.A.D.M. International Union of Associations of Doctor-Motorists
I.U.A.I. International Union of Aviation Insurers
I.U.A.J. International Union of Agricultural Journalists
I.U.A.O. International Union for Applied Ornithology
I.U.A.S. International Union of Agricultural Sciences
I.U.A.T. International Union Against Tuberculosis

I.U.B. International Union of Biochemistry

International Universities Bureau

I.U.B.S. International Union of Biological Sciences

I.U.C. International University Contact for Management Education

I.U.C.A.F. Inter-Union Committee on Frequency Allocations for Radio Astronomy and Space Science

I.U.C.N. International Union for Conservation of Nature and Natural Resources

I.U.Cr. International Union of Crystallography

I.U.C.W. International Union for Child Welfare

I.U.D. Intra-Uterine Devices

I.U.D.W.& C. Irish Union of Distributive Workers and Clerks

I.U.E.F. International University Exchange Fund

I.U.F. International Union of Food and Allied Workers' Associations

I.U.F.D.T. International Union of Food, Drink and Tobacco Workers' Associations

I.U.F.O. International Union of Family Organisations

I.U.F.R.O. International Union of Forest Research Organisations

I.U.G.G. International Union of Geodesy and Geophysics

I.U.G.S. International Union of Geological Sciences

I.U.H.P.S. International Union of the History and Philosophy of Science

I.U.H.R. International Union of Hotel, Restaurant and Bar Workers (*now merged with* I.U.F.)

I.U.K.P. Internationale Union der Katholischen Presse (International Catholic Press Union)

I.U.L.A. International Union of Local Authorities

I.U.L.C.S. International Union of Leather Chemists' Societies

I.U.L.C.W. International Union of Liberal Christian Women

I.U.M.I. International Union of Marine Insurance

I.U.N.S. International Union of Nutritional Sciences

I.U.O.T.O. International Union of Official Travel Organisations

I.U.P.A. International Union of Practitioners in Advertising

I.U.P.A.C. International Union of Pure and Applied Chemistry

I.U.P.A.P. International Union of Pure and Applied Physics

I.U.P.M. International Union for Protecting Public Morality

I.U.P.S. International Union of Physiological Sciences

I.U.R. International University of Radiophonics and Television

I.U.R.N. Institut unifié de recherches nucléaires (Joint Institute for Nuclear Research)

I.U.S. International Union of Students

I.U.S.D.T. International Union of Social Democratic Teachers

I.U.S.P. International Union of Scientific Psychology

I.U.S.S.I. International Union for the Study of Social Insects

I.U.S.Y. International Union of Socialist Youth

I.U.T.A.M. International Union of Theoretical and Applied Mechanics

I.U.V.D.T. International Union Against the Venereal Diseases and the Treponematoses

I.U.V.S.T.A. International Union for Vacum Science, Technique and Applications

I.U.W.D.S. International Ursigrams and World Days Service

i.v. increased value
initial velocity
in verbo (under the word)
invoice value

I.V.A. Internationale Vereinigung der Anschlussgeleise-Benützer (International Association of Users of Private Sidings)

I.V.A.K.V. Internationale Vereinigung Ärztlicher Kraftfahrer-Verbände (International Union of Associations of Doctor-Motorists)

I.V.B.F. International Volley-Ball Federation

I.V.B.H. Internationale Vereinigung für Brückenbau und Hochbau (International Association for Bridge and Structural Engineering)

I.V.C. International Veterinary Congress

I.V.E. Institute of Vitreous Enamellers
Internationale Vereinigung der Eisenwaren und Eisenhändlerverbände (International Federation of Ironmongers' and Iron Merchants' Associations)

I.V.F. Inter-Varsity Fellowship of Evangelical Unions

I.V.F.Z. International Veterinary Federation of Zootechnics

I.V.J.H. Internationale Vereinigung für Jugendhilfe (International Union for Child Welfare)

I.V.K.M. Internationaler Verband der Katholischen Mädchenschutzvereine (International Catholic Girls' Society)

I.V.L. Internationale Vereinigung für theoretische und angewandte Limnologie (International Association of Theoretical and Applied Limnology)

I.V.L.D. Internationale Vereinigung der Organisationen von Lebensmittel-Detaillisten (International Federation of Grocers' Associations)

I.V.M.B. Internationale Vereinigung der Musikbibliotheken (International Association of Music Libraries)

I.V.R. Internationale Vereinigung des Rheinschiffsregisters (International Association for the Rhine Ships Register)

I.V.S. Internationale Verbindung für Schalentragwerke (International Association for Shell Structures)
International Voluntary Service
I.V.S.S. Internationale Vereinigung für Soziale Sicherheit (International Social Security Association)
I.V.S.U. International Veterinary Students' Union
I.V.T. Internationale Vereinigung der Textileinkaufsverbände (International Association of Textile Purchasing Societies)
I.V.U. International Vegetarian Union
I.V.W.S.R. Internationale Verband für Wohnungswesen, Städtebau und Raumordnung (International Federation for Housing and Planning)
I.W. Inspector of Works
Isle of Wight
i.W. innere Weite (inside diameter)
i.w. inside width
I.W.A. Indian Workers' Association
Inland Waterways Association
International Wheat Agreement
International Women's Auxiliary to the Veterinary Profession
I.W.& D. Inland Waterways and Docks
I.W.C. International Whaling Commission
International Wheat Council
I.W.D. Inland Waterways and Docks
I.W.D.S. International World Days Service
I.W.E. Institution of Water Engineers
I.W.G.C. Imperial War Graves Commission
I.W.H.S. Institute of Works and Highway Superintendents
I.W.M. Institution of Works Managers
I.W.O. International Vine and Wine Office

I.W.R.B. International Wildfowl Research Bureau
I.W.R.M.A. Irish Wholesale Ryegrass Machiners' Association
I.W.R.P.F. International Waste Rubber and Plastic Federation
I.W.S. Industrial Welfare Society (*now* **I.S.**)
Institute of Wood Science
International Wool Secretariat
I.W.S.A. International Water Supply Association
International Workers' Sport Association
I.W.Sc. Institute of Wood Science
I.W.S.G. International Wool Study Group
I.W.S.I. Irish Work Study Institute
I.W.T. Inland Water Transport
I.W.T.(D.) Inland Water Transport (Department)
I.W.T.O. International Wool Textile Organisation
I.W.V. Internationale Warenhaus-Vereinigung (International Association of Department Stores)
I.W.W. Industrial Workers of the World (U.S.)
I.W.Y.F. International World Youth Friendship
I.X. Iesus Christus (Jesus Christ)
I.Y. Imperial Yeomanry
I.Y.C.S. International Young Christian Students
I.Y.E.O. Institute of Youth Employment Officers
I.Y.H.F. International Youth Hostel Federation
I.Y.R.U. International Yacht Racing Union
I.Z. I Zingari
I.Z.D. Internationaler Zivildienst (International Voluntary Service)

J

J. Jack
Jahr (year)
Jew(ish)
Joule
Judge
Justice
j. jour (day)
journal
jus (law)
juris (of law
one
J.A. Joint Account
Judge Advocate
Jac. Jacobean
Jacobus (James)
J.A.C.A.R.I. Joint Action Committee Against Racial Interference
J.A.C.T. Joint Association of Classical Teachers

J.Adv. Judge Advocate
J.A.F. Judge Advocate of the Fleet
J.A.G. Judge Advocate-General
J.A.L. Japan Air Lines
Jam. Epistle of Saint James
Jamaica
Jan. January
J.& K. Jammu and Kashmir
j. & w.o. jettison and washing overboard
Janv. Janvier (January)
Jap. Japan(ese)
jap. japanned
J.A.S. Junior Astronomical Society
J.A.T.C.C. Joint Aviation Telecommunications Co-ordination Committee
j.a.t.o. jet assisted take-off
Jav. Java(nese)

J.A.Y.F. Jersey Association of Youth and Friendship
J.B. John Bull
Jurum Baccalaureus (Bachelor of Laws)
J.B.C.P.S. Journeyman Bakers' and Confectioners' Pension Society
J.B.G. Jewish Board of Guardians
J.B.L. Journal of Business Law
Junior Bird League
Jc. Junction
J.C. Jesus Christ
Jockey Club
Julius Caesar
Juris-consultus (jurisconsult)
Justice-Clerk
Justiciary Cases
Juvenile Court
J.C.A.R. Joint Commission of Applied Radioactivity
J.C.B. Juris Canonici Baccalaureus (Bachelor of Canon Law)
Juris Civilis Baccalaureus (Bachelor of Civil Law)
J.C.B.M.I. Joint Committee for the British Monumental Industry
J.C.C. Joint Consultative Committee
J.C.D. John Chard Decoration
Juris Canonici Doctor (Doctor of Canon Law)
Juris Civilis Doctor (Doctor of Civil Law)
J.C.I. Junior Chamber International
J.C.L. Juris Canonici Licentiatus (Licentiate in Canon Law)
Juris Civilis Licentiatus (Licentiate in Civil Law)
J.C.R. Junior Common Room
J.C.S. Joint Chiefs of Staff
Joint Commonwealth Societies
Journal of the Chemical Society
jd. joined
j.D. Diploma in Journalism
Junior Deacon
Junior Dean(s)
Jurum Doctor (Doctor of Jurisprudence)
J.d. Jordan dinar(s)
J.D.L. Junior Drama League
J.D.R.E.M.C. Joint Departmental Radio and Electronics Measurements Committee
j.e.a. joint export agent
J.E.C.C. Joint Egyptian Cotton Committee
J.E.C.I. Jeunesse étudiante catholique internationale (International Young Catholic Students)
J.E.F. Jeunesses européennes fédéralistes (Young European Federalists)
Jeho. Jehosaphat
J.E.L. Jeunesses européennes libérales (Young European Liberals)
J.E.M. Jerusalem and the East Mission
Jer. Jeremiah
Jeremias
Jerusalem
Jes. Jesus
Jes. Coll. Jesus College (Oxford or Cambridge)
Jew. Jewelry
Jewish

J.F.K. John Fitzgerald Kennedy
J.F.M. Jeunesses fédéralistes mondiales (Young World Federalists) (now W.F.Y.)
J.F.R.O. Joint Fire Research Organization
J.F.T.C. Joint Fur Trade Committee
J.F.U. Jersey Farmers' Union
j.g. junior grade
J.G.R. Jamaica Government Railway
J.G.T.C. Junior Girls' Training Corps
J.G.W. Junior Grand Warden
J.H.D.A. Junior Hospital Doctors Association Ltd.
J.H.M.O. Junior Hospital Medical Officer
J.H.U. Johns Hopkins University (U.S.)
JHVH Jehovah
J.I. Institute of Journalists
J.I.B. Joint Intelligence Bureau
J.I.C. John Innes Cuttings Compost
Joint Industrial Council
Joint Intelligence Committee
Joint Iron Council
J.I.C.T.A.R. Joint Industry Committee for Television Advertising Research
J.I.E. Junior Institution of Engineers
J.I.N.R. Joint Institute for Nuclear Research
J.Inst.E. Junior Institution of Engineers
J.I.O.A. Joint Intelligence Objectives Agency
J.I.P. John Innes Potting Compost
J.I.S. John Innes Seed Compost
Joint Intelligence Staff
JJ. Justices
J.L.B. Jewish Lads' Brigade
J.L.P. Jamaica Labour Party
jls. journals
J.M.A. Joinery Managers' Association
J.M.B. J. M. Barrie
J.M.C.Y. Joseph Malins Crusade of Youth
J.M.J. Jesus, Mary and Joseph
J.M.R.P. Joint Meteorological Radio Propagation Sub-Committee
J.M.S.O. Joint Meetings of Seafarers' Organisations
Jn(c). Junction
J.N.C. Joint Negotiating Committee
J.N.D. Just Noticeable Difference
J.N.F. Jewish National Fund
Jnl(s). Journal(s)
Jnr. Junior
Jnt. Joint
Jo. Joachim
J.O. Journal Officiel (Official Gazette
Jo. Bapt. John the Baptist
J.O.B.S. Job Opportunities in Business Sectors (U.S.)
Jo'burg Johannesburg
joc. jocose(ly)
jocular(ly)
J.O.C. Jeunesse ouvrière chrétienne internationale (International Young Christian Workers)
Jo. Div. John the Divine
Jo. Evang. John the Evangelist
J.O.G. Junior Offshore Group
join. joinery
J.O.T. Joint Observer Team

Jour. Journal
jour. journalist
J.P. Justice of the Peace
j.p. jet-propelled
 jet propulsion
J.P.A. Jamaica Press Association
 Joint Palestine Appeal
J.P.B. Joint Production Board
J.P.C. Joint Production Council
 Judge of the Prize Court
J.P.C.A.C. Joint Production, Consultative and Advisory Committee
J.P.L. Jet Propulsion Laboratory, Pasadena
 Journal of Planning Law
J.P.S. Joint Parliamentary Secretary
 Joint Planning Staff
 Junior Philatelic Society
Jr. Journal
 Junior
 Juror
J.R. Jacobus Rex (King James)
 Judges' Rules
 Jurist Reports
J.R.C. Junior Red Cross
Jr.Gr. Junior Grade
J.S. Johnson Society
 Junior Secondary
J.S.A.W.C. Joint Services Amphibious Warfare Centre
j.s.c. Qualified at a Junior Staff Course or the equivalent
J.S.D. Doctor of Juristic Science
J.S.L.S. Joint Services Liaison Staff
J.S.S.C. Joint Services Staff College
j.s.s.c. Officers who have completed a course at the Joint Services Staff College
jt. joint
J.T.C. Junior Training Corps

J.T.S. Joint Tactical School
J.T.U.A.C. Joint Trade Union Advisory Committee
Ju. June
J.U. Jeunesse universelle (World Youth)
J.U.C.S.P.A. Joint University Council for Social and Public Administration
Jud. Judge(s)
jud. judicial
J.U.D. Juris utriusque Doctor (Doctor of Civil and Canon Law)
Judg. Judge(s)
Jul. July
Jun. June
 Junius
jun. junior
Junc. Junction
Jup. Jupiter
Jur.D. Juris Doctor (Doctor of Law)
Juris. Jurisprudence
jurisd. jurisdiction
Jus. Justice
J.U.S.M.A.G. Joint United States Military Advisory Group
J.U.S.M.A.P. Joint United States Military Advisory and Planning Group
Juss. Jussive
Just. Justinian
Juv. Juvenal
 Juvenile
J.W. Jehovah's Witness(es)
 Junior Warden
J.W.B. Jewish Welfare Board
 Joint Wages Board
J.W.E.F. Joinery and Woodwork Employers' Federation
jwlr. jeweller
J.W.S. Joint Warfare Staff
Jy. July

K

K Kalium
K. Capacity
 Caret
 Kalends
 Kelvin (scale)
 King(s)
 Knight
 Knit
 Kompagnie (Company)
k. cumulus
 keel
 killed
 kilo(s)
 knot
Ka. Komppania (Company)
K.A. King of Arms
 Knight of the Order of Saint Andrew
K.A.D.U. Kenya African Democratic Union
K.A.E. Keighley Association of Engineers

Kal. Kalends
Kan. Kansas
k. & b. kitchen and bathroom
K. & E.S.R.A. Kent and East Sussex Railway Association
K.A.N.T.A.F.U. Kenya African National Traders' and Farmers' Union
K.A.N.U. Kenya African National Union
K.A.R. King's African Rifles
K.A.S. Kent Archaeological Society
K.B. King's Bench
 King's Bishop
 Knight Bachelor
 Knight of the Order of the Bath
 Kolster-Brandes, Limited
 Kommanditbolaget (limited partnership)
K.B.A. Knight of the Order of Saint Benedict of Aviz
K.B.C. King's Bench Court
K.B.D. King's Bench Division

K.B.E. Knight Commander of the Order of the British Empire
Knight of the Order of the Black Eagle

kc. kilocycle(s)

K.C. Kansas City
Kennel Club
King's College
King's Counsel
King's Cross
Knight of Columbus
Knight Commander

K.C.B. Knight Commander of the Order of the Bath

K.C.C. Knight Commander of the Order of the Crown and the Congo Free State
King's College, Cambridge

K.C.H. King's College Hospital
Knight Commander of the Hanoverian Guelphic Order

K.C.H.S. Knight Commander of the Order of the Holy Sepulchre

K.C.I.E. Knight Commander of the Order of the Indian Empire

K.C.L. King's College, London

K.C.L.Y. Kent and County of London Yeomanry

K.C.M.G. Knight Commander of the Order of Saint Michael and Saint George

K.C.N.S. King's College, Nova Scotia

K.C.P. Knight Commander of the Order of Pius IX

K.C.S. King's College School

K.C.S.G. Knight Commander of the Order of Saint Gregory the Great

K.C.S.I. Knight Commander of the Order of the Star of India

K.C.S.S. Knight Commander of Saint Silvester

K.C.V.O. Knight Commander of the Royal Victorian Order

kd. killed

K.D. Knocked Down
Kongeriget Danmark (Kingdom of Denmark)
Kriegsdekoration (War Decoration)

K.d. Kuwait dinar(s)

K.D.F. Kraft durch Freude (Strength through Joy)

K.D.G. King's Dragoon Guards

k.d.l.c.l. knocked down in less than carloads

K.E. Kinetic Energy

Keb. Coll. Keble College, Oxford

K.E.H. King Edward's Horse

K.E.H.F. King Edward's Hospital Fund

K.E.L.I. Kristana Esperantista Ligo Internacia (Christian Esperanto International Association)

Ken. Kentucky

Kes. Keskusosuusliike (Co-operative society)

K.E.V. Kilo Electron Volt(s)

K.F.A. Keep Fit Association
Kenya Farmers' Association

kg. kilogramme(s)

K.G. Knight of the Order of the Garter
Kommanditgesellschaft (limited partnership)

K.Ga.A. Kommanditgesellschaft auf Aktien (limited partnership on share basis)

K.G.B. Komitet Gosudarstvennoi Bezopasnosti (Committee of State Security (Russia))

K.G.C. Knight of the Golden Circle

K.G.C.B. Knight Grand Cross of the Order of the Bath

K.G.C.S.G. Knight Grand Cross of the Order of Saint Gregory the Great

K.G.E. Knight of the Order of the Golden Eagle

Kgf. Kriegsgefangener (Prisoner of War)

K.G.F. Knight of the Order of the Golden Fleece

K.G.F.S. King George's Fund for Sailors

K.G.K. Kabuskiki Goshi Kaisha (joint stock limited partnership)

kgl. königlich (royal)

kg.m. kilogrammetre(s)

Kgs. Kings

K.G.St.J. Knight of Grace of the Order of Saint John of Jerusalem (now K.St.J.)

K.H. Kelvin and Hughes Company, Limited
Knight of the Royal Guelphic Order of Hanover

K.H.C. Honorary Chaplain to the King

K.H.D.S. Honorary Dental Surgeon to the King

K.H.M. King's Harbour Master

K.H.N.S. Honorary Nursing Sister to the King

K.H.P. Honorary Physician to the King

K.H.S. Honorary Surgeon to the King
Knight of the Holy Sepulchre

K.I.A. Killed in Action

K.i.H. Kaisar-i-Hind (Emperor of India)

kil. kilderkin(s)

Kild. Kildare

Kilk. Kilkenny

kilo. kilogram(s)

Kinc. Kincardine

Kinr. Kinross

Kirk. Kirkcudbright

kit. kitchen

K.J.St.J. Knight of Justice of the Order of Saint John of Jerusalem (now K.St.J.)

K.J.V. Kartell Juedischer Verbindungen in Great Britain (Jewish Association in Great Britain)

K.K. Kabushiki Kaisha (Joint stock company)

k.k. kaiserlich-königlich (imperial-royal)

K.K.K. Ku-Klux-Klan

K.Kt. King's Knight

Kl. Klasse (class)

kl. kilolitre(s)

K.L. King Lear (Shakespeare)

K.L.A. Kingdom of Libya Airlines

K.L.J. Knight of Justice of the Order of Saint Lazarus of Jerusalem

K.L.M. Koninklijke Luchtvaart Maatschappij (Dutch Air Lines)

K.M. King's Medal
King's Messenger
Knight of Malta
km. kilometre(s)
K.M.A. Incorporated Association of Kinematograph Manufacturers
K.M.J. Knight of the Military Order of Maximilian Joseph
K.M.O.M. Knight Magistral of the Order of Malta
K.N.L. Knight of the Order of the Netherlands Lion
K.N.S. Knight of the Order of the Royal Northern Star
Knt. Knight
K.O. King's Own
k.o. keep off *or* out
kick-off
knock out
K.O.C. Knight of the Order of the Oak Crown
K. of C. Knight of Columbus
K. of L. Knights of Labor
K. of P. Knights of Pythias
K.O.R.R. King's Own Royal Regiment
K.O.S.B. King's Own Scottish Borderers
K.O.Y.L.I. King's Own Yorkshire Light Infantry
Kp. Kochpunkt (boiling point)
K.P. King's Parade
King's Pawn
Kitchen Police
Knight of Pythias
Knight of the Order of Saint Patrick
➤ **K.P.D.** Kommunistische Partei Deutschlands (German Communist Party)
➤ **K.P.D.R.** Korean People's Democratic Republic
K.P.E. Kenya Preliminary Examination
K.P.F.S.M. King's Police and Fire Service Medal
k.p.h. kilometre(s) per hour
K.P.M. King's Police Medal
K.P.P. Keeper of the Privy Purse
Kr Krypton
Kr. Kreuzer
Krone
K.R. King's Regiment
King's Regulations
King's Rook
Knight of the Order of the Redeemer
Knowledge of results
K.R.A. Kentish Ragstone Association
K.R. & A.L. King's Regulations and Admiralty Instructions
K.R.E. Knight of the Order of the Red Eagle

K.R.R. King's Royal Rifles
K.R.R.C. King's Royal Rifle Corps
K.R.S. Kinematograph Renters' Society
K.S. Keep Type Standing
King's School
King's Scholar
Kitchener Scholar
Kommanditselskabet (limited partnership)
K.S.A. Knight of Saint Anne
K.S.C. King's School, Canterbury
K.S.E. Knight of the Order of Saint-Esprit (Holy Ghost)
K.S.F.M. Knight of the Order of Saint Ferdinand and Merit
K.S.G. Knight of the Order of Saint George
Knight of the Order of Saint Gregory the Great
K.S.H. Knight of the Order of Saint Hubert
K.S.L. Knight of the Order of the Sun and Lion
K.S.L.I. King's Shropshire Light Infantry
K.Soc. Kamashastra Society
K.S.P. Knight of the Order of Saint Stanislaus of Poland
K.S.S. Knight of the Southern Star
K.St.J. Knight Commander of the Order of Saint John of Jerusalem
K.S.V. Knight of the Order of Saint Vladimir
Kt. Knight
kt. knot
K.T. Knight of the Order of the Thistle
Knight Templar
Kt.Bach. Knight Bachelor
K.T.D.F. Knitted Textile Dyers Federation
kts. knots
K.T.S. Knight of the Order of the Tower and Sword
k.V. kilovolt(s)
k.V.A. kilovolt-ampère(s)
k.V.A.h. kilovolt-ampère hour(s)
K.v.K. Kriegsverdienstkreuz (War Merit Cross, Germany)
K.W. Knight of the Order of William
k.W. kilowatt(s)
K.W.E. Knight of the Order of the White Eagle
k.W.h. Kilowatt hour(s)
K.W.I.C. Keyword-in-Context
Ky. Kentucky
ky. kyat
Kybd. Keyboard

L

L Fifty (Roman numerals)
Inductance
latent heat per molecule
L. Labour
Lambert
Latin
Learner
Lethal
Leu
Liber (book)
Liberal
Licentiate
Lieutenant
Light colour
Linnaeus
Lire
London
Lord
Luxembourg
Pound Sterling
l. elbow
lady
lake
lambda
large
latitude
law
leaf
league
left
legitimate
length
light
lightning
line(s)
link
literate
litre(s)
little
livre (book)
locus (place)
long
lost
low
lumen
pound
La Lanthanum
La. Louisiana
la. last
L.A. Law Agent
Leave Allowance
Legal Adviser
Legislative Assembly
Library Association
Licensing Act
Lieutenant-at-Arms
Light Alloy
Literate in Arts
Liverpool Academy
Lloyd's Agent
Local Association
Local Authority
Long Acting
Los Angeles
Low Altitude
L/A. Letter of Authority
l.a. lege artis (by the rules of the art)
local agent

l/a. letter of advice
L.A.A. Lancashire Authors' Association
Lieutenant-at-Arms
Light Anti-Aircraft
London Angling Association
L.A.A.O.H. Ladies' Auxiliary, Ancient Order of Hibernians
Lab. Labour Party
Labrador
lab. laboratory
labour(er)
L.A.B. Laboratory Animals Bureau
Low Altitude Bombing
L.A.C. Licentiate of the Apothecaries' Company
Leading Aircraftman
London Athletic Club
L.A.C.I. London Association of Conference Interpreters
L.A.C.W. Leading Aircraftwoman
L.A.D. Light Aid Detachment
L.A.D.H.M.A. Leicester and District Hosiery Manufacturers' Association Ltd.
Ladp. Ladyship
L.A.D.S.I.R.L.A.C. Liverpool and District Scientific, Industrial and Research Library Advisory Council
L.Adv. Lord Advocate
L.A.E. London Association of Engineers
laev. laevus (left)
La.F. Louisiana French
L.A.F.C. Latin-American Forestry Commission
L.A.-F.C. London Anti-Fluoridation Campaign
L.A.F.D. London Association of Funeral Directors
L.A.F.T.A. Latin-American Free Trade Association
L.A.G.B. Linguistics Association of Great Britain
L.A.H. Licentiate of the Apothecaries' Hall
L.A.H.S. Leicestershire Archaeological and Historical Society
L.A.I. Library Association of Ireland
Lam. Lamark
Lamentations
lam. laminated
L.A.M. Liberalium Artium Magister (Master of the Liberal Arts)
London Academy of Music and Dramatic Art
L.A.M.A. Locomotive and Allied Manufacturers' Association of Great Britain
L.A.M.D. London Association of Master Decorators
L.A.M.D.A. London Academy of Music and Dramatic Art
L.A.M.G. Laban Art of Movement Guild
L.A.M.I.D.A. Lancashire and Merseyside Industrial Development Association
L.A.M.I.T. Local Authorities Mutual Investment Trust

L.A.M.P. Liaison of Actors, Management and Playwrights
L.A.M.P.S. London Area Mobile Physiotherapy Service, Ltd.
L.A.M.S. London Association of Master Stonemasons
L.A.M.S.A.C. Local Authorities Management Service and Computer Committee
L.A.N. Local Apparent Noon
Lanc. Lancerast
Lancs. Lancashire
L.& D. Loans and Discounts
    Loss and Damage
L.& I.D. London and India Docks
L. & N.R.R. Louisville and Nashville Railroad
L.& N.W.R. London and North-Western Railway
L.& S.W.R. London and South-Western Railway (*became* S.R. *until nationalization*)
Landw. Landwirtschaft (agriculture)
L.& W. Living and Well
L. & Y.R. Lancashire and Yorkshire Railway (*became* L.M.S.R. *until nationalization*)
Lang. Language(s)
    Languedoc
Lan.R.(P.W.V.) Lancashire Regiment (Prince of Wales' Volunteers)
L.A.O. Licentiate of Obstetric Science
L.A.O.S.A. Librarianship and Archives Old Students' Association
Lap. Lapland
L.A.P. London Airport
L.A.P.A. London Adventure Playground Association
L.A.P.E.S. Low Altitude Parachute Extraction System
Lapp. Lappish
L.A.P.T. London Association for Protection of Trade
L.A.R.C. Libyan-American Reconstruction Commission
larg. largeur (width)
    largamente (broadly)
Laryngol. Laryngology
L.A.S. Land Agents' Society
    Licentiate of the Society of Apothecaries
    London Appreciation Society
    Lord Advocate of Scotland
L.A.S.A. Laboratory Animal Science Association
L.A.S.E.R. Light amplification by stimulated emission of radiation
Lash lighter-aboard-ship
L.A.S.R.A. Leather and Shoe Research Association (New Zealand)
L.A.S.S.A. Licensed Animal Slaughterers and Salvage Association
L.A.S.T. London Association of Science Teachers
Lat. Latin
    Latitude
    Latvia
lat. lateral
    latus (wide)
L.A.T. Local Apparent Time
L.A.T.A. Land Amenities and Transport Association

L.A.T.C.R.S. London Air Traffic Control Radar Station
latd. latitude
lat. ht. latent heat
Latv. Latvia
L.A.U.A. Lloyd's Aviation Underwriters' Association
law. lawyer
L.A.W. League of American Wheelmen
Laz. Lazarus
lb. libra (pound)
L.B. Baccalaureus Litterarum (Bachelor of Letters)
    Lavatory Basin
    Lectori Benevolo (to the kind reader)
    Left Back
    Light Bomber
    Local Board
l.b. leg bye
    letter box
L.B.A. London Boroughs Association
L.B. & S.C.R. London, Brighton, and South Coast Railway (*became* S.R. *until nationalization*)
L.B.B.A. London Beer Bottlers' Association
L.B.C. Land Bank Commission
    London Builders' Conference
L.B.C.H. London Bankers' Clearing House
L.B.C.M. London Board of Congregational Ministers
L.Bdr. Lance-Bombadier
L.B.D. Little black dress
L.B.F.A. London Builder's Foremen's Association
L.B.H. Length, Breadth, Height
L.B.H.A.S.A. London Business Houses Amateur Sports Association
lb.-in. pound-inch
L.B.J. Lyndon Baines Johnson
L.B.P. Length Between Perpendiculars
L.B.P.C. London Building Productivity Committee
Lbr. Lance-Bombardier
lbs. pounds
L.b.s. Lectori benevolo salutem (to the kind reader, greeting)
lb.t. pound troy
L.B.V. Late Bottled Vintage
l.b.w. leg before wicket
L.C. Lance Corporal
    Landing Craft
    Leander Club
    Left Centre
    Legislative Council
    Level Crossing
    Library of Congress (U.S.)
    Lieutenant Commander
    Livestock Commissioner
    London Cheque
    London Clause
    Lord Chamberlain
    Lord Chancellor
    A Lover's Complaint (Shakespeare)
    Lower Canada
    Lutheran Council of Great Britain
    Scottish Land Court Reports

L/C. Letter of Credit
l.c. label clause
    law courts
    lead covered
    leading cases
    legal currency
    letter card
    loco citato (in the passage already quoted)
    lower case
L.C.A. Licensed Company Auditor
    Liverpool Cotton Association
    London Choir Association
L.C.B. Liquor Control Board
    Lord Chief Baron
l.c.b. longitudinal centre of buoyancy
L.C.C. Lancashire Cotton Corporation, Ltd.
    London Chamber of Commerce
    London County Council(lor) (*now* G.L.C.)
L.C.D. London College of Divinity
    Lord Chamberlain's Department
    Lord Chancellor's Department
    Lower Court Decisions
l.c.d. lowest common denominator
L.C.E. Licentiate in Civil Engineering
l.c.f. longitudinal centre of flotation
    lowest common factor
L.C.F.T.A. London Cattle Food Trade Association
l.c.g. longitudinal centre of gravity
L.C.G.B. Locomotive Club of Great Britain
L.Ch. Licentiatus Chirurgiae (Licentiate in Surgery)
L.C.I.G.B. Locomotive and Carriage Institution of Great Britain and Ireland
L.C.J. Lord Chief Justice
L.C.L. Licentiate of Civil Law
l.c.l. less than carload lots
L.C.M. Landing Craft Mechanized
    London College of Music
l.c.m. lowest common multiple
L.C.N. Local Civil Noon
L.C.O. Landing Craft Officer
L. Col. Lieutenant-Colonel
L.-Corp. Lance Corporal
L.C.P. Last Complete Programme
    Licentiate of the College of Preceptors
    London College of Printing
    Low Cost Production
L.C.P. & S.A. Licentiate of the College of Physicians and Surgeons of America
L.C.P. & S.O. Licentiate of the College of Physicians and Surgeons of Ontario
L.Cpl. Lance Corporal
L.Cr. Lieutenant-Commander
l/cr. letter of credit
L.C.S. Left of Centre Society
L.C.S.G. London Construction Safety Group
L.C.S.S. London Council of Social Service
L.C.T. Landing Craft Tank
    Local Civil Time
L.C.T.A. London Continuative Teachers' Association   *cont.*

    London Corn Trade Association Ltd.
L.C.U. Large Close Up
L.C.V. Licentiate of the College of Violinists
L.C.W.I.O. Liaison Committee of Women's International Organisations
Ld. Limited
    Lord
ld. land
    lead
    load
L.D. Doctor of Letters
    Lady Day
    Laus Deo (Praise be to God)
    lepide dictum (wittily said)
    Lethal Dose
    Licentiate in Divinity
    Light Dragoons
    London Docks
    Low Dutch
l.d. lethal dose
    light difference
    line of departure
    line of duty
lda. limitada (limited)
L.D.A. Lead Development Association —
L.D.C. Less Developed Countries
l.d.c. lower dead centre
ldg. landing
    leading
    loading
    lodging
ldg. & dely. landing and delivery
ldgs. lodgings
L.d'H. Légion d'Honneur (Legion of Honour)
L.Div. Licentiate in Divinity
L.D.M.A. London Discount Market Association
Ldn. London
L.D.O.S. Lord's Day Observance Society
Ldp. Ladyship
    Lordship
L.D.P.D. Liberal-Demokratische Partei Deutschlands (Liberal Democratic Party of East Germany)
Ldr. Leader
ldr. ledger
ldry. laundry
Lds. Lords
lds. loads
L.D.S. Lakeland Dialect Society
    Latter Day Saints
    Licentiate in Dental Surgery
L.D.V. Litter defence volunteers
    Local Defence Volunteers (*later* H.G.)
L.D.X. Long Distance Xerography
L.D.Y. Leicestershire and Derbyshire Yeomanry
L.E. Labour Exchange
    Left Eye
l.e. library edition
    limited edition
lea. league
    leather
    leave
L.E.A. Local Education Authority
L.E.A.P. Loan and Educational Aid Programme

L.E.A.P.S. London Electronic Agency for Pay and Statistics
Leb. Lebanon
L.E.B. London Electricity Board
L.E.C. Local Employment Committee
L.E.C.E. Ligue européenne de coopération économique (European League for Economic Cooperation)
lect. lectio (lesson)
    lecture
L.E.C.T. League for the Exchange of Commonwealth Teachers
lectr. lecturer
led. ledger
L.E.D.C. Lighting Equipment Development Council
l.e.f. liberté, égalité, fraternité (liberty, equality, fraternity)
Leg. Legation
    Legierung (alloy)
    Legislative
    Legislature
leg. legato
    legal
    legit (he *or* she reads)
    legunt (they read)
legg. leggiero (light and rapid)
legis. legislative
    legislature
legisl. legislative
legit. legitimate
leichtl. leichtlöslich (easily soluble)
Leics. Leicestershire
Leip. Leipzig
Le.Is. Leeward Islands
Leit. Leitrim
L.E.L. Laureate in English Literature
    League of Empire Loyalists
Lem. Lempira
L. en D. Licencié en droit (Licentiate of Law)
L.Ens. Licencié en enseignement (Licentiate in Teaching)
L.E.O. Lyons Electronic Office
LEPRA British Leprosy Relief Association
L.E.S. Liverpool Engineering Society
    Licensing Executives Society
L. ès L. Licencié ès lettres (Licentiate in Letters)
L. ès. Sc. Licencié ès sciences (Licentiate in Science)
let. letter
L.E.T.A.T.A. Light Edge Tool and Allied Trades Association
L. et C(h). Loir-et-Cher
L. et G. Lot-et-Garonne
Lett. Lettish
Lev. Levant
    Leviticus
L.E.V. Lunar Excursion Vehicle
Lex. Lexicon
Lexicog. Lexicography
lexicog. lexicographical
    lexicographer
L.E.Y. Liberal European Youth
Leyd. Leyden
lf. leaf
L.F. Lancashire Fusiliers
l.f. ledger folio
    light face
    low frequency

L.F.A. London Floorcovering Association
    London Football Association
l.f.a. local freight agent
L.F.B. London Fire Brigade
L.F.B.C. London Federation of Boys' Clubs
L.F.C. London Fencing Club
    Lutheran Free Church
l.f.c. low frequency current
Lfd. Longford
lfd. laufend (current)
L.F.D. Least Fatal Dose
    Low Fat Diet
L.F.D.C. Light Façades Development Council
L.F.E. London Fixtures Exchange
    London Fur Exchange
lfg. lieferung (portion)
L.F.M. London and South Eastern Furniture Manufacturers' Association
L.F.P.S. Licentiate of the Faculty of Physicians and Surgeons
L.F.P.S. (G.) Licentiate of the Faculty of Physicians and Surgeons (Glasgow)
lft. leaflet
l.ft. linear foot *or* feet
L.F.T.A. London Flour Trade Association
lg. long
L.G. Landing Ground
    Large Grain
    Lewis Gun
    Life Guards
    Lloyd George
    London Gazette
    Low German
L.G.A.R. Ladies of the Grand Army of the Republic (U.S.)
L.G.B. Local Government Board
L.G.C. Laboratory of the Government Chemist
lge. large
L.G.E.B. Local Government Examination Board
L.-Gen. Lieutenant-General
L.-Ger. Low-German
L.G.I.O. Local Government Information Office for England and Wales
L.G.M. Lloyd's Gold Medal
L.G.O.C. London General Omnibus Company
L.-Gr. Low-Greek
L.G.R. Local Government Reports
L.G.S.M. Licentiate of the Guildhall School of Music
lgth. length
lg.tn. long ton
L.G.U. Ladies' Golf Union
L.H. Left Hand
    Left Half
    Legion of Honour
    Licensing Hours
    Licentiate of Hygiene
    Light Horse
l.h. left hand
L.H.A. Local Health Authority
    London Hemp Association
    Lord High Admiral
    Lower Hour Angle
L.H.A.R. London, Hull, Antwerp, or Rotterdam

l.h.b. left halfback
L.H.C. Lord High Chancellor
L.H.D. Litterarum Humaniorum Doctor (Doctor of the more humane letters)
L.Heb. Late Hebrew
L.H.I. Ligue homéopathique internationale (International Homeopathic League)
L.H.M.C. London Hospital Medical College
L.H.O. Livestock Husbandry Officer
l.hr. lumen hour
L.H.S. Left Hand Side
L.H.T. Lord High Treasurer
Li. Lithium
li. link
   lira
L.I. Leeward Islands
   Liberal International (World Liberal Union)
   Licentiate of Instruction
   Light Infantry
   Ligue internationale de la représentation commerciale (International League of Commercial Travellers and Agents)
   Long Island
l.i. letter of introduction
   longitudinal interval
Lib. Liberal Party
   Liberia
   Librarian
   Library
L.I.B.A. Lloyd's Insurance Brokers' Association
lib.cat. library catalogue
Lib.Cong. Library of Congress (U.S.)
L.I.B.E. Ligo Internacia de Blindaj Esperantistoj (International League of Blind Esperantists)
Lic. Licenciado (Attorney)
L.I.C.C.D. Ligue internationale contre la concurrence déloyale (International League Against Unfair Competition)
L.I.Ceram. Licentiate of the Institute of Ceramics
Lic. Med. Licentiate in Medicine
Lic. Theol. Licentiate in Theology
L.I.D.A.S.E. Lecturer in Design and Analysis of Scientific Experiments
L.I.D.C. Lead Industries Development Council
L.I.D.H. Ligue internationale des droits de l'homme (International League for the Rights of Man)
L.I.D.I.A. Liaison internationale des industries de l'alimentation (International Liaison for the Food Industries)
L.I.E.N. Ligue internationale pour l'éducation nouvelle (New Education Fellowship (International))
Lieut. Lieutenant
L.I.F. Lighting Industry Federation Ltd.
L.I.Fire E. Licentiate of the Institution of Fire Engineers
L.I.F.O. Last in, First out

L.I.F.P.L. Ligue internationale de femmes pour la paix et la liberté (Women's International League for Peace and Freedom)
Lig. Liguria
   Limoges
L.I.H.G. Ligue internationale de hockey sur glace (International Ice Hockey Federation)
L.I.L. Laporte Industries Limited
L.I.L.A. Ligue internationale de la librairie ancienne (International League of Antiquarian Booksellers)
L.I.L.O. Last in, Last out
Lim. Limerick
   Limit
L.I.M.P.L. Liga Internacional de Mujeres pro Paz y Libertad (Women's International League for Peace and Freedom)
lin. lineal
   linear
   lines
   liniment
Linc.Coll. Lincoln College, Oxford
Lincs. Lincolnshire
Lindl. Lindley
L.Infre. Loire-Inférieure
lin.ft. linear foot or feet
ling. linguistics
Linn. Linnaeus
   Linnean
Lino. Linotype
lino. linoleum
   linotype
L.I.O.B. Licentiate of the Institute of Building
L.I.P. London International Press, Ltd.
l.i.p. life insurance policy
liq. liquid
   liquor
L.I.R.A. Lambeg Industrial Research Association
   Linen Industry Research Association
L.I.R.I. Leather Industries Research Institute (South Africa)
L.I.R.R. Long Island Railroad Company
L.I.S. List and Index Society
Lit. Literally
   Literary
   Litterae (Letters)
lit. literature
Lit.D. Litterarum Doctor (Doctor of Letters)
Lith. Lithuania(n)
Litho. Lithography
Lithog. Lithographical
Lit.Hum. Litterae Humaniores (the Humanities)
lit(s). literal(s)
Litt.B. Litterarum Baccalaureus (Bachelor of Letters)
Litt.D. Litterarum Doctor (Doctor of Letters)
Litt.D.(Econ.) Doctor of Letters in Economic Studies
Litt.M. Litterarum Magister (Master of Letters)
Liturg. Liturgies
   Liturgical

Liv. Liverpool
    Livre (book)
    Livy (Titus Livius)
    pound
liv.st. livre sterling (pound sterling)
L.J. Lord Justice
l.j. laufenden Jahres (current year)
L.J.A. London Jute Association
L.J.C. London Juvenile Courts
L.JJ. Lords Justices
L.J.S. London Judo Society
Lk. Luke
L.K.A. Ladies' Kennel Association
lkg.& bkg. leakage and breakage
L.K.Q.C.P.I. Licentiate of the King and Queen's College of Physicians, Ireland (*now* L.R.C.P.I.)
lkr. locker
ll. leaves
    leges (laws)
    lines
    not to end a line
L.L. Late Latin
    Law List
    Lending Library
    Lend-Lease
    Limited Liability
    Lord Lieutenant
    Lower Limb
    Loyalist League of Rights
L.-L. Low Latin
l.l. loco laudato (in the place quoted)
L.L.A. Lady Literate in Arts
LL.AA.II. Leurs Altesses Impériales (Their Imperial Highnesses)
LL.AA.RR. Leurs Altesses Royales (Their Royal Highnesses)
LL.B. Legum Baccalaureus (Bachelor of Laws)
L.L.C.M. Licentiate of the London College of Music
LL.D. Legum Doctor (Doctor of Laws)
LL.EE. Leurs Excellences (Their Excellencies)
LL.ÉÉ. Leurs Éminences (Their Eminences)
L.Lett. Licentiate of Letters
L.L.I. Lord-Lieutenant of Ireland
L.LL. Licentiate in Laws
L.L.L. Loose Leaf Ledger
    Love's Labour's Lost (Shakespeare)
LL.M. Legum Magister (Master of Laws)
LL.MM. Leurs Majestés (Their Majesties)
L.L.S.B.A. Leicester Longwool Sheepbreeders' Association
L.L.U. Lending Library Unit
L.L.V. Lunar Logistic Vehicle
L.M. Legion of Merit
    Licentiate in Medicine
    Licentiate in Midwifery
    Licentiate in Music
    London Museum
    Long Metre
    Lord Mayor
l.M. laufenden Monats (of the current month)
l.m. locus monumenti (place of the monument)

L.M.A. Linoleum Manufacturers' Association
    London Mayors Association
L.M.A.G.B. Locomotive and Allied Manufacturers' Association of Great Britain
L.M.B.A. London Master Builders' Association
L.M.B.B.I. London Master Bakers' Benevolent Institution
L.M.C. Lloyd's Machinery Certificate
    London Musical Club
l.m.c. low middling clause
L.M.C.A. Lorry Mounted Crane Association
L.M.C.C. Licentiate of the Medical Council of Canada
L.M.D. Local Medical Doctor
    Long Metre Double
L.M.E. London Metal Exchange
L.Med. Licentiate in Medicine
L.M.F.A. Light Metal Founders' Association
L.M.G. Light Machine-Gun
L.M.H. Lady Margaret Hall, Oxford
lm.hr. lumen hour(s)
L.M.M.A. London Wholesale Millinery Manufacturers' Association
L.M.P.A. London Master Plasterers' Association
    London Master Printers' Alliance
L.M.P.F.A. London and Middlesex Playing Fields Association
L.M.R. London Midland Region (British Rail)
L.M.R.C.P. Licentiate in Midwifery of the Royal College of Physicians
L.M.R.S.H. Licentiate Member of the Royal Society for the Promotion of Health
L.M.S. Licentiate in Medicine and Surgery
    London Mathematical Society
    London, Midland and Scottish Railway (*before nationalization*)
    London Missionary Society
    London Municipal Society
L.M.S.S.A. Licentiate in Medicine and Surgery of the Society of Apothecaries
L.M.T. Length, Mass, Time
    Local Mean Time
L.M.T.A. London Master Typefounders' Association
L.M.T.P.I. Legal Member of the Town Planning Institute
L.M.U.A. Lloyd's Motor Underwriters' Association
L.Mus. Licentiate of Music
L.Mus.T.C.L. Licentiate in Music of the Trinity College of Music, London
L.Nat. Liberal National
L.N.C. League of Nations Covenant
L.N.E.R. London and North Eastern Railway (*before nationalization*)
L.N.H.S. London Natural History Society
L.N.P.I.B. Loch Ness Phenomena Investigation Bureau

Lnrk. Lanark
L.N.U. League of Nations Union
L.O. Liaison Officer
    Local Oscillator
l.o. leur ordre (their order)
    lubricating oil
L.O.A. Leave of Absence
    Life Officers' Association
l.o.a. length over all
loadg. & dischg. loading and discharging
L.O.A.S. Loyal Order of Ancient Shepherds
L.O.B. Location of Offices Bureau
loc. local
    location
    locative
L.O.C. Library of Congress (U.S.)
    Lines of Communications
l.o.c. letter of credit
loc.cit. loco citato (at the place mentioned)
loc.laud. loco laudato (in the place cited)
locn. location
loco. locomotive
loc. primo cit. loco primo citato (in the place first cited)
L.O.D. The Little Oxford Dictionary
L.O.F.A. Leisure and Outdoor Furniture Association
L. of C. Library of Congress (U.S.)
    Lines of Communication
L. of N. League of Nations
L. of P. Lodge of Perfection
log. logarithm
    logic
    logistic(s)
Lond. London
    Londonderry
Londin. Londoninensis (of London)
Lond. Off. Bishop of London's Office
Long. Longford
    Longitude
Longl. Longitudinal
L.O.O.M. Loyal Order of Moose
loq. loquitur (he *or* she speaks)
L.Or. Licencié en orientation (Licentiate in Orientation)
L.O.S. Latin Old Style
lösl. löslich (soluble)
lot. lotion
Lot-et-Gar. Lot-et-Garonne
Lou. Louisiana
    Louth
LOX Liquid Oxygen
    Liquid Oxygen Explosive
Loz. Lozère
Lp. Ladyship
    Lordship
lp. limp
L.P. Labour Party
    Large Paper
    Large Post
    Last Post
    Legal Procurator
    Liberal Party
    Life Policy
    Liquid Petroleum
    Long Playing
    Lord Provost
L./P. Letterpress

l.p. large paper
    low pressure
L.P.A. Leather Producers' Association for England
L.P.A.A. London Poster Advertising Association
L.P. & K.T.F. London Printing and Kindred Trades' Federation
L.P.C. Lord President of the Council
L.P.C.M. London Police Court Mission
L.Ped. Licentiate of Pedagogy
L.P.F.A. Laminated Plastics Fabricators Association
L.P.F.S. London Playing Fields Society
    London Public Fur Sales
L.Ph. Licentiate of Philosophy
L.P.M. Long Particular Metre
L.P.M.A. Methodist Local Preachers' Mutual Aid Association
L.P.N. Legio Patria Nostra (The Legion is our Fatherland)
    Licenced Practical Nurse
L.P.O. Liberal Party Organisation
    Local Posts Officer
    Local Purchasing Officer
    London Philharmonic Orchestra
L'pool Liverpool
L.P.P.T.F.S. London and Provincial Printing Trades' Friendly Society
L.P.S. London Philharmonic Society
    Lord Privy Seal
L.Ps.Péd. Licencié en psycho-pédagogie de l'enfance inadaptée (Licentiate in Psychoeducation of Handicapped Children)
L.Ps.Sc. Licencié en psychologie scolaire (Licentiate in Psychoeducation Counselling)
L.P.T.B. London Passenger Transport Board (*now* L.T.E.)
l.p.w. lumens per watt
Lpz. Leipzig
L.Q.R. Law Quarterly Review
L.Q.T. Liverpool Quay Terms
Lr. Lira
L.R. Land Registry
    Law Report(s)
    Long Range
    Loyal Regiment
    Lowland Regiment
l.R. laufende Rechnung (current account)
l.r. log run
L.R.A. Lace Research Association
    Local Radio Association
L.R.A.C. Law Reports, Appeal Cases
L.R.A.D. Licentiate of the Royal Academy of Dancing
L.R.A.M. Licentiate of the Royal Academy of Music
L.R.B. London Rifle Brigade
L.R.C. Labour Representation Committee
    Leander Rowing Club
    London Rowing Club
L.R.C.A. London Retail Credit Association
L.R.Ch. Law Reports, Chancery Division
L.R.C.M. Licentiate of the Roya lAcademy of Music

L.R.C.P. Licentiate of the Royal College of Physicians

L.R.C.P.E. Licentiate of the Royal College of Physicians of Edinburgh

L.R.C.P.Ed. Licentiate of the Royal College of Physicians of Edinburgh

L.R.C.P.I. Licentiate of the Royal College of Physicians of Ireland

L.R.C.S. League of Red Cross Societies
Licentiate of the Royal College of Surgeons

L.R.C.S.E. Licentiate of the Royal College of Surgeons of Edinburgh

L.R.C.S.Ed. Licentiate of the Royal College of Surgeons of Edinburgh

L.R.C.S.I. Licentiate of the Royal College of Surgeons of Ireland

L.R.C.V.S. Licentiate of Royal College of Veterinary Surgeons

L.R.D. Labour Research Department

L.R.F.P.S. Licentiate of the Royal Faculty of Physicians and Surgeons

L.R.H.L. Law Reports, House of Lords

L.R.I.B.A. Licentiate of the Royal Institute of British Architects

L.R.Ind.App. Law Reports, Indian Appeals

L.R.K.B. Law Reports, King's Bench

L.R.O.C. Land-Rover Owners' Club

L.R.P. Law Reports, Probate Division

L.R.P.S. London Railway Preservation Society

L.R.Q.B. Law Reports, Queen's Bench

Lrs. Lancers

L.R.S. Land Registry Stamp
Lincoln Record Society
Lloyd's Register of Shipping

L.R.S.M. Licentiate of the Royal Schools of Music

L.R.T.L. Light Railway Transport League

L.R.W.E.S. Long Range Weapons Experimental Station

L.S. Law Society
Leading Seaman
Letter Service
Licensed Surveyor
Licentiate in Surgery
Linnean Society
locus sigilli (place of the seal)
London Scottish
Long Shot
Loud Speaker

L.s. Letter (not autograph) signed

l.s. latitude sud (south latitude)
left side
local sunset
locus sigilli (place of the seal)
long sight

L.S.A. Land Settlement Association
Licentiate of Science in Agriculture
Licentiate of the Society of Apothecaries, London
London Sisal Association

L.S.& G.C.M. Long Service and Good Conduct Medal

L.S.B. London School Board

L.S.B.A. Leading Sick-Bay Attendant

L.S.C. Licentiate of Sciences
London Salvage Corps
Lower School Certificate

l.s.c. loco supra citato (in the place before cited)

L.Sc.Act. Licentiate of Acturial Science

L.S.C.B.A. London and Southern Counties Bowling Association

L.Sc.Com. Licencié en sciences commerciales (Licentiate of Commercial Sciences)

L.S.C.I.A. London and Southern Counties Ironmongers' Association

L.Sc.O. Licencié en sciences-optométrie (Licentiate of Optometry)

L.Sc.Pol. Licencié ès sciences politiques (Licentiate in Political Sciences)

LSD lysergic acid diethylamide - 25

L.S.D. League of Safe Drivers
Librae, Solidi, Denarii (pounds, shillings and pence)
Lightermen, Stevedores, Dockers

£.s.d. Librae, solidi, denarii (pounds shillings, pence)

lsd.li. leased line

L.S.E. London School of Economics and Political Science
London Stock Exchange

l.s.e. limited signed edition

Lsg. Lösung (solution)

L.Sgt. Lance Sergeant

L.S.H.T.M. London School of Hygiene and Tropical Medicine

L.S.J.M. Laus sit Jesu et Mariae (Praise be to Jesus and Mary)

L.S.L. Linnean Society of London

l.s.m. litera scripta manet (the written word remains)

L.S.O. London Symphony Orchestra

L.S.P.C. Lead Sheet and Pipe Council (now B.L.M.A.)

L.S.P.G.A. London School of Printing and Graphic Arts

L.S.R.F.U.R. London Society of Rugby Football Referees

L.S.T. Landing Ship Tank
Licentiate in Sacred Theology
Local Standard Time

L.S.W. Licensed Shorthand Writer

Lt. Lieutenant
Light

lt. laut (in accordance with)
lieutenant
light

L.T. Lawn Tennis
Leading Telegraphist
Letter Telegram
Licentiate in Teaching
Licentiate in Theology
Lira Turca (Turkish Pound)
Low Tension

L.t. Long ton(s)

l.t. landed terms
local time
locum tenens (substitute)
low tension

L.T.A. Lawn Tennis Association
London Teachers' Association

L.T.B. London Transport Board (now L.T.E.)

l.t.b. low tension battery

L.T.B.C. Lawn Tennis Ball Convention

L.T.C. Lawn Tennis Club
L.T.C.L. Licentiate of the Trinity College of Music, London
Lt.-Col. Lieutenant-Colonel
Lt.-Comm. Lieutenant Commander
Ltd. Limited
L.T.E. London Transport Executive
L.T.F. Lithographic Technical Foundation
ltg. lettering
L.T.G. Little Theatre Guild of Great Britain
ltge. lighterage
Lt.-Gen. Lieutenant-General
Lt.Gov. Lieutenant Governor
L.Th. Licentiate in Theology
L.T.I.B. Lead Technical Information Bureau
Lt. Inf. Light Infantry
l.t.l. less than truckload
L.T.M. Licentiate of Tropical Medicine
Little Theatre Movement
ltn. lightning
ltng. arr. lightning arrester
L.T.O. Leading Torpedo Operator
L.T.O.S. Law Times, Old Series
ltr. letter
lighter
L.T.R.A. Lands Tribunal Rating Appeals
Lt.R.N. Lieutenant, Royal Navy
L.T.R.S. Low Temperature Research Station
L.T.S. London Topographical Society
London Typographical Society
L.T.S.B. London Trustee Savings Bank
L.T.S.C. Licentiate of the Tonic Solfa College
Lu Lutetium
Lu. Lucerne
L.U. Ligue universelle (espérantiste) (Universal Esperantist League)
Liberal Unionist
L.U.A. Linotype Users' Association
Liverpool Underwriters' Association
lubr. lubricant
lubricate
lubricator
L.U.C. London Union Catalogue
Lucr. Lucretius
The Rape of Lucrece (Shakespeare)
l.u.e. left upper entrance
lu. h. lumen hour(s)
L.U.H.F. Lowest Useful High Frequency
L.U.L.O.P. London Union List of Periodicals
L.U.O.T.C. London University Officers' Training Corps
L.U.S. Land Utilisation Survey (Great Britain)
Luth. Lutheran
Lux. Luxembourg
L.V. Largest Vessel
Licensed Victualler
Low velocity
Luncheon Vouchers
l.v. low voltage
L.V.A. Licenced Victuallers' Association
L.V.C. London Visitors' Club
L.V.D.L. Licensed Victuallers' Defence League of England and Wales
L.V.I. Laus Verbo Incarnato (Praise to the Incarnate Word)
L.V.N.D.L. Licensed Victuallers' National Defence League (*now* N.F.L.V.)
lvs. leaves
L.V.T. Landing Vehicle Tracked
L.W. Left Wing
Long Wave
Low Water
l.W. lichte Weite (internal diameter)
l.w. lumens per watt
L.W.A. London Welsh Association
l.w.b. long wheel base
L.W.C. London Weather Centre
L.W.C.A. London Wholesale Confectioners' Association
L.W.E.S.T. Low Water Equinoctial Spring Tide
L.W.F. Lutheran World Federation
L.W.L. Length on Water Line
Load Waterline
L.W.M. Low Water Mark
L.W.M.M.A. London Wholesale Millinery Manufacturers' Association
L.W.O.N.T. Low Water Ordinary Neap Tide
L.W.O.S.T. Low Water Ordinary Spring Tide
L.W.S. London Wargames Section
L.W.T. London Weekend Television
L.W.T.M.A. London Wool Terminal Market Association
lx. lux (light)
LXX Septuagint
Ly. Lyon
L.Y. Queen's Own Lowland Yeomanry
L.Y.C.C. Lancashire Yorkshire Canary Club
lyr. lyric(al)
L.Z. Landing Zone
L.Zug. Luxus-Zug (German luxury railway train)

M

M One Thousand (Roman numerals)
Magister (Master)
M. Magistrate
Main colour
Majesty
Manipulus (handful)
Mano (hand)
Manual
Marquis *or* Marquess
Martyr
Mate
Medal
Medical
Medicine
Member
Methodist
Metronome
Metropolitan
Mezzo *or* Mezza (half)
Middle
Militia
Minesweeper
Misce (mix)
Missing
Mitte (send)
Mix
Moderate
Monday
Monsieur
Moon
Mother
Mountain
m. maiden (over)
male
manipulus (a handful)
manual
mark
married
masculine
mass
measure
medicine
memorandum
meridian
metre(s)
midday
mile(s)
mille (thousand)
minim
minimum
minor
minute
mist
mixture
molar
month
morning
mort(o) (dead)
Ma Masurium
Ma. Mater (mother)
M.A. Magister Artium (Master of Arts)
Magistrates' Association
Mathematical Association
Mental Age
Middle Ages
Military Academy
Military Aviation   *cont.*

Missionarius Apostolicus (Apostolic Missionary)
Mountaineering Association
m.a. milliampère(s)
m/a. my account
M.A.A. Manufacturers' Agents' Association of Great Britain
Master-at-Arms
Mathematical Association of America
Member of the Architectural Association
Midlands Association for the Arts
Motor Agents' Association
M.A.A.C. Mastic Asphalt Advisory Council
M.A. (Adm. Hosp.) Maître ès arts (administration hospitalière) (Master of Arts (Hospital Administration))
M.A.A.F. Mediterranean Allied Air Force(s)
M.A.A.G. Military Assistance Advisory Group
M.A.A.G.B. Medical Artists' Association of Great Britain
M.A. & F. Ministry of Agriculture and Fisheries (*now* M.A.A.F.)
M.A.A.R.A. Midlands Asthma and Allergy Research Association
M.A.(Arch.) Master of Arts (Architecture)
M.A.A.S. Member of the American Academy of Arts and Sciences
M.A.B. Menswear Association of Britain Ltd.
Metropolitan Asylums Board
M.A.B.S. Manchester Association of Beauty Specialists
mac. macadam
M.A.C. Military aid to the community
Macb. Macbeth (Shakespeare)
Macc. Maccabees
M.A.C.C. Military Aid to the Civilian Community
M.A.C.E. Member of the Australian College of Education
Maced. Macedonia(n)
mach. machine(ry)
machinist
M.A.C.I. Member of the American Concrete Institute
M.A.C.S. Member of the American Chemical Society
M.A.C.T. Member of the Association of Occupational Therapists
M.A.C.V. Military Assistance Command Vietnam (U.S.A.)
Mad. Madame
MADAM Manchester Automatic Digital Machine
M.Admin. Master of Administration
Madr. Madras
Madrid
Mad. Univ. Madison University
Madras University
Ma.E. Master in Engineering

M.A.E. Manchester Association of Engineers

M.A.(Econ.) Master of Arts in Economic Studies

M.A.(Ed.) Master of Arts in Education

M.A.E.E. Marine Aircraft Experimental Establishment

M.A.E.F. Mastic Asphalt Employers' Federation

Maesto. Maestoso majestic and stately)

M.A.F.A. Manchester Academy of Fine Arts

M.A.F.F. Ministry of Agriculture, Fisheries and Food

Mag Magnesium

Mag. Magnetic
Magyar

mag. magazine
magnetic
magnetism
magneto
magnus (great)

M.Ag. Master of Agriculture

M.A.G.B. Microfilm Association of Great Britain

Magd. Magdalen College, Oxford
Magdalene College, Cambridge

M.Ag.Ec. Master of Agricultural Economics

Magg. Maggio (May)

MAGGI Million Ampère Generator

magn. magnus (great)

M.Agr. Master of Agriculture

M.Agr.Sc. Master of Agricultural Science

M.Agr.Sc.(Dairy Tech.) Master of Agricultural Science (Dairy Technology)

M.Agr.Sc.(Hort.) Master of Agricultural Science (Horticulture)

mah. mahogany

M.A.H. Maître en administration hospitalière (Master of Hospital Administration)

M.A. (Hons.) Master of Arts with Honours

M.A.I. Magister in Arte Ingeniaria (Master of Engineering)

M.A.I.Ch.E. Member of the American Institute of Chemical Engineers

M.A.I.E.E. Member of the American Institute of Electrical Engineers

MAILLEUROP Secrétariat des industries de la maille des pays de la C.E.E. (Secretariat of the Knitting and Weaving Industries of the E.E.C. Countries)

M.A.I.M.E. Member of the American Institute of Mining and Metallurgical Engineers

maint. maintenance

Maj. Major(ity)

Maj.-Gen. Major-General

Mal. Malachi
Malaysia(n)
Malta
Maréchal (Marshal)

M.A.L.D. Master of Arts in Law and Diplomacy

M.A.(Lib.Sc.) Master of Library Science

mall. malleable

m. à m. mot à mot (word for word)

M.A.M.P.E. Midland and South Western Association of Master Process Engravers

M.Am.Soc.C.E. Member of the American Society of Civil Engineers

Man. Manager
Manchester
Manila
Manitoba
manufactured

man. management
manual
manufactured

M.A.N. Maschinenfabrik Augsburg-Nürnberg A.G.

M.A.N.A. Music Advisers' National Association

M.Anaes. Master of Anaesthesiology

manc. mancando (gradually softer)

Manch. Manchester
Manchuria(n)

mand. mandamus (we command)

Mand.ap. mandatum apostolicum (apostolic mandate)

M. & B. May and Baker, Limited
Mitchells and Butlers, Limited
Mild and Bitter

M. and D. Medicine and Duty

Man. Dir. Managing Director

M. & O. Managers' and Overlookers' Society

M.& S. Marks and Spencer, Limited

M.& V. Meat and Vegetable

Man. Ed. Managing Editor

manf. manufacturer

M.A.N.F. May, August, November, February

Mang.B. Manganese Bronze

Manit. Manitoba

Man.L.R. Manitoba Law Reports

Man. op. Manually operated

Mans. Mansions

M.A.N.S. Member of the Academy o Natural Sciences (U.S.)

M.A.N.S.A. Man-made Soling Association, Ltd.

manuf. manufacture
manufacturing

manufg. manufacturing

manufs. manufacturers

M.A.N.W.E.B. Merseyside and North Wales Electricity Board

M.A.O. Master of Obstetrics

m.a.o. med andra ord (in other words)

M.A.O.T. Member of the Association of Occupational Therapists

M.A.O.U. Member of the American Ornithologists' Union

M.A.P. Maximum Average Price
Medical Aid Post
Minimum Association Price
Ministry of Aircraft Production
Modified American Plan

M.A.(Ph.) Maître ès arts (philosophie) (Master of Arts (Philosophy))

M.App.Sc. Master of Applied Science

M.A.Public Admin. Master of Arts in Public Administration

M.A.Q. Monmouthshire Associated Quarries, Ltd.

Mar. March
Marine
Maritime
mar. married
M.Ar. Master of Architecture
marc. marcato (marked)
March. Marchioness
M.Arch. Master of Architecture
M.Arch.(C.P.) Master of Architecture (Community Planning)
marg. margin(al)
marg.trans. marginal translation
marit. maritime
mar.lic. marriage licence
Marq. Marquis *or* Marquess
M.A.R.S. Manuel Astronautical Research Station, San Diego
mar.settl. marriage settlement
Mart. Martial
mart. market
martyr
mas. masculine
M.A.S. Master of Applied Science(s) Military Agency for Standardization
M.a.S. Milliampère-second(s)
masc. masculine
M.A.Sc. Master of Applied Science
M.A.S.C.E. Member of the American Society of Civil Engineers
M.A.S.E.R. Microwave Amplification by Stimulated Emission of Radiation
M.A.S.E.S. Management Association of South East Scotland
M.A.S.M.E. Member of the American Society of Mechanical Engineers
Mass. Massachusetts
M.A.(S.S.) Master of Arts in Social Science
Mat. Maternity
mat. matinée
matins
maturity
M.A.T. Manual Arts Therapist
M.A.T.A. Museums Association of Tropical Africa
Math. Mathematical
math. mathematician
mathematical
mathematics
Maths. Mathematics
matr. matrimonium (marriage)
matric. matriculated
matriculation
M.A.T.S. Military Air Transport Service
Matt. Matthew
matut. matutinus (in the morning)
Maur. Mauritius
max. maxim(um)
max. cap. maximum capacity
M.A.Y.C. Methodist Association of Youth Clubs
mb. (millibars)
M.B. Magnetic Bearing
Maritime Board
Marketing Board
Master Bookbinders' Alliance of London
Medical Board
Medicinae Baccalaureus (Bachelor of Medicine) *cont.*

Medium Bomber
Metropolitan *or* Municipal Borough
Milk Bars Association of Great Britain and Ireland, Ltd.
Motor Barge *or* Boat
Musicae Baccalaureus (Bachelor of Music)
m.b. misce bene (mix well)
M.B.A. Marine Biological Association of the United Kingdom
Master of Business Administration
M.B.A.C. Member of the British Association of Chemists
M.B.A.L. Master Bookbinders' Alliance of London
M.B.A.U.K. Marine Biological Association of the United Kingdom
M.B.C. Metropolitan *or* Municipal Borough Council
M.B.C.P.E. Member of the British College of Physical Education
M.B.E. Member of the Order of the British Empire
M.B.F. Master Builders' Federation
Musicians' Benovelent Fund
M.B.F. et H. Magna Britannia, Francia, et Hibernia (Great Britain, France and Ireland)
m.b.H. mit beschränkter Haftung (limited liability)
M.B.I.M. Member of the British Institute of Management
M.B.K. Missing, believed killed
M.B.L. Marine Biological Laboratory
M.B.M. Master of Business Management
M.B.O. Management by objection
M.B.O.U. Member of the British Ornithologists' Union
M.B.P. Mean Blood Pressure
Mbr. Member
M.Bret. Middle Breton
M.Brit.I.R.E. Member of the British Institution of Radio Engineers
M.B.S. Mutual Broadcasting System
M.B.Sc. Master of Business Science
M.B.S.I. Member of the British Boot and Shoe Institution
M.B.T. Main Battle Tank
M.B.W. Metropolitan Board of Works (*later* L.C.C. *now* G.L.C.)
mc. megacycle(s)
millecurie(s)
M.C. Machinery Certificate
Magister Chirurgiae (Master of Surgery)
Magistrates' Court
Magnetic Course
Marine Corps (U.S.)
Maritime Commission (U.S.)
Marked Capacity
Marriage Certificate
Master Commandant
Master of Ceremonies
Master of Congress
Medical Certificate
Medical College
Medical Corps
Member of Congress
Member of Council *cont.*

149

Mennonite Church
Mess Committee
Methodist Church
Millicurie(s)
Military College
Military Committee
Military Cross
Morse Code
Motor Contact
Motor-cycle
M.-C. Medico-Chirurgical
M/C. Marginal Credit
m.c. mois courant (current month)
motor-cycle
M.C.A. Malayan-Chinese Association
Malaysian Commercial Association
Management Consultants' Association
Manufacturing Chemists' Association
Manufactured Copper Association
Matrimonial Causes Act
Ministry of Civil Aviation (now M.o.A.)
M.C.A.A.A. Midland Counties Amateur Athletic Association
M.C. & T.S. Monotype Casters' and Typefounders' Society
M.C.B. Methodist College, Belfast
M.C.C. Mains Cable Council
Marylebone Cricket Club
Meteorological Communications Centre
M.C.C.C. Middlesex County Cricket Club
M.C.C.T.A. Manufacturing Confectioners' Commercial Travellers Association
M.C.D. Doctor of Comparative Medicine
Master of Civic Design
M.C.E. Master of Civil Engineering
Mch. March
M.Ch. Magister Chirurgiae (Master of Surgery)
M.Ch.D. Magister Chirurgiae Dentalis (Master of Dental Surgery)
M.Ch.E. Master of Chemical Engineering
M.Chir. Magister Chirurgiae (Master of Surgery)
M.Ch.Orth. Magister Chirurgiae Orthopaedicae (Master of Orthopaedic Surgery)
M.Chrom. Master of Chromatics
mcht. merchant
m.c.i. malleable cast iron
M.C.I.E. Midland Counties Institution of Engineers
M.C.L. Master of Civil Law
M.Clin. Psychol. Master of Clinical Psychology
M.C.L.O.S.A. Member of the Continental Law Office Society of America
M.Cl.Sc. Master of Clinical Science
M.C.M.A. Mains Cable Manufacturers' Association
M.C.M.E.S. Member of the Civil and Mechanical Engineers' Society
Mco. Morocco

M.C.O. Motor Contact Officer
Movement Control Officer
M.C.O.D.A. Motor Cab Owner-Drivers' Association
M.Coll.H. Member of the College of Handicrafts
M.Com. Master of Commerce
Minister of Commerce
M.Cons.E. Member of the Association of Consulting Engineers
M.C.P. Malayan Communist Party
Master of City Planning
Member of the College of Preceptors
M.C.P.A. Member of the College of Pathologists of Australia
mc.p.s. megacycles per second
M.C.P.S. Mechanical Copyright Protection Society
Member of the College of Physicians and Surgeons
M.C.Q.S. Member of the Chapter of Quantity Surveyors of the South African Institute of Architects
M.C.R. Mass Communications Research
M.C.R.A. Member of the College of Radiologists, Australasia
Montgomery County Recreation Association
M.C.R.S.S.A. Midland Cold Rolled Steel Strip Association
M.C.S. Madras Civil Service
Malayan Civil Service
Master of Commercial Science
Medium Close Shot
M.C.S.P. Member of the Chartered Society of Physiotherapy
M.C.S.T. Manchester College of Science and Technology
M.C.T. Member of the College of Technologists
M.C.U. Modern Churchmen's Union
M.C.W. Maternity and Child Welfare
m.c.w. modulated continuous wave
M.C.W.A.A.A. Midland Counties Women's Amateur Athletic Association
Md Mendelivium
Md. Maryland
md. marchand (dealer)
M.D. Managing Director
Map Distance
Market Day
Medical Department
Medicinae Doctor (Doctor of Medicine)
Memorandum of Deposit
Mentally Deficient
Message-dropping
Mess Deck
Meteorology Department
Middle Dutch
Military District
Monroe Doctrine
Months after Date
Musical Director
m.d. mano destra (right hand)
month's date
more dicto (as directed)
M.D.A. Millinery Distributors Association *cont.*

Muscular Dystrophy Association

M.D.A.P. Mutual Defense Assistance Program (U.S.)

M.D.C. Mechanical Development Committee

Mddx. Middlesex

M.D.E. Master of Domestic Economy

M.Des. Master of Design

M.D.G. Medical Director General

M.D.H.B. Mersey Docks and Harbour Board

M.Di. Master of Didactics

M.D.I.C. Multilateral Disarmament Information Centre

m.dict. more dicto (in the manner directed)

M.Dip. Master of Diplomacy

M.Div. Master of Divinity

mdl. model

Mdlle. Mademoiselle

Mdme. Madame

mdnt. midnight

M.D.P.C.A. Manchester and District Packing Casemakers' Association

m.d.r. minimum daily requirement

Mds. Mesdames

M.D.S. Main Dressing Station
Master of Dental Surgery
Metropolitan Dairymen's Society

M.D.Sc. Master of Dental Science

mdse. merchandise

M.D.S.T. Mountain Daylight Saving Time

M.Du. Middle Dutch

M.D.U. Medical Defence Union

M.D.V. Doctor of Veterinary Medicine

M.D.W. Military Defence Works

Me. Maine
Maître
Messerschmitt

M.E. Marbled Edges
Marine Engineer
Master of Elements
Master of Engineering
Mechanical Engineer
Methodist Episcopal
Middle East(ern)
Military Engineer
Mill Edge
Mining Engineer
Most Excellent
Mottled Edges
Mouvement européen (European Movement)

M.-E. Middle English

m.E. meines Erachtens (in my opinion)

M.E.A. Metropolitan Entertainers' Association
Middle East Airlines

M.E.A.F. Middle East Air Force

meas. measurable
measure
measuring

M.E.(Auto.) Master of Automobile Engineering

M.E.B. Midlands Electricity Board

M.Ec. Master of Economics

M.E.C. Master of Engineering Chemistry
Member of the Executive Council

M.E.C.A.S. Middle East Centre for Arab Studies

M.E.C.C.A. Missionary and Ecumenical Council of the Church Assembly

Mech. Mechanic(al)
Mechanized

M.E.Ch. Methodist Episcopal Church

Mech. E. Mechanical Engineer

M.E.(Chem.) Master of Engineering (Chemical)

M.Econ. Master of Economics

M.Econ.S. Master of Economic Science

Med. Medallist
Medical
Medieval
Mediterranean
Medium

med. median
medical
medicine

M.Ed. Master of Education

M.E.D. Master of Elementary Didactics
Minimal Effective Dose

M.E.D.D. Middle East Development Division

MEDICO Medical International Cooperation

Medit. Mediterranean

Med. Jur. Medical Jurisprudence

M.E.D.L.A.R.S. Medical Literature Analysis and Retrieval System

Med.L(at). Medieval Latin

Med.R.C. Medical Reserve Corps

M.Ed.S. Maître en éducation sanitaire (Master of Health Education)

Med. Sch. Medical School

Med. Tech. Medical Technician
Medical Technologist
Medical Technology

M.E.E. Master of Electrical Engineering

M.E. (Elec.) Master of Engineering (Electrical)

M.E.F. Middle East Force
Mediterranean Expeditionary Force

M.E.G.H.P. Most Excellent Grand High Priest

M.E.I.C. Member of the Engineering Institute of Canada

Mej. Mejuffrouw

M.E.L. Master or Mistress of English Literature

Melan. Melanesia(n)

Melb. Melbourne

M.E.L.F. Middle East Land Force(s)

Mem. Member
Memorial

mem. member
memento (remember)
memorandum

M.E.M.A. Marine Engine and Equipment Manufacturers' Association

M.E.(Mech.) Master of Engineering (Mechanical)

memo. memorandum or memoranda

M.E.N.A. Mixed manned element in Nato's armament

M.Eng. Master of Engineering

M.Eng. and P.A. Master in Engineering and Public Administration

M.Eng.Sc. Master of Engineering Science

M.Ens. Maître en enseignement (Master of Teaching)

Mensur. Mensuration

mentd. mentioned

m.e.p. mean effective pressure

M.E.(Pub.Health) Master of Engineering (Public Health)

Mer. Mercury
    Meridian
    Merioneth(shire)

mer. mercantile
    merchandise
    meridian

M.E.R.B. Mechanical Engineering Research Board

merc. mercantile
    mercurial

M.E.R.L. Mechanical Engineering Research Laboratory

MERLIN Medium Energy Reactor Light Water Industrial Neutron Source

M.E.R.R.A. Middle East Refugee and Relief Administration (*incorporated with U.N.R.R.A.*)

Mert. Merton College, Oxford

M.E.R.U. Mechanical Engineering Research Unit (South Africa)

M. ès A. Maître ès arts (Master of Arts)

Mesd. Mesdames

Messrs. Messieurs

Met. Metaphysical
    Metaphysics
    Meteorological
    Meteorology
    Metronome
    Metropolitan

met. metaphor
    metallurgical

M.E.T. Maître en enseignement technique (Master in Technical Teaching)

M.E.T.A. Model Engineering Trade Association

Metal. Metallurgy

metaph metaphysics
    metaphor(ical(ly))

metath. metathesis
    metathetic

met. bor. metropolitan borough

Met.E. Metallurgical Engineer

Meteor. Meteorology
    Meteorological

Meth. Methodist

meth(s). methylated spirits

M.-et-L. Maine-et-Loire

M.-et-M. Meurthe-et-Moselle

M. et n. mane et nocte (morning and night)

Met. O. Meteorological Officer

M.E.T.O. Middle East Treaty Organisation (*now* CENTO)

meton. metonymy

Met.R. Metropolitan Railway

Metro. Metropolitan Railway

Metrol. Metrology

metrol. metrological

Met.-Vic. Metropolitan-Vickers

Mev. Mevrouw

M.E.V. Mega Electron Volt(s)

M.E.W. Microwave Early Warning
    Ministry of Economic Warfare

Mex. Mexican
    Mexico

M.E.X.E. Military Engineering Experimental Establishment

Mex. Sp. Mexican Spanish

mez. mezzo (half, medium)

M.E.Z. Mitteleuropäische Zeit (Middle European Zone Time)

mezzo. mezzotint

mF. microfarad(s)

mf. millifarad(s)

M.F. Malvern Festival
    Master of Forestry
    Mill-finish
    Minister of Food

m.f. machine finish
    medium frequency
    mezzo-forte (medium loud)
    mill-finish
    moyenne fréquence (intermediate frequency)

m/f. my favour

M.F.A. Master of Fine Arts
    Metal Finishing Association (*now* B.J.A.)
    Metal Fixing Association for Ceiling Systems
    Motor Factors' Association

M.F.A.B.I. Metal Fixing Association for Building Insulation (*now* M.F.A.)

M.F.A.Mus. Master of Fine Arts in Music

M.F.A.R.C.S. Member of the Faculty of Anaesthetists of the Royal College of Surgeons

M.F.B. Metropolitan Fire Brigade (*now* L.F.B.)

M.F.B.T.E. Midland Federation of Building Trades Employers

M.F.C. Mouvement familial chrétien (Christian Family Movement)

mfd. manufactured
    microfarad(s)

M.F.D. Mennonitischer Freiwilligen-Dienst (Mennonite Voluntary Service)
    Minimum Fatal Dose

M.F.E. Mouvement fédéraliste européen (European Federalist Movement)

M.Fed. Miners' Federation

mfg. manufacturing

mfgr. manufacturer

M.F.H. Master of Foxhounds
    Mobile Field Hospital

M.F.H.A. Masters of Foxhounds Association

M.F.Hom. Member of the Faculty of Homoeopathy

m. fl. med flera (with others)

M.Flem. Middle Flemish

M.F.N. Most Favoured Nation

M.F.N.O. Midland Federation of Newspaper Owners

M. for M. Measure for Measure (Shakespeare)

mfr. manufacturer

M.-Fr. Middle French
mfre. manufacture
mfrs. manufacturers
M.F.S. Master of Foreign Study
M.F.S.S. Manchester Federation of Scientific Societies
mfst. manifest
M.ft. Mistura fiat (let a mixture be made)
m.f.t. motor freight tariff
m. ft. m. misce fiat mistura (mix to make a mixture)
M.F.V. Motor Fleet Vessel
Mg Magnesium
Molekulargewicht (molecular weight)
mg. morning
M.G. Machine Glazed
Main Gauche (left hand)
Major-General
Master-General
Medical Gymnast
Morris Garages
M.-G. Middle German
m.G. méridien de Greenwich (Greenwich Meridian)
m.g. machine gun
main gauche (left hand)
milligram
mixed grain
motor generator
m/g. manufacturing
M.G.A. Major-General, Administration
Marble and Granite Association
Midland Gravels Association
Mushroom Growers' Association
M.G.B. Ministerstvo Gosudarstvennoi Bezopasnosti (Ministry of State Security (Russia))
Motor Gunboat
M.G.C. Machine Gun Corps
Marriage Guidance Council
mge. message
M.G.G.S. Major-General, General Staff
M.G.I. Member of the Institute of Certificated Grocers
Mining and Geological Institute of India
M.Gk. Middle *or* Modern Greek
M.G.M. Metro-Goldwyn-Mayer
M.G.M.S. Manchester Geological and Mining Society
M.G.O. Master-General of Ordnance
Master of Gynaecology and Obstetrics
M.Goth. Meso-Gothic
Mgr. Manager
Monseigneur
Monsignor
mgr. manager
M.Gr. Middle Greek
M.G.R.A. Major-General, Royal Artillery
M.G.S. Manchester Grammar School
m.g.s. metre-gram-second(s)
mh. millihenry
M.H. Master of Horse
Master of Horticulture
Master of Hygiene
Medal of Honour   *cont.*

Military Hospital
Ministry of Health
M.H.A. Manila Hemp Association
Mansion House Association on Transport, Inc.
Master of Hospital Administration
Member of the House of Assembly
Mental Health Administration (U.S.)
Methodist Homes for the Aged
Mutual Households Association, Ltd.
M.H.C.I. Member of the Hotel and Catering Institute
m.h.cp. mean horizontal candlepower
M.H.D. magneto-hydro-dynamics
M.H.E.A. Mechanical Handling Engineers' Association
M.Heb. Middle Hebrew
M.H.G. Middle High German
M.H.K. Member of the House of Keys
M.H.L.G. Ministry of Housing and Local Government
mho. unit of conductance
M.Hon. Most Honourable
M.H.R. Member of the House of Representatives
M.H.R.A. Modern Humanities Research Association
M.H.R.F. Mental Health Research Fund
M.H.R.I. Mental Health Research Institute
M.H.S. Medical History Sheet
Member of the Historical Society
Military Historical Society
M.H.Sc. Master of Home Science
m.h.t. med hensyn til (as regards)
M.H.T.A. Midland Home Timber Association
M.H.W. Mean High Water
M.H.W.N.T. Mean High Water Neap Tide
M.H.W.S.T. Mean High Water Spring Tide
M.Hy. Master of Hygiene
Mi. Minor
Mississippi
mi. mile(s)
mill
minute
M.I. Malleable Iron
Metal Industries
Military Intelligence
Minister of Information
Monumental Inscription
Mounted Infantry
m.i. monumental inscription
M.I.A. Malleable Ironfounders' Association
Manitoba Institute of Agrologists
Member of the South African Institute of Architects
Missing in action
M.I.A.E. Member of the Institution of Automobile Engineers
M.I.Ae.E. Member of the Institute of Aeronautical Engineers

L

M.I.A.M.A. Member of the Incorporated Advertising Managers' Association

M.I.B. Metal Information Bureau, Limited

M.I.B.E. Member of the Institute of British Embalmers

M.I.B.F. Member of the Institute of British Foundrymen

M.I.Biol. Member of the Institute of Biology

Mic. Micah

M.I.C. Magnesium Industry Council
Malayan Indian Congress

M.I.C.A. Member of the Institute of Chartered Accountants in England and Wales

M.I.C.E. Member of the Institution of Civil Engineers

M.I.C.E.I. Member of the Institution of Civil Engineers of Ireland

Mich. Michaelmas
Michigan

M.I.Chem.E. Member of the Institution of Chemical Engineers

mic. pan. mica panis (crumb of bread)

M.I.C.R. Magnetic Ink Character Recognition

micro. microscope

Micros. Microscopy

Mid. Midlands
Midshipman

mid. middle
midnight

MIDAS Missile Defence Alarm System

M.I.D.A.S. Measurement Information and Data Analysis System
Media Investment Decision Analysis Systems

Middx. Middlesex

M.I.D.E.C. Middle East Industrial Development Projects Corporation

M.I.D.E.(S.A.) Member of the Institute of Diesel Engineers (South Africa)

Midl. Midlothian

Mid. Lat. Middle Latin

M.I.E. Member of the Institute of Engineers (South Africa)

M.I.E.Aust. Member of the Institution of Engineers of Australia

M.I.E.C. Pax Romana, mouvement international des étudiants catholiques (Pax Romana, International Movement of Catholic Students)

M.I.E.D. Member of the Institution of Engineering Designers

M.I.E.E. Member of the Institution of Electrical Engineers

M.I.E.I. Member of the Institution of Engineering Inspection

M.I.E.(Ind.) Member of the Institution of Engineers (India)

M.I.E.R.E. Member of the British Institute of Electronic and Radio Engineers

M.I.E.S. Member of the Institution of Engineers and Shipbuilders in Scotland

M.I.Ex. Member of the Institute of Export

M.I.F. Miners' International Federation

M.I.Fire E. Member of the Institution of Fire Engineers

M.I.G. Mikoyan and Gurevich
Minimum income guarantee

M.I.G.B. Millinery Institute of Great Britain

M.I.G.E. Member of the Institution of Gas Engineers

M.I.G.S. Music Industries Golfing Society

m.i.h. miles in the hour

M.I.H.V.E. Member of the Institution of Heating and Ventilating Engineers

M.I.I.A. Member of the Institute of Industrial Administration (*now* B.I.M.*)

M.I.I.C. Pax Romana, mouvement international des intellectuels catholiques (Pax Romana, International Catholic Movement for Intellectual and Cultural Affairs)

M.I.I.E. Member of the Institution of Industrial Engineers

M.I.I.S. Member of the Institute of Industrial Supervisors

Mij. Maatschapij (joint stock company)

M.I.J.A.R.C. Mouvement international de la jeunesse agricole et rurale catholique (International Movement of Catholic Agricultural and Rural Youth)

Mil. Military

mil. mileage
military
millilitre(s)

Mil. Att. Military Attaché

M.I.L.E. Member of the Institution of Locomotive Engineers

Milit. Military
Militia

mill. million

M.I.Loco.E. Member of the Institution of Locomotive Engineers

Milt. Milton

M.I.Mar.E. Member of the Institute of Marine Engineers

M.I.M.E. Member of the Institution of Mining Engineers
Midland Institute of Mining Engineers

M.I.Mech.E. Member of the Institution of Mechanical Engineers

M.I.M.I. Member of the Institute of the Motor Industry

M.I.Min.E. Member of the Institution of Mining Engineers

M.I.M.M. Member of the Institution of Mining and Metallurgy

M.I.M.S. The Monthly Index of Medical Specialties

M.I.M.T. Member of the Institute of the Motor Trade

M.I.Mun.E. Member of the Institution of Municipal Engineers

Min. Mineralogical
Mineralogy
Minister(ial)
Ministry

min. minim(um)
mining
minister   *cont.*

ministry
minor
minute

M.I.N. Member of the Institute of Navigation

M.I.N.A. Member of the Institution of Naval Architects (*now* M.R.I.N.A.)

Min.Can. Minor Canon

Min. Counc. Mining Councillor

Minn. Minnesota

mino. ministro (minister)

min. pen. minimum premium

Min. Plen. Minister Plenipotentiary

Min. Res. Minister Resident

mins. minutes

M.Inst.B.E. Member of the Institution of British Engineers

M.Inst.C.E. Member of the Institution of Civil Engineers

M.Inst.F. Member of the Institute of Fuel

M.Inst.Gas E. Member of the Institution of Gas Engineers

M.Inst.H.E. Member of the Institution of Highway Engineers

M.Inst.J. Member of the Institute of Journalists

M.Inst.Met. Member of the Institute of Metals

M.Inst.M.M. Member of the Institution of Mining and Metallurgy

M.Inst.M.S.M. Member of Institute of Marketing and Sales Management

M.Inst.N.A. Member of the Institution of Naval Architects (*now* M.R. Inst. N.A.)

M.Inst.P.I. Member of the Institute of Patentees and Inventors

M.Inst.R. Member of the Institute of Refrigation

M.Inst.R.A. Member of the Institute of Registered Architects

M.Inst.S.P. Member of the Institution of Sewage Purification

M.Inst.T. Member of the Institute of Transport

M.Inst.W.E. Member of the Institution of Water Engineers (*now* M.I.W.E.)

M.I.Nuc.E. Member of the Institution of Nuclear Engineers

min. wt. minimum weight

M.I.O.B. Member of the Institute of Building

M.I.P. Marine Insurance Policy

m.i.p. mean indicated pressure

M.I.P.E. Member of the Institution of Production Engineers (*now* M.I. Prod. E.)

M.I.Pet. Member of the Institute of Petroleum

M.I.P.H.E. Member of the Institution of Public Health Engineers

M.I.Plant E. Member of the Institution of Plant Engineers

M.I.P.R. Member of the Institute of Public Relations

M.I.Prod.E. Member of the Institution of Production Engineers (*formerly* M.I.P.E.)

M.I.Ptg.M. Member of the Institute of Printing Management

M.I.Q. Member of the Institute of Quarrying

M.Ir. Middle Irish

M.I.R.A. Member of the Institute of Registered Architects
Motor Industry Research Association

M.I.R.E. Member of the British Institution of Radio Engineers
Member of the Institution of Railway Signal Engineers

M.I.R.T.E. Member of Institute of Road Transport Engineers

M.I.R.V. Multiple Independent Re-Entry Vehicle

Mis. Missouri

M.I.S. Mining Institute of Scotland

misc. miscellaneous
miscellany

Misc. Doc. Miscellaneous Document(s)

miscend. miscendus (to be mixed)

M.I.S.I. Member of the Iron and Steel Institute

M.I.S.(India) Member of the Institution of Surveyors (India)

Miss. Mission(ary)
Missioner
Mississippi

M.I.S.S. Member of the Institute of Industrial Supervisors

mist. mistura (mixture)

mistrans. mistranslation

M.I.Struct.E. Member of the Institution of Structural Engineers

M.I.S.W. Member of the Institute of Shorthand Writers (practising in High Court of Justice)

M.It. Middle Italian

M.I.T. Massachusetts Institute of Technology

Mitt. Mitteilung (report)

mitt. mitte (send)

M.I.W.E. Member of the Institution of Water Engineers

mix. mixed
mixing

mixt. mixture

M.J. Ministry of Justice
Monkey Jacket

M.J.A. Merchant Jewellers' Association, Ltd.

M.J.I. Member of the Institute of Journalists

M.J.I.E. Member of the Junior Institution of Engineers

M.J.S. Member of the Japan Society

M.J.S.D. March, June, September, December

Mk. Mark

mkd. marked

m.kg. metre kilogramme(s)

mkr. mikroskopisch (microscopic

mks. marks

m.k.s. metre-kilogramme-second(s)

Mkt. Market

M.K.W. Military Knight of Windsor

Ml. Matmazel

mL. millilambert(s)

ml. millilitre(s)

M.L. Licentiate in Midwifery
Master of Law
Master of Letters
Medicinae Licentiatus (Licentiate in Medicine) *cont.*

Medieval Latin
Middle Latin
Ministry of Labour
Motor Launch
Muzzle-loading
M/L. Mine Layer
m.l. mean level
M.L.A. Master in Landscape Architecture
Master of the Liberal Arts
Medical Library Association
Member of the Legislative Assembly
Modern Language Association
M.L.A.G.B. Muzzle Loaders' Association of Great Britain
M.L.C. Meat and Livestock Commission
Member of the Legislative Council
mld. moulded
M.L.D. Master of Landscape Design
Maximum *or* Minimum Lethal Dose
mldg. moulding
mldr. moulder
mle. modèle (pattern)
m.l.e. maximum loss expectancy
M.L.E.U. Mouvement libéral pour l'Europe unie (Liberal Movement for a United Europe)
M.L.F. Multilateral Nuclear Force
M.L.G. Middle Low German
Ministry of Labour Gazette
M.Lib. Master of Library Science
M.Lib.Sc. Master of Library Science
M.Litt. Master of Letters
Master of Literature
M.L.J. Madras Law Journal
M.L.L. Manned Lunar Landing
Mlle. Mademoiselle
M.L.M.A. Miners' Lamp Manufacturer's Association
M.L.N.S. Ministry of Labour and National Service (*now* M.L.)
M.L.O. Midland Light Orchestra
Military Liaison Officer
M.L.R. Modern Law Review
m.l.r. muzzle-loading rifle
M.L.R.G. Muzzle-loading Rifled Gun
M.L.S. Master of Library Science
Medium Long Shot
Member of the Linnean Society
M.L.S.A. Ministry of Labour Staff Association
M.L.V. Medal for Labour Valour
M.L.W. Mean Low Water
M.L.W.N.T. Mean Low Water Neap Tide
M.L.W.S.T. Mean Low Water Spring Tide
MM. (Their) Majesties
Messieurs (Gentlemen)
Mm. Martyrs
mm. millimetre(s)
M.M. Maelzel's Metronome
Master Mason
Medal of Merit
Mercantile Marine
Military Medal
Mille Miglia (1000 Miles)   *cont.*

Minister of Mines
Ministry of Munitions
Music Master
m.m. made merchantable
med mera (and so forth)
mutatis mutandis (with the necessary changes)
M.M.A. Manitoba Medical Association
Meter Manufacturers' Association
Music Masters' Association
M.M.B. Milk Marketing Board
M.M.B.F.O.A. Midland Merchant Blast Furnace Owners' Association
M.M.C. Mars and Mercury Club
M. Mde. Marine Marchande (Merchant Marine)
Mme. Madame
M.M.E. Master of Mechanical Engineering
Master of Mining Engineering
Midlands Mathematical Experiment
M.Mech.E. Master of Mechanical Engineering
M.Med. Master of Medicine
M.Med.Sc. Master of Medical Science
M.M.E.G. Meter Manufacturers' Export Group
Mmes. Mesdames
M.Met. Master of Metallurgy
M.Met.E. Master of Metallurgical Engineering
mmf. magnetomagnetic force
magnetomotive force
M.M.F. Member of the Medical Faculty
mmfd. micromicrofarad
M.M.G. Medium Machine Gun
M.M.G.I. Member of the Mining, Geological and Metallurgical Institute of India
M.M.I. Materials Management International, Ltd.
m.mk. material mark
mmm. millimicron(s)
M.M.M. Mark Master Mason
Mouvement mondial des mères (World Movement of Mothers)
M.M.P. Master Music Printers and Engravers Association
Military Mounted Police
M.M.P.A. Midland Master Printers Alliance
M.M.P.I. Minnesota Multiphase Personality Inventory
M.M.R. Mass Miniature Radiography
M.M.R.A. Maritime Marshland Rehabilitation Administration (Canada)
M.M.R.B.M. Mobile Medium Range Ballistic Missile
M.M.S. Moravian Missionary Society
Methodist Missionary Society
Motor Mine Sweeper
M.M.S.A. Master of Midwifery of the Society of Apothecaries
Mercantile Marine Service Association
M.Mus. Master of Music

Mn. Midnight
Montenegro
Mn Manganese
mn. maison (house)
M.N. Magnetic North
Master of Nursing
Merchant Navy
m.n. mutato nomine (the name being changed)
m/n. moneda nacional (national money)
M.N.A.S. Member of the National Academy of Sciences (U.S.)
M.N.D. A Midsummer Night's Dream (Shakespeare)
Minister of National Defence
mng. managing
mngmt. management
mngr. manager
M.N.I. Madras Native Infantry
Ministry of National Insurance (now M.P.N.I.)
Mnl. Manila
mnm. minimum
M.N.A.O.A. Merchant Navy and Airline Officers' Association
M.N.P. Malay Nationalist Party
Mnr. Mijnheer
M.N.S. Member of the Numismatical Society (U.S.)
M.N.T. Mean Neap Tide
M.N.Z.I.E. Member of the New Zealand Institution of Engineers
Mo Molybdenum
Mo. Missouri
Moderato
M.O. Mail Order
Manually Operated
Mass Observation
Master of Obstetrics
Master of Oratory
Master Oscillator
Medical Officer
Meteorological Office
Method of Operation
Money Order
Monthly Order
Motor Operated
Municipal Officer
mo. month
m.-o. months old
M.o.A. Ministry of Aviation
M.O. & G. Master of Obstetrics and Gynaecology
mob. mobile
mobilization
mobilized
Mobizn. Mobilization
M.O.C. Mother of the Chapel
Mod. Moderate
Moderato
M.O.D. Mail Order Department
Ministry of Defence
mod. modern
modification
modified
mod. con(s). modern conveniences
Mod.E. Modern English
modif. modification
Mods. Moderations
M.O.D.S. Manned Orbital Development System
M.o.E. Ministry of Education

M.o.F. Ministry of Food (now M. of A.)
M. of A. Ministry of Agriculture (Fisheries and Food)
M. of E. Ministry of Education
M. of P. Ministry of Pensions (and National Insurance)
Ministry of Power
M. of R.A.F. Marshal of the Royal Air Force
M. of V. The Merchant of Venice (Shakespeare)
M. of W. Ministry of Works (now M.P.B. and W.)
M.O.G. Master of Obstetrics and Gynaecology
Moh. Mohammedan(ism)
M.O.H. Master of Otter Hounds
Medical Officer of Health
Ministry of Health
M.o.H. Ministry of Housing (and Local Government)
Moham. Mohammedan(ism)
M.O.H.L.G. Ministry of Housing and Local Government
M.O.I. Military Operations and Intelligence
Ministry of Information
Ministry of the Interior
m.o.i.v. mechanically operated inlet valve
M.O.J.M.R.P. Meteorological Office, Joint Meteorological Radio Propagation Sub-Committee
mol. molecule
M.O.L. Master of Oriental Learning
M.o.L. Ministry of Labour
M.o.l. Manned orbiting laboratory
Mold. Moldavia(n)
M.O.L.N.S. Ministry of Labour and National Service (now M.L.)
mol. wt. molecular weight
M.O.M. Milk of Magnesia
m.o.m. middle of month
Mon. Monaco
Monaghan
Monastery
Monday
Monitor
Monmouthshire
Montana
mon. maison (house)
monastery
monastic
monetary
Mong. Mongol(ia)
Monm. Monmouthshire
mono. monotype
monog. monograph
Mons. Monsieur
Monsig. Monsignor
Mont. Montana
Montgomeryshire
Montgom. Montgomeryshire
Montr. Montreal
M.O.O. Money Order Office
Moore's Adj. Moore's International Adjudications
Moore's Arb. Moore's International Arbitrations
Moore's Dig. Moore's Digest of International Law

M.o.P. Member of Parliament
Ministry of Pensions (*now* M.P.N.I.*)
Ministry of Power
Ministry of Production
m.o.p. mother-of-pearl
moped motorized pedal cycle
M.O.P.H. Military Order of the Purple Heart (U.S.)
Mor. Morendo
Moroccan
Morocco
M.O.R. Ministry of Reconstruction
M.O.R.A.D.E. Movement for Rethinking Art and Design
Morb. Morbihan
M.O.R.C. Medical Officers Reserve Corps
mor. dict. more dicto (in the manner directed)
morn. morning
Morph. Morphology
mor. sol. more solito (in the usual manner)
mort. mortgage
mortuary
Mos. Moselle
mos. months
M.O.S. Ministry of Supply
M.O.S.A. Medical Officers of Schools Association
M.O.S.I.D. Ministry of Supply Inspection Department
mot. motor(ized)
M.O.T. Ministry of Transport
M.O.T.C.P. Ministry of Town and Country Planning
mot.op. motor-operated
M.O.U.S.E. Minimum Orbital Unmanned Satellite of the Earth
M.O.W. Ministry of Works (*now* M.P.B. and W.)
M.O.W.T. Ministry of War Transport
moy. money
Moz. Mozambique
M.P. Madhya Pradesh
Master of Painting
Master of Planning
Meeting Point
Member of Parliament
Mercator's Projection
Methodist Protestant
Metropolitan Police
Mille Passuum (thousand paces)
Military Police
Minister-Plenipotentiary
Municipal Police (U.S.)
M/P. Memorandum of Partnership
M.-P. Mandat-Poste (Postal Money Order)
m.p. medium pattern
medium pressure
melting point
melting pot
mezzo piano (moderately soft
mile post
mille passuum (thousand paces)
months after payment
mooring post
M.P.A. Master of Public Administration *cont.*

Master Photographers' Association of Great Britain
Merseyside Productivity Association
Metropolitan Pensions Association
Music Publishers' Association
M.P.A.G.B. Modern Pentathlon Association of Great Britain
M.P.B. and W. Ministry of Public Building and Works
M.P.C. Member of Parliament, Canada
Metropolitan Police College
Metropolitan Police Commissioner
m.p.c. mathematics, physics, chemistry
M.P.C.E.F. Manchester Packing Case Employers Federation
M.Pd. Master of Pedagogy
M.P.D. Maximum Permissible Dose
M. pdo. meses pasado (last month)
M.P.E. Master of Physical Education
M.Pen. Ministry of Pensions (*now* M.P.N.I.)
M.Per. Middle Persian
m.p.f. multi-purpose food
m.p.g. miles per gallon
M.P.G.A. Metropolitan Public Gardens Association
M.Ph. Master of Philosophy
M.P.H. Master in Public Health
m.p.h. miles per hour
M.Pharm. Maître en pharmacie (Master of Pharmacy)
M.Phil. Master of Philosophy
m.p.i. mean point of impact
Mpl. Montpellier
M.P.L. Master of Patent Law
Master of Polite Literature
Maximum Permissible Level
m.p.m. metres per minute
multi purpose meal
M.P.M.A. Motion Picture Museum Association
M.P.N.I. Ministry of Pensions and National Insurance
M.P.O. Metropolitan Police Office
Milk Production Officer
Military Post Office
Mobile Printing Office
Mobile Publishing Office
M.P.P. Member of Provincial Parliament
M.P.P.A. Music Publishers' Protective Association
M.P.R. Maritime Provinces Reports, Canada
Mongolian People's Republic
M.Prof.Acc. Master of Professional Accountancy
M.P.S. Medical Protection Society, Limited
Member of the Pharmaceutical Society of Great Britain
Member of the Philological Society
m.p.s. metres per second
M.P.S.C. Military Provost Staff Corps (U.S.)
M.Ps.Sc. Master of Psychological Science

M.P.T.A. Municipal Passenger Transport Association

M.P.U. Medical Practitioners' Union

Mpy. Maatschappij (company)

M.Q.B. Mining Qualifications Board

Mqe. Martinique

Mr. Master
Mister

M.R. Map Reference
Master of the Rolls
Mauritius Decisions
Middlesex Regiment
Minister-Residentiary
Ministry of Reconstruction
Motorways Traffic Regulations
Municipal Reform

M/R. Mate's Receipt

m.r. mill run
memorandum receipt
moment of resistance

m/r. mi remesa (my shipment)

M.R.A. Maritime Royal Artillery
Moral Re-armament

M.R.A.C. Member of the Royal Agricultural College

M.R.A.C.P. Member of the Royal Australasian College of Physicians

M.Rad. Master of Radiology

M.R.Ae.S. Member of the Royal Aeronautical Society

M.R.A.F. Marshal of the Royal Air Force

M.R.A.I.C. Member of the Royal Architectural Institute of Canada

M.R.A.S. Member of the Royal Asiatic Society of Great Britain and Ireland
Member of the Royal Astronomical Society

M.R.B. Mersey River Board

M.R.B.M. Medium Range Ballistic Missile

M.R.C. Medical Registration Council
Medical Research Council
Medical Reserve Corps
Model Railway Club

M.R.C.C. Member of the Royal College of Chemistry

M.R.C.I. Medical Registration Council of Ireland

M.R.C.O. Member of the Royal College of Organists

M.R.C.O.G. Member of the Royal College of Obstetricians and Gynaecologists

M.R.C.P. Member of the Royal College of Physicians

M.R.C.P.E. Member of the Royal College of Physicians of Edinburgh

M.R.C.P.Ed. Member of the Royal College of Physicians of Edinburgh

M.R.C.P.I. Member of the Royal College of Physicians of Ireland

M.R.C.S. Member of Royal College of Surgeons

M.R.C.S.E. Member of Royal College of Surgeons of Edinburgh

M.R.C.S.I. Member of Royal College of Surgeons of Ireland

M.R.C.V.S. Member of Royal College of Veterinary Surgeons

M.R.D. Microbiological Research Department

M.R.E. Master of Religious Education
Microbiological Research Establishment
Mining Research Establishment

M.R.Emp.S. Member of the Royal Empire Society (*now* R.C.S.)

M.R.F.B. Malayan Rubber Fund Board

M.R.Flight Meteorological Research Flight

M.R.G. Management Research Groups
Minorities Research Group

M.R.G.S. Member of the Royal Geographical Society

M.R.H. Member of the Royal Household

M.R.I. Maître en relations industrielles (Master of Industrial Relations)
Member of the Royal Institution

M.R.I.A. Member of the Royal Irish Academy

M.R.I.A.I. Member of the Royal Institute of the Architects of Ireland

M.R.I.A.S. Manchester Region Industrial Archaeology Society

M.R.I.C.S. Member of the Royal Institution of Chartered Surveyors

M.R.I.N.A. Member of Royal Institution of Naval Architects

M.R.Inst.N.A. Member of the Royal Institution of Naval Architects

M.R.I.P.H.H. Member of the Royal Institute of Public Health and Hygiene

M.R.O. Member of the Register of Osteopaths

M.R.P. Master in Regional Planning
Mouvement Républicain Populaire (Popular Republican Movement)

Mrs. Messieurs
Mistress

M.R.S. Market Research Society

M.R.San.I. Member of the Royal Sanitary Institute (*now* M.R.S.H.)

M.R.Sc. Master of Rural Science

M.R.S.H. Member of the Royal Society for the Promotion of Health

M.R.S.L. Member of the Royal Society of Literature

M.R.S.M. Member of Royal Society of Medicine
Member of the Royal Society of Musicians of Great Britain

M.R.S.M.P. Member of the Royal Society of Miniature Painters, Sculptors and Gravers

M.R.S.P.E. Member of the Royal Society of Painter-Etchers and Engravers

M.R.S.P.P. Member of the Royal Society of Portrait Painters

M.R.S.T. Member of the Royal Society of Teachers

M.R.S.W. Member of the Royal Society of Scottish Painters and Watercolours

M.R.T.S. Member of the Royal Television Society

M.R.U. Mobile Repair Unit

M.R.U.A. Mobile Radio Users' Association

M.Rur.Sc. Master of Rural Science

M.R.U.S.I. Member of the Royal United Service Institution

MS. Manuscript

M.S. Master of Science
Master of Surgery
Medical Staff
Medium Shot
Memoriae Sacrum (sacred to the memory of)
Mess Sergeant
Metric System
Military Secretary
Mine Sweeper
Minister for Science
Ministry of Supply
Missionaries of La Salette
Motor Ship
Multiple Sclerosis

M/s. Month's sight

m.s. machinery survey
mail steamer
margin of safety
maximum stress
medium steel
mild steel

m/s. metres per second

M.S.A. Manchester Society of Architects
Master of Science in Agriculture
Member of the Society of Apothecaries
Member of the Society of Architects
Motorists Security Association
Motor Schools' Association of Great Britain
Mutual Security Agency (U.S.A.)

m.s.a. misce secundum artem (mix skilfully)

M.S.A.E. Member of the Society of Automotive Engineers (U.S.A.)

M.S.Agr. Master of Science in Agriculture

M.S.Agr.Eng. Master of Science in Agricultural Engineering

M.S.Agr.Ex. Master of Science in Agricultural Extension

M.(S.A.)I.C.E. Member of the South African Institution of Civil Engineers

M.(S.A.)I.E.E. Member of the South African Institute of Electrical Engineers

M.(S.A.)I.M.E. Member of the South African Institution of Mechanical Engineers

M.S.A.Inst.M.M. Member South African Institute of Mining and Metallurgy

M.S.A.I.T. Member of the South African Institute of Translators

M.S.A.I.V. Member of the South African Institute of Valuers

M.S.A.P.S. Member the South African Pharmaceutical Society

M.S.& R. Merchant Shipbuilding and Repairs

M.S.Arch. Master of Science in Architecture

M.S.A.Soc.C.E. Member the South African Society of Civil Engineers

M.S.Aut.E. Member of the Society of Automotive Engineers (U.S.)

M.S.B.A. Master of Science in Business Administration

M.S.Bus. Master of Science in Business

msc. miscellaneous

M.Sc. Master of Science

M.S.C. Madras Staff Corps
Management Studies Centre, Ltd.
Manchester Ship Canal
Medical Staff Corps
Mediterranean Sub-Commission (Food and Agriculture Organization)
Meteorological Service of Canada
Metropolitan Special Constabulary
Missionarii Sacratissima Cordis Jesu (Missionaries of the Most Sacred Heart of Jesus)

m.s.c. mandatum sine clausula (authority without restriction)
moved, seconded and carried

M.Sc.Agr. Master of Science in Agriculture

M.Sc.(Agric.Eng.) Master of Science in Agricultural Engineering

M.Sc.(A.H.) Master of Science (Animal Husbandry)

M.Sc.App. Master of Applied Science

M.Sc.(Appl.) Master of Science (Applied)

M.S.C.C. Manchester Ship Canal Company

M.Sc.C.E. Master of Science in Civil Engineering

M.Sc.(Cer.) Master of Science in Ceramics

M.Sc.Chem.Tech. Master of Science in Chemical Technology

M.Sc.(C.P.) Master of Science (Community Planning)

M.Sc.D. Master of Dental Science

M.Sc.(Dairy Tech.) Master of Science (Dairy Technology)

M.Sc.(Dent.) Master of Science in Dentistry

M.Sc.(Econ.) Master of Science in Economics

M.Sc.(Elec.) Master of Science (Electronics)

M.Sc.Eng. Master of Science in Engineering

M.Sc.(Est.Man.) Master of Science (Estate Management)

M.Sc.F. Master of the Science of Forestry

M.S.Ch.E. Master of Science in Chemical Engineering

M.S.Chem. Master of Science in Chemistry

M.Sc.(Home Sc.) Master of Science (Home Science)

M.Sc.(Hort.) Master of Science in Horticulture

M.Sc.(Ind.Chem.)Tech. Master of Science in Technology (Industrial Chemistry)

M.Sc.Med. Master of Science in Medicine

M.Sc.(Med.Sc.) Master of Science in Medical Science

M.Sc.(Min.) Master of Science in Mining

M.Sc.N. Master of Science in Nursing

M.Sc.(Nutr.) Master of Science (Nutrition)

M.S.Com. Maître en sciences commerciales (Master of Commerce)
    Maître en sciences comptables (Master of Accountancy)
    Master of Science in Commerce

M.S.C.P. Mean Spherical Candlepower

M.Sc.Phm. Master of Science in Pharmacy

M.Sc.Rel. Maître en sciences religieuses (Master of Religious Science)

M.Sc.Soc. Maître en sciences sociales (Master of Social Sciences)

M.Sc.Sur. Master of Science in Land Surveying

M.Sc.Tech. Master of Technical Science

M.S.D. Doctor of Medical Science
    Master of Scientific Didactics
    Master Surgeon Dentist

M.S.Dent. Master of Science in Dentistry

M.S.E. Master of Science in Engineering
    Member of the Society of Engineers

m.sec. millisecond(s)

M.S.Ed. Master of Science in Education

M.S.E.E. Master of Science in Electrical Engineering

M.S.E.M. Master of Science in Engineering Mechanics

M.Serv.Soc. Maître en service social (Master of Social Service)

mses. marchandises (goods)

M.S.E.U.E. Mouvement socialiste pour les États Unis d'Europe (Socialist Movement for the United States of Europe)

M.S.F. Master of Science in Forestry
    Mine-Sweeping Flotilla
    Multiple Shops Federation

M.S.F.S. Missionaries of Saint Francis de Sales

msg. message

Msgr. Monsignor

msgr. messenger

M.Sgt. Master Sergeant

M.S.H. Master of Staghounds

M.S.H.Ec. Master of Science in Home Economics

M.S.Hyg. Master of Science in Hygiene

M.S.I. Movimento Sociale Italiano (Italian Social Movement)

M.S.I.A. Member of the Society of Industrial Artists and Designers

M.S.Ind.E. Master of Science in Industrial Engineering

M.S.I.T. Member of the Society of Instrument Technology

M.S.J. Master of Science in Journalism

m.s.l. mean sea-level

M.S.L.S. Master of Science in Library Science

M.S.M. Master of Medical Science
    Master of Sacred Music
    Meritorious Service Medal

M.S.M.A. Member of the Sales Managers' Association of Southern Africa
    Master Sign Makers' Association

M.S.M.E. Master of Science in Mechanical Engineering

M.S.Med. Master of Medical Science

M.S.Mus. Master of Science in Music

M.S.N.E. Master of Science in Nursing Education

msngr. messenger

M.S.Nurs. Master of Science in Nursing

M.Soc.Sc. Master of Social Science

M.Soc.St. Master of Social Studies

M.Soc.(S.W.) Master of Social Science (Social Welfare)

M.Soc.Wk. Master of Social Work

M.S.(Ophthal.) Master of Surgery (Ophthalmology)

M.S.(Ortho.) Master of Orthopaedic Surgery

M.S.P. Master of Science in Pharmacy
    Minimum Sterling Proportion
    Mutual Security Program (U.S.)

M.S.P.E. Master of Science in Physical Education

M.S.P.H. Master of Science in Public Health

M.S.Phar. Master of Science in Pharmacy

M.S.P.H.E. Master of Science in Public Health Engineering

M.S.P.S.M. Master of Science in Public School Music

M.S.Public Adm. Master of Science in Public Administration

M.S.R. Member of the Society of Radiographers

M.S.R.A. Multiple Shoe Retailers' Association

M.S.Ret. Master of Science in Retailing

M.S.R.G. Member of the Society for Remedial Gymnasts

MSS. Manuscripts

M.S.S. Maître en service social (Master of Social Work)
    Manchester Statistical Society
    Medical Superintendents' Society

M.S.S.E. Master of Science in Sanitary Engineering

M.S.S.G.B. Motion Study Society of Great Britain

M.S.S.I.G. Manchester Statistical Society Industrial Group

M.S.S.R.C. Mediterranean Social Sciences Research Council

M.S.S.S. Master of Science in Social Service

M.S.S.V.D. Medical Society for the Study of Venereal Diseases
M.S.S.W. Master of Science in Social Work
mst. measurement
M.S.T. Master of Sacred Theology
Mean Spring Tide
Mountain Standard Time (U.S.)
M.S.Tech. Magister Scientiae Technicae (Master of Technical Science)
M.S.Trans. Master of Science in Transportation
M.S.Trans.E. Master of Science in Transportation Engineering
Mstr.Mech. Master Mechanic
M.S.U.L. Medical Schools of the University of London
M.Surgery Master in Surgery
M.Surv. Master of Surveying
M.Sw. Middle Swedish
M.S.W. Master of Social Work
Mt. Mount(ain)
M.T. Mandated Territory
Masoretic Text
Master of Teaching
Mean Time
Mechanical Transport
Middle Temple
Motor Tanker
Motor Transport
m.t. metric ton(s)
M.T.A. Mica Trade Association
Motor Traders' Association (*now* B.M.T.A.)
Multiple Tailors' Association
Music Teachers' Association
Music Trades' Association
M.T.B. Motor Torpedo Boat
M.T.C. Marcus Tullius Cicero
Mechanical Transport Corps
Music Teacher's Certificate
M.T.C.A. Ministry of Transport and Civil Aviation (*now* M.O.T. *and* M.O.A.*)
M.T.C.P. Ministry of Town and Country Planning
Mtd. Mounted
M.T.D. Mean Temperature Difference
Midwife Teacher's Diploma
M.T.D.E. Maintenance Technique Development Establishment
M.Tech. Master in Technology
M.Tel.E. Master of Telecommunications Engineering
M.Text. Master of Textiles
mtg. meeting
mortgage
mounting
M.T.G. Multiple Tobacconists' Group
mtgee. mortgagee
mtgor. mortgagor
mth. month
M.Th. Master of Theology
M.T.H. Master of Trinity House
M.T.I.R.A. Machine Tool Industry Research Association
mtl. material
m.t.l. mean tidal level
M.T.M. Methods-Time Measurement
M.T.M.A.-U.K. Methods - Time Measurement Association of the United Kingdom

162

M.T.M.S. Manchester Transport Museum Society
M.T.O. Mechanical Transport Officer
Mediterranean Theatre of Operations
M.T.P. Master of Town Planning
M.T.P.I. Member of the Town Planning Institute
mtr. meter
Mt.Rev. Most Reverend
M.T.R.P. Master of Town and Regional Planning
M.Ts. Machine-tools
M.T.S. Machine Tractor Station
Merchant Taylors' School
Missions to Seamen
Motor Transport Service
M.T.T.A. Machine Tools Trades' Association
M.T.U.C. Malay Trade Union Congress
M.T.V. Motor Torpedo Vessel
mu. micron(s)
millimicron(s)
M.U. Maintenance Unit
Mass Unit
Monetary Unit
Mothers' Union
Musicians' Union
M.U.A. Machinery Users' Association
Monotype Users' Association
M.U.C. Missionary Union of the Clergy
M.U.F. Maximum Usable Frequency
M.U.F.M. Mouvement universel pour une fédération mondiale (World Association of World Federalists)
Munic. Municipal
Mus. Music(al)
mus. musician
museum
M.U.S.A. Multiple-Unit Steerable Antenna
Mus.B. Musicae Baccalaureus (Bachelor of Music)
Mus.D. Musicae Doctor (Doctor of Music)
Mus.M. Musicae Magister (Master of Music)
mut. mutilated
mutual
mv. millivolt(s)
M.V. Medicus Veterinarius (Veterinary Physician)
Merchant Vessel
The Merchant of Venice (Shakespeare)
mezza voce (at half power of voice)
m.v. market value
mean variation
medium voltage
motor vessel
muzzle velocity
M.V.D. Doctor of Veterinary Medicine
M.V.D.A. Motor Vehicle Dismantlers' Association of Great Britain
M.Vet.Med. Master of Veterinary Medecine
M.V.G. Medal for Victory over Germany
M.V.O. Member of the Royal Victorian Order

M.V.S. Master of Veterinary Science
Master of Veterinary Surgery
Mennonite Voluntary Service
M.V.Sc. Master of Veterinary Science
mvt. movement
M.W. Medium Wave
Middle Welsh
Molecular Weight
Most Worshipful
Most Worthy
M.W. meines Wissens (to my knowledge)
M/W. Midwife
m.w. megawatt(s)
milliwatt(s)
M.W.A. Metal Window Association
Modern Woodmen of America
M.W.B. Metropolitan Water Board
Ministry of Works and Buildings (*now* M.P.B. and W.)
M.W.D. Military Works Department
M.Weld.I. Member of the Welding Institute
M.W.F. Medical Women's Federation
m.w.g. music wire gauge
M.W.G.C.P. Most Worthy Grand Chief Patriarch
M.W.G.M. Most Worthy *or* Worshipful Grand Master

mWh megawatt hour
M.W.I. Ministry of War Information (U.S.)
M.W.I.A. Medical Women's International Association
M.W.N. Madras Weekly Notes
M.W.N.T. Mean Water Neap Tide
M.W.P. Mechanical Wood Pulp
Most Worthy Patriarch
M.W.P.A. Married Women's Property Act
M.W.W. The Merry Wives of Windsor (Shakespeare)
Mx. Middlesex
mxd. mixed
mxm. maximum
My. Maatschappij (Company
my. myopia
M.Y. Motor Yacht
mycol. mycological
mycology
M.Y.D. Methodist Youth Department
M.Y.O.B. Mind Your Own Business
myst. mysteries
mystery
Myth. Mythological
Mythology
mythol. mythology
m.Z. mangels Zahlung (for nonpayment)

N

N Nitrogen
N. Name(s)
Nationalist
Navigation
Navy
Near
Noon
Norse
North(ern)
Norway
Nurse
Nursing
n. nails
name
natus (born)
navy
near
nephew
net
neuter
new
nocte (at night)
nominative
noon
normal
note
notre (our)
noun
number
Na Natrium (sodium)
N.A. National Academician
National Academy   *cont.*

National Assembly
Nautical Almanac
Naval Architect
Naval Attaché
Naval Auxiliary
North America
Nursing Auxiliary
N/A. No Account
No Advice
N/a. Non-acceptance
n.a. nota del autor (author's note)
N.A.A. National Aeronautic Association (U.S.)
National Assistance Act
National Automobile Association (U.S.)
n.a.a. not always afloat
N.A.A.B.C. National Association of American Business Clubs
N.A.A.C. National Association of Agricultural Contractors
N.A.A.C.P. National Association for the Advancement of Colored People (U.S.)
N.A.A.F. North-African Air Force
N.A.A.F.I. Navy, Army and Air Force Institute
Naafi No ambition and fractional interest (*Parliamentary Dining Club*)
N.A.A.R. National Association of Advertising Representatives

N.A.A.S. National Agricultural Advisory Service

N.A.A.W. National Association of Amateur Winemakers

N.A.B. National Assistance Board
National Association of Bookmakers, Ltd.

N.A.B.B.A. National Amateur Bodybuilders Association

N.A.B.B.C. National Association of Brass Band Conductors

N.A.B.C. National Association of Bingo Clubs
National Association of Boys' Clubs

N.A.B.E. National Association for Business Education

N.A.B.M. National Association of British Manufacturers (*now* C.B.I.)

N.A.B.M.A. National Association of British Market Authorities

N.A.B.S. National Advertising Benevolent Society
Nuclear-Armed Bombardment Satellite

N.A.C. National Advisory Council
National Air Council
National Amusements Council
National Archives Council
National Association of Choirs
Naval Aircraftman
North Atlantic Coast

N.A.C.A. National Advisory Committee for Aeronautics (U.S.) (*now* N.A.S.A.)
National Athletic and Cycling Association

N.A.C.A.M. National Association of Corn and Agricultural Merchants

N.A.C.C.G. National Association of Crankshaft and Cylinder Grinders

N.A.C.F. National Art Collections Fund
National Association of Church Furnishers

Nachf. Nachfolger (successor)

nachm. nachmittags (in the afternoon)

N.A.C.M. National Association of Charcoal Manufacturers
National Association of Cider Makers

N.A.C.O.D.S. National Association of Colliery Overmen, Deputies and Shotfirers

N.A.C.P. National Association of Creamery Proprietors and Wholesale Dairymen, Inc.

N.A.C.R.O. National Association for the Care and Resettlement of Offenders

N.A.C.T. National Association of Craftsman Tailors

N.A.C.T.S.T. National Advisory Council on the Training and Supply of Teachers

N.Ad. Naval Adviser

N.A.D. National Academy of Design (U.S.)
National Association for the Deaf *cont.*

Naval Air Division
Naval Aircraft Department
Nothing Abnormal Detected

n.a.d. no appreciable disease

N.A.D.A. National Association of Drama Advisers

N.A.D.C. Naval Aide-de-Camp

N.A.D.E.E. National Association of Divisional Executives for Education

N.A.D.F.S. National Association of Drop Forgers and Stampers

N.A.D.G.E. Nato Air Defence Ground Environment

N.A.D.P.A.S. National Association of Discharged Prisoners' Aid Societies

N.A.E. National Academy of Engineering (U.S.)
Naval Aircraft Establishment

N.A.E.A. National Association of Estate Agents

N.A.E.C. National Aeronautical Establishment, Canada
National Association of Exhibition Contractors

N.A.E.D.S. National Association of Engravers and Diestampers

N.A.E.T. National Association of Educational Technicians

N.A.F.A.S. National Association of Flower Arrangement Societies of Great Britain

N.A.F.D. National Association of Funeral Directors

N.A.F.E.P. National Association of Frozen Egg Packers Ltd.

N.A.F.F.P. National Association of Frozen Food Producers

N.A.F.O. National Association of Fire Officers

N.A.F.S.A. National Fire Services Association of Great Britain

N.A.F.T.A. North Atlantic Free Trade Area

N.A.F.W.R. National Association of Furniture Warehousemen and Removers

N.A.G. National Association of Goldsmiths
National Association o Groundsmen
Northern Army Group

N.A.G.C. National Association for Gifted Children

N.A.G.M. National Association of Glove Manufacturers

N.A.G.S. National Allotments and Gardens Society

Nah. Nahum

N.A.H.S.O. National Association of Hospital Supplies Officers

N.A.H.T. National Association of Head Teachers

N.A.I.C. National Association of Investment Clubs

N.A.I.D.A. National Agricultural and Industrial Development Association

N.A.I.E.O. National Association of Inspectors of Schools and Educational Organisers

N.A.I.W.C. National Association of Inland Waterway Carriers

N.A.L. National Air Lines Incorporated

N.A.L.G.O. National and Local Government Officers' Association

N.A.L.M. National Association of Lift Makers

N.A.L.O. National Association of Laundrette Owners

N.A.L.S.A.T. National Association of Land Settlement Association Tenants

N.A.L.S.O. National Association of Labour Student Organisations

N.Am. North America

N.A.M. National Association of Manufacturers (U.S.)

N.A.M.B. National Association of Master Bakers

N.A.M.E. National Association of Marine Engine Builders
National Association of Marine Engineers of Canada

N.A.M.H. National Association for Mental Health

N.A.M.I. National Association of Malleable Ironfounders

N.A.M.M. National Association of Master Masons

N.A.M.M.C. Natural Asphalt Mineowners' and Manufacturers' Council

N. and Q. Notes and Queries

N.A.N.F.M. National Association of Non-Ferrous Scrap Metal Merchants

N.A.N.T.I.S. Nottingham and Nottinghamshire Technical Information Service

N.A.N.U. National Association of Non-Unionists

N.A.O. National Accordion Organization of Great Britain
National Association of Outfitters

N.A.O.P. National Association of Operative Plasterers

Nap. Napoleon

N.A.P. National Association for the Paralysed
Niger Agricultural Project

N.A.P.A. National Association of Park Administrators

N.A.P.A.E.O. National Association of Principal Agricultural Educational Officers

N.A.P.C. National Association of Parish Councils

N.A.P.D. National Association of Pharmaceutical Distributors

N.A.P.E. National Association of Port Employers

N.A.P.G.C. National Association of Public Golf Courses

Naph. Naphtha

N.A.P.M. National Association of Paper Merchants

N.A.P.O. National Association of Probation Officers

N.A.P.P. National Association of Poultry Packers Ltd.

N.A.P.R. National Association of Pram Retailers

N.A.P.S. National Association of Personal Secretaries

N.A.P.T. National Association for the Prevention of Tuberculosis (*now* C.H.A.*)

N.A.P.V. National Association of Prison Visitors

N.A.R.F. National Association of Retail Furnishers

N.A.R.I. Natal Agricultural Research Institute

narr. narratio (complaint)

NARTEL North Atlantic Radio Telephone Committee

N.A.R.T.M. National Association of Rope and Twine Merchants

N.A.S. National Academy of Science (U.S.)
National Adoption Society
National Association of Schoolmasters
National Association of Shopfitters
Naval Air Station
Noise Abatement Society
Nursing Auxiliary Service

N.A.S.A. National Aeronautics and Space Administration (U.S.)

N.A.S.B.A. National Automobile Safety Belt Association

N.A.S.D. National Amalgamated Stevedores and Dockers

N.A.S.D.E.C. National Assets and Services Development Export Consortium

N.A.S.D.U. National Amalgamated Stevedores and Dockers Union

N.A.S.E.N. National Association of State Enrolled Nurses

N.A.S.M. National Association of School Magazines

N.A.S.M.A.R. National Association of Sack Merchants and Reclaimers Ltd.

N.A.S.P.M. National Association of Seed Potato Merchants

Nass. Nassau

N.A.S.S. National Association of Steel Stockholders
Naval Air Signal School

N.A.S.U. National Adult School Union

N.A.S.W.M. National Association of Scottish Woollen Manufacturers

Nat. Natal
Nathan
National(ist)
Natural(ist)

nat. native
naturalized

N.At. North Atlantic

N.A.T. National Arbitration Tribunal

Nat.Absten. National Abstentionalist

natat. natation

N.A.T.B. National Automobile Theft Bureau

N.A.T.C.G. National Association of Training Corps for Girls

N.A.T.D. National Association of Teachers of Dancing Ltd.
National Association of Tool Dealers

Nat.Dem. National Democrats

N.A.T.E. National Association for the Teaching of English

Nat.Fed. National Federation

165

N.A.T.G.A. National Amateur Tobacco Growers' Association
Nat.Gal. National Gallery
Nat.Hist. Natural History
Nativ. Nativity
N.A.T.K.E. National Association of Theatrical and Kine Employees
Natl. National
Nat.Lib. National Liberal
N.A.T.M.H. National Association of Teachers of the Mentally Handicapped
N.A.T.N. National Association of Theatre Nurses
N.A.T.O. National Association of Temperance Officials
    North Atlantic Treaty Organisation
Nat.Ord. Natural Order
N.A.T.O.U.S.A. Northern African Theatre of Operations, U.S. Army
Nat.Phil. Natural Philosophy
Nat.Prov. National Provincial Bank
N.A.T.R. National Association of Tenants and Residents
    National Association of Toy Retailers
Nat.Sc. Natural Science
Nat.Sc.D. Doctor of Natural Science
N.A.T.S.O.P.A. National Society of Operative Printers and Assistants
N.Att. Naval Attaché
natur. naturalist
N.A.U.A. National Automobile Underwriters' Association (U.S.)
Naut. Nautical
nav. naval
    navigation
    navigator
N.A.V.A.C. National Audio-Visual Aids Centre
Nav.Constr. Naval Constructor
N.A.V.H. National Association of Voluntary Hostels
navig. navigation
    navigator
N.A.V.L. National Anti-Vaccination League
N.A.V.S. National Anti-Vivisection Society
N.A.W.B. National Association of Workshops for the Blind Incorporated
N.A.W.C. National Association of Women's Clubs
N.A.W.C.H. National Association for the Welfare of Children in Hospital
N.A.W.D.C. National Association of Waste Disposal Contractors Ltd.
N.A.W.D.O.F.F. National Association of Wholesale Distributors of Frozen Foods
N.A.W.N.D. National Association of Wholesale Newspaper Distributors
N.A.W.P. National Association of Women Pharmacists
N.A.W.P.M. National Association of Wholesale Paint Merchants
N.A.Y.C. National Association of Youth Clubs
N.A.Y.O. National Association of Youth Orchestras

Nazi National Socialist German Workers' Party
Nb Nimbus
    Niobium
N.B. Naval Base
    New Brunswick
    North Borneo
    North Britain
    North British
    Nota Bene (mark well)
n.b. no ball (cricket)
N.B.A. National Benzole and Allied Products Association
    National Brassfoundry Association
    Net Book Agreement
    North British Academy
N.B.B.C. National Brass Band Club
N.B.A.H.M.F. National Building and Allied Hardware Manufacturers Federation
N.B.E.E. National Board for Bakery Education
N.B.C. National Book Council (now N.B.L.)
    National Broadcasting Council
    National Broadcasting Company (U.S.)
N.B.D.C. National Broadcasting Development Committee
N.b.E. North by East
N.B.E.R. National Bureau of Economic Research
N.B.F. National Bedding Federation Ltd.
N.B.G. No bloody good
N.B.I. National Benevolent Institution
N.B.L. National Book League (formerly N.B.C.)
    Not bloody likely
N.B.P.I. National Board for Prices and Incomes
n. Br. nördliche Breite (north latitude)
n. br. naval brass
N.B.R. National Buildings Record
N.B.R.I. National Building Research Institute (South Africa)
N.B.S. National Bakery School
    National Broadcasting Service (of New Zealand)
    National Bureau of Standards (U.S.)
N.B.S.S. National Bible Society of Scotland
    National British Softball Society
nb.st. nimbo-stratus
N.B.T.P.I. National Book Trade Provident Institution
N.b.W. North by West
N.C. National Certificate
    National Congress
    National Council
    Nature Conservancy
    New Church
    Newspaper Conference
    Nitro-cellulose
    North Carolina
    Northern Command
n.c. new charter
    north country

N.C.A. National Council of Aviculture
National Cricket Association
No Copies Available
N.C.A.A. National Collegiate Athletic Association (U.S.)
Northern Counties Athletic Association
N.C.A.B. National Citizen's Advice Bureaux Committee
N.C.A.C.C. National Civil Aviation Consultative Committee
N.C.A.I. National Congress of American Indians
N.C.A.V.A.E. National Committee for Audio-Visual Aids in Education
N.C.A.W. National Council for Animal's Welfare
N.C.B. National Coal Board
N.C.B.A. National Cattle Breeders' Association
N.C.B.F.C.C. Northern Counties Border Fancy Canary Club
N.C.B.M.P. National Council of Building Material Producers
N.C.C. National Caravan Council, Ltd.
National Computing Centre
National Coursing Club
Non-Combatant Corps
Northern Counties Committee (Northern Ireland)
N.C.C.A. National Club Cricket Association
N.C.C.I. National Committee for Commonwealth Immigrants
N.C.C.L. National Council for Civil Liberties
N.C.C.M. National Council of Catholic Men
N.C.C.O.P. National Corporation for the Care of Old People
N.C.C.P.C. National Cervical Cancer Prevention Campaign
N.C.C.T. National Council for Civic Theatres Ltd.
N.C.C.W. National Council of Catholic Women
N.C.D. Naval Construction Department
No can do
N.C.D.L. National Canine Defence League
N.C.E.C. National Christian Education Council
N.C.E.T. National Council for Educational Technology
N.C.F.S. National Conference of Friendly Societies
N.C.H. National Children's Home
n.Chr. nach Christo (after Christ)
N.C.H.S.O. National Committee of Hungarian Student Organisation(s)
n.c.i. no common interest
N.C.I.C. National Cancer Institute of Canada
N.C.I.T. National Council on Inland Transport
N.C.L. National Central Library
National Chemical Laboratory (now merged with N.P.L., Teddington)
National Church League
N.C.L.C. National Council of Labour Colleges

N.C.M. National College of Music
N.C.M.U.A. National Committee of the Monotype Users' Associations
N.C.N. National Council of Nurses
N.C.N.C. National Council of Nigerian Citizens
N.C.O. Non-Commissioned Officer
N.C.O.I. National Council for the Omnibus Industry
N.C.P. National Cycling Proficiency
n.c.p. normal circular pitch
N.C.P.P.L. National Committee on Prisons and Prison Labour
N.C.P.S. Non-contributory Pension Scheme
N.C.Q.R. National Council for Quality and Reliability
N.C.R. National Cash Register Company
No Carbon Required
N.C.R.D. National Council for Research and Development, Israel
N.C.R.E. Naval Construction Research Establishment
N.C.R.L. National Chemical Research Laboratory (South Africa)
N.C.R.T. National College of Rubber Technology
N.C.S. National Chrysanthemum Society
N.C.S.S. National Cactus and Succulent Society
National Council of Social Service
N.C.T. National Chamber of Trade
National Childbirth Trust
N.C.T.D. National College of Teachers of the Deaf (Inc.)
N.C.T.F. National Check Traders' Federation
N.C.T.L. National Commercial Temperance League
N.C.U. National Cyclists' Union
N.C.U.M.C. National Council for the Unmarried Mother and her Child
n.c.v. no commercial value
N.C.W. National Council of Women (of Great Britain)
N.C.W.A. National Children's Wear Association
N.C.W.G.B. National Council of Women of Great Britain
Nd Neodymium
nd. niederdruck (low pressure)
N.D. National Debt
National Diploma
North Dakota
Notre Dame (Our Lady)
N.d. No(t) date(d)
N.D.A. National Dairymen's Association
National Diploma in Agriculture
n.d.a. not dated at all
N.Dak. North Dakota
N.D.B.I. National Dairymen's Benevolent Institution
N.D.C.S. National Deaf Children's Society
N.D.D. National Diploma in Dairying
National Diploma in Design

cont.

Navigation and Direction Division

N.D.D.T. National Diploma in Dairy Technology

N.D.E.A. National Display Equipment Association

N.D.F.A. National Drama Festivals Association

N.D.F. National Diploma in Forestry

N.D.H. National Diploma in Horticulture

Ndl. Nederland (The Netherlands)

N.D.L. Norddeutscher Lloyd

N.D.M.B. National Defense Mediation Board (U.S.)

N.D.O. National Debt Office
Northern Dance Orchestra (B.B.C.)

N.D.O.A. National Dog Owners' Association

N.D.P. National Diploma in Poultry Husbandry

n.d.p. normal diametric pitch

N.D.P.A. National Dairy Producers' Association

N.D.P.K.C. National Domestic Poultry Keepers' Council

N.D.P.S. National Data Processing Service

N.D.R.C. National Defence Research Committee

N.D.S. National Dahlia Society

N.D.S.B. Narcotic Drugs Supervisory Body (U.N.)

N.D.T. non-destructive testing

n.d.t. note du traducteur (translator's note)

N.D.T.S. Non-Destructive Testing Society of Great Britain

N.D.U. Notre-Dame University

Ne Neon

Ne. Neuchatel

N.E. National Executive
Naval Engineer
New Edition
New England
News Editor
North-East(erly)
North-Eastern

N/E. No Effects

n.e. not essential
not exceeding

N.E.A. National Education Association
National Enterprise Association

N.E.A.C. New English Art Club

N.E.A.F. Near East Air Force

N.E.A.H.I. Near East Animal Health Institute

N.E.A.R. National Emergency Alarm Repeater (U.S.)

Neb. Nebraska

N.E.B. New English Bible

Nebr. Nebraska

N.E.B.S.S. National Examinations Board in Supervisory Studies

N.E. by E. North East by East

N.E. by N. North East by North

N.E.C. National Executive Committee

n.e.c. not elsewhere classified

N.E.C.I.E.S. North East Coast Institution of Engineers and Shipbuilders

N.E.C.T.A. National Electrical Contractors' Trading Association

necy. necessary
necessity

N.E.D. New English Dictionary

N.E.D.C. National Economic Development Council
North-East Development Council

N.E.D.O. National Economic Development Office

N.E.E.B. North-East Engineering Bureau
North Eastern Electricity Board

N.E.E.T.U. National Engineering and Electrical Trade Union

N.E.F. New Education Fellowship

N.E.F.A. North East Frontier Agency

N.E.F.C. Near East Forestry Commission

neg. negation
negative(ly)
negotiate

N.E.G.B. North Eastern Gas Board

N.E.G.I. National Federation of Engineering and General Ironfounders

negt. négociant (merchant)

Neh. Nehemiah

N.E.I. Netherlands East Indies
Nouvelles Équipes Internationales (Union of Christian Democrats)

n.e.i. non est inventus (he, she *or* it has not been found)
not elsewhere indicated

N.E.I.M.M.E. North of England Institute of Mining and Mechanical Engineering

N.E.L. National Engineering Laboratory

nem.con. nemine contradicente (nobody contradicting)

nem.dis. nemine dissentiente (nobody dissenting)

N.E.M.P.A. North-Eastern Master Printers' Alliance

N.Eng. New England

neol. neologism

N.E.O.P.A.C. North East Overseas Publicity Advisory Committee

Nep. Nepal
Neptune

N.E.P. New Economic Policy (Russia)

n.e.p. new edition pending

N.E.P.A.L. National Egg Packer's Association, Ltd.

N.E.P.C. Northern Economic Planning Council

N.E.P.P. National Egg and Poultry Promotion

N.E.P.R.A. National Egg Producers Retailers Association Ltd.

N.E.R. North Eastern Region

N.E.R.A. National Emergency Relief Administration (U.S.)

N.E.R.C. National Electronic Research Council
National English Rabbit Club
Natural Environment Research Council

NERO Sodium (Na) Experimental Reactor of Zero power

N.E.R.V.A. Nuclear Engine for Rocket Vehicle Application

N.E.S. National Extension Service (India)
Naval Education Service

n.e.s. not elsewhere specified

N.E.S.C. Nuclear Engineering and Science Conference

NESTOR Neutron Source Thermal Reactor

net netto (not subject to deduction)

n.e.t. not earlier than

N.E.T.A.C. Nuclear Energy Trade Associations' Conference

Neth. Netherlands

n. et m. nocte et mane (night and morning)

neut. neuter
neutral

Nev. Nevada

news. newsagency

N.F. National Formula
Newfoundland
Newfoundland Law Reports
New Forest
New French
No Funds
Norman French
Northumberland Fusiliers

N.-F. Norman-French

n.F. neue Folge (new series)

n.f. noun feminine

N.F.A. National Farmers' Association
National Federation of Anglers

n.f.a. no further action

N.F.A.C. National Federation of Aerial Contractors Ltd.

N.F.B.Ca. National Film Bureau of Canada

N.F.B.P.M. National Federation of Builders' and Plumbers' Merchants

N.F.B.S.S. National Federation of Bakery Students' Societies

N.F.B.T.E. National Federation of Building Trades' Employers

N.F.B.T.O. National Federation of Building Trades' Operatives (*now* N.F.C.U.)

N.F.C.D.A. National Federation of Civil Defence Associations of Great Britain and the Commonwealth

N.F.C.D.S. National Federation of Clubs for the Divorced and Separated

N.F.C.G. National Federation of Consumer Groups

N.F.C.G.A. National Federation of Constructional Glass Associations

N.F.C.I. National Federation of Clay Industries

N.F.C.S. National Federation of Construction Supervisors

N.F.C.S.I.T. National Federation of Cold Storage and Ice Trades

N.F.C.T.A. National Federation of Corn Trade Associations

N.F.C.T.C. National Foundry Craft Training Centre

N.F.C.U. National Federation of Construction Unions

N.F.D. National Federation of Drapers and Allied Traders, Ltd.

N.F.D.C. National Federation of Demolition Contractors

N.F.E.A. National Federated Electrical Association

N.F.E.R. National Foundation for Educational Research

N.F.E.T.M. National Federation of Engineers' Tool Manufacturers

N.F.F. National Froebel Foundation

N.F.F.C. National Film Finance Corporation

N.F.F.F. National Federation of Fish Friers Ltd.

N.F.F.P.T. National Federation of Fruit and Potato Trades, Ltd.

N.F.F.Q.O. National Federation of Freestone Quarry Owners

N.F.F.T.U. National Federation of Furniture Trade Unions

Nfg. Nachfolger (successor)

N.F.G.S. National Federation of Gramaphone Societies Ltd.

N.F.H.S. National Federation of Housing Societies

N.F.I. National Federation of Ironmongers

N.F.I.S.M. National Federation of Iron and Steel Merchants

N.F.L.T.M.P. Nuffield Foreign Language Materials Teaching Project

N.F.L.V. National Federation of Licensed Victuallers

N.F.M.A. National Fireplace Makers Association

N.F.M.A. Needleloom Felt Manufacturers' Association

N.F.M.P. National Federation of Master Painters and Decorators of England and Wales

N.F.M.P.S. National Federation of Master Printers in Scotland

N.F.M.S. National Federation of Music Societies

N.F.M.S.L.C.E. National Federation of Master Steeplejacks and Lightning Conductor Engineers

N.F.M.T.A. National Federation of Meat Traders' Associations

N.F.O. National Freight Organization

N.F.O.A.P.A. National Federation of Old-Age Pensioners' Associations

N.F.O.H.A. National Federation of Off-Licence Holders Associations of England and Wales

N.F.O.O. Naval Forward Observing Officer

N.F.P. & D.H.E. National Federation of Plumbers and Domestic Heating Engineers

N.F.P.C. National Federation of Plastering Contractors

N.F.P.H.C. National Federation of Permanent Holiday Camps

N.F.P.R. National Fund for Research into Poliomyelitis and other Crippling Diseases

N.F.P.T.A. National Federation of Parent-Teacher Associations

N.F.P.W. National Federation of Professional Workers

N.F.R.C. National Federation of Roofing Contractors
N.F.R.N. National Federation of Retail Newsagents, Booksellers and Stationers
N.F.S. National Fire Service
N.F.S.A. National Fire Services' Associations
National Federation of Sea Anglers
N.F.S.H. National Federation of Spiritual Healers
N.F.T. National Film Theatre
N.F.T.A. National Fillings Trades Association
N.F.T.M.S. National Federation of Terrazzo-Mosaic Specialists
N.F.T.W.M.A. National Federation of Textile Works Managers' Association
N.F.U. National Farmers' Unions
N.F.U.S. National Farmers Union of Scotland
N.F.V.T. National Federation of Vehicle Trades
N.F.W.I. National Federation of Women's Institutes
N.F.W.P.M. National Federation of Wholesale Poultry Merchants
N.F.Y.F.C. National Federation of Young Farmers' Clubs
Ng. Norwegian
N.G. National Gallery
National Government
National Guard
National Guardsman
New Grenada
New Guinea
No good
Noble Grand
North German
n.g. new genus
not given
n.-g. nitro-glycerine
N.G.A. National Graphical Association
N.G.A.C. National Guard Air Corps (U.S.)
N.G.B. Northern Gas Board
N.G.C. National Guild of Co-operators
New General Catalogue (Astronomy)
N.gen. New genus
N.G.F. National Grocers' Federation
N.Gk. New Greek
N.Gmc. North Germanic
N.G.O. Non-governmental Organisations
N.Gr. New Greek
N.G.R.C. National Greyhound Racing Club
N.G.R.S. Narrow Gauge Railway Society
National Greyhound Racing Society of Great Britain Limited
N.G.S. National Gardens Scheme
ngt. négociant (merchant)
N.G.T. National Guild of Telephonists
N.G.T.E. National Gas Turbine Establishment
N.G.U.T. National Group of Unit Trusts

N.H. National Hunt
Naval Hospital
New Hampshire
Northumberland Hussars
N.H.A. National Hardware Alliance, Ltd.
National Horse Association of Great Britain
N.H.B.R.C. National House-Builders' Registration Council
N.H.C. National Hamster Council
National Hunt Committee
N.H.D. Doctor of Natural History
N.Heb. New Hebrew
N.-Heb. New Hebrides
N.H.F. National Hairdressers' Federation
N.H.G. New High German
N.H.I. National Health Insurance
N.H.M.R.C.A. National Health and Medical Research Council of Australia
n.h.p. nominal horsepower
N.H.R. National Hunt Rules
N.H.R.A. National Roller Hockey Association of Great Britain
N.H.R.P. National Hurricane Research Project
N.H.R.U. National Home Reading Union
N.H.S. National Health Service
N.H.S.R. National Hospital Service Reserve
N.H.T.P.C. National Housing and Town Planning Council
Ni Nickel
N.I. National Insurance
Native Infantry
Naval Instructor
Naval Intelligence
Northern Ireland
Northern Ireland Law Reports
Nuclear Institute
N.I.A.A.A. Northern Ireland Amateur Athletic Association
N.I.A.B. National Institute of Agricultural Botany
N.I.A.B.C. Northern Ireland Association of Boys' Clubs
N.I.A.E. National Institute of Adult Education
National Institute of Agricultural Engineering
N.I.B. National Institute for the Blind (*now* R.N.I.B.)
Nibmar no independence before majority African rule
Nic. Nicaragua
N.I.C. National Incomes Commission
N.I.C.A.P. National Investigating Committee for Aerial Phenomena
N.I.C.B. National Industrial Conference Board
N.I.C.E.I.C. National Inspection Council for Electrical Installation Contracting
N.I.C.F. Northern Ireland Cycling Federation
North of Ireland Cricket and Football Club
N.I.C.H.A. Northern Ireland Chest and Heart Association

N.I.C.I.A. Northern Ireland Coal Importers' Association
N.I.C.S.S. Northern Ireland Council of Social Services
N.I.D. National Institute for the Deaf (now R.N.I.D.)
  Naval Intelligence Division
  Northern Ireland District
N.I.D.C. Northern Ireland Development Council
N.I.D.F.A. National Independent Drama Festivals Association
niedr. neidrig (low)
N.I.E.F. National Ironfounding Employers' Federation
N.I.E.S.R. National Institute of Economic and Social Research
N.I.F.E.S. National Industrial Fuel Efficiency Service
Nig. Nigeria(n)
N.I.G.A. North of Ireland Grocers' Association
N.I.G.F.C.C. Northern Ireland Gloster Fancy Canary Club
N.I.H. National Institute of Hardware
  North Irish Horse
N.I.I.P. National Institute of Industrial Psychology
N.I.M.H. National Institute of Medical Herbalists Ltd.
n. imp. new impression
N.I.M.R. National Institute for Medical Research
N.I.O. National Institute of Oceanography
N.I.O.C. National Iranian Oil Company
N.I.P.H. National Institute of Poultry Husbandry
N.I.P.R. National Institute of Personnel Research (South Africa)
ni.pri. nisi prius (unless previously)
N. Ir. Northern Ireland
N.I.R.D. National Institute for Research in Dairying
N.I.R.N.S. National Institute for Research in Nuclear Science
N.I.S.C. National Industrial Space Committee
N.I.S.E.R. Nigerian Institute for Social and Economic Research
N.I.T. None in Town
N.I.T.A. Nicophilic Institute of Tobacco Antiquarians Ltd.
N.I.W.A.A.A. Northern Ireland Women's Amateur Athletic Association
N.J. New Jersey
N.J.A. National Jewellers' Association
N.J.A.B. National Joint Apprenticeship Board for the Building Industry
N.J.A.C. National Joint Advisory Council
N.J.C. National Joint Council
N.J.C.B.I. National Joint Council for the Building Industry Administrative Council
N.J.C.C. National Joint Consultative Committee
N.J.F. Nordiske Jordbrugsforskeres Forening (Scandinavian Agricultural Research Workers' Association)

N.J.I.C. National Joint Industrial Council
N.J.N.C. National Joint Negotiating Committee
N.K. Not known
N.K.G.B. Norodny Komitet Gosudarstvennoi Bezopasnosti (People's Commissariat of State Security (Russia))
N.K.V.D. Norodny Komitet Vnutrennih Del (People's Commissariat of Internal Affairs (Russia))
Nl. National
N.L. National Labour
  National Liberal
  Navy League
  Navy List
  non liquet (it is not clear)
  North Latitude
N.-L. New Latin
n.l. new line
  nicht löslich (not soluble)
  non licet (it is not permitted)
  non longue (not far)
N.Lat. North Latitude
N.L.B. National Labor Board (U.S.)
  National Library for the Blind
N.L.C. National Liberal Club
N.L.C.A. Norwegian Lutheran Church of America
N.L.C.I.F. National Light Castings Ironfounders' Federation
N.L.F. National Labour Federation
  National Liberal Federation
N.L.I. National Library of Ireland
  National Lifeboat Institution (now R.N.L.I.)
N.L.L. National Lending Library for Science and Technology
N.L.M.C. National Labour Management Council
N.L.O. National Liberal Organization
  Naval Liaison Officer
N.L.O.G.F. National Lubricating Oi' and Grease Federation
N.L.R. Newfoundland Law Reports
  Nigeria Law Reports
  Nyasaland Law Reports
N.L.R.B. National Labor Relations Board (U.S.)
N.L.S. National Library of Scotland
n.l.t. not later than
N.L.W. National Library of Wales
Nly. Northerly
N.L.Y.L. National League of Young Liberals
nm. nutmeg
N.M. National Marketing
  New Mexico
n.m. nautical miles
  nocte et mane (night and morning)
  noun masculine
n/m. no mark
N.M.A. Lloyd's Underwriters' Non-Marine Association
  Needle Makers' Association
N.M.B. National Maritime Board
N.M.B.L.A. North Midland Branch of the Library Association
N.M.C. National Marketing Council
  National Mouse Club
n.m.c. no more credit

N.M.E. National Military Establishment (U.S.)
N.-Mex. New Mexico
N.M.G.C. National Marriage Guidance Council
N.M.H.R.A. National Mobile Homes Residents Association
N.M.H.T.A. North Midland Home Timber Association
N.M.I.S. Newspapers Mutual Insurance Society, Ltd.
N.M.P.A. National Marine Paint Association
N.M.P.C. National Milk Publicity Council
N.M.R. National Military Representatives with S.H.A.P.E.
National Milk Record
N.M.S.S.A. Nato Maintenance Supply Services Agency
N.M.S.U. Naval Motion Study Unit
N.M.T. National Maritime Trust
N.M.T.F. National Market Traders' Federation
N.M.T.F.A. National Master Tile Fixers' Association
N.M.T.S. National Milk Testing Service
N.M.U. National Maritime Union
nn. names
nouns
N.N. Neurotics Nomine
n.n. neutralization number
no name
N.N.E. North North-East
N.N.F. Northern Nurses' Federation
N.N.I. Noise and nuisance index
Noise and Number Index
N.N.R.C. Neutral Nations Repatriation Commission
N.N.S.C. Neutral Nations Supervisory Commission
N.N.W. North North-West
No Norium
No. Numero (number)
no. nuero (number)
N.O. Natural Order
Naval Officer
Naval Operations
Navigation Officer
New Orleans
N/O. No Orders
n.o. not out
nob. nobis (for or on our part)
noble
n.o.c. not otherwise classified
N.O.D. Naval Ordnance Department
N.O.D.A. National Operatic and Dramatic Association
n.o.e. not otherwise enumerated
n.o.h.p. not otherwise herein provided
n.o.i.b.n. not otherwise indexed by name
N.O.I.C. Naval Officer in Charge
N.O.I.L. Naval Ordnance Inspection Laboratory
nol. pros. nolle prosequi (will not prosecute)
nom. nomenclature
nominal
nominative
Nomm. Nomination
172

nom. nov. nomen novum (new name)
Non-Coll. Non-Collegiate
Non-Com. Non-Commissioned
Noncon. Noncomformist
non cul. non culpabilis (not guilty)
non pros. non prosequitur (he or she does not prosecute)
non res. non resident
non seq. non sequitur (it does not follow)
nonstand. nonstandard
n.o.p. not otherwise provided (for)
N.O.P.W.C. National Old People's Welfare Council
Nor. Norman
Norway
Norwegian
Norwich
nor. normal
north(ern)
NORAD North American Air Defense Command
NORDFORSK Nordiska Samarbetsorganisationen för Teknisk-Naturvetenskaplig Forening (Scandinavian Council for Applied Research)
Norf. Norfolk
norm. normalised
NORTHAG Northern Army Group
Northants. Northamptonshire
Northumb. Northumberland
Norvic. Norvicensis (of Norwich)
Norw. Norwegian
nos. numbers
n.o.s. not otherwise specified
Not. Notary
not. notice
N.O.T.B. National Ophthalmic Treatment Board
Nottm. Nottingham
Notts. Nottinghamshire
notwg. notwithstanding
Nov. November
nov. novel
novice
novitiate
n.o.y. not out yet
Np Neptunium
N.P. New Paragraph
New Pattern
New Providence
Nitro-proof
Nobel Prize
Norwegian Patent
Notary Public
N.p. No place, publisher, printer
n.p. net personality
net proceeds
new paragraph
nickel-plated
non participating
normal pitch
n/p. net proceeds
N.P.A. National Parks Association (U.S.)
National Pawnbrokers' Association, Inc.
National Pigeon Association
National Port Authority
National Production Authority
Newspaper Publishers' Association

N.P.A.C.I. National Production Advisory Council on Industry
N.P.B. National Provincial Bank
N.P.B.A. National Pig Breeders' Association
N.P.C. National Peace Council
 Nato Parliamentarians' Conference
 Naval Personnel Committee
 Northern People's Congress (Nigeria)
N.P.D. North Polar Distance
N.P.F. Newspaper Press Fund
n.p.f. not provided for
N.P.F.A. National Playing Fields Association
N.Ph. Nuclear Physics
N.P.I.P.F. Newspaper and Printing Industries' Pension Fund
n.pl. noun plural
N.P.L. National Physical Laboratory
n.p.n.a. no protest for nonacceptance
N.P.O. New Philharmonic Orchestra
n.p. or d. no place or date
n.p.p. no passed proof
N.P.P.T.B. National Pig Progeny Testing Board
N.P.S. National Philatelic Society
 National Pony Society
 National Portrait Society
N.P.T. Nuclear non-proliferation treaty
n.p.t. normal pressure and temperature
N.P.T.A. National Paper Trade Association (U.S.)
N.P.U. National Pharmaceutical Union
n.p.v. no par value
N.P.W.A. National Pure Water Association (for the prevention of water pollution)
N.P.Y. National Productivity Year
n.q.a. net quick assets
Nr. Near
 Number
nr. near
N.R. National Register
 Naval Rating
 Navy Regulations
 Northern Rhodesia
 North Riding
N./R. No risk
n.r. net register
 no risk
 non repetatur (not to be repeated)
N.R.A. National Recovery Act (U.S.)
 National Reclamation Association
 National Rifle Association
 National Rounders Association
n.r.a.d. no risk after discharge
N.R.C. National Recreation Centre
 National Research Council
 Northern Railfans' Club
N.R.C.C. National Republican Congressional Committee (U.S.)
N.R.C.S. National Roller Canary Society
N.R.D. National Register of Designers
 Naval Recruiting Department
N.R.D.B. Natural Rubber Development Board
N.R.D.C. National Research Development Corporation *cont.*

 National Retail Distributive Certificate
N.R.E.S.A. National Rural and Environmental Studies Association
N.R.F. National Relief Fund
 Nouvelle Revue Française
N.R.G.S. Narrow Gauge Railway Society
N.R.H.A. National Roller Hockey Association
N.R.I.A.D. National Register of Industrial Art Designers
N.R.L. National Reference Library of Science and Invention
 Nelson Research Laboratory
N.R.L.B. Northern Regional Library Bureau
N.R.L.R. Northern Rhodesia Law Reports
N.R.N.L.R. Northern Region of Nigeria Law Reports
Nro. Numero (number)
N.R.P.R.A. Natural Rubber Producers' Research Association
N.R.R. Northern Rhodesia Regiment
N.R.S. National Rose Society
 Naval Recruiting Service
 Navy Records Society
N.R.S.A. National Rural Studies Association (*now* N.R.E.S.A.)
n.r.t. net registered tonnage
Ns. Nimbostratus
N.S. National Service
 National Society
 Natural Science
 Naval Service
 Newcomen Society
 New School
 New Series
 Newspaper Society
 New Style
 Not Sufficient
 Notre Seigneur (Our Lord)
 Nova Scotia
 Numismatic Society
N.-S. Notre-Seigneur (Our Lord)
N/S. Not Sufficient
n.s. Graduate of the Royal Naval Staff College, Greenwich
 near side
 nickel steel
 not specified
N.S.A. National Service Acts
 National Sheep Association
 National Skating Association
 National Sawmilling Association
 New Society of Artists
 Nursery School Association of Great Britain and Northern Ireland
N.S.A.A. National Sulphuric Acid Association
N.S.A.C. National Society for Autistic Children
N.S.A.C.S. National Society for the Abolition of Cruel Sports
N.S.A.E. National Society for Art Education
N.S.A.F.A. National Service Armed-Forces Act

173

N.S.A.S. National Smoke Abatement Society
N.S.B.A. National Sheep Breeders' Association
National Silica Brickmakers' Association
.S.B.B.A. National School Brass Band Association
N.S.B.S.S.A. National Strict Baptist Sunday School Association
N.S.B.Y. North Somerset and Bristol Yeomanry
N.S.C. National Safety Council
National Savings Committee
National Security Council (U.S.)
National Sporting Club
N.S.C.A. National Society for Clean Air
N.S.C.M.A. Natural Sausage Casings Manufacturers Association
N.S.C.R. National Society for Cancer Relief
N.S.D. Naval Stores Department
N.S.C.N. National Society of Children's Nurseries
N.S.E. Nottingham Society of Engineers
N.S.E.S. National Society of Electrotypers and Stereotypers
n.s.f. not sufficient funds
N.S.F.G.B. National Ski Federation of Great Britain
N.S.G.P.M.A. National Salt Glazed Pipe Manufacturers' Association
N.S.G.T. Non-Self-Governing Territories
N.S.H.E.B. North of Scotland Hydro-Electric Board
N.S.I.C. Noster Salvator Iesus Christus (Our Saviour Jesus Christ)
N.S.I.M.E. North Staffordshire Institute of Mining Engineers
n. sing. noun singular
N.S.I.S. National Softwood Importers' Section of the Timber Trade Federation
N.S.J. Nuestro Señor Jesucristo (Our Lord Jesus Christ)
N.-S.J.-C. Notre-Seigneur Jésus-Christ (Our Lord Jesus Christ)
N.S.K.K. Nationalistisches Sozialistisches Kraftfahrkorps (Nazi German Automobile Corps)
N.S.L. National Service League
National Sporting League
National Sunday League
N.S.M. National Savings Movement
National Socialist Movement
N.S.M.H.C. National Society for Mentally Handicapped Children
N.S.M.M. National Society of Metal Mechanics
N.S.M.P. National Society of Master Patternmakers
N.S.O. Naval Staff Officer
n.sp. new species
N.S.P.A. National Students' Press Association
Nova Scotia Pharmaceutical Association
N.S.P.C.A. National Society for the Prevention of Cruelty to Animals (*now* R.S.P.C.A.)

N.S.P.C.C. National Society for the Prevention of Cruelty to Children
n.s.p.f. not specially provided for
N.S.P.S. National Sweet Pea Society
N.S.P.S.E. National Society of Painters, Sculptors and Engravers
n.sr. notre sieur (our lord)
N.S.R.A. National Small-Bore Rifle Association
N.S.R.C. National Shoe Retailers' Council
N.S.R.F. Nova Scotia Research Foundation
N.S.S. New Shakespeare Society
N.S.S.U. National Sunday School Union and Christian Youth Service
N.S.T.C. Nova Scotia Technical College
N.S.T.I.C. Naval Scientific and Technical Information Centre
N.S.Trip. Natural Science Tripos
N.S.W. New South Wales
N.S.W.L.V.R. New South Wales Land Valuation Reports
N.S.W.S.R. New South Wales State Reports
N.S.Y. New Scotland Yard
Nt Nitron
N.T. National Theatre
National Trust
Neap Tide
New Testament
New Translation
Northern Territory
Not Titled
No Trumps
n.t. net tonnage
normal temperature
N.T.A. Natal Society of Artists
National Therapeutics Association
National Trolleybus Association
Nurse Teachers' Association
N.T.C. Nigerian Tobacco Company
n.t.c. negative temperature coefficient
N.T.C.H.A. National Taxi and Car Hire Association
N.T.D.A. National Trade Development Association
National Tyre Distributors' Association
N.T.D.S. Naval Tactical Data System
N.T.E.C. National Traction Engine Club
N.T.E.T.A. National Traction Engine and Traction Association, Inc.
ntfy. notify
N.T.G.B. North Thames Gas Board
N.T. Gk. New Testament Greek
Nthb. Northumberland
nthn. northern
n.t.m. net ton mile
N.T.O. Naval Transport Officer
n.t.o. not taken out
N.T.P. Normal Temperature and Progress
n.t.p. normal temperature and blood pressure
no title page
N.T.P.S. National Turf Protection Society

N.T.R.L. National Telecommunications Research Laboratory (South Africa)

N.T.S. Naradno-Trudovoy Soyuz (Popular Labour Alliance)
National Trust for Scotland
Naval Transport Service (U.S.)
Nevada Test Site

n.t.s. not to scale

nt. wt. net weight

N.U. Name Unknown
National Union
Nations Unies (United Nations)
Naval Unit
Northern Union

n.u. name unknown

N.U.A.T. Nordisk Union för Alkoholfri Trafik (Scandinavian Union for Non-Alcoholic Traffic)

N.U.A.W. National Union of Agricultural Workers

N.U.B.E. National Union of Bank Employees

N.U.B.S.O. National Union of Boot and Shoe Operatives

N.U.C.O. National Union of Co-operative Officials

N.U.C.U.A. National Union of Conservative and Unionist Associations

N.U.D.B.T.W. National Union of Dyers, Bleachers and Textile Workers

N.U.F.C.W. National Union of Funeral and Cemetery Workers (*now* N.U.F.S.O.)

N.U.F.L.A.T. National Union of the Footwear, Leather and Allied Trades

N.U.F.S.O. National Union of Funeral Service Operators

N.U.G.M.W. National Union of General and Municipal Workers

N.U.G.S.A.T. National Union of Gold, Silver and Allied Trades

N.U.H.W. National Union of Hosiery Workers

N.U.I. National University of Ireland

N.U.I.W. National Union of Insurance Workers

N.U.J. National Union of Journalists

N.U.J.M.B. Northern Universities Joint Matriculation Board

N.U.L. & M.W. National Union of Lock and Metal Workers

N.U.L.O. National Union of Labour Organisers

N.U.L.W. & A.T. National Union of Leather Workers and Allied Trades

Num. Numbers

num. number
numerals

N.U.M. National Union of Manufacturers
National Union of Mineworkers

Numis. Numismatics

N.U.P. National Union of Protestants

N.U.P.B.P.W. National Union of Printing, Bookbinding and Paper Workers

N.U.P.E. National Union of Public Employees

N.U.P.T. National Union of Press Telegraphists

N.U.R. National Union of Railwaymen

N.U.R.A. National Union of Ratepayers' Associations

N.U.R.C. National Union of Retail Confectioners

N.U.R.T. National Union of Retail Tobacconists

N.U.S. National Union of Seamen
National Union of Students

N.U.S.A.S. National Union of South African Students

N.U.S.S. National Union of Small Shopkeepers

N.U.S.U.K. National Union of Students of the United Kingdom

N.U.T. National Union of Teachers

N.-u.-T. Newcastle-upon-Tyne

N.U.T. & G.W. National Union of Tailors and Garment Workers

N.U.T.G. National Union of Townswomen's Guilds

N.U.T.N. National Union of Trained Nurses

N.U.T.S. National Union of Track Statisticians

N.U.V.B. National Union of Vehicle Builders

N.U.W.A. National Unemployed Workers Association

N.U.W.W. National Union of Women Workers

Nv. Nonvoting

N.V. Naamloze Vennootschap (limited liability company)
New Versian

N.V.A. National Villa Association

N.V.B. National Volunteer Brigade

N.V.M. Nativity of the Virgin Mary

n.v.m. non-volatile matter

N.V.M.A. National Veterinary Medical Association

N.V.O. Northern Variety Orchestra (B.B.C.)

N.V.R.S. National Vegetable Research Station

N.W. North Wales
North-West(erly)
North-Western

n.w. net weight

N.W.A. North-West Africa(n)

N.W. by N. North-West by North

N.W. by W. North-West by West

N.W.C.A. National Wholesale Confectioners' Association
National Women Citizens' Association

N.W.E.A.B.I. North Western Educational Association for the Building Industry

N.W.E.B. North Western Electricity Board

N.W.F.P. North West Frontier Province

n.w.g. national wire gauge

N.W.G.A. National Wholesale Grocers Alliance Ltd.
National Wool Growers' Association

N.W.G.B. North Western Gas Board

N.W.I. Netherlands West Indies

n.w.l. natural wave-length

N.W.M.P. North-West Mounted Police (*now* R.C.M.P.)
N.W.M.P.A. North Wales Master Printers' Alliance
North-Western Master Printers' Alliance
N.W.P. North-Western Polytechnic
North-West Provinces
N.W.R.L.S. North Western Regional Library System
n.w.s. normal water surface
N.W.S.A. National Women's Suffrage Association
N.W.S.D. Naval Weather Service Department
n. wt. net weight
N.W.T. North-Western Territories
n.w.t. non watertight
n.w.t.d. non watertight door
N.W.T.E.C. National Wool Textile Export Corporation
N.Y. New Year
New York
N.Y.C. New York Central Railway
New York City
n.y.d. not yet diagnosed
N.Y.H.A. National Yacht Harbour Association
N.Y.H.S. New York Historical Society
nyk. nykyinen (current)
N.Y.L.C. National Young Life Campaign
Ny.L.R. Nyasaland Law Reports
N.Y.O. National Youth Orchestra of Great Britain
n.y.p. not yet published
N.Y.S. New York State
N.Y.S.A. New York State Assembly
N.Y.S.A.C. New York State Athletic Commission
N.Y.T. National Youth Theatre
New York Times
N.Y.T.C. National Youth Temperance Council
N.Z. Neutrality Zone
New Zealand

N.Z.A.B. New Zealand Association of Bacteriologists
N.Z.A.Sc. New Zealand Association of Scientists
N.Z.B.S. New Zealand Broadcasting Service
N.Z.C.E.R. New Zealand Council for Educational Research
N.Z.D. New Zealand Division
N.Z.D.A. New Zealand Department of Agriculture
New Zealand Dietetic Association
N.Z.D.C.S. New Zealand Department of Census and Statistics
N.Z.D.L.S. New Zealand Department of Lands and Survey
N.Z.D.S.I.R. New Zealand Department of Scientific and Industrial Research
N.Z.E.F. New Zealand Expeditionary Force
N.Z.E.I. New Zealand Electronics Institute
N.Z.E.S. New Zealand Ecological Society
N.Z.F.R.I. New Zealand Forest Research Institute
N.Z.F.S. New Zealand Forest Service
N.Z.Gen.S. New Zealand Genetics Society
N.Z.G.S. New Zealand Geographical Society
N.Z.I.C. New Zealand Institute of Chemistry
N.Z.I.E. New Zealand Institution of Engineers
N.Z.J.C.B. New Zealand Joint Communications Board
N.Z.L.A. New Zealand Library Association
N.Z.L.R. New Zealand Law Reports
N.Z.M.S. New Zealand Meteorological Service
N.Z.S.A. New Zealand Statistical Association
N.Z.V.A. New Zealand Veterinary Association

O

O Oxygen
O. Observe(r)
Occupation
Ocean
Octavo
October
Oculus (eye)
Office(r)
Ohio
Ontario
Operations
Orange
Order
Ordinary
Orient

Osten (East)
Ouest (West)
Owner
o. occasional
octavo
off
ohm
old
only
optimus (best)
organ
ortho
over
overcast
overseer

cont.

O.A. Océan Atlantique (Atlantic Ocean)
Office Address
Officier d'Académie
Officers' Association
Ordnance Artificer
Over All
O/A. On Account of
o.a. onder andere (among others)
O.A.A. Organisation des Nations Unies
pour l'alimentation et l'agri-
culture (United Nations Food
and Agriculture Organisation)
Old Age Assistance
O.A. & H.S. Oxford Architectural and
Historical Society
O.A.B.E.T.A. Office Appliance and
Business Equipment Trades' Asso-
ciation (*now* B.E.T.A.)
O.A.C. Outdoor Advertising Council
O.A.C.I. Organisation de l'aviation
civile internationale (International
Civil Aviation Organisation)
O.A.H. Organization of American His-
torians
O.A.I.A. Organisation des agences d'in-
formation d'Asie (Organisation of
Asian News Agencies)
O.A.M.A. Oil Appliance Manufac-
turers' Association
O.A.M.D.G. Omnia ad Majorem Dei
Gloriam (All to the Greater Glory of
God)
O.A.N.A. Organisation of Asian News
Agencies
O.& A. October and April
O.& C. Onset and Course (*of a disease*)
O.& E. Operations and Engineering
O.& M. Organisation and Methods
O.A.O. Orbiting Astronomical Observ-
atories
O.A.P. Old Age Pension
O.A.S. Old Age Security
On Active Service
Organisation de l'Armée Sec-
rète (Secret Army Organis-
ation, France)
Organisation of American States
O.A.S.I. Old Age and Survivors' In-
surance
OASP Organic Acid Soluble Phos-
phorus
O.A.T.C. Ocean Air Traffic Control
O.A.U. Organisation of African Unity
Ob. Obadiah
ob. obiit (died)
obligation
oboe
O.B. Observed Bearing
Oil Bomb
Old Bailey
Old Boy
Order of Battle
Ordnance Board
Outside Broadcast
O.B.A.A. Oil Burning Apparatus As-
sociation
Obad. Obadiah
obbl. obbligato
O.B.C. Old Boys' Club
O.B.C.H. Overseas Booksellers' Clear-
ing House
obdt. obedient

O.B.E. Officer of the Order of the
British Empire
O.B.I. Order of British India
obj. object(ion)
objective
objn. objection
Obl. Oblong
obl. obligation
oblique
oblong
oblat. oblatum (cachet)
O.B.L.I. Oxford and Buckinghamshire
Light Infantry
O.B.O. Oil, bulk and ore
Ob. Ph. Oblique Photography
O.B.R.A. Overseas Broadcasting Representatives' Association
Obre. Octobre (October)
Obs. The Observer
obs. obscure
observation
observatory
observe(r)
obsolete
obsol. obsolescent
ob.s.p. obiit sine prole (died without
issue)
O.B.S.P. Old Bailey Sessions Papers
Obstet. Obstetrics
obstet. obstetrical
obstetrician
obt. obedient
O.B.T.A. Oak Bark Tanners' Associa-
tion
obtd. obtained
O.B.U. Oriental Boxing Union
O.Bul. Old Bulgarian
O.B.V. Ocean Boarding Vessel
obv. obverse
oc. overcharge
O.C. Observer Corps
Officer Commanding
Old Carthusian
Old Catholic
Old Cheltonian
Old Comrade(s)
Order in Council
Order of Carmelites
Order of the Coif
Ordo Cistercium (Cistercian
Order)
Ordo Charitatis (Order of Charity)
Oslo Convention
Ottawa Convention
O/c. Old charter
Old crop
Overcharge
o.c. office copy
official classification
only child
open charter
open cover
opere citato (in the work cited)
over the counter
o'c. o'clock
O.C.A. Old Comrades Association
O.Carm. Order of Carmelites
O.Cart. Order of Carthusians
O.C.A.S. Organisation of Central Am-
erican States
O.Catal. Old Catalan
Oc.B/L. Ocean Bill of Lading

occ. occasion(ally)
  occurrence
  occidental
O.C.C.A. Oil and Colour Chemists' Association
occas. occasionally
occn. occasion
O.C.D. Office of Civil Defense (U.S.)
  Orden de Carmelitas Descalzas (Order of Discalced Carmelite Nuns)
O.C.D.E. Organisation de coopération et de développement économiques (Organisation for Economic Co-operation and Development)
Oceanog. Oceanography
O.C.F. Officiating Chaplain to the Forces
O.C.F.R. Oxford Committee for Famine Relief
O.C.I.C. Office catholique international du cinéma (International Catholic Film Office)
O.C.M.A. Oil Companies' Materials Association
O.C.M.I. Organisation consultative maritime inter-gouvernementale (Inter-Governmental Maritime Consultative Organisation)
O.Corn. Old Cornish
O.C.P.C.A. Oil and Chemical Pant Constructors Association
O.C.R. Office for Civilian Requirements (U.S.)
  Officer of the Order of the Crown of Rumania
  Optical Character Reading
  Ordinis Cistercianorum Reformatorum (Order of Reformed Cistercians)
O.C.S. Officer Candidate School
  Organe de contrôle des stupéfiants (Drug Supervisory Body)
  Oriental Ceramic Society
O.C.S.O. Order of the Cistercians of the Strict Observance
Oct. Octavius
  Octavo
  October
oct. octave
  octavo
O.C.T.I. Office central des transports internationaux par chemins de fer (Central Office for International Railway Transport)
O.C.T.U. Officer Cadets' Training Unit
octupl. octuplicate
O.C.U.C. Oxford and Cambridge Universities' Club
ocul. oculis (to the eyes)
Od. Odyssey
od. oder (or)
O.D. Doctor of Optometry
  Officer of the Day
  Old Danish
  Old Dutch
  Operations Division
  Ordnance Data
  Ordnance Datum   *cont.*

  Ordnance Department
  Ordnance Depot
O/D. Overdraft
  Overdrawn
o.d. outside diameter
o/d. on demand
O.D.A. Owner-Drivers' Association
O. Dan. Old Danish
O.D.C. Order of Discalced Carmelites
O.D.Ch. Chaplain for Other Denominations
O.D.E.C.A. Organización de Estados Centroamericanos (Organisation of Central American States)
O.D.I. Open Door International (for the Economic Emancipation of the Women Worker)
  Overseas Development Institute, Ltd.
O.D.P. Open Door Policy
O.Ds. Other Denominations
O.D.S.B.A. Oxford Down Sheep Breeders' Association
O.E. Old English
  Old Etonian
  Omissions Excepted
  Original Equipment
  Original Error
O.E.A. Orchestral Employers' Association
  Organisation des états américains (Organisation of American States)
O.E.C.D. Organization for Economic Co-operation and Development (*formerly* O.E.E.C.)
O.E.C.E. Organisation européenne de coopération économique (Organisation for European Economic Co-operation *now* O.E.C.D.)
O.E.C.Q. Organisation européenne pour le contrôle de la qualité (European Organisation for Quality Control)
O.E.D. Oxford English Dictionary
O.E.E.C. Organisation for European Economic Co-operation (*now* O.E.C.D.)
O.E.F. Organisation of Employers Federation and Employers in Developing Countries
O.E.I. Oficina de Educación Iberoamericana (Ibero-American Bureau of Education)
O.E.O. Office of Economic Opportunity (U.S.A.)
  Ordnance Engineer Overseer
O.E.P.P. Organisation européenne et méditerranéenne pour la protection des plantes (European and Mediterranean Plant Protection Organisation)
O.E.R. Officers' Emergency Reserve
O.E.R.S. Organisation européenne de recherches spatiales (European Space Research Organisation)
O.E.S. Order of the Eastern Star
O.F. Odd Fellow
  Old Face
O.-F. Old French
o.f. Oil fired
O.F.A. Oil Fired Appliances (see N.F. B.P.M.)

O.F.B.E.C. Office Franco-Britannique d'Études et de Commerce
O.F.C. Overseas Food Corporation
O.F.C.F. Overseas Farmers' Co-operative Federation, Ltd.
off. (offered)
   office
   official
offg. officiating
offic. official(ly)
Offr. Officer
O.F.M. Order of Friars Minor (Franciscans)
O.F.M.Cap. Order of Friars Minor Capuchin
O.F.M.Conv. Order of Friars Minor Conventual
O.Fr. Old French
O. Fris. Old Frisian
O. Frk. Old Frankish
O.F.S. Orange Free State
O.G. Officer of the Guard
   Ogee
   Olympic Games
   Outside Guard
O. Gael. Old Gaelic
O.G.M. Ordinary General Meeting
O.G.O. Orbiting Geophysical Observatory
O.G.P.U. Obedenennoye Gosudarstvennoye Politicheskoe Upravleniye (Unified State Political Administration, (Russia))
O.G.S. Oratory of the Good Shepherd
O.H. Order of Hospitallers
O/H. Overzuche Handelsmaatschappij (foreign trade company)
o.h. omni hora (hourly)
   open hearth
O.H.B.M.S. On His *or* Her Britannic Majesty's Service
O.H.D. Organic Heart Disease
O.H.E. Office of Health Economics
O.H.G. Old High German
O.H.I.O. Over the hill in October
O.H.M.S. On His *or* Her Majesty's Service
O.H.S. Oxford Historical Society
O.I.A.T. Osteopathic Institute of Applied Technique
O.I. Old Irish
O.I.C. Organisation inter-américaine du café (Inter-American Coffee Organisation)
   Organisation Internationale Catholique (International Catholic Organization)
   Organisation internationale du commerce (International Trade Organisation)
O.i/c. Officer in charge
O.Icel. Old Icelandic
O.I.C.I. Organización Interamericana de Cooperación Intermunicipal (Inter-American Municipal Organisation)
O.I.E. Office international des épizooties (International Office of Epizootics)
   Organisation internationale des employeurs (International Organisation of Employers)

O.I.E.C. Office international de l'enseignement catholique (Catholic International Education Office)
O.I.G. Ophthalmic Industrial Group
   Organisation intergouvernementale (Inter-Governmental Organisation)
O.I.J. Organisation internationale des journalistes (International Organisation of Journalists)
O.I.M.L. Organisation Internationale de Métrologie Légale (International Organization for Legal Metrology)
O.I.N.G. Organisation internationale non gouvernementale (International Non-Governmental Organisation)
O.I.P. Organización Internacional de Periodistas (International Organisation of Journalists)
   Oxford India Paper
O.I.P.C. Organisation internationale de police criminelle (International Criminal Police Organisation (Interpol))
   Organisation internationale de protection civile (International Civil Defence Organisation)
O.Ir. Old Irish
O.I.R.T. Organisation internationale de radiodiffusion et télévision (International Radio and Television Organisation)
O.I.S.S. Organisation ibéro-américaine de sécurité sociale (Ibero-American Social Security Organisation)
O.I.S.T.V. Organisation internationale pour la science et la technique du vide (International Organisation for Vacuum Science and Technology)
O.It. Old Italian
O.I.T. Organisation internationale du travail (International Labour Organisation)
O.I.T.A.F. Organizzazione Internationale dei Transport a Fune (International Organisation for Transportation by Rope)
O.I.V. Office international de la vigne et du vin (International Vine and Wine Office)
O.I.V.S.T. Organisation Internationale pour la Science et la Technique du Vide (International Organization for Vacuum Science and Technology)
O.J.A.J. October, January, April, July
O.K. Orl K'rect (all correct)
o.K. ohne Kosten (without cost)
Okla. Oklahoma
Ol. Olympiad
   Olympic
ol. oil
O.L. Officer of the Order of Leopold (Belgium)
   Oil Lighter
   Ordnance Lieutenant
   Outside Left
O.-L. Old Latin
o.l. overhead line
   overflow level

O.L.Cr. Ordnance Lieutenant-Commander
old-fash. old-fashioned
O.L.G. Old Low German
O.L.M.R. Organic Liquid Moderated Reactor
O.L.Q. Officer-like Qualities
Om. Oman
O.M. Member of the Order of Merit
  Optimus Maximus (Greatest and Best)
  Ordnance Map
  Organization and Methods
o.m. old measurement
  omni mane (every morning)
O.M.A. Oilskin Manufacturers Association of Great Britian
  Overall Manufacturers' Association of Great Britain
  Overseas Mining Association
O.M.A.I. Organisation mondiale Agudas Israel (Agudas Israel World Organisation)
O.M.C.I. Organisation intergouvernementale consultative de la navigation maritime (Inter-Governmental Maritime Consultative Organisation)
O.M.E. Ordnance Mechanical Engineer
O.M.E.F. Office Machines and Equipment Federation
O.M.E.P. Organisation mondiale pour l'éducation préscolaire (World Organisation for Early Childhood Education)
O. Merced. Ordo Beatae Mariae de Mercede Redemptionis Captivorum (Order of Our Lady of Mercy for the Ransom of Captives)
O.M.G.E. Organisation mondiale de gastroentérologie (World Organisation of Gastroenterology)
O.M.I. Oblates of Mary Immaculate
O.M.M. Organisation météorologique mondiale (World Meteorological Organisation)
omn. bih. omni bihora (every two hours)
omn. hor. omni hora (every hour)
omn. noct. omni nocte (every night)
omn. quad. hor. omni quadrante hora (every quarter of an hour)
O.M.O. One man operated
OMPA Octamethyl pyrophosphoramide
O.M.P.A. One man pension arrangement
O.M.P.S.A. Organisation mondiale pour la protection sociale des aveugles (World Council for the Welfare of the Blind)
O.M.S. Organisation mondiale de la santé (World Health Organisation)
O.M.T. Old Merchant Taylors'
On. Onorevole (Honorable)
O.N. Old Norse
  Orthopaedic Nurse
o.n. omni nocte (every night)
on app(ro). on approval
O.N.C. Ordinary National Certificate
  Orthopaedic Nursing Certificate

O.N.D. Ophthalmic Nursing Diploma
  Ordinary National Diploma
O.N.F. Old Norman French
  Old Northern French
ong. ongeveer (about)
O.N.G. Organisation non gouvernementale (Non-Governmental Organisation)
o.n.o. or near offer
onomat. onomatopoeia
  onomatopoeic
O. Norw. Old Norwegian
O.N.R. Official Naval Reporter
Ont. Ontario
O.N.T. Ordinary Neap Tide
O.N.U. Organisation des Nations Unies (United Nations Organisation)
O.N.U.C. Opération des Nations Unies au Congo (United Nations Operation in the Congo)
O.O. Observation Officer
  Operation Order
  Order of Owls
  Orderly Officer
o/o. on order
  order of
O.O.D. Officer of the Day
O.O.G. Officer of the Guard
O.O.Q. Officer of the Quarters
O.O.W. Officer of the Watch
Op. Opaque
  Operator
op. operation
  optime
  optimus (excellent)
  opinion
  opus (a work)
O.P. Observation Post
  Old Pattern
  Old Persian
  Old Playgoers' Club
  Open Policy
  Order of Preachers
  Other People's
  Out of Print
O/P. Out of Print
o.p. open pattern
  opposite the prompter's side
  order policy
  original policy
  over proof
O.P.C. Out-patient Clinic
  Overseas Press Club of America
op. cit. opere citato (in the work quoted)
O.P.E.C. Organization of Petroleum Exporting Countries
O.P.E.G. O.E.E.C. Petroleum Emergency Group
O.P.E.P. Organisations des pays exportateurs de pétrole (Organisation of Petroleum Exporting Countries)
O.Per. Old Persian
OPEX Operational, Executive and Administrative Personnel (U.N.)
O.Pg. Old Portuguese
Ophth. Ophthalmic
Opm. Opmerking (remark)
O.P.M. Office of Production Management (U.S.)
O.P.M.A. Overseas Press and Media Association, Ltd.

Opmac. Operations for Military Aid to the Community
opn. operation
    opinion
    option
o.p.n. ora pro nobis (pray for us)
O.Pol. Old Polish
opp. opposed
    opposite
    opportunity
O.P.P. Out of print at Present
oppy. opportunity
opr. operator
O.Prov. Old Provençal
O.Pruss. Old Prussian
ops. operations
O.P.S. Organisation panaméricaine de la santé (Pan-American Health Organisation)
opt. optative
    optical
    optician
    optics
    optime
    option
Opt. D. Doctor of Optometry
O.P.W. Office of Public Works
Or. Oregon
    Oriel College, Oxford
    Orient(al)
    Original
or. oratorio
    other
O.R. Official Receiver
    Official Referee
    Old Roman
    Operational Research
    Orderly Room
    Other Ranks
    Outside Right
o.r. owner's risk
O.R.A.P. Organisation régionale de l'Orient pour l'administration publique (Eastern Regional Organisation for Public Administration)
orat. oratorical(ly)
o.r.b. owner's risk of breakage
O.R.C. Old Roman Catholic Church (English Rite)
    Order of the Red Cross
    Orange River Colony (now O.F.S.)
    Overseas Research Council
O.R.C.A. European Organisation for Research on Flourine and Dental Caries Prevention
    Ocean Resources Conservation Association
Orch. Orchestra
orchl. orchestral
Ord. Ordained
    Order
    Ordinary
    Ordnance
ord. order
    ordinal
    ordinary
    ordnance
o.r.d. owner's risk of damage
Ord. Bd. Ordnance Board
Ord. Dept. Ordnance Department U.S.)

Ord. Sgt. Ordnance Sergeant
O.R.E. Office for Research and Experiments of the International Union of Railways
    Organisation régionale européenne de la Confédération internationale des syndicats libres (European Regional Organisation of the International Confederation of Free Trade Unions)
Oreg. Oregon
ORESCO Overseas Research Council
o.r.f. owner's risk of fire
Or. F. S. Orange Free State
Org. Organization
org. organ(ic)
    organism
    organist
    organized
O.R.G. Operations Research Group
ORGALIME Organisme de liaison des industries métalliques européennes (Liaison Group for the European Metal Industries)
organ. organic
    organization
Orgzn. Organization
Orig. Original
orig. origin(ally)
    originated
O.R.I.T. Organización Regional Interamericana de Trabajadores (Inter-American Regional Organisation of Workers of the International Confederation of Free Trade Unions)
Ork. Orkney Islands
o.r.l. owner's risk of leakage
Orn. Ornithology
orn. ornament
Ornith. Ornithological
    Ornithology
orph. orphan(age)
o.r.r. owner's risk rates
ors. others
O.R.S. Operational Research Society Ltd.
    Oxfordshire Record Society
O.R.S.A. Order of Recollects of Saint Augustine
orse. otherwise
O.R.T. Organisation for Rehabilitation by Training
O.R.T.F. Office de la Radio Télévision Française
Orth. Orthography
    Orthopaedic
O.R.T.P.A. Oven-Ready Turkey Producers' Association
O.Russ. Old Russian
Os Osmium
O.S. Old Saxon
    Old School
    Old Series
    Old Style
    Omnibus Society
    Ordinary Seaman
    Ordnance Survey
    Out of Stock
    Output Secondary
    Outsize

o.s. ocean station
only son
on spot
o/s. on sale
out of standing
out of stock
O.S.A. Official Secrets Act(s)
Old Style Antique
Order of Saint Augustine
O.S.A.S. Overseas Service Aid Scheme
O.Sax. Old Saxon
O.S.B. Order of Saint Benedict
O.S.B.M. Ordo Sancti Basilii Magni
(Order of Saint Basil the Great)
Osc. Oscan
osc. oscillating
O.S.C. Old Water Colour Society's
Club
Order of Saint Charles
O.S.Cam. Order of Saint Camillus
O.Scan. Old Scandinavian
O.S.C.A.R. Orbital Satellite Carrying
Amateur Radio
Oxygen Steelmaking Com-
puter and Recorder
O.S.D. Ordnance Survey Department
Sisters of the Order of Saint
Dominic
O'seas Overseas
O.S.F. Order of Saint Francis
O.S.F.S. Oblates of Saint Francis of
Sales
o.s.h. omni singula hora (every hour)
O.S.J. Oblates of Saint Joseph
Order of Saint Jerome (Hierony-
mites)
O.S.J.D. Ordo Hospitalarius Sancti
Joannis de Deo (Order of Brothers
Hospitallers of Saint John of God)
O.Sl. Old Slavonic
O.S.L. Old Style Latin
Ordnance Sub-Lieutenant
O.Slav. Old Slavic
O.S.M. Order of the Servants of Mary
(Servites)
O.S.O. Orbiting Solar Observatory
O.Sp. Old Spanish
O.S.P. Order of Saint Paul
o.s.p. oblit sine prole (died without
issue)
O.S.P.A. Organisation de la Santé
Panaméricaine (Pan-Amer-
can Health Organisation)
Overseas Service Pensioners'
Association
O.S.R. Old Style Roman
O.S.R.B. Overseas Service Resettle-
ment Bureau
O.S.R.D. Office of Scientific Research
and Development (U.S.)
O.S.S. Office of Strategic Services
(U.S.)
O.S.S.R. Order of the Most Holy Re-
deemer
O.SS.T. Ordo Sanctissimae Trinitatis
Redemptionis Captivorum (Order of
the Most Holy Trinity for the Ransom
of Prisoners)
o.s.t. ordinary spring tide
osteo. osteopath(y)

O.S.T.I. Office of Scientific and Tech-
nical Information
Organisation for Scientific and
Technical Information
O.S.T.I.V. Organisation scientifique et
technique internationale du vol à
voile (International Technical and
Scientific Organisation for Soaring
Flight)
O.St.J. Officer of the Order of Saint
John of Jerusalem
O.S.T.S. Official Seed Testing Station
O.S.U.K. Ophthalmological Society of
the United Kingdom
o.s.v. och sa vidare (and so forth)
O.Sw. Old Swedish
O.T. Off Time
Old Testament
Old Teutonic
Overseas Trade
Overtime
O.T.A. Organisation mondiale du tour-
isme et de l'automobile (World Tour-
ing and Automobile Organisation)
O.T.A.N. Organisation du traité de
l'Antlantique nord (North Atlantic
Treaty Organisation)
O.T.A.S.E. Organisation du traité de
défense collective pour l'Asie du sud-
est (South-East Asia Treaty Organ-
isation)
otbd. outboard
O.T.C. Officers' Training Corps (*now*
C.C.F.)
Officers' Transit Camp
Over-the-Counter
O.T.D. Ocean Travel Development
Overseas Travel Development
O.Teut. Old Teutonic
Oth. Othello (Shakespeare)
O.T.H. Over-the-horizon radar
O.T.M. Old Turkey Mill
otol. otological
O.T.S. Officers' Training School
ott. ottava (octave)
O.T.U. Operational Training Unit
O.Turk. Old Turkish
O.U. Official Use
Oxford University
O/U Over and under
O.U.A. Order of United Americans
O.U.A.C. Oxford University Appoint-
ments Committee
Oxford University Athletic
Club
O.U.A.F.C. Oxford University Associa-
tion Football Club
O.U.A.M. Order of United American
Mechanics
O.U.A.S. Oxford University Air
Squadron
Oxford University Archaeo-
logical Society
O.U.B.C. Oxford University Boat Club
O.U.C.C. Oxford University Cricket
Club
O.U.D.S. Oxford University Dramatic
Society
O.U.G.C. Oxford University Golf
Club

O.U.H.C. Oxford University Hockey Club
O.U.L.C. Oxford University Lacrosse Club
O.U.L.T.C. Oxford University Lawn Tennis Club
O.U.M. Oxford University Mission
O.U.P. Oxford University Press
O.U.R.C. Oxford University Rifle Club
O.U.R.F.C. Oxford University Rugby Football Club
O.U.S.C. Oxford University Swimming Club
O.U.Y.C. Oxford University Yacht Club
Ov. Ovid
ov. ovary
 overture
O.V.A.C. Overseas Visual Aids Centre
O.V.A.H. Overseas Visual Aids Centres
O.V.P. Österreichische Volkspartei (Austrian People's Party)

O.W. Office of Works
 Old Welsh
O/W. Oil in Water
o.W. ohne Wert (without value)
o.w. one way
O.W.A.E.C. Organisation for West African Economic Co-operation
O.W.E. Office of Wages Councils
O.W.F. Optimum Working Frequency
O.W.I. Office of War Information (U.S.)
O.W.S. Ocean Weather Ship Service
 Old Water-colour Society
Oxf. Oxford(shire)
OXFAM Oxford Committee for Famine Relief
Oxf. Bucks. Oxfordshire and Buckinghamshire Light Infantry
Oxon. Oxoniensis (of Oxford)
oz(s). ounce(s)
oz. t. ounce troy

P

P. Page(s)
 Pale
 Papa (the Pope)
 Park
 Parson
 Part
 Passed
 Pastor
 Pater (father)
 Pawn
 Penny
 Percussion
 Père (Father)
 Period
 Person(nel)
 Pipe
 Pitch
 Pole
 Pondere (by weight)
 Pontifex (bishop)
 Port(ugal)
 Positive
 Post
 Prestbyterian
 President
 Pressure
 Priest
 Prince
 Probate
 Probation
 Proconsul
 Progressive
 Protestant
 Pupil
 Purl
p. page
 paragraph
 park
 particle
 partim (in part)

 pass(ed)
 past
 pawn
 peak
 pectoral
 per (by)
 perch
 peso(s)
 piano
 pied (foot)
 pint(s)
 pius (holy)
 poco (little)
 population
 pouce (inch)
 pour (for)
 power
 pressure
 primus (first)
 professional
Pa Protoactinium
Pa. Pennsylvania
P.A. Paintmakers' Association of Great Britain
 Pakistan Army
 Particular Average
 Personal Assistant
 Post Adjutant
 Power of Attorney
 Prefect Apostolic
 Press Agent
 Press Association
 Press Attaché
 Provisional Allowance
 Public Accountant
 Public Address system
 Public Analyst
 Publishers' Association
P/A. Private Account
p.A. per Adresse (care of)

cont.

183

p.a. par avion (by air (mail))
    participle adjective
    per annum (yearly)
    poids atomique (atomic weight)
    progression arithmétique (arithmetical progression)

p/a. put away

P.A.A. Pan-American World Airways Incorporated
    Paper Agents' Association
    Phonetic Alphabet Association

p.a.a. parti affectae applicandus (to be applied to the affected part)

P.A.A.D.C. Principal Air Aide-de-Camp

P.A.B.X. Private Automatic Branch Exchange

Pac. Pacific

P.A.C. Pan-African Congress
    Pan-American Congress
    Political Action Committee
    Public Accounts Committee
    Public Assistance Committee

p.a.c. Passed final examination of the advanced class, Military College of Science

P.A.C.E. Precision Analogue Computing Equipment

P.A.C.H. Publishers' Accounts Clearing House

P.A.D. Passive Air Defence
    Payable After Death

P.A.D.L. Performing and Captive Animals Defence League

p.ae. partes aequales (equal parts)

p.a.f. puissance au frein (brake-horsepower)

PAFMECA Pan-American Freedom Movement of East and Central Africa (now OAU)

P.A.G.B. Proprietary Association of Great Britain

P.A.G.C. Port Area Grain Committee

P.A.H.O. Pan-American Health Organisation

P.A.I.G.H. Pan-American Institute of Geography and History

paint. painting

Pak. Pakistan

Pal. Palace
    Palaeology
    Palaeontology
    Palestine

P.A.L. Phase Alternating Line
    Philippine Air Lines Incorporated

Palaeob. Palaeobotany

palaeob. palaeobotanical

Palaeog. Palaeography

palaeog. palaeographical

Palaeont. Palaeontology

Palm. Palmistry

pam. pamphlet

p.a.m. pulse amplitude modulation

P.A.M.A. Pan-American Medical Association
    Press Advertisement Managers' Association

P.A.M.C. Pakistan Army Medical Corps

P.A.M.E.T.R.A.D.A. Parsons and Marine Engineering Turbine Research and Development Association

pamph. pamphlet

Pan. Panama

pan. panchromatic
    panoramic

Pan. Am. Pan-American
    Pan-American World Airways Incorporated

Panam. Pan-American World Airways Incorporated

P. & C.R. Planning and Compensation Reports

P. & G.W.A. Pottery and Glass Wholesalers' Association

P. & L. Profit and Loss

P. & O. Peninsular and Oriental Steam Navigation Company Limited

p.& p. postage and packing

P. & R.T. Physical and Recreational Training

P.A.N.S. Procedures for Air Navigation Services

PANSDOC Pakistan National Scientific and Technical Documentation Centre

Panto. Pantomime

P.A.O. Poultry Advisory Officer

P.A.O.A. Pan-American Odontological Association

Pap. Papua

pa. p. past participle

P.A.P. People's Action Party (Singapore)

P.A.P.C. Poster Advertising Planning Committee

p.app. puissance apparente (apparent power)

Par. Paralipomenon

par. paragraph
    parallax
    parallel(ogram)
    paraphrase
    parenthesis
    parish
    parochial

Para. Paraguay(an)

P.A.R.A.D.A. Preparatory Academy for the Royal Academy of Dramatic Art

Paras. Parachute troops

parch. parchment

Par. Ch. Parish Church

parens. parentheses

Parl. Parliament(ary)

Parl.S. Parliamentary Secretary

Parlt. Parliament

pars. paragraphs

part. participating
    participle
    particular
    partner

part. adj. participle adjective

partn. partnership

Pas. Terminus Paschae (Easter Term)

P.A.S. Public Address System

P.A.S.B. Pan-American Sanitary Bureau (now P.A.H.O.)

P.A.S.I. Professional Associate of the Chartered Surveyors' Institution (now A.R.I.C.S.)

P.A.S.O. Pan-American Sanitary Organisation (*now* P.A.H.O.)
Pass. Passage
    Passenger(s)
    Passover
pass. passim (here and there)
    passive
pass. tr. passenger train
pat. patent(ed)
    pattern
pa.t. past tense
p.-à-.t. pied-à-terre (an occasional lodging)
Pata. Patagonia(n)
P.A.T.A. Pacific Area Travel Association
    Proprietary Articles' Trade Association
patd. patented
Path. Pathology
    Pathological
Pat.Off. Patent Office
P.A.T.R.A. Printing, Packaging and Allied Trades' Research Association (*now* Pira)
patt. pattern
P.A.T.W.A. Professional and Technical Workers' Aliyah
P.A.U. Pan-American Union
paul. paullum (a little)
Pav. Pavilion
P.A.W.A. Pan-American Women's Association (*now* Pan American Workers Congress)
    Pan-American World Airways Incorporated
pax pax vobiscum (peace be with you)
P.A.X. Private Automatic Exchange
P.A.Y.E. Pay As You Earn
Paymr. Paymaster
Pb Plumbum (lead)
P.B. Permanent Base
    Philosophiae Baccalaureus (Bachelor of Philosophy)
    Picket Boat
    Plymouth Brethren
    Pocket Book
    Prayer Book
    Premium Bond
    Primitive Baptists
    Provisional Battalion
    Publications Board (U.S.)
P.B.A. Poor Bloody Assistant
    Public Buildings Administration (U.S.)
P.B.C. Prayer Book Catholic
P.B.C.P. Political Bureau of the Communist Party
P.B.I. Poor Bloody Infantry
P.B.K.T.O.A. Printing, Bookbinding and Kindred Trades Overseers' Association
P.B.L. Public Broadcast Laboratory (U.S.A.)
P.B.M. Principal Beach Master
P.boat Patrol boat
P.b.P. Person before Place
P.b.S. Place before Subject
P.B.T. President of the Board of Trade
P.B.T.B. Paper Bag Trade Board (U.S.)   *cont.*

    Paper Box Trade Board (U.S.)
P.B.X. Private Branch Exchange
pc. piece
P.C. Panama Canal
    Parish Council(lor)
    Patres Conscripti (Senators)
    Paymaster Captain
    Peace Commissioner
    Perpetual Curate
    Pioneer Corps
    Police Constable
    Polo Club
    Première classe (First Class)
    Preparatory Commission
    Press Club
    Press Council
    Printing Cylinder
    Prison Commission
    Privy Council(lor)
    Provincial Commission
    Publicity Club
    The Publishers Circular
p.c. per centum (by the hundred)
    petty cash
    point de congélation (freezing point)
    postcard
    post cibum (after meals)
    prices current
P.C.A. Parliamentary Commissioner for Administration
    Parochial Clergy Association
    Permanent Court of Arbitration
    Printers' Costing Association
    Proprietary Cremation Association
P.C.A.C. Professional Classes Aid Council
P.C.B. Petty Cash Book
P.C.C. Parochial Church Council
    Prerogative Court of Canterbury
    Privy Council Cases
P.C.C.C. Pakistan Central Cotton Committee
P.C.C.E.M.R.S.P. Permanent Commission for the Conservation and Exploitation of the Maritime Resources of the South Pacific
P.C.D.G. Prestressed Concrete Development Group
P.C.E.M. Parlimentary Council of the European Movement
P.C.G.N. Permanent Committee on Geographical Names
P.Ch. Parish Church
P.C.H. Presbyterian Church House
P.C.I.F.C. Permanent Commission of the International Fisheries Convention
P.C.I.I. Potato Chip Institute International
P.C.I.Z.C. Permanent Committee of International Zoological Congresses
pcl. parcel
p.c.m. pulse code modulation
P.C.M.A. Plaited Cordage Manufacturers' Association
    Plastics Crate Manufacturers Association
P.C.M.O. Principal Colonial Medical Officer

N

P.C.M.S. Pattern Card Makers' Society
P.C.O.B. Permanent Central Opium Board
P.C.P. Past Chief Patriarch
——Progressive Constitutional Party (Malta)
P.Cr. Paymaster Commander
P.C.R.C. Poor Clergy Relief Corporation
P.C.R.S. Poor Clergy Relief Society
P.C.S. Principal Clerk of Session
P.C.S.I.R. Pakistan Council of Scientific and Industrial Research
P.C.W. Presbyterian Church of Wales
P.Cyc. Penny Cyclopedia
Pd Palladium
pd. paid
passed
pied (foot)
P.D. Pharmaciae Doctor (Doctor of Pharmacy)
Pharmacopoeia Dublinensis (Dublin Pharmacopoeia)
Philosophiae Doctor (Doctor of Philosophy)
Plans Division
Polar Distance
Postal District
Potential Difference
Preventive Detention
Printer's Devil
p.d. per diem (by the day)
port dues
position doubtful
potential difference
printer's devil
p/d. post dated
P.D.A. Photographic Dealers' Association
p.d.a. pour dire adieu (to say goodbye)
P.D.A.D. Probate, Divorce, and Admiralty Division
Pd.B. Pedagogiae Baccalaureus (Bachelor of Pedagogy)
P.D.C. Personnel Despatch Centre
Personnel Dispersal Centre
P.d.c. public dividend capital
Pd.D. Pedagogiae Doctor (Doctor of Pedagogy)
P.D.E. Projectile Development Establishment
P. de C. Pas de Calais
P.-de-D. Puy-de-Dôme
P.D.G.W. Principal Director of Guided Weapons
Pd.M. Pedagogiae Magister (Master of Pedagogy)
p.d.m. pulse duration modulation
P.D.M.H.S. Peak District Mines Historical Society
p.d.q. pretty damned quick
pdr. pounder
P.D.S. Parkinson's Disease Society of the United Kingdom Ltd.
P.D.S.A. People's Dispensary for Sick Animals
P.D.S.R. Principal Director of Scientific Research
Pe Pelopium

P.E. Permissible Error
Pharmacopoeia Edinburgensis (Edinburgh Pharmacopoeia)
Physical Education
Pocket Edition
Port Elizabeth
Presiding Elder
Protestant Episcopal
P/E. Port of Embarkation
Price/Earnings ratio
p.e. personal estate
point d'ébullition (boiling point)
P.E.A. Physical Education Association of Great Britain and Northern Ireland
Portuguese East Africa
P.E.A.B. Professional Engineers' Appointments Bureau
P.E.A.T. Programme élargi d'assistance technique des Nations Unies (United Nations Expanded Programme of Technical Assistance)
Pe.B. Pediatriae Baccalaureus (Bachelor of Pediatrics)
P.E.C. Photo Electric Cell
ped. pedal
pedestrian
Ped.B. Pedagogiae Baccalaureus (Bachelor of Pedagogy)
Ped.D. Pedagogiae Doctor (Doctor of Pedagogy)
P.E.E.P. Pilot's Electronic Eye Level Presentation
P.E.F. Palestine Exploration Fund
P.E.I. Prince Edward Island
Pek. Pekingese
Pem(b). Pembroke
Pembrokeshire
Pem.Yeo. Pembroke Yeomanry
Pen. Peninsular
Penitentiary
P.E.N. Poets, Playrights, Editors, Essayists, Novelists
P.Eng. Registered Professional Engineer (Canada)
Penn. Pennsylvania
Penol. Penology
Pent. Pentateuch
Pentecost
pent. pentagon
P.E.O. Programme Evaluation Organization (India)
Pe.P. Principal of Pedagogics
P.E.P. Political and Economic Planning
P.E.P.S.U. Patiala and East Punjab States Union
Per. Pericles (Shakespeare)
per. period
person
P.E.R.A. Production Engineering Research Association of Great Britain
per an. per annum (yearly)
perc. percussion
perd. perdendosi (dying away)
perf. perfect
perforated
perforation
performance
perh. perhaps
Perm. Permanent
Permission

perp. perpendicular
perpetual
per pro. per procurationem (by proxy)
Pers. Persian
pers. persons
perspective
persp. perspective
pert. pertaining
P.E.R.T. Programme Evaluation and Review Technique
Peruv. Peruvian
Pes. Peso(s)
P.E.S.C. Public Expenditure Survey Committee
P.E.S.T. Pressure for Economic and Social Toryism
Pet. Peterhouse, Cambridge
Petronius
P.E.T. Paper Equilibrium Tester
P.E.T.M.A. Portable Electric Tool Manufacturers' Association
petn. petition
Petriburg. Petriburgensis (of Peterborough)
p.ex. par exemple (for example)
Pf. Pfennig(s)
pf. perfect
preferred
proof
P.F. Panchromatic Film
Procurator Fiscal
P.f. Pianoforte
p.f. pour féliciter (to congratulate)
P.F.A. Popular Flying Association
Professional Footballers' Association
Pulverized Fuel Ash
P.F.B. Petroleum Films Bureau
P.f.c. Private first class (U.S.)
p.f.c. passed Flying College
pfd. preferred
P.F.D. Position Fixing Device
pfg. pfennig(s)
p.f.m. pulse frequency modulation
P.F.M.A. Pet Food Manufacturers' Association
Pressed Felt Manufacturers' Association
P.F.P.A. Pitch Fibre Pipe Association of Great Britain
p.f.s.a. pour faire ses adieux (to say goodbye)
Pft.Acct. Pianoforte Accompaniment
p.f.v. pour faire visite (to make a call)
pfx. prefix
Pg. Portugal
Portuguese
P.G. Pharmacopoeia Germanica (German Pharmacopoeia)
Paying Guest
Post Graduate
Preacher General
Procurator-General
P.G.A. Plate Glass Association
Professional Golfers' Association
Public General Acts
P.G.A.D. Past Grand Arch Druidess
P.G.C. Patent Glazing Conference
P.G.D. Past Grand Deacon
P.G.J.D. Past Grand Junior Deacon
P.G.L. Provincial Grand Lodge

P.G.M. Past Grand Master
P.G.M.A. Private Grocers' Merchandising Association
Pgn. Pigeon
P.G.R.O. Pea Growing Research Organization
P.G.S.D. Past Grand Senior Deacon
P.G.S.W. Past Grand Senior Warden
Ph. Philosophy
ph. phase
pH Hydrogen ion concentration
P.H. Purple Heart
P.H.A. Public Health Act
Public Housing Administration (U.S.)
Phar. Pharmaceutical
Pharmacist
Pharmacy
Pharmacopoeia
Phar.B. Pharmaciae Baccalaureus (Bachelor of Pharmacy)
Phar.C. Pharmaceutical Chemist
Phar.D. Pharmaciae Doctor (Doctor of Pharmacy)
Pharm. Pharmaceutical
Pharmacology
Pharmacy
Phar.M. Pharmaciae Magister (Master of Pharmacy)
Pharmac. Pharmacological
Pharm.D. Pharmaciae Doctor (Doctor of Pharmacy)
Pharm.M. Pharmaciae Magister (Master of Pharmacy)
Ph.B. Philosophiae Baccalaureus (Bachelor of Philosophy)
Ph.B.J. Bachelor of Philosophy in Journalism (U.S.)
Ph.B.Sp. Bachelor of Philosophy in Speech (U.S.)
Ph.C. Pharmaceutical Chemist
P.H.C.A. Pig Health Control Association
Ph.D. Pharmaciae Doctor (Doctor of Pharmacy)
Philosophiae Doctor (Doctor of Philosophy)
P.H.D. Doctor of Public Health
Ph.D.Ed. Doctor of Philosophy in Education
Ph.G. Graduate in Pharmacy (U.S.)
Pharmacopoeia Germanica (German Pharmacopoeia)
P.H.G. Postmen Higher Grade
Ph.I. Pharmacopoeia Internationalis (International Pharmacopoeia)
Phil. Philadelphia
Philharmonic
Philippians
Philippine Islands
Philological
Philology
Philosophical
Philosophy
Phila. Philadelphia
Philem. Philemon
Phil. Is. Philippine Islands
Philol. Philology
Philos. Philosopher
Philosophy
philos. philosophical

Phil. Soc. Philosophical Society of England
Philological Society
Phil.Sp. Philippine Spanish
Phil. Trans. Philosophical Transactions
Ph.L. Pharmaciae Licentiatus (Licentiate of Pharmacy)
P.H.L.S. Public Health Laboratory Service
Ph.M. Philosophiae Magister (Master of Philosophy)
P.H.N. Public Health Nursing
PHOENIX Plasma Heating Obtained by Energetic Neutral Injection Experiment
Phon. Phonetics
phot. photograph(ic)
photostat
photog. photograph(er)
photom. photometry
p.h.p. pump horse power
phr. phrase(ology)
Phren. Phrenological
Phrenology
P.H.S. Printing House Square
Public Health Service (U.S.)
P.H.T.S. Psychiatric Home Treatment Service (U.S.)
Phys. Physical
Physician
Physics
Physiology
Phys.Ed. Physical Education
Physiol. Physiology
Phys.Sc. Physical Science
P.I. Pasteur Institute
Pharmacopoeia Internationalis (International Pharmacopoeia)
Philippine Islands
Photographic Interpretation
Plastics Institute
Protocol International (International protocol)
P.I.A. Pakistan International Airlines Corporation
Photographic Importers' Association
P.I.A.C. Petroleum Industry Advisory Committee
P.I.A.N.C. Permanent International Association of Navigation Congresses
P.I.A.R.C. Permanent International Association of Road Congresses
P.I.A.T. Projector, Infantry, Anti-tank
P.I.B. National Board for Prices and Incomes (*dissolved*)
Petroleum Information Bureau
P.I.B.A.C. Permanent International Bureau of Analytical Chemistry of Human and Animal Food
Pic. Pictorial
P.I.C. Paint Industries Club
Programmed Instruction Centre
P.I.C.A.O. Provisional International Civil Aviation Organization (*now* I.C.A.O.)
P.I.C.G.C. Permanent International Committee on Genetic Congresses
P.I.C.I.C. Pakistan Industrial Credit and Investment Corporation

P.I.C.M. Permanent International Committee of Mothers
Pict. Pictorial
P.I.C.U.T.P. Permanent and International Committee of Underground Town Planning
P.I.D.A. Pig Industry Development Authority (*now* M.L.C.)
P.I.D.C. Pakistan Industrial Development Corporation (*now* E.P.I.D.C. *and* W.P.I.D.C.)
P.I.E. Pulmonary Infiltration associated with blood Eosinophilia
P.I.E.G. Pianoforte Industries Export Group
P.I.G. Pipeline Industries Guild
pil. pilula (pellet *or* pill)
P.I.L. Pest Infestation Laboratory
PINAC Permanent International Association of Navigation Congresses
P.-in-C. Priest-in-Charge
Pind. Pindar
P.I.O. Photographic Interpretation Officer
P.I.O.S.A. Pan-Indian Ocean Science Association
Pira Research Association for the Paper and Board, Printing and Packaging Industries
P.I.T.A.C. Pakistan Industrial Technical Assistance Centre
Pizz. Pizzicato (plucked)
P.J. Police Justice
Presiding Justice
Probate Judge
Pk. Park
pk. peck
P.K. Psychokinesis
pkg. package
packing
pkt. packet
pocket
P.K.T.F. Printing and Kindred Trades Federation
pl. place
plain
plate
platoon
plural
P.L. Paradise Lost
Parliamentary Labour Party
Paymaster Lieutenant
Pharmacopoeia Londinensis (London Pharmacopoeia)
Plimsoll Line
Poet Laureate
Position Line
Primrose League
Public Law
Public Library
P/L Profit and Loss
P.l. Partial loss
Pla. Place
Plaza
P.L.A. People's Liberation Army (China)
Port of London Authority
Private Libraries' Association
plat. platonic
Plaut. Plautus
P.L.B. Poor Law Board

P.L.C. Poeta Laureatus Caesareus (Imperial Poet Laureate)
Poor Law Commissioners
Plen. Plenipotentiary
plf(f). plaintiff
P.L.G. Poor Law Guardian
p.l.m. pulse length modulation
pl.-n. place name
P.L.R.A. Photo Litho Reproducers' Association
Pl.Sgt. Platoon Sergeant
plstr. plasterer
plu. plural
plup. pluperfect
PLUTO Pipe Line Under The Ocean
Pm Promethium
Pm. Premium
P.M. Pacific Mail
Parachute Mine
Past Master
Paymaster
Peculiar Metre
Piae Memoriae (of pious memory)
Police Magistrate
Pope and Martyr
Postmaster
Post Meridiem (after noon)
Post Mortem (after death)
Prime Minister
Provost Marshal
p.m. phase modulation
poids moléculaire (molecular weight)
post meridiem (after noon)
P.M.A. Permanent Magnet Association
Pianoforte Manufacturers' Association, Ltd.
P.M.& A.T.A. Paint Manufacturers' and Allied Trades Association
P.M.& O.A. Printers Managers' and Overseers' Association
P.M.&R. Physical Medicine and Rehabilitation
P.M.A.S.A. Printers' Medical Aid and Sanatoria Association
P.M.B. Pigs Marketing Board
Potato Marketing Board
P.M.C. President of the Mess Committee
P.M.G. Pall Mall Gazette
Postmaster General
p.m.h. production per man hour
P.M.L. Prime Minister's List
P.M.L.O. Principal Military Landing Officer
P.M.M.T.S. Printing Machine Managers' Trade Society (*now* L.T.S.)
P.M.O. Principal Medical Officer
pmr. paymaster
P.M.R. Pacific Missile Range
Private Milk Records
P.M.R.A.F.N.S. Princess Mary's Royal Air Force Nursing Service
P.M.X. Private Manual Exchange
P.N. Pakistan Navy
P/N. Promissory Note
P.N.dB Perceived Noise Decibel(s)
P.N.E. Preston North End
pneu. pneumatic(s)
P.N.E.U. Parents' National Educational Union

p.n.g. persona non grata (undesirable person)
P.N.P. People's National Party (Jamaica)
Pnr. Pioneer
P.N.T.O. Principal Naval Transport Officer
Po Polonium
P.O. Parcels Office
Par ordre (by order)
Patent Office
Petty Officer
Pilot Officer
Planning Office(r)
Postal Order
Post Office
Power-Operated
Province of Ontario
Pyrénées-Orientales
P.O.A. Phonograph Operators' Association Ltd.
Police Offices' Association
Prison Officers' Association
Purchasing Officers' Association
P.O.B. Post-Office Book
p.o.c. port of call
P.O.D. Pay on Delivery
Pocket Oxford Dictionary
Post Office Department
P.O.E.D. Post Office Engineering Department
Provincial Officer of Establishment Division
poenit. poenitentia (penance)
poet. poetic(al)
poetry
P.O.E.U. Post Office Engineering Union
P. of J. Princes of Jerusalem
P.O.G.O. Polar Orbiting Geophysical Observatories
Pol. Poland
Polish
Political
Politics
pol. polished
politically
politician
P.O.L. Patent Office Library
Pol. Econ. Political Economics
Political Economy
Polio. Poliomyelitis
polit. political
Poly. Polytechnic
Polyb. Polybius
Polyn. Polynesia
Pont. Max. Pontifex Maximus (Supreme Pontiff)
P.O.O. Post Office Order
pop. popular
population
P.O.P. Post Office Preferred
Printing-out Paper
por. portion
P.O.R. Personnel Occurrence Report
p.o.r. pay on receipt
pay on return
P.O.R.I.S. Post Office Radio Interference Station
Port. Portrait
Portugal
Portuguese

port(s). portrait(s)
pos. apostrophe
    position
    positive
P.O.S.B. Post Office Savings Bank
P.O.S.D. Post Office Savings Department
posn. position
poss. possession
    possessive case
    possible
possn. possession
posthum. posthumous(ly
pot. potassium
    potential
P.O.U.C. Post Office Users' Council
P.O.W. Please Oblige With
    Prince of Wales
    Prisoner of War
pp pianissimo (very softly)
PP. Patres (Fathers)
pp. pages
P.P. Parcel Post
    Parish Priest
    The Passionate Pilgrim (Shakespeare)
    Past President
    Pastor Pastorum (Shepherd of the Shepherds)
    Pater Patriae (Father of his Country)
    Permanent Pass
    Petrol Point
    Pilotless Plane
    Port Pipe
    Privately Printed
    Proportional Part
p.p. passive participle
    past participle
    per procurationem (by authority of)
    post paid
    privately printed
P.P.A. Peat Producers Association of Great Britain and Ireland
    Periodical Publishers' Association
    Pianoforte Publicity Association, Ltd.
    Pre-school Playgroups Association
    Printers' Provident Association
    Produce Packers' Association, Ltd.
Ppb. Pappband (bound in paper boards)
P.P.B. Planning – Programming – Budgeting
    Private Posting Box
P.P.B.S. Planning, Programming, Budgeting System
P.P.C. Printers' Pension Corporation
    Publishers' Publicity Circle
p.p.c. pour prendre congé (to take leave)
P.P.C.L.I. Princess Patricia's Canadian Light Infantry
P.P.C.S. Primary Producers' Cooperative Society (New Zealand)
p.pd. post paid
    prepaid
P.P.D.A. Produce Packaging Development Association
P.P.E. Philosophy, Politics and Economics

P.P.I. Plan Position Indicator
p.p.i. policy proof of interest
P.P.Inst.R.A. Past President of the Institute of Registered Architects
P.P.L.O. pleuropneumonia-like organisms
p.p.m. parts per million
    pulse position modulation
P.P.M.S. Plastic Pipe Manufacturers' Society
ppp pianissimo (as softly as possible)
Ppr. Proper
P.P.R. Polish People's Republic
    Principal Probate Registry
    Printed Paper Rate
P.P.R.A. Past President of the Royal Academy of Arts
P.P.S. Parliamentary Private Secretary
    Principal Private Secretary
p.p.s. post post scriptum (an additional postscript)
P.P.S.A. Pan-Pacific Surgical Association
P.P.S.E.A.W.A. Pan-Pacific and South-East Asia Women's Association
P.P.T.P.I. Past President of the Town Planning Institute
P.P.U. Peace Pledge Union
P.Q. Parliamentary Question
    Previous or Preceding Question
    Province of Quebec
Pr Praseodymium
Pr. Prayer
    Preferred Stock
    Price
    Priest
    Prince
    Printer
    Protestant
    Provençal
    Provincial
pr. painter
    pair
    pounder
    present
    pressure
    price
    print(ed)
    printer
    pronoun
    proper
    proved
P.R. Paradise Regained
    Plotting and Radar
    Populus Romanus (the Roman People)
    Postal Regulations
    Pre-Raphaelite
    Press Representative
    Prize Ring
    Proportional Representation
    Public Relations
    Puerto Rico
p.r. parcel receipt
P.R.A. Paymaster Rear-Admiral
    People's Republic of Albania
    President of the Royal Academy
P.R.A.C. Pyrethrum Research Advisory Committee (Kenya)
prand. prandium (dinner)
P.R.A.T.R.A. Philippines Relief and Trade Rehabilitation Administration

P.R.B. People's Republic of Bulgaria
Pre-Raphaelite Brotherhood
P.R.C. People's Republic of China
Post Romam Conditam (after the founding of Rome)
Price Regulation Committee (U.S.)
P.R.C.A. President of the Royal Cambrian Academy
P.R.C.P. President of the Royal College of Physicians
P.R.C.S. President of the Royal College of Surgeons of England
P.R.E. Fédération européenne des fabricants de produits réfractaires (European Federation of Refractory Material Producers)
Preb. Prebend(ary)
Prec. Precentor
pred. Predicative(ly)
Pref. Preface
Prefect
Preference
Preferred
pref. preferably
preference
preferred
prefix
prefab. prefabricated
prehist. prehistoric(al)
prehistory
prelim. preliminaries
preliminary
prelims. preliminaries
Prem. Premium
Prep. Preparatory
prep. preparation
preposition
Pres. Presbyter(ian)
Presentation
Presidency
President
pres. present
presumptive
Presby. Presbyterian
pres. part. present participle
pret. preterite
prev. previous(ly)
p.r.f. pulse repetition frequency
P.R.H. Petrol Railhead
P.R.H.A. People's Refreshment House Association
President of the Royal Hibernian Academy
P.R.I. President of the Royal Institute of Painters in Water Colours
La prévention routière internationale (International Prevention of Road Accidents)
Public Relations Institute of Ireland
P.R.I.A. President of the Royal Irish Academy
P.R.I.B.A. President of the Royal Institute of British Architects
Prim. Primate(s)
prim. primary
primitive
Prin. Principal(ity)
prism. prismatic
priv. privative

P.R.L. Prairie Research Laboratory (Canada)
Price Reduction League
prm. premium
Pr. Man. Prayer of Manasseh
P.R.N. pro re nata (according to the occasion)
Pro. Provost
pro. professional
prostitute
P.R.O. Press Officer
P.R.O. Public Record Office
Public Relations Officer
Prob. Probate
prob. probability
probable
probably
problem
Proc. Proctor
proc. proceedings
Procop. Procopius
prod. produced
producer
production
prods. producers
Prof. Professor
prof. profession
prog. progressive
P.R.O.I. President of the Royal Institute of Oil Painters
Prol. Prologue
Prom. Promenade
Promenade Concert
Promontory
Promotion
Proms. Promenade Concerts
pron. pronoun(ced)
pronunciation
pron.a. pronominal adjective
prond. pronounced
pronunc. pronunciation
Prop. Propertius
Proprietor
prop. propeller
proper(ly)
proposition
proprietary
propl. proportional
propn. proportion
Propr. Proprietor
propr. proprietary
props. properties
P.R.O.R.M. Pay and Records Office, Royal Marines
pros. prosodical
prosody
Pros.Atty. Prosecuting Attorney
Prot. Protestant
protem. pro tempore (for the time being)
Prov. Provençal
Provence
Proverbs
Province
Provost
prov. proverb
proverbial(ly)
provincial
provisional
Prov.G.M. Provincial Grand Master
prox. proximus (next)

prox. acc. proxime accessit (next in order of merit)
P.R.P. Petrol Refilling Point
Prs. Printers
P.R.S. Paint Research Station
Performing Right Society
President of the Royal Society
Protestant Reformation Society
P.R.S.A. President of the Royal Scottish Academy
P.R.S.E. President of the Royal Society of Edinburgh
Pr.S.T. Prairie Standard Time (U.S.)
Pru. Prudential Assurance Company
P.R.U. Civil Service Pay Research Unit
Photographic Reconnaissance Unit(s)
Pruss. Prussia
p.r.v. pour rendre une visite (to return a call)
P.R.W.S. President of the Royal Society of Painters in Water Colours
Ps. Peseta(s)
Psalm(s)
P.S. Paddle Steamer
Parade State
Parliamentary Secretary
Pastel Society
Penal Servitude
Permanent Secretary
Pharmaceutical Society of Great Britain
Philological Society
Philosophical Society of England
Physical Society
Physiological Society
Police Sergeant
Postscriptum (postscript)
Press Secretary
Privy Seal
Prompt Side
Provost Sergeant
p.s. poids spécifique (specific weight)
P.S.A. Pacific Science Association
Photographic Society of America
Pleasant Sunday Afternoon(s)
Political Studies Association of the United Kingdom
Poultry Stock Association, Ltd.
President of the Society of Antiquaries
P.S.A.B. Public Schools Appointments Bureau
P.S.B.A. Public Schools Bursars' Association
P.S.B.O. Premium Savings Bond Office
P.S.C. Pacific Science Council
Public Service Commission
p.s.c. passed Staff College
P.S.C.D. Patrol Service Central Depot
P.S.C.J. Societas Presbyterorum Sacratissimi Cordis Jesu de Bètharram (Priests of the Sacred Heart of Jesus of Bètharram)
P.S.D. Pay Supply Depot
Personal Services Department
Petty Sessional Division
P.S.D.A. Paper Sack Development Association Ltd.
Pseud. Pseudonym(ous)
P.S.G.B. Pharmaceutical Society of Great Britain

P.S.H.F.A. Public Servants' Housing and Finance Association
P.S.I. Pharmaceutical Society of Ireland
President of the Service Institute
Public Services International
p.s.i. per square inch
pounds per square inch
P.S.I.P. Poultry Stock Improvement Plan
P.S.L. Paymaster Sub-Lieutenant
p.s.m. passed Royal Military School of Music
P.S.M.A. President of the Society of Marine Artists
P.S.M.S.L. Permanent Service for Mean Sea Level
P.S.N.I. Pharmaceutical Society of Northern Ireland
P.S.O. Personnel Selection Officer
Principal Scientific Officer
PSP phenol-sulphone-phthalein
pss. postscripta (postscripts)
P.S.S. Printing and Stationery Service
Professor of Sacred Scripture
P.S.S.C. Pious Society of the Missionaries of Saint Charles
p.s.s.o. pass slipped stitch over
P.S.T. Pacific Standard Time
P.S.T.O. Principal Sea Transport Officer
P.Surg. Plastic Surgery
P.S.V. Public Service Vehicle
P.S.V.A.C. Public Service Vehicle Advertising Committee
P.S.W. Psychiatric Social Worker
P.S.W.B. Patented Steel Wire Bureau
Psych. Psychic
Psychol. Psychological
Psychology
Pt Platinum
Pt. Part
Point
Port
pt. part
payment
pint(s)
P.T. The Phoenix and the Turtle (Shakespeare)
Physical Training
Post Town
Preferential Treatment
Public Trustee
Pupil Teacher
Purchase Tax
p.t. part time
past tense
pro tempore (for the time being)
P.T.A. Paper Towel Association
Parent Teacher Association
Pianoforte Tuners' Association
Printing Trades Alliance
Public Transport Association, Inc.
Public Transport Authorities
P.T.A.S. Productivity and Technical Assistance Secretariat
P.T.C. Personnel Transit Centre
Photographic Type Composition
Primary Training Centre
Ptd. Printed
Pte. Private

pt.ex(ch). part exchange
ptg. printing
P.T.I. Physical Training Instructor
P.T.I.D.G. Presentation of Technical Information Discussion Group
P.T.M.C.A. Pit Tub and Mine Car Manufacturers' Association
P.T.O. Please Turn Over
　　　Power Take-off
　　　Public Trustee Office
ptr. printer
P.T.S. Pali Text Society
　　　Philatelic Traders' Society
　　　Printing Technical School
P.T.T. Postes, Télégraphes et Téléphones (Mail, Telegraphs and Telephones)
P.T.T.I. Postal, Telegraph and Telephone International
P.T.U. Plumbing Trades Union
Pty. Proprietary
pty. party
　　　proprietary
Pu Plutonium
P.U. Public Utilities
p.u. paid up
P.U.A.S. Postal Union of the Americas and Spain
pub. public(an)
　　　publish(ed)
　　　publisher
pubd. published
Pub.Doc. Public Documents
publ. publication
pubn. publication
P.U.C. Papers under Consideration
　　　Pick-up Car
　　　Post Urbem Conditam (after the building of the city)
　　　Public Utilities Commission (U.S.)
pud. pudding
PULHEEMS Physical capacity, Upper limbs, Locomotion, Hearing, Eyesight, Mental capacity, Emotional capacity
p.u.m.s. permanently unfit for military service
punc. punctuation
P.U.O. Pyrexia of Unknown Origin
P.U.P. People's United Party (British Honduras)

pur. purchase
Purp. Purple
P.U.S. Parents' Union School
　　　Parliamentary Under-Secretary
　　　Permanent Under-Secretary
　　　Pharmacopoeia of the United States
p.u.s. permanently unfit for service
Puy-de-D. Puy-de-Dôme
P.V. Paravane
　　　Patrol Vessel
　　　Petite Vitesse (freight train)
　　　Piccola Velocità (slow train)
　　　Porte de Versailles
　　　Positive Vetting
　　　Priest Vicar
p.v. post village
　　　priest vicar
PVA Polyvinyl Alcohol
Pv.B. Bachelor of Pedagogy
PVC Polyvinyl-chloride
P.V.O. Principal Veterinary Officer
PVP Polyvinylpyrrolidone
P.V.P.M.P.C. Perpetual Vice-President and Member of the Pickwick Club (Pickwick Papers—Dickens)
Pvt. Private
p.v.t. par voie télégraphique (by telegraph)
p.w. purlwise
P.W.A. Public Works Administration (U.S.)
P.W.C. Peoples' World Convention
P.W.D. Public Works Department
P.W.I.F. Plantation Workers' International Federation
P.W.L.B. Public Works Loan Board
P.W.N.D.A. Provincial Wholesale Newspaper Distributors' Association
P.W.O. Prince of Wales' Own
P.W.R. Police War Reserve
　　　Pressurised Water Reactor
pwt. pennyweight
P.W.T. Pacific War Time
P.X. Please Exchange
　　　Post Exchange (U.S.)
　　　Private Exchange
Pyr.-Or. Pyrénées-Orientales
P.Z.T. Photographic Zenith Tube

Q

Q. Quadrans (farthing)
　　　Quantity
　　　Quartermaster
　　　Quebec
　　　Queen(sland)
　　　Question
　　　Quintal
　　　Quotient
　　　Sir Arthur Quiller-Couch
q. quaere (inquire)
　　　quart
　　　quarter(ly)
　　　quarto

quasi (almost)
queen
query
question
quire
Q.A.B. Queen Anne's Bounty
Q.A.I.M.N.S. Queen Alexandra's Imperial Military Nursing Service (*now* Q.A.R.A.N.C.*)
Q.A.L.A.S. Qualified Associate of the Chartered Land Agents' Society
Q.A.R.A.N.C. Queen Alexandra's Royal Army Nursing Corps

cont.

Q.A.R.N.N.S. Queen Alexandra's Royal Naval Nursing Service
Q.B. Quarterback
    Queen's Bays
    Queen's Bench
    Queen's Bishop
Q.B.D. Queen's Bench Division
Q.B.S.M. que besa su mano (who kisses your hand)
q.b.s.p. que besa sus pies (who kisses your feet)
Q.C. Queen's College
    Queen's Counsel
Q.C.I.M. Quarterly Cumulative Index Medicus
Q.C.Is. Queen Charlotte Islands
Q.C.L.L.R. Queensland Crown Lands Law Reports
q.d. quaque die (every day)
    quasi dicat (as if one should say)
    quasi dictum (as if said)
q.d.D.g. que de Dios goce (may he be in God's keeping)
Q.D.G. Queen's Dragoon Guards
q.e. quod est (which is)
Q.E.A. Quantas Empire Airways Limited
Q.E.D. quod erat demonstrandum (which was to be proved)
Q.E.F. quod erat faciendum (which was to be done)
Q.E.I. quod erat inveniendum (which was to be found)
Q.F. Quick-firing
Q.F.S.M. Queen's Fire Service Medal
Q.G. Quartier-Général (Headquarters)
Q.H. Queen's Hall
q.h. quaque hora (every hour)
Q.H.C. Queen's Honorary Chaplain
Q.H.N.S. Queen's Honorary Nursing Sister
Q.H.P. Queen's Honorary Physician
Q.H.S. Queen's Honorary Surgeon
q.i.d. quater in die (four times a day)
Q.I.D.N. Queen's Institute of District Nursing
Q.I.P. Quiescat in Pace (rest in peace)
Q.J.P.R. Queensland Justice of the Peace Reports
Q.Kt. Queen's Knight
Q.Kt.P. Queen's Knight's Pawn
ql. quintal
q.l. quantum libet (as much as you please)
Qld. Queensland
qlty. quality
Qm. quomodo (by what means)
Q.M. Quartermaster
    Queen's Messenger(s)
Q.M.A.A.C. Queen Mary's Army Auxiliary Corps (*now* W.R.A.C.)
Q.M.C. Queen Mary College, London
Q.Mess. Queen's Messenger(s)
Q.M.G. Quartermaster-General
Q.M.G.F. Quartermaster-General to the Forces
Qmr. Quartermaster
Q.M.S. Quartermaster-Sergeant
Qn. Queen
qn. question
    quotation

q.n. quaque nocte (every night)
Q.N.S. Quantity not Sufficient
Qns. Coll. Queen's College
Qnty. Quantity
Q.O.C.H. Queen's Own Cameron Highlanders
Q.O.H. Queen's Own Hussars
Q.O.R. Quebec Official Reports
Q.P. Qualification Pay
    Queen's Pawn
q.p. quantum placet (as much as you please)
Q.P.M. Queen's Police Medal
Q.P.R. Quebec Practice Reports
    Queen's Park Rangers
qq. questions
qq.v. quantum vis (as much as you wish
qr. quadrans (farthing)
    quarter
    quire
Q.R. Queen's Rook
Q.R.I.H. Queens' Royal Irish Hussars
Q.R.P. Queen's Rook's Pawn
Q.R.R. Queen's Royal Rifles
qrs. quarters
Q.R.S.C. Quebec Reports, Superior Court
Q.S. Quarter Section
    Quarter Sessions
    Queen's Scholar
q.s. quantum sufficit (as much as is sufficient)
Q.S.R. Quasi-stellar Radio Sources
qt. quantity
    quart
qto. quarto
qtr. quarter(ly)
qts. quarts
qty. quantity
Qu. Queen
qu. quarter
    quasi (almost)
    query
    question
quad. quadrangle
    quadrant
    quadrat
    quadruple(t)
    quadruplicate
quadrupl. quadruplicate
qual. qualified
    quality
quant. suff. quantum sufficit (as much as is sufficient)
quar. quarter(ly)
Q.U.B. Queen's University, Belfast
Que. Quebec
Queensl. Queensland
ques. question
questn. questionnaire
quint. quintuplicate
quor. quorum
quot. quotation
    quoted
q.v. quantum vis (as much as you wish)
    quod vide (which see)
Q.V.C.F. Queen Victoria Clergy Fund
Q.V.R. Queen Victoria's Rifles
Q.W.N. Queensland Law Reporter and Weekly Notes
Qy. Query

R

R radioactive mineral
R. Ohms
Rabbi
Radical
Radiologist
Radiology
Radius
Railway
Rapido (fast train)
Réaumur
Recht (law)
Rechnung (bill *or* invoice)
Recipe
Rector
Regiment
Regina (Queen)
Registered
Regular
Remotum (far)
Republican
Reserve
Resistance
Retard(er)
Retired
Reward
Rex (King)
Rifles
Right
River
Road
Rod
Roman
Rome
Rook
Rosary
Rouble(s)
Royal
Rue (street)
Rumania
Rupee(s)
r. radius
rain
rare
ratio
recipe
recto
reply
reserve(d)
residence
right
rises
river
rod
rood
runs
rupee(s)
Ra Radium
R.A. Ramblers' Association
Ratepayers' Association
Rear Admiral
Recidivists Anonymous
Referees Association
Regular Army (U.S.)
Republica Argentina (Argentine Republic)
Resettlement Administration (U.S.)
Right Arch *cont.*

Right Ascension
Royal Academician
Royal Academy
Royal and Ancient Golf Club
Royal Arch
Royal Artillery
Russian America
R/A. Refer to Acceptor
Return to Author
R.A.A. Royal Academy of Arts
Royal Artillery Association
Royal Australian Artillery
R.A.(A). Rear-Admiral of Aircraft Carriers
R.A.A.F. Royal Australian Air Force
R.A.A.M.C. Royal Australian Army Medical Corps
R.A.A.N.C. Royal Australian Army Nursing Corps
R.A.A.S. Racial Adjustment Action Society
Royal Amateur Art Society
Rabb. Rabbinical
R.A.B.D.F. Royal Association of British Dairy Farmers
R.A.B.F.M. Research Association of British Flour Millers
R.A.B.I. Royal Agricultural Benevolent Institution
R.A.C. Regional Advisory Council(s)
Royal Aero Club
Royal Agricultural College
Royal Arch Chapter
Royal Armoured Corps
Royal Automobile Club
R.A.C.A. Royal Automobile Club of Australia
R.A.Ch.D. Royal Army Chaplains' Department
R.A.C.I. Royal Australian Chemical Institute
R.A.C.P. Royal Australasian College of Physicians
R.A.C.S. Royal Australasian College of Surgeons
R.A.C.V. Royal Automobile Club of Victoria
Rad. Radar
Radical
Radio
Radiologist
Radiology
Radiotherapist
Radiotherapy
Radnorshire
rad. radius
radix (root)
R.A.D. Royal Academy of Dancing
Royal Albert Docks
R.A.(D). Rear Admiral of Destroyers
R.A.D.A. Royal Academy of Dramatic Art
RADAR Radio Detection and Ranging
R.A.D.C. Royal Army Dental Corps
R.A.D.D. Royal Association in Aid of the Deaf and Dumb
Raddol. Raddolcendo (growing softer)
R.A.Dks. Royal Albert Docks

R.Adm. Rear Admiral
radn. radian
R.A.E. Royal Aircraft Establishment(s)
R.Ae.C. Royal Aero Club
R.A.E.C. Royal Army Educational Corps
Ra.Em. Radium Emanation
R.Ae.S. Royal Aeronautical Society
R.A.F. Royal Aircraft Factory
　　Royal Air Force
R.A.F.A. Royal Air Force Association
R.A.F.B.F. Royal Air Force Benevolent Fund
R.A.F.E.S. Royal Air Force Educational Service
R.A.F.F.C. Royal Air Force Ferry Command (*now* R.A.F.T.C.)
R.A.F.G.S.A. Royal Air Force Gliding and Soaring Association
R.A.F.M.S. Royal Air Force Medical Services
R.A.F.O. Reserve of Air Force Officers (*now* R.A.F.R.O.)
R.A.F.R. Royal Air Force Regiment
R.A.F.R.O. Royal Air Force Reserve of Officers
R.A.F.S.A. Royal Air Force Sailing Association
R.A.F.S.C. Royal Air Force Staff College
R.A.F.T.C. Royal Air Force Transport Command
R.A.F.V.R. Royal Air Force Volunteer Reserve
R.A.G.B. Refractories Association of Great Britain
R.A.G.C. Royal and Ancient Golf Club, Saint Andrews
R.A.H. Royal Albert Hall
R.A.H.S. Royal Australian Historical Society
R.A.I. Royal Albert Institution
　　Royal Anthropological Institute
　　Royal Archaeological Institute
R.A.I.A. Royal Australian Institute of Architects
R.A.I.C. Royal Architectural Institute of Canada
rall. rallentando (gradually slower)
R.A.M. Radical Action Movement
　　Revolutionary Action Movement (U.S.)
　　Right Ascension of the Meridian
　　Royal Academy of Music
　　Royal Arch Masons
RAMAC Radio Marine Associated Companies
R.A.M.C. Royal Army Medical Corps
R.A.M.N.A.C. Radio Aids to Marine Navigation Application Committee
R.A.M.S. Right Ascension of the Mean Sun
R.A.N. Royal Australian Navy
R.& A. Royal and Ancient Golf Club, Saint Andrews
R.& B. Rhythm and Blues
r.& c.c. riots and civil commotions
R. and C.H.S. Railway and Canal Historical Society
R. & N. Rhodesia and Nyasaland Law Reports

R.& S.M. Royal and Select Masters
R.& V.A. Rating and Valuation Association
R.& V.R. Rating and Valuation Reports
R.A.N.V.R. Royal Australian Naval Volunteer Reserve
R.A.O.B. Royal Antediluvian Order of Buffaloes
R.A.O.C. Royal Army Ordnance Corps
R.A.O.T.A. Radio Amateur Old Timers Association
R.A.O.U. Royal Australasian Ornithologists' Union
rap. rapid
R.A.P.C. Royal Army Pay Corps
R.A.P.R.A. Rubber and Plastics Research Association of Great Britain
R.A.R.D.E. Royal Armament Research and Development Establishment
R.A.R.O. Regular Army Reserve of Officers
R.A.S. Replenishment at sea
　　Royal Aeronautical Society
　　Royal Agricultural Society
　　Royal Albert School
　　Royal Asiatic Society
　　Royal Astronomical Society
R.A.S.B. Royal Asiatic Society of Bengal
R.A.S.C. Royal Army Service Corps (*now* R.C.T.)
　　Royal Astronomical Society of Canada
R.A.S.E. Royal Agricultural Society of England
R.A.S.K. Royal Agricultural Society of Kenya
rat. rations
R.A.T.O. Rocket Assisted Take-Off
R.A.T.P. Régie autonome des transports parisiens (Paris municipal transport control)
R.Aux.A.F. Royal Auxiliary Air Force
R.A.V.C. Royal Army Veterinary Corps
Rb Rubidium
R.B. Republica Boliviana (Republic of Bolivia)
　　Rifle Brigade
　　Right Back
　　River Board
r.b. rubber band
R.B.A. Refined Bitumen Association (formerly Road Bitumen Association)
　　Retail Book, Stationery and Allied Trades Employees' Association
　　River Boards Association
　　Roads Beautifying Association
　　Royal Society of British Artists
R.B.A.I. Royal Belfast Academical Institution
R.B.E. Relative Biological Efficiency
R.Berks. Royal Berkshire Regiment
R.B.L. Royal British Legion
R.Bn. Radio Beacon
R.B.N. Registry of Business Names
R.B.N.A. Royal British Nurses' Association
R.B.S. Royal Society of British Sculptors

R.B.S.A. Royal Birmingham Society of Artists
R.C. Red Cross
　　Reformed Church
　　Republican Convention (U.S.)
　　Research Centre
　　Right Centre
　　Roman Catholic
　　Royal College
　　Royal Commission
r.c. release clause
R.C.A. Racecourse Association
　　Radio Corporation of America ✔
　　Reinforced Concrete Association ✔
　　Royal Canadian Academy of Arts
　　Royal College of Art ✔
　　Royal Company of Archers
R.C.A.A. Royal Cambrian Academy of Art
　　Royal Canadian Academy of Arts
R.C.A.F. Royal Canadian Air Force
R.Cam.A. Royal Cambrian Academy of Art
R.C.A.M.C. Royal Canadian Army Medical Corps
R.C.A.S. Royal Central Asia Society
R.C.A.S.C. Royal Canadian Army Service Corps
R.C.A.T. Royal College of Advanced Technology
R.C.C. Radiochemical Centre at Amersham
　　Rescue Co-ordination Centre
　　Roman Catholic Chaplain
　　Roman Catholic Church
　　Royal Canoe Club
　　Rubber Cable Council
R.C.C.C. Royal Caledonian Curling Club
R.C.Ch. Roman Catholic Church
R.C.C.D. Regional Co-operation for Development
R.C.D.S. Royal Scottish Country Dance Society
R.C.G.S. Royal Canadian Geographical Society
R.C.H. Railway Clearing House
R.C.H.S. Railway and Canal Historical Society
R.C.I. Royal Colonial Institute (*now* R.C.S.)
R.C.J. Royal Courts of Justice
R.C.L. Railway Conversion League
　　Ruling Case Law
R.C.M. Radar Counter Measures
　　Regimental Corporal-Major
　　Regimental Court Martial
　　Republica de los Ciudadanos del Mundo (Commonwealth of World Citizens)
　　Royal College of Midwives
　　Royal College of Music
R.C.M.P. Royal Canadian Mounted Police
R.C.N. Royal Canadian Navy
　　Royal College of Nursing
R.C.N.C. Royal Corps of Naval Constructors

R.C.N.R. Royal Canadian Naval Reserve
R.C.N.V.R. Royal Canadian Naval Volunteer Reserve
R.C.O. Royal College of Organists
R.C.O.C. Royal Canadian Ordnance Corps
R.C.O.G. Royal College of Obstetricians and Gynaecologists
R.C.P. Royal College of Physicians
rcpt. receipt
R.C.R.D.C. Radio Components Research and Development Committee
R.C.R.F. Rei Cretariae Romanae Fautores (Association of Roman Ceramic Archaeologists)
R.C.S. Royal Choral Society
　　Royal College of Science
　　Royal College of Surgeons of England
　　Royal Commonwealth Society
　　Royal Corps of Signals
　　Royal Counties Show
R.C.S.C. Radio Components Standardization Committee
R.C.S.E. Royal College of Surgeons of Edinburgh
R.C.S.(I.) Royal College of Surgeons of Ireland
R.C.S.T. Royal College of Science and Technology
rct. recruit
R.C.T. Royal Corps of Transport
R.C.T.S. Railway Correspondence and Travel Society
R.C.U. Road Construction Unit(s)
R.C.V.S. Royal College of Veterinary Surgeons
R.Cy.N. Royal Ceylon Navy
Rd Radium
Rd. Road
　　Round
R.D. Republic Dominicana (Dominican Republic)
　　Research Department
　　Rive Droite (right bank)
　　Royal Dragoons
　　Royal Naval Reserve Decoration
　　Rural Dean
R/D. Refer to Drawer
R.D.A. Retail Distributors' Association
　　Royal Docks Association
R.D.C. Red Deer Commission
　　Rural District Council
　　Universal Esperanto Association Research and Documentation Centre
R.D.C.A. Rural District Councils Association
R.D.E. Research and Development Establishment
R.D.F. Radio Direction-Finding
　　Royal Dublin Fusiliers
rd.hd. round head
R.D.I. Royal Designer for Industry
R.D.S. Religious Drama Society of Great Britain
　　Royal Drawing Society
　　Royal Dublin Society
R.Dy. Royal Dockyard
Re Rhenium

Re. Rupee(s)
Fellow of Royal Society of Painter
Etchers and Engravers
R.E. Reformed Episcopal
Revised Edition
Right Excellent
Right Eye
Royal Engineers
Royal Exchange
Royal Society of Painter-Etchers
and Engravers
R.e. Red edges
Réaum. Réaumur
rec. receipt
received
recens (fresh)
recent
recipe
record(er)
R.E.C. Railway Enthusiasts' Club
Railway Executive Committee
recap. recapitulate
recapitulation
Recce. Reconnaissance
recd. received
recep. reception
recip. reciprocal
reciprocity
Recit. Recitative
Recitativo
recit. recitation
R.E.C.M.F. Radio and Electronic
Component Manufacturers' Federation
R.Econ.S. Royal Economic Society
recr. receiver
Rec. Sec. Recording Secretary
Rect. Rector
rect. rectangle
rectified
red. reduced
redisc. rediscount
redup. reduplication
Ref. Referee
Reformation
Refraction
ref. referee
reference
referred
reformed
refused
Ref. Ch. Reformed Church
refd. referred
refl. reflex
Reform. Reformatory
Ref. Pres. Reformed Presbyterian
Refrig. Refrigerate(d)
Refrigeration
Reg. Regent
Regiment
Regina (Queen)
Register
Registrar
Registry
Regulation
reg. region
register
regular(ly)
regd. registered
Reg.-Gen. Registrar-General
Reg. Prof. Regius Professor
Regr. Registrar

Regs. Regulations
Regt. Regiment
Regtl. Regimental
Reg.T.M. Registered Trade Mark
R.E.I. Rat der Europäischen Indust-
rieverbände (Council of European
Industrial Federations)
Rel. Religion
Religious
rel. relative(ly)
relic
religion
reliure (binding)
Relig. Religion
Religious
Rel. Pron. Relative Pronoun
Rem. Remittance
Remitted
R.E.M.C. Radio and Electronics Mea-
surements Committee
R.E.M.E. Royal Electrical and Mechan-
ical Engineers
R.E.M.P. Research Group for Euro-
pean Migration Problems
Ren. Renaissance
Renf. Renfrewshire
R.E.N.F.E. Red Nacional de los Ferro-
carriles Espanoles (National System
of Spanish Railways)
Rep. Repertory
Republic(an)
rep. repeat
report(er)
representative
representing
R.E.P. Regional Employment Premium
repr. represent(atives)
repro. reproduction
Repub. Republic(an)
req. request
require
requisition
R.E.R.O. Royal Engineers Reserve of
Officers
Res. Research
Reserve(d)
Residence
Resident
res. research
reserve(d)
residence
resident
resigned
R.E.S. Royal Economic Society
Royal Empire Society (*now*
R.C.S.)
Royal Entomological Society
resgnd. resigned
resp. respectively
respondent
Res. Sec. Resident Secretary
rest. restaurant
Ret. Retired
ret. retired
returned
R. et I. Regina et Imperatrix (Queen
and Empress)
Rex et Imperator (King and
Emperor)
retnr. retainer
Ret. P. Retired Pay

Rev. Revelations
Reverend
Review
Revised
rev. revenue
reverse
review
revise
revision
revolution
rev. ed. revised edition
revs. revolutions
Rev. Stat. Revised Statutes
Rev. Ver. Revised Version
R.F. Rainer Foundation
Range Finder
Rapid Fire
Regular Forces
République Française (the French Republic)
Rheumatic Fever
Rockefeller Foundation
Royal Fusiliers
Rugby Football
r.f. radio frequency
R.F.A. Royal Field Artillery
Royal Fleet Auxiliary
R.F.A.C. Royal Fine Art Commission
R.F.C. Radio Frequency Choke
Royal Flying Corps (*now* R.A.F.)
Rugby Football Club
R.F.D. Rural Free Delivery (U.S.)
R.F.E. Radio Free Europe
R.F.E.A. Regular Forces Employment Association
R.F.H. Royal Festival Hall, London
R.F.L. Rugby Football League
Rfn. Rifleman
R.F.N. Registered Fever Nurse
r.f.p. retired full pay
R.F.P.S.(G.) Royal Faculty of Physicians and Surgeons of Glasgow
R.F.R. Royal Fleet Reserve
rfrd. referred to
R.F.S. Registry of Friendly Societies
Royal Forestry Society of England and Wales
R.F.U. Rugby Football Union
R.F.Y.C. Royal Forth Yacht Club
R.G. Rive Gauche (Left Bank)
R.G.A. Royal Garrison Artillery
Royal Guernsey Artillery
Rubber Growers' Association
R.G.A.H.S. Royal Guernsey Agricultural and Horticultural Society
rgd. registered
R.G.D. Radio Gramophone Development Company, Limited
R.G.D.A.T.A. Retail Grocery, Dairy and Allied Trades Association
R.G.E. Rat der Gemeinden Europas (Council of European Municipalities)
R.-Genl. Registrar-General
R.G.H. Royal Gloucestershire Hussars
R.G.I. Royal Glasgow Institute of the Fine Arts
R.G.O. Royal Greenwich Observatory
R.G.N. Registered General Nurse
R.G.S. Royal Geographical Society
R.G.S.A. Royal Geographical Society of Australasia

Rgt. Regiment
R.G.T.F. Royal General Theatrical Fund
Rgtl. Regimental
Rh Rhesus
Rhodium
R.H. Relative Humidity
Right Half
Right Hand
Royal Highlanders
Royal Highness
Royal Hospital
R.H.A. Road Haulage Association
Royal Hibernian Academy
Royal Horse Artillery
R.Hamps. Royal Hampshire Regiment
R.H.B. Regional Hospital Board
R.H.C. Road Haulage Cases
R.H.D.S. Romney Hythe and Dymchurch Light Railway
R.H.E. Road Haulage Executive
Rhet. Rhetorical
R.H.F. Royal Highland Fusiliers
R.H.G. Royal Horse Guards
rhino. rhinoceros
R.Hist.S. Royal Historical Society
R.H.M.S. Royal Hibernian Military School
R.H.R. Royal Highland Regiment
R.H.S. Royal Historical Society
Royal Horticultural Society
Royal Humane Society
R.H.S.I. Royal Horticultural Society of Ireland
R.I. Regimental Institute
Regina et Imperatrix (Queen and Empress)
Reinsurance
Religious Instruction
Rex et Imperator (King and Emperor)
Rhode Island
Rotary International
Royal Institution
Member of the Royal Institute of Painters in Water Colours
R.I.A. Royal Irish Academy
R.I.A.C. Royal Irish Automobile Club
R.I.A.I. Royal Institute of the Architects of Ireland
R.I.A.M. Royal Irish Academy of Music
R.I.A.S. Royal Incorporation of Architects in Scotland
R.I.B. Rural Industries Bureau
R.I.B.A. Royal Institute of British Architects
R.I.B.I. Rotary International in Great Britain and Ireland
R.I.C. Radio Industry Council
Royal Institute of Chemistry
Royal Irish Constabulary
Union Internationale des Voitures et Fourgons (International Carriage and Van Union)
R.I.C.M. Registre international des citoyens du monde (International Registry of World Citizens)
R.I.C.S. Royal Institution of Chartered Surveyors

R.I.F. Resistance Inducing Factor
    Royal Irish Fusiliers
R.I.I.A. Royal Institute of International Affairs
R.I.L.E.M. Réunion internationale des laboratoires d'essais et de recherches sur les matériaux et les constructions (International Union of Testing and Research Laboratories for Materials and Structures)
R.I.N.A. Royal Institution of Naval Architects
R.I.O.P. Royal Institute of Oil Painters
R.I.P. Requiescat in Pace (may he *or* she rest in peace)
R.I.P.A. Royal Institute of Public Administration
R.I.P.H.H. Royal Institute of Public Health and Hygiene
R.I.P.P.L.E. Radioactive Isotope Powered Pulsed Light Equipment
R.Ir.F. Royal Irish Fusiliers
R.I.S. Railway Invigoration Society
    Research Information Service
R.I.S.C.O. Rhodesian Iron and Steel Company
R.I.S.D. Rural Institutions and Services Division of the Food and Agriculture Organization
rit. ritardando (decrease pace)
riten. ritenuto (with restraint)
RITENA Réunión Internacional de Técnicos de la Nutrición Animal (International Meeting of Animal Nutrition Experts)
Riv. River
R.I.V. Regolamento Internazionale Veicoli (International Railway Wagon Union)
    Repayment Issue Voucher
R.J.A. Royal Jersey Artillery
R.J.A.H.S. Royal Jersey Agricultural and Horticultural Society
R.J.L.I. Royal Jersey Light Infantry
R.J.M. Royal Jersey Militia
R.J.O. Rapports Judiciaires Officiels (Quebec Official Law Reports)
R.K.O. Radio-Keith-Orpheum
Rl. Rouble
R.L. Reference Library
    Rocket Launcher
    Rugby League
R.L.B.W.M. Regional Library Bureau, West Midlands
R.L.I. Rhodes-Livingstone Institute (Zambia)
R. Lincolns. Royal Lincolnshire Regiment
R.L.O. Railway Liaison Officer
    Returned Letter Office
R.L.P.A.S. Royal London Prisoners' Aid Society
Rls. Roubles
R.L.S. Robert Louis Stevenson
R.L.S.S. Royal Life Saving Society
Rly. Railway
rm. ream(s)
    room
R.M. Registered Midwife
    Resident Magistrate
    Royal Mail
    Royal Marines

R.M.A. Retread Manufacturers' Association
    Royal Malta Artillery
    Royal Marine Artillery
    Royal Marines Association
    Royal Military Academy, Sandhurst (*formerly* Woolwich)
    Royal Musical Association
R.M.A.I. Radio Manufacturers' Association of India
R.M.C. Radio Modifications Committee
    Royal Military College, Sandhurst (*now* R.M.A.)
R.M.C.C. Royal Military College of Canada
R.M.C.S. Royal Military College of Science
R.Met.S. Royal Meteorological Society
R.M.F.V.R. Royal Marine Forces, Volunteer Reserves
R.M.L.I. Royal Marine Light Infantry
R.M.N. Registered Mental Nurse
    Royal Malaysian Navy
R.M.O. Regional Medical Officer
    Resident Medical Officer
    Royal Marine Office
R.Mon.R.E. (M.) Royal Monmouthshire Royal Engineers (Militia)
R.M.P. Corps of Royal Military Police
R.M.P.A. Royal Medico-Psychological Association
R.M.S. Royal Mail Steamer
    Royal Medical Society
    Royal Meteorological Society
    Royal Microscopical Society
    Royal Society of Miniature Painters, Sculptors and Gravers
R.M.S.A. Rural Music Schools Association
R.M.Sch.Mus. Royal Marines School of Music
R.M.S.M. Royal Military School of Music
R.M.S.P. Royal Mail Steam Packet Company
R.M.Y.C. Royal Motor Yacht Club
Rn Radon
R.N. Registered Nurse
    Royal Naval
    Royal Navy
RNA Ribonucleic Acid
R.N.A. Romantic Novelists' Association
R.N.A.F. Royal Naval Air Force (*now* F.A.A.)
R.N.A.S. Royal Naval Air Service (*now* F.A.A.)
    Royal Naval Air Station
R.N.A.V. Royal Naval Artillery Volunteers
R.N.A.W. Royal Naval Aircraft Workshop
R.N.A.Y. Royal Naval Aircraft Yard
R.N.B. Royal Naval Barracks
R.N.B.T. Royal Naval Benevolent Trust
R.N.C(oll). Royal Naval College
rnd. round
R.N.D. Royal Naval Division

R.N.E.C(oll). Royal Naval Engineering College
R.N.F. Royal Northumberland Fusiliers
R.N.F.U. Rhodesia National Farmers' Union
R.N.H.U. Royal National Homing Union
R.N.I.B. Royal National Institute for the Blind
R.N.I.D. Royal National Institute for the Deaf
R.N.L.I. Royal National Lifeboat Institution
R.N.L.O. Royal Naval Liaison Officer
R.N.M.D. Registered Nurse for Mental Defectives
R.N.M.D.S.F. Royal National Mission to Deep Sea Fishermen
R.N.M.S. Royal Naval Medical School
R.N.M.W.S. Royal Naval Minewatching Service
R.N.O. Riddare af Nordstjerne Orden (Knight of the Order of the Pole Star)
R. Norfolk Royal Norfolk Regiment
R.N.P.F.N. Royal National Pension Fund for Nurses
R.N.P.L. Royal Naval Physiological Laboratory
R.N.R. Royal Naval Reserve
R.N.R.A. Royal Naval Rifle Association
R.N.R.S. Royal National Rose Society
R.N.S. Royal Numismatic Society
R.N.S.A. Royal Naval Sailing Association
R.N.S.C. Royal Naval Staff College
R.N.S.R. Royal Naval Special Reserve
R.N.S.S. Royal Naval Scientific Service
R.N.T.E. Royal Naval Training Establishment(s)
R.N.T.U. Royal Naval Training Unit
R.N.V.R. Royal Naval Volunteer Reserve
R.N.V.S.R. Royal Naval Volunteer Supplementary Reserve
R.N.W.A.R. Royal Naval Wireless Auxiliary Reserve
R.N.Y.C. Royal Northern Yacht Club
R.N.Z.A.F. Royal New Zealand Air Force
R.N.Z.A.S. Royal Astronomical Society of New Zealand
R.N.Z.N. Royal New Zealand Navy
Ro. Recto
ro. recto
 rood
R.O. Receiving Officer
 Receiving Order
 Record Office
 Registered Office
 Reserve Occupation
 Returning Officer
 Routine Order
 Royal Observatory
R.O.A. Roller Owners' Association
R.O.C. Royal Observer Corps
R.O.F. Royal Ordnance Factory
R. of O. Reserve of Officers
R.O.H. Royal Opera House
R.O.I. Royal Institute of Oil Painters
R.O.K. Republic of Korea
Rom. Roman(s)
 Romance

rom. roman type
R.O.M. Record Office Memorandum
R.O.O. Railhead Ordnance Officer
r.o.p. run of paper
R.O.R.C. Royal Ocean Racing Club
Ros. Rosary
 Roscommon
R.O.S.C. Road Operators' Safety Council
R.O.S.L.A. Raising of school leaving age
RoSPA Royal Society for the Prevention of Accidents
rot. rotary
 rotation
 rotor
R.O.T.C. Reserve Officers' Training Corps (U.S.)
R.O.U. Radio Officers' Union
R.O.W. Right of Way
Rox. Roxburgh
Roy. Royal
Rp. Rupiah(s)
R.P. Reformed Presbyterian
 Regimental Police
 Regius Professor
 Reprint(ing)
 Res publica (the State)
 Révérend Père (Reverend Father)
 Royal Society of Portrait Painters
 Rules of Procedure
r.p. reply paid
R.P.A. Regional port authorities
 Registered Plumbers' Association
 Rubber Proofers' Association
R.P.C. Readers' Pensions Committee
 Reports of Patent Cases
 Republican Party Conference (U.S.)
 Request Pleasure of your Company
 Royal Pioneer Corps
R.P.D. Regional Port Director
 Regius Professor of Divinity
 Rerum Politicarum Doctor (Doctor of Political Science)
 Rocket Propulsion Department
 Royal Purple Degree
R.P.E. Radio Production Executive
 Reformed Protestant Episcopal
 Relative price effect
 Rocket Propulsion Establishment
R.P.F. Rassemblement du Peuple Français (Rally of the French People)
R.P.F.M.A. Rubber and Plastics Footwear Manufacturers' Association
r.p.g. rounds per gun
r.p.h. revolutions per hour
R.Phil.S. Royal Philharmonic Society
R.P.M. Resale Price Maintenance
r.p.m. revolutions per minute
 rounds per minute
R.P.O. Railway Post Office
 Regional Personnel Officer
 Royal Philharmonic Orchestra
R.P.R. Rumanian People's Republic
R.P.S. Royal Philatelic Society
 Royal Philharmonic Society
 Royal Photographic Society
 Royal Pinner School

O

r.p.s. revolutions per second
Rpt. Report
rpt. repeat
    reprint
R.P.T. Registered Physical Therapist
R.Q.M.S. Regimental Quartermaster-Sergeant
Rr. Rare
R.R. Radiation Resistance
    Railroad
    Ready Reckoner
    Research Reactor
    Right Reverend
    Rolls-Royce
    Rural Route (Canada)
R.R.A. Royal Regiment of Artillery
R.R.A.F. Royal Rhodesian Air Force
R.R.B. Radio Research Board
R.R.C. Royal Red Cross
R.R.E. Royal Radar Establishment
R.R.F. Royal Regiment of Fusiliers
R.R.I. Rowett Research Institute
    Rubber Research Institute (Malaya)
R.R.I.C. Rubber Research Institute of Ceylon
R.R.L. Registered Record Librarian
    Road Research Laboratory
RR.PP. Révérends Pères (Reverend Fathers)
R.R.S. Radio Research Station (*now* R.S.R.S.)
    Royal Research Ship
Rs. Rupees
R.S. Recording Secretary
    Recruiting Service
    Research Station
    Revised Statutes
    Rolls Series
    Royal Society
    Royal Scots
R/S. Rejection Slip
r.s. right side
R.S.A. Radical Student Alliance
    Royal Scottish Academician
    Royal Scottish Academy
    Royal Society for the Encouragement of Arts, Manufactures and Commerce
    Royal Society of Australia
R.S.A.C. Royal Scottish Automobile Club
R.S.A.F. Royal Small Arms Factory
R.S.A.I. Royal Society of Antiquaries of Ireland
R.S.A.M. Royal Scottish Academy of Music
R.San.I. Royal Sanitary Institute *now* R.S.H.)
R.S.A.S. Royal Sanitary Association of Scotland
    Royal Surgical Aid Society
R.S.A.S.A. Royal South Australian Society of Arts
R.S.B. Regimental Stretcher-Bearer
R.S.C. Royal Society of Canada
    Rules of the Supreme Court
R.S.C.J. Virgines Religiosae Societatis Sacratissimi Cordis Jesus (Nuns of the Most Sacred Heart of Jesus)
R.S.C.M. Royal School of Church Music

R.S.C.N. Registered Sick Children's Nurse
R.S.D. Returned Stores Department
    Royal Society of Dublin
R.S.D.L.P. (b.) Russian Social Democratic Labour Party (Bolsheviks)
R.S.E. Royal Society of Edinburgh
R.S.F. Royal Scots Fusiliers
R.S.F.S. Royal Scottish Forestry Society
R.S.F.S.R. Russian Soviet Federated Socialist Republic
R.S.G. Regional Seats of Government
    Royal Scots Greys
R.S.G.B. Radio Society of Great Britain
R.S.G.S. Royal Scottish Geographical Society
R.S.H. Royal Society for the Promotion of Health
R.S.H.M. Religious of the Sacred Heart of Mary
R.S.I. Royal Sanitary Institute R.S.H.)
    Royal Signals Institution
R.Sigs. Royal Corps of Signals
R.S.L. Royal Society of Literature
R.S.L.A. Raising school leaving age
R.S.M. Regimental Sergeant Major
    Royal School of Mines
    Royal Society of Medicine
    Royal Society of Musicians of Great Britain
R.S.N.A. Royal Society of Northern Antiquaries
R.S.N.Z. Royal Society of New Zealand
R.S.O. Railway Sorting Office
    Railway Sub-Office
    Recruiting Staff Officer
    Resident Surgical Officer
    Rural Sub-Office
R.S.P.B. Royal Society for the Protection of Birds
R.S.P.C.A. Royal Society for the Prevention of Cruelty to Animals
R.S.P.C.C. Royal Scottish Society for the Prevention of Cruelty to Children
R.S.P.E. Royal Society of Painter-Etchers and Engravers
R.S.P.P. Royal Society of Portrait Painters
R.S.R.S. Radio and Space Research Station
R.S.S. Regiae Societatis Sodalis *or* Socius (Fellow of the Royal Society)
    Royal Statistical Society
R.S.S.A.I.L.A. Returned Sailors', Soldiers' and Airmen's Imperial League of Australia
R.S.T. Rhodesian Selection Trust
    Royal Shakespeare Theatre
    Royal Society of Teachers
R.S.T.M. & H. Royal Society of Tropical Medicine and Hygiene
R.S.U.A. Royal Society of Ulster Architects
R. Sussex Royal Sussex Regiment
R.S.V. Revised Standard Version
R.S.V.P. répondez s'il vous plaît (please reply)

R.S.W. Royal Scottish Society of Painters in Water Colours
R.S.Y.C. Royal Southern Yacht Club
rt. right
R.T. Radio Telegraphy
    Radio Telephone
    Radio Telephony
    Radio Times
    Return Ticket
R.T.A. Reciprocal Trade Agreements
    Rhodesian Tobacco Association
    Road Traffic Act
    Rubber Trade Association of London
R.T.A.M.A. Railway Tyre and Axle Manufacturers Association
R.T.B. Richard Thomas and Baldwins, Limited
R.T.B.I. National Association of Round Tables of Great Britain and Ireland
R.T.C.E.G. Rubber and Thermoplastic Cables Export Group
R.T.C.H. National Conference of Road Transport Clearing Houses
R.T.D. Religion Through Drama
R.T.E. Radio-Telefis Eireann
R.T.E.B. Radio Trades Examination Board
R.T.E.C. Retail Trades' Education Council
Rt. Hon. Right Honourable
R.T.I. Round Table International
R. Tks. Royal Tank Regiment
R.T.O. Railway Transport Officer
R.T.R. Royal Tank Regiment
R.T.R.A. Radio and Television Retailers' Association
Rt. Rev. Right Reverend
R.T.S. Religious Tract Society
    Reserve Tug Service
    Royal Toxophilite Society
R.T.S.A. Retail Trading Standards Association Incorporated
R.T.V. Re-entry Test Vehicle
R.T.W. Road Tank Wagons
R.T.Y.C. Royal Thames Yacht Club
Ru Ruthenium
R.U. Readers' Union
    Rugby Football Union
R.U.A. Royal Ulster Academy of Painting, Sculpture and Architecture
R.U.A.S. Royal Ulster Agricultural Society
R.U.C. Royal Ulster Constabulary
R.U.E. Right Upper Entrance
R.U.K.B.A. Royal United Kingdom Beneficent Association
Rum. Rumania(n)
R.U.R. Rossum's Universal Robots
    Royal Ulster Rifles
R.U.S.I. Royal United Service Institution
R.U.S.M. Royal United Service Museum
Russ. Russia(n)

Rv. Rendezvous
R.V. Revised Version
    Rifle Volunteers
R.V.A. Rating and Valuation Association
    Regular Veterans' Association of the United States
R.V.C. Rifle Volunteer Corps
    Royal Veterinary College
    Royal Victorian Chain
R.V.C.I. Royal Veterinary College of Ireland
R.V.I.A. Royal Victoria Institute of Architects (Australia)
R.V.O. Royal Victorian Order
R.V.R. Runway Visual Range
R.V.S.V.P. répondez vite s'il vous plaît (please reply quickly)
R.W. Right of Way
    Right Worshipful
    Right Worthy
    Royal Warrant
R.W.A. Member of the Royal West of England Academy
R.W.A.F.F. Royal West African Frontier Force
R.War.R. Royal Warwickshire Regiment
R.W.A.S. Royal Welsh Agricultural Society
R.W.D.G.M. Right Worshipful Deputy Grand Master
R.W.E.A. Royal West of England Academy
R.W.F. Radio Wholesalers' Federation
    Royal Welch Fusiliers
R.W.G.M. Right Worshipful Grand Master
R.W.G.R. Right Worthy Grand Representative
R.W.G.S. Right Worthy Grand Secretary
R.W.G.T. Right Worthy Grand Templar
R.W.G.W. Right Worthy Grand Warden
R.Wilts.Yeo. Royal Wiltshire Yeomanry
R.W.J.G.W. Right Worthy Junior Grand Warden
R.W.K. Queen's Own Royal West Kent Regiment
R.W.O. Riddare af Wasa Orden (Knight of the Order of Vasa)
R.W.S. Royal Society of Painters in Water Colours
R.W.S.G.W. Right Worshipful Senior Grand Warden
Ry. Railway
R.Y.A. Royal Yachting Association
R.Y.S. Royal Yacht Squadron
R.Z.Scot. Royal Zoological Society of Scotland
R.Z.S.I. Royal Zoological Society of Ireland

S

S Scalar
Sulphur

S. Sabbath
Saint
Saturday
Saxon
School
Scotch
Scottish
Scribe
Sea
Sears
Secondary
Secret
Secretary
Section
Segno (repeat from *or* to this sign)
Seite (page)
Senate
Señor
Sepultus (buried)
Series
Servius
Sextus
Ship
Signaller
Signor
Singular
Sister
Socialist
Society
Socius (Fellow)
Sodalis (Fellow)
Solar
Solo
Soprano
South(ern)
Staff
Statute
Stem
Submarine
Succeeded
Summer
Sun
Sunday
Surplus
Sweden

s. second
section
see
semi
sermon
set
shilling(s)
sign
singular
sinistra (left hand)
snow
solo
son
south(ern)
spades
spherical
stratus cloud
suit
sunny

Sa Samarium

Sa. Sable
Saturday

S.A. Salvation Army
Semi-annual
Services Adviser
Sex-appeal
Shops Act
Small Arms
Sociedad Anónima (Corporation)
Societas Adunatonis (Franciscans of the Atonement)
Society of Antiquaries
Society of Authors
Son Altesse (His *or* Her Highness)
South Africa
South America
South Australia
Sturm-Abteilung (Nazi Storm Troops)
Supply Assistant

s.a. safe arrival
secundum artem (according to the art)
see also
sine anno (undated)
special agent
sub anno (under the year)
subject to approval

S.A.A. Screen Advertising Association, Ltd.
Small Arms Ammunition
South African Airways
South Arabian Army
Standards Association of Australia
Surface Active Agents

S.A.A.A. Scottish Amateur Athletic Association

S.A.A.D. Small-Arms Ammunition Depot
Society for the Advancement of Anaesthesia in Dentistry

S.A.A.F. South African Air Force

S.A.A.T.C. Southern African Air Transport Council

S.A.A.U. South African Agricultural Union

Sab. Sabbath

S.A.B. Science Advisory Board
Society of American Bacteriologists
Soprano, Alto, Bass

S.A.B.A. Scottish Amateur Boxing Association

S.A.B.C. South African Broadcasting Corporation

S.A.B.E.N.A. Société anonyme belge d'exploitation de la navigation aérienne (Belgian World Air Lines)

S.A.B.R.A. South African Bureau of Racial Affairs

Sabrita South Africa-Britain Trade Association

S.A.B.S. South African Bureau of Standards

S.A.C. Scientific Advisory Council
Scottish Automobile Club *cont.*

Senior Aircraftman
Société africaine de culture (Society of African Culture)
Society for Analytical Chemistry
South Atlantic Coast
State Athletic Commission (U.S.)
Strategic Air Command (U.S.)
Sud Aviation Corporation
s.a.c. qualified at a Small Arms Technical Long Course
S.A.C.A. Supreme Allied Commander Atlantic
S.A.C.A.N.G.O. Southern Africa Committee on Air Navigation and Ground Operation
S. Acc. Società Accomandita (limited partnership)
SACEUR Supreme Allied Commander Europe
S.A.C.K. School and Community Kits
SACLANT Supreme Allied Commander Atlantic
Sacr. Sacrist
S.A.C.S.E.A. Supreme Allied Command South East Asia
S.A.C.S.I.R. South African Council for Scientific and Industrial Research
S.A.C.T.U. South African Congress of Trade Unions
S.A.D.A.S. Sperry Airborne Data Acquisition System
S.A.D.F. South African Defence Forces
S.A.D.G. Société des architectes diplômés par le gouvernement (Society of Government-certified Architects)
S.Ad.O. Station *or* Senior Administrative Officer
S.A.E. Society of American Etchers
Society of Automotive Engineers (U.S.)
s.a.e. stamped addressed envelope
saec. saeculum (century)
S.A.E.P.K.T. Scottish Alliance of Employers in the Printing and Kindred Trades
S.A.F. Strategic Air Force (U.S.)
S.A.F.A. South Africa Freedom Association
S. Afr. South Africa
S.Afr.D. South African Dutch
S.A.F.U. Scottish Amateur Fencing Union
S.A.G.A. Society of American Graphic Artists
S.A.G.A.G.B. Sand and Gravel Association of Great Britain
S.A.G.B. Spiritualist Association of Great Britain Limited
S.A.G.E. Semi-Automatic Ground Environment
S.A.G.G.A. Scout and Guide Graduate Association
S.A.H. Supreme Allied Headquarters
S.A.H.R. Society for Army Historical Research
S.A.I. Scottish Agricultural Industries, Ltd.
Società Anonima Italiana (Incorporated Company)
Son Altesse Impériale (His *or* Her Imperial Highness)

S.A.I.A. South Australian Institute of Architects
S.A.I.F. South African Industrial Federation
S.A.I.M.R. South African Institute of Medical Research
S.A.I.R.R. South African Institute of Race Relations
S.A.K.I. Self-organizing Automatic Keyboard Instructor
sal. salary
s.a.l. secundum artis leges (according to the rules of art)
S.A.L.A. South African Library Association
S.A.L.J. South African Law Journal
Sall. Sallust
Salop Shropshire
S.A.L.P. South African Labour Party
S.A.L.R. South African Law Reports
S.A.L.T. Strategic Arms Limitation Talks
Salv. Salvador
Sam. Samaria
Samaritan
Samoa
Samuel
S. Am. South America(n)
S.A.M. Social Accounting Matrix
Surface-to-Air Missile
S.A.M.A. Scottish Agricultural Machinery Association
Samar. Samaritan
S.A.M.B. Scottish Association of Master Bakers
S.A.M.C. Scottish Association of Manufacturing Coppersmiths
South African Medical Corps
S.A.M.H. Scottish Association for Mental Health
Sami Socially Acceptable Monitoring Instrument
S.A.M.S. South American Missionary Society
S.A.M.S.A. Silica and Moulding Sands Association
san. sanitary
S.A.N. Society of Antiquaries of Newcastle upon Tyne
Sanat. Sanatorium
S.A.N.B. South African National Bibliography
S.A.N.C.A.D. Scottish Association for National Certificate and Diplomas
San. D. Doctor of Sanitation
S. & D.T.U. Sign and Display Trades Union
S. & F.A. Shipping and Forwarding Agents
S. & M. Bishop of Sodor and Man
s.& m. sausages and mash
S.& T. Supply and Transport
San Fran. San Francisco
s.a.n.r. subject to approval, no risk
S.A.N.R.O.C. South African Non-Racial Olympics Committee
Sans. Sanskrit
Sans Serif
S.A.N.S. South African Naval Service
S.A.N.T.A. South African National Tuberculosis Association

S.A.O. Senior Accountant Officer
⸺ Scottish Association of Opticians
Squadron Accountant Officer
S.A.O.S. Scottish Agricultural Organisation Society
S.A.P. South African Police
s.a.p. soon as possible
S.A.P.M. Scottish Association of Paint Manufacturers
Sar. Sarawak
Sardinia
S.A.R. Search and Rescue
Son Altesse Royale (His *or* Her Royal Highness)
Sons of the American Revolution
South African Republic
South Australian Industrial Court Reports
Standardised Abnormality Ratio
S.A.R.A.H. Search and Rescue and Homing
S.A.R. & H. South African Railways and Harbours
S.A.R.B.E. Search and Rescue Beacon Equipment
S.A.R.C.C.U.S. South African Regional Committee for the Conservation and Utilisation of the Soil
S.A.R.L. Société à responsabilité limitée (Limited Liability Company)
S.A.S. Scandinavian Airlines System
Son Altesse Sérénissime (His *or* Her Serene Highness)
Special Air Service Regiment
S.A.S.C. Small Arms School Corps
Sask. Saskatchewan
S.A.S.L.O. South African Scientific Liaison Office
S.A.S.O. Senior Air Staff Officer
S.A.S.R. South Australian State Reports
Special Air Service Regiment
Sat. Satellite
Saturday
Saturn
sat. saturated
S. At. South Atlantic
S.A.T. Sennacieca Asocio Tutmonda (Nationless Worldwide Association)
Ship's Apparent Time
⸺ Society for Acoustic Technology
S.A.T.A.F. Second Allied Tactical Air Force
S.A.T.B. Soprano, Alto, Tenor, Bass
S.A.T.C.C. Southern Air Traffic Control Centre
SATCO Signal Automatic Air Traffic Control
SATEX Semi-Automatic Telegraph Exchange
S.A.T.I.P.S. Society of Assistants Teaching in Preparatory Schools
S.A.T.O. South American Travel Organization
S.A.T.R.A. Shoe and Allied Trades' Research Association
S.A.T.U. South African Typographical Union
S.A.U. Schools Action Union

S.Aus. South Australia
Sav. Savoie
s.a.v. stock at valuation
S.A.V.S. Scottish Anti-Vivisection Society
S.A.W.A. Screen Advertising World Association
Sax. Saxon(y)
sax. saxophone
S.A.Y.F.C. Scottish Association of Young Farmers' Clubs
Sb Stibium (antimony)
sb. substantive
S.B. Sales Book
Sam Browne
Savings Bank
Scientiae Baccalaureus (Bachelor of Science)
Serving Brother
Sick Bay
Signal Book
Signal Boatswain
Simultaneous Broadcast(ing)
Single Barrelled
Single Breasted
Smooth Bore
Special Branch
Spring Back
Statute Book
Stretcher Bearer
s.b. single breasted
small bore
S.B.A. Scottish Beekeepers' Association
Sick-Bay Attendant
Small Business Administration (U.S.)
Smaller Businesses Association
S.B.A.C. Society of British Aerospace Companies
S.B.B.N.F. Ship and Boat Builders' National Federation
S.B.C. School Broadcasting Council
Signal Books Correct
Southern Baptist Convention (U.S.)
Supplementary Benefits Commission
S.B.Chem. Bachelor of Science in Chemistry
S.B.Comm. Bachelor of Science in Commerce
S.B.C.P.O. Sick Bay Chief Petty Officer
S.B.Ed. Bachelor of Science in Education
S.B.Engin. Bachelor of Science in Engineering
S.B.Geol. Bachelor of Science in Geology
S.B.G.I. Society of British Gas Industries
S.B.M. Strict Baptist Mission
S.B.M.A. Stock Brick Manufacturers' Association
S.B.N. Standard Book Number
S.B.N.O. Senior British Naval Officer
S.B.N.S. Society of British Neurological Surgeons
S.B.O.T. Sacred Books of the Old Testament
S.B.Pharm. Bachelor of Science in Pharmacy

S.B.P.I.M. Society of British Printing Ink Manufacturers
S.B.R. Society for Biological Rhythm
S.B.S. Scottish Budgerigar Society
S.B.S.A. Standard Bank of South Africa
S.B.St.J. Serving Brother of the Order of Saint John of Jerusalem
S.B.U. Sociedades Bíblicas Unidas (United Bible Societies)
S. by E. South by East
S. by W. South by West
Sc Scandium
Sc. Scandinavia(n)
   Scene
   Science
   Scotland
   Scots
   Scottish
   Sculptor
sc. science
   scilicet (namely)
   screw
   scruple
   sculpsit (he carved *or* engraved it)
S.C. Sailing Club
   Salvage Corps
   Same Case
   School Certificate
   Senatus Consultum (Decree of the Senate)
   Senior Counsel
   Service Certificate
   Session Cases
   Shooting Club
   Short Course
   Skating Club
   Sking Club
   Small Craft
   Social Club
   South Carolina
   Southern Command
   Special Constable
   Special Constabulary
   Sports Club
   Staff Captain
   Staff College
   Staff Corps
   Standing Committee
   Statutory Committee
   Suffolk and Cambridgeshire Regiment
   Supreme Court
   Swimming Club
s.c. self contained
   single column
   small capital(s)
   steel casting
S.C.A. Society of Catholic Apostolate
S.C.A.A.A. Southern Counties Amateur Athletic Association
S.C.A.A.P. Special Commonwealth African Assistance Plan
S.C.A.D. Subsonic Cruise Armed Decoy
S.C.A.F. Supreme Commander of Allied Forces
SCAN Stockmarket Computer Answering Network
Scan(d). Scandinavia(n)
Sc. & T. Science and Technology
scan. mag. scandalum magnatum (libellous expressions)

S.C.A.O. Senior Civil Affairs Officer
S.C.A.P. Supreme Command Allied Powers
S.C.A.P.A. Society for Checking the Abuses of Public Advertising
s. caps. small capital letters
S.C.A.R. Scandinavian Council for Applied Research
   Scientific Committee on Antarctic Research
S.C.A.S. Southern Counties Archery Society
S.C.A.S.A. Southern Counties Amateur Swimming Association
S.C.A.T.S. Southern Counties Agricultural Trading Society
Sc.B. Scientiae Baccalaureus (Bachelor of Science)
S.C.B. Society of Craftsmen Bakers
S.C.B.C. Somerset Cattle Breeding Centre
Sc. C. Scottish Command
S.C.C. Scottish Churches Council
   Sea Cadet Corps
   Society of Cosmetic Chemists of Great Britain
S.C.C.A.P.E. Scottish Council for Commercial, Administrative and Professional Education
S.C.C.P.A.E. Scottish Council for Commercial Professional and Administrative Education
Scd. Scheduled
Sc.D. Scientiae Doctor (Doctor of Science)
S.C.D.A. Scottish Community Drama Association
   Standing Conference of Drama Associations
S.C.E. Scottish Certificate of Education
S.C.E.A.R. Scientific Committee on the Effects of Radiation (U.S.A.)
S.C.E.L. Standing Committee on Education in Librarianship
S.C.F. Save the Children Fund
   Senior Chaplain to the Forces
scg. scoring
S.C.G. Screen Cartoonists' Guild
   Social Credit Group
Sc.Gael. Scottish Gaelic
S.C.G.B. Ski Club of Great Britain
S.C.G.R.L. Signal Corps General Research Laboratory
S.C.G.S.A. Signal Corps Ground Signal Agency
S.C.G.S.S. Signal Corps Ground Signal Service
Sch. Scholar
   School
sch. scholarship
   scholium (note)
   schooner
S.C.H. Safe Course home
S.C.H. Student/Community/Housing
sched. schedule
Scherz. Scherzando (lively)
S.C.(H.L.) Sessions Cases (House of Lords)
Sch. M. School Master
Sch.Mist. School Mistress
schol. scholar
   scholastic

Sci. Science
sci. scientific
S.C.I. Service Civil International (International Voluntary Service)
Society of Chemical Industry
s.c.i. single-column inch
S.C.I.B.P. Special Committee for the International Biological Programme
sci. fa. scire facias (please make known)
scil. scilicet (namely)
Sci. M. Science Master
Sci. Mist. Science Mistress
S.C.J. Societas Cordis Jesu (Society of Priests of the Sacred Heart of Jesus)
S.C.(J.) Sessions Cases (Judiciary Reports)
S.C.L. Scottish Central Library
Student of Civil Law
S.C.L.H. Standing Conference for Local History
S.C.L.I. Somerset and Cornwall Light Infantry
Sc.M. Scientiae Magister (Master of Science)
S.C.M. Sacra Caesarea Majestas (Sacred Imperial Majesty)
State Certified Midwife
Student Christian Movement of Great Britain and Ireland
Summary Court-Martial
S.C.M.A. Society of Cinema Managers of Great Britain and Ireland (Amalgamated)
S.C.N.O. Senior Canadian Naval Officer
S.C.N.V.Y.O. Standing Conference of National Voluntary Youth Organisations
S.C.O.L.A. Second Consortium of Local Authorities
S. Coll. Staff College
S.C.O.L.M.A. Standing Conference on Library Materials on Africa
S. Coln. Supply Column
s. con. self contained
S.C.O.N.U.L. Standing Conference of National and University Libraries
SCOPE Southern Committee on Political Ethics
S.C.O.R. Special Committee on Oceanic Research (International Council of Scientific Unions)
SCORPIO Subcritical Carbon Moderated Reactor Assembly for Plutonium Investigations
Scot. Scotland
Scotsman
Scottish
S.C.O.T.A.P.L.L. Standing Conference of Theological and Philosophical Libraries in London
Scotbec Scottish Business Education Council
Scotec Scottish Technician Education Council
Scotus Supreme Court of the United States
S.C.P. Social Credit Party (Canada)
S.C.P.R. Scottish Council of Physical Recreation
Scr. Scruple
scr. scrip

S.C.R. Senior Common Room
Silicone Controlled Rectifier
Society for Cultural Relations with the U.S.S.R.
S.C.R.C.C. Soil Conservation and Rivers Control Council (N.Z.)
S.C.R.E. Scottish Council for Research in Education
Scrip. Scriptural
Scripture
S.C.R.L. Signal Corps Radar Laboratory
Scrt. Sanscrit
S.C.S. Society of Civil Servants
Space Communications Systems
S.C.S.D. Schools Construction Systems Development (U.S.A.)
S.C.S.S. Scottish Council of Social Service
S.C.T. Society of Commercial Teachers
Society of County Treasurers
S.C.T.R. Standing Conference on Telecommunications Research
S.C.T.U. Security Council Truce Commission (Palestine)
S.C.U. Scottish Cricket Union
Scottish Cycling Union
S.C.U.A. Scottish Conservative and Unionist Association
Suez Canal Users' Association
S.C.U.B.A. Self-contained Underwater Breathing Apparatus
S.C.U.E. Standing Conference on University Entrance
sculp. sculpsit (he carved or engraved it)
sculptor
sculptural
sculpture
S.C.V. Stato Città del Vaticano (Vatican City)
S.C.W.S. Scottish Co-operative Wholesale Society
S.C.Y.A. Scottish Christian Youth Assembly
Sd. Sound
sd. said
sewed
S.D. Diploma in Statistics
Scientiae Doctor (Doctor of Science)
Senatus Decreto (by decree of the senate)
Senior Deacon
Service Dress
Sight Draft
Signal Department
Signal Division
South Dakota
Special Duty
Staff Duties
Standard Displacement
State Department (U.S.)
Submarine Detector
Supply Department or Depot
s.d. safe deposit
same date
semi-detached
semi-diameter
semi-double
several dates
sine die (without date)

S.D.A. Scottish Dinghy Association
Seventh Day Adventist(s)
S. Dak. South Dakota
S.D.& T. Staff Duties and Training
S.D.B. Salesians of Don Bosco
S.D.B.L. Sight Draft, Bill of Lading
S.D.C. St. David's College
Society of Dyers and Colourists
s. det. semi-detached
S.D.F. Social Democratic Federation
Sudan Defence Force
S.D.G. Soli Deo Gloria (Glory to God Alone)
S.D.L. Special Duties List
S.D.M.A. Surgical Dressing Manufacturers' Association
S.D.M.J. September, December, March, June
S.D.N. Société des Nations (League of Nations)
S.D.N.S. Scottish Daily Newspaper Society
S.D.O. Senior Dental Officer
Senior Duty Officer
Signal Distributing Office
Squadron Dental Officer
Station Duty Officer
S. Doc. Senate Document
S.D.P. Social Democratic Party
S.Dpo. Stores Depot
S.D.R. Special Despatch Rider
special drawing rights
S.D.S. Salvatorians (Society of the Divine Saviour)
Sisters of the Divine Saviour
Students for a Democratic Society (U.S.)
S.D.T. Society of Dairy Technology
S.D.T.U. Sign and Display Trades Union
S.D.U.K. Society for the Diffusion of Useful Knowledge
Se Selenium
S.E. Sanitary Engineering
Society of Engineers
Son Eminence (His Eminence)
Son Excellence (His Excellency)
South-East
South-Easterly
South-Eastern
Staff Engineer
Stock Exchange
s.e. single entry
S.E.A. Shipbuilding Exports Association
Society for Education Through Art
S.E.A.A.C. South-East Asia Air Command
S.E.A.C. South-East Asia Command
South-Eastern Architects' Collaboration
Sea. H. Seaforth Highlanders
S.E.A.L.F. South-East Asia Land Forces
S.E.A.N. State Enrolled Assistant Nurse
S.E.A.T.O. South-East Asia Treaty Organisation
S.E.B. Southern Electricity Board
S.E.B.T. South-Eastern Brick and Tile Federation

S.E. by E. South-East by East
S.E. by S. South-East by South
Sec. Section
Secretary
sec. secant
second(ed)
secundum (according to)
S.E.C. Securities Exchange Commission (U.S.)
Simple Electronic Computer
Société européenne de culture (European Society of Culture)
South-Eastern Command
SECAM Sequential couleur à mémoire (colour sequence by memory: colour television system)
sec. art. secundum artem (according to the art)
Sec. Gen. Secretary General
Sec. Leg. Secretary of the Legation
sec. leg. secundum legem (according to law)
sec. nat. secundum naturam (according to nature)
sec. reg. secundum regulam (according to rule)
secs. seconds
Sect. Section
Sector
Secy. Secretary
S.E.D. Scottish Education Department
S.E.E. Senior Electrical Engineer
Signals Experimental Establishment
Société d'études et d'expansion (Studies and Expansion Society)
Society of Environmental Engineers
S.E.E.A. Société européenne d'énergie atomique (European Atomic Energy Society)
S.E.E.B. South-Eastern Electricity Board
S.E.E.C.A. South Eastern Electricity Commercial Association
S.E.e.O. Salvis Erroribus et Omissis (errors and omissions excepted)
S.E.F. Shipbuilding Employers' Federation
S.E.F.A. Scottish Educational Film Association
S.E.F.E.L. Secrétariat européen des fabricants d'emballages métalliques légers (European Secretariat for Manufacturers of Light Metallic Packings)
S.E.F.T. Society for Education in Film and Television
seg. segment
S.E.G.B. South Eastern Gas Board
S.E.H. Société européenne d'hématologie (European Society of Haematology)
S.E.H.M.F. South of England Hat Manufacturers' Federation
S.E.I.F.S.A. Steel and Engineering Industries' Federation of South Africa
Sel. Selwyn College, Cambridge
sel. selected
selection
selig (deceased)

S.E.L. Scouts' Esperanto League
Selk. Selkirk
Selw. Selwyn College, Cambridge
Sem. Seminary
Semitic
Sempre (continuous)
sem. il semble (it seems)
semicolon
S.E.M.A. Spray Equipment Manufacturers' Association
S.E.M.F.A. Scottish Electrical Manufacturers' and Factors' Association
semi. semicolon
Sen. Senate
Senator
Seneca
Senior
S.E.N. State Enrolled Nurse
S. en C. Société en Commandite (limited partnership)
Sen. Cd. Senior Commissioned
sen. clk. senior clerk
Sen. Doc. Senate Document
S.Eng.O. Senior Engineering Officer
Sen.M. Senior Master
Sen.Mist. Senior Mistress
S. en N.C. Société en nom collectif (joint stock company)
Sen.Opt. Senior Optime
sent. sentence
Sen. Wt. O. Senior Warrant Officer
S.E.O. Senior Equipment Officer
Senior Executive Officer
Senior Experimental Officer
s.e.o.o. sauf erreurs ou omissions (errors and ommissions excepted)
Sep. September
Septuagint
sep. separate
S.E.P. The Saturday Evening Post
Selective employment payment(s)
separ. separately
Sept. September
Septuagint
sept. septem (seven)
septupl. septuplicate
seq. sequens (the following)
sequente (and in what follows)
sequitur (it follows)
seq. luce sequenti luce (the following day)
seqq. sequentes *or* sequentia (the following)
sequentibus (in the following places)
ser. serial
series
Serb. Serbia(n)
Serg. Sergeant
Sergt. Sergeant
Serj. Serjeant
Serjt. Serjeant
S.E.R.L. Services Electronics Research Laboratory
S.E.R.L.B. South Eastern Regional Library Bureau
Serv. Servia(n)
Service(s)
servt. servant
S.E.S. Seafarers' Education Service
Studies and Expansion Society

S.E.S.O. Senior Equipment Staff Officer
S.E.S.R. Société européenne de sociologie rurale (European Society for Rural Sociology)
Sess. Session(s)
S.E.T. Selective employment tax
Setis Société Européene pour l'Étude et l'Intégration des Systèmes Spatiaux
S.-et-.M. Seine-et-Marne
S.-et-.O. Seine-et-Oise
S.E.T.S. Scottish Electrical Training Scheme
Sett. Settembre (September)
sev. several
sevl. several
S.E.W. *or* **S/E/W.** Safety Equipment Worker
Sexag. Sexagesima
sf. sforzando (with sudden stress)
S.F. San Francisco
Science Fiction
Senior Fellow
Sherwood Foresters
Shipping Federation
Sinn Fein (Ireland)
Sinking Fund
Socialist Fellowship
Society of Friends
S.f. Science fiction
s.f. signal frequency
sub finem (towards the end)
surface foot *or* feet
s.-f. science fiction
S.F.A. Scientific Film Association (*now* B.I.S.F.A.)
Scottish Football Association
Soroptimist Federation of the Americas
Stourbridge Firebrick Association
Sweet Fanny Adams (i.e. nothing at all)
S.F.B. Society of Furnace Builders (*now* S.I.F.B.)
S.F.C. Scottish Film Council
Standing Federation Committee (West Indies)
S.f.c. Sergeant first class
S.F.E.A. Scottish Further Education Association
S.F.G. Studien und Förderungsgesellschaft (Studies and Expansion Society)
S.F.I. Société financière internationale (International Finance Corporation)
S.F.M.A. School Furniture Manufacturers' Association
S.F.M.S. Shipwrecked Fishermen and Mariners Royal Benevolent Society
S.F.M.T.A. Scottish Federation of Meat Trades Associations
S.F.O. Senior Flag Officer
S.F.O.B. Special Forces Operating Base
S.F.O.R.S.A. School Furniture Operation Raising School-leaving Age
S.F.R.Y. Socialist Federal Republic of Yugoslavia
S.F.S. Society for Freedom in Science
S.F.S.A. Scottish Field Studies Association Limited
S.F.T.A. Society of Film and Television Arts

S.F.T.C.D. Senior Fellow Trinity College, Dublin
S.F.T.S.A. Scottish Forest Tree Seed Association
S.F.U. Signals Flying Unit
sfz. sforzando (with sudden stress)
Sg. Surgeon
S.G. Sa Grâce (His *or* Her Grace)
    Sa Grandeur (His *or* Her Highness)
    Salutis Gratia (for the sake of safety)
    Scots Guards
    Society of Genealogists
    Solicitor General
    Specific Gravity
    Surgeon General
s.g. specific gravity
S.G.A. Society of Graphic Artists
S.G.B. Scottish Gas Board
    Southern Gas Board
S.G.B.I. Schoolmistresses' and Governesses' Benevolent Institution
Sg.C. Surgeon Captain
Sg.Cr. Surgeon Commander
Sgd. Signed
S.G.D. Senior Grand Deacon
s.g.d.g. sans garantie du gouvernement (without Government guarantee)
S.G.F. Scottish Grocers' Federation
S.G.F.S. Scottish Girls Friendly Society
S.G.H.W. Steam Generating Heavy-Water Moderated Reactor
sgl. single
Sg.L.Cr. Surgeon Lieutenant-Commander
S.G.M. Scripture Gift Mission
    Sea Gallantry Medal
S.G.O. Squadron Gunnery Officer
Sg.R.A. Surgeon Rear-Admiral
S.G.Rep. Standing Group Representative
S.G.S. Stage Golfing Society
Sgt. Sergeant
S.G.T. Society of Glass Technology
Sgt. Maj. Sergeant Major
S.G.U. Scottish Gliding Union
Sg.V.A. Surgeon Vice-Admiral
S.G.W. Senior Grand Warden
Sh. Shilling(s)
    Shipwright
sh. shall
    shilling(s)
    shower(s)
S.H. Schleswig-Holstein
    School House
    Scottish Horse
    Staghounds
s.h. second-hand
S.H.A. Sidereal Hour Angle
S.H.A.E.F. Supreme Headquarters Allied Expeditionary Force
Shak(s). Shakespeare
S.H.& M.A. Scottish Horse and Motormen's Association
S.H.A.P.E. Supreme Headquarters Allied Powers in Europe
S.H.C.J. Society of the Holy Child Jesus
shd. should

S.H.D. Scottish Home Department
    State Hydro-electric Department (N.Z.)
Shef(f). Sheffield
Shet. Shetland Islands
s.h.f. super-high frequency
S.H.F.F. Scottish House Furnishers' Federation
S.H.H.D. Scottish Home and Health Department
shipt. shipment
Sh.L. Shipwright Lieutenant
S.H.L.M. Society of Hospital Laundry Managers
S.H.M. Society of Housing Managers
S.H.M.O. Senior Hospital Medical Officer
S.H.O. Senior House Officer
s.h.p. shaft horsepower
S.H.Q. Supreme Headquarters
Shrops. Shropshire
Shrops. Yeo. Shropshire Yeomanry
S.H.S. Shire Horse Society
    Societatis Historicae Socius (Fellow of the Historical Society)
s.h.v. sub hac voce (under this word)
    sub hoc verbo (under this word)
Si Silicon
S.I. Order of the Star of India
    Sandwich Islands
    Seine-Inférieure
    Shetland Isles
    Staff Inspector
    Staten Island
    Statutory Instrument
S.I.A. Saskatchewan Institute of Agrologists
    Société internationale d'acupuncture (International Acupuncture Society)
    Society of Industrial Artists (*now* S.I.A.D.)
    Soroptimist International Association
    Structural Insulation Association
S.I.A.D. Society of Industrial Artists and Designers
S.I.A.P. Sociedad Interamericana de Planificación (Inter-American Planning Society)
Sib. Siberia(n)
S.I.B. Shipbuilding Industry Board
    Special Investigation Branch
S.I.B.C. Société internationale de biologie clinique (International Society of Clinical Biology)
Sic. Sicily
    Sicilian
sic. siccus (dry)
S.I.C. Specific Inductive Capacity
    Société internationale de cardiologie (International Society of Cardiology)
    Société internationale de chirurgie (International Society of Surgery)
S.I.C.A. Society of Industrial and Cost Accountants of Canada

S.I.C.O.T. Société internationale de chirurgie orthopédique et de traumatologie (International Society of Orthopaedic Surgery and Traumatology)

S.I.D. Spiritus in Deo (his spirit is with God)
Sudden Ionospheric Disturbances

S.I.D.S. Société internationale de défense sociale (International Society of Social Defence)
Société internationale de droit du travail et de la sécurité sociale (International Society for Labour Law and Social Legislation)

S.I.E.C. Société internationale pour l'enseignement commercial (International Society for Business Education)

S.I.E.E. Student of the Institution of Electrical Engineers

S.I.E.S. Soils and Irrigation Extension Service (Australia)

S.I.F.B. Society of Industrial Furnace Builders

Sig. Signal(ler)
Signalman
Signals
Signature
Signor(a)

sig. signature
signifies
signification

S.I.G.E.S.O. Sub-committee, Intelligence German Electronics Signals Organization

sigill. sigillum (seal)

Sig.L. Signal Lieutenant

SIGMA Science in General Management

Sigma Science in General Management

S.I.G.M.A. Station Internationale de Géobotanique Méditerranéene et Alpine (International Station for Mediterranean and Alpine Geobotany)

Sigmn. Signalman

sign. signature

sig. n. pro. signa nomine proprio (label with the proper name)

Sig.O. Signal Officer

Sigs. Signals

S.I.H. Société internationale d'hématologie (International Society of Haematology)
Society for Italic Handwriting

S.I.I.A.E.C. Secrétariat international des ingénieurs, des agronomes et des cadres économiques catholiques (International Secretariat of Catholic Technologists, Agriculturalists and Economists)

S.I.I.C. Secrétariat international des groupements professionnels des industries chimiques des pays de la C.E.E. (International Secretariat of Professional Groups in the Chemical Industries of the E.E.C. Countries)

Sil. Silesia

S.I.L. Société internationale de la lèpre (International Leprosy Association)

sim. similar(ly)
simile

S.I.M. Self Inflicted Mutilation
Sergeant Instructor of Musketry
Société internationale de la Moselle (International Moselle Company)
Société internationale de musicologie (International Musicological Society)

S.I.M.A. Scientific Instrument Manufacturers' Association of Great Britain
Steel Industry Management Association

S.I.M.C. Société internationale de médecine cybernatique (International Society of Cybernetic Medicine)
Société internationale pour la musique contemporaine (International Society for Contemporary Music)

S.I.M.H.A. Société internationale de mycologie humaine et animale (International Society for Human and Animal Mycology)

S.I.M.P.L. Scientific, Industrial and Medical Photographic Laboratories

Sin. Sine

sin. sinecure
sinistra (left hand)

S.-Infre. Seine-Inférieure

Sing. Singapore

sing. singular

S.I.N.S. Ships Inertial Navigationa System

SINTO Sheffield Interchange Organisation

S.I.P. Société interaméricaine de psychologie (Inter-American Society of Psychology)

S.I.P.G. Société internationale de pathologie géographique (International Society of Geographical Pathology)

S.I.P.R.C. Society of Independent Public Relations Consultants

S.I.O. Senior Intelligence Officer

S.I.R. Service International de Recherches (International Research Service of the International Committee of the Red Cross)

S.I.R.A. Scientific Instrument Research Association

Sis. Sister

S.I.S.S. Société internationale de la science du sol (International Society of Soil Science)

S.I.S.T.E.R. Special Institutions for Scientific and Technological Education and Research

sit. sitting-room
situation

S.I.T. Singapore Improvement Trust
Society of Instrument Technology

s.i.t. stopping in transit
storing in transit

S.I.T.A. Société Internationale des Télécommunications Aéronautiques (International Society of Aeronautical Telecommunications) *cont.*

Students' International Travel Association

S.I.T.C. Standard International Trade Classification

S.I.T.R.A. South India Textile Research Association

S.I.T.S. Société internationale de transfusion sanguine (International Society of Blood Transfusion)

sitt. sitting-room

S.I.U. Société internationale d'urologie (International Society of Urology)

S.I.W. Self-Inflicted Wound

S.J. Society of Jesus (Jesuits)
Solicitors' Journal

s.j. sub judice (under consideration)

S.J.A.A. Saint John Ambulance Association

S.J.A.B. Saint John Ambulance Brigade

S.J.C. Standing Joint Committee

S.J.D. Scientiae Juridicae Doctor (Doctor of Juridical Science)

S.K.C. Scottish Kennel Club

S.Ken. South Kensington

S.K.K.C.A. Supreme Knight of the Knights of Columbus (U.S.)

s.k.p.o. slip one, knit one, pass slipped stich over

Skr. Sanskrit
Skipper

S.K.R. South Korean Republic

Skrt. Sanskrit

sks. sacks

Skt. Sanskrit

sl. slip

S.L. Salvage Loss
Saône-et-Loire
Sea Level
Searchlight
Second Lieutenant
Security List
Serjeant-at-Law
Solicitor-at-Law
South Latitude
Southern League
Squadron Leader
Sub-Lieutenant
Supplementary List

S.l. Sine loco (no place of publication)

s.l. secundum legem (according to the law)
seditious libel

S.L.A. School Library Association
Scottish Library Association
Special Libraries Association (U.S.)

S.L.A.D.E. Society of Lithographic Artists, Designers, Engravers and Process Workers

S.L.A.E.T. Society of Licenced Aircraft Engineers and Technologists

s.l.a.n. sine loco, anno, vel nomine (without place, year or name of printer)

s.l.& c. shipper's load and count

S.Lan.R. South Lancashire Regiment

S.L.A.S.H. Scottish Local Authorities Special Housing Group

S.lat. South latitude

Slav. Slavonic

S.L.C. Statute Law Committee
Surgeon Lieutenant Commander

S.L.C.R. Scottish Land Court Reports

sld. sailed
sealed

Sld. Sold
Solid

S.L.D. Scottish Land Development, Ltd.

S.Ldr. Squadron Leader

S.L.E.A.T. Society of Laundry Engineers and Allied Trades, Ltd.

s. l. et a. sine loco et anno (without place and year of publication)

S.L.F. Skandinaviska Lackteknikers Förbund (Federation of Scandinavian Paint and Varnish Technicians)

s.l.f. straight line frequency

S.L.G.B. Society of Local Government Barristers

S.L.I.M. South London Industrial Mission

s.l.n.d. sine loco nec data (without indication of place or date of printing)

S.L.O. Senior Liaison Officer

slp. slip

S.L.P. Socialist Labour Party

s.l.p. sine legitima prole (without lawful issue)

S.L.P.F. Scottish Locomotive Preservation Fund

S.L.P.P. Sierra Leone People's Party

S.L.R. Scottish Land Reports
Statute Law Revision Act

S.L.Rev. Scottish Law Review

S.L.S. Stephenson Locomotive Society

S.Lt. Sub-Lieutenant

S.L.T. Scots Law Times

S.L.T.A. Scottish Licensed Trade Association

S.L.T.C. Society of Leather Trades Chemists

S.L.T.E.A. Sheffield Lighter Trades Employers' Association

Sly. Southerly

Sm Samarium

Sm. Small

S.M. Sa Majesté (His or Her Majesty)
Sanctae Memoriae (of holy memory)
Scientiae Magister (Master of Science)
Senior Magistrate
Sergeant-Major
Short Metre
Silver Medallist
Sisters of Mercy
Society of Miniaturists
Sons of Malta
State Militia (U.S.)
Station Master
Stipendiary Magistrate
Surgeon-Major

s.m. short metre

S.M.A. Saw Manufacturers' Association
Sheffield Metallurgical and Engineering Association
Socialist Medical Association
Society of Medieval Archaeology
Society of Marine Artists
Solder Makers' Association
Supermarket Association *cont.*

Superphosphate Manufacturers' Association

S.M.A.A. Society of Members of the Advertising Association

S.M.A.C. Standing Medical Advisory Committee

S.M.A.E. Society of Model Aeronautical Engineers

S.M.B. Sa Majesté Britannique (His *or* Her Britannic Majesty)

S.M.C. Sa Majesté Catholique (His *or* Her Catholic Majesty)

Sealant Manufacturers Conference of the Federation of British Rubber and Allied Manufacturers

Worshipful Company of Spectacle Makers

S.M.C.C.L. Society of Municipal and County Chief Librarians

S.M.D. Short Metre Double

Sony Magnetic Diode

Superintendent of Mine Design

S.M.D.A. Sewing Machine Dealers' Association Limited

S.M.E. Sancta Mater Ecclesia (Holy Mother Church)

School of Military Engineering

S.M.E.E. Society of Model and Experimental Engineers

S.M.E.G. Spring Makers' Export Group

S.M.E.R. Société Médicale Internationale d'Endoscopie et de Radio-Cinématographie (International Medical Society for Endoscopy and Radioscopic Cinematography)

SMERSH Smert Shpionam (Death to Spies (Russia))

S.Met.O. Senior Meteorological Officer

S.M.F.U.A. Silk and Man-made Fibre Users' Association

S.M.I. Sa Majesté Impériale (His *or* Her Imperial Majesty)

S.M.I.A. Sheet Metal Industries Association

Smith. Inst. Smithsonian Institution (U.S.)

S.M.J. Sisters of Mary and Joseph

S.M.L. Science Museum Library

S.M.L.E. Short Magazine Lee-Enfield

S.M.M. Sancta Mater Maria (Holy Mother Mary)

S.M.M.B. Scottish Milk Marketing Board

S.M.M.T. Society of Motor Manufacturers and Traders

S.M.O. Senior Medical Officer

Squadron Medical Officer

S.M.P. School Mathematics Project

Society of Mural Painters

s.m.p. sine mascula prole (without male issue)

S.M.P.C. Scottish Milk Publicity Council

S.M.P.M.F. Scottish Metal and Plumbers' Merchants' Federation

S.M.P.S. Society of Master Printers of Scotland

S.M.R. Sa Majesté Royale (His *or* Her Royal Majesty)

Standardised Mortality Ratio

S.M.R.A. Spring Manufacturers' Research Association

S.M.R.E. Safety in Mines Research Establishment

S.M.R.I. Sugar Milling Research Institute (South Africa)

S.M.S. Seiner Majestät Schiff (His Majesty's Ship)

S.M.S.O. Senior Maintenance Staff Officer

S.M.T. Scottish Motor Traction Company

Ship's Mean Time

S.M.T.A. Scottish Motor Trade Association

S.M.T.C. Sa Majesté très Chrétienne (His Most Christian Majesty)

S.M.T.F. Scottish Milk Trade Federation

S.M.T.O. Senior Mechanical Transport Officer

S.M.T.S. Scottish Machinery Testing Station

S.M.U.S.E. Socialist Movement for the United States of Europe

S.M.W. Standard Metal Window

S.M.Y.C. Royal Scottish Motor Yacht Club

Sn Stannum (tin)

S.N. Sergeant Navigator

Shipping Note

S/N. Signal to Noise Ratio

s.n. secundum naturam (according to nature)

sine nomine (without name)

S.N.A. Steel Nail Association (*dissolved*)

S.N.A.P. Society of National Air Passengers

S.N.B.T.F. Scottish National Building Trades Federation (Employers)

S.N.C.F. Société nationale des chemins de fer français (National French Railways)

Snd. Sound

S.N.D.A. Sunday Newspaper Distributing Association

S.N.F.U. National Farmers' Union of Scotland

s.n.g. sans notre garantie (without our guarantee)

S.N.H.T.P.C. Scottish National Housing and Town Planning Council

Snick Student non-violent coordinating committee (U.S.)

S.N.I.W.B. Scottish National Institute for War-Blinded

S.N.L.R. Services No Longer Required

S.N.O. Scottish National Orchestra

Senior Naval Officer

Senior Navigation Officer

S.N.P. Scottish National Party

S.N.P.A. Scottish Newspaper Proprietors' Association

Sñr. Señor

S.N.R. Society for Nautical Research

Sñra. Señora

Snrta. Senhorita

S.N.S.O. Superintending Naval Stores Officer

S.N.T.P.C. Scottish National Town Planning Council

S.N.T.S. Studiorum Novi Testamenti Societas (Society for the Study of the New Testament)
So. South(ern)
S.O. Scottish Office
    Section Officer
    Senior Officer
    Signals Officer
    Sorting Office
    Staff Officer
    Standing Order(s)
    Stationery Office
    Statistical Office
    Sub-Office
    Supply Officer
    Symphony Orchestra
s.o. seller's option
S.O.A. Staff Officer, Administration
S.O.A.A. Solus Outdoor Advertising Association
S.O.A.D. Staff Officer, Air Defence
S.O.A.S. School of Oriental and African Studies
S.O.B. Senate Office Building
    Silly Old Blighter
    Society of Bookmen
    Son of a Bitch
    State Office Building
Soc. Social(ist)
    Society
    Socrates
soc. social
S.O.C. Scottish Ornithologists' Club
    Slightly off Colour
Soc.Dem. Social Democrat
S.O.C.E.M. Society of Objectors to Compulsory Egg Marketing
S.O.C.G.P.A. Seed, Oil Cake and General Produce Association
Sociol. Sociology
sociol. sociological
    sociologist
    sociology
Soc.Isl. Society Islands
Socy. Society
S.O.E. Special Operations Executive
S.O.E.D. Shorter Oxford English Dictionary
S. of M. School of Musketry
S. of S. Secretary of State
S. of T. Sons of Temperance
S. of T.T. School of Technical Training
S.O.G.A.T. Society of Graphical and Allied Trades
S.O.G.S. Save our Grammar Schools Committees
S.O.(I.) Staff Officer (Intelligence)
S.O.-in-C. Signal Officer-in-Chief
Sol. Solar
    Solicitor
    Solomon
sol. soluble
    solution
s.o.l. ship owner's liability
sol.aq. solution aqueuse (aqueous solution)
Sol.G(en). Solicitor General
Sol.J. Solicitors' Journal
soln. solution
Solrs. Solicitors
Som. Somersetshire

S.O.M. Society of Occupational Medicine
S.O.M.E. Senior Ordnance Mechanical Engineer
somet. sometimes
Som.L.I. Somerset Light Infantry
Soms. Somersetshire
Son. Sonnets
SONAR Sound Navigation and Ranging
S.O.(O.) Staff Officer (Operations)
S.O.O.B.E. self operating outside broadcasting equipment
Sop. Soprano
S.O.P. Sleeping-out Pass
Soph. Sophocles
S.O.R. Sale or Return
S.O.R.F.O. Society of Rural Financial Offices
S.O.S. Save Our Souls
    Secretary of State
    Senior Officers' School
    Services of Supply
s.o.s. si opus sit (if necessary)
S.O.S.B. Congregatio Silvestrina Ordinis Sancti Benedicti (Sylvestrine Order of Saint Benedict)
sost. sostenuto (sustained)
Soton. Southampton
S.O.T.S. Society for Old Testament Study
sov(s). sovereign(s)
Sp. Spain
    Spanish
    Specialist
    Spring
sp. special
    species
    specific
    specimen
    speed
    spelling
    spirit
    sport
    sposa (wife)
S.P. Santo Padre (Holy Father)
    Service Police
    Shore Patrol
    Sisters of Providence
    Small Paper
    Staff Paymaster
    Stop Press
    Supply Point
    Supreme Pontiff
s.p. self-propelled
    short page
    signal publication
    sine prole (without issue)
    single phase
    single pole
    small paper
    starting point
    starting price
    stop payment
S.P.A. Society of Saint Peter the Apostle for Native Clergy
S.p.A. Società per Azioni (stock company)
S.P.A.B. Society for the Protection of Ancient Buildings
SPADATS Space Detection and Tracking System

Span. Spanish
S.P.A.R. Super Precision Approach Radar
S.P.A.S. Societatis Philosophicae Americanae Socius (Fellow of the American Philosophical Society)
S.P.A.T.C. South Pacific Air Transport Council
S.P.C. Society for the Prevention of Crime (U.S.)
South Pacific Commission
S.P.C.K. Society for Promoting Christian Knowledge
S.P.D. South Polar Distance
S.P.D.C. Spare Parts Distributing Centre
spec. special(ly)
specification
spectrum
speculation
spec.appt. special appointment
spec.emp. specially employed
special. specialised
specif. specific(ally)
specification
specs. spectacles
speedo. speedometer
S.P.G. Society for the Propagation of the Gospel (*now* U.S.P.G.)
Special Patrol Group
S.P.G.A. Scottish Professional Golfers' Association
S.P.G.B. Socialist Party of Great Britain
sp. gr. specific gravity
Sp. ht. Specific heat
S.P.I. Secrétariats professionnels internationaux (International Trade Secretariats)
S.P.I.E. Secrétariat professionnel international de l'enseignement (International Federation of Free Teachers' Unions)
Spirit. Spiritualism
Spiritualistic
S.P.I.W. Special Purposes Individual Weapon
S.P.K. Stowarzyszenie Polskich Kombatantow (Polish Ex-Combatants' Association)
S.P.K.C. Small Pig Keepers' Council
s.p.l. sine prole legitima (without legitimate issue)
S.P.L.S.M. Single Position Letter Sorting machine
S.P.M. Saint-Pierre et Miquelon
Short Particular Metre
s.p.m. sine prole mascula (without male issue)
S.P.M.A. Sewage Plant Manufacturers' Association
s.p.m.s. sine prole mascula superstite (without surviving male issue)
S.P.M.U. Society of Professional Musicians in Ulster
S.P.N. Stop Press News
S.P.N.M. Society for the Promotion of New Music
S.P.N.R. Society for the Promotion of Nature Reserves

S.P.O. Senior Press Officer
Socialistische Partei Österreichs (Austrian Socialist Party)
Stoker Petty Officer
s.p.o. sausages potatoes and onions
S.P.O.E. Society of Post Office Engineers
spot. spotlight
S.P.Q.R. Senatus Populusque Romanus (the Roman Senate and People)
Small Profits - Quick Returns
Spr. Sapper
Sprinkled
S.P.R. Semi-permanent Repellent
Society for Psychical Research
S.P.R.C. Society for the Prevention and Relief of Cancer
S.P.R.I. Scott Polar Research Institute
S.P.R.L. Society for the Promotion of Religion and Learning
S.P.S. Scottish Painters' Society
s.p.s. sine prole supersite (without surviving issue)
S.P.S.L. Society for the Protection of Science and Learning
S.P.S.O. Senior Personnel Staff Officer
Senior Principal Scientific Officer
S.P.S.P. Saint Peter and Saint Paul
Spt. Seaport
sptg. sporting
S.P.T.L. Society of Public Teachers of Law
S.P.U. Salaried Pharmacists' Union
S.P.V.D. Society for the Prevention of Venereal Disease
Sq. et sequentes *or* et sequentia (the following)
Squadron
Square
S.Q. Sick Quarters
Survival Quotient
Sqdn. Squadron
Sqdn.-Ldr. Squadron-Leader
sq. ft. square foot *or* feet
sq. in(s). square inch(es)
sq. m. square mile(s)
S.Q.M.S. Staff Quartermaster-Sergeant
sqn. Squadron
Sqn. Ldr. Squadron-Leader
Sqn. Q.M.S. Squadron Quartermaster-Sergeant
Sqn.S.M. Squadron Sergeant-Major
Sq. O. Squadron Officer
sq.rd(s). square rod(s)
sq.yd(s). square yard(s)
Sr Strontium
Sr. Senior
Señor
S.R. Scottish Region, British Railways
Self Raising
Senate Resolution
Service Rifle
Socialist Revolutionaries
Society of Radiographers
Southern Region (of British Rail)
Southern Rhodesia
Special Reserve
Supplementary Reserve

s.r. shipping receipt
short rate
Sra. Señora
S.R.A. Squash Rackets Association
Surgeon Rear-Admiral
S.R. & O. Statutory Rules and Orders
S.R.B.M. Short Range Ballistic Missile
S.R.C. Sacra Rituum Congregatio (Sacred Congregation of Rites)
Santa Romana Chiesa (Holy Roman Church)
Science Research Council
Student Representative Council
s.r.c.c. strikes, riots, and civil commotions
S.R.C.M.A. Steel Radiator and Convector Manufacturers' Association
S.R.D. Service Rum Diluted
Society for the Relief of Distress
S.R.D.A. Scottish Retail Drapers Association
S.R.D.C. Shopfitting Research and Development Council
S.R.D.E. Signals Research and Development Establishment
S.R.E. Sancta Romana Ecclesia (Holy Roman Church)
Scientific Research and Experiments Department
S.R.F.O. Society of Rural Financial Officers
S.Rg. Sound-Ranging
S.R.H. Supply Railhead
S.R.I. Sacrum Romanum Imperium (Holy Roman Empire)
srio. secretario (secretary)
S.R.L. Società a Responsabilità Limitata (limited liability company)
S.R.N. State Registered Nurse
S.R. (N.S.W.) State Reports, New South Wales
S.R.O. Squadron Recreation Officer
Statutory Rules and Orders
Supplementary Reserve of Officers
S.R.P. Supply Refuelling Point
S.R.P.S. Scottish Railway Preservation Society
S.R.P.T.A. Scottish Road Passenger Transport Association
S.R.Q. State Reports, Queensland
S.R.R. Supplementary Reserve Regulations
S.R.R.A. Scottish Radio Retailers' Association
S.R.T.S. Steam Railway Traction Society
S.R.S. Societatis Regiae Socius (Fellow of the Royal Society)
Soil Research Station
S.R.U. Scottish Rugby Union
S.R.U.B.L.U.K. Society for the Reinvigoration of Unremunerative Branch Lines in the United Kingdom
S.R.Y. Sherwood Rangers Yeomanry
SS. Saints
Sanctissimus (Most Holy)
S.S. Royal Statistical Society
Sacra Scriptura (Holy Scripture)
Santa Sede (Holy See)
Sa Sainteté (His Holiness) *cont.*

Schutzstaffel (Storm Troops)
Secondary School
Secretary of State
Selden Society
Senior Sister
Short Sleeves
Sidney Sussex College, Cambridge
Silver Star
Social Security
Social Survey
Staff Surgeon
Standard Size
Steam Ship
Strada Statale (National Highway)
Straits Settlements
Sunday School
Supply and Secretariat
Su Señoria (His Lordship)
S/S. Side by Side
Silk Screen
s.S. siehe Seite (see page)
s.s. senza sordini (without mutes)
simplified spelling
sworn statement
S.S.A. Scottish Schoolmasters' Association
Secretary of State for Air
Senior Service Accountant
Society for the Study of Addiction (to Alcohol and other Drugs)
Social Security Administration (U.S.)
Society of Scottish Artists
SS.AA.II. Ses Altesses Impériales (Their Imperial Highnesses)
SS.AA RR. Ses Altesses Royales (Their Royal Highnesses)
S.S.A.C. Scottish Sub-Aqua Club
S.S.A.F.A. Soldiers', Sailors' and Airmen's Families Association
S.S.B. Sacrae Scripturae Baccalaureus (Bachelor of Sacred Scripture)
s.s.b. single sideband
S.S.C. Scottish Schoolboys' Club
Scottish Ski-Club
Sculptors' Society of Canada
Societas Sanctae Crucis (Society of the Holy Cross)
SS.D. Sanctissimus Dominus (Most Holy Lord)
S.S.D. Sacrae Scripturae Doctor (Doctor of Sacred Scripture)
S.S.D.A. Self Service Development Association
S.S.E. Society of Saint Edmund
Society of Shipping Executives
South-South-East
S.S.E.B. South of Scotland Electricity Board
S.S.E.C. Secondary School Examinations Council
S.S.F. Single-seater Fighter
Society of Saint Francis
S.S.F.A. Scottish Schools' Football Association
Scottish Steel Founders' Association
Stainless Steel Fabricators' Association of Great Britain
S.S.F.F. Solid Smokeless Fuels Federation

P

S.Sgt. Staff Sergeant
S.S.H.A. Scottish Special Housing Association, Ltd.
S.S.I. Service social international (International Social Service)
Sites of Scientific Importance
Society of Scribes and Illuminators
S.S.I.D.A. Steel Sheet Information and Development Association
S.S.I.M.E. South Staffordshire and Warwickshire Institute of Mining Engineers
S.S.I.S.I. Statistical and Social Inquiry Society of Ireland
S.S.J.E. Society of Saint John the Evangelist
S.S.K.T.P. Society for Spreading Knowledge of True Prayer
S.S.L. Sacrae Scripturae Licentiatus (Licentiate of Sacred Scripture)
S.S.M. Severely sub-normal
Society of the Sacred Mission
Squadron Sergeant-Major
Staff Sergeant-Major
Surface to Surface Missile
S.S.M.A. Scottish Steel Makers' Association
State Servants (and Allied) Motoring Association Limited
SS.MM. Sus Majestades (Their *or* Your Majesties)
S.S.N. Sociétaire de la Société Nationale des Beaux Arts (Member of the National Society of Fine Arts)
S.S.O. Senior Scientific Officer
Senior Supply Officer
Squadron Signals Officer
Special Service Officer
Staff Signals Officer
Station Staff Officer
S.S.P. Pious Society of Saint Paul
S.S.P.C.A. Scottish Society for the Prevention of Cruelty to Animals
SS.PP. Sancti Patres (Holy Fathers)
S.S.P.V. Scottish Society for the Prevention of Vivisection
S.S.Q. Station Sick Quarters
S.S.R. Soviet Socialist Republic
S.S.R.A. Scottish Squash Rackets Association
S.S.R.C. Social Science Research Council
S.S.S. Secretary of State for Scotland
Selective Service System
Single Screw Ship
Societas Sanctissimi Sacramenti (Congregation of the Most Blessed Sacrament)
su seguro servidor (your faithful servant)
S.S.S.C. Soft-sized, Super-calendered
S.S.S.I. Sites of Special Scientific Importance
S.S.S.R. Soyuz Sovietskikh Sotsialisticheskikh Respublik (Union of Soviet Socialist Republics)
S.S.St.J. Serving Sister, Order of Saint John of Jerusalem
S.S.T. Supersonic Travel
S.S.T.A. Scottish Secondary Teachers' Association

S.S.T.O. Superintending Sea Transport Officer
S.S.W. Secretary of State for War
South-South-West
S.S.W.A. Scottish Society of Women Artists
St. Saint
Strait
Street
Strophe
st. stanza
stem
stet (let it stand)
stitch
stone
stumped
S.T. Shock Troops
Spring Tide
Standard Time
Summer Time
The Sunday Times
s.t. short ton
Sta. Station
S.T.A. Sail Training Association
Swimming Teachers' Association
Scottish Typographical Association
Seed Trade Association of the United Kingdom
stacc. staccato (abrupt)
S.T.A.C.O. Society of Telecommunications Administrative and Controlling Officers
S.T.A.E. Stoke-on-Trent Association of Engineers
Staffs. Staffordshire
stand. standard
Stat. Statics
Statistics
Statuary
Statute(s)
stat. static
stationary
statistical
statistics
Stat. Hall. Stationers' Hall
S.T.A.U.K. Seed Trade Association of the United Kingdom
S.T.B. Sacrae Theologiae Baccalaureus (Bachelor of Sacred Theology)
stbt. steamboat
S.T.C. Samuel Taylor Coleridge
Senior Training Corps
Short Title Catalogue of Books Printed in England, Scotland and Ireland, and of English Books Printed Abroad, 1477-1640
Society of Town Clerks
S.T.C.S. Society of Technical Civil Servants
Std. Stunde (hour)
std. standard
started
S.T.D. Sacrae Theologiae Doctor (Doctor of Sacred Theology)
Sea Transport Department
Society of Typographic Designers
Subscriber Trunk Dialling

218

Ste. Sainte (female saint)
Sté Société (Company)
S.T.E. Society of Telecommunications Engineers
S.T.E.C.C. Scottish Technical Educational Consultative Council
S.T.E.L.O. Studenta Tutmonda Esperantista Ligo (World League of Esperanto-Speaking Students)
stereo. stereophonic
      stereotype(d)
sterl. sterling
St. Ex. Stock Exchange
stg. sterling
S.T.G.W.U. Scottish Transport and General Workers' Union
Sth. South
S.Th. Scholar in Theology
Sthn. Southern
S.T.I.B. Scientific and Technical Intelligence Branch
stip. stipend(iary)
Stir. Stirling
s.t.i.r. surplus to immediate requirements
stk. stock
S.T.L. Sacrae Theologiae Licentiatus (Licentiate of Sacred Theology)
      Standard Telecommunications Laboratories
S.T.M. Sacrae Theologiae Magister (Master of Sacred Theology)
S.T.M.S.A. Scottish Timber Merchants' and Sawmillers' Association
S.T.O.P.P. Society of Teachers Opposed to Physical Punishment
S.T.P.M.A. Scottish Theatrical Proprietors' and Managers' Association
stn. station
Sto. Stoker
S.T.O. Sea Transport Officer
      Senior Technical Officer
S.T.O.L. Short Take-off and Landing
S'ton. Southampton
S. to S. Ship to Shore
      Station to Station
S.T.P. Sacrosanctae or Sacrae Theologiae Professor (Professor of Sacred Theology)
      Scientific and Technical Potential
S.T.P.T.C. Standardization of Tar Products Test Committee
Str. Street
str. seater
      steamer
      streptococcus
      string(er)
      stroke
S.T.R. Society for Theatre Research
s.t.r. surplus to requirements
STRAC Strategic Air Command (U.S.)
S.T.R.A.D. Signal Transmitting, Receiving and Distribution
Sts. Saints
      Straits
sts. stitches
      streets
S.T.S. Scottish Text Society
      Spring Trapmakers' Society

S.T.S.D. Society of Teachers of Speech and Drama
S.T.S.O. Senior Technical Staff Officer
st. st. stocking stitch
S.T.T.A. Scottish Table Tennis Association
S.Tube Steel Tubing
S.T.U.C. Scottish Trades Union Congress
Stuka Sturzkampf-Flugzeug (Dive Bomber)
S.T.U.T.I.S. Secondary, Technical and University Teachers' Insurance Society
S.T.V. Single Transferable Vote
      Scottish Television Limited
Su. Sunday
S.U. Scripture Union
      Soviet Union
      Strontium Unit
s.u. set up
      siehe unten (see below)
Sub. Subaltern
sub. sub-editor
      subject
      subjunctive
      submarine
      subscription
      substitute
      suburb(an)
      subway
S.U.B.A.N. Scottish Union of Bakers and Allied Workers
subd. subdivision
sub.-ed. sub-editor
subj. subject
      subjunctive
Sub.L. Sub-Lieutenant
subs. subscription
      subsidiary
      subsistence
      substantive
      substitute(d)
subsec. subsection
subsq. subsequently
subst. substantive
      substitute
substand. substandard
Sub.U. Substitution Unit
Suc. sucre (Sugar)
suc. succeeded
      successor
      suction
succ. succeeded
      success
S.U.C.E.E. Socialist Union of Central Eastern Europe
S.U.C.S.E. Scottish Universities Council on Studies in Education
S.U.E.B. Scottish Universities Entrance Board
Suet. Suetonius
suf. suffix
Suff. Suffolk
      Suffragan
suff. sufficient
      suffix
Suff. B. Suffragan Bishop
Suffr. Suffragan
sug. suggested
      suggestion
sugend. sugendus (to be sucked)

Suid. Suidas
S.U.I.T. Scottish and Universal Investment Trust
suiv. suivant (following)
Sult. Sultan(a)
sum. summary
S.U.M. Surface-to-Underwater Missile
sums. summons
Sun. Sunday
S.U.N. Support the United Nations
Sund. Sunday
S.U.N.F.E.D. Special United Nations Fund for Economic Development
Sup. Supply
sup. superfine
    superior
    superlative
    supine
    supra (above)
Sup. Dpo. Supply Depot
Supdt. Superintendent
Super. Superintendent
super. superficial
    superfine
    superior
    supernumerary
superl. superlative
sup.lint. super linteum (on lint)
Sup.O. Supply Officer
Supp. Supplement
Sup.P. Supply Point
suppl. supplement(ary)
supr. superior
    supreme
Supt. Superintendent
Supvr. Supervisor
sur. surplus
Surg. Surgeon
    Surgery
    Surgical
Surg-Comdr. Surgeon-Commander
Surg.-Gen. Surgeon-General
Surg-Lt.Comdr. Surgeon-Lieutenant Commander
Surg-Maj. Surgeon-Major
Surr(o). Surrogate
Surv. Survey(or)
surv. surveying
    surveyor
    surviving
Surv.-Gen. Surveyor-General
S.U.S. Scottish Union of Students
susp. suspend(ed)
sus.per.coll. suspendatur or suspensio per collum (let him be hanged or hanging by the neck)
Suss. Sussex
S.U.S.T.A. Scottish Union of Students' Travel Association
Suth. Sutherland
S.V. Sailing Vessel
    Sancta Virgo (Holy Virgin)
    Sanctitas Vestra (Your Holiness)
s.v. sailing vessel
    sub voce or verbo (under a word or heading)
S.V.D. Fathers of the Divine Word
S.V.M. Service volontaire ménnonite (Mennonite Voluntary Service)
S.V.O. Scottish Variety Orchestra
    Superintending Veterinary Officer

S.V.P. Small Vessels Pool
s.v.p. s'il vous plaît (please)
S.V.S. Society for Visiting Scientists
s.v.t. spiritus vini tenuior (proof spirit of wine)
s.v.v. sit venia verbo (forgive the expression)
Svy. Survey
Sw. Sweden
    Swedish
    Swiss
S.W. Senior Warden
    Short Wave
    South Wales
    South-West(erly)
    South-Western
s.w. small women
    specific weight
s/w. seaworthy
S.W.A.P.O. South West Africa People's Organisation
S.W.A.S. Social Work Advisory Service
S.W.B. South Wales Borderers
Swbd. Switchboard
s.w.b.s. south-west by south
s.w.b.w. south-west by west
Swd. Sewed
S.W.D.A. Scottish Wholesale Druggists' Association
S.W.E.B. South Wales Electricity Board
    South Western Electricity Board
Swed. Sweden
    Swedish
S.W.E.T.M. Society of West End Theatre Managers
S.W.F.B.T.E. South Wales and Monmouthshire Federation of Building Trades Employers
S.W.G. Standard Wire Gauge
S.W.G.B. South Western Gas Board
S.W.I.A. South Wales Institute of Architects
S.W.I.E. South Wales Institute of Engineers
Switz. Switzerland
S.W.M.A. Steel Wool Manufacturers' Association
S.W.M.F. South Wales Miners' Federation
S.W.O. Squadron Wireless Officer
    Station Warrant Officer
S.W.O.A. Scottish Woodland Owners Association, Ltd.
S.W.P.A. Steel Works Plant Association (now B.M.P.M.A.)
S.W.P.F. Social Workers' Pension Fund
S.W.R.I. Scottish Women's Rural Institutes
S.W.R.L.S. South Western Regional Library System
S.W.S. Static Water Supply
S.W.T. School of Welding Technology
S.W.T.E.A. Scottish Woollen Trade Employers' Association
S.W.T.M.A. Scottish Woollen Trade Mark Association
S.W.W.J. Society of Women Writers and Journalists
S.W.W.S. Scottish Wayfarers' Welfare Society

Sx. Sussex
Sy. Seychelles
Supply
Surrey
S.Y. Steam Yacht
Syd. Sydney
S.Yd. Scotland Yard
Syd.L.R. Sydney Law Review
S.Y.H.A. Scottish Youth Hostels Association
syl. syllable
sym. symbol(ic)
symmetrical
symmetry
symphony

symb. symbol(ic)
Symp. Symposium
Symph. Symphony
syn. synchronizing
synonym
synonymous
synthetic
S.Y.P. Society of Young Publishers
Sy.P.O. Supply Petty Officer
Syr. Syria(c)
Syrian
syr. syrup
syst. system
sz. size

T

T. Tace(te) (be silent
Tanker
Target
Teacher
Teeth
Telegraph(ic)
Telephone
Temperature
Temporary
Tempore (in the time of)
Tenor
Terminal
Territorial
Territory
Testament
Thermometer
Tiler
Time
Titus
Tome
Topical
Torpedo
Transport(ation)
Treasury
Trinity
Troy
Tuesday
Tullius
Turkish
Tutti (all instruments)
t. taken
tempo
tempore (in the time of
tense
terminal
that
thunder
time
tome
ton
town(ship)
transitive
troy
tun
turn
Ta Tantalum
ta. tableau
tablet

T.A. Telegraphic Address
Territorial Army
Tithe Annuity
Traffic Agent
Traffic Auditor
Translators' Association
Typographical Association (*now* N.G.A.)
T/A. Temporary Assistant
t.a. testantibus actis (as the acts show)
T.A.A. Territorial and Auxiliary Forces Association
tab. table(t)
tabulate
T.A.B. Technical Assistance Board
Typhoid, paratyphoid A and paratyphoid B vaccine
T.A.B.A. Timber Agents' and Brokers' Association of the United Kingdom
Tac. Tacitus
T.A.C. Tactical Air Command
Tanganyika Agricultural Corporation
Technical Assistance Committee (U.N.)
Television Advisory Committee
Tobacco Advisory Committee
Trades Advisory Council
T.A.F. Tactical Air Force
Tag. Tagalog
T.A.G. The Adjutant-General (U.S.)
Telegraphist Air Gunner
Tai. Taiwan
Tal. Talmud(ic)
tal. talis (such)
T.A.L.I.C. Tyneside Association of Libraries for Industry and Commerce
tal. qual. talis qualis (as they come
Tam. Tamil
T.A.M. Tactical Air Missile
Television Audience Measurement Limited
tan. tangent
T.& A.F.A. Territorial and Auxiliary Forces Association
t.& g. tongued and grooved
T.& G.W.U. Transport and General Workers' Union

t. & o.

t.& o. taken and offered
T.& S. Transport and Supply
T.& S.G. Television and Screen Writers' Guild
Tang. Tanganyika
T.A.N.S. Territorial Army Nursing Service (*now* Q.A.R.A.N.C.)
T.A.N.U. Tanganyika African National Union
T.A.O. Technical Assistance Operations (U.N.)
T.A.P. Technical Assistance Program (U.S.)
T.A.R. Territorial Army Regulations
T.A.R.A. Technical Assistant, Royal Artillery
    Territorial Army Rifle Association
TARFU Things are really fouled up
Tarmac. Tar Macadam
T.A.R.O. Territorial Army Reserve of Officers
T.A.R.S. Technical Assistance Recruitment Service (U.N.)
Tart. Tartaric
Tas. Tasmania(n)
T.A.S.I. Time Assignment Speech Interpolation
Tasm. Tasmania(n)
T.A.S.S. Telegrafnoye Agenstvo Sovetskovo Soyuza (Telegraphic Agency of the Soviet Union)
    Transport Aircraft Servicing Specialist (R.A.F.)
Tas.Univ.L.Rev. Tasmanian University Law Review
T.A.T. Transatlantic Telephone Cable
T.A.U.N. Technical Assistance of the United Nations
taut. tautological
    tautology
t.a.w. twice a week
Tb Terbium
Tb. Tuberculosis
T.B. Torpedo Boat *or* Bomber
    Training Battalion
    Treasury Bill
    Trial Balance
    True Bearing
    Tubercle Bacillus
t.b. trial balance
T.B.D. Torpedo Boat Destroyer
T.B.E. Fédération européenne des fabricants de tuiles et de briques (European Federation of Tile and Brick Manufacturers)
T.B.L. Through Bill of Lading
t.b.l. through back of loops
T.B.M. Tactical Ballistic Missile
T.B.M.A. Timber Building Manufacturers' Association of Great Britain
T.B.N. The Times Business News
Tbsp. tablespoon(ful)
Tc Technetium
tc. tierce
T.C. Tank Corps
    Tax Cases
    Technical College
    Temporary Clerk
    Temporary Constable
    Tennis Club
    Thames Conservancy   *cont.*

    Touring Club
    Town Clerk
    Town Council(lor)
    Training Centre
    Training Corps
    Transport Command
    Traveller's Cheque
    Treble Chance
    Trinity College
    Trusteeship Council (U.N.)
t.c. till cancelled
T.C.A. Trans-Canada Airlines (*now* Air Canada)
T.C.B. Thames Conservancy Board
    Title Certificate Book
T.C.C. Temporary Council Committee (N.A.T.O.)
    Transport and Communications Commission (U.N.)
    Troop Carrier Command (U.S.)
T.C.D. Trinity College, Dublin
T.C.E.A. Training Centre for Experimental Aerodynamics
T.C.F. Temporary Chaplain to the Forces
    Time Correction Factor
    Touring Club de France
T.C.F.B. Transcontinental Freight Bureau
Tchg. Teaching
Tchr. Teacher
T.C.I. Touring Club Italiano (Italian Touring Club)
T.C.J.C.C. Trades Councils' Joint Consultative Committee
T.C.M. Trinity College of Music
T.C.M.A. Telephone Cable Makers' Association
    Tufted Carpet Manufacturers' Association
T.C.M.B. Tomato and Cucumber Marketing Board
T.C.O. Trinity College, Oxford
TCP tricresyl phosphate
    trichloro-phenyl-iodo-methyl-salicyl
T.C.P. Traffic-Control Post
T.C.P.A. Town and Country Planning Association
td. tod
T.D. Tactical Division
    Tealto Dail (Member of the Dail) (Eire)
    Technical Development
    Telegraph Department
    Telephone Department
    Territorial Decoration
    Torpedo Depot
    Traffic Director
    Treasury Decisions
    Treasury Department
    True Democratic
t.d. ter die (three times daily)
    tractor-drawn
T.D.A. Textile Distributors' Association
    Timber Development Association
T.D.B. Total Disability Benefit
T.D.C. Top Dead Centre
T.D.D. Tuberculous Diseases Diploma
T.D.G. Twist Drill Gauge**

t.d.r. tous droits réservés (all rights reserved)
t.d.s. ter die sumendum (to be taken three times a day)
Te Tellurium
T.E. passed Telecommunications Engineering course
    Topographical Engineer
t/e. time-expired
    twin-engined
T.E.A.L. Tasman Empire Airways Limited
T.E.A.M. The European-Atlantic Movement
    Top European Advertising Media
Tech. Technical
    Technology
tech. technical
    technics
techn. technical
    technician
    technology
technol. technological(ly)
    technology
Tech.Sgt. Technical Sergeant
T.E.D. Territorial Efficiency Medal
T.E.E. Torpedo Experimental Establishment
    Trans-Europe Express
T.e.g. Top edge(s) gilt
T.E.J.A. Tutmonda Esperantista Jurnalista Asocio (World Association of Esperantist Journalists)
T.E.J.O. Tutmonda Esperantista Junulara Organizo (World Esperantist Youth Organisation)
Tel. Telugu
tel. telegram
    telegraph(ic)
    telegraphist
    telephone
Tel.Bn. Telegraph Battalion
tele. telegram
    telegraphy
telecom. telecommunications
teleg. telegram
    telegraphy
teleph. telephone
    telephony
telg. telegram
Tel. No. Telephone Number
tem. temperature
T.E.M.A. Telecommunication Engineering and Manufacturing Association
Temp. The Tempest (Shakespeare)
    Temporary
temp. temperance
    temperate
    temperature
    temporal
    temporary
    tempore (in the time of)
temp. dext. tempori dextro (to the right temple)
temp. sinist. tempori sinistro (to the left temple)
tempy. temporary
Ten. Tenor

ten. tenement
    tenor
    tenuto (sustained)
Tenn. Tennessee
    Tennyson
T.E.P. Tetraethyl-Pyrophosphate
Ter. Terrace
    Terence
    Territory
ter. tere (rub)
Terat. Teratology
Term. Terminology
    Termite
term. terminal
    termination
    terminology
Terr. Terrace
    Territorial
    Territory
ter. sim. tere simul (rub together)
T.E.S. Technical Enquiries Section
    The Times Educational Supplement
Test. Testament
    Testator
test. testament(ary)
    testator
    testimonial
testo. testigo (witness)
T.-et-G. Tarn-et-Garonne
T.E.T.O.C. Technical Education and Training for Overseas Countries
Teut. Teuton(ic)
T.E.W.T. Tactical Exercise without Troops
Tex. Texan
    Texas
text. textile
text.rec. textus receptus (the received text)
T.F. Task Force
    Technological Forecasting
    Territorial Force
tfg. typefounding
tfr. transfer
T.F.R. Territorial Force Reserve
T.F.T.A. Textile Finishing Trades Association
T.F.U. Telecommunications Flying Unit
T.G. Tate Gallery
    Theatre Guild (U.S.)
    Theosophische Gesellschaft (Theosophical Society)
    Townswomen's Guilds (see N.U.T.G.)
    Training Group
t.g. type genus
t.g.b. tongued, grooved and beaded
T.G.M. Torpedo Gunner's Mate
T.G.O. Timber Growers' Organisation
T.G.R. Theatregoround (Royal Shakespeare Company)
T.G.V. The Two Gentlemen of Verona (Shakespeare)
T.G.W.U. Transport and General Workers' Union
Th Thorium
Th. Theatre
    Theology
    Thermal
    Thursday

th. thermal
T.H. Transport House
    Trinity House
    Toynbee Hall
Th.A. Theological Association
T.H.A. Trade Hemstitchers' Association
Thai. Thailand
Th.B. Theologiae Baccalaureus (Bachelor of Theology)
Th.D. Theologiae Doctor (Doctor of Theology)
theat. theatre
    theatrical
T.H.E.L.M.A. The Linoleum Manufacturers Association
Theo. Theologian
    Theological
    Theology
Theoc. Theocritus
Theol. Theologian
    Theological
    Theology
Theoph. Theophilus
    Theophrastus
theor. theorum(s)
    theory
theoret. theoretical(ly)
Theos. Theosophical
    Theosophist
    Theosophy
Therap. Therapeutic(s)
therm. thermometer
Thermochem. Thermochemistry
Thermodyn. Thermodynamics
thes. thesis
Thess. Thessalonians
    Thessaly
T.H.H.M. Trinity House High Water Mark
t.h.i. time handed in
Thk. Thick
Th.L. Theological Licentiate
Th.M. Theologiae Magister (Master of Theology)
thoro. thoroughfare
thou. thousand(th)
thr. their
    through
T.H.R.A. Tasmanian Historical Research Association
Thro.B.L. Through Bill of Lading
Thuc. Thucydides
Thur(s). Thursday
Ti Titanium
Ti. Tiberius
    Tibet
    Tibullus
T.I. Technical Institute
    Textile Industry
    Textile Institute
T/I. Target Indicator
T.I.C. Tyne Improvement Commission
T.I.C.A. Thermal Insulation Contractors' Association
t.i.d. ter in die (three times a day)
T.I.D.U. Technical Information and Documents Unit
T.I.E. totally integrated environment
tier. tierce
T.I.F.R. Tata Institute of Fundamental Research, Bombay

T.I.H. Their Imperial Highnesses
T.I.I.A.L. The International Institute of Applied Linguistics
T.I.L.S. Technical Information and Library Service
Tim. Timothy
t.i.m. time is money
timp. timpani
T.I.M.S. The Institute of Management Sciences
tinc(t). tincture
T.I.O. Technical Information Officer
Tip. Tipperary
T.I.P.S. Tune Index of Performance and Sales
T.I.R.C. Tobacco Industry Research Committee
T.I.R.O.S. Television and Infra-Red Observation Satellite
Tis. Tissue
T.I.S. Technical Information Service
Tit. Titus
tit. title
    titular
Tk. Tank(s)
t.k.o. technical knockout
tks. thanks
Tl Thallium
T.L. Torpedo Lieutenant
T.-L. Thermoluminescence dating
T/L. Telegraphist Lieutenant
t.l. time loan
    total loss
T.L.G. Theatrical Ladies' Guild of Charity
T.L.O. Technical Liaison Officer
t.l.o. total loss only
T.L.P. Tasmanian Labour Party
tlr. trailer
T.L.R. Tasmania Law Reports
    Tanganyika Law Reports
    The Times Law Reports
T.L.S. Territorial Long Service Medal
    The Times Literary Supplement
T.L.s. Typed letter, signed
T.L.W.M. Trinity House Low Water Mark
Tm Thulium
T.M. Traffic Manager
    Trained Man
    Training Memorandum
    Trench mortar
    Tropical Medicine
t.m. trade mark
    trench mortar
T.M.A. Theatrical Management Association
    Twine Manufacturers' Association
T.M.A.M.A. Textile Machinery and Accessory Manufacturers' Association
T.M.B. Travelling Medical Board
T.M.C. Tyre Manufacturers' Conference
tmkpr. timekeeper
T.M.L. Three Mile Limit
T.M.M.G. Teacher of Massage and Medical Gymnastics
T.M.O. Telegraph Money Order(s)
T.M.S. Tramway Museum Society
T.M.S.C. Tobacco Manufacturers' Standing Committee

Tn. Town(ship)
    Transportation
tn. ton
T.N. True North
    Twelfth Night (Shakespeare)
t.n. telephone number
T.N.C. Theatres National Committee
Tn.I.O.B. Technician of the Institute
    of Building
T.N.M. Tactical Nuclear Missile
T.N.P.G. The Nuclear Power Group
TNT Trinitrotoluene
TNX Trinitroxylene
T.O. Technical Officer
    Telegraph Office
    Telegraphic Order
    Telephone Office
    Telephone Order
    Torpedo Officer
    Trained Operator
    Transport Officer
    Turn Over
t.o. tinctura opii (tincture of opium)
    traditional orthography
Tob. Tobit
tob. tobacco
T.O.B. Temporary Office Building
Toch. Tocharian
Toc.H. Talbot House
Toch.A. Tocharian A
Toch.B. Tocharian B
T.O.D. Trade and Operations Division
T.O.E.T. Test(s) of Elementary Train-
    ing
T. of A. Timon of Athens (Shakespeare)
tog. together
togr. together
T.O.L. Tower of London
tom. tome
tonn. tonnage
t.o.o. time of origin
T.O.P. Temporarily Out of Print
topog. topographer
    topographical
    topography
Tor. Toronto
T.O.R. Third Order Regular of Saint
    Francis
t.o.r. time of reception
tor. dep. torpedo depot
Torp. Torpedo
T.O.S.D. Third Order of Saint Dominic
T.O.S.F. Third Order of Saint Francis
tot. total
tour. tourist
toxicol. toxicological
    toxicologist
    toxicology
Tp. Township
    Troop
T.P. Tax Payer
    Teaching Practice
    Technical Pool
    Technical Publications
    Teleprinter
    Tempo Primo
    Title Page
    Translucent Paper
    Transvaal Province
t.p. timbre(s)-poste(s) (postage
    stamp(s))
    title page   *cont.*

    toilet paper
    to pay
T.P.A. Technical Publications Associa-
    tion
T.P.F. Toilet Preparations Federation
T.P.I. Town Planning Institute
    Tropical Products Institute
t.p.i. teeth per inch
    threads per inch
    tons per inch
    turns per inch
T.P.O. Travelling Post Office
Tpr. Trooper
t.p.r. temperature, pulse, respiration
T.P.R.I. Tropical Pesticides Research
    Institute
tps. troops
T.P.S. Télégraphie par le soleil (tele-
    graphy by the sun)
tpt. transport
tptr. trumpeter
t.p.w. title page wanting
Tr Terbium
Tr. Transaction
    Treasurer
    Trustee
tr. trace
    track
    tragedy
    train
    transaction(s)
    transfer
    transitive
    translated
    translation
    translator
    transport(ation)
    transpose
    treble
    troop
    truck
    trustee
T.R. Tariff Reform
    Taxation Reports
    Territorial Reserve
    Tons Registered
    Trust Receipt
T/R. Transmitter-Receiver
trad. tradition
    traditional(ly)
    traduction (translation)
T.R.A.D.A. Timber Research and
    Development Association
trag. tragedy
    tragic(al)
Trans. Transvaal
trans. transaction
    transfer(red)
    transitive
    transistorized
    transitory
    translated
    translation
    translator
    transport(ation)
    transpose
    transverse
transf. transfer(red)
    transference
Transl. Translated
    Translation
    Translator

translit. transliterated
transliteration
transp. transportation
trav. traveller
travels
Trb. Tribune
T.R.C. Thames Rowing Club
Tithe Rent Charge
Tobacco Research Council
Tr.Co. Trust Company
Tr.Coll. Training College
Tre. Treasurer
Treasury
T.R.E. Telecommunications Research
Establishment
Treas. Treasurer
Treasury
tree. trustee
Trem. Tremolando (tremulous)
trf. tariff
T.R.F. Tuned Radio Frequency
T.R.H. Their Royal Highnesses
T.R.I. Tea Research Institute (Ceylon)
Television Reporters Inter-
national
Tin Research Institute
United Nations Department of
Trusteeship and Information
from Non-Self-Governing
Territories
Trib. Tribune
trib. tribal
tributaries
tributary
trid. triduum (three days)
T.R.I.E.A. Tea Research Institute o
East Africa
Trig. Trigonometrical
Trigonometry
trig. trigger
TRIGA Trigger Reactor
Trigon. Trigonometry
trim. trimestre (quarter of a year)
Trin. Trinidad
Trinity
Trin. H. Trinity Hall, Cambridge
Trip. Tripos
trip(l). triplicate
Trit. Triturate
Tr.L.R. Trinidad Law Reports
Trng. Training
T.R.O. Temporary Restraining Order
trom. trombone
Tromp. Trompette (trumpet)
Trop. Tropic(al)
Trop.Med. Tropical Medicine
T.R.P.S. Talyllyn Railway Preservation
Society
Trs. Transpose
Trustees
trs. transfer(red)
transpose
trustees
T.R.S. Tobacco Research Station (New
Zealand)
Torry Research Station
trsd. transferred
transposed
T.R.T.A. Traders' Road Transport
Association
Truron. Truronesie (of Truro)
226

T.S. Television Society
Tensile Strength
Theosophical Society
Tool Steel
Tough situation
Training Ship
Treasury Solicitor
Typescript
t.s. tensile strength
till sale
turbine steamship
twin screw
typescript
T.S.A. Tasmanian State Archives
T.S.B. Trustee Savings Bank(s)
T.S.B.A. Trustee Savings Banks Asso-
ciation
t.s.c. passed a Territorial Army course
in staff duties
T.S.D.S. Two-Speed Destroyer
Sweeper
T.S.F. Two-seater Fighter
t.s.f. télégraphie sans fil (wireless
telegraphy)
T.S.H. Their Serene Highnesses
T.S.O. Town Sub-Office
T.S.O.A. Triumph Sports Owners'
Association
tsp. teaspoon(ful)
T.S.R. Tactical Strike Reconnaissance
Torpedo-Spotter Reconnaiss-
ance
Trans-Siberian Railway
TSS. Typescripts
T.S.S. Turbine Steamship
Twin-Screw Steamer
T.S.S.A. Transport Salaried Staffs'
Association
t.s.u. this side up
t.s.v.p. tournez s'il vous plaît (please
turn over)
TSX Telecommunications Satellite
Experiment
T.T. Technical Training
Teetotaller
Telegraphic Transfer
Torpedo Tube(s)
Tourist Trophy
Tuberculin Tested
T.t. Tank top
Telegraph transfer
t.t. tank technology
T.T.A. Theatrical Traders Association,
Ltd.
Travel Trade Association
T.T.B.S. Timber Trades' Benevolent
Society
T.T.C. Technical Training Command
(R.A.F.)
T.T.E. Tropical Testing Establishment
T.T.F. Timber Trade Federation of the
United Kingdom
T.T.J.C. Tyre Trade Joint Committee
T.T.L. To Take Leave
T.T.S. Teletypesetting
T.T.T. Tyne Tees Television Limited
T.T.T.A. Tobacco Trade Travellers'
Association
T.T.T.C. Technical Teachers Training
College
Tu Thulium

Tu. Tuesday
T.U. temps universel (Universal Time)
    Trade(s) Union(s)
T.U.A.C. Trade Union Advisory
    Committee to the O.E.C.D.
Tuberc. Tuberculosis
T.U.C. Trades Union Congress
T.U.C.C. Transport Users' Consulta-
    tive Council
T.U.C.G.C. Trades Union Congress
    General Council
T.U.C.S.A. Trades Union Council of
    South Africa
Tues. Tuesday
T.U.F.E.C. Thailand-U.N.E.S.C.O.
    Fundamental Education Centre
T.U.I.A.F.W. Trade Unions Inter-
    national of Agricultural and Forestry
    Workers
T.U.M. Trades Union Movement
Turk. Turkey
    Turkish
Turkn. Turkistan
turp. turpentine
tus. tussis (cough)
T.V. Television
    Terminal Velocity
T.V.A. Tax Value Added
    Tennessee Valley Authority
T.V.C. Technical Valve Committee
Tvl. Transvaal
T.V.R. Temperature Variation of
    Resistance
T.W.A. Trans-World Airlines
T.W.A.R.O. Textile Workers' Asian
    Regional Organisation

T.W.C. Tail Waggers' Club
T.W.I. Training of Supervisors within
    Industry
T.W.I.M.C. To Whom It May Concern
T.W.O. This Week Only
twp. township
T.W.P.D. Tactical and Weapons Policy
    Division
T.W.S. Timed Wire Service
tw.-sc. twin-screw
T.W.T. Travelling-wave Tube
T.W.U. Tobacco Workers' Union
T.W.U.A. Transport Workers' Union
    of America
T.W.W. Television Wales and West
    Limited
twy. twenty
tx. tax
Ty. Territory
    Truly
T.Y.C. Thames Yacht Club
    Two-Year-old Course
t.y.o. two-year-old
Typ. Typographical
    Typography
typ. type
    typical
    typographer
    typographical
    typography
typw. typewriter
    typewriting
    typewritten
Tyr. Tyrone

U

U Uranium
U. Uhr (clock, o'clock)
    Union(ist)
    United
    Universal
    University
    Upper
    Utah
u. ugly
    uncle
    und (and)
    upper
U.A. Ulster Association
    United Artists Corporation
    United Society of Artists
    University Actors
U/A. Underwriting Account
u.a. under age
    usque ad (as far as)
U.A.B. Universities Appointments
    Board
U.A.B.S. Union of American Biological
    Societies
U.A.C. Ulster Automobile Club
    United Africa Company

U.A.C.E.E. Union de l'artisanat de la
    C.E.E. (Union of Master-Craftsmen
    of the E.E.C.)
U.A.Co. United Africa Company
U.A.D.W. Universal Alliance of Dia-
    mond Workers
U.A.E. Union of Arab Emirates
U.A.I. Union académique internation-
    ale (International Union of
    Academies)
    Union astronomique inter-
    nationale (International Astro-
    nomical Union)
    Union des associations inter-
    nationales (Union of Inter-
    national Associations)
U.A.L. United Air Lines
U.A.M. Underwater-to-Air Missile
    Union africaine et malgache
    (African and Malagasy Union
    (Brazzaville Group))
U.A.M.P.T. Union africaine et
    malgache des postes et télécommuni-
    cations (African and Malagasy Postal
    and Telecommunications Union)

U.A.N.A. Unión Amateur de Natación de Las Americas (Amateur Swimming Union of the Americas)

u.& o. use and occupancy

U.A.O.D. United Ancient Order of Druids

U.A.O.S. Ulster Agricultural Organisation Society

U.A.R. United Arab Republic

U.A.S. University Air Squadron

U.A.T.I. Union des associations techniques internationales (Union of International Engineering Organisations)

U.A.T.P. Universal Air Travel Plan

U.A.U. Universities Athletic Union

U.A.W. United Automobile Workers (U.S.)

u.A.w.g. um Antwort wird gebeten (an answer is requested)

U.B. United Brethren
Upper Bench

U.B.B.S. University of Basutoland, Bechuanaland Protectorate and Swaziland

U.B.F. Union of British Fascists

U.M.B. Union mondiale de billard (World Billiards Union)

U.-boat Unterseeboot (submarine)

U.B.S. United Bible Societies

U.C. University College
Urban Council
Urbe Condita (the city being built)

u.c. upper case
una corda (on one string)

U.C.A. Ulster Chemists' Association
United Chemists' Association Limited

U.C.A.E. Universities' Council for Adult Education

U.C.B. Unemployment Compensation Board (U.S.)

U.C.C. University College, Cork

U.C.C.A. Universities' Central Council on Admissions

U.C.C.E. Union des Capitales de la Communauté Européenne (Union of Capitals in the European Community)

U.C.D. University College, Dublin

U.C.D.E.C. Union chrétienne démocrate d'Europe centrale (Christian Democratic Union of Central Europe)

U.C.F. Union Culturelle Française
United Counties Farmers, Ltd.

U.C.G. University College, Galway

U.C.H. University College Hospital

U.C.H.D. Usual Childhood Diseases

U.C.I. Union cycliste internationale (International Cyclists' Union)

U.C.I.S.S. Union catholique internationale de service social (Catholic International Union for Social Service)

U.C.J.G. Alliance universelle des unions chrétiennes de jeunes gens (World Alliance of Young Men's Christian Associations)

U.C.L. University College, London

U.C.L.A. University of California at Los Angeles

U.C.M.D.S. Unilever Companies Management Development Scheme

U.C.N.W. University College of North Wales

U.C.P. United Country Party (Australia)

U.C.P.A. Universal Coloured People's Association

U.C.P.T.E. Union pour la coordination de la production et du transport de l'électricité (Union for Co-ordinating Production and Distribution of Electricity)

U.C.S. University College School
Upper Clyde Shipbuilders

U.C.S.W. University College of South Wales

U.C.T.A. United Commercial Travellers' Association of Great Britain and Ireland

U.C.W. University College of Wales

U.C.W.R.E. Under-Water Counter-Measures and Weapons Research Establishment

U.D. United Dairies

u.d. ut dictum (as directed)

U.D.C. Union of Democratic Control
Universal Decimal Classification
Urban District Council

u.d.c. upper dead centre

U.D.C.A. Urban District Councils Association

U.D.E. Under-Water Development Establishment

UDECEVER Union européenne des détaillants en céramique et verrerie (European Union of Ceramic and Glassware Retailers)

U.D.F. Union Defence Forces (South Africa)

u.d.f. und die folgenden (and those following)

U.D.I. Unilateral Declaration of Independence
Unione Donne Italiane (Italian Womens' Association)

UDMH Unsymmetrical Dimenthyl Hydrazine

U.D.S. United Drapery Stores Limited

U.D.T. United Dominions Trust

U.E. University Extension

ue. unexpired

U.E.A. Union européenne de l'ameublement (European Furniture Federation)
Universal Esperanto Association

U.E.C. Union européenne de la carrosserie (European Union of Coachbuilders)
Union européenne des experts comptables économiques et financiers (European Union of Accountants)

U.E.C.B. Union européenne des commerces du bétail (European Cattle Trade Union)

U.E.C.L. Union européenne des constructeurs de logements (secteur privé) (European Union of Independent Building Contractors)

U.E.F. Union européenne des fédéral-
istes (European Union of
Federalists)
Union européenne féminine
(European Union of Women)
U.E.F.A. Union of European Football
Associations
U.E.I. Union of Educational Institu-
tions
U.E.I.C. United East India Company
U.E.M.S. Union européenne de méde-
cine sociale (European
Association of Social Medi-
cine)
Union européenne des méde-
cins spécialistes (European
Union of Medical Special-
ists)
U.E.N.C.P.B. Union européenne des
négociants en cuirs et peaux bruts
(European Union of Hide and Skin
Merchants)
U.E.O. Union de l'Europe occidentale
(Western European Union)
Unit Educational Officer
U.E.P. Union européenne de paiements
(European Payments Union)
Union européenne de pédo-
psychiatres (European Union
for Child Psychiatry)
U.E.R. Union européenne de radio-
diffusion (European Broad-
casting Union)
University Entrance Require-
ments
U.F. United Free Church
U.F.A. Universal-Film-Aktiengesell-
schaft (Universal Film Company)
U.F.A.W. Universities Federation for
Animal Welfare
U.F.C. United Free Church (of Scot-
land)
U.F.C.E. Union fédéraliste des com-
munautés ethniques européennes
(Federal Union of European Nation-
alities)
U.F.E. Union des groupements pro-
fessionnels de l'industrie de la fécu-
lerie de pommes de terre de la C.E.E.
(Union of Specialist Groups of the
Potato-Starch Industry of the E.E.C.)
U.F.E.R. Mouvement international
pour l'union fraternelle entre les
races et les peuples (International
Movement for Fraternal Union
Among Races and Peoples)
Uff. Ufficiale (Official)
U.F.I. Union des foires internationales
(Union of International Fairs)
U.F.L.C. Union internationale des
femmes libérales chrétiennes (Inter-
national Union of Liberal Christian
Women)
U.F.M.A.T. Union des fédérations
nationales des négociants en matériaux
de construction de la C.E.E. (Union
of National Federations of Building
Merchants in the E.E.C.)
U.F.N.E. Unión Federalista de Nacion-
alidades Europeas (Federal Union of
European Nationalities)

U.F.O. Unidentified Flying Object
Unlimited Freak Out
u.f.p. unemployed full pay
U.F.U. Ulster Farmers' Union
u/g. underground
Ugan. Uganda
U.G.C. University Grants Committee
U.G.G.I. Union géodésique et géo-
physique internationale (International
Union of Geodesy and Geophysics)
U.G.I. Union géographique inter-
nationale (International Geographical
Union)
U.G.L.E. United Grand Lodge of
England
U.G.S.S.S. Union of Girls' Schools for
Social Service
U.H. Upper Half
U.H.A. Union House of Assembly
(South Africa)
U.H.C.C. Upper House of the Convo-
cation of Canterbury
U.H.C.Y. Upper House of the Convo-
cation of York
u.h.f. ultra-high frequency
U.H.T. Ultra High Temperature
u.i. ut infra (as below)
u/i. under instruction
U.I.A. Union internationale contre
l'alcoolisme (International
Union Against Alcoholism)
Union internationale des archi-
tectes (International Union of
Architects)
Union internationale des avocats
(International Association of
Lawyers)
Union internationale des travailleurs des industries alimentaires et connexes (International Union of Food and
Allied Workers Associations)
Union of International Associations
U.I.A.A. Union internationale des asso-
ciations d'alpinisme (Inter-
national Union of Alpine
Associations)
Union internationale des asso-
ciations d'annonceurs (International Union of Adver-
tisers' Associations)
U.I.A.C.M. Union internationale des
automobile-clubs médicaux (International Union of Associations of
Doctor-Motorists)
U.I.A.P.M.E. Union internationale de
l'artisanat et des petites et moyennes
entreprises (International Association
of Crafts and Small and Medium-
Sized Enterprises)
U.I.A.T. Union internationale des syndicats des industries de l'alimentation
et des tabacs (International Union of
Food, Drink and Tobacco Workers'
Associations)
U.I.B. Union internationale des maitres
boulangers (International Union of
Master Bakers)
U.I.B.W.M. Trade Unions Internation-
al of Workers of Building Wood and
the Building Materials Industries

U.I.C. Union internationale des chemins de fer (International Union of Railways)

U.I.C.C. Union internationale contre le cancer (International Union Against Cancer)

U.I.C.G.F. Union internationale du commerce en gros de la fleur (International Union for the Wholesale Flower Trade)

U.I.C.M. Union internationale catholique des classes moyennes (International Catholic Union of the Middle Classes)

U.I.C.N. Union internationale pour la conservation de la nature et de ses ressources (International Union for Conservation of Nature and Natural Resources)

U.I.C.P.A. Union internationale de chimie pure et appliquée (International Union of Pure and Applied Chemistry)

U.I.C.T. Union internationale contre la tuberculose (International Union Against Tuberculosis)

U.I.D.A. Union internationale des organisations de détaillants de la branche alimentaire (International Federation of Grocers' Associations)

U.I.E. Union internationale d'électrothermie (International Union for Electroheat)

Union Internationale des Éditeurs (International Publishers' Union)

Union internationale des étudiants (International Union of Students

U.I.E.C. Union internationale de l'exploitation cinématographique (International Union of Cinematograph Exhibitors)

U.I.E.I.S. Union internationale pour l'étude des insectes sociaux (International Union for the Study of Social Insects)

U.I.E.O. Union of International Engineering Organisations

U.I.E.P. Union internationale des entrepreneurs de peinture (International Union of Housepainting Contractors)

U.I.E.S. Union Internationale d'Études Sociales (International Union for Social Studies)

Union internationale pour l'éducation sanitaire (International Union for Health Education)

U.I.F.I. Union internationale des fabricants d'imperméables (International Rainwear Council)

U.I.H.L. Union internationale de l'humanisme laique (International Humanist and Ethical Union)

U.I.H.P.S. Union internationale d'histoire et de philosphie des sciences (International Union of the History and Philosophy of Science)

U.I.I.G. Union internationale de l'industrie du gaz (International Gas Union)

U.I.J.S. Unino internationale de la jeunesse socialiste (International Union of Socialist Youth)

U.I.L. Unione Italiana del Lavoro (Italian Workers' Association)

U.I.L.E. Union internationale pour la liberté d'enseignement (International Union for the Freedom of Education)

U.I.M. Union internationale motonautique (International Union for Motorboating)

U.I.M.C. Union internationale des services médicaux des chemins de fer (International Union of Railway Medical Services)

U.I.M.J. Union Internationale des Maisons de Jeunesse (International Union of Young People's Hostels)

U.I.M.P. Union internationale pour la protection de la moralité publique (International Union for Protecting Public Morality)

U.I.N.F. Union internationale de la navigation fluviale (Internationale Union for Inland Navigation)

U.I.N.L. Union Internationale du notariat latin (International Union of Latin Notaries)

U.I.O. Union internationale des orientalistes (International Union of Orientalists)

U.I.O.F. Union internationale des organismes familiaux (International Union of Family Organisations)

U.I.O.O.T. Union internationale des organismes officiels de tourisme (International Union of Official Travel Organisations)

U.I.O.T. Unione Internazionale Organizzatori Turismo (Touring Organizer's International Association)

U.I.P. Union internationale d'associations de propriétaires de wagons de particuliers (International Union of Private Railway Truck Owners' Associations)

Union internationale de patinage (International Skating Union)

Union internationale de physique pure et appliquée (International Union of Pure and Applied Physics)

Union internationale des publicitaires (International Union of Practitioners in Advertising)

Union interparlementaire (Inter-Parliamentary Union)

U.I.P.C. Union internationale de la presse catholique (International Catholic Press Union)

U.I.P.C.G. Union internationale de la pâtisserie, confiserie, glacerie (International Union of Bakers and Confectioners)

U.I.P.E. Union internationale de protection de l'enfance (International Union for Child Welfare)

U.I.P.F.B. Union internationale de la propriété foncière bâtie (International Union of Landed Property Owners)

U.I.P.M. Union internationale de la presse médicale (International Union of the Medical Press)
Union internationale de pentathlon moderne (International Modern Pentathlon Union)

U.I.P.P.I. Union internationale pour la protection de la propriété industrielle (International Union for the Protection of Industrial Property)

U.I.P.V.T. Union internationale contre le péril vénérien et les tréponématoses (International Union Against Venereal Diseases and Treponematoses)

U.I.R.D. Union internationale de la résistance et de la déportation (International Union of Resistance and Deportee Movements)

U.I.S. Union internationale de secours (International Relief Union)

U.I.S.A.E. Union internationale des sciences anthropologiques et ethnologiques (International Union of Anthropological and Ethnological Sciences)

U.I.S.B. Union internationale des sciences biologiques (International Union of Biological Sciences)

U.I.S.E. Union internationale de secours aux enfants (International Union for Child Welfare)

U.I.S.M. Union internationale des syndicats des mineurs (Miners' Trade Unions International)

U.I.S.M.M. Union internationale des syndicats des industries métallurgiques et mécaniques (Trade Unions International of Metal and Engineering Industries)

U.I.S.N. Union internationale des sciences de la nutrition (International Union of Nutritional Sciences)

U.I.S.P.P. Union internationale des sciences préhistoriques et protohistoriques (International Union of Prehistoric and Protohistoric Sciences)

U.I.S.T.A.F. Union internationale des syndicats des travailleurs agricoles et forestiers (Trade Unions International of Agricultural and Forestry Workers)

U.I.S.T.C. Union internationale des syndicats des travailleurs du commerce (Trade Unions International of Workers in Commerce)

U.I.T. Union internationale des télécommunications (International Telecommunication Union)

U.I.T.A. Unión Internacional de Asociaciones de Trabajadores de Alimentos y Ramos Afines (International Union of Food and Allied Workers' Associations)

U.I.T.A.M. Union internationale de mécanique théorique et appliquée (International Union of Theoretical and Applied Mechanics)

U.I.T.B.B. Union internationale des syndicats des travailleurs du bâtiment, du bois et des matériaux de construction (Trade Unions International of Workers of the Building Wood and Building Materials Industries)

U.I.T.P. Union internationale des transports publics (International Union of Public Transport)

U.I.U.S.D. Union internationale universitaire socialiste et démocratique (International Union of Social Democratic Teachers)

U.I.V. Union internationale des villes et pouvoirs locaux (International Union of Local Authorities)

U.J. Union Jack

U.J.C. Union Jack Club

U.J.D. Utriusque Juris Doctor (Doctor of Civil and Canon Law)

U.K. United Kingdom of Great Britain and Northern Ireland

U.K.A. United Kingdom Alliance

U.K.A.C. United Kingdom Automation Council

U.K.A.E.A. United Kingdom Atomic Energy Authority

U.K.A.P.E. United Kingdom Association of Professional Engineers

U.K.B.G. United Kingdom Bartenders' Guild

U.K.C.A.T.R. United Kingdom Civil Aviation Telecommunications Representative

U.K.C.B.D.A. United Kingdom Carbon Block Distributors' Association

U.K.C.O.S.A. United Kingdom Council for Overseas Student Affairs

U.K.C.S.M.A. United Kingdom Cutlery and Silverware Manufacturers Association

U.K.C.T.A. United Kingdom Commercial Travellers' Association

U.K.D.A. United Kingdom Dairy Association

U.K.G.P.A. United Kingdom Glycerine Producers' Association

U.K.J.G.A. United Kingdom Jute Goods Association

U.K.M.A.N.Z.R.A. United Kingdom Manufacturers and New Zealand Representatives Association

U.K.O.B.A. United Kingdom Outboard Boating Association

U.K.P.A. United Kingdom Pilots' Association

Ukr. Ukraine
Ukrainian

U.K.R.A.S. United Kingdom Railway Advisory Service

U.K.S.M. United Kingdom Scientific Mission

U.K.S.M.A. United Kingdom Sugar Merchants' Association

U.L. Universal League
University Library
Upper Limb

U.L.A.J.E. Unión Latino Américana de Juventudes Evangélicas (Union of Latin-American Evangelical Youth)

U.L.A.P.C. Unión Latino Americana de Prensa Católica (Latin-American Catholic Press Union)
U.L.A.S.T. Unión Latino Americana de Sociedades de Tisiologia (Latin-American Union of Societies of Phthisiology)
U.L.F. Upper Limiting Frequency
U.L.I. Union pour la langue internationale Ido (Union for the International Language Ido)
U.L.P. University of London Press
U.L.R. Uganda Law Reports
U.L.S. Union of Liberal Students
ult. ultimate
    ultimo (in the preceding month)
U.L.T. United Lodge of Theosophists
ult. praes. ultimum praescriptus (last prescribed)
U.L.U. University of London Union
um. unmarried
U.M. Union Movement
u.m. under-mentioned
U.M.B. Union mondiale de billard (World Billiards Union)
Umbr. Umbria(n)
U.M.C.A. Universities Mission to Central Africa (now U.S.P.G.)
U.M.E.C. Union mondiale des enseignants catholiques (World Union of Catholic Teachers)
U.M.E.J. Union mondiale des étudiants juifs (World Union of Jewish Students)
U.M.F.C. United Methodist Free Church(es)
UMFIA Union médicale latine (Latin Medical Union)
U.M.H.P. Union mondiale des sociétés d'histoire pharmaceutique (World Organisation of Societies of Pharmaceutical History)
U.M.N.O. United Malays National Organisation
U.M.O.F.C. Union mondiale des organisations féminines catholiques (World Union of Catholic Women's Organisations)
U.M.O.S.B.E.S.L. Union mondiale des organisations syndicales sur base économique et sociale libérale (World Union of Liberal Trade Union Organisations)
U.M.O.S.E.A. Union mondiale des organismes pour la sauvegarde de l'enfance et de l'adolescence (World Union of Organiations for the Safeguard of Youth)
ump. umpire
U.M.S. Unfederated Malay States
U.M.W.A. United Mine Workers of America
un. unified
    union
    united
U.N. United Nations
U.N.A. United Nations Association
unab. unabridged
unan. unanimous
U.N.A.T. Unione Nazionale Artisti Teatrali (Theatre Actors' National Association)
unatt. unattached

Unb. Unbound
unc. uncertain
U.N.C. United Nations Command in Korea
U.N.C.C.P. United Nations Conciliation Commission for Palestine
U.N.C.I.O. United Nations Conference on International Organisation
U.N.C.I.P. United Nations Commission on India and Pakistan
U.N.C.O. United Nations Civilian Operations Mission (Congo Republic)
U.N.C.O.K. United Nations Commission on Korea
uncond. unconditioned
uncor. uncorrected
U.N.C.P. United Nations Conference of Plenipotentiaries
unct. unctus (smeared)
U.N.C.T.A.D. United Nations Conference on Trade and Development
U.N.C.U.R.K. United Nations Commission for the Unification and Rehabilitation of Korea
U.N.D.A. Association catholique internationale pour la radiodiffusion et la télévision (International Catholic Association for Radio and Television)
undsgd. undersigned
undtkr. undertaker
U.N.E.C. United Nations Education Conference
U.N.E.C.A. United Nations Economic Commission for Asia
UNECOLAIT Union européenne du commerce laitier (European Milk Trade Union)
U.N.E.D.A. United Nations Economic Development Administration
U.N.E.F. United Nations Emergency Force
U.N.E.S.C.O. United Nations Educational Scientific and Cultural Organization
U.N.E.S.E.M. Union européenne des sources d'eaux minérales naturelles du Marché Commun (European Union of Natural Mineral Water Sources of the Common Market)
unexpl. unexplained
    unexploded
    unexplored
U.N.F.A.O. United Nations Food and Agricultural Organization
U.N.F.B. United Nations Film Board
U.N.F.C. United Nations Food Conference
UNFICYP United Nations Force in Cyprus
U.N.G.A. United Nations General Assembly
U.N.H.C.R. United Nations High Commissioner for Refugees
U.N.H.Q. United Nations Headquarters
U.N.I.A.D.U.S.E.C. Union Internationale des Associations de Diplômés Universitaires en Sciences Economiques et Commerciales (International Union of Associations of University Graduates in Science and Commerce)

U.N.I.A.P.C. Union Internationale des Associations Patronales Catholiques (International Union of Catholic Employers' Associations)

U.N.I.A.T.E.C. Union Internationale des Associations Techniques et Cinématographiques (International Union of Technical Cinematographic Associations)

U.N.I.C. United Nations Information Centre

UNICA Union internationale du cinéma d'amateurs (International Union of Amateur Cinema)

UNICE Union des industries de la communauté européenne (Union of Industries of the European Community)

U.N.I.C.E.F. United Nations Children's Fund (*formerly* United Nations International Children's Emergency Fund)

UNICHAL Union internationale des distributeurs de chaleur (International Union of Heating Distributors)

U.N.I.D.O. United Nations Industrial Development Organisation

UNIDROIT Institut international pour l'unification du droit privé (International Institute for the Unification of Private Law)

UNIMA Union internationale de grands magasins (International Union of Department Stores)

U.N.I.O. United Nations Information Organization

UNIPEDE Union internationale des producteurs et distributeurs d'énergie électrique (International Union of Producers and Distributors of Electrical Energy)

U.N.I.S. United Nations Information Service

United Nations International School

U.N.I.S.C.A.T. United Nations Expert Committee on the Application of Science and Technology

UNISCAN Anglo-Scandinavian Economic Committee

Unit. Unitarian

U.N.I.T.A.R. United Nations Institute for Training and Research

Univ. University
Universitarian

univ. universal(ist)
university

Univ.Q.L.J. University of Queensland Law Journal

U.N.J.S.P.B. United Nations Joint Staff Pension Board

unkn. unknown

U.N.K.R.A. United Nations Korean Reconstruction Agency

U.N.L.C. United Nations Liaison Committee

unm. unmarried

U.N.M.C. United Nations Mediterranean Commission

U.N.M.O.G.I.P. United Nations Military Observer Group in India and Pakistan

U.N.O. United Nations Organization

unop. unopposed

U.N.P.A. United Nations Postal Administration

U.N.P.C. United Nations Palestine Commission

U.N.P.C.C. United Nations Conciliation Commission for Palestine

U.N.P.O.C. United Nations Peace Observation Commission

unpub. unpublished

U.N.R. Union pour la Nouvelle République

U.N.R.E.F. United Nations Refugee Emergency Fund

U.N.R.P.R. United Nations Relief for Palestine Refugees

U.N.R.R.A. United Nations Relief and Rehabilitation Administration

U.N.R.W.A. United Nations Relief and Works Agency for Palestine Refugees in the Near East

U.N.R.W.A.P.R.N.E. United Nations Relief and Works Agency for Palestine Refugees in the Near East

U.N.S.C. United Nations Security Council
United Nations Social Commission

U.N.S.C.C. United Nations Standards Co-ordinating Committee

U.N.S.C.C.U.R. United Nations Scientific Conference on the Conservation and Utilization of Resources

U.N.S.C.E.A.R. United Nations Scientific Committee on the Effects of Atomic Radiation

U.N.S.C.O.B. United Nations Special Committee on the Balkans

U.N.S.C.O.P. United Nations Special Committee on Palestine

U.N.S.F. United Nations Special Fund

U.N.S.G. United Nations Secretary General

U.N.S.R. United Nations Space Registry

U.N.T.A. United Nations Technical Assistance

U.N.T.A.A. United Nations Technical Assistance Administration

U.N.T.A.B. United Nations Technical Assistance Board

U.N.T.A.M. United Nations Technical Assistance Mission

U.N.T.C. United Nations Trusteeship Council

U.N.T.C.O.K. United Nations Temporary Commission on Korea

U.N.T.E.A. United Nations Temporary Executive Authority West New Guinea

U.N.T.S.O. United Nations Truce Supervision Organization

U.N.T.T. United Nations Trust Territory

U.N.W.C.C. United Nations War Crimes Commission

U.N.Y.O.M. United Nations Yemen Observation Mission
U. of A. University of Alaska
U. of S. University of Saskatchewan
U.O.F.S. University of the Orange Free State
U.P. Ulster Parliament
    Under Proof
    Union Pacific
    United Party (Ghana)
    United Presbyterian
    United Press
    United Provinces (India)
    University of Pennsylvania
up. upper
U.P.A. Union postale arabe (Arab Postal Union)
    United Pattern Makers' Association
U.P.A.D.I. Unión Panamericana de Asociaciones de Ingenieros (Pan-American Federation of Engineering Societies)
U.P.A.E. Union postale des Amériques et de l'Espagne (Postal Union of the Americas and Spain)
U.P.C. United Presbyterian Church
    Universal Postal Convention
U.P.C.S. United Pastrycook's and Confectioners' Society
Upd. Unpaid
uphol. upholsterer
    upholstery
U.P.I. United Press International, Inc.
U.P.I.G.O. Union professionnelle internationale des gynécologues et obstétriciens (International Union of Professional Gynaecologists and Obstetricians)
U.P.O.A. Ulster Public Officers' Association
U.P.O.W. Union of Post Office Workers
U.P.R. Union Pacific Railway
U.P.S. Union of Progressive Students
U.P.T.C. Union panafricaine des travailleurs croyants (Pan-African Workers Congress)
U.P.U. Universal Postal Union
U.P.W. Union of Post Office Workers
U.R. Uniform Regulations
u.r. uti rogas (be it as you desire)
urb. urban
U.R.B.M. Ultimate Range Ballistic Missile
U.R.C. United Ratepayers' Campaign
U.R.F. Union des services routiers des chemins de fer européens (Union of European Railways Road Services)
U.R.I. Université radiophonique et télévisuelle internationale (International Radio-Television University)
Urol. Urology
U.R.P.E. Union des résistants pour une Europe unie (Union of Resistance Veterans for a United Europe)
U.R.S.I. Union radio-scientifique internationale (International Scientific Radio Union)
U.R.S.S. Union des Républiques Socialistes Soviétiques (Union of Socialist Soviet Republics)

U.R.T.U. United Road Transport Union
Uru. Uruguay
U.S. Under Secretary
    United Services
    United States
U/S. Unserviceable
u.s. ut supra (as above)
U.S.A. United States Army
    United States of America
U.S.A.A.C. United States Army Air Corps (*now* U.S.A.A.F.)
U.S.A.A.F. United States Army Air Force(s)
U.S.A.E.C. United States Atomic Energy Commission
U.S.A.F. United States Air Force
U.S.A.F.I. United States Armed Forces Institute
U.S.A.Med.S. United States Army Medical Service
U.S.A.R. United States Army Reserve
U.S.A.T. United States Army Transport
U.S.B.C. United States Bureau of the Census
U.S.C. Ulster Special Constabulary
    United Service Corps
    United Services Club
    United States Code
    United States of Colombia
    Up Stage Centre
U.S.C.A. United States Code Annotated
U.S.C.C. United States Circuit Court
U.S.C.C.A. United States Circuit Court of Appeals
U.S.C.C.P.A. United States Court of Customs and Patent Appeals
U.S.C.G. United States Coast Guard
U.S.C.G.R. United States Coast Guard Reserve
U.S.C.L. United Society for Christian Literature
U.S.Corps United Services Corps
U.S.C.S.C. United States Civil Service Commission
U.S.C.Supp. United States Code Supplement
U.S.C.V. Union scientifique continentale du verre (European Union for the Scientific Study of Glass)
U.S.D.A. United States Department of Agriculture
U.S.D.A.W. Union of Shop, Distributive and Allied Workers
U.S.D.H.E. & W. United States Department of Health, Education and Welfare
U/Sec. Under Secretary
U.S.F. United States Forces
U.S.G. United States Government
    United States Standard Guage
U.S.H.L. United States Hygienic Laboratory
U.S.I United Schools International
    United Services Institution
    United States Industries
U.S.I.A. United States Information Agency
U.S.I.S. United States Information Service

U.S.L. United States Legation
United States Lines
U.S.L.T.A. United States Lawn Tennis Association
U.S.M. Underwater-to-Surface Missile
United States Mail
United States Marines
United States Mint
U.S.M.A. Underfeed Stoker Makers' Association
United States Military Academy
U.S.M.C. United States Marine Corps
United States Maritime Commission
U.S.M.H. United States Marine Hospital
U.S.M.S. United States Maritime Service
U.S.N. United States Navy
U.S.N.A. United States Naval Academy
U.S.N.G. United States National Guard
U.S.N.R. United States Naval Reserve
U.S.O. United Services Organization
U.S.O.M. United States Operations Mission
U.S.P. United States Patent
United States Pharmacopoeia
U.S.Pat. United States Patent
U.S.P.C.A. Ulster Society for the Prevention of Cruelty to Animals, Inc.
U.S.P.G. United Society for the Propagation of the Gospel
U.S.Phar. United States Pharmacopoeia
U.S.P.H.S. United States Public Health Service
U.S.P.O. United States Post Office
U.S.R. United States Reserves
Usher of the Scarlet Rod
U.S.S. United States Senate
United States Ship
United States Standard Thread
U.S.S.A.F. United States Strategic Air Force
U.S.-S.A.L.E.P. United States-South Africa Leader Exchange Programme
U.S.S.C. United States Supreme Court
U.S.S.R. Union of Soviet Socialist Republics
U.S.S.S. United States Steamship
ust. ustus (burnt)
U.S.T.C. United States Tariff Commission

U.S.T.S. United States Travel Service
usu. usual(ly)
usurp. usurpandus (to be used)
U.S.V. United States Volunteers
U.S.V.B. United States Veterans' Bureau
U.S.V.H. United States Veterans' Hospital
u.s.w. und so weiter (and so forth)
U.S.W.D. Undersurface Warfare Division
U.S.W.P. Ultra Short Wave Propagation Panel
U.S.W.V. United Spanish War Veterans
Ut. Utah
ut. utility
U.T. Utah Territory
Unit Trust
Universal Time
U.T.A. Ulster Transport Authority
U.T.C. University Training Corps
U.T.C.P.T. Union internationale des organismes touristiques et culturels des postes et des télécommunications (International Union of Tourist and Cultural Associations in the Postal and Telecommunications Services)
Utd. United
U.T.D.A. Ulster Tourist Development Association
ut dict. ut dictum (as directed)
utend. utendus (to be used)
utend. mor. sol. utendus more solito (to be used in the usual manner)
ut inf. ut infra (as below)
U.T.O. United Town Organisation
ut sup. ut supra (as above)
U.U. Ulster Unionist
u.ü.V. unter üblichem Vorbehalt (with the usual proviso)
U.V. Ultra Violet
U.V.Co. United Veterans' Council (U.S.)
U.V.F. Ulster Volunteer Force
U/w. Underwriter
U.W.C.E. Under-Water Weapons and Counter-Measures Establishment
U.W.H.C. Ulster Women's Hockey Union
ux. uxor (wife)
u.x.b. unexploded bomb
U.Y. Universal Youth

V

V Five (Roman Numerals)
Vanadium
Volt(s)
v volt(s)
V. Vector
Venerable
Vergeltungswaffe (reprisal weapon)
Version   *cont.*

Vespers
Vicar(age)
Vice
Victoria
Victory
Vide (See)
Viscount
Volunteer

v. valve
vector
vel (or)
velocity
ventral
verb
verse
version
versus (against)
vertical
very
via (by way of)
vicar
vide (see)
village
violin
voice
volume
von (of)
votre (your)
Va. Viola
Virginia
V.A. Venus and Adonis (Shakespeare)
Veterans' Administration (U.S.)
Vicar Apostolic
Vice-Admiral
Voice of America
Vuestra Alteza (Your Highness)
v.a. verb active
verbal adjective
vixit annos . . . (he *or* she lived . . .
years)
volt ampère(s)
V.A.B.F. Variety Artistes' Benevolent
Fund
vac. vacancy
vacant
vacation
vacuum
vacc. vaccination
Vacemp Vacation Employment Agency
V.A.D. Voluntary Aid Detachment
V.Adm. Vice-Admiral
V.A.F. Variety Artistes' Federation
V.A.H. Veterans' Administration Hospital (U.S.)
val. value
valvular
V.A.L.A. National Viewers' and Listeners' Association
V. & A. Royal Order of Victoria and
Albert
Victoria and Albert Museum
V. & M. Virgin and Martyr
v. & m.m. vandalism and malicious
mischief
Var. Variation
Variety
var. variant
variation
variety
various
V.A.R. Visual-Aural Radio Range
Votre Altesse Royale (Your
Royal Highness)
var. lect. varia lectio (different reading)
V.A.S.C.A. Electronic Valve and Semi-Conductor Manufacturers' Association
vas vit. vas vitreum (a glass vessel)
Vat. Vatican
V.A.T. Value Added Tax

Vaud. Vaudeville
v.aux. verb auxiliary
vb. verb
V.B. Volunteer Battalion
vbl. verbal
vb.n. verbal noun
V.B.R.A. Vehicle Builders' and Repairers' Association
V.C. Veterinary Corps (U.S.)
Vice-Chairman
Vice-Chamberlain
Vice-Chancellor
Vice-Consul
Victoria Cross
Vietcong
Vir Clarissimus (Most famous
man)
v.c. valuation clause
verbi causa (for example)
V.C.A. Vegetarian Catering Association
V.C.A.S. Vice-Chief of the Air Staff
V.C.C. Veteran Car Club of Great Britain
v.cel. vir celeberrimus (most celebrated man)
V.C.G. Vertical Centre of Gravity
vch. vehicle
V.C.H. Victoria County History *or*
Histories
v. Chr. vor Christus (before Christ)
V.C.I.G.S. Vice-Chief of the Imperial
General Staff
v. cl. vir clarissimus (most famous
man)
V.C.N.S. Vice-Chief of the Naval Staff
V.C.O.A.D. Voluntary Committee on
Overseas Aid and Development
V.C.R. Viva Cristo Rey (Long Live
Christ the King)
Vd. Vaud
V.D. Royal Naval Volunteer Reserve
Decoration (*now* V.R.D.)
Veneral Disease
v.d. vapour density
various dates
v.def. verb defective
v.dep. verb deponent
V.D.H. Valvular Disease of the Heart
V.D.L. Van Diemen's Land
V.D.M. Verbi Dei Minister (Preacher
of the Word of God)
V.D.M.I.E. Verbum Domini Manet in
Eternum (The word of the Lord
endureth for ever)
V.D.R.L. Venereal Disease Research
Laboratory
ve. veuve (widow)
V.E. Vocational Education
Votre Éminence (Your Eminence)
Vuestra Excelencia (Your Excellency)
V.E. Day Victory in Europe Day (8
June, 1945)
V.E.D.C. Vitreous Enamel Development Council
veg. vegetable
vel. velocity
Ven. Venerable
Venezuela
Venetian
Venice
Venus

Venet. Venetian
Venez. Venezuela
V.E.N.I.S.S. Visual Education National Information Service for Schools
Vent. Ventriloquist
vent. ventilation
Ver. Verein (Association *or* Company)
ver. verse
V.E.R.A. Versatile Experimental Reactor Assembly
Vision Electronic Recording Apparatus
verb. sap. verbum sapienti (a word to the wise)
Verm. Vermont
verm. vermillion
vern. vernacular
Ver. St. Vereinigte Staaten (United States)
ves. vessel
vestry
vesica (bladder)
vesicula (blister)
vespere (in the evening)
Vet. Veteran
Veterinary
Vet. Admin. Veterans' Administration (U.S.)
Vet. Sci. Veterinary Science
V.F. Vicar Forane
v.f. very fair
voice frequency
V.F.O. Variable-Frequency Oscillator
V.F.R. Visual Flight Rules
V.F.W. Veterans of Foreign Wars (U.S.)
V.G. verbi gratia (for the sake of example)
Vicar General
Votre Grâce (Your Grace)
V.g. Very good
V.G.A. Vocational Guidance Association
v.g.c. very good condition
V.H.C. Voluntary Hostels Conference
V.H.F. Very High Fidelity
Very High Frequency
v.h.f. very high frequency
Vi Virginium
V.I. Vertical Interval
Virgin Islands
v.i. verb intransitive
vide infra (see below)
Vic. Vicar(age)
vic. vices (times)
Vic.Ap. Vicar Apostolic
V.I.Corp. Virgin Islands Corporation
Vict. Victoria
vid. vide (see)
vig. vignette
vil. village
V.i.m. Vertical improved mail
v.imp. verb impersonal
v. imper. verb imperative
V.I.O. Veterinary Investigation Officer
V.I.P. Very Important Person
vir. viridis (green)
V.I.R. Victoria Imperatrix Regina (Victoria Empress and Queen)
Virg. Virgil
v.irr. verb irregular

Vis. Viscount
vis. visibility
visual
V.I.S. Veterinary Investigation Service
Visc(t). Viscount
vit. ov. sol. vitello ovi solutus (dissolved in yolk of egg)
Vitr. Vitruvius
vitr. vitreum (glass)
Viv. Vivace (quickly)
vix. vixit (he *or* she lived)
viz. videlicet (namely)
V.J. Day Victory in Japan Day (15 August, 1945)
V.L. Vulgar Latin
v.l. varia lectio (different reading)
v.l.f. very low frequency
V.L.R. Victorian Law Reports, Australia
V.M. Victory Medal
V.m. Vuestra merced (Your Worship)
v.M. vorigen Monats (last month)
v.m. voormiddag (ante meridian)
v/m. volts per metre
volts per mile
V.M.A. Voice of Methodism Association
V.M.A.I. Veterinary Medical Association of Ireland
V.M.D. Veterinariae Medicinae Doctor (Doctor of Veterinary Medicine)
V.M.H. Victoria Medal of Honour
V.N. Vietnam
v.n. verb neuter
vo. verso
V.O. Valuation Officer
Very Old
Veterinary Officer
V.O.A. Voice of America
voc. vocation
vocative
vocal
V.O.C. Vehicle Observer Corps
vocab. vocabulary
V.O.C.O.S.S. Voluntary Organisations Co-operating in Overseas Social Service
Voit. Voiture (wagon *or* truck)
Vol. Volume
Volunteer
vol. volatile
volume
voluntary
volunteer
volc. volcanic
volcano
vols. volumes
V.O.L.S. Voluntary Overseas Library Service
volvend. volvendus (to be rolled)
V.O.P. Very Oldest Procurable
V.O.W. Voice of Women
vox pop. vox populi (voice of the people)
V.P. Vice-President
Vice-Principal
Victory Points
v.p. vapour pressure
V.P.A. Village Produce Association
V.P.S.C. Varsities and Public Schools Camps

V.Q.M.G. Vice-Quartermaster-General
V.R. Vicar Rural
    Victoria Regina (Queen Victoria)
    Victoria Reports
    Volunteer Reserve
v.r. verb reflexive
V.R.C. Volunteer Rifle Corps
V.R.D. Royal Naval Volunteer Reserve Decoration
v. refl. verb reflexive
V.R. et I. Victoria Regina et Imperatrix (Victoria Queen and Empress)
V.Rev. Very Reverend
V.R.P. Vestra Reverendissima Paternitas (Your Most Reverend Paternity)
Vs. Venesection
vs. versus (against)
V.S. Vegetarian Society of the United Kingdom Ltd.
    Veterinary School
    Veterinary Surgeon
    Virgil Society
v.s. variable speed
    vide supra (see above)
    vieux style (old style)
    volta subito (turn over quickly)
Vs.B. venaesectio brachii (bleeding in the arm)
V.S.C. Volunteer Staff Corps
V.S.O. Vienna State Opera
    Voluntary Service Overseas
    Very Superior Old
V.S.O.P. Very Special Old Pale
V.S.Q. Very Special Quality

V.S.R. Very Special Reserve
V/S.T.O.L. Vertical/Short Take-Off and Landing
Vt. Vermont
V.T. Variable Time
    Vetus Testamentum (Old Testament)
v.t. variable time
    variable transmission
    verb transitive
V.T.C. Volunteer Training Corps
    Voting Trust Certificate
V.T.O. Vertical Take-off
V.T.O.L. Vertical Take-Off and Landing
v.u. von unten (from the bottom)
Vulg. Vulgate
vulg. vulgar(ly)
vv. verbs
    verses
    violins
v.v. vice versa
    viva voce (spoken aloud)
V.V.B.F. Victoria Veterinary Benevolent Fund
Vv.ll variae lectiones (different readings).
V.V.O. Very Very Old
V.W. Very Worshipful
V.W.H. Vale of the White Horse
vy. very
V.Y. Victualling Yard
v.y. various years
Vy. Rev. Very Reverend

W

W Wolfram
W. Wales
    Warden
    Water
    Watt(s)
    Wednesday
    Weight
    Welch
    Welsh
    Wesleyan
    West(erly)
    Western
    White
    Widow(er)
    Width
w. waist
    water
    watt(s)
    week(s)
    weight
    wet dew
    white
    wicket
    wide
    width
    wife
    with
    woman
    wrong

W.A. West Africa
    Western Approaches
    Western Australia
W.A.A.A. Women's Amateur Athletic Association
W.A.A.A.F. Women's Australian Auxiliary Air Force (now W.R.A.A.F.)
W.A.A.C. War Artists' Advisory Committee
    Women's Army Auxiliary Corps (now W.R.A.C.)
W.A.A.F. Women's Auxiliary Air Force (now W.R.A.F.)
W.A.C. Women's Advisory Committee of the British Standards Institution
    Women's Army Corps (U.S.)
W.A.C.A. West Africa Court of Appeal Reports
W.A.C.B. World Association for Christian Broadcasting
W.A.C.I. Women's Army Corps of India
WACY 2000 World Association for the Celebration of the Year Two Thousand
Wad. Wadham College, Oxford
W.A.E.C. War Agricultural Executive Committee

W.A.F. West African Forces
    Women in the Air Force (U.S.)
w.a.f. with all faults
W.A.F.F. West African Frontier Force
W.Afr. West Africa(n)
W.Afr.R. West African Regiment
W.A.F.S. Women's Auxiliary Ferrying
    Squadron (U.S.)
W.A.G.B.I. Wildfowlers' Association
of Great Britain and Ireland
W.A.G.G.G.S. World Association of
Girl Guides and Girl Scouts
W.A.I.S. Wechsler's Adult Intelligence
Scale
W.A.I.T.R. West African Institute for
Trypanosomiasis Research
W.A.L.A. West African Library Association
Wall. Walloon
W.A.L.R. Western Australian Law
Reports
W.A.M. Working Association of
Mothers
W.A.M.R.A.C. World Association of
Methodist Radio Amateurs and
Clubs
W.A.M.R.U. West African Maize Research Unit
W. & L. Washington and Lee University (U.S.)
W. & M. William and Mary
w. & s. whisky and soda
W.A.N.S. Women's Australian National
Service
W.A.O.S. Welsh Agricultural Organisation Society
W.A.P.C. Women's Auxiliary Police
Corps
W.A.P.D.A. Water and Power Development Authority (Pakistan)
W.A.P.O.R. World Association for
Public Opinion Research
War. Warwickshire
W.A.R. West Africa Regiment
W.A.R.C. Women's Amateur Rowing
Council
W.A.R.I. Waite Agricultural Research
Institute (Australia)
W.A.R.R.S. West African Rice Research Station
Warw(icks). Warwickshire
W.A.S.A. Welsh Amateur Swimming
Association
Wash. Washington
W.A.S.P. White Anglo-Saxon Protestant (U.S.)
    Women Auxiliary Service
    Pilots (U.S.)
Wass. Wassermann Test
W.A.S.U. West African Students' Union
Wat. Waterford
W.A.T.A. World Association of Travel
Agencies
W.Aus(t). Western Australia
W.A.V.E.S. Women Accepted for Volunteer Emergency Service (U.S.)
W.A.W.F. World Association of World
Federalists
W.A.Y. World Assembly of Youth
W.A.Y.C. Welsh Association of Youth
Clubs

W.B. Warner Brothers Pictures Incorporated
    Water Board
    Washable Base
    Way-Bill
    Weather Bureau
    Wet Bulb
    World Bank
    World Brotherhood
W/B. Warehouse Book
    Way-Bill
w.b. waste ballast
    wave-band
    wool back
W.B.A. West Bromwich Albion Football Club, Ltd.
W.B.B.G. Weltbund der Bibelgesellschaften (United Bible Societies)
W.B.C. White Blood Cells
W.B.H. Welsh Board of Health
W.b.N. West by North
W.b.S. West by South
W.B.T. Wet Bulb Temperature
W.C. War Cabinet
    War Communications
    War Council
    War Credits
    Watch Committee
    Water Closet
    Wesleyan Chapel
    West Central
    Western Command
    Wheel Chair
    Whitley Council
    Workmen's Circle
w.c. water closet
    without charge
W.C.A. Wholesale Confectioners' Alliance
    Women Citizens' Association
    Women's Cricket Association
    World Calendar Association
    Workmen's Compensation Act
W.C.C. War Crimes Commission
    World Council of Churches
W.C.C.B. World Committee for Christian Broadcasting
W.C.C.E.S.S.A. World Council of
Christian Education and Sunday
School Association
W.Cdr. Wing-Commander
W.C.E.U. World's Christian Endeavour
Union
W.C.F. Workers' Christian Fellowship
    World Congress of Faiths
W.C.F.T.S. West Cumberland Farmers' Trading Society Ltd.
W.C.M.A. Wiping Cloth Manufacturers' Association
W.Comm. Wing-Commander
W.C.O.T.P. World Confederation of
Organisations of the Teaching Profession
W.C.P.T. World Confederation for
Physical Therapy
W.C.P.W.C. World Council for the
People's World Convention
W.C.R. (N.S.W.) Workers' Compensation Reports (New South Wales)
W.C.W.B. World Council for the Welfare of the Blind

W.C.Y.M.S.C. World Council of Young Men's Service Clubs
wd. ward
   warranted
   word
   would
W.D. War Department
   Works Department
W/D. Wind Direction
w/d. well developed
W.D.C. War Damage Commission
   War Damage Contribution
   World Data Centre
Wdr. Wardmaster
Wdr.L. Wardmaster Lieutenant
wds. words
wd.sc. wood screw
W.E. War Establishment
w.e. watch error
   week end(ing)
   white edge(s)
W.E.A. Royal West of England Academy
   Workers' Educational Association
W.E. & F.A. Welsh Engineers' and Founders' Association
W.E.C. Worldwide Evangelization Crusade
Wed. Wednesday
W.E.D.A. Wholesale Engineering Distributors' Association
Wedy. Wednesday
W.E.F. War Emergency Formula
   Women's Employment Federation
w.e.f. with effect from
W.E.G. War Emergency Grant
W.E.M.A. Winding Engine Manufacturers' Association
Wes. Wesleyan
W.E.S. War Equipment Scale
   Women's Engineering Society
   World Economic Survey
W.E.S.P.A.D. West End Steamship Passenger Agents' Dinner
Westm. Westmeath
   Westminster
Westmd. Westmorland
Westmr. Westminster
Wes. Univ. Wesleyan University
W.E.T.U.C. Workers' Educational Trade Union Committee
W.E.U. Western European Union
Wex. Wexford
W.F. White Fathers
w.f. wrong fount
W.F.A. White Fish Authority
W.F.A.L.W. Weltbund Freiheitlicher Arbeitnehmerverbände auf Liberaler Wirtschaftsgrundlage (World Union of Liberal Trade Union Organisations)
W.F.B. World Fellowship of Buddhists
W.F.C.Y.W.G. World Federation of Catholic Young Women and Girls
w.fd. wool forward
W.F.D. World Federation of the Deaf
W.F.D.A. Wholesale Floorcovering Distributors' Association
   Wholesale Footwear Distributors' Association

W.F.D.Y. World Federation of Democratic Youth
w.f.e. with food element
W.F.F. World Friendship Federation
W.F.G.A. Women's Farm and Garden Association
W.F.I.J.I. World Federation of International Juridical Institutions
W.F.L. Women's Freedom League
W.F.M.H. World Federation for Mental Health
W.F.M.W. World Federation of Methodist Women
W.F.O.T. World Federation of Occupational Therapists
W.F.P. World Food Programme
W.F.P.A. World Federation for the Protection of Animals
W.Fris. West Frisian
W.F.S.A. World Federation of Societies of Anaesthesiologists
W.F.S.W. World Federation of Scientific Workers
W.F.T.U. World Federation of Trade Unions
W.F.U.N.A. World Federation of United Nations Associations
W.F.W. Weltföderation der Wissenschaftler (World Federation of Scientific Workers)
W.F.Y. World Federalist Youth
Wg. Wing
W.G. Welsh Guards
   West German(ic)
   The Westminster Gazette
   William Gilbert Grace
W.-G. West German(ic)
w.g. weight guaranteed
   wire guage
W.G.B. Wales Gas Board
   Weltgewerkschaftsbund (World Federation of Trade Unions)
W.G.C. Worthy Grand Chaplain
   Worthy Grand Conductor
Wg.-Comdr. Wing-Commander
W.Ger. West German(ic)
W.G.F. Womens' Gas Federation
W.G.G. Worthy Grand Guardian
   Worthy Grand Guide
W.G.H. Worthy Grand Herald
W.G.I. World Geophysical Interval
W.G.M. Worthy Grand Master
W. Gmc. West Germanic
W.G.S. Worthy Grand Sentinel
Wh. Watt-hour(s)
wh. wharf
   which
   whispered
   white
W.H.A. Welsh Hockey Association
W'hampton Wolverhampton
Wh.Ex. Whitworth Exhibitioner
whf. wharf
W.H.M. Women's Home Mission
W.H.O. World Health Organisation
w.h.p. water horse-power
whr. whether
W.H.R.A. Welwyn Hall Research Association
W.I.A. Willow Importers' Association

W.I.A.C. Women's International Art Club
W.I.C. West India Committee
Wh.Sc. Whitworth Scholar
whsle. wholesale
w.h.y. what have you
W.I. West India(n)
    West Indies
    When Issued
    Windward Islands
    Women's Institute
w.i. wrought iron
Wick. Wicklow
wid. widow(er)
W.I.D. West India Docks, London
W.I.D.F. Women's International Democratic Federation
W.I.F. West Indies Federation
W.I.L.P.F. Women's International League for Peace and Freedom
Wilts. Wiltshire
Wilts.R. Wiltshire Regiment
Wind.I. Windward Islands
W.I.N.S. Women's Industrial and National Service Corps
W. Inst. Women's Institute
Winton. Wintoniensis (of Winchester)
W.I.O. Women's International Ort
W.I.P.O. World Intellectual Property Organisation
W.I.R. Weekly Intelligence Report
    West India Regiment
    West Indian Reports
W.I.R.A. Wool Industries Research Association
Wis(c). Wisconsin
W.I.S.C. West Indian Standing Conference
    Women's Information and Study Centre
Wisd. Wisdom
wisd. wisdom
W.I.T.B. Wool Industry Training Board
Wits. Witwatersrand
W.I.V.A.B. Women's Inter-Varsity Athletic Board
W.I.Z.O. Women's International Zionist Organisation
W.J.C. World Jewish Congress
W.J.C.B. World Jersey Cattle Bureau
W.J.E.C. Welsh Joint Education Committee
wk. week
    work
w.k. well-known
wkly. weekly
Wkr. Worker
wks. weeks
    works
wkt(s). wicket(s)
W.L. Waiting List
    Wagon-lit
    Wave Length
    West Lothian
W.L.A. Women's Land Army
W.L.B. War Labor Board (U.S.)
W.L.D. War Load Displacement
W.L.F. Women's Liberal Federation
wl.fwd. wool forward
W.lon(g). West longitude
W.L.P.S.A. Wild Life Preservation Society of Australia

W.L.R. Weekly Law Reports
W.L.T.B.U. Watermen, Lightermen, Tugmen and Bargemen's Union
W.L.U.S. World Land Use Survey
Wly. Westerly
W.L.Y. Welsh League of Youth
W.M. White Metal
    Worshipful Master
W.M.A. Webbing Manufacturers' Association
    Women's Missionary Auxiliary
    Workers' Music Association
    World Medical Association
W.M.C. World Methodist Council
    Working Men's Club
    Working Men's College
W.M.C.I.U. Working Men's Club and Institute Union Limited
W.M.G.B. West Midlands Gas Board
wmk. watermark
W.M.M. World Movement of Mothers
W.M.M.A. Wholesale Memorial Manufacturers' Association
W.M.O. World Meteorological Organisation
W.M.O.A.S. Women's Migration and Oversea Appointments Society
W.M.P. With Much Pleasure
W.M.S. Wesleyan Missionary Society
W.M.T.C. Women's Mechanized Transport Corps
W.N.E. Welsh National Eisteddfod
W.N.L. Within Normal Limits
W.N. (N.S.W.) Weekly Notes, New South Wales
W.N.O.C. Welsh National Opera Company, Ltd.
W.N.P. Welsh Nationalist Party
W.N.W. West-North-West
W.O. Walk-Over
    War Office
    Warrant Officer
    Welfare Officer
    Wireless Operator
    Written Order
w.o. walk-over
w/o without
w.o.b. washed overboard
w.o.c. without compensation
W.O.C.C.I. War Office Central Card Index
W.O.C.L. War Office Casualty List
w.o.g. with other goods
W.O.L. War Office Letter
w.o.l. wharf-owner's liability
W.O.M. Wireless Operator Mechanic
w.o.n. wool on needle
W.O.O. Warrant Ordnance Officer
Wor. Worshipful
Worc.R. Worcestershire Regiment
Worcs. Worcestershire
Words. Wordsworth
W.O.S.B. War Office Selection Board
W.O.W. Women Ordnance Workers
    Woodmen of the World (U.S.)
Wp. Worship
W.P. Weather Permitting
    West Point
    White Paper
    Worthy Patriarch
    Worthy President

w.p. waste paper
 weather permitting
w/p. without prejudice
W.P.A. Western Provident Association
 for Hospital and Nursing
 Home Services
 Wire Products Association
 World Parliament Association
 World Presbyterian Alliance
W.P.B. War Production Board
w.p.b. waste-paper basket
W.P.B.S. Welsh Plant Breeding Station
W.P.C. War Pension(s) Committee
 Woman Police Constable
 World Petroleum Congress
 World Power Conference
W.P.F. World Prohibition Federation
W.P.F.A. Wholesale Photo Finishers'
 Association
W.P.F.L. West Pakistan Federation of
 Labour
W.P.I.D.C. West Pakistan Industrial
 Development Corporation
w.p.m. words per minute
W.P.N. World's Press News
W.P.O. World Ploughing Organisation
W.P.R.A. Wall Paper Merchants' As-
 sociations of Great Britain
 Waste Paper Recovery As-
 sociation
W.P.R.L. Water Pollution Research
 Laboratory
W.P.Sc.A. World's Poultry Science
 Association
W.P.S.M.A. Welsh Plate and Steel
 Manufacturers' Association (*dissolved*)
W.R. Ward Room
 War Reserve
 Western Region
 West Riding
 Willelmus Rex (King William)
w.r. war risk
W.R.A. Water Research Association
W.R.A.A.F. Women's Royal Australian
 Air Force
W.R.A.C. Women's Royal Army Corps
 (*formerly* W.A.A.C.*)
W.R.A.F. Women's Royal Air Force
 (*formerly* W.A.A.F.*)
W.R.A.P. Committee for Writing and
 Reading Aids for the Paralysed
W.R.C. Water-Retention Coefficient
 Wire Rod Conference
W.R.E. Weapons Research Establish-
 ment
W.R.I. War Resisters International
 War Risks Insurance
w.r.n. wool round needle
W.R.N.L.R. Western Region of Nigeria
 Law Reports
W.R.N.R. Women's Royal Naval Re-
 serve
W.R.N.S. Womens' Royal Naval Ser-
 vice
W.R.P.M.A. Waste Rubber and Plastics
 Merchants' Association of Great
 Britain
W.R.U. Welsh Rugby Union
 Wesleyan Reform Union
W.R.V.S. Women's Royal Voluntary
 Service
W.R.Y. World Refugee Year

W.S. War Scale
 War-Substantive
 Water Soluble
 West Saxon
 Writer to the Signet
W.S.C. Women Speakers for the
 Commonwealth
W.S.C.F. World Student Christian
 Federation
W.S.I.S.I. West of Scotland Iron and
 Steel Institute
W.S.L. Warren Spring Laboratory
 (Ministry of Technology)
W.S.O.C. Wider Share Ownership
 Council
W.S.P.U. Women's Social and Political
 Union
W.S.R.A. Women's Squash Rackets
 Association
W.S.S.A. Welsh Secondary Schools
 Association
W.S.W. West-South-West
Wt. Warrant
wt. weight
 without
W.T. Warrant Telegraphist
 War Transport
 Watch Time
 The Winter's Tale (Shakespeare)
 Wireless Technology
 Wireless Telegraphy
 Wireless Telephony
w.t. watertight
W.T.A. World Transport Agency
W.T.A.A. World Trade Alliance Assoc-
 iation
W.T.B.A. Water-Tube Boilermakers'
 Association
W.T.C. Women's Timber Corps
W.T.D. War Trade Department
 Wool Textile Delegation
W.T.E. World Tapes for Education
W.T.G. Welt-Tierärztegesellschaft
 (World Veterinary Association)
W.T.H.B. Welsh Tourist and Holidays
 Board
W.T.M.H. Watertight Manhole
W.T.P. World Tape Pals
Wtr. Writer
wtr. winter
 writer
W.T.R.C. Wool Textile Research Coun-
 cil
W.T.S. Women's Transport Service
W.T.T.A. Wholesale Tobacco Trade
 Association of Great Britain and
 Northern Ireland
W.T.U.C. World Trade Union Con-
 ference
W.U.C.T. World Union of Catholic
 Teachers
W.U.C.W.O. World Union of Catholic
 Women's Organisations
W.U.F. World Union of Freethinkers
W.U.I. Workers' Union of Ireland
W.U.J.S. World Union of Jewish
 Students
W.U.L.T.U.O. World Union of Liberal
 Trade Union Organisations
W.U.P.J. World Union for Progressive
 Judaism

W.U.R. World University Round Table
W.U.S. World University Service
W.U.S.L. Women's United Service League
W.Va. West Virginia
W.V.A. World Veterinary Association
W.V.D. Wereldverbond van Diamantbewerkers (Universal Alliance of Diamond Workers)
W.V.F. World Veterans' Federation
W.V.P.A. World Veterinary Poultry Association
W.V.R.A. Westerham Valley Railway Association
W.V.S. Women's Voluntary Service (*now* W.R.V.S.)
W.W. Warrant Writer
   Who's Who
   World War

W/W. Warehouse Warrant
W.W.C.P. Walking Wounded Collecting Post
W.W.C.T.U. World's Woman's Christian Temperance Union
W.Wdr. Warrant Wardmaster
W.W.F. World Wildlife Fund
W.W.O. Wing Warrant Officer
W.W.R. Western Weekly Reports
W.W.W. Who Was Who
W.W.Y. Queen's Own Warwickshire and Worcestershire Yeomanry
W.X. Women's Extra
Wy(o). Wyoming
W.Y.R. West Yorkshire Regiment
W.Y.S. Wildlife Youth Service
W.Z. Weltzeit (Universal Time)

X

X Reactance
   Ten (Roman numerals)
   Unknown Quantity
   Xenon
x unknown quantity
   xylonite
X. Christ(ian)
   Cross
   Explosive
   Extension
x. extr a
xbre. décembre (December)
x.c.l. excess current liabilities
x.cp. not including right to coupon
x.cut cross cut
x.d. not including right to dividend
x.div. not including right to dividend
Xe Xenon
Xen. Xenophon
xg. crossing
x.i(nt). not including right to next interest
Xmas Christmas
xmtr. transmitter
Xn. Christian

x.n. not including right to new shares
Xnty. Christianity
x.o. examination officer
x. out cross out
x.p. express paid
x.p.p. exprès payé lettre (express paid letter)
x.p.t. exprès payé télégraphe (express paid telegraph)
x.q. cross question
X.R. External Relations Service (U.N. E.S.C.O.)
x.ref. cross reference
x.roads cross roads
x.rts. without rights (securities)
Xt. Christ
Xtian. Christian
xtry. extraordinary
Xty. Christianity
XX (Ales of) double strength
xx double strength
XXX (Ales of) triple strength
xxx treble strength
xylo. xylophone

Y

Y Yttrium
Y. Year
   Yellow
   Yen
   Young
   Yugoslavia
y. yacht
   yard

cont.

   year
   youngest
Y.A. York-Antwerp Rules
Y. & L. York and Lancaster Regiment
Y.A.S.G.B. Youth Association of Synagogues in Great Britain
Y.A.S. Yorkshire Agricultural Society
Yb Ytterbium

Y.B. Year Book
Y.C. Young Conservative
    Young Conservative and Unionist
    Organisation
    Youth Club
Y.C.A. Youth Camping Association
Y.C. & U.O. Young Conservative and Unionist Organisation
Y.C.F.E. Yorkshire Council for Further Education
Y.C.L. Young Communist League
Y.C.N.D. Youth Campaign for Nuclear Disarmament
Y.C.S. International Young Catholic Students
    Young Christian Students
Y.C.W. International Young Christian Workers
yd. yard
y'day yesterday
ydg. yarding
yds. yards
Y.E. Yellow Edge(s)
Y.E.A.B.I. Yorkshire Educational Association for the Building Industry
Y.E.B. Yorkshire Electricity Board
Yeo. Yeoman
    Yeomanry
Y.E.O. Youth Employment Officer
Y.E.S. Youth Employment Service
yesty. yesterday
Y.E.W.T.I.C. Yorkshire East and West, Technical Information Centre
Y.F.B.T.E. Yorkshire Federation of Building Trades Employers
Y.F.C. Young Farmers' Club
Y.F.C.U. Young Farmers' Clubs of Ulster
Y.G.S. Yorkshire Grassland Society
Y.H. Youth Hostel
Y.H.A. Youth Hostels' Association
Y.H.A.N.I. Youth Hostels Association of Northern Ireland
Yid. Yiddish
Yks. Yorkshire
Y.L. Young Liberals
Y.L.I. Yorkshire Light Infantry
Y.L.M. Young Launderers' Movement
y.m. yannä muuta (et cetera)

Y.M.B.A. Yacht and Motor Boat Association
Y.M.C.A. Young Men's Christian Association
Y.M.Cath.A. Young Men's Catholic Association
Y.M.H.A. Young Men's Hebrew Association
Y.M.P. Young Master Printer
Y.M.P.A. Young Master Printers' Alliance
Y.N.A. Young Newspapermen's Association
y.o. year old
Yorks. Yorkshire
Y.P. Young People
y.p. yield point
Y.P.S.C.E. Young People's Society for Christian Endeavour
yr. year
    your
    younger
Y.R.A. Yacht Racing Association
Yr.B. Year Book
Y.R.L.S. Yorkshire Regional Library System
yrs. years
    yours
yrs. ty. yours truly
Y.S. Young Soldier(s)
y.s. yard super
    yield strength
Y.S.L. Young Sowers' League
yst. youngest
Y.T. Yukon Territory
y.t.b. yarn to back
y.t.f. yarn to front
Y.T.N. Yorkshire Television Network
Y.U. Yale University (U.S.)
Yugo. Yugoslavia
Y.V.F.F. Young Volunteer Force Foundation
Y.W.C.A. Young Women's Christian Association
Y.W.F. Young World Federalists (*now* W.F.Y.)
Y.W.H.A. Young Women's Hebrew Association
Y.W.S. Young Wales Society

Z

Z Atomic number symbol
Z. Zero
    Zoll (customs (duty))
    Zone
    Zuckung (contraction)
z. zenith distance
    zero
    zone
za. zirka (approximately)
Z.A. Zéro absolu (Absolute Zero)
    Zuid Afrika (South Africa)
Z.A.D.C.A. Zinc Alloy Die Casters' Association

Zan. Zanzibar
Z.A.N.U. Zimbabwe African National Union (Rhodesia)
Z.A.P.U. Zimbabwe African People's Union (Rhodesia)
Z.A.S.P. Polska Macierz Szkolna (Union of Polish Stage Artists Abroad)
z.B. zum Beispiel (for example)
Z.C. Zionist Congress
Z.D. Zenith Distance
z.d. zenith distance
Z.D.A. Zinc Development Association

Z.E.B.R.A. Zero Energy Breeder Reactor Assembly
Zech. Zechariah
ZENITH Zero Energy Nitrogen Heated Thermal Reactor
Zeph. Zephaniah
Z.E.T.A. Zero Energy Thermonuclear Apparatus
Z.E.T.R. Zero Energy Thermal Reactor
Z.F. Zone of Fire
Z.F.G.B.I. Zionist Federation of Great Britain and Ireland
Z.F.V. Deutsche Zentrale für Fremdenverkehr (German Central Tourist Association)
Zg. Zug (Switzerland)
Z.G. Zoological Gardens
Z.Hr. Zero Hour
Z.I. Zone interdite (Prohibited zone)
Z.I.P. Zoning Improvement Plan
Zl. Zloty
Zn. Zinc
Zod. Zodiac
Z. of I. Zone of Interior

Zoochem. Zoochemical Zoochemistry
Zoogeog. Zoogeography
Zool. Zoological Zoologist Zoology
Zooph. Zoophytology
Z.P.D.A. Zinc Pigment Development Association
Zr Zirconium
Z.S. Zoological Society
Z.S.F. Zero Skip Frequency
Z.S.I. Zoological Society of Ireland
Z.S.L. Zoological Society of London
Z.S.T. Zone Standard Time
Z.T. Zone Time
z.T. zum Teil (in part)
Ztg. Zeitung (newspaper)
Ztr. Zentner (hundred-weight)
Zulu. Zululand
Zv. Zollverein (Customs Union)
zw. zwischen (between)
Zz. Zingiber (ginger)
z.Z. zur Zeit (at present *or* acting)